D0854636

PHILIP RODWAY

AND

A TALE OF TWO THEATRES

PHILIP RODWAY

THE THEATRE ROYAL & PRINCE OF WALES THEATRE
BIRMINGHAM
From a painting by Bernard Munns, R.B.S.A.
Exhibited at the Royal Birmingham Society of Artists, Autumn, 1934

PHILIP RODWAY

AND

A TALE OF TWO THEATRES

by

HIS DAUGHTERS

PHYLLIS PHILIP RODWAY

AND

LOIS RODWAY SLINGSBY, B.A. (Hons.)

BIRMINGHAM

CORNISH BROTHERS LTD.

1934

Dedicated
TO MOTHER

The Woodlands
Edgbaston.
Birmingham.

A letter I received from Sir Charles Grant Robertson, Principal and Vice-Chancellor of the University of Birmingham, on February 3rd, 1932, was one of the spurs for this book. His words were instinct with consolation and inspiration. He wrote:

"*It is not surprising that Philip Rodway was a powerful personality not merely in Birmingham but in Great Britain. He had a fine position in his profession, and everyone admired his devotion to the theatre, his integrity, high principles and artistry. He did much to keep our theatres on a high level, and he will be sorely missed. But he leaves the kind of tradition of which his daughters can be proud. And you who shared his life can feel that his life has done much for thousands who never knew him.*"

That Phyllis and Lois are indeed proud of that tradition I know—that I may entrust the recording of it, and of their father's life, into their hands I have complete confidence.

To Sir Frank Benson's tribute to him as an outstanding example of all a man should be as a citizen and a friend, we would add our tribute to a beloved father and husband.

Ethel Rodway.

October. 21st, 1934.

Introduction by Mr. R. CROMPTON RHODES ("R.C.R.")

Epilogue by SIR FRANK BENSON

First Published, Christmas, 1934

Copyright — All rights reserved

Printed in England at The Kynoch Press, Birmingham

"Philip Rodway and Pantomime"

Birmingham Post, February 6th, 1932

"They look forlorn and cold in the grey morning light, those models of pantomime scenes which stand in a dressing-room at the top of the Prince of Wales Theatre. They had been packed away when Philip Rodway left the Theatre Royal four years ago, but shortly before his death he had them built up, and they stand there as he looked at them for the last time. As I gazed at them I recalled in Philip Rodway something which few suspected, despite his sound judgment and his sense of theatrical values—it was, I think, a vein of poetry. One evening, long ago, I first discovered it. We were talking, as ever, of plays and players, when I happened to mention some phrase from *Samson Agonistes*. While I was searching my mind for the exact word, he surprised me by reciting a long passage, a little shyly at first, but afterwards in sonorous tones which caught the magnificence that lies beneath the abrupt staccato periods of Milton.

"He was not, in the ordinary way, a reading man, and by no means a writing-man, so his poetry found expression in what may seem a strange way—the transformation scenes of his four-and-twenty pantomimes at the Theatre Royal. In Melbourne—or perhaps destroyed long ago—is the model of the scene which he loved best of all. It was the old-world garden of *Puss in Boots*, beautifully painted by Mr. W. R. Young, who was so happy in the Warwickshire landscapes that Philip Rodway loved so well. Night after night he used to steal into his box, or at the back of the dress circle, to watch it, and when he came out his eyes were always full of tears. Like all true men of the theatre, he had a touch of the sentimentalist.

"Some years ago, when I was writing a history of the Theatre Royal, we often fell to talking over pantomime. He used to amaze me by the tenacity and exactitude of his memory, for sometimes, when I could only recall the sense of something I had written, he would give me the very words. The one scene in pantomime to which he always reverted was not one of his transformations, but the episode of George Robey and Fred Emney in the kitchen. I suppose nobody who saw it can ever have forgotten it, for Robey came on in a huge collier's suit, with a vast watch-chain, and, while Emney, as his wife, nagged and nagged and nagged, he sat in a chair, never speaking a word, glaring murderously at his nails and biting his lips.

"It was a scene with a history; at first Fred Emney could see nothing in it, and brought with him to rehearsal his tame author, and it took all the diplomacy of Philip Rodway to persuade him that it had even a chance of success. Emney left the last private rehearsal in despair, and he sat for an hour with me, discussing it earnestly, despondently. He thought George Robey ought to have had something to say in reply to the old woman's exasperating remarks—like, 'It's your bath-night, and you keep putting it off and putting it off.' At the first public performance there was no doubt of its complete success, for the audience rocked and shouted with laughter. Long afterwards, Mr. Rodway admitted to me that he sighed with relief when the first roar of laughter came—and such is the resilience of human nature, and the fallibility of human recollection, that when I met Fred Emney on the last night of *Sinbad the Sailor*—he solemnly assured me he knew the kitchen-scene was bound to be a 'riot' from the very first time he read it in 'scrip.'

"It was Philip Rodway's favourite comic scene, which he never missed watching. One night he escorted me on my annual visit behind the scenes, and up in the flies—his old head flyman used to tell me that 'Mr. Rodway says as ourn are the best flies in the providences'—we looked at it from this unaccustomed angle. It was not only we who were watching it, for in the orchestra below the band were to be seen, standing up with beaming faces, and the flymen themselves were leaning over, as they did every night. I never wondered that Mr. Rodway glowed with amused pride as he recalled this scene as the greatest piece of comedy he had ever known in pantomime.

"I do not suppose there are half a dozen people who knew that Philip Rodway, in his callow youth, made an appearance in a little village hall as the dame in an amateur pantomime. It was that effort which convinced him that acting was not his vocation, but inspired him with the ambition of becoming a producer of pantomimes. His first chance came in 1904, with *Babes in the Wood*, the first pantomime in the New Theatre Royal, which was prematurely produced and threatened to become a disastrous failure. After a few days, he took it in hand himself, and reconstructed it, and from that time for almost a quarter of a century his was the guiding mind in the pantomimes of the Theatre Royal.

"When I looked at these models they were eloquent of the care Mr. Rodway used to lavish upon his productions. No sooner was one first night over than he began to think of next year's show. He knew exactly what he wanted, and the scenery progressed from rough sketch to working model, from working model to framework, from framework to painted scene, with many conferences and much brooding. There is a model, not easy to work, of a lovely transformation which was called 'The Four Seasons.' It suggests the graceful foliage and flowers that Mr. W. R. Young reproduced in their own beauty. The lilacs of springtime, the cornfield of summer, the wine-dark roses of autumn, the frosty landscape of winter— I can see them as they were. A rising sun, I know, is missing; and I remember it because of Mr. Rodway's intense indignation when once the synchronisation was wrong by a fraction of a second.

"I suppose no producer of pantomime can have planned more carefully than Philip Rodway. If it was *Sinbad the Sailor* he would read again and again the story as it was told in the *Arabian Nights*, and he loved to find some old version of a fairy-tale. If it was a story of his own invention, like *Little Miss Muffet* or *Old King Cole*, he would let his fancy play freely in the realms of pantomime. He discovered an old version of *Puss in Boots*, played in the first year of Queen Victoria's reign, with a frontispiece of Charles Matthews as the cat and Madam Vestris as Colin, and from that he got his idea of playing Billy Merson as the cat.

"It was always his joy to show me the mechanical ingenuity employed in perfecting his great scenic changes—to point to the dozens of stage-hands moving softly about in felt shoes, often working in the dark with the occasional flash of a torchlight. Not a sound of their movements escaped to the front, and they worked with the speed and precision of a gun team. Then, perhaps, he would find for me the picture which had first suggested his transformation, and I knew that what had been to you and me just a scene in pantomime was to Philip Rodway a dream come true.

"R.C.R."

PREFACE

Philip Rodway was essentially and resolutely a "provincial manager." It was one of the problems that we propounded and left unsolved as to who was the first person to speak of "the provinces" as such in their theatrical sense: my theory was that it was some London actor, some adventurer of the early nineteenth century, some refulgent star who made a triumphal progress from country playhouse to country playhouse, imposing himself upon their stock-companies, and regarding their areas, with a fine old Roman satisfaction, as territory to be conquered and annexed. Perhaps it was Philip Rodway's remote and grandiloquent predecessor at the Theatre Royal, Birmingham, Robert William Elliston, who always announced that he "proposed to open the summer campaign" at Birmingham with such-and-such a play. I do not mean that the problem of etymology ever obsessed Philip Rodway, but he had his own very decided ideals and very decided opinions as to what was the function of a "provincial manager."

This biography, by his daughters Phyllis and Lois, gives so full an account of the twenty years during which I knew him that it leaves me but little to say by way of preface—especially as it incorporates some of the things that I have written elsewhere upon his favourite subject of pantomime. Of the earlier stages of his management, from the time when he entered the box office at the Theatre Royal in 1897, I knew very little at first-hand, for my acquaintance with him began in the September of 1913, when his success was firmly established: he had "produced" his first pantomime, in the sense that for the first time his direction had been publicly acknowledged; and (also for the first time in its history) the new Theatre Royal, the twentieth century playhouse, had paid a dividend to its shareholders; and he had been rewarded by the position of managing director of the theatre whose staff he had joined as "box office keeper."

Philip Rodway was very proud of the traditions of the Birmingham Theatre Royal, and to think of the managers who had preceded him since 1774. His particular joy was to hear stories of these his predecessors, a strange and remarkable company, which included Old Dicky Yates, the original Oliver Surface in "The School for Scandal"; that redoubtable Milesian, the elder Macready, R. W. Elliston; Alfred Bunn, known in Birmingham as "Hot Cross Bunn," and afterwards to "Punch" as "Poet Bunn," from his authorship of divers libretti like "The Bohemian Girl"; the Mercer Simpsons, father and son, whose management covered nearly sixty years between them; and Charles Dornton, who made a fortune out of touring "The Two Orphans." He collected their playbills, which adorned the corridors of the Theatre Royal until the end of his management, when they were discarded as "junk" by his successors.

He used to love the pompous advertisements of the famous Elliston, whose *régime* was neither long nor profitable. Yet it had left stories that had been handed down for more than a century. He was always delighted to quote Lamb's lines on his forerunner: ". . . wherever Elliston walked, sate or stood still, there was the theatre. He carried about with him his pit, boxes, and galleries, and set up his portable playhouse at corners of streets, and in the market places. Upon flintiest pavements he trod the boards still; and if his theme chanced to be passionate, the green baize carpet of tragedy spontaneously rose beneath his feet."

But there was certainly nothing of the Elliston in his own make-up. He preferred to dress and comport himself as a business man, not wearing unnecessarily the managerial livery of evening dress—profoundly interested in the business of the theatre, yet anxious in every way to avoid the appearance of being a showman.

Pantomime was his greatest interest, the outlet of his creative energy. In this he was following the example of his predecessors from the days of the elder Mercer Simpson who produced the first Christmas pantomime at the Theatre Royal in 1840. It is difficult for those who have not known them to realise what a part pantomime has played, and plays even now, in the social life of a great provincial city. As James Agate, looking back on half a century since he saw his first pantomime at Manchester, has recently said in his "First Nights": "Clearing our minds of cant, let it be said that London Pantomime has never been a patch upon its provincial brother, a fact which would have been recognized aeons ago but for the astounding genius of Dan Leno, and the fatness of unfunny Herbert Campbell." For this reason, pantomime figures largely in these pages. Philip Rodway was resolutely a Birmingham manager. Occasionally he was interested in a touring venture, but he resisted all attempts to induce him to take any financial part in London productions. He gratified all his theatrical ambitions except two, I believe; one was to receive and accept an unsolicited invitation to direct a pantomime at the Theatre Royal, Drury Lane, and the other, curiously enough, was to stage the three parts of Shakespeare's "King Henry VI" with proper heraldic appointments. I know, however, that on one occasion he was tempted to make a London venture financially—after the first production at the Birmingham Repertory Theatre, in 1916, of "The Farmer's Wife," by Eden Phillpotts, and H. B. Irving had purchased an option, which afterwards lapsed. When the play was printed, Philip Rodway borrowed my copy and tried to persuade several of his business friends to interest themselves in a production, but they could see no merit in it, and it therefore remained on the shelf until Barry Jackson decided that he himself would revive it at his own theatre, with a young actor named Cedric Hardwicke in the part of Churdles Ash.

In the twenty years of our acquaintance we talked, I am sure, over every aspect of the theatre except "the figures," and every play except his own "current attraction." I have never been interested in how much they "did on the week" at South Shields, or at the Theatre Royal, Birmingham; and Philip Rodway used to say drily, "It's just as well, because you'd rarely hear the truth." In the history of his own Theatre Royal he was much interested, but he was in no sense an antiquary—yet in preparing a pantomime he would go to vast trouble over costumes to study the correct "period," discover its essentials, and then "pantomime" them, as he called the process.

Philip Rodway loved to dandle the oddities of man. He used to look forward with the greatest delight to the annual visits of "A Royal Divorce," that relic of the early nineties, which made between fifty and sixty appearances at the Theatre since Mercer Simpson's time. When I first saw this Napoleonic drama, in the Whitsuntide of 1914, it was so familiar to the staff of the Theatre Royal that the attendants would stand at the back of the Dress Circle reciting it sotto voce, a line ahead of the actors, like the prompter in the Italian theatre. It was a holiday piece, which brought strange visitors to the house, and "Manager Kelly," always resplendent in his silk hat, was always ready to stand on the theatre steps inviting the astonished passers-by to enter— that is, until Philip Rodway caught him at it, and insisted that, while these methods were all very well outside the travelling booth, they were quite unfitted to the Theatre Royal, Birmingham.

So far as I know he was not superstitious, yet when he was being asked as to the form a certain souvenir should take, he said that he would leave it to the other man so long as he did not adorn it with peacocks; then he produced the history of the old Theatre Royal, written by the late Edgar Pemberton, and pointed out a dado of peacocks on the title page. He solemnly regarded this bird of ill omen as the cause of the misfortunes that followed in the next decade.

This biography is love's labour. Every page of it attests the care and diligence with which Lois and Phyllis Rodway have set themselves to reconstruct the story of their father's life. No theatrical memoir, at least to my knowledge, has had such attention paid to the illustrations, which, like the book itself, concern themselves partly with the side of Philip Rodway which we did not see in the theatre. It is a melancholy thought to me that only in two subjects in all our acquaintance did he try to convert me, and then he failed dismally. After much persuasion, I once consented to go fishing with him to Harvington, where he sat contentedly all day without a single bite, and was rather hurt that I chose to spend two hours in the more exciting pastime of watching the swallows entering and leaving a ruined barn. He also tried, by long and awful sermons, to break me of a regrettable addiction to cigars and cigarettes, and, after very discreet and elaborate explanations that his gift was not to be regarded as an attempt at "bribery and corruption," presented me with a case *of pipes. I never had the heart to tell him that within two days I had dropped both the pipes and broken the stems. Otherwise, we always talked of "plays and players," and there never seemed to be any need of another subject— especially as the conversations happened to cover, by reason of the nature of drama itself, every other subject under the sun.*

R. CROMPTON RHODES.

ACKNOWLEDGEMENTS

We offer our sincerest thanks:

To the many who have contributed to the making of this book, not only to those who have aided materially by their recollections and reminiscences, but to those who, by their goodwill and enthusiasm, have given us so much encouragement;

To Sir Francis H. Pepper, chairman of the Prince of Wales Theatre (Birmingham) Ltd., and our friends of the "Two Theatres";

To Mr. R. Crompton Rhodes for his preface, Sir Frank Benson for his epilogue, Mr. W. Bridges Adams and Mr. W. H. Savery of the Stratford-upon-Avon Festival Company, for their help in regard to the Shakespearean side of our story;

To the many leading personalities of the stage whose names appear within these pages, and especially those associated with the pantomimes—Wee Georgie Wood, Clarkson Rose, Hal Bryan, George M. Slater . . .

To Mr. Bernard Munns, R.B.S.A., for the infinite care he has expended on the portraits of Philip Rodway.

For personal interest and co-operation our thanks are due to Mr. H. V. Davis of the Kynoch Press, Mr. E. A. Bierman of Messrs. Siviter Smith & Co. Ltd., and Mr. Martyn Pollack of Messrs. Cornish Brothers Ltd., our publishers.

For permission to include extracts from copyright music, to the publishers, Messrs. Boosey and Hawkes Ltd., London.

For their courtesy in allowing us to reproduce cartoons, photographs, etc., to the many newspapers and periodicals concerned.

To Mr. M. F. K. Fraser, whose valuable advice, untiring assistance, and unfailing interest have been with us from the beginnings of this book;

To Charles, for his legal guidance;

And, above all, to Mother, our "Art Editor," for her encouraging influence and the endless help she has given, particularly in the early chapters, and in the arduous work of proof-reading.

P.R.
L.R.S.

A*

CONTENTS

CHAPTER 15
(1913-14)

1913 Season—Philip Rodway becomes Managing Director—*Little Miss Muffet*, 1913-14; Ernie Mayne, Ella Retford, Maidie Scott, Fred Allandale—P.R. gives Jack Buchanan his first engagement—George M. Slater's reminiscences—A Robb Wilton story—Some anecdotes—Wee Georgie Wood adds a commentary—Lord Mayor's Ball: an 1840 Dandy; the Philip Rodway none of us knew.

CHAPTER 16
(1914-15)

A new influence, R. Crompton Rhodes—1914 Season—The licensing regulations— August 4th, 1914—War—The news at Welford-on-Avon—P.R. inaugurates the twice-nightly system—*Sinbad the Sailor*, 1914-15; George Robey and Fred Emney—The famous "Kitchen Scene"; "The Valley of Diamonds"—1915 Season—Seymour Hicks in *Wild Thyme*—A story of *The Chinese Honeymoon*—Henry Hallatt's recollections.

CHAPTER 17
(1915-16)

The House that Jack Built; Billy Merson and Clarice Mayne—*Jingle Johnnie*—a Graham Squiers' story—"Blossomland," "The Waterfall," and "The Snow-clad Hills"—Special entertainments to wounded soldiers—"The Tale of a Timepiece"—Mr. Howard Jaques —Zeppelins over Birmingham—1916 Season—Parties at the Botanical Gardens—Mr. Neville Chamberlain.

CHAPTER 18
(1916-17)

Boy Blue, 1916-17; Dorothy Ward, Shaun Glenville, and Jay Laurier—The Harlequinade —Souvenir album presented by the Bishop of Birmingham—1917 Season—The annual meeting—First Mary Anderson matinée at the Royal—*Cinderella*, 1917-18; Billy Merson and Clarice Mayne—"The Enchanted Lake"—The Tank Bank Race.

CHAPTER 19
(1918)

1918 Season—Sunday entertainments for wounded—P.R.'s lecture "Producing a Play" —Theatre Royal takes over Prince of Wales Theatre; Birmingham now keystone of touring system—Second Mary Anderson charity matinée, £6,200 raised—Philip Rodway becomes sole Managing Director of the two theatres.

CHAPTER 20

Characteristics—His bookshelf; Dickens, Conan Doyle, George Borrow, Edgar Allan Poe—Sense of humour—Generosity—Simplicity—Religion—Some comparisons—P.R. and his pipe—His friends speak; Sir Charles Grant Robertson, Gerald Forty. . . .

CHAPTER 21

Hobbies: Billiards; Mr. H. F. Harvey's recollections—The Midland Club—The Press Club—A Gerald Lawrence story—Our own billiards room—The window over the garden —"The great C major of this Life"—Cricket; County Ground and home—Fishing; Harvington—Mr. J. J. Noble's angle.

CHAPTER 22
(1918-20)

Babes in the Wood, 1918-19; Wee Georgie Wood, Ella Retford, Robb Wilton, Fred Allandale—"Meccanoland"—Some letters and stories—Reminiscences—1919 Season— Messager's *Monsieur Beaucaire*—Annual meeting—*Dick Whittington and his Cat*, 1919-20; Billy Merson and Clarice Mayne.

LIST OF COLOUR PLATES

LIST OF ILLUSTRATIONS

AUTHORS' NOTE

Events, both theatrical and personal, have been dealt
with in chronological order; the "seasons" at the two
theatres are tabulated for ease of reference, and the
records bring up to date the histories of that ancient
and distinguished playhouse, the Birmingham Theatre
Royal, and its younger rival, the Prince of Wales
Theatre.

We have had no diaries or personal memoranda of
Daddy's on which to work, but the idea for the title
of this biography came from a chance remark of his in
which he said, "If ever I were to write a book of my
reminiscences I should call it *A Tale of Two Theatres.*"

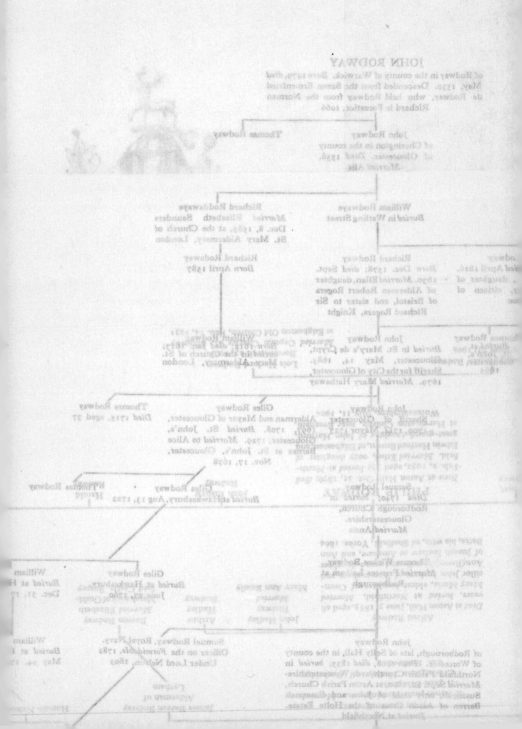

Stephen Rodway
Born April 1564

Nicholas Rodway

William
Born Oct. 1590?
Married Rebecca
Randal, Mania...
Lon...

William Rodway
Buried at Hawkesbury,
June 13, 1700; aged...

Edward Rodway,
Married at Hawkesbury,
Gloucestershire, 1656

Stephen Rodway

Edward Rodway
of Hawkesbury. Fought
for King Charles II at
Worcester, 1651

Stephen Rodway
of Frome. Fought at the Battle
of Sedgemoor, for the Duke of
Monmouth. Banished to the
Barbados by order of King
James II, 1685

William Rodway
Buried at Hawkesbury,
1734

George
Rodway

John
Rodway

Major William
Henry Rodway,
Trinidad, 1804

Henry
Barton Rodway,
Adelaide,
South Australia

HIS FATHER

CHAPTER 1

(1080-1876)

The Genealogical Record—Origin of the name of Rodway—Doomsday Book, 1080—Saxon descent—De Loges, Lords of Rodway—The Manor of Rodway, in the county of Warwick, 1325—Gloucestershire connections— John Rodway of Rodway, 1539—Sedgemoor, Edgehill, and Worcester— Arden and Hathaway—Lord Nelson and "the gallant Rodway"—Selly Hall and our great-great-grandfather—The Barrons; and the Fitzgeralds, Earls of Kildare—Major Rodway, founder of the Volunteer Movement— The inventive Inshaw—Aston Hall—And so to Philip.

"The family of *Rodway*" (wrote Philip Rodway's eldest brother, the heraldic expert) "takes its name from the village of *Rodway*, now called Radway, near Kineton, in Warwickshire. William Camden, the learned antiquary, in his *Britannica* (1586) says:

" 'Of ye redy soil comes the name of *Rodway*, yea and a great part of the verie Vale is thereupon termed the Vale of the Red Horse!' In John Speed's map published in 1606, with his *Theatre of Great Britain* it is marked *Rodway*. A copy of the map is in my possession.

"In the Doomsday Book (A.D. 1080) the Saxon *Ermenfried de Rodway* holds *Rodwei* from the great Norman Richard le Forestier. This powerful nobleman held lands in Arden and the Chase of Cannock. It was usual in early days for tenants to assume (with permission) a portion of the arms of their overlords, hence the similarity between the arms of all the families who were fiefs of the le Forestiers (now corrupted into Forster and Foster). The great German family of Forster bears the bugle-horn, the Rodways bear roses (from the Greek 'roda'—roses). Rodville (Rodavilla) bore 'azure, semee of roses or.' The de Loges, Lords of Rodway tempus Edward II, bore a golden roebuck in a blue canton as denoting their office."

The names Rodway, Rodawaye, Rodeway, and Radway are to be found near Trowbridge, Wilts, also at Road, near Frome, and there is a Rodway Hill in Gloucestershire. The name exists in Saxony as Rodewig. In Ancient German (eighth century) it is Hrodwig, Ruodwah.

B

The Genealogical Record prepared in 1904 by Alfred Rodway,* for his brother Philip on the occasion of his marriage, will be found near the title page, and shows clearly enough the descent of Philip Rodway from the old Saxon Ermenfried de Rodway. From the time of that *John Rodway*, of Rodway in the County of Warwick, who died in May 1539, the track is unbroken. Members of the various generations found their way into business life in London: established commercial and civic prestige in Gloucestershire: soldiered and sailored here, there, and everywhere; but always the Warwickshire connection has been maintained.

In some of our earliest records we find "Thomas de Rodway, Lord of the Manor of Rodway, 1325," and again, "Nicholas de Rodway, Incumbent of Wormleighton 1328, and Thomas de Rodway, Incumbent of Rodway, 1328."

At an early stage in the descent the Gloucester interest is created, and here may we pause for a moment to show you the Will of that first John, with its quaint, old-world phrasing:

"*WILL of John Rodway of North Cerney in the County of Gloucester.*

"*I bequeath my soole to Almighty Gode and to the m'cy of hys passyene and my bodye to be berydde in the church-yarde of North C'ney. To servant Thomas Curteys viij scheppe. Wife Agnes and sons Robert and Thomas to be executors. She to have halfe of ev'ythinge. The Will to be fulfilled to the plesur of Gode and the welth of my soole.*

"*Witnessed by Wm. Trindor*
        John Moyse ye elder
        Richarde Reddinge
        John Grene
        Robert Rodway
        Thomas Rodway
        John Rodway
        William Pynchyn
"*Proved at Cirencester, May 6th, 1539.*"

John's son, John, of Cherington, who died in 1556, left two

*Fellow of The Royal Historical Society, and of the Society of Antiquaries, Canada.

sons, of whom the younger, Richard Roddawaye, gave the name an alternative spelling, which reverted to Rodway in his grandson. The elder, in whom our present purpose is more concerned, contented himself with adding an 'e'— William Rodwaye, who died in 1604.

Of his four sons, the eldest, Stephen, was the grandfather of an adventurous namesake who fought for James Duke of Monmouth at Sedgemoor, and was consequently tried by the notorious Judge Jeffreys. His name appears in Sir William Booth's list of prisoners as one of "77 rebels banished to Barbadoes from Bristol in the ship *John Frigatt* in 1685." Years later there is record of an estate called Rodway in Barbados, so he may not have come off so badly. Sir Arthur Conan Doyle mentions him in his novel *Micah Clarke, a Tale of Sedgemoor*.

The second son, Nicholas, had a daughter who married into the Shropshire Sandfords. The third, William, concerns us not, but the youngest, Richard, is our man. He married Ellen, daughter of Alderman Robert Rogers, of Bristol, and sister of Sir Richard Rogers. They again carried on the name with four sons, and once more the descent continues through the youngest.

All had Gloucestershire connections. The eldest, Edward, supported Charles I at Edgehill in 1642, and had a cavalier son who fought for Charles II at Worcester in 1651. The second, William, lived to be eighty-one, and was buried at Hawkesbury, where Edward had been married. The third, Thomas, was buried in St. John's, Gloucester; and the youngest, John, our next link, was buried in St. Mary's de Crypt in the same city. He was a Sheriff of Gloucester in 1679.

This John married Mary Hathaway, concerning which marriage the record runs:

"The family of Hathaway is a most ancient one upon the borderland of Warwickshire and Gloucestershire. Shakespeare's wife, Anne Hathaway, is presumed by some antiquaries to have been of the Gloucestershire branch. Shakespeare himself was of course familiar with the district wherein this family lived, vide his frequent allusions to Gloucestershire, Justice Shallow, etc."

Digressing, we may note that in 1584, at Stourton Church in Wiltshire, a Thomas Rodwaye married a Maud Arden.

Shakespeare's mother was an Arden, his wife a Hathaway. There we must leave the coincidence, if it is no more (*cf. Arms of Hathaway*), and resume the trail of the Gloucestershire Rodways.

There were numerous sons towards the middle of the 18th century, and no doubt a fair proportion of daughters. We find many of the name living, marrying, dying, in Hawkesbury, Avening, Rodborough, and other Gloucestershire places during the eighty or so years following the death, in 1685, of Mary Hathaway's husband Sheriff John Rodway.

Two of his sons figure in the Genealogical Record as eminent citizens and city fathers of Gloucester. John, the eldest, was a mercer, Sheriff in 1709 and 1714, and Mayor in 1723. Giles, the second, was also a mercer, also a Sheriff, and twice Mayor (in 1697 and 1708).

From Mayor John Rodway we descend via Samuel and Thomas Wickes Rodway (both Rodborough men) to another John, in whom for the first time we find a link with the Birmingham neighbourhood. There was not very much of Birmingham in 1768, when this significant John was born. Though he is described as of Rodborough, he is also said to be "late of Selly Hall in the County of Worcestershire," and was buried in the churchyard of Northfield, where has ever since been the family vault, on which the first inscription is "In memory of John Rodway, gentleman, late of this parish, who died November 21, 1833, age 65 years."

In this John Rodway we find our great-great-grandfather. His young brother, Samuel, who went into the Royal Navy, was associated with the Lord Viscount Nelson. Duncan's

Life of Lord Nelson, published by Milner and Sowerby, Halifax, contains the passage:

"Captain Rusbrigh stood on this occasion as undaunted on the quarter-deck of the *Vagrien*, as when a lieutenant on board the *Formidable* under the gallant Rodway on the 12th of April, 1782."

"The gallant Rodway" introduced his great commander's name into the family by calling his son Horatio Nelson Rodway, and at the time when the record was prepared there was a Samuel Horatio Rodway, a direct descendant, living at Selly Oak.

We must go back once more to John Rodway "of Rodborough, late of Selly Hall,"—great-great-grandfather Rodway. His importance as a branch of the family tree is intensified by the fact that his wife, whom he married on September 22nd, 1800, at Aston Parish Church, was Susannah, only child of John and Susannah Barron, of Aston Cross. The Barrons were a very ancient family, descended from the Fitzgeralds, Earls of Kildare (forbears of the Dukes of Leinster), and originally from the Geraldini or Gherardini of Italy. A Barron was esquire to Henry VI, as we learn from Fuller's *Worthies*. Susannah Barron's parents were tenants of the Holte Estate, and it was the noble family of Holte who formerly held Aston Hall, where Philip Rodway was born.

Selly Hall, which was great-great-grandfather John's residence, is still standing, but has been built into the Convent of Saint Paul at Selly Oak.

John Rodway and his wife Susannah had three sons, the eldest of whom was our great-grandfather, John Barron Rodway. Samuel, the sailor, also had a son named John, and thereby hangs a tale, for while our great-grandfather as a boy did a great deal of travelling in Wales, Holland, France, etc., his cousin stayed at home; and John the elder, instead of his own son, took into partnership his nephew, who became a shining light in both business and civic affairs. In

Birmingham's first Municipal Elections he was returned at the top of the poll in the Radical interest for St. Martin's Ward, subsequently receiving an aldermancy. A street, not now existent, was named after him.

It is perhaps not surprising that great-grandfather let slip the opportunity of joining his father in business, for his tastes ran on different lines. From uncle Alfred's notes we find that this John was one of the bucks of the Regency period, and that his diaries contain references to his friendship with the Prince Regent, Lord Brougham, and others.

The second son of John and Susannah, James, attained the dignity of an Alderman of Lytham, and the third, Major Henry Barron Rodway, settled at Torquay.

This military great-great-uncle of ours had a special claim to distinction, as may be judged from the following extract from *The Times* of March 4th, 1881, which refers to "Major Rodway, D.V.R., the originator of the Volunteer Movement":

> "In 1852, seven years before the Volunteer Movement became general, Mr. Rodway, at the desire of the Duke of Somerset, Earl Fortescue and other gentlemen, raised a company of riflemen under Royal warrant. In 1853 he received his commission as captain of this company."

He died at Vale Lodge, Torquay, at the age of seventy. (His wife, Elizabeth Allin, before her marriage had lived for some time in a curious old house known as the "Flag," on the site of the present Council House, Birmingham.) Their son, Major William Henry Rodway, also held a commission in the Devon Regiment. This he received on May 8th, 1858, and was "with several of the young nobility and gentry on the staff of Sir James Brooke, Rajah of Sarawak."

Incidentally, our grandfather and his cousin Barron were among the earliest members of the Birmingham volunteers. Dr. Langford, in his treatise upon Birmingham, speaks of "the excellent shooting of Mr. Rodway."

Thus from John Rodway, our great-grandfather, and his

wife Margaret Hadley of Penkridge, Staffordshire, continues our descent. He died on January 29th, 1869, and sleeps with his fathers at Northfield. He left a family of three sons and several daughters, one of whom married a direct descendant of the famous Vice-Admiral John Benbow (1650-1702).

His eldest son, our grandfather, (the first Rodway, so far as we have traced, to be named Alfred,) was born at a small country estate, Pil Glas, near Llanstephan, in Carmarthenshire, on November 18th, 1836, where for his Godfather he had Alderman John Palmer, afterwards Mayor of Birmingham.

When he married Mary Maria, eldest daughter of Councillor John Inshaw of Birmingham, he also endowed us with a brilliantly clever great-grandfather. The Inshaws—originally Ainshaw or Aynshaw, an ancient Yorkshire family—were related to the late Rt. Rev. Edward Benson, Archbishop of Canterbury, Primate of all England.

Great-grandfather Inshaw was recognised as one of the foremost authorities of the day on mechanical engineering—sure of a place in history if only by one of his many inventions, the twin screw. His obituary notices give some of his most interesting achievements, which we feel should be included since they went to the making of Midland history. His death took place on January 13th, 1893, at Laburnam Cottage, Aston, in his eighty-sixth year.

"Councillor Inshaw from his earliest youth" (we quote from the *Birmingham Daily Post*) "manifested a keen interest in the utilisation of mechanical forces, and especially in the earlier developments of the steam engine. He invented a steam pressure gauge and tried a number of experiments with a view to promoting the use of steam for canal boats: but owing to the destructive operation of the wash upon the banks, the employment of steamers upon the narrow canals had been discouraged. Prior to the construction of the Stour Valley Railway, he carried on a series of 'fly boats' on the canal between Birmingham and Wolverhampton on special occasions such as the Wolverhampton races.

For this purpose, in 1853, he built some boats with a screw propeller upon each side of the rudder—*the original twin screw*. One of these boats won for the inventor a prize of 100 guineas in a contest which was held on the Regent's Canal in London. The great fête which took place at Aston Hall in aid of the General Hospital funds, in 1856, owed much of its success to Mr. Inshaw,* who brought the whole of the visitors from the Black Country to Aston by boats, as he also did two years later on the occasion of the official opening of Aston Park and Hall by Queen Victoria and the Prince Consort."

Grandfather Rodway, who married the daughter of this notable engineer, was a well-known figure in the public life of Birmingham for many years. When a boy, he was apprenticed to his prospective father-in-law with a view to learning the theory of engineering, but he never took kindly to cog-wheels, pistons, and mathematical calculations, although he was a facile draughtsman. His bent was towards art and literature, natural history and botany.

After his marriage to Mary Inshaw, in 1864, he took up his official residence in Aston Hall, holding the appointment which soon after his death was split up into three, Sir Whitworth Wallis becoming the Keeper of the Museums and Art Gallery (the position now held by Mr. S. C. Kaines Smith), Mr. J. Cox the Superintendent of Baths, and Mr. Samuel Hearne the Keeper of the Parks.

In 1880 he received, "in recognition of his valuable services to the borough," a gold watch and chain, and grandmother was presented with "a suite of jewellery." The *Gridiron* of August 14th published the following tribute:

"Mr. Rodway was, we believe, the first curator of Aston Hall under the Corporation, and so well did he perform the duties of that office that he won the confidence of the Baths and Parks Committee, and was appointed Superintendent of Parks, a position which is no sinecure, when we consider how wide apart the various parks and recreation grounds lie, and that they are considerably over 200 acres in extent.

"As one wanders through the rooms of Aston Hall, glancing

*Appendix.

THE ARMS OF PHILIP RODWAY, ESQ.,

of Birmingham, in ye County of Warwick

A.D. 1903

The Arms of Rodway, formerly Lords of the Manor of Rodway in the County of Warwick, are entered in the Books of His Majesty's College of Arms.

Arms. 1st and 4th for Rodway. Argent on a fesse azure. Three roses or between three bugle-horns stringed sable.

2nd and 3rd. Gules a cheveron argent, between three garbs or.

The shield is differenced in the fesse point with an annulet argent for Philip Rodway the fifth son.

Crest. A roebuck trippant proper.

Motto. Dum Spiro Spero.

Ye Arms of
Alderman Giles Rodway,
twice Mayor of the City of Gloucester,
A.D. 1697, 1708
(*cf.* De Rodway, Lords of Rodway,
1086)

Le Forestier,
Hunter to the King,
Overlord of Rodway
and Arden,
1086

De Loges,
Lords of Rodway,
Temp. Edward II

The Rose of Rodway

The affinity will be observed between all these, also with the Arms of De Wyrley, Sub Venators or under Foresters, Lords of Cannock. The Rodway Arms were originally minus the horns, which were added as a badge of office. The roebuck which is the Crest of the present Rodways appears on the Arms of De Loges for the Honour of Rodway.

but carelessly, perhaps, at the thousands of small shells and insects so neatly arranged in the glass cases, but little thought is given to those by whose busy hands and intelligent care they have been preserved and classified. That this is no light labour, all those who know the condition of the collection once existing in the museum of Queen's College as it was handed over to Mr. Rodway, and as it is now, will bear testimony. This collection had been allowed to fall into decay, every specimen bore evidences of neglect, and it was only by such loving care as we seldom, unfortunately, find, that Mr. Rodway was enabled to preserve that portion of the collection which is now looked upon as one of the greatest treasures of Aston Hall.*

"Then a stroll through Cannon Hill Park or Small Heath Park creates a feeling of surprise at the results obtained from the comparatively small yearly sum allowed the Baths and Parks Committee for the purposes of floral decoration. Wherever we turn in our public parks, the impress of Mr. Rodway's care and example may be witnessed, care which no money wage can purchase, and which it is therefore well to recognise in some other manner.

"Several years ago we read, with much interest, a novel written by Mr. Rodway, and so highly pleased were we with its excellent lessons that we had hoped ere this to have had the opportunity of reading something more from his pen. If this was the author's first attempt at public writing, let us assure him that it was equal to his supervision of Parks and Museums, and if he can find time for another attempt, we advise him to make it."

Incidentally, we have a long poem of his—*An Ode on the Death of General Havelock*—written, and printed, at the age of twenty-two.

For twenty years he lived at Aston Hall, and it was there on June 5th, 1885, that he died, when only forty-six, from a chill caught while making the rounds of the various parks under his supervision. His funeral was an impressive ceremony—the cortège the longest within memory. Eight representatives of the eight parks then owned by the Borough bore him to the family grave at Northfield, and many civic leaders, amongst them Aldermen White and Barrow, and Councillors Godfree, Clark, and Shannon, followed.

---

*This was the nucleus of our present Art Gallery.

And so we come at last to Philip Rodway's own generation. He was one of fifteen children—eight sons and seven daughters. The eldest and the youngest died, Ada when only five years old, and little Digby at six months—they, too, rest at Northfield.

Philip was the fifth son; Alfred, Will, George, and Gilbert his seniors, and John, Harold, and Digby his younger brothers; of his sisters, Ada, the eldest, he never saw; then came Laura, Rose, Lily, Annie, Violet, and Daisy . . . but of the children's early life in Aston Hall you may read, if you will, in the next chapter.

If we seem to have lingered overlong with our Family Tree, we must advance the plea that delineation of the background of any picture is an essential to its composition. We need have no regrets if by its medium we are able to make the central figure on our canvas stand forth more clearly.

Heredity goes a long way towards making the man, and our purpose has been to show that the form of Philip Rodway, imposed on this ancestral background, was likely to take on a strong, definite, many-sided character. In his veins ran the blood of men who had helped to write English history; the sturdy Saxon stock had been enriched by alliance with bold fighters, men of science, men of art. He had true title to all that is meant by tradition in the best sense.

From a pen and ink drawing by his father, 1871

ASTON HALL

Where Philip Rodway was born

1876

CHAPTER 2
(1876-1885)

The curtain rises on Aston Hall—Conan Doyle attends the birth of Philip
Rodway—Atmosphere of the old Hall—Glimpses into its historic past; Sir
Thomas Holte; King Charles I; Washington Irving and Bracebridge Hall—
Early childhood days—Some ghost stories—The swinging chair; claustro-
phobia—His father's death, June, 1885—Rhododendrons—The funeral
procession—Good-bye to the Hall.

*The curtain rises on Aston Hall in the year 1876. It is October
21st—Trafalgar's Day—and in a room in the great south wing is set
the first scene of our play.*

Many are the tales of adventure which the late Sir Arthur
Conan Doyle has given to us, yet when, as a young and
almost unknown doctor, he ushered on to the stage of the world
that autumn morning the little Philip Rodway, he was bringing into existence a life which was to be as full of romance as
one of his own stories.

And the setting—Aston Hall! History and strange adventure at every turn of twilit staircase and creaking landing; an
atmosphere so charged with tradition, so instinct with memories, that it could not but cast its spell over the least sensitive
among us. How, then, might it colour the impressionable
mind of youth; how even more intensely could it influence
so imaginative and contemplative a nature as that of the young
Philip Rodway.

History hid in the half-light of years! Slip quietly back
into the past with us, and know, then, that even before the
Norman Conquest, the Manor of Aston—in those days Estone
or East Town—was possessed by Edwin Earl of Mercia.
William the Conqueror bestowed it upon William Fitz Ans-
culf, lord of the neighbouring castle of Dudley, and the lords
of Dudley held it for several generations before it was given
by one of them, Ralph Someri, in the beginning of the reign
of King John, to William de Erdington and his heirs for ever.
And therewith went the curious grant "That the manor
house should be held by him . . . by the service of a pair of
gilt spurs payable yearly at Easter."

From the de Erdingtons, through the Maidenhaches, whose daughter Sibel conveyed it by marriage to Adam de Grymesurwe, it came in 1367 to John Atte Holt, of Duddeston, near Birmingham, and by his family it was held for the next 400 years.

The Aston Hall of to-day still carries the imprint of its founder, who in 1602 received his baronetcy, and thereupon began the enclosing of the park and later the erection of the hall—which took him seventeen years to complete. Even to-day above the doorway one may trace the inscription:

"Sir Thomas Holte of Duddeston in the Countie of Warwick, Knight and Baronet, began to build this house in Aprill Anno Domini 1618: in the 16th yeare of the raigne of King James of England, and of Scotland the One and Fiftieth; and the sa de Sir Thomas Holte came to dwell in this house in May Anno Domini 1631, in the seaventh yeare of the raigne of our sovereign Lord King Charles, and he did finish this house in Aprill Anno Domini 1635 in the eleventh yeare of the raigne of the sayde King Charles.

"Laus Deo."

With its lofty towers, capped by the closed ogee roofs, its embayed windows with their pierced parapets, and the groups of octagonal chimneys, it remains a fine example of the style of architecture developed in the reign of England's Maiden Queen, and it may well be that the centre and two side wings are indeed emblematic of the initial letter of Elizabeth.

It is this same Sir Thomas of whom the story runs that one day, being displeased with the dish set before him at dinner, he promptly "tooke a cleever and hytt hys cooke with the same cleever uppon the heade, and clave his head; that one syde fell uppone one of his shoulders, and the other syde on the other shoulder."

Dame Rumour has it that the Bloody Hand which appears in the armorial bearings of the Holtes had reference to this incident, but, as is not unusual, she is misinformed. It is actually the Red Hand of Ulster, which the Holtes had received permission to incorporate, and which is itself the centre of another legendary story of the time of that first O'Neill, who approaching Ulster from the sea, laid claim to it by the drastic expedient of cutting off his own hand and throwing it on to the shore, thereby fulfilling the condition that "he whose hand shall first touch land" should be the rightful owner.

It was in October, 1642, on the nights of Sunday and Monday, the 16th and 17th, that Charles I, whose army was marching from Shrewsbury to relieve Banbury Castle, stayed at Aston as the guest of the loyal old Baronet; and this visit has invested the hall with an undying interest, as identifying it with the fortunes of the ill-fated King.

The people of Birmingham warmly supported the Parliamentary cause, and the day after King Charles left Aston they seized the carriages containing his plate and other articles, which they carried for security to Warwick Castle.

On the 3rd of April the following year they resisted Prince Rupert, who with a force of 1,800 men was marching towards Lichfield on his way to the north, but they were defeated with considerable loss. This, however, did not damp their zeal, and rumours of danger the next December led Sir Thomas Holte to apply to Colonel Leveson, Governor of Dudley Castle, for a guard of soldiers for protection, so that on the 18th of that month forty musketeers were placed in the Hall.

On the 26th the townspeople of Birmingham, numbering 1,200, commenced their attack upon the Hall. The marks of the cannonading are still visible on the walls of the south-west wing, and show that it must have been very severe. The array brought against the Hall was probably assisted by a detachment of gunners and soldiers of Cromwell's party, as the choice of ground for the attack showed much more skill than an undisciplined assembly, unacquainted with the science of gunnery, could have possessed.

The attack continued on the 27th, and on the 28th, after

twelve of the Royalists had been killed, the gallant defenders surrendered their fortress—though not before they had inflicted a loss of sixty on the enemy. On the day of the surrender five of the Royalists killed during the defence of the Hall were buried in Aston Churchyard.

The old Baronet suffered severely for his loyalty. Immediately after its surrender the Hall was plundered, many of the family papers lost, and Sir Thomas himself imprisoned. His household goods were confiscated for the second time, his estates decimated, and contributions forced from him to the amount of £20,000.

When he died, in November, 1654, he was succeeded to the title and estates by his grandson, Sir Robert Holte, who, according to the provisions contained in his will, built the almshouses in the village of Aston.

He in turn was succeeded by his son, Sir Charles, in whose time the Hall again became the centre of military occupation, though happily of a more peaceful nature. Sir Charles was a warm but cautious adherent of James II, and in the troublous times of the revolution soldiers were twice quartered at Aston, in the November of 1688, possibly to watch the inhabitants of Birmingham, and at the same time to protect the family, as Sir Charles himself was absent—presumably in concealment.

The hall remained in the possession of the Holtes until, on the death of Sir Charles in 1782, the estates reverted to Mr. Legge, who after the death of the Dowager Lady Holte took up his abode there till 1817, when an act of Parliament was obtained to sanction the sale of the estate.

Within a few years Washington Irving, the famous American writer, had been so charmed with the old Hall on his visit there that he had given it a new immortality in his book *Bracebridge Hall*. A Bracebridge had married a Holte, (1775—Abraham Bracebridge of Atherstone married Mary Elizabeth, the only child and heiress of Sir Charles Holte,) and the hospitality their family showed to Irving during the

Christmas season, with its typical English revels, made a lasting impressing on the creator of *Rip Van Winkle*.

Some years after this James Watt, the son of the great engineer, lived at Aston Hall, where he died on June 2nd, 1848. Eventually, subscribed for by the Corporation and benefactors, the Park and Hall were formally opened and inaugurated by Queen Victoria and the Prince Consort, on June 15th, 1858, as a "Free Hall and Park for ever."

And so, a year or two later, it came about that Alfred Rodway took up his official residence at the Hall, from which he controlled the Museum, Parks, and Baths of the Borough of Birmingham.

*   *   *

Such, then, is the story of Aston Hall; such the atmosphere of legend and tradition into which the little Philip Rodway was born.

There he spent his childhood; played in the Long Gallery; marshalled imaginary soldiers in what was once the guard-room of the forty musketeers; explored by many a twilight the fearsome regions of Dick's Garret. . . .

A happy family of brothers and sisters they were: seven boys and six girls, and for their games or study were all the wonderful possibilities of the rambling old hall, wherein the magic of make-believe was with them all the while.

Their sweet but strong-minded little mother, and their tall black-browed father they adored—though with the awe and reverence expected of children in those days, when to be seen and not heard was the first counsel of perfection.

And of this there is a touching little episode. . . .

The family used to assemble at a great round table for their meals. Fifteen to be served! It is hardly surprising that somebody *might* on occasion be forgotten. And once somebody was. It happened to be Philip—and it was his favourite pudding!

Endeavouring to live up to the ideal of "never speak until you're spoken to," little Phil watched with growing hopelessness the rapidly diminishing rhubarb pie on the plates of his more fortunate brothers and sisters.

It was no use. Nobody would ever notice him. Two big tears slowly ran down his cheeks and dropped upon the white table cloth before him.

"Why, Philip, old man!" At last his father's eye had found him, and watched by fourteen pairs of eyes he now received in state his own particular piece of pie.

Their father called the children his "Knights of the Round Table," and he had little wooden swords made for them, with which they used to drill and parade. At that time there was a local paper called the *Aston Chronicle*, the editor of which, William Hughes, would often visit the Hall and make up poetry about the family. One poem, composed

> *"To celebrate*
> *Young Philip Rodway's Birth,"*

naturally made a special appeal to its little hero, and he would trot it out at all times, seemly and unseemly, in a most dramatic style, with his quaint little lisp:

> *"A go-cart thoon will make him thtrong,*
> *And then with thord in hand*
> *In brave defenth of Athton Hall*
> *He'll with the otherth thtand."*

(A go-cart was a contraption to teach babies to walk.)

He used to stand in the Long Gallery and declaim the three stanzas long before he wore suits.

Philip was always rather different from the others in the contemplative and reflective side of his nature, which from the first was very strongly developed. Often he would be found in the old chapel, chin in hand, gazing into space, his mind worlds away.

His eldest sister used to say to him:

"What are you thinking about, Philip?"

"Well, you thee," he lisped, "I am thinking thum thecret thingth, and if I tell you I shall not have them come to me again, and they are tho utheful to me."

HIS FATHER AND MOTHER

1864

It must have been one of these thoughts being useful to him that prompted him to ask:

"Pleath, could you give me a ha'penny, tho that I could make my fortune?"

"Why, Philip, how could a ha'penny make your fortune?"

"Well, you thee, I could buy a ha'penny nurley* and learn to play football with it and be the bethth player in all the world and make my fortune and then I thould give you your ha'penny back."

He was a cheery little soul, so brown and dark and fat that his father used to call him "Cetewayo" after the South African chief. He had black curly hair, blue eyes, a wide frank smile, and an unbounded optimism, with his fair share of the love of mischief.

One of his great games came at bath time, when the twelve children, with their eldest sister in charge of affairs, would line up for their nightly tub. His particular joy was never to wait for his turn, but to keep bobbing backward and forward and appearing at the head of the queue, generally upsetting the sequence and anything else he happened to pass.

Laura, her mother's right hand, and the most devoted elder sister children ever had, must have found her hands full every second of the day. Even to know where everyone was would have been a whole-time job in itself.

One afternoon they were playing hide-and-seek, running more or less wild over the entire Hall. There were wonderful opportunities for concealment, and of course the more blood-curdling the *locale* the better.

There was the tiny room in the roof, lit only by the narrowest of slit-windows, where a century before some mad member of the Holte family was kept confined. So the story ran, with the sometime alternative that it was the youngest daughter of the house, who for years had been kept shut up there because she would not marry the man of her parents' choice.

---

*A little wooden ball.

C

There was the one-time guardroom of the forty musketeers, whose shades must surely still patrol the old Hall in whose defence they fought against the Roundheads, so many sleeping years ago; and the Long Gallery, where ancestral portraits looked down upon the world from the angle of eternity. . . .

There was that gruesome garret in the Clock Tower—long and low and dark—and thereby hangs a sinister tale, that tells of the hanging from one of the beams of the manservant Dick, who by taking his life has given his name to those attic regions as long as they may exist.

There was the landing where legend will have it the white lady walks in the quiet of the night; and King Charles's bedchamber, huge and forbidding; and loneliness growing in room beyond room; dark turns and twists in the great oaken staircases; cupboards and crannies that lurk in the wall; and big open fireplaces, lost in a blackness as deep as—the secret "hide" under the stairs!

For this was the greatest thrill of all—the swinging chair that covered a secret hiding place of olden days. Whether at one time it may have been a Roman Catholic priest-hole, or whether it was simply an extraordinarily ingenious contrivance of the original builder, no one knows—but against the dark oak panelling of the hall, below the third section of the staircase, stands an exquisitely carved arm-chair of heavy oak, and this, on the removal of a pin near the floor, swings silently aside to reveal a hidden room.

It is a tiny chamber, only six feet by ten, lying in eerie darkness behind its closed chair door. Until a very few years ago the skeleton of an unknown woman, whose bones were discovered under the floor of the little chapel, used to sit in a corner, so that one may imagine the potential horrors of the place. (We shall meet this skeleton in another chapter!)

On the afternoon in question, then, the children, tiring of hide-and-seek, invented a variation. One of the hiders, just for fun, shut the seeker into the secret room, and in the excitement of the game promptly forgot all about him.

THE SWINGING CHAIR
THE SECRET HIDE IN ASTON HALL
In which Philip was shut as a child in 1883

It was Philip again! For how long he was mislaid was never known, but some hours elapsed before he was eventually discovered, and when at last he did emerge into the light once more, for ever after he was to bear the mental imprint of that incident in the *claustrophobia* which never left him throughout his life. So intensely do our earliest experiences affect us; so is it that the joke thoughtlessly played upon a six-year-old may go echoing down the years, to find its last grim expression in the Press of half a century later, when after his death appeared the dramatic posters "Birmingham Theatre Magnate's Fear of Burial Alive."*

The entire atmosphere of the old Hall was conducive to a complete sense of unreality, "full of noises, sounds, and strange airs" which, if they did not, like those of Prospero's island, "give delight and hurt not," could create a good many uncanny situations.

As when, in the dead of night, once was heard from the kitchen regions a sound of ghostly clanking, faint, but distinct, as if of chains or steel; then silence, then a weird and dismal wailing. . . . And did not thoughts fly back two hundred years and more to that first Sir Thomas Holte who took hys cleever and hytt hys cooke? . . . And was the spirit of that unlucky cooke doomed perhaps to haunt those same kitchens, for ever spoiling that same dish and being hytt with that same cleever?

Now the clanks and muffled wails were mingled together in an awe-ful harmony, and ghost or no ghost, grandfather felt it was time to investigate. Downstairs he went, near and nearer to the mystifying sounds. On the threshold of the great kitchen he stopped abruptly.

There, in a pool of moonlight and milk, his head firmly fixed in the top of a can, was Tiddles, the family tortoiseshell cat, hopelessly, helplessly banging about, howling dismally the while, and with every clank becoming more tightly jammed.

---

*This referred to a clause in his Will.

A simple explanation, but——it might not have been so! And to this day uncle Gilbert tells us the story of how he and Philip slept together in a room of which the door would open slowly—and a little old man, hooded and cloaked, would peer at them gravely and slowly vanish again.

But speaking of simple explanations . . .

The children often used to play together the game called "Speculation" for nuts. One day Philip was having very bad luck, which was most unusual for him.

Suddenly he got up from his place and went across the room, saying "Wait a minute." He stood solemnly by the window, apparently lost in thought. Then he returned to the table with a beaming face, and his luck, from the moment he sat down again, was amazing.

"Why did you go over there?" asked Laura, curiously.

"I will tell you when I go to bed," he replied.

And at bedtime he whispered to his sister; "I thaid, pleath God make me win thum nuths and He thaid, 'All right Philip, I will;' and He did."

His sense of honour and of right and wrong was always a very strong point with him. But there were times when he was sorely tried; for instance, one blazing July afternoon, aged about five, he had been entrusted with a penny and sent to fetch an ice-cream. He got there safely and duly exchanged the coin clenched in his hot little fist for a chilly ice-cream.

He started back. The sun shone strongly; the ice started to melt. It began to run over the side of its wafer. It seemed a pity to let it fall and be wasted. Better lick it off. A tentative tongue tidied up the softening wafer. Again it overflowed; again was trimmed down smaller and yet smaller by careful licking of the boundaries, "to prevent it," as he argued to himself, "from melting away." And so Philip arrived back at the Hall. Arrived alone—for of that ice-cream with which he started home there now was nothing left.

How could he possibly explain? He looked up at his sister despairingly. "You thee—" he began.

"Yes, I see, Philip," she replied quietly. Of course at that he confessed, and was forgiven, but it was a long time before he forgave himself.

One of the saddest notes of childhood days was sounded for them, ironically enough, once more in the midst of laughter and play.

In the great barn there was fixed to a rafter in the roof a pulley with a rope. They devised a plan whereby they could attach a big basket to this rope, and give each other rides up and down. Everything was well for the first few times, and the thrill and novelty of the thing went right to their heads.

Daisy, the baby, was as a great privilege allowed her turn, and amid shrieks of excitement was hauled up to the ceiling, with their big collie dog in the basket beside her.

No one knew how it happened; something went wrong; the basket descended with a rush. Little Daisy hit the floor heavily, and her spine was injured. And so she became the Peter Pan of the family, never to attain her full height, save in sweetness of disposition and depth of character, in which daily she grew more and still more; for throughout her life her love and sympathy were ever ready for those who had the slightest need.

For a few more happy years Philip Rodway's childhood was spent in Aston Hall, until the chord of tragedy was struck which was to alter the whole course of his life.

His father had so much increased the scope of his work that all the parks and grounds belonging to the Borough of Birmingham had long since come under his supervision, and were laid out under his direction (even to the minutest detail, for it was he who caused to be planted the ivy which made picturesque the severed trunk of every old felled tree). It happened one day that he had taken Philip with him, in the high two-wheeled gig which was the official vehicle of that time, he himself driving the chestnut mare. There was no hood to the carriage—and it began to rain. It poured incessantly during the whole of their journey from Aston Hall to Calthorpe Park, from Calthorpe Park to Rednal and the Lickey Hills, and thence to Sutton Park and back again to Aston. They arrived home at the Hall soaked through, and his father had caught the chill from which he was never to recover. He was then scarcely forty-six years old.

And so it was that while little Philip was playing in the old gardens among the flaming rhododendrons, in the June of '85, there was brought to him the news of his father's death. For ever after he almost dreaded those brilliant flowers, and he never again saw them in bloom without remembering and speaking of that tragic June 5th.

His youthful feelings were harrowed to the uttermost. The imaginative child was spared nothing; he and all his brothers and sisters—thirteen children—were taken in coaches to their father's burial, and the length and misery of that journey from the Hall to Northfield can better be imagined than described.

A little while more of the saddest memories . . . and they left the old Hall amid scenes of the deepest gloom. His father and his happy childhood days were gone for ever, and the silence of the centuries descended upon the home he had loved so well.

Such were Philip Rodway's early days; so is it that his daughters hold in even greater reverence the history and memories enshrined in Aston Hall.

CHAPTER 3

(1885-1890)

Then the schoolboy—His early years—Prize lists—Amateur theatricals;
W. S. Gilbert, Dickens, and Shakespeare—A prophetic Dame; P.R. as
Mrs. Squeers—The Technical School—*Enter* Ethel Brown.

> " . . . *with his satchel*
> *And shining morning face . . ."*
> —*As You Like It.*

Jaques' schoolboy crept like snail unwillingly to school, but
not so the little Philip Rodway, so eager, so pathetically eager,
for the knowledge that his father's death had put so much
further from his grasp. He was a voracious reader, and no
doubt smiled ironically at Jaques' laggard scholar before he
was ten years of age.

His mother, left with the large family of children to
bring up, did her utmost for them, and the boys and girls
helped with all their will; but at the very best it was a poor
travesty of the sheltered and protected homelife in which
they had revelled. But a family united cannot fall. Though
their beloved father had gone, they stuck staunchly together,
with much roughing it, few comforts, and never a luxury for
a long time to come. They were sad years, so widely different
from the years they would have enjoyed at Aston Hall. But
hope never left them, and gradually their fortunes took a
turn for the better as the children grew older and added their
early salaries to the family exchequer.

From the brighter moments of Philip's schooldays we have
chosen the following extracts. The Rev. G. H. Moore (Chaplain for thirty years of the Queen's Hospital) writes:

"The memories of an old schoolmaster are very tender, but so
full of the intimacies of family life that it is by no means an easy
matter to write dispassionately on any one character.

"We met as master and pupil in 1886, and I can well recall the
boy, Phil Rodway, as a human personality, full of unknown
elements of power and possibilities of achievement.

"My real joy and pride in his friendship came twenty years later, when he gave me the right hand of fellowship, and spoke of me to his friends as 'My old schoolmaster.' A pedagogue has, or had, few material returns for his labour, yet he gains a rich reward if he be found worthy enough to retain the sweet gratitude and simple affection of youth.

"Other links in the golden chain of mutual appreciation deepened the friendship which had been engendered in earlier years. Such influences never die—they may change, but their effect is still the same. The friendship of master and pupil became the brotherhood of the Press Club, and later the pride of the master who sees his pupil occupying the master's chair."

To the courtesy of two more of his schoolmasters, Mr. Yoxall and Mr. R. A. Clarke, we owe our records of Philip at the age of ten, when he entered the Old Meeting School in April, 1887. Not far away in the same register are the names of Walter and Charles Hyde; who would have guessed that years later, as a noted operatic tenor, Walter would be singing in a theatre of which his erstwhile playfellow had become managing director?

In the light of his later place in the world of the stage we were interested to find (interspersed with the prize lists: 1888, Class VII, Philip Rodway. Silvio Pellico, *Merchant of Venice.* Easter 1889, Philip Rodway. The Redfern Prize, Tennyson's Poems, etc.), some treasured old programmes, and a cutting from the *Inquirer* of November 29th, 1890, which under the heading of "Birmingham Old Meeting Schools" remarks:

"During the winter the pupils of these schools, with their parents and friends, are given some very pleasant concerts. The programme of the latest concert, which took place on November 19th in the large schoolroom before a dense audience, shows that the plan has been adopted of making juveniles perform in the same concert with their elders. The teachers, who hold these entertainments about every two months, may be congratulated on the high character of their programmes, and on winning the approval of very large audiences by performances which are educative as well as enjoyable.

". . . The Dogberry scenes from *Much Ado About Nothing* were capitally rendered by boys. In addition to recitations and music, there was a most amusing finale in the shape of a dramatic version of the good old story of 'I vant deux fly,' the unfortunate Frenchman being cleverly represented by Philip Rodway, another boy of these schools, *who exhibits unusual power over audiences*."

That particular sketch must have been one after his own heart, so dearly did he love his fishing. The programme ran:

FARCE IN ONE ACT
FLY FISHING
Scene at Redditch

Monsieur de la Gudgeon (French prisoner out on parole).....Philip Rodway
John Bull-y-head (Proprietor of shop).........................Thos. J. Stevens
Mary Jane Fisher (Servant to above)...............................Lizzie Leach
Alderman de Worms (Mayor of Redditch)...................Herbert Simpson
Bobby Katch-em-alive (Chief Constable of the plaice)........Albert Knight

In the programmes of all these concerts—whether at the "Scholars' Christmas Party, on Monday, December 20th, 1889; tea at 5, and after tea a concert, followed by carols, and the presentation of New Year cards," or "at Kingswood Chapel, Holywood, in the New Lecture Hall"—Philip's name appears, either in some of his beloved Thomas Hood's poems, or possibly in a Dickensian sketch, such as *Bob Sawyer's Party*.

Apparently his star turns in the recitation line were *The Jackdaw of Rheims* by Thomas Barham (of the *Ingoldsby Legends*), followed closely by Mark Twain's *The Difficulty about that Dog*, Hood's *Pain in a Pleasure Boat*, W. S. Gilbert's *Ode to the Terrestrial Globe*, and that little poem which even now catches at the heartstrings:

> "*I remember, I remember,*
> *The house where I was born,*
> *The little window where the sun*
> *Came peeping in at morn. . . .*"

How often have we heard the story of the very first of these recitations. The great night arrived; so did the audience. The curtains were drawn apart, and Phil marched on to the stage, made his bow, and said his little piece. It was rewarded with its round of applause. He bowed again . . . and—stayed where he was! There he remained in the centre of the stage until he was literally dragged off. As he plaintively used to explain—"I knew how to go on, and how to say my little piece, but nobody had ever said anything to me about going off."

On Sunday, June 8th, 1890, he read the lesson (Psalm XIX) at the Church service, and it is noted that "great interest was shown by both schools"!

The Stage, however, soon claimed him again from the Church, for the next entry shows him as Jack Hopkins in a sketch from *The Pickwick Papers*, while his following appearance was as Mrs. Squeers in scenes from *Nicholas Nickleby*. (Had his first, and so far as we know only, venture in skirts any bearing on the Dame types which were to lend such distinction to his best pantomimes?)

His next step, at the age of fourteen, was to pass into the Technical School, where——*but an imperious knocking is coming from the next chapter!*

A very young lady demands admittance, and since she is to play a most important rôle in our story, we must let her in at once.

Enter Ethel Brown.

ETHEL BROWN

1895

CHAPTER 4
(1890-96)

"Who ever loved that loved not at first sight?"—*As You Like It.*

It was a sweet spring morning in the early nineties. Under
the two old oak trees which used to stand just inside the gates
of Calthorpe Park, in Speedwell Road opposite her home, a
little girl was playing happily with her dolls.

She was dressed, after the fashion of children in those days,
in a little navy blue sailor frock, anchors on its wide white
collar and cuffs, a short kilted skirt, from beneath which
appeared the neatest little legs and the trimmest ankles; and
a jaunty round sailor cap, with *H.M.S. Victory* in gold letters
on its band, perched on the fair curls which fell to her shoulders.

A dark, very serious schoolboy was walking thoughtfully
past. He caught sight of this pretty child, fell in love at first
sight, and then and there, from that very moment, decided
he would marry her and no one else.

From this decision he never wavered. He gravely informed
his mother of his determination, and this characteristic attitude of making up his mind and never changing it was ever
one of the strongest forces of his life.

The fact that he never spoke to her for two years had not
the slightest effect on the situation. He worshipped literally
from afar.

The fact that she did not love him until years after did not
alter the position in the least. She coloured his entire existence, and was his inspiration for the rest of his life.

Daddy (for you will have guessed it was he) persuaded
Mother (you knew it was she) always to save that little cap,
and it still reposes, with its faded legend, in the loft among
the memories of the past. How often have we heard him
tell the story of how, every morning after that first meeting,

he would run from the other side of the town, breakfastless, just to see her leave her home for school at half-past eight, and walk all the way on the other side of the road, without expecting, or getting, even a look, for she was quite unconscious of his existence.

And he would always finish up the story of this one-sided romance (sitting, as he usually did, on the edge of one of our beds, on his return home from the theatre after the play), "If ever woman was worshipped by man, that woman was your Mother." Sometimes, as an afterthought, he would add with a twinkle, "Why, God knows!"

(*Here the curtain must be lowered for a few minutes to denote the lapse of time.*)

We are back in the early nineties.

Queen Victoria on the throne; England peaceful and prosperous. It was the day of the hansom cab, when the sole means of getting to town was by a one-horse bus, known as the Royal Blue, leaving once each hour, holding about twelve passengers, and smelling strongly of the straw which was the only floor covering.

Think of it! No telephone, no wireless, no cinema nor gramophone, not an aeroplane, not a single motor car on the roads, no electricity, and even gas still in its infancy. The magic lantern and musical evenings at home were, except for a very occasional visit to a theatre, the only possible recreations (and in those days there were two theatres, perhaps a music hall and, of course, no picture houses of any kind).

Schooldays were passing, stormy and full of stress for Philip, while life was proving an easy and happy adventure for the little girl of the sailor frock. He had long since managed to effect an introduction to her, and she now accepted his adoration and gifts as a matter of course, though with his tiny allowance it was very often actual self-sacrifice —a box of chocolates for her usually meant no lunch for him.

It was about this time that cycling came in,* and Mother,

---

*Mother's diary records a new song of this period: "Daisy, Daisy, "or "A bicycle made for two"!

greatly daring, allowed herself to be given lessons by him. She had a machine (one of the new free wheels!) enamelled chocolate colour to match the very long and very full brown velvet dress which she wore for riding.

Although she could usually start, and in fact became quite an expert cyclist, she never really managed to get off, in the accepted sense of the word, alone and unaided, and always had to fall off into Daddy's, or, we regret to say, anyone else's arms with whom she happened to be riding.

Her diaries of the cycling period suggest that her time was fully occupied with this and other activities. It must have been the need for rigid economy of the fleeting moments that would account for words giving place to letters in certain places, and at times they become much too involved for her daughters to follow: Thus: "P.K.M.W.I.F.O." The last four letters, we think, may possibly stand for "When I fell off"— but why should Phil have *kicked* her? She was so obviously doing her best.

He was also privileged, together with a number of other honorary instructors, to teach her skating on Edgbaston Pool. In this young edition of the Gay Nineties set we read of Lal Hoskins, Hamilton Gray, Rose Davies, and Carl Metz, together with Jeannie Ettwell, Charlie Macpherson, and Harold and Ethel Stembridge. On a February day recorded in her diary, the gates of Edgbaston Hall were rushed and broken down by crowds impatient of delay, bonfires were lit on the banks, chestnuts roasted and coffee brewed, and the stars were paling when the last of the revellers returned home.

Ethel Brown may have been an apt pupil, but she was certainly a very ungrateful one, for her diary says, *Phil Rodway skates no better than I do. Too many jerks and starts.*

That same year the Thames was frozen over, and in Birmingham, as elsewhere, the water carts came round, a little bucket of fire in front, and a row of swinging buckets of water behind, these last to be sold for $1\frac{1}{2}$d. each.

They skated, too, on the pool at Cottesmore Priory, that

tragic pool which lies beyond the meadow-lands where are now the Priory Lawn Tennis Club's courts. There the young brother of their old friend Mrs. Sheffield, who owned the Priory, was drowned while skating when home for his holidays from Cambridge, and there her husband met his death many years afterwards. . . .

Philip had by now become a declared suitor. So, too, had a dozen others. We cannot attempt to keep pace with Mother's diaries.

He had become a habit; wherever she was, whatever she was doing, he was always there in the background. It was a mystery how he managed it. Summer holidays in those days of early excursion trains often meant getting up at an unearthly hour. On one occasion, at 4.30 in the morning, when she was getting into the cab with her mother and father to catch the 5 o'clock train to Aberystwyth, he was observed watching, as usual, from his vantage point of the same old oaks in Calthorpe Park. When they arrived at New Street station he was walking casually up and down the platform.

How did he do it?

If she was at a dance, although he disliked it on principle and never danced himself, he would appear from behind some pillar or in a doorway, watching her with gloomy disapproval, ready to see her safely home if he was allowed (which he generally wasn't). If he was, he invariably ruined his opportunities and her evening's enjoyment by a lecture on the evils of the world in general, and dancing in particular. Probably he was especially serious because the background of his life at this time, through the loss of his father, was sad coloured too.

But he was full of courage, initiative, and ambition, and concentrated all his energies in getting on; to be above all things thorough and conscientious. He undoubtedly had the brains of an organiser, and the personality of a leader.

He left the Technical School with high honours, and entered the solicitor's office of Herd and Nutt with the idea of becoming a barrister. The law and logic had always appealed to

ETHEL BROWN
(*Mother*)
AND HER PARENTS

him—but it was not to be. It was decided that funds would not run to it, and his hopes had to be abandoned.

About this time Philip effected one of his strategical moves. For some time his family had been discussing moving house; he saw to it that the new environment should be Edgbaston, and the house itself only a moment's walk from the home of Ethel Brown (and incidentally within a few minutes of our present home, The Woodlands). Needless to say, his family were quite unaware of any purpose underlying their choice.

Meanwhile, Mother had completed her studies at King Edward's Grammar School (Camp Hill), and Mason's College (now the University of Birmingham), and passed all her examinations qualifying her to be a teacher. One afternoon she was giving a lecture and illustrating it with sketches on the blackboard, when Mr. Airey, then head of the Education Department, happened to come in to listen. After it was over he went up to her on the platform, patted her on the shoulder and said, "Young lady, your drawing is being wasted here. You ought to be at the School of Art."

And if there is anything in heredity, he was right. She was the only daughter of that delightful old artist Edwin Harford Brown, who was for many years head lithographer to Sir J. T. Middlemore (of the family who founded the Middlemore Homes). Of her father, Philip always used to say "*he was like a pencil sketch himself*," fragile and delicate, full of a quiet gentleness and kindly tranquillity that was charming and restful in the extreme.

Had the comparison been continued he might have seen in her mother the likeness to an oil painting, in the rich colouring, strength of purpose, and depth of character in every line and tone.

And romance once more steps out of the past in the figure of her grandmother, Emma Harford,* who eloped at the age of sixteen from the Select Academy for Young Ladies at Bromsgrove, and ran away to Ireland with her young husband.

*See appendix: Lois's "*Story of the Sampler*."

And so Ethel Harford Brown inherited from her ancestors many qualities not often blended: the artistic temperament, in its true sense (so many have the temperament, so few the art); balancing it, most unusually, an intensely practical mind and a sure instinct for the value of things; and withal a love of adventure and a complete fearlessness of anything or anybody.

It is not surprising, therefore, that her artistic powers should at last proclaim themselves, striving to find an outlet, and that she, with her restless spirit and dislike of being tied down to the imparting of knowledge in other subjects to other people, should welcome the chance of studying what she loved best in all the world.

She sat for an entrance examination for the School of Art, gained a scholarship with flying colours, and from then onward spent her whole time there, sailing through all her examinations, and each subsequent year winning two or three overlapping scholarships.

"*You ought to be at the School of Art.*"

So strange are the ways of Fate. If that remark had not been made on that particular afternoon, the world of the Theatre might never have known Philip Rodway.

Solely so that he could see her coming out of the School of Art in the evenings, he looked round for something to occupy the time until 9.15, when her classes finished. His chief, Mr. James Herd, the solicitor, suggested that his friend Mr. "Tommy" Foster needed a clerk in the box office at the Prince of Wales Theatre, and that Philip might apply. He did so and was accepted for the post.

And so began his theatrical career, in the box office of the theatre to which, twenty-one years later, he was to return as managing director.

It was the first step on the road to honour and success, and it was the finger-post of romance that had pointed the way.

HARVINGTON

"Thatcholm" and "The Thatchways," now our country cottages

Leaves from an artist's sketchbook

CHAPTER 5

(1896-97)

It was towards the end of the pantomime season of 1896-97
that Philip Rodway broke into the gloriously uncertain,
hazardously attractive business which was to absorb the rest
of his working life. (The pantomime was *Cinderella*, in which
Eugene Stratton's magnetic singing and thistledown dancing
in Leslie Stuart's *Lily of Laguna* made him immediately the
idol of the city.)

Captain Rodgers was nearing the close of his distinguished
régime, and under him, as manager, was the genial "Tommy"
Foster, widely known and loved throughout the profession.
"My father" (writes Miss Elizabeth Foster) "was manager
when your late father came as a slim young man, indeed
almost a youth, to be in the box office. My father was
always very proud of his pupil. . . . I think it may be
said that each in his own particular day graced and enriched the profession he loved so well. We have the happiest
memories of Mr. Rodway's unfailing courtesy towards his
old chief and the members of his family."

The history of the Prince of Wales Theatre up to this time
is comparatively brief. It was originally intended as a "hall
for music," and equipped with a magnificent organ, when
it was built at a cost of £12,000 in 1856. Madame Clara
Novello, Sims Reeves, and Adelina Patti appeared on its
boards, but musical appreciation at that period was not
sufficient to carry it on, and in seven years an application for
a theatrical licence was made by James Scott of the Belfast
Theatre. After a very short ownership it was taken over by
W. H. Swanborough of the Royal Strand Theatre, and formally opened as "The Royal Music Hall and Operetta House."

D

In 1863, in honour of the marriage of the Prince of Wales, afterwards King Edward VII, it became "The Prince of Wales Operetta House," and soon afterwards it acquired its present name, "The Prince of Wales Theatre."

Mr. James Rodgers became lessee in 1866, and started a series of pantomimes and other productions. Ten years later the house was entirely reconstructed, and became the acknowledged home in Birmingham of D'Oyly Carte's companies in Gilbert and Sullivan operas, the late Sir Augustus Harris's famous spectacular burlesques, and George Edwardes' Gaiety productions.

After the death of James Rodgers the theatre was carried on by his son, Captain Rodgers, and it was during his régime that Philip Rodway's connection began. His post in the box office was naturally not a very remunerative one, but the extra money he earned must have been a godsend on top of the small salary paid him in the solicitor's office for his daytime services. It meant that he could add more to the family finances, and yet allow himself the little extra which made all the difference.

Beyond all that, it opened the door to a future which, though still vague, held promise of wonderful possibilities.

*　　*　　*

Now we must make our return to the School of Art, for, as we have shown at the close of the last chapter, it had everything to do with Philip Rodway entering the theatrical profession; and, for the next few years until he and Ethel Brown were married, many of their friends were "School of Art friends," and many of their activities its activities. Released from the rôle of student-teacher at Mason's College, now the University of Birmingham, she knew some of the happiest years of her life at the Central School of Art in Margaret Street. She was doing work (if indeed so much happiness could be called work) she loved, among surroundings and people she loved. There was even a charming symbolism in her walk there, along Paradise Street and through Eden Place.

"There was a star danced, and under that was I born," says Beatrice in *Much Ado about Nothing*, in extenuation of her vivacity. Another star must have danced on April 27th, 1880, for surely never was more vitality put into one small person than into the Ethel Brown of those days. Nor has it abated one jot in Mrs. Philip Rodway. Everything she does well she does quickly. So in those days she romped through her examinations, and scholarships fell to her nimble fingers. Her criticisms of painting and design were of extreme value and help to Daddy as a producer, and so the list of classes she attended is of interest. She took every subject from architecture to modelling in clay, painting from still life to figure drawing from life, cloisonné enamel work to historic ornament, miniature painting on ivory to landscape painting, illustrating in black and white to poster work in colour, and naturally geometry, perspective, and anatomy.

In this last class she actually used (without recognising it as such) the same skeleton which had been kept in the secret hide in Aston Hall in which Philip was shut when a little boy of six, and which had terrified her a few years later when she was taken to the Hall. It was only in after years that she was told its history. It appears that the guide in charge had a habit of suddenly slipping off the skull and placing it in the hands of the unsuspecting visitor. On one occasion he presented it to a young and impressionable American lady, who promptly dropped it and fainted, whereupon it was removed to the anatomy class at the School of Art, there to fulfil a more useful if less spectacular existence. Ethel Brown used to unhinge its arm and leg bones and thread up its vertebrae with the nonchalance born of familiarity.

Two of her early designs for stained glass windows, which used to hang upon our nursery wall, were the inspiration of the *Jack and Jill* and *Little Miss Muffet* pantomimes.

Her father, grandfather, and great-grandfather had all been

artists, and so hers was a lucky inheritance. When she married she lost the time to carry on her work, although never the interest in the paintings of others. With never a word of regret, she turned her energies into other channels; seeing that we children were preserved intact from the whirl of accident which she believed surrounded us, and that Daddy had every assistance possible to carry on his arduous work. She gave us three her unremitting attention, and it is but a slight return to acknowledge this, for there is little doubt that for us she let slip away a future of artistic possibilities. She even allowed to become a password of gaiety in the house her "Seventeen First Class Certificates" from South Kensington, each one a potential stepping stone to success.

It may be that in this book this is the only tribute we shall pay to the quaint humour, the loyalty, and the unselfishness of Mother. We want one figure, that of Daddy, to stand out from the canvas; but half discernible, there should always be close by (if only by implication), another figure hand in hand with his. Could Daddy know of this biography, he would wish it so. For she was everything to him, and he worked hard and long for her praise alone.

Ethel Brown of the dancing star is by nature a gay inconsequential person, who deliberately displays to the world the more frivolous elements in her character, and will hide from all but the most discerning the strength that lies at bedrock.

On the stage, charming modern inconsequences are always spoken by a friendly, petite actress, a Marion Lorne, or an Iris Hoey. They cultivate their natural talent for these, and the audience loves it. So it came about that in later years Daddy often likened Mother to this type. There must be an aptitude, an unconscious flair (for a forced inconsequentiality would be a most embarrassing thing). But these three ladies have the art to perfection, and that is possibly why they make such incomparable adjuncts to a party.

We have watched in imagination a fourteen-year-old Philip Rodway playing in *Nicholas Nickleby*. So at that early age he already knew his Dickens and his Ethel Brown; in his own mind then, and later in actual fact, her aptitude for astonishingly out-of-the-way references led to Daddy calling her his Mrs. Nickleby. Like that charming lady, she rarely reached the point of a story by the straight path, but in sight of the goal would strike off at a tangent to the complete bewilderment of the listener. Bewilderment, yes; but we must admit that she makes the side track so interesting that we find ourselves wandering down the bypaths too, and likely as not we forget the projected end of the journey.

(How Daddy loved the Dickens chapter containing "some romantic passages between Mrs. Nickleby and the Gentleman next door." How often has he quoted:

" 'My dear,' said Mrs. Nickleby, 'I don't know why it is, but a fine warm summer day like this, with the birds singing in every direction, always puts me in mind of roast pig, with sage and onion sauce and made gravy.' . . .

" 'That's a curious association of ideas, is it not, Mama?' ")

You see how it is! Already in her company we have wandered down a side path a long way from Eden Place and Margaret Street, and we must hurry back or we shall miss the century.

It is a truism that parents say "Things are not what they were in my young days." They never were. But there is some special meaning in the phrase when Mother tells us of her School of Art adventures, a charming laxity about the rules in those dear dead days almost too good to be true. Yet there are many who will vouch for their veracity. For instance, on a Monday afternoon Philip would often send over the Theatre Royal call-boy with a little package for Ethel Brown. This call-boy, in his green and gold uniform and brass buttons, was actually allowed to go into the classroom and up to her easel and deliver the precious packet into her own hands. Inside were passports to an enchanted evening, or, in plain terms, complimentary tickets for that night's performance. (In those days "orders" were rather more

freely distributed to "dress the house"—"little wondrous talismans, slight keys, and insignificant to outward sight, but
opening to me more than Arabian Paradises" wrote Charles
Lamb, himself an inveterate theatre-goer of a century before.)
It is very pleasant, "for a dreamwhile or so, to imagine a
world with no meddling restrictions," and so we can picture
in our minds the class practically breaking up from that
moment, and discussing, in the common room over an early
tea—The Play To-night!

For enjoyment proper, we moderns are losing the key. It is
the whole business of theatre-going that is the secret of its
charm: as much as you give to it, so much shall you be
rewarded. We should still do it in the grand manner of the
nineties; we should go home and change into full evening
dress, and float (can we float nowadays?) up the broad flight
of stairs to the dress circle, with flowers in our hair, to feel the
true thrill of enjoyment. Once there, Ethel Brown and a
round dozen of her friends would settle down with a lost
froufrou of taffeta skirts, and a lost swirl of tulle scarves; and
who shall say that Philip Rodway did not find urgent business
calling him many times in the course of the evening to the
front row (there were only four rows in those days) of the
dress circle?

Such then were the theatre nights. A little later we shall
have the excursions, and a contemporary sketch of Ethel
Brown. But one moment must be given for the serious side
of her studies, for there was not a lesson attended that was not
loved and appreciated. She learned two things superlatively
well in those days, to appreciate and to enjoy.

She studied water colour painting under Mr. J. V. Jelley
(now President of the Royal Birmingham Society of Artists).
The Life Class was taken by Mr. Edward S. Harper, the
distinguished artist and portrait painter, and father of Mr.
Edward (Teddy) Steel-Harper, now the brilliant exponent of
the Italian method of "wet-white" painting.

Other well-loved masters of those days (under Mr. Edward

Taylor, headmaster)* included Mr. Jackson, Mr. Charles
Morgan, Mr. Meteyard, Mr. Gaskin, Mr. Bidlake, Mr. Payne,
and Mr. William Midgley. It is to Mr. Midgley that the
Royal Birmingham Society of Artists owes the possession of
its present lease, though in those days his chief claim to fame
in Ethel Brown's eyes was as an inspired giver of parties, and
she still saves amongst her souvenirs an invitation to a dance,
given by him jointly with Mr. Alderson and Mr. J. Moore, in
his Studio, No. 1 Newhall Street, "Near the Sky."

In this happy band of students, to which Philip Rodway
always had admittance as an honorary member, were Eric
Heathcote, Teddy Steel-Harper and Estelle Lermit (who
were afterwards married, as were Ethel May and Murray
Bladon), Ivy Harper, Sarah Bastick, Mabel Radcliffe, Harold
Round, with Ernest Cotton, Ben Warren, and the three
Greatbach girls Ada, Maud, and Frances.

Of these Elysian days Stella Steel-Harper (the indefatigable
organiser of the Midland Arts Fellowship) writes with charming compliment:

"Looking back into those student days, certain things stand
out very vividly—we were such a happy group of young Art
students, working under that fine old master, Edward R. Taylor.
We were keen on our studies, but found time and opportunity for
recreation too. Our favourite amusements were outings, 'architect-
ural' and otherwise, to various interesting places round about Birmingham. To facilitate this we formed a Cycle Club, which included
girls as well as boys, decidedly an innovation for those days.

"An outstanding figure of this happy group was a student
called Ethel Brown. Everyone spoke of her as 'Ethel Brown,'
never 'Ethel' or 'Miss Brown.' This continued long after her
marriage, for when speaking of her among ourselves, or seeing
her in her stage box at the theatre, we always said 'Look, there's
Ethel Brown!' Perhaps it was because the name suited her so
well. She generally dressed in brown velvet, and had large brown
eyes, and the prettiest soft brown, curly hair. Those stray curls
required a great deal of attention to keep them in order, and we
laughingly used to say that if there was a mirror within a mile
of her, she would discover it! Not that she was vain, but she

---

*The present headmaster is Mr. H. H. Holden.

was so pretty and dainty and neat, that she must always be assuring herself that everything was exactly right and trim. One felt that her home would be just the same, charmingly arranged and not a pin out of place. In spite of this, there was a something about her that suggested there might be at least one drawer in a delightful muddle, to contrast with tidiness!

"She was great fun, pretty and witty, and had a way of saying unexpected things and causing much amusement. Of course she was much sought after, and was always accompanied by one escort (more often two) on our excursions, to the considerable annoyance of an interesting looking youth, slim and dark, named Phil Rodway. He was not an Art student, but came in a friendly way on our various excursions. He also waited at the School in Margaret Street to escort a certain tantalising damsel home, and, we suspected, to prevent anyone else doing so. We often wondered which of all the swains would be the chosen one, and remarking that the dark youth showed signs of a masterful disposition, we were not altogether surprised to hear that Ethel Brown was to become Mrs. Philip Rodway, when she slipped away from us all into that fascinating world of the Theatre.

"Just two vignettes from those happy old days.

"An evening cycle ride in the days of fixed wheels, before the free wheel was invented. A particularly steep incline which I was struggling to negotiate, when by me sailed Ethel Brown, her feet on the footrests of her front wheel, and a cavalier cycling on either side of her, holding her by an arm and propelling her up the hill!! As she passed, I caught this fragment of conversation:

"ETHEL. 'Really ——, it's surprising how strong Ken is. Now he *can* push.'

"And so poor —— redoubled his efforts as he panted past me.

"One of our picnic parties in Sutton Park; fifteen or twenty tired but contented cyclists seated on the ground in a circle, Ethel Brown and Philip Rodway among them. She is looking particularly charming in a new fashioned hat called 'The Pork Pie.' A jolly boy named Harold Round officiating at the teapot, and pouring out at a tray of cups held up for him. A momentary inattention to his task, and he finds to his dismay and horror he has poured the contents of the teapot into the Precious Hat of Ethel Brown seated just below. His dismay quickly turns to terror as the damsel, without the slightest hesitation, retaliates by hurling the contents of the sugar basin at his head. The untimely end of her fascinating creation lends aim to her arm, and the laughter which

The Miniature
of
Ethel Brown
1900

has arisen at the Alice in Wonderland nature of the picnic grows even louder at his collapse.

"During the summer of 1900 Ethel Brown was asked to sit for her portrait at the School of Art. Altogether some twenty or so students painted her head, most of them in oils, a few in water colours, and several on ivory as miniatures.

"One of these miniatures was exhibited in the Autumn Exhibition of the Royal Birmingham Society of Artists of that year. Great excitement prevailed one day in the Life Class. The miniature had vanished from its case in the Exhibition! 'A gentleman bought it; no name,' was all that could be extracted from the authorities.

"Our speculative interest in some unknown fairy prince waned a little after a week or two, but it revived again when we heard that on Christmas morning a mysterious little sealed package had arrived at Ethel Brown's house, labelled 'Fragile, with great care.'

"It was the miniature!

"With it was the message from ———, telling her that he had taken the liberty of having a copy made for himself, which, if anything, excelled the original."

And Mother herself adds:

"I still cherish that little miniature as a souvenir of one of the most romantic periods of my life.

"In those early days Phil always took me out to tea every afternoon, and he and I invariably strolled for an hour or two afterwards in the Art Gallery, more or less absorbing its art treasures, during the interval between tea and the evening class or the theatre. I suppose I ought to admit that there was really nowhere else for us to go! Cinemas were unheard of, there were no motor cars for a little run out for tea in some country inn—a hansom as far as Harborne was the farthest we ever got! In those days Harborne was just a tiny village of lovely lanes. . . ."

*   *   *

But before long another village of lovelier lanes was to cast its spell over their lives; a little village by the Avon, lost in the orchards of the Vale of Evesham. Half-timbered black and white cottages lift thatched roofs from the blaze of summer gardens, and the way of the willow trees leads to an ancient paved ford, with the picturesque old "Fish and

Anchor" Inn beyond. The sound of the weir makes drowsy melody, and the village church still chimes across the fields, with a quaintly inquiring air, its peal of six bells. . . .

Harvington!

There the young Philip Rodway took a tiny cottage as a fishing retreat—and how many a morning has seen him climbing the stile, setting off through the cherry orchard for the old mill and the river. Maybe he sang *The Angler's Song*, of Piscator; he might have written it himself, so truly did it picture him:

> *"I care not, I, to fish in seas,*
> *Fresh rivers best my mind do please,*
> *Whose sweet calm course I contemplate*
> *And seek in life to imitate."*

Sometimes on summer afternoons a merry party of School of Art students would race down the hill at Cleeve Prior and, appearing on the river bank, delightfully disturb the lonely angler, who speedily exchanged his rod and line for a pair of sculls, and proceeded to exhibit his undoubted prowess as an oarsman for the benefit of a certain young lady who had condescended to grace his craft.

How many happy days have Mother and Daddy spent there, she with her School of Art sketch book, he with his rods and his reels. A picture of just such carefree days is drawn by Fred E. Weatherley in those simple, pleasant verses:

> *"There's a bend of the river, the trees bending o'er,*
> *And an old boat is moored to the green shady shore,*
> *And someone is fishing, the long summer day,*
> *By the bend of the river, so the folks say.*
> *But what has he caught through the long summer day?*
>
> *"There's a pathway that leads from the old village hill*
> *To the bend of the river, cool, shady, and still,*
> *And someone sits painting the long summer day,*
> *By the bend of the river, so the folks say.*
> *But what has she painted the long summer day?*

"And what if they sit side by side in a dream,
And his fishing rod's floating away down the stream?
They have found what they wanted the long summer day,
By the side of the river, so the folks say.
Their hearts are as bright as the long summer day."

And the water meadows that lay beside that lovely stretch of river between Harvington and Cleeve Prior became for Philip Rodway fields Elysian fairer still.

O changeless heart of England! There are yet quiet corners undisturbed, where time stands still, and we may hear again the tinkle of the hammer on the anvil, the sound of the scythe on the whetstone, the gentle lowing of cattle at the water's edge. These are our England . . . "in Avons of the heart her rivers run."

So little altered is that village of Harvington, and so unspoilt. We still keep our double outrigger, as Philip did his fishing punt, at the old mill, and we still use the old landing stage opposite the weir. It is as if we step back more than a quarter of a century, and the atmosphere of the past closes around us. The old familiar names are there: Bomford, Malins, Stratton, and Hodgkinson; Mr. and Mrs. Grice of the Mill, Mrs. Bullock of the Manor Farm, Mr. and Mrs. Towers. . . . Walker at the Shakespeare Inn, Bromley at the Coach and Horses. . . . And Jack White and his wife, of the Shakespeare Cottages, who gardened and cooked for Philip Rodway more than thirty-five years ago, carry out the same duties for us, in the same cottage, to this very day.

And of those early days we have discovered in an old book —like that first small octavo edition of *The Compleat Angler* "thumbed into nothingness, after enduring much from May showers, July suns, and fishy companionship"—a story written by Philip Rodway on one of his beloved fishing expeditions. Doubtless he never dreamed any but himself would see it; but how much better is it to have his own description of one of his fishing days.

THE FISHING STORY

"To many men there are few delights which surpass those of a good day's angling, and pike angling in particular. When, added to the excitement and uncertainty of the sport, one can have glorious scenery and quietness, the opportunity is one not to be neglected. Let me describe such a day as I have in my mind—a day's real holiday which may be enjoyed by going a very few miles from Birmingham and its smoke and noise.

"My companion, a bluff old fisherman (old only in that his knowledge of fresh-water fish and their habits is based on years' experience), is one of those happy, breezy men whose presence seems to make bright the dullest days, and whose never-failing humour amuses and interests us even when the fish are in a quiet mood. He is a man of ample proportions, and to see him with his large broad-brimmed hat, and his tackle slung over his shoulders, one might imagine he was taking the whole of his household effects with him. Inside his huge basket is everything a fisherman can need—tackles of all kinds, lines, reels, hooks, wax, floats, pipes, cigars, and plenty of food for discussion at the river bank.

"The village—our starting place—is not far from the river, and how we enjoy the walk to the Avon in the beautiful October morning. Down the hill we go, through the sleepy railway station and across the line. Along the edge of an extensive hopfield, now with its poles bare and deserted, we march along to a small fishing hut on the river bank. My friend Jack produces a key from his everlasting basket and reaches out the oars. We are at last in the punt and my hearty companion pulls in leisurely fashion down stream towards the weir.

"Now we begin our first try to take a pike. Putting a spinning bait—that is, an imitation fish—at the end of the line, and seeing that the bait is well provided with swivels so that it may turn properly, we gently allow it to spin behind the punt. Gradually the line runs off the reel, and after letting thirty yards or more out the check is applied and the rod is held firmly.

"We have been on the water for perhaps ten minutes when there is a sudden pull at the rod, the top joint bends nearly double —a quick jerk, and the splash and commotion in the water tell me that a pike is hooked. Now is the chance for my jolly companion. Many are the directions he shouts—but at last we have our fish safely in the well of the punt. It is a moderate-sized jack, and this early success puts us on good terms with ourselves. We have no further triumphs, however, until we reach the mill water,

though the row down takes us through some of the prettiest
scenery it is possible to imagine, and yet quite deserted, although
so near to a large city.

"Now we anchor our punt close to the weir. The rushing water
bubbles and swirls all round us, threatening to carry our boat
away from its moorings in its splendid rush. My friend Jack has
now his tackle ready and has baited his hooks with a shining
roach. Carefully he adjusts his float, and lets the bait go with the
swiftly moving water. We both try this plan a few times, but not
meeting with much success we change our quarters and make for
a small island round which the water moves slowly, and where
the river is shallow and clear. Baiting our lines afresh we throw
them out, rest our rods across the punt, light our pipes and await
results.

"It is perhaps a long time before anything happens, but when
a pike 'runs' it is unmistakable. Yet the wait is not at all irksome.
The day is fairly warm, the surroundings are glorious, and the
sound of the water rushing over the weir is Nature's own music.

"Just as we are contemplating another move one of the floats
begins to bob in a most erratic fashion; suddenly it disappears,
and circle after circle forms on the surface of the water. With a
sudden jerk the hooks are driven into the pike and the fight begins.
The float is only a few yards from us, and we can see the large
and hungry jaws quite plainly. Shakespeare himself might have
fished in this same river at Stratford and noticed the same thing,
for does he not say:

> 'The pleasant'st angling is to see the fish
> Cut with her golden oars the silver stream,
> And greedily devour the treacherous bait.'

"After a keen struggle, in which Jack's hat goes overboard and
slowly drifts downstream, the fish is landed. After recovering the
oft-soaked Garibaldi, we carefully fish all round the islands,
taking two or three more pike and losing one—of course the
largest of the day. *How often an angler is chaffed because he says the
fish that breaks away is the largest of the day. And yet how very easy it
is to understand that the larger the fish the more likely he is to escape.*

"We stay all afternoon near this beautiful spot, until it is almost
time to return. As I row back Jack packs up the tackle and regales
me with a few stories—perfectly true ones, of that I am certain,
for Jack always tells the truth—about fish! We reach the hut,
and after locking up the punt and the oars we start for the village.

"It is growing dark, but we know the way through the hopfields well, and the old church spire is our landmark and guide. Jack, more heavily laden than ever, with five respectable pike fastened with a piece of wire thrust through their gills, tramps along ahead, and we soon reach the village, ready to do full justice to the meal set before us.

"By no means the least pleasant part of our outing is to sit in the cosy parlour of the Shakespeare Inn, and listen to the opinions of the villagers on questions of the hour. They have strong views on the politics of the day, these brawny sons of toil, and their admiration for Mr. Joseph Chamberlain is unbounded.

"At last the church clock strikes ten. With a cheery 'goodnight' the good-natured countrymen leave us one by one and we start for our own beds a short distance away.

"The air is sweet and clear, the lights twinkle from the windows of the pretty half-timbered old cottages, the echoes of a fine old English song, with which some of the yokels are beguiling their walk home, sound fainter and fainter . . . and we ourselves are soon asleep, to dream of mighty catches and pike of impossible size."

* * *

P.R.'s evening post in the box office of the Prince of Wales Theatre was proving an unqualified success. He still carried on his work at the solicitor's office during the daytime, but within a few months the chance came for him to consolidate his position at the theatre.

A new syndicate, under the style of Rodgers Ltd., was formed to take over from Captain Rodgers, and its principals offered Philip Rodway a whole time engagement in charge of the box office. A simultaneous offer of an identical post came from the Theatre Royal.

Thus came the momentous choice; which should he accept? Momentous, because although at the time both positions were very similar, in reality the Fates had ordained that a complete change of staff was to overtake the Prince of Wales within six months. Had he known it, his career and his fortunes were to hang on his decision.

Was it sound judgment, or intuition, or both, that influenced him to take up his position under the Royal banner? We reproduce (facing next page) in facsimile the letter, carefully phrased and beautifully penned, which he wrote to Mr. Charles Dornton at that time.

And so Philip Rodway was another step on his way; in July, 1897, he began his career at the Theatre Royal. . . .

CHAPTER 6

(1897-1902)

Theatre Royal, 1774-1897—Yates—Theatre fired by incendiaries, 1792—
Matthew Boulton's petition—Macready—Elliston—Bunn—The second fire,
1820—The Mercer Simpson régime—1900. P.R. becomes the youngest
acting manager in England—Betrothal of marriage—Benson and Shakespeare—The Royal to be demolished—Last night of the old theatre,
January 4th, 1902—Ghosts.

"In the meadows where Temple Street now stands" the playhouse
in New Street had its first beginning; our Birmingham historian Hutton traces it back even before 1730. Records of
actual advertisements date from 1741, but it was not until
Richard Yates, the famous comedian, visiting the city with
his company of "His Majesty's Servants from the Theatres
Royal in London," ordered to be built for him two theatres,
that any attempt was made to provide a worthy playhouse
for the city. One was in 1751, in King Street, where now
thunder the trains of New Street station, and the other, with
which our present purpose is concerned, was erected in New
Street twenty-three years later.

So that it was in 1774, when George III was King of England, that its footlights first flickered. No doubt, as Mr. T.
Edgar Pemberton reminds us, they did so in more senses
than one, for in those days the theatres were illuminated by
tallow, and continually the candle-snuffer went his greasy
rounds.

"At the Theatre in New Street, Birmingham, this present
Monday, June 20th, 1774, will be presented a Concert of Music.
Boxes 3s., Pit 2s., Gallery 1s. . . . Between the several Parts of the
Concert will be presented (gratis) by a Company of His Majesty's
Comedians from the Theatres Royal in London, a Comedy called
As You Like It (Touchstone, Mr. Yates) and an Occasional Pro-
logue to be spoken by Mr. Yates. To which will be added *Miss in
her Teens*."

To the handsomely appointed building there was added,
in 1780, the "superb portico," whereat Hutton declared it
to be one of the first theatres in Europe. "Two busts," he
wrote, "in relief, of excellent workmanship, are elevated over

[?] Road
Edgbaston
1st July 1897

Dear Sir

In compliance with the desire which you expressed this morning, that I should write to you and again bring before your notice the subject of your conversation with Mr James Herd, I beg to submit my qualifications. I am twenty years of age and have been with Mr James Herd ever since I left school nearly six years ago. During that period most of my time has been spent in dealing with the general office correspondence and accounts — the former principally. I am engaged at the Box Office of the Prince of Wales Theatre in the evenings, and have by this time become thoroughly accustomed to the methods of conducting business usual in Theatres.

Yours truly
Philip Rodway

Chas Dornton Esq
Theatre Royal
Birmingham

Facsimile Letter from Philip Rodway to Charles Dornton

the attic-windows; one is the father, the other the refiner, of the British stage—Shakespeare and Garrick."

These two medallion portraits, which have looked down upon Birmingham playgoers for a century and a half, were bought by Philip Rodway when the theatre was demolished in 1902, and it was he who caused them to be built into the wall of the present dress-circle staircase—the sole surviving relics of that first theatre of 1774.

The most notable of the seasons under Yates, says Mr. R. Crompton Rhodes, was his third, in which Mrs. Siddons—then unknown to fame—appeared. For Sarah Siddons Birmingham must have held many memories. It was there that she met and loved the handsome William Siddons, when they were both members of her father's, Roger Kemble's, strolling company, and long before her name was of any account. Her father forbad her to marry an actor, but his equally strong minded daughter finally had her way, and in November, 1773, at Holy Trinity Church, Coventry, she became Mrs. Siddons.

In 1777 the burning question in Birmingham was whether or not the city should be allowed to have a licensed theatre. There were already two unlicensed theatres, but they only existed by toleration, and Yates' desire to have a playhouse sanctioned by Royal patent was quite a different matter.

The Earl of Dartmouth Manuscripts, Vol. III, as issued by the Historical Manuscripts Commission, recalls an interesting episode of that time. The objectors to the licensing were so strongly organised that they took a poll of the inhabitants, and presented the result to his Lordship, accounting therein for 2,449 ratepayers, of whom 1,468 were against, 124 in favour, 192 neuter, and 665 "not at home when called upon"!

The great objection appeared to be that a licensed theatre "must be productive of idleness and dissipation." Matthew Boulton of Soho, a firm supporter of the cause, raised many ingenious arguments in its favour, pointing out that "all well-regulated states have found it expedient to indulge the people

E

with amusements of some kind or other," and that the theatre
was an improvement on the previous century, when the popular
diversions were "bull-baitings, cock-fightings, boxing matches
and abominable drunkenness with all its train." He followed
on with the piquant and practical argument that "of late
years, Birmingham hath been visited much in the summer
season by persons of fashion, and it is some inducement to
prolong their stay when their evenings can be spent at a
commodious, airy theatre. This is a fact I mention from
experience, and it is certainly our interest to bring company
to Birmingham, as it contributes much to the public good,
not only from the money they leave behind them, but from
their explaining their wants to the manufacturers themselves,
and from their correcting the taste and giving hints for
various improvements, which nothing promotes so much as
an intercourse with persons from different parts of the world."
Boulton's sensible and insinuative logic was ineffective at
the time, for the bill was defeated in the House of Commons
on the second reading, in spite of the strong support of Fox,
Wilkes, and Edmund Burke. It was then that the last named
orator launched his famous description of Birmingham as
"*the great toy-shop of Europe*," urging that on that very account
it was the most proper place in England to have a licensed
house.

During these prolonged Parliamentary proceedings local
enemies were plotting mischief, and on August 17th, 1792,
the very day which was announced for the return of Mrs.
Siddons with the most notable play of the season, the theatre,
fired by incendiaries, lay in smoking ruins. With it went the
whole of the scenery and wardrobe which Yates had been
getting together for the past forty years. He himself died
four years later—in a fit of temper because he had not been
given the stewed eels he ordered for breakfast!

Yates' last great performance was that of Ben the Sailor in
Congreve's *Love for Love*, with Dorothy Jordan as Prue. With
her in the stock company was that famous comedian Dicky

Suett, whom Charles Lamb pictures so vividly: "Thousands of hearts yet respond to the chuckling 'O la!' of Dicky Suett . . . he drolled upon the stock of these two syllables richer than the cuckoo. Shakespeare foresaw him when he framed his fools and jesters. They have all the true Suett stamp, a loose and shambling gait, a slippery tongue."

In less than three years the Theatre Royal was rebuilt. It reopened in 1795 under the control of Macready, father of the subsequently famous tragedian. The opening night was so great an event that the theatre was actually "illuminated with wax"! Macready set to work wholeheartedly, engaging the best stars and stock company of the year: Mrs. Siddons; the stately John Philip Kemble, her brother; George Frederick Cooke, one of the greatest and most disappointing of English tragedians. . . .

One Monday night in the August of 1802 Lord Nelson, accompanied by Sir William and Lady Hamilton, attended a performance at the Theatre Royal of *The Merry Wives of Windsor*, and on the next evening, "by desire of Lord Nelson," *King Henry IV, or the Humours of Sir John Falstaff*, was played. Nelson congratulated Macready upon the universal esteem in which his character was held, and the sum which he paid for his box was used to buy a souvenir piece of plate.

In 1804 Macready engaged the amazing young Henry West Betty, who at the age of twelve had already created a furore in Ireland and Scotland. Macready, doubting his capabilities, altered his contract on to a divisional-profit basis, but very soon realised his mistake, since Betty was such a phenomenal success that under the new arrangements he received five or six times as much as his first terms gave him!

Early in 1807 Matthew Boulton and others again petitioned the House of Commons for letters patent to be granted to the theatre. This time, after a struggle which had lasted thirty years, it was granted, and the playhouse in New Street became "The Theatre Royal."

That same year Mrs. Siddons "took leave of her provincial friends previous to her retirement from the stage."

In 1808, Mr. Watson, manager of the Theatre Royal, Cheltenham, brought a company which opened with the comedy *Speed the Plough*, the small part of Henry being played by a "Mr. Kean." This was the famous Edmund Kean, then a poor and struggling young man. Macready's son, William, home from Rugby School for the holidays, records his impressions of the pantomime in which Kean appeared:

"How little did I know, or could guess, that under that shabby green satin dress (worn by Alonzo) was hidden one of the most extraordinary theatrical geniuses that have ever illustrated the dramatic poetry of England. When some years afterwards public enthusiasm was excited to the highest pitch by the appearance at Drury Lane of an actor of the name of Kean, my astonishment may easily be conceived in discovering that the little insignificant Alonzo the Brave was the grandly impassioned impersonator of Othello, Richard, and Shylock."

It was in 1808, too, that the great Grimaldi (as Charles Dickens tells us in his fascinating memoirs of the King of Clowns) "received permission from Mr. Kemble, who then reigned at Covent Garden, to play for his sister-in-law's benefit at the Birmingham theatre, which was then under the management of Macready."

In 1810 the elder Macready brought his son from school to assist in the management, and this youngster, destined to become one of the leading tragedians of the day, was only 18 when for his first performance on any stage he played Romeo at the Theatre Royal.

In 1813 the Theatre Royal lease was taken over by the delightful, mercurial manager, Robert William Elliston. This amusingly pushing comedian lives again for us in Charles Lamb's perfect pen picture:

"Wherever Elliston walked, sat, or stood still, there was the theatre. He carried about with him his pit, boxes, and galleries, and set up his portable playhouse at corners of streets and in the market places. Upon flintiest pavements he trod the boards still;

and if his theme chanced to be passionate, the green baize carpet of tragedy spontaneously rose beneath his feet."

William Hazlitt, however, severely criticises his many and varied pranks and schemes, and speaks of him as "dressed in a little brief authority, and playing such fantastic tricks before high heaven as to make his own candle-snuffers laugh and his own scene-shifters blush." On the boards, though, Leigh Hunt considered him "not only with respect to his versatility, but in his general excellence, and in the perfection to which he brought some of his characters, the greatest actor of the present day."

In 1814 Edmund Kean, now in the full flood of his fame, appeared at the Royal. The high-spirited actor-manager Elliston had been going on cheerfully for some time past in his usual frivolous way, but it was not a way likely to fill his coffers, so that the arrival of Edmund Kean came as a boon. The great actor played his finest parts (Coleridge compared his performances to reading Shakespeare by flashes of lightning) and the failing exchequer was replenished.

It was Elliston who established the "Fashionable Night," and it is worth while giving this suggestion of his from an address:

"One evening, at least, in the week to be considered fashionable for theatrical amusements. On this evening, without inconvenience, perhaps, to any individual, an expectation might be held out that the best company, or that a considerable portion of the best company, of Birmingham and its neighbourhood, would be collected at the Theatre. An elegant place of periodic assemblage might be thus established. If that night were to be distinguished in the manner I have pointed out, all persons coming to the Theatre on the Friday would be assured of beholding an interesting performance, and of being surrounded by those they know, and might be pleased to meet."

Spectators were allowed to sit on the stage for the last time during Elliston's management, when "seats were provided in front of the proscenium, and the places as regularly let as in the boxes." An attempt at its revival was made in 1823, but the pit and gallery became so annoyed that the benches were hastily removed.

Elliston, in spite of his buoyancy and ever-flowing stream of advertisement, could not make the theatre pay, and in 1819 he was succeeded by the hardly less enterprising and self-assertive Alfred Bunn. But for Bunn real disaster lay in wait. The second great tragedy in the old theatre's history is graphically recorded by our local historian, Mr. R. K. Dent:

"On the 6th of January, 1820, Sheridan's *Pizarro* was played, and the performance having concluded at an earlier hour than usual, the theatre was in darkness by half-past eleven o'clock, and the actors had left it for the night—and for ever. The echoes of applause had scarcely died away in the deserted building, when vast columns of smoke and flame were seen breaking out from the windows and issuing from the roof. Thousands of the inhabitants came out to see the old playhouse once more perish in the flames. All attempts to save it were vain; amid the drizzling rain the roof fell in with a crash which shook the ground for some distance around, and in three hours nothing was left but the bare walls and (curiously enough) the original façade which thus braved the fury of two destructive fires."

Before the year was out the theatre was rebuilt. One of the new stars to appear therein was Madame Vestris, who, on the first Fashionable Night, played Susannah in *The Marriage of Figaro*.

From a criticism of those times we have extracted this comment:

"Mr. Bunn: Manager. In the farce of *Bombastes Furioso*, on Friday last, the wing of a palace was left during an entire scene in a cottage. Pray, when are we to expect the stage machinery for the wings to be used; and how long are we to see the dirty fingers of your scene-shifters pushing them along the grooves, frequently without being able to move them in time?"

Parallel paragraph with this last, we cannot but recall "R.C.R." writing in the *Birmingham Post* in 1930:

"At the old Theatre Royal pantomimes of Mr. Philip Rodway I have on several occasions had the privilege of watching a change of setting. On the stage there have been, perhaps, a couple of people singing a duet, while behind there were fully a hundred men working in absolute silence and almost in darkness, striking one scene and setting another. It was most impressive. . . ."

In spite of difficulties Alfred Bunn continued as manager until he was succeeded in 1825 by Warde, under whose régime William Charles Macready, now a recognised London actor, and on his way to fulfil lucrative American engagements, appeared, also the popular T. P. Cooke, the great Liston (originator of Paul Pry), Charles Kemble and his daughter Fanny, and Charles Kean, son of the famous Edmund.

In 1826 Brunton became manager, and five years later Watson, of the Theatre Royal, Cheltenham. There follow several brief and luckless managements, and it was not until 1837 that Fortune began to smile upon the theatre. Mr. Monro took over, with "Stage Manager, Mr. Simpson; Leader of the Band, Mr. A. Mellon; Ballet Master, Mr. William Rignold." These were Mercer H. Simpson, who joined Monro in management in 1840; Alfred Mellon, one of the first musical directors of his generation; and Rignold, the founder of the well-known theatrical family.

On Boxing Day, 1843, Mercer Simpson became sole lessee and manager. During the first years of his régime a sound stock company was organised. Many of the young actors there rose to great heights, and made much of their early training, as when, in 1852, *The Heir at Law* was given at the National Theatre, Boston, and Douglas Stewart appeared as "from the Theatre Royal, Birmingham; his first appearance in America"; and when *Our American Cousin* was given for the first time in England at the Haymarket Theatre in 1861, Lord Dundreary was described as "Mr. E. A. Sothern, formerly of the Theatre Royal, Birmingham."

In 1864 Mercer Simpson, sen., retired, and was succeeded by his son, also Mercer, who in 1887 celebrated the fiftieth year of his and his father's régime by a series of performances for charity, in which F. R. Benson made his first local appearance. Four years later the management was taken over by Charles Dornton, who seventeen years before had been a member of the theatre's stock company, and under his control we find it when, direct from the rival box office, Philip Rodway took up his new position.

He entered a theatre steeped in honourable tradition. Since 1774 all the leading actors and actresses had appeared on its stage. The long régime of the Mercer Simpsons was distinguished by such great names as G. V. Brooke, Madge Robertson (Mrs. Kendal), Irving, Toole, Brough, Ellen Terry, G. H. Macdermott, George Alexander, John Hare, and those "splendid strollers" who toured with Charles Dickens in 1846.

For the young recruit, Philip Rodway, fresh from a house with little history and few traditions, the very stones of the Royal held inspiration and encouragement. He responded with his wonted eagerness to their call, throwing himself heart and soul into every phase of his work.

Virtue, for once, was not alone its own reward. The "divinity that shapes our ends" ordained that opportunities for advancement should come his way more speedily than he could have anticipated—but it was his own industry that fitted him to accept them. The circumstances were that Charles Dornton, almost from the day of Philip Rodway's arrival, had to diminish his own activities owing to ill-health, and soon to abandon them altogether. Thus the nominal box office clerk was acting manager in all but name from a very early date. The actual title fell to him some months before Dornton's death in the May of 1900, and he became, at twenty-two, the youngest acting manager in England.

*   *   *

To Philip Rodway the attainment of this settled position was the signal for another important step. His contract for the acting managership was safely in his pocket when he went down Speedwell Road to interview the father of Ethel Brown. Prospects were reviewed and approved, and when he came away he had the official sanction to the engagement which in his own mind had been pre-ordained from the first. It was perhaps the happiest and most momentous day so far in his life.

*   *   *

Our great friend, Mr. W. R. Young, who as chief scenic artist at the Royal was closely associated with many of P.R.'s pantomime triumphs, sends us an interesting little reminiscence. Philip Rodway had hardly been in the theatre ten minutes before he found his way to the paint room. A *Cinderella* palace scene was on the stocks, and he immediately asked Mr. Young if he would be good enough to explain the working of it. "I thought at the time," writes "W.R.Y.," "that this young man would make a name for himself."

As acting manager, during the eventful years of the Boer War, there were several occasions when, without notice, it became necessary for him to go before the footlights to make an announcement. Of these were the Relief of Ladysmith on February 28th, 1900, and Mafeking on May 17th, when the whole house, like the town, went wild with delight, in such a spontaneous outburst of national joy as can hardly ever be surpassed.

How widely different from that night of January 22nd the following year, when the tragic duty of announcing the death of Queen Victoria fell to his lot. It was during the run of the pantomime *Dick Whittington*, and the news meant the immediate closing of the theatre halfway through the show. Mother well recalls the hush that fell on the audience as they heard his words, and the deathly quiet as they rose and filed slowly out.

The four or five years from 1897 provided Philip Rodway with many and varied experiences. In October, 1898, he organised the first Shakespeare subscription season for Frank Benson. Tangible proof of F.R.B.'s "gratitude for much courtesy and kind assistance" is contained in his gift of a silver cigarette case.

The pantomimes with which P.R. was associated at the old Royal were *The Forty Thieves* (1897-98), *Cinderella* (1898-99), *Babes in the Wood* (1899-1900), with George Robey, Maggie Duggan, and Tom Murray; and *Dick Whittington and his Cat* (1900-01), with Vesta Tilley and George Mozart. Even in the first of these—*The Forty Thieves* season—the advertisements ran "*Address all communications to Mr. P. Rodway.*"

His own first "benefit night," which inaugurated a famous series dealt with in later pages, came on March 7th, 1900, just after he had become acting manager in name as well as in practice. The history of his special nights is unique in many respects, but in none so strikingly as in the evidence it gives of generous appreciation of work well done.

Stars who visited the Royal in the dramatic seasons about this period included Charles Wyndham, John Hare, the Kendals, Lewis Waller, Edward and Fred Terry, and Charles Sugden and his wife. In the latter half of 1899 Forbes Robertson and Mrs. Patrick Campbell came with *For the Crown*, a production of which Mr. Arthur Llewellyn Matthison has written entertainingly in his book published not long ago.

After Dornton's death his widow carried on until January, 1902, and then, Mr. F. S. Bolton having acquired the lease, accepted the inevitable necessity of giving up the attempt to maintain a theatre which, owing to structural defects in the auditorium, was entirely out of date, inconvenient, and un-economic. From a great number of seats it was impossible to get even a glimpse of the stage, and with the music-halls rapidly becoming stern competitors, it was plainly a case of the Royal shutting up and being reconstructed, before it fell so deeply into the background that any prospects of new existence in a modernised state had fallen through.

A survey of the box-plan (prepared and initialled by Philip Rodway in 1902) which accompanies this chapter, will explain better than words what was wrong with the auditorium.
    *   *   *

And so yet another phase of the Theatre Royal's history was about to be closed. In the winter of 1901-02, for the first time since that of 1840-41, no pantomime was produced. Instead there was a short season of Shakespeare's *Midsummer Night's Dream*, by Frank Benson's splendid company—splendid indeed, as the programme shows:

Theseus (Duke of Athens)	Mr. Alfred Brydone
Egeus (Father of Hermia)	Mr. B. Iden Payne
Lysander (in love with Hermia) ...	Mr. F. R. Benson
Demetrius	Mr. E. Harcourt Williams
Philostrate (Master of the Revels) ...	Mr. Walter Hampden
Quince (a carpenter)	Mr. Arthur Whitby
Bottom (a weaver)	Mr. George R. Weir
Flute (a bellows mender)	Mr. C. Croker King
Snug (a joiner)	Mr. Matheson Lang
Snout (a tinker)	Mr. Charles Bibby
Starveling (a tailor)	Mr. H. O. Nicholson
Helena (in love with Demetrius) ...	Miss Francis Dillon
Hermia (in love with Lysander) ...	Miss Hutin Britton
Hippolyta (Queen of the Amazons)...	Miss Olive Noble
Oberon (King of the Fairies) ...	Mr. Henry Ainley
Titania (Queen of the Fairies) ...	Mrs. F. R. Benson
Puck (or Robin Goodfellow) ...	Miss Dorothy Marsdin
First Singing Fairy	Miss Cissie Saumerez
Fairy	Miss Leah Hanman

Almost every name in the cast is, or has been, a household word among theatre goers. We are particularly interested to see that the small part of Egeus was played by Mr. B. Iden Payne, for he is the same Ben Iden Payne, now everywhere accepted as America's leading authority on Shakespeare production (but an Englishman for all that) who has been appointed to succeed Bridges Adams as Director of the Stratford Festival.

This "company of earnest and capable actors" having fulfilled their term of eleven nights and four matinées from December 16th, 1901; there came the grand finale.

To Charles Wyndham, soon to be knighted by King

Edward on the occasion of his coronation, fell the sad distinction of closing the old house. In the last week he produced three plays, with three different leading ladies in Lena Ashwell, Mrs. Bernard Beere, and Mary Moore (who later became Lady Wyndham).

January 4th, 1902, saw the last performance in the old theatre—*David Garrick*—and the names of many of those who were in the theatre on this historic night may be read from the box plan opposite. Surely one of the most interested of the spectators there was Ethel Brown, the fiancée of the young acting-manager. Her name, in Philip Rodway's own writing, is soon deciphered over the three stalls in the second row which she and her parents occupied.

The play ended, Charles Wyndham delivered a gracious speech of farewell. Looking round at the old walls, he said:

"Each brick in them is instinct with its own proud memory, carrying hidden in its cells, burnt in with the sacred fire of genius, every shade of tone and colour that has played its fitful light upon these boards throughout the brilliant era, the Victorian age. Each rafter, at the touch of the magician's wand, would ring out again with the passion of a Kemble, and a Siddons, and a Kean—the elocution of a Macready, the laughter of a Nisbett, the gentle tenderness of a Faucit, the humour of a Harley, Farren's dignity, Dundreary's problems, and the art of all those who strove to keep the Drama's torch alive. All these are passing now before us in stately procession, giving back ghostly echoes of the plaudits that greeted them in olden times; plaudits from now vanished hands and lips that are silent. Well, though the Muse of this theatre, like other charming ladies, once changed her name in early life; though the poor thing was once burnt out of house and home and had to build another, the fact remains that on this spot she has lived and flourished since her birth on that distant day when the British realms were ruled over by George III and the British stage by David Garrick."

Players and audience joined in *Auld Lang Syne*, and so ended the last performance in the old Theatre Royal.

*   *   *

No sooner had the curtain fallen than pandemonium broke

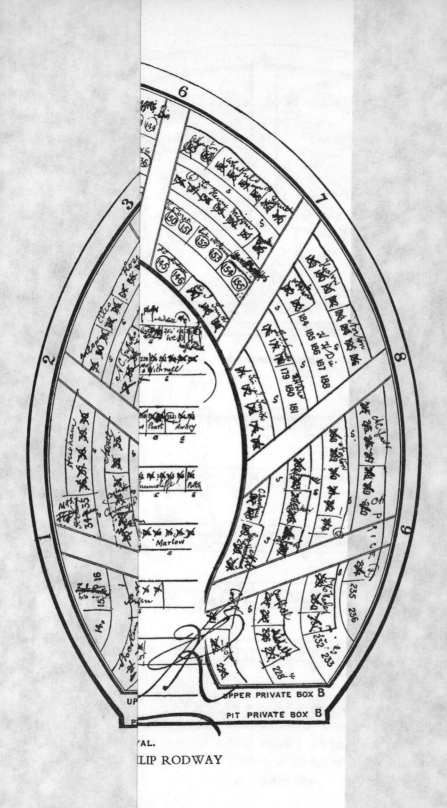

PHILIP RODWAY

loose. Members of the audience were transformed into ruth-less souvenir hunters, who tore off parts of the fittings, chipped the very plaster from the walls, and made more than a good beginning for those destined to complete the demolition of the building.

For Philip Rodway the occasion, sad as it could not fail to be, was in some measure lightened; his short period of manage-ment had already gained him many friends among the journalists of Birmingham, and in the old theatre there was to be enacted yet one more scene.

On January 5th, 1902, in the old green room, as a result of a conference of the representatives of the whole of the daily newspapers of Birmingham, two presentations were made to him: a marble clock and a gold pencil case.

As a matter of reminiscent interest, the names of those journal-ists were: J. Fennell, Girdlestone, H. F. Harvey, F. H. Henshaw, Hicks, D. Evans, and J. Trevor Jones of the *Daily Post;* J. C. Walters, H. H. Doe, E. H. Rann, G. H. Kynaston, C. Jenkins, W. Webb, A. Franks, C. Gray, and F. Ward of the *Daily Gazette;* G. H. Bywater, H. A. Botwood, T. Brown, W. Whittell, E. G. Busbridge, and Oscar Pollack of the *Daily Mail;* H. A. Gray, F. Ormerod, T. Lloyd, and Horton of the *Daily Argus;* and W. H. Garbutt, W. McAliece, W. Downing, and Wimbury of the *Daily Express.*

Mr. H. F. Harvey is now the distinguished editor of the *Birmingham Mail,* and Mr. Trevor Jones an invaluable mem-ber of his staff. Mr. Dudley Evans is secretary of the Birming-ham Iron and Steel Exchange. Mr. Busbridge, Mr. Whittell, and Mr. "Freddie" Henshaw are still much in evidence though no longer in the journalistic sphere.

In this way was concluded the last official ceremony within the walls of the old Royal.

* * *

There was one more ritual to take place in the old doomed theatre. Here was no casual business man's abrupt adieu to a business house. It was the goodbye which Philip Rodway made to the home of tradition which he had learned to love so well. On the night following the final performance, he and his future wife explored for the last time the deserted stage and auditorium. Together they passed through the corridors to take a last farewell of his forlorn little office. Each lonely corner, each twist of the staircase is instinct with memories, and unseen ghosts hide behind the red velvet curtains and pull the folds closer as the two pass.

If we knew that to-morrow a beloved spot would have disappeared, or, almost worse, would be desecrated by gradual demolition, how doubly dear would it become. Then indeed would the "last time" come upon us with the suddenness of a blow. There could never again be that revisiting of favourite haunts which we promise ourselves in the limbo of someday and sometime. It must be now or never.

Even a prosaic house grows almost beautiful when the hand of desolation hangs over it. The ruins of a dwelling, be it cottage or castle, are always unutterably pathetic. But for a theatre, whose boards have been trodden by the greatest actors of all time, how doubly tragic is the fate. Whither will their ghosts, who have so long been sheltered within these walls, take flight? Where will the shades take rest as sacrilegious hands lay bare their haunts?

All this is in Philip Rodway's mind as he takes his bunch of keys and unlocks the way through the old green room— the last green room, for there is no space allowed for pleasant meetings in the new theatre's plan. Through the pass door— (that sacred door that divides the stage from the front of the house—but of what account are doors to spirits?)—to the front hall, and they stand for a moment by the box office where Charles Dornton first engaged him. They turn their steps to the staircase and make their way along the winding corridor to the dress circle; there they allow themselves the sweet sorrow, a moment to sit again in the two front seats from which she had seen the curtain rise so many times on brilliant spectacle and enchanting scene. As they stare out this night into the silence and darkness, they can but re-echo:

"Old 'house,' you must not die;
　You came to us so readily,
　You lived with us so steadily,
Old 'house,' you shall not die.

"Old 'house' you must not go;
　So long as you have been with us
　Such joy as you have seen with us,
Old 'house' you shall not go.

"Old 'house' you shall not die;
　We did so laugh and cry with you,
　I've half a mind to die with you,
Old 'house' if you must die."

How could the new theatre, be it never so modern and gilded, have such dear associations? Why, even the new dress circle, in its pride of many rows, will bear no relation to this dear quaint old thing.

The shabby little old dressing rooms all seem to know they, too, have failed in a test of Modernism too difficult for them; the doors and curtains seem, in the deep gloom, to ask for a reprieve. It is no fault of theirs they are outworn. Cannot they be spared?

"Shake hands before you die,
　Old 'house,' we'll dearly rue for you,
　What is it we can do for you?
Speak out before you die."

As he feels the mute appeal of these dear inanimate things Philip Rodway wishes with all his heart that it was in his power to give them their reprieve. He is as heartbroken as though he is losing his dearest friend. He makes a vow to himself that at the sale of the old Royal, when all its glories are dismantled, he will try and preserve some relic of its fame to carry on to the new house. This is the least that Loyalty can do for Tradition; and he swears that he will purchase for his own keeping some small memento as a due to memory.

As his hand unwillingly turns out the last faint gas jet and the whole house sinks into blackness, as the door slams behind them, the old Royal knows that its last hour is upon it.

MEDALLIONS OF GARRICK AND SHAKESPEARE

The only surviving relics of the Theatre Royal of 1774

Bought by Philip Rodway when the old theatre was demolished in 1902, and given by him to be built into the dress-circle staircase of the present Theatre Royal

CHAPTER 7

(1902-04)

Demolition of the Old Royal—Superstition of the peacocks—Difficulties—
Stories of the contents sale—The Two Medallions—More difficulties; all
work suspended—The position is explained—Rebuilding begun at last—
The marriage at Harvington, July 11th, 1904.

The next three years were anxious ones for Philip Rodway,
as they were, indeed, for everyone connected with the Theatre
Royal that had been, or for the Theatre Royal that was to
be. For many months Birmingham was left in doubt whether
any of the various schemes for the re-creation of the ancient
playhouse would fructify. What the difficulties were and why
the original schemes fell through will be fully explained in
due course. Meanwhile the closed building, partially demolished, stood in gaunt and lonely idleness, while the public
were assailed on all sides with disturbing reports as to the
failure of successive negotiations. There were those who un-
easily recalled the title page of the *Souvenir* which had been
presented to players and audience on the last night of the old
theatre. Had it not been decorated with a design of peacocks? And were these not birds of ill-omen, especially in the
theatrical profession? Maybe the superstition was already
beginning to fulfil itself!

The chief stumbling block was undoubtedly cost. Syndicate
after syndicate was attracted by the obvious possibilities of the
proposition, but again and again they were frightened away
by the list of heavy "dead" charges.

Sir Charles Wyndham (as he had become since the closing
night of the old house) had said in his farewell speech that the
new theatre would probably be built within twelve months.
How far out was his estimate! The Moss and Thornton
combination, the United Theatres Company (then interested
in the Prince of Wales Theatre) and other groups threw out
more or less tentative feelers, but each time the financial
barrier intruded.

A favourite story of P.R.'s in later years was of an incident

F

which happened during the sale of the contents of the old theatre. When the metal gallery railing—quite a valuable lot—was put up for auction, the old dealer who made the final bid of half-a-crown or so thought he had secured a bargain.

There was a condition of sale that everything bought should be removed within three days, so, having noticed that the uprights were concreted in to the gallery flooring, the buyer came back next day with a basket carrier, a couple of small hammers, and a little boy to hold his coat. He hammered away for hour after hour without making the slightest impression, so on the second day he returned with more tools, two men, and the boy. Four hours later he had a free fight in the gallery with his helpers, and sacked the lot. Next day he returned with three more, and this time they managed to clear the concrete from the bases of the uprights. Would they lift out? They would not—because those same supports ran down through the pillars of the upper circle, through the pillars of the dress circle, through to the pit floor, and down, down, down to the very basement of the theatre!

P.R. gently reminded him that time was nearly up, whereupon he addressed Daddy, the rails, and the theatre in terms far from Shakespearean, threw his hammers into the pit, and stood not upon the order of his going.

Another purchase at the same sale (says Mr. Harry Carter, that staunch friend of the theatre) also outran the original expectations of the buyer. He had bought a property hobby horse belonging to a previous pantomime; lent it for the Coronation Day procession; and when next he heard of it it was miles away with hundreds of boys chasing the rider! In the acquisition of a property giant this purchaser was similarly unfortunate. Again he lent it, and a member of the committee who was arranging the celebration decided to wear the unwieldy contraption himself. Only an expert should have handled it, and that fact, coupled with the crowd's exuberance; nearly resulted in disaster both for the giant and his inmate.

The two medallions which may be seen to-day in the stair-case wall leading out of the foyer are themselves the centre of another story. Philip Rodway had set his heart on buying these himself and saving them for a connecting link between the old and new theatres. Noticing at the auction sale which was taking place on the stage, that Mr. Carter was always lucky in his frequent bids, he approached the footlights and looking down, announced that he was going to bid for the next lot; whereupon the erstwhile bidder gallantly turned his back on stage and auctioneer, and P.R. was able to secure the medallions for himself and give them as a heritage to the new Royal.

Among the mementoes which he bought for his new home were the great flower stands which had appeared on the stage when Charles Wyndham played David Garrick on the last night of the old theatre. Still more significant, he acquired the centre knob of the gallery rail; that centre knob to which many hundred hands had clung in their struggle to secure the pride of place in the old days of "rushing the gallery."

For long after the sale the theatre stood month by month in partial ruins. Mother tells us how, during the years of their engagement, she and Daddy used to walk along Bristol Road to New Street each morning to look at the old building, and watch almost every brick as it was pulled down, just as later on they watched almost every stone and brick going up. Long before the roof was on they chose "their box." It helped during the lengthy waiting to feel that there was some place in that shell of a building which had a special meaning and interest for them; which they could almost regard as their own. And so on the dress circle tier, the box nearest the stage* was chosen. It became Box B.4. From it Mother was to watch every first and last night of importance during Philip Rodway's thirty years' régime. From it she beheld comedy and tragedy, and later, with the greatest interest of all, his pantomime productions. It became at nights a second

*On the "prompt" side.

enthralling home for us all. That box with its little anteroom was to be the scene of momentous excitement in the days of the early pantomimes; of sure enjoyment on the later Boxing Days; and of tragic intensity on the last night of his last pantomime. By the courtesy of the later managements she occupies it still, but it can never be quite the same as when a familiar figure used to slip in quietly and say "Are you enjoying it?"

But in those days, before the box existed, there was Daddy fretting about the terms of the contract which kept him "rusting," as he called it—preventing his taking up any other position elsewhere. He loathed idleness, chafed at inaction, and felt that he was uselessly frittering away valuable time.

Early in 1903, however, when the most optimistic had almost given up hope of good news, a new personality entered the lists. It was Mr. Tom B. Davis, then much in the public eye as the sponsor of *Florodora*, an extremely successful play of the period. To him more than to any other Birmingham owes it that a theatre stands on the Royal site to-day.

A shrewd Londoner, less than forty years old, he had been in management only about five years, but during that period he had made an impressive mark in the world of what the Americans call "musicals." In April, 1899, he had introduced the famous Evie Greene to London in *L'Amour Mouille*, and six months later the king of melody-makers, Leslie Stuart, had written *Florodora* for him to present at the Lyric Theatre. It ran for 455 performances from November 1899, which carried it well into the new century. Then Mr. Davis sent out a number of touring companies, so that by the February of 1903 he was a busy man.

Not too busy, though, to have heard about the half-demolished theatre standing idle on Birmingham's best site, and to make up his mind that something ought to be done about it. Before February ended it was publicly announced that the aggravating obstacles (still to be authoritatively described) which had so long been blocking the way, had all been removed, and bright hopes of the new house being opened by Christmas 1903, were held out.

A significant postscript to the announcement was that the theatre would reopen with Mr. Philip Rodway as acting manager.

But even "Tom B.," with his tremendous fund of energy and acumen, found the going hard. The expectations that the housebreakers would soon be at work again demolishing the remnants of the old Royal were tardy of fulfilment; so tardy that by mid-June there was again a confirmed opinion extant that the latest negotiations had failed at the old familiar obstacles.

Whereupon Mr. G. W. Hubbard, then editor of the *Birmingham Daily Mail*, got into communication with Mr. Davis, and in reply to a straight question received a telegram:

"Not exactly fallen through at present but extremely probable I and my friends shall have to abandon project as terms insisted on by landlord prove to be as a result of valuation prohibitive. Matters so far have never got beyond our respective lawyers, and of course I cannot do my part until preliminaries can be mutually agreed by the professional men."

The newspaper went on to explain that the property had been acquired by Mr. F. S. Bolton of the Broad Street Metal Works, after the closing in 1902, with the intention of immediate reconstruction, but that circumstances had persuaded him to put it back on the market.

"The value of the site is so great, and the ground rent so heavy, that capitalists have hesitated to embark on the venture," added the *Mail*. "Another very important element is a condition which secures the retention of Mr. Philip Rodway as acting manager, at a considerable salary."

The paper, hitherto optimistic, now took the general and fully understandable view that Mr. Davis, having closely investigated the finances of the proposition, had been forced to the same conclusion as his predecessors in the field. It estimated that the ground rent on any new theatre would be at least £3,500 a year, to which had to be added £1,800 a year in rates and taxes and £2,000 in interest on capital; altogether £8,600 a year would have to be allowed for fixed charges before a halfpenny could be used for running the enterprise. No syndicate, it was declared, would accept these very heavy overhead charges without some hesitation.

"The question naturally arises whether, in these circumstances, we have seen the last of the Theatre Royal. Is it possible to surmount the difficulties? One cannot prophesy with any great confidence, but we have reason to believe that the position is not altogether hopeless. Although it seems highly probable that Mr. Davis will be unable to see his way to acquire the property, it is not unreasonable to anticipate that arrangements may ultimately be made which will clear away the difficulties that prevented one of the previous negotiators from concluding a bargain. *In any case, it is pretty certain that Birmingham will have another first-class theatre, although it may not be built upon the Theatre Royal site. It is in fact stated that at the present time one of the best known London managers is making preliminary enquiries with a view to erecting a theatre, if eventually all hope of rebuilding the Theatre Royal has to be abandoned.*"

And there was Philip, all this time, with his future as a manager at stake, and his prospects extremely uncertain. The complications that had arisen to jeopardise these latest negotiations must have shaken even his youthful optimism, tremendous as it was, for Mother tells us that at about this time he would often wonder audibly whether the theatre would ever be rebuilt. It could not help being trying for him, moreover, to read of himself and his "considerable salary" as constituting one of the barriers to reconstruction, when he knew how trivial the item was in comparison with others involved.

The matter lay in abeyance for some three months. At least, that was how it appeared to the public, but Tom B. was not to be baulked. Quietly but assiduously, with P.R.'s help, he went on pulling strings, adjusting figures, revising estimates, negotiating, negotiating, negotiating. Full as were his hands with *Florodora* and other profitable ventures, the Royal was his paramount concern throughout the summer of 1903.

There were many interests to be reckoned with. The communications between ground landlords, lessees, sub-lessees, and so forth, formed a regular labyrinth, dear, perhaps, to the legal mind, but enough to damp the determination of the average plain business man. Tom B. explored the labyrinth with imperturbable resolution, until at last, in September, he was able once more to announce that the end of the struggle was in sight.

By mid-November he had things almost perfectly cut and dried—nearly two years having elapsed since the old house was closed. At about this time the public, always eagerly interested in information about Birmingham's most popular institution, were for the first time given a detailed explanation of the position in all its bearings.

It appeared that the freehold of the familiar site bounded by New Street, Colonnade Passage, Stephenson Street, and Lower Temple Street, occupying about 4,000 square yards, was vested in the Birmingham Theatre Royal Estate Company, the principal shareholder of which was the General Hospital. The freeholders, from whom the land was held by various lessees, had given notice in 1900 that when the theatre lease expired in 1907 they would prefer one tenant to several. As a consequence, the whole of the property, including the residue of the current leases, had been acquired by Mr. Francis Seddon Bolton, of the Broad Street Metal Works, to whom a new lease of ninety-nine years from 1900 had been granted.

Mr. Bolton's aim was to clear the site of all its buildings and to erect a new theatre, a suite of shops, offices, and an arcade at an estimated cost of £125,000, of which £30,000 was earmarked for the theatre, exclusive of furniture and fittings. He had not got far with the demolition work, however, when his brother's death brought about certain difficulties, which persisted until 1903.

Mr. Davis, it was now explained, had been the last of various persons approached for co-operation towards the completion of the scheme. He had been willing to talk business, but not willing to go outside his sphere of theatrical management and undertake the considerable property speculation contemplated by Mr. Bolton. Aware that Birmingham's chief theatre must be a large, imposing building, erected on modern principles and perfect in every detail, he realised also that such an establishment would be seriously handicapped by the heavy ground rent apportioned to it as part of the elaborate scheme.

So, through many interviews between the parties, Mr. Davis stuck to it that he would only take so much of the site as he needed for the theatre of his imagination. It was not until this offer had been accepted, and the ground rent fixed at a figure he regarded as reasonable, that terms were concluded.

Negotiations with Mr. Bolton and with the Midland Trust—the body which collaborated with Tom B. in financing his scheme—had taken nearly eighteen months when the prospectus of the Theatre Royal Birmingham, Limited, was published on December 17th, 1903. A month earlier, Mr. Davis had assured the public that the company would not be burdened with the usual promoters' profit, his anxiety being to see Birmingham citizens widely represented on the share-roll of Birmingham's chief theatre.

"All who are willing to subscribe will be able to do so on exceptional terms," he said. "I and my friends will obtain our reward solely in deferred shares. That is all we are asking for, and they will not bring us any profit at all until the ordinary shareholders have had a satisfactory return."

In thus expressing the willingness of himself and his associates to work for nothing if the company did not succeed, Tom B. let it be clearly understood that he did not see much risk. From the start he was convinced that the new Royal would be a great success.

The issue of the prospectus was delayed a week beyond the intended date by a curious circumstance. The promoters had announced their intention of incorporating the word "Royal" in the title—and on the eve of issue they were told that this word could not be applied to any new place of amusement without the King's permission. No doubt this would have been readily given, but in the end there was no need to seek it, because enquiry revealed that the "Royal" in the title of the old building could legitimately be carried forward to the new.

When the prospectus *did* come out, it bore the names, as directors, of:

Mr. E. J. Abbott, F.C.A. (Messrs. Abbott, Deeley, Hill & Co.), Birmingham, chartered accountant (managing trustee of the Midland Trust, Limited), chairman.

Mr. Tom B. Davis, Lyric and Apollo Theatres, London, managing director.

Mr. William R. Cobay (Messrs. Smee & Cobay), 139 New Bond Street, London, W., furnishing contractor.

Mr. Arthur Oliphant Burton, Laleham, Middlesex (director of New Gaiety Hotel and Restaurant Company Limited, London), stockbroker.

Mr. Isaac Myers (Messrs. Myers Bros.), 117 Vyse Street, Birmingham, Colonial merchant, member of the City Council.

Philip Rodway was the acting manager, and Mr. Walter E. Alldritt, a Birmingham chartered accountant, was given *pro tem.* the office of secretary. It is worth recording here that Walter Alldritt remained P.R.'s constant friend and associate throughout the existence of the company to the end of his life.

The share capital was fixed at £55,000, divided into 50,000 preferred ordinary shares of £1 each, entitled to a cumulative preference dividend of 5 per cent. per annum and also to half the surplus net profits available for distribution; and 5,000 deferred shares of £1 each, entitled to the remaining half of the available surplus.

In addition there was an authorised debenture issue of £30,000 in 300 first mortgage bonds of £100 each, carrying 5 per cent. interest per annum and secured by a trust deed.

There were offered for sale at par 34,000 preferred shares and 150 debenture bonds.

A few extracts from the body of the prospectus may usefully be given here, both as evidence of the promoters' plans and hopes and as a matter of reminiscent interest:

"The system on which the theatre will be conducted will be that in vogue throughout the Provinces, namely the booking of touring companies to visit the theatre—usually for a week at a time—on what are known as sharing terms; that is to say, this company divides the gross receipts with the visiting company in proportions varying with the status of the latter. There will also be an annual pantomime season, at Christmas, for about twelve weeks.

"The directors have concluded a most satisfactory arrangement with Mr. Tom B. Davis, of the Lyric and Apollo Theatres, London, to act as managing director for a period of six years at a salary of £500 a year. The services of a London manager of Mr. Tom B. Davis's standing should be of great benefit to this company.

"The cost of building, fitting, decorating, lighting, furnishing and equipping the theatre ready for opening, including architects' and surveyors' fees, has been carefully gone into, and the directors have obtained an estimate with regard thereto from Messrs. Ernest Runtz and Ford (who were the architects for the New Gaiety and the Adelphi Theatres, London, the Crown Theatre, Peckham, and other theatres in the Provinces) based on preliminary plans made by them, which estimate, including shops and premises, amounts to £51,960, say £52,000.

"The directors have made arrangements with Mr. Henry Lovatt (one of the largest and best known contractors in England) to build the theatre, shops, and premises, in accordance with plans, specifications, and quantities to be prepared by the company's architects and surveyors, and on which the price to be paid to Mr. Lovatt will be based." (Mr. Lovatt, we note, agreed to take £18,000 of his money in debentures, and the amounts due under other contracts for furnishing, fitting, and equipping the theatre were also to be partly satisfied in this way.)

Tom B. Davis's expert report on the financial probabilities followed. He estimated that for twelve weeks of the year the gross receipts in respect of touring attractions would average £1,200 weekly, total £14,400; for twelve weeks £860 weekly, total £10,200; for six weeks £600, total £3,600; and for eight summer weeks £400, total £3,200. That gave a gross for thirty-eight weeks of £31,400, to which he added £18,000 for twelve weeks of pantomime at £1,500 a week, making a yearly gross, allowing for two blank weeks, of £49,400.

The running expenses for the thirty-eight weeks were put at £5,180, and £18,840 was allowed as the visiting companies' proportion. Then he estimated that the cost of producing and running the pantomime would be £12,180, giving an esti-mated annual deduction, in all, of £36,200, and leaving an estimated disposable balance of £13,200.

His figures, he said, were based on practical experience of presenting attractions at the old Theatre Royal and on accounts supplied by Mr. Philip Rodway. From these it would appear that during the old theatre's last year, first-class attractions had always drawn profitable houses, having aver-aged £930 a week for sixteen weeks, though some were not novelties and several had visited the theatre twice during the year. On six specified weeks the average had been £1,300, and in one case £1,623 had been taken.

An estimate which came down to an average of £820 for thirty-eight weeks could thus be called nothing if not con-servative, especially as Tom B. had taken no account of the higher prices usually charged for the visits of stars. In fact his highest figure, £1,200 a week for twelve weeks, was not much above half the old theatre's capacity of £2,100. Similarly, in regard to the pantomime, he had ascertained that *Dick Whittington*, the last production (1900-1901), had averaged £1,478 a week for four weeks, until the death of her Majesty Queen Victoria had caused a temporary cessation of theatrical business throughout the country.

The figures, it was emphasised, ignored also the facts that a new up-to-date house would secure a larger number of powerful attractions, and that an increased holding capacity would make higher receipts possible on "capacity" occasions.

Nor had he reckoned, so far, the possibilities of revenue from the bars, programmes, advertisements, *et cetera*, and the income likely to be derived from reproducing the company's pantomimes in other towns. He put the former group of revenue-making side-lines at an annual value of £1,500, and again one could hardly call him over-optimistic.

The great stumbling block in any of the rebuilding schemes, we must here recall, had been the ground rent of £8,500, covering the entire site held on ninety-nine years' lease by Mr. Bolton. This incubus had been the subject of protracted "conversations," and Mr. Davis had eventually secured the following highly favourable terms:

That Mr. Bolton would assign to the new company a lease of the land required for the theatre scheme, in return for £9,500 fully-paid preferred ordinary shares and a small cash settlement for his expenses;

That the company would pay a ground rent, under the new lease, of £2,200 annually until the end of 1908, and thereafter of £4,200 annually;

That Mr. Bolton would take from the company a sub-lease of the shops and premises to be erected as an integral part of the theatre scheme, for the remainder of the ninety-nine years, at a rent of £2,200 a year—the company thus getting the site rent free for some years, and at £2,000 a year thereafter.

At the same time it was arranged with the Birmingham Corporation that a strip of land urgently needed for the widening of New Street at this point be sold by Mr. Bolton to the Corporation at the price of £50 per square yard.

Mr. Ernest Runtz, the architect named in the prospectus, had already evolved a plan for the new Royal. As was to be expected from a theatrical architect of his repute, his vision was of a perfectly up-to-date house, to be built of red brick and stone, and—what was more important from the public viewpoint—to give an uninterrupted view of the stage from every seat. The main entrance was placed on New Street, "at the corner of Colonnade Passage," and the four shops which Mr. Bolton had agreed to take on a sub-lease were to be on the remainder of the frontage.

The design indicated a free treatment of the Renaissance style. The theatre was to rise five stories, with a glass-roofed arcade in Colonnade Passage for the shelter of pit and upper circle patrons.

We interrupt ourselves here to say we are well aware that Mr. Runtz's first plan was considerably amended, but we think that both for its points of agreement with, and its aspects of divergence from, the final design, it is worth a detailed description. The ground-plan published at the time showed a wide, sweeping corridor round the stalls, just as it was eventually constructed, and a clever alternation of exits and entrances in Colonnade Passage and Stephenson Street.

The first schedule of accommodation allowed for 2,450 seats, 500 more than in the old building, with a money capacity of about £300 in a full house, as against a former £258. There were to be 250 orchestra stalls at 4/- each, 230 pit-stalls at 2/6, 420 pit seats at 1/-, 320 dress-circle seats at 5/-, 490 upper circle seats at 2/-, 700 places in the gallery at 6d., and eight boxes averaging a guinea and a half each.

The big innovation in this lay-out was the provision of numbered bookable pit-stalls at half-a-crown, a concession for which theatrical Birmingham, to judge from letters frequently addressed to the Press, had long been desirous. Tom B. himself received many similar requests as soon as his intention to build was announced.

Birmingham received with profound satisfaction the news that somebody was at last going to do something about the Royal. The citizens' warm personal and collective concern in the fortunes of the play-house was well expressed by the leader-writer of the *Birmingham Daily Mail*, who said that, while the public bestowed its patronage largely on a business basis, it would be a mistake to assume that this fact embodied the whole of the relations existing between the management of a first-class theatre and the play-going public. The traditions of the old Theatre Royal held a very different story. On occasion plays had been staged there, not because they

were likely to be financially successful, but because it was felt
that the regular patrons wished to see them.

Corresponding with this managerial generosity there had
been a very genuine love for the old house and its associations.
Many Birmingham people felt that it had been mixed up
with the leading events of their lives.

"In it they saw their first pantomime. It figured in some of the
red-letter days of their youth. It sheltered them on many a blissful
evening prior to marriage. It gave the young husband and wife
welcome respite from domestic problems; and it provided the
children, in turn, with many a treat."

This friendly commentator was full of praise for the architect's intention to let every patron have a full and free view
of the stage, and he described as noteworthy the concession
of reserved pit-stalls. Of course, he remarked, it was not sheer
altruism, as half-a-crown was more than a shilling, but the
new "reserves" might counterbalance the gain in receipts by
seriously competing with the orchestra stalls. In any case the
public would gain by the greater choice of reserved seats
afforded.

Tom B. quickly became a figure in local life. He proved
an admirable subject for interview by the reporters, and was
never slow to claim the freedom of the newspaper columns
when he felt that any point needed elucidation or emphasis.
One of his first items of news was that if the theatre could be
ready by early November, 1904, Sir Herbert (then Mr.)
Beerbohm Tree had definitely promised to open it: a prospect
which, as we know, did not mature.

Mr. and Mrs. Citizen showed that they were every bit
as interested in this matter of rebuilding the Royal as was
the company itself. Every announcement evoked lavish correspondence in the local press—all very good publicity, of
course, but, beyond that, evidence that for Birmingham this
venture was something above a mere commercial enterprise
in entertainment catering.

The concession of bookable pit-stalls was received with
gratitude, but not generally accepted as going far enough.

For those who wanted more it was urged that the whole of the pit should be numbered off and bookable for an extra sixpence, instead of an early-door fee being charged.

"Pit patrons," said their spokesman, "can't afford half-a-crown often. It is to be hoped some astute manager will yet appear to grant them the boon they ask. He will tap a goldmine, for the great majority can now go either seldom or not at all, as we cannot stand *en queue*, endangering our health and wasting our time."

Such letters bear a familiar ring in their similarity to those written more recently, as often as the same controversy has arisen. Tom B. didn't mind what people wrote or how hard they criticised his plans. He kept a keen eye on the correspondence columns and made it abundantly clear that his attitude towards suggestions was "the more the merrier." It was his desire, he proclaimed, to arrange the accommodation as far as practicable to suit the wishes of Birmingham play-goers in preference to his own or his architect's views.

Thus encouraged, the good people of Birmingham bombarded Mr. Davis with advice *via* the newspapers. Several put in a heartfelt plea for reasonable knee-room in the pit. Another asked for more space in the auditorium and less in the bars—with a rider that temperance drinks as well as alcohol be sold. From one side he was urged to build a theatre immune from draughts, from another to ensure a constant passage of fresh air! To each and every one he gave the same answer: "Thanks for the tip; if what you suggest can be done, done it shall be."

Whether in deference to his many local advisers or not, his plans were certainly modified in various details within the next few weeks. Up to quite a late stage it was still intended to put the main entrance at the Colonnade Passage end of the block, with a stairway on the right of the foyer leading to the dress circle, and one on the left to the stalls (just the opposite of the arrangement actually carried out). The proscenium opening was to be 34 ft., and the stage 73 ft. wide by 48 ft. deep, wider than but not quite so deep as the stage of the old

Royal, which had been the largest, with the exception of Drury Lane, in England.

With the plans more or less definite, the directors eager to go ahead, the public no less eager to see "the historic temple of Thespis rise upon its ashes more handsome and imposing than ever before" (as a contemporary writer expressed it), the plainest of plain sailing for the enterprise was indicated.

The only thing lacking was a prompt and generous response to the prospectus! On December 19th, 1903, when the subscription list closed, by no means all the capital had been subscribed. Delay in going to allotment caused a renewal of public uneasiness, but Tom B. cleared the air with a categoric statement that the directors would supply any necessary capital not subscribed, and would certainly go to allotment after Christmas.

They actually did so on New Year's Day, 1904. On that date they were still some thousands short of the £34,000 preference capital for which they had asked, but they had managed to make a new arrangement with the vendors, who now consented to leave in the company's hands 1,700 of the deferred ordinary shares which were to have been allotted to them. These shares the directors decided to offer at par to the preference shareholders, in the ratio of one preferred share for every twenty preference shares held.

At the same time they propounded a scheme whereby each original subscriber of £250 was entitled to a season ticket for the theatre during his lifetime, or so long as he held those shares, while an applicant for 1,000 shares was entitled to two season tickets. Sir Francis H. Pepper, the company's solicitor, tells us that these tickets admitted the holder to the auditorium and to a seat if there was one vacant. Not a great many were ever issued, and of course they became merely souvenirs when the Royal was sold to Moss Empires Ltd.

On January 14th, 1904, all doubt was finally removed by the announcement that the necessary capital was guaranteed, and on January 22nd the work of demolishing the old

Photo by Whitlock

PHILIP RODWAY

1904

building was at long last restarted. A week later the plans were submitted to the Birmingham magistrates and unanimously approved.

Constructive work began early in March, and simultaneously an important alteration in the lay-out was announced. This did not affect the internal arrangements to any extent, but was the changing of the principal entrance from the corner of Colonnade Passage to its present position, opposite Bennett's Hill. It was done by wish of the licensing justices, who considered it would allow more space in the foyer, and also relieve congestion in Colonnade Passage, where the various other entrances were placed. When this alteration was reported to the magistrates by their sub-committee, they expressed great appreciation of the way their wishes had been met in every respect by the directors. It is necessary to add that Mr. Bolton's consent to the change was readily forthcoming, and that his agreement in regard to the shops on the frontage was modified accordingly.

That the Birmingham magistrates, long famous for superlative carefulness over the construction of places intended for public assembly, would give even more than their customary painstaking consideration to the plans of the new Royal, will be appreciated when we remind our readers that the Chicago fire disaster at the Iroquois Theatre had happened not long before—the tragic holocaust of which Vesta Tilley writes so movingly in her reminiscences:

"The theatre," she says, "was quite new (having been only recently opened) and the latest thing in amusement palaces. The contractors had finished the interior, but had still to complete the iron staircases outside the building, which served as emergency escapes in case of accident. Unfortunately the stairway leading from the top gallery was only half finished, and stopped abruptly half way down. When the alarm of fire was raised the gallery audience made a rush for the emergency exit, and the poor wretches discovered that the stairway ended in the air. Forced onward by the mass of people behind them, dozens were hurled into the street, many meeting a violent death. I had just left the

G

matinée performance of *Algy*, and found the road packed with fire-
men and the excited crowd. I saw bodies being lifted and placed
on the window slab of a butcher's shop in the neighbourhood. I
was deathly ill and was hurried away from the gruesome scene.
I pray that I may never see such a sight again."

In many reports of magistrates' meetings at about this time,
whenever reference is made to licensing matters, there is
repeated testimony to their sense of their responsibility for the
public safety "in view of the disaster in the United States."

The Royal plans, indeed, were considered by a special
sub-committee of the magistrates, which remained in being
throughout the period of the reconstruction, and made frequent reports. One consequence of the Chicago fire was that
to the general conditions, laid down by the Licensing Justices
in 1902, was now added a clause requiring theatres and
similar buildings to be equipped with sprinklers. The new
Royal, we assume, was the first Birmingham theatre to be
thus equipped—the first, that is, to be fitted throughout with
a network of piping from which water would be automatically
sprayed over any part of the house in which a fire started.

Progress was rapidly made by Mr. Lovatt's industrious
workmen, of whom 150 were engaged on the job. They had
a trifle of 1,100,000 bricks to lay! The walls of the new
auditorium were reared while the shell of the old dress-circle
still stood on the site, so that the area of the building was
slightly curtailed.

It was just about this time that Ethel Brown, having
accompanied Philip on his daily tour of the skeleton theatre,
witnessed what was nearly an untimely end to all their planning, for an accident almost cost him his life. He had climbed
the scaffolding to examine the construction of the new roof,
she waiting below, and was making his way precariously
across the planks high above the vast space of the auditorium,
when his foot slipped, and he only saved himself from crashing
a hundred feet by clutching a jutting girder as he fell.

By June Mr. Runtz, speaking from thirty years' experience

HARVINGTON CHURCH

as a playhouse architect, was able to aver that he had never known a contract of this character go ahead so quickly. Mr. and Mrs. John Citizen, with all the little citizens, retained their almost proprietorial interest in the venture, and it became fashionable to make daily visits to see how the Royal was going on.

It was now definitely settled that Philip Rodway would resume his position as acting manager under the new régime.

"Mr. Tom B. Davis, alert to have around him the best possible assistance in the conduct of his Birmingham enterprise," said the *Evening Despatch*, "has naturally secured the services of Mr. Rodway as his right-hand man, a fact on which we congratulate both.

"Upon the share which he had in the delicate negotiations leading up to the formation of the new company, Mr. Philip Rodway, the acting manager of the new house, as he was of the old, deserves, as he will no doubt receive, the hearty congratulations of all who are interested in the undertaking; and some apologies are due to him from those who were wont to suggest that the task was beyond his powers. He has shown that youth and enthusiasm can make light even of such difficulties as confronted the promoters."

* * *

Thus secured as to his future, Philip Rodway did what he had resolved that spring morning in the early nineties. He married Ethel Brown. The wedding took place in the little village church at Harvington, the beloved spot which had been a haven of peace and rest in the anxious thirty months now happily concluded.

The marriage was solemnised on July 11th, 1904. . . .

CHAPTER 8

July 11th, 1904

"In sweetest season when each flower. . . .
The earth did fresh arraye
So fresh they seemed as day
Even as their Brydale day. . . .
Sweete Thames, runne softly till I end my song."

So sang Edmund Spenser in perhaps the world's most beautiful celebration of a riverside wedding day, and on the wedding eve the loveliest flowers were gathered and all was preparation for the following morning.

By the side of the Avon, sister river to Spenser's Thames, preparations for another bridal day were being made, in golden summer weather.

With the clash of the bells, gaiety is released.

"Hear the mellow wedding bells,
Golden bells!
What a world of happiness their harmony foretells."

Elizabethan England! Twentieth century England. There is little difference when a wedding is afoot, and so throughout the village of Harvington all is high holiday and festival. The bridegroom has promised that all who come to the "Shakespeare Inn" or "The Coach and Horses" shall drink his bride's health as often as they please—a very popular fisherman is the bridegroom. And the villagers, doubly delighted that their little village has been chosen for the wedding, have made, as a surprise, arches of flowers and green ferns from church door to gate.

It is July 11th, the year 1904, and the glory of a whole summer is in the space of one day. The air is ashimmer with sun and warmth and scent. The tiny station is the scene of great excitement, where the guests and flowers are arriving by the one and only morning train, reaching Harvington in leisurely fashion at noon.

From the painting by Edward Steel-Harper

HARVINGTON

Blossom-time in the Vale of Evesham

Soon after the hour the bride, on her father's arm, and carrying her bouquet of lilies of the valley, walks down the gardens of the lovely old Georgian house, until she comes to the wall-gates opposite the church. They cross the little country road and pass through the flowers to the church door. The groom is already standing by the altar rails.

Somewhere the Recorder of Fulfilled Vows prepares to set his seal. The fulfilment of a young knight's vow made fourteen years before, to love one lady only, and to marry her, is no small feat when twenty-seven is the sum total of the groom's age. No bride could ever have been happier in the knowledge of a steadfast devotion, or ever have had her faith more justified.

She walks up the aisle, the service is read, the bells clash out, their peals waking the echoes in the summer air, and Philip Rodway and his wife pass under the flowered arches to begin their life together. He had long dreamed of his wedding, and wished it to take place in the beauty of the Avon country he loved. Perhaps even he had not imagined Harvington could look as beautiful as in the July radiance of that day.

> *"Ring ye the bells*
> *And leave your wonted labours for this day.*
> *Make feast therefore now all this livelong day."*

They recross the road to the old red house, the guests following, the delighted villagers cheering. The wedding breakfast is set with roast ducks from the Manor Farm, with all their green accompaniments in the best village tradition; under the big cherry tree on the lawn tea is laid, and through the yew hedges if you look you can see the bobbing, interested heads of Most of the Village.

There are the usual speeches, the usual good wishes and congratulations. At last the bride leaves the sunlit lawn and goes up the old oak staircase to change from her wedding dress. When she comes down she is wearing a pale biscuit-coloured costume, with what is to become almost a tradition

in the Rodway family—a cape. Three neat Highwayman
capes, in point of fact; and a huge Leghorn hat with roses
has been exchanged for the white chiffon bonnet with its
satin ribbons—the whole charmingly reminiscent of the
wedding costume in *La Poupée*.

The bridal party walk down the little hill to the station
(and all the village too, to see that they get there safely). So
that there shall be no chance of a mistake, once in their
reserved carriage, the handles of the doors are firmly tied
with the laces of the proverbial wedding shoes. And just in
case the newly-married pair should wish to say anything to
each other without interruption, once the guard says "Right-
away," thoughtful friends (in collusion with the railway
officials) have put fog signals and detonators at frequent
intervals all the way along the line to Evesham. The train
starts off with a puff of importance on its nerve shattering
and noisy career. At Evesham Mr. and Mrs. Philip Rodway
are released from their carriage and catch the boat train to
Southampton.

They embarked on the s.s. *Alberta* for the Channel Isles,
and that evening their boat encountered one of the worst storms
within memory, one of those strange, swift storms that sometimes sweep the Channel in midsummer, with vivid lightning
flashes and heavy claps of thunder. The next morning was
as fair and lovely as ever, with only a sparkling ripple on
the sunny waters as together they gazed at the Casquets, that
cruel reef of rocks on which a year or two before, the s.s. *Stella*,
taking the very same course, had foundered and gone down
with nearly everyone on board, only a few of the two hundred
passengers being saved. (*Heavens! thought Mother, was that the
bottom of the paddle steamer scraping already?*)

They sailed safely past the fatal Casquets and, hours late
from the storm, the boat steamed into the harbour of St.
Helier, and they drove to their Jersey hotel. They had a few
weeks of idyllic happiness on the island, which was quite
unspoiled and very lovely in those days; each bay as they

drove round in their little one-horse brougham (of course there were no cars) seemed more beautiful than the last.

There were halcyon hours at St. Aubyn—that delightful bay where they fished on the beach with long sticks for the razor-fish which are deeply buried in the sand; there were long drives round St. Brelades Bay; scrambles over the rocks to La Corbière Lighthouse, where they marvelled at the view from its tower; they explored the fine ruins of Mont Orgueil Castle; and were carried by sailors across the waters dividing the Caves of the Devil's Hole.

After three weeks they returned to Guernsey; and thence to Whichford Mill, hidden in the heart of the Cotswolds, where the pleasant trout stream meanders for miles among the hills.

CHAPTER 9

(1904-05)

Theatre Royal reopens on December 17th with *The Babes in the Wood;* —"Ring up the Curtain"—Nightmare rehearsals—P.R. takes over—Settling down to it—The 1905 Season—Martin Harvey—Some W. W. Kelly stories— P.R. introduces the Promenade Concerts and turns the tide thereby— Sarah Bernhardt in *Pelléas and Mélisande*—Phyllis's birth.

The new Theatre Royal opened on December 16th, 1904, with a pantomime production *The Babes in the Wood.* During the past few months Philip Rodway had been occupied with the thousand and one administrative details which were the responsibility of the acting manager now that the new Theatre Royal was at last an imminent fact.

On the day previous to the opening a private view for Press representatives from London and Birmingham was arranged, and afterwards a luncheon party at the Grand Hotel. Guests on that occasion, besides the journalists, included Alderman Jarvis (chairman of the Watch Committee), Councillors Myers and Brooks, Mr. W. R. Cobay, Mr. Ernest Runtz, Mr. W. Barradale (clerk to the Justices), Mr. C. H. Rafter (Chief Constable, now Sir Charles), Mr. J. Price (City Surveyor), Mr. A. Tozer (Superintendent of the Fire Brigade), Mr. Francis H. Pepper (since knighted and chairman nowadays of the Prince of Wales Theatre Ltd.), Messrs. M. Morris, G. H. Cartland, F. W. Rinder (so long famous as the arbiter of Aston Villa's fortunes), R. Dawson, Guy Jones (the musical director, brother of Sidney Jones), J. P. Callan (newly appointed as stage-manager), and the new manager Philip Rodway.

Alderman Jarvis gave "Success to the Theatre Royal," observing that although a tinge of regret might be felt at the parting from the old, hearty congratulations must be expressed at the opening of the new Royal. "Admirable and safe" he styled the new building, "excellently managed and perfect in its arrangements."

Tom B. Davis, in reply, complimented all who had worked for the project, "reserving a few special superlatives for Mr. Philip Rodway, the local manager."

Mr. Runtz made the interesting statement that the Royal, with its 2,200 seats, had been built in a quarter the time taken to build the then new Gaiety Theatre in London, with its 1,300 seats. This record had been possible only with the helpful co-operation of the local authorities, who had set an example of promptitude worth commending to the London County Council!

"When the public are admitted to-morrow night" (said the local press) "there will be a chorus of praise which will be the beginning of the reward which Mr. Davis and Mr. Rodway have so thoroughly earned."

From a contemporary report we learn that many new buildings had been erected in Birmingham recently, but none had attracted so much attention as the Theatre Royal. It was almost three years since the old theatre, so closely associated with the names of Mercer Simpson and Charles Dornton, had been closed, and now from its historic ashes had arisen a house which would be worthy of the city and of the inhabitants who loved the drama in its various aspects. The work of reconstruction had occupied only about nine months, and within that period a beautiful building, designed in the semi-classic style of the period of George III, had been set up which would be one of the city's landmarks.

It was declared that there could be no two opinions as to the merits of the internal arrangements. There had sprung up a five-storey building, with an elevation of about 69 ft. and a height of 70 to 80 ft. The floor was divided into orchestra stalls, pit stalls, and pit, while rising in deep tiers were dress circle, upper circle, and gallery.

It is interesting to compare the seating accommodation with the original plan suggested. The new theatre's capacity was about 2,200, composed of 380 seats in the dress circle, 350 in the upper circle, 550 in the gallery, 116 in the pit stalls,

166 in the orchestra stalls, 72 in the boxes, and 550 in the pit, and, so different from the old Royal, there was a clear view obtainable from every seat.

The decorative and upholstering schemes had been carried out in green, white, and gold, and the effect was both rich and restful. Behind the scenes there was ample dressing room accommodation, and the stage accessories were of the latest invention. The overhead arrangements for lighting the stage embodied the most recent improvements, few provincial theatres, if any, being able to boast so complete and satisfactory a system. As to the "house lights," they were both electric and gas. That every precaution had been taken against fire and panic was shown by the number, the very large number, of entrances and exits provided. The cost of building was stated at about £50,000.

* * *

"Come then, Ring up the Curtain."

It is the evening of December 17th, 1904. Mr. Tom B. Davis presents "on a scale of magnificence never before attempted in Birmingham," the pantomime, *The Babes in the Wood*. He has announced a posse of collaborators as numerous as those employed in preparing a modern revue. He has had the "book" written by two famous men in A. M. Thompson ("Dangle" of the *Sunday Chronicle*) and Robert Courtneidge (father of the brilliant Cicely). His scenery has been made and painted by Stafford Hall, T. Holmes, R. C. McLeery, E. H. Ryan, and Philip Howden. The dresses, designed by Wilhelm, have been executed by Landolf of Paris. Guy Jones is in charge of the orchestra. J. P. Callan, the stage-manager, has produced the pantomime under Tom B.'s supervision.

It is nearly seven o'clock. The auditorium is packed out with enthusiasts. Never has a Birmingham theatre held a more fashionable audience for a pantomime. Every bookable seat was sold days ago, and to-night the unreserved places have been eagerly competed for by a crowd far too big to obtain admission. "Standing Room Only" has been displayed by the box offices this half-hour or more, and now the triumphant signs "House Full" are out.

Many of the reserved seat holders have been here longer than the victors from the queues, because they wanted time to inspect the interior of the building, and to see and be seen by everyone there. Amid the animated chatter we hear repeated expressions of approval and admiration at the erection of so handsome and well-appointed an edifice.

The hour of seven is about to strike. Let us see who is here. The young Mrs. Philip Rodway is in her box; in another we note that distinguished photographic genius Sir Benjamin Stone, with Lady Stone. Near them, in the front row of the dress circle, are Mr. Jesse Collings, another M.P., and his wife. City fathers who catch the eye include Alderman Lawley Parker, chairman of the Water Committee, with his wife; Alderman Jarvis, chairman of the Watch Committee (we met him at luncheon yesterday); and Councillors Murray, Freeman, Brooks, Myers, Walthall, and D. Davis (later Alderman Sir David Davis). We see also Lieutenant-General Phelps, Mr. W. L. Powell, Mr. Ashton Smith, Mr. G. H. Cartland, Mr. Edward Rowlands, Mr. W. Barradale, Mr. C. A. Carter, Mr. (now Sir) F. H. Pepper, Mr. H. H. Horsfall, Mr. (later Sir) Whitworth Wallis, Keeper of the Art Gallery, and a hundred others whose names make local news. The directors of the company, of course, are here in force. These parts of the house form a picturesque and animated scene, as the soft lights shine on the elaborate costumes and coiffures of the ladies, accentuated by the black and white of their cavaliers.

And in pit-stalls, pit, upper circle, and gallery are the hundreds upon hundreds of Birmingham playgoers whose names may never get into the papers, but who represent the great theatre-supporting public relied upon by the directors to keep the venture alive when the newness is worn off.

Seven o'clock! Guy Jones taps imperatively on the conductor's desk. A roll of drums brings the house to its feet, the

National Anthem is played, and at last the curtain rises. Could it ascend under happier auspices?

And now, the show's the thing! Let us study the judgment of the always generous *Birmingham Daily Post* before we proceed to less congenial considerations. The subject of the pantomime, we gather, is a good one. The first performance, all things considered, is "eminently satisfactory." With every stage appliance new, it can hardly be expected that "slight delays in the manipulation of the mechanical arrangements" should not occur, but the production, if somewhat slow, passes off with remarkable smoothness.

The *Daily Post*, it is true, finds the pantomime far too long. No wonder, seeing that it takes four and a half hours to unfold, with a consequent marring of the last scene through over-anxiety. Still, we have detected a similar note in the criticisms of pantomime first nights on other occasions, and we know that to-morrow morning will see the necessary cuts ruthlessly made. Nor need we give much thought to the gentle suggestion that the "book," while allowing ample scope for the players to shine brightly, is at present deficient in humour, for the comedians, if they know their work, will very soon remedy this.

Praise is lavished on the rich and colourful settings for Nottingham Market Place; for the Archery Tournament, the Town of Toyland, the Barons' Emporium, and the gorgeous final scene in Robin Hood's Palace (for which the audience, unfortunately, has to wait until nearly midnight). H. E. Haines's music is "above the average in merit," and the orchestra "performs its share of the work admirably."

In Lily Iris the critic saw a notable Robin Hood, though, having regard to what appears elsewhere in this volume about incongruities in modern pantomime, we might here make a note that in one scene Robin Hood, without the slightest warning, became a Japanese naval officer, and held forth with the song *Little Yo-San!*

Gladys Ward, the Maid Marian, had a "Dixie" song, while

Bert Gilbert was a great success as the Baron. Mabel Lait and Monica Sayer were second boy and girl. Nowadays these parts are not so prominent in pantomime, but in pre-war times, when subsidiary salaries were negligible, it was customary to cast them, and often even third boy and third girl, each pair with at least one song between them.

The Babes were Maidie Andrews and Phyllis Dare, the latter then only fourteen years old, and having already been four years on the stage. Mabel Lait's vaudeville partner, Daly Cooper, was one robber, with Henry Wright as the other, and J. F. McArdle as the nurse, Flossie, with *It's All Right in the Summer Time* for his best song. Fred Farren won hearty praise for his faithful study of the collie dog, Towser, and Fred Walton, who played a toy soldier, became a huge favourite.

Reading the extremely flattering comments of the local press, one finds it hard to realise that the pantomime was what is expressively called "a flop." Yet that is the cold truth. Birmingham, with its critical faculty sharpened by over a century of great pantomime tradition, would not put up with a hotch-potch, "thrown-together" production, which was just what Tom B. had unfortunately presented to the city. It is with no idea of depreciating his services to the company, but solely in order to maintain a correct perspective, that it must be recorded how nearly he came to ruining at the outset the venture he had laboured so diligently to launch.

The pantomime, in fact, was prematurely produced, and might as well never have seen the light for all the value it had in either cash or good-will. No doubt Mr. Davis had his own reasons, seemingly valid to him, for insisting on a pre-Christmas opening. He may have expected the reconstruction work to have been completed in good time to allow for adequate rehearsal of the artists, the lighting and the mechanical arrangements. He may have thought that the advantage of opening well ahead of the other Christmas productions in the city, and thus obtaining an "exclusive press," outweighed the patent disadvantages of an un-prepared show. Whatever his reasons, he went ahead despite the warnings of Philip Rodway, whose local knowledge told him that Christmas was the only propitious time for producing a pantomime in Birmingham. P.R. did everything humanly possible to persuade Tom B. to postpone it, but in vain. The pantomime was a failure. Birmingham *wanted* to be friendly, but it would not—will not —accept a half-finished pantomime. A prominent producer of to-day we hope will forgive our saying that this truth was exemplified by the fate of his *Goldilocks* in the same theatre, and in much the same circumstances, nearly thirty years later.

Babes in the Wood never had a chance, and its failure dealt the newly born enterprise a blow from which, as we shall show, it took many years to recover. Apart from missing the Christmas tide, the pantomime of 1904 lacked the one great essential—a director really expert in this type of entertainment. Tom B. himself could not fill the bill, and his attempts to do so achieved some fatal results. He actually ordered (at immense cost) full sets for all the scenes, instead of arranging the necessary alternation of full, half-stage, and front cloth sets. George M. Slater, one of P.R.'s oldest associates, tells us that cartloads of unnecessary and expensive scenery had to be sent away before they had even been unpacked, or else kept eating their heads off in the stores!

The rehearsals, for which nothing like adequate time was allowed, were what Sean O'Casey's "Paycock" would describe as "chass."* They began and ended at all hours of the day and night, but no amount of hard work could force the artists into the skins of their parts (always excepting Farren as the dog) or familiarise the stage staff with the intricacies of the new and elaborate plant. Everyone concerned was naturally full of apprehension as December 17th approached, and even the generous forbearance of the press could not blind them to the conviction, on the actual night, that the show was all wrong.

Philip Rodway knew better than anyone that a tragic

---

*Chaos.

failure was foredoomed. As acting manager he was primarily responsible for the business management of the theatre—but in those days "acting manager" covered a much wider range, especially at the Royal, where he was the only resident functionary with any knowledge or vision. It was his knowledge that warned him of the almost certain disaster ahead, and his vision that impelled him to take all possible steps to avert or soften it.

He had the dress rehearsal called for six o'clock on the evening before production date. Mother and a few privileged guests were invited to see it. We have her heartfelt assurance that it was the most appalling travesty of a dress rehearsal ever staged. Even the dresses were not all ready, and much of the essential scenery had not reached the theatre. It began at about half-past six. At half-past midnight, when the unhappy company had struggled through, hit or miss, to the end of the first half, Mother went home.

Home, and to bed—but not to sleep. Philip had assured her "he wouldn't be long," but she knew that behind his imperturbability was a mounting anxiety. What with this, and the longing to know how things were going, is it to be wondered that she lay awake through the small hours?

Four o'clock passed, and five. No Philip! and of course no telephone either. At six o'clock she could stand inaction no longer, and she began to dress. She had determined to walk back to the Royal and learn the worst, but just as she got to the front door it opened, and Philip, white and worn, walked in. The rehearsal had ended after twelve hours' torture, and the certainty of a fiasco was confirmed.

"Who sympathises with a manager in his difficulties or his failures? No one outside his domestic circle." The public who see the finished production of a pantomime go home contentedly to their beds at eleven o'clock. They do not remember—if indeed they know—that on the fall of the curtain immediate revision is taking place on the stage. The producer, actors, orchestra, and stage hands work at top speed for hours to get the acts which have not run smoothly straightened out. And when at three or four o'clock they at last leave wearily for home, questions, hopes, fears, and impossible gags all revolve in the manager's mind, and contrive to render the short remainder of the night sleepless. The public naturally pay to see the finished article, and give no heed to what goes before or after. Only the "domestic circle" knows the twenty-four hour day, the apparently insuperable difficulties, which attend production. In later years, by careful planning and concentrated work for months ahead, Daddy was able to avoid late night rehearsals for his cast at pantomime time, and the company would disperse secure in the knowledge of a smoothly running show. Every pantomime he put on was carefully timed at rehearsals. The result was that the curtain usually fell on the opening night at the very minute he intended it should, and cuts for the subsequent performances were, therefore, rarely necessary. Not only was the pantomime timed as a whole, but each song, dance, and speciality act as well. In actual fact, all the difficulties had been faced up to and surmounted previous to production; but in the Christmas of 1904-05 these all-night sittings were the rule rather than the exception.

Subsequent events show that Tom B., having seen the theatre opened, left the entire charge to P.R., and he, by instituting regular rehearsals at reasonable hours, managed gradually to get the pantomime pulled into some sort of coherence. But throughout the run, Mother says, the magnificent costumes of the finale were never seen by more than a handful of people, because the show ran to such an inordinate length. The cost to the management was prodigious. It took years of uphill fighting to regain lost ground and put the theatre on a sound financial basis.

The Babes in the Wood ran for thirteen weeks. After a fortnight of continuous work by P.R. it had become almost a new production, to which by rigorous pruning, the introduction of new business and songs, and a general remodelling

H G GAWTHORN

Photo by Vandyk

SIR JOHN MARTIN HARVEY

of the dialogue, he had managed to give some claims to quality, though the mischief had been done.

The "special nights" which were a special feature of P.R.'s long régime were early inaugurated with a visit from students of the University of Birmingham. The Medicals were so keen to match their spirits to the atmosphere of pantomime that they arrayed themselves in the most outlandish fancy costumes, and, as one example of their effervescent enthusiasm, invaded the stage and provided a chorus of nearly forty for *Navahoe*. More of their contributions to the programme made the evening a riotous success, and at the end they showered gifts on the performers and the young acting manager.

Next followed his own special night, and the run closed on March 11th, 1905, the *Daily Post* paying Philip Rodway the compliment that, in spite of Tom B. having produced before it was ready, *The Babes* had developed into one of the best pantomimes Birmingham had ever seen. Tom B. came down from London for the last night.

* * *

H

Season 1905

To Mr. Martin Harvey (as Sir John was then) fell the distinction of inaugurating the first dramatic season in the new Royal. This was on March 13th, 1905, with Martin Harvey as Reresby the Rat in *The Breed of the Treshams*, and his wife, Nina de Silva, as Batty. On the first night he made a little speech congratulating Birmingham on its fine new playhouse, and its manager, Mr. Rodway.

The next few attractions present no interest at this distance of time, except that Nellie Wigley, the principal boy of the 1912-13 pantomime, appeared in March, 1905, as Princess Soo-Soo in *A Chinese Honeymoon*. Early May brought a Shakespeare company in *The Tempest*, with Iris Hoey as Ariel, while later in the same month Stanley Cooke came in *Charley's Aunt*.

On June 12th *A Royal Divorce*, the Bank Holiday standby and sure winner for many years, played at the new theatre for the first time, although it had already been seen often enough at the old house in the preceding fifteen or sixteen years. Edith Cole, the only imaginable Josephine for most people, was in her familiar rôle.

Miss Cole, of course, was the wife of the late W. W. Kelly, "The Barnum of the Theatre," and proprietor of *A Royal Divorce*. She met her death a few years ago through being burned while cleaning a pair of white kid gloves. Few people knew that in real life she was a woman of the most intensely brooding type, her soul weighted down by private sorrows—but it is all expressed in a volume of poems and stories called *Scarlet and Grey* which bore her name as authoress.

Poor Josephine! she had a difficult Napoleon in W. W. Kelly, the genial American-born Lancastrian whose recent death released a flood of stories about his showmanship, his quaint blend of simplicity, astuteness, overweening arrogance, vanity, and love of personal display. As a stunter he has rarely been equalled, never surpassed. His famous melodrama was a farrago of sentimental nonsense, yet he made money out of it for forty years, thanks to the flamboyance with which he introduced and presented it.

The newspaper advertising for the Whit Week visit in 1905 was typical. On the Friday evening Miss Cole took her benefit, for which it was announced that "The Famous Edgbaston Military Band" would play on the stage "with limelight and scenic effects." But that was nothing; for the Saturday he advertised "A Grand Gala night in honour of the Anniversary of the Battle of Waterloo, which was fought on the 1st June, 1815. In order to celebrate appropriately the occasion The Famous Edgbaston Military Band will play again on the stage Eckersberg's descriptive music *The Battle of Waterloo*."

Kelly lived (theatrically speaking) in a freakish world of superlatives. Limelight was his passion. He valued above everything the traditions that grew up around his top-hat, his frock-coat, and his huge buttonhole. When he was in the town he loved to be the centre of an admiring circle in the theatre saloon, and sooner or later, if there was a stranger present, the "Kelly Mallet" was sure to appear.

About this mallet there is a story which, while simple to the point of fatuity, so well illustrates Kelly's character that it must be told once more. He always carried a little gavel, or hammer, with a detachable handle. By unscrewing a portion of the stem he revealed a cavity containing a silver coin of small value. As soon as he found an opening, he would turn the conversation to this toy, and loudly express his conviction that the Kelly luck was moulded in the coin.

As the conversation went on, he would replace the handle. A few minutes later he would manage to be called from the room, leaving the mallet on the table. During his absence someone "in the know" would say "Let's have a lark with W.W.; let's take his precious coin out, screw the thing up again, and pull his leg when he comes back." So it would be fixed, with the unsuspicious stranger deputed to act as the leg-puller.

In due time back would come Kelly, and soon the mallet would crop up again. The would-be leg-puller would then put in his oar with, "That's all very well, Mr. Kelly. You talk a lot about your mallet and your luck—but I don't believe there's a coin in it at all." An argument, carefully worked up on both sides to fever pitch, would follow, and at last Kelly—or the other man—would exclaim, "Well, look here, I'll just bet you drinks and cigars all round!"

The wager made, Kelly would solemnly detach the handle, unscrew the section, gaze into the empty cavity. At this stage his opponent would be congratulating himself on having caught W.W. napping, but not for long—because Kelly, unscrewing a *second* section, would show a *second* cavity, with a *second* coin, and throatily chuckle "You pay, my boy!"

Does it sound utterly childish? Well, he was in some sort a great man, and great ones, as we all know, have their follies. Mark the sequel. Daddy, whose position brought him closest into touch with W.W., was often the confederate in this quite harmless confidence trick. One evening, when Kelly had gone out of the room as usual, and the stage was being set for the climax, "Look here, you chaps," Daddy said, "I'm getting a bit tired of old W.W. and his 'You pay, my boy!' Can't we change the finale a bit?" . . . (interval for counter-plot).

Kelly came in again, and the old farce went on . . . "Drinks all round?" "And cigars?" "Done!" Kelly detached the handle. Kelly unscrewed the first section. Kelly unscrewed the second section. Kelly's face fell when he saw, instead of the expected coin, a screwed-up piece of paper which, on being unfolded, was found to bear the words "You pay, my boy—for once!"

Generations of playgoers will remember Napoleon's "spirited white charger," which figured so prominently in the Waterloo scenes, and thereby hangs another tale. Instead of "travelling" a horse, W.W. used to hire one in each town. In Birmingham, for several years running, he had the same one, a

docile animal normally engaged in pulling a bus. Daddy
would often tell us how this particular horse could never be
induced to take the stage until someone in the opposite wings
had given the "right away" with two strokes on a bell—and
that a similar signal was absolutely essential before it would
consent to move off! (One is reminded of the schoolboy's
expressive description: "The elephant is a docile creature,
but when infuriated he would not do so!")

P.R. had *A Royal Divorce* at the Royal annually, and some
times twice or thrice in one year, until after the war. He
might have given it further bookings, only one Whit Monday
morning, while he was watching the run-through, it struck
him that for some years the production had been getting
cheaper and cheaper.

"Look here, W.W.," he said, "this isn't quite the game, is
it? I mean to say, four supers and two pans of red fire for the
Battle of Waterloo——"

"Quite right, my boy, quite right," rumbled Kelly. "Jones,
set off a couple more pans of red fire!"

So P.R. decided that on the whole he had better say farewell to *A Royal Divorce* while it still had some style about it.

Thus having digressed, we return to the Royal in 1905.
The drama season ended at Whitsun, and the directors were
faced with the uncomfortable knowledge that so far their
brave new venture had been very expensive. A few weeks
earlier it had been decided to close from Whitsun to August
Bank Holiday, in the hope of cutting losses, but Philip
Rodway fought strongly against a step which he felt would
still further impoverish the theatre's goodwill.

"What on earth is the alternative?" asked Tom B.

P.R. had it pat—an alternative which might not make
money, might lose money, but would certainly create prestige,
increase goodwill, and attract a wide range of new patronage.
He reminded Tom B. that years earlier, in the old Royal,
a series of Promenade Concerts had been given by a band
drawn partly from Birmingham and partly from Manchester,

with visiting conductors and soloists. That series was a failure.

"So it may have been," argued P.R. "But we have a house much better adapted for the purpose, and we can do the thing on really bold lines. It *must* be better than closing six months after opening, when so far we've given the public nothing to like!"

So Tom B. and the Board (which is to say, Tom B.) decided to let him have his head, and P.R. went all out to make the "Proms" not merely worth while to Birmingham's genuine music-lovers, but likely also to intrigue and attract the general public.

He turned the ground floor into a real promenade, with easy chairs and lounges in place of the formal rows of seats, a built-up centre piece of ferns, palms, and flowers, and attractive fairy lighting. With the hearty co-operation of the late Mr. Max Mossel he was able to secure Sir (then Mr.) Landon Ronald to direct an orchestra of seventy-five performers. He worked out all the details of a season of four weeks' duration with concerts every night, and a special matinée by a visiting star each Thursday.

One of those stars was Mischa Elman, then a very young Russian violinist. At the first Thursday matinée he took the place, at short notice, of Kubelik, who fell ill, and a fortnight later he again took the principal position. Another was Marie Tempest; our generation thinks of her only as a queen of comedy acting, but her matinée at the Royal on July 20th, 1905, is a reminder that she had studied at the Royal Academy of Music under Manuel Garcia, and taken gold and silver medals. Her fame up to 1905, it is true, had been chiefly made in light musical fare, though she had sung in opera in America. The *Daily Post* commented on her "transition from the stage to the concert platform," but actually it was nothing of the kind: merely an interlude. All the same, she was recognised as a highly accomplished vocalist, and later appeared at leading London concerts, while in 1906 she earned a very large salary as a singer at the Palace Theatre.

On one afternoon during this month a variation was furnished by a flying matinée—with the divine Sarah Bernhardt at the head of the cast—of Maeterlinck's *Pelléas and Mélisande*.

*   *   *

It was during this first Promenade Concert season, on Tuesday, June 27th, that Phyllis was born. As it was the month of roses, everyone brought baskets of them, crimson, cream and white; Mother remembers that the house was a perfect bower of flowers, that even the chintz curtains and frills and covers in her room had roses on them, and how much the picturesque effect pleased her.

As the first child of the first manager of the new Theatre Royal, presents were showered on "Miss Baby Rodway"—a little gold bracelet from the staff of the theatre; silver christening mugs from Fred Terry and Julia Neilson; silver spoons from Councillor Myers, Mrs. Charles Dornton and others.

A month old, in robes about five feet long, she was taken by Mother and Daddy in what must have been one of the first motor-cars. It had no hood, and Daddy held a sunshade over them the whole way from Edgbaston to Knightwick-on-Teme.

The summer of 1905 was a very lovely one; the heat grew more and more intense, and on many a night during their holiday at the old black and white house at Knightwick they heard the horns blown in the woods around, to keep off the foxes. Just as one of Mother's most vivid memories is the chattering of the blackbirds under her windows during the weeks before Phyllis was born, so, in those summer months that followed, came the song of the nightingale, for which that part of the country is famous. Mother and Daddy, after a long day on the river, often sat up till midnight just for the sheer joy of listening, and the words of the most compleat angler of all must have found an echo in their hearts, for there "the Nightingale breathes such sweet loud musick out of her little instrumental throat, that it might make mankind to think miracles are not ceased. He that at midnight, when the very labourer sleeps securely, should hear, as I have very often, the clear airs, the sweet descants, the natural rising and falling, the doubling and redoubling of her voice, might well be lifted above earth, and say, 'Lord, what musick hast thou provided in Heaven, when thou affordest such musick on Earth!' "

*　　*　　*

From the melody of the nightingale we return to the melodies of the Promenade Concerts. *O Lovely Night*, from his song-cycle *Summertime*, is the inscription on the portrait which Landon Ronald gave to Daddy at the end of the season:

> "To that clever, courteous, and kind acting manager, Mr. Philip Rodway, in remembrance of a month's pleasant work done together during the Promenade Concerts at the Theatre Royal, Birmingham."

The "Proms" over, things settle down again into the ordinary routine of a first-class provincial theatre. Most of the popular attractions and leading artists of the day included the Royal on their provincial round—Oscar Asche and Lily Brayton in *The Taming of the Shrew*, Fred Terry and Julia Neilson in the first Birmingham visit of *The Scarlet Pimpernel*, Edward Terry in *The Magistrate*, *Sweet Lavender*, and other plays, James Welch in *Mr. Hopkinson*, Mr. and Mrs. F. R. Benson, as they then were, with H. O. Nicholson, George Weir and Tita Brand in Shakespeare, Robert Michaelis in *Veronique*, were examples of the quality achieved.

PHYLLIS

*A miniature painted on ivory by
Mrs. Philip Rodway,*
1906

MRS. PHILIP RODWAY

A miniature by Mabel Delmé-Radcliffe,
1904

The outstanding feature of this autumn, however, was *The Catch of the Season*, which Seymour Hicks and Ellaline Terriss brought here for the first time. Sidney Fairbrother was in the cast, and it opened to a record house, both for the theatre and for the play. Said a critic: "Our new-old theatre certainly never looked better or more pleased with itself."

The 1905 season ended with the appearance of Godfrey Tearle as Ferdinand and Iris Hoey as Ariel in a lovely production of *The Tempest*.

CHAPTER 10

(1905-08)

PANTOMIME 1905-06
ALADDIN

The second pantomime under the new régime was *Aladdin*, a production by Robert Arthur, who in the old theatre had produced *Dick Whittington*. The mistake of a premature opening was not repeated, and so on Boxing Day, 1905, the Royal, with Philip Rodway in command, settled down once more to follow its ancient tradition.

Aladdin was an extremely picturesque and ingenious production, with Ada Reeve, many people's ideal principal boy, as the hero; Harry Tate as Abanazar the Magician, and Fanny Dango as the Princess So-Shi. Ada Reeve, to quote Mr. Crompton Rhodes, was "the only principal boy who can be named in the same breath as Jenny Hill and Vesta Tilley . . . in pantomime her personality amounts to genius." Harry Tate is still famous in music-hall circles for his wonderfully mobile moustache and his uproarious skits on various pastimes, from golf to billiards. Fanny Dango, a Birmingham girl, was one of the five Rudge sisters—Letty Lind, Lydia Flopp, Adelaide Astor (Mrs. George Grossmith), and Millie Hilton being the others. Regan and Ryan appeared as Chinese policemen, and Harry Brayne was Widow Twankey.

The pantomime had one piece of bad luck. It ran into the general election of January, 1906. In those days general elections were longer-drawn affairs so far as the polling went, than they are nowadays, and the pantomime, like other shows everywhere, suffered from the distraction of public interest. After the Birmingham polling day (January 18th), however, it recovered splendidly, "house full" boards becoming a regular evening display.

Harry Tate's sketches were a tremendous success, especially those which introduced his remarkable motor-car. In one scene it had a madcap career across mountains and through buildings. In another, which showed Abanazar and Aladdin flying by motor-car to the treasure cave, the infant art of cinematography was employed to perfect the illusion. Harry Tate also introduced his golfing skit, with Ernest Leno, son of the famous Dan, as the phlegmatic caddie.

Harry Brayne, the Widow Twankey of the production, recalls that a "United Pantomimes Midnight Fancy Dress Carousal" was held in the cellars of the Trocadero during the run. Only men were eligible to attend, and Mr. Brayne, who defied the rule by turning up as "Mrs. Edwards' Desiccated Old Cook," was penalised by the loss of his share of the Christmas pudding. Philip Rodway went as Charles Surface, Lester Collingwood (of the Alexandra) as Charles the First, Albert Bushell (of the old Gaiety) as John Bull, Harry Tate as Tony Lumpkin, Ernest Leno as Claude Duval, George Lashwood as Orlando, and Joe Graham (of the Prince of Wales) as a courtier.

The students of Birmingham University held their night on March 2nd, and gave to P.R. a beautifully engraved gold pencil as a souvenir.

Many of our readers must have wondered what becomes of the innumerable presents which a popular theatre manager receives, during the course of thirty years, from artists and friends on anniversary and other special occasions. Obviously he cannot wear all the tie-pins, carry all the pencils, match-boxes, cigarette-cases, and Russian-leather wallets, or use all the hair-brushes, fountain pens, attaché cases, and umbrellas handed over the footlights or presented "on behalf of the principals, chorus, orchestra, and staff."

What *does* become of them? Well, P.R. followed the practice customary among frequent recipients, of admiring his gifts for a few days, and then tucking them away in some desk, or cabinet. Not all, of course, for some found place and utility in his pocket, or in the home. Actually, in our case, the vast majority went down for safety to the bank where they still remain.

It is an instinct of the human race to give presents, and in theatrical circles this instinct is most strongly developed. After all, the joy of giving and receiving lies not so much in the gift as in the sentiment that prompts it. At home to-day are scores of such souvenirs of bygone special occasions, and still within them gleams the friendly appreciation of services rendered, efforts made, or success achieved.

P.R.'s own night followed ten days later, when a crowded house saw a prolonged programme, to which extra turns were contributed by Lelia Rose, Dorothy Ward, May Moore Duprez, "The Jolly Dutch Girl," and others. Dorothy Ward, the star of many pantomimes and musical comedies in the last twenty years, was then a young Birmingham girl playing Zenobia in *Bluebeard* at the Alexandra—her first stage engagement. P.R. on this occasion received among other presentations a gift from the late Lester Collingwood (then proprietor of the Alexandra Theatre and chairman of the Benefit committee), as "a mark of the appreciation in which he is held by his colleagues in the profession."

These presents (said the *Daily Post* next day) were evidence of the fact that during the past decade he had made many friends among the play-going public by his courtesy and kindness. After the performance he gave a supper to the working staff of the theatre at the Colonnade Hotel (now the Chamber of Commerce), where, in the intervals between toasts and songs, he received further gifts—a pair of silver-backed hair-brushes, a standard lamp, a turquoise and diamond pendant for Mrs. Philip Rodway, and (happy inspiration!) a tiny pendant for their little daughter. He himself gave presents to various members of the theatre and pantomime executive.

Another pleasant function of a different kind, during the pantomime run, was a party given by Ada Reeve and her husband, Wilfred Cotton, at the Edgbaston Assembly Rooms on Friday, March 2nd, from 11-30 p.m. to 4 a.m., "to sup, to dance, and to usher in the . . . anniversary of Mrs. Cotton's birthday." With the reticence popularly attributed to our sex, Mrs. Cotton omitted to specify her age on the invitations, but somebody filled the blank on Mother's and Daddy's card with the utterly libellous figures 84! Ada Reeve was in fact thirty. She had been on the stage since 1882 when, as a child of six, she made the traditional début of the later Victorian era by playing little Willie in *East Lynne.*

Mother's dance programme contains a list of nine valses—one, "Many Happy Returns," by Hudson, dedicated to the hostess; there were three Lancers, a barn dance, and a galop.

Aladdin ran for twelve weeks, and was generally acknowledged one of the most successful pantomimes in England that year.

* * *

Season 1906

Again Martin Harvey opened the spring season, this time with *Hamlet* and other plays. The next attraction was *The Spring Chicken*, with George Gregory leading the Gaiety Company. Nelson Keys, who had not then made his name, had a small part not considered worth noticing by the critics. *Charley's Aunt*, the ever-green, followed on, a point of interest being that Brandon Thomas, the author, played Sir Francis Chesney.

The other important features of the season were the first production on any stage of Bernstein's *The Whirlwind*—Mrs. Patrick Campbell playing lead—and the first Birmingham production, by the Moody-Manners Opera Company, of *The Marriage of Figaro*. It was during the Company's fortnight this year that Mr. Charles Manners revealed that he had thrice vainly sought to secure P.R. as his manager.

And so to the second series of "Proms," under Max Mossel's direction. The previous year's experience dictated an earlier season, and various alterations in method were introduced. An influential local sub-committee was formed, and a guarantee fund established. Landon Ronald was again engaged to conduct an orchestra seventy strong, with principals drawn from among the best instrumentalists of the day, but the bulk of the players were recruited locally. The stage was transformed into an orchestral platform, and the pit cleared for promenade purposes, but the orchestra stalls remained in position, since in 1905 the patrons had shown little disposition to venture into the great open spaces. P.R. enthusiastically made all the arrangements.

The season lasted three weeks from May 14th. Each Tuesday was a Wagner Night, each Thursday a Tchaikowsky Night. There was also a "British Night," devoted to the works of Sir Edward German, Hubert Bedford, Sir Landon Ronald, Sir Edward Elgar, and Sir Arthur Sullivan—though the public then as now, were shy of British music when presented wholesale.

There was practically no promenading. The *Daily Post* critic was impelled to remark that "There must be some mysterious influence at work to attract all sorts of people to take their musical pleasures standing."

A feature of the season was the first performance in England of August Enna's Festival Overture. On the final night (June 2nd) "The Theatre Royal presented a truly brilliant aspect, crowded as it was from floor to ceiling. The enormous audience was a conclusive testimony to the attractive power of the Promenade Concerts, and the increasing desire on the part of the public to hear orchestral music, one of the highest forms of musical art, in the best possible conditions and amidst such pleasant surroundings as the Theatre Royal is able to offer. . . . A word of acknowledgment is due to Mr. Philip Rodway for the admirable way in which the theatre was managed during the concert season."

The next notable event was the visit of Lewis Waller (Othello), H. B. Irving (Iago), Evelyn Millard (Desdemona),

Henry Ainley, Edith Wynne Matthison, etc., in *Othello*. Miss Wynne Matthison, incidentally, is the Birmingham-born actress who, with her husband (Charles Rann Kennedy), has done such distinguished work in the American theatre.

A two months' closure ended with the inevitable return of *A Royal Divorce* on August Bank Holiday. H. B. Irving was soon back again, bringing *The Lyons Mail*, and—for the first time in Birmingham—*Paolo and Francesca*, himself playing Alexander's old part of Giovanni Malatesta; his wife, Dorothea Baird (the original Trilby), playing Francesca, Harcourt Williams Paolo, and Maud Milton Lucrezia.

Julia Neilson and Fred Terry in *Dorothy o' the Hall*, Willie Edouin and Pollie Emery, Martin Harvey and Nina de Silva, Beerbohm Tree and Constance Collier, Olga Nethersole, the Moody Manners Opera Company and other more or less regular tourists filled the Autumn season. Martin Harvey brought *Boy O'Carroll*, in which he forsook the vein of Byronic tragedy for that of Irish comedy. Miss Nethersole played the title rôles in *Sappho*, *The Second Mrs. Tanqueray*, *Carmen*, and *Camille*. Mr. Tree brought *The Newcomes*, an adaptation from Thackeray.

Tannhauser was given by the Moody Manners Company in the version arranged by Wagner for Paris in 1861. This was the first performance of the Paris version in Birmingham, and for some reason the principals were supported by fifty-five members of the Sheffield Amateur Grand Opera Society.

This November (1906) Daddy lost a close friend in Mr. William Lemon Sheffield, of Cottesmore Priory, Edgbaston, who was found drowned in the lake in his grounds. There had always been a close friendship between the families, and Sheffield's firm, the famous bill-posters, with Uptons, the equally well-known printers, did all the work of this kind for the theatres with which P.R. was connected.

Only two days before the tragedy Daddy and Mother had lunched with Mr. and Mrs. Sheffield at Cottesmore Priory and spent the afternoon in their lovely grounds, Daddy fishing in the pool. Driving back to town in the smart high dog-cart with the bay mare, Mr. Sheffield remarked to him: "You know, if anybody got into that pool, he'd never get out again—the mud is too deep and thick."

On hearing the news of the tragedy Daddy's first words to Mother were: "Upton will never get over this—he'll be the next."

At times he possessed an uncanny knack of foreseeing events. His premonition came true. Upton *was* the next; within a few months he was found lying dead across the threshold of his beautiful home, Berry Hall,* Solihull. His gun, which had gone off accidentally, was lying by his side.

The name of Herbert Clayton, later so well known as Jack Waller's partner in the very successful productions of musical comedy at Drury Lane after the war, crops up in 1906. He was then an actor, touring with Florence Smithson ("the song-bird of Old Drury") and Bert Gilbert in *The Blue Moon*.

Camille Clifford came in December for what used to be called a "flying matinée." This was just after her marriage to the Hon. H. L. Bruce, which gained great prominence from the fact that it was almost the first stage marriage into the peerage. A Danish girl who had taken to the stage in New York, she had figured prominently in London in *The Prince of Pilsen*, *The Catch of the Season*, and *The Belle of Mayfair* with Seymour Hicks. She personified the type of American beauty then popular, known as *The Gibson Girl*, (created by the famous artist, Charles Dana Gibson,) the distinctive essentials of which were height and a magnificent carriage, striking looks, dark hair piled high on the head, and a very long and tightly fitting gown of black velvet swathed and moulded to the figure.

*   *   *

PANTOMIME 1906-07
THE QUEEN OF HEARTS

December 26th, 1906, saw the production of *The Queen of*

*Appendix.

With all good wishes

H. B. Irving as Hamlet. Henry Irving

Hearts, with George Robey as the Queen. This was the third pantomime which the eye-browed "Prime Minister of Mirth" played at the Royal, and he was destined to star in another three. His full record was *Dick Whittington* (1897-98), *The Babes in the Wood* (1899-1900), *The Queen of Hearts* (1906-07), *Jack and the Beanstalk* (1909-10), *Goody-Two-Shoes* (1912-13), and *Sinbad the Sailor* (1914-15)—six star comedy engagements at the same theatre in fourteen years, not counting the three closed seasons. Besides "G.R.," there were dear old Tom Shale as the King of Hearts, Edward Lewis as the Knave, Tom Hearn as the Grand Slam, Millie Lindon as Prince Florizel, Ethel Haydon (Mrs. George Robey) as Fortuna, and Helen Cecile as Armida.

Robey's gifts were brilliantly displayed; it was impossible to say in which scene he was best, and difficult to think of him at any time except in superlatives.

Shale's King was a quaint, eminently apt blend of dignity and burlesque, with taking songs in *Dandy Pete* and *Sailing in my Balloon*. Teddy Lewis's chief number was *It's a different girl again*. Tom Hearn's part had no very obvious connection with the play, but his juggling act was worth inclusion on any terms. Millie Lindon was handsome and gallant as the Prince, though throughout the run she was unable to do herself justice because of her recent illness. Her song, *The Girl in the Picture Frame*, was written by Mr. W. Jackson Houlston, of Erdington, who has for upwards of thirty years directed a remarkable amateur stage organisation, and who in those days was well-known as a writer of songs and scenes for professional productions. Valli Valli was a dainty principal girl, making a sure hit with *By the Side of the Zuyder Zee*. The scenery was beautiful, especially for the transformation scene at the end of the first act, Poppyland.

Later George Robey put in a typical song, *I said "Oh,"* sung with true Robeyan unction, and Edward Lewis introduced *Leave 'em alone and they'll play for hours*. The show was

I

billed as "The pantomime success of the country," and really did very excellent business.

George Robey, always a keen footballer, collected a team of professional talent to meet Aston Villa's full league team at Aston in February, for the benefit of local charities. He himself played centre-forward, and after the match, which Aston Villa won 4-3, gave a dinner to all concerned at the Stork Hotel. The same night, on the stage, he presented gold medals to the players, and a cup to the winners' captain, Joe Bache. P.R. announced that £350 had been raised by this sporting diversion.

Before the pantomime ended on March 16th, after the twelve weeks' run—the full period allowed—he added a Harlequinade, with George Robey as the Clown, and all the other principals in character.

Students' Night was observed with customary enthusiasm— "Methinks devilment is rife," murmured "G.R." as he surveyed the kaleidoscopic invasion. The University students had taken great pains in rehearsing various choruses and dances, their poets had put in extra verses, and their wits had contrived topical jokes. They frequently overflowed on to the stage to help the performance along.

P.R.'s own night was on Monday, March 11th, when a packed house and many gifts emphasised the position he had gained in public and professional esteem. Extra turns were contributed among others by the star of the previous pantomime, Ada Reeve, who sang a new song, *June*, specially composed for the occasion by Guy Jones, the theatre's musical director. George Robey and his wife gave a clever little sketch called *Business and Pleasure Combined*, and George's solo "extras" included a laughter-making impersonation of Paderewski. Among the new material interpolated by the other principals, the best idea was Tom Hearn's, who promised a Protean sketch embodying imitations of his fellow artists. For several minutes the deception was kept up—only for the audience to be made aware, eventually, that the merry

Messrs. Lewis, Shale, and Robey had been their own impersonators!

A *Queen of Hearts* Commemoration Supper was given that same night by Mr. Harry Lewis, the genial Yorkshireman (still living, but unhappily a confirmed invalid) who had succeeded to the chairmanship of the Board on the death of Mr. Abbott. The fare (if we are to believe the menu which Mother kept), included:

Salmon Mayonnaise à la Haydon . . . Sauce Robey

Braised Lamb Cutlets with
Shale-ots

Teddies à la Lewis   Turret Tops à l' Hearn

Tongue à la Mrs. Simpkins

———

Poularde en Cecile

———

Frozen Hearts en Soufflet à la Valli Valli

Tarts of Trouble

———

Laitances à la Lindon

Stilton, "Ark."   Gorgonzola, "Listen!!"

and so on.

In an article of his which appeared in the press, P.R. observed: "*The Queen of Hearts* is the most successful pantomime I can remember at the Royal. When making a rough calculation the other day, I found that it was witnessed by over a quarter of a million people—and it may be interesting to note that some of them came as many as a dozen times." . . .

One story of that particular pantomime which he used to tell us concerned the theatre cat, which in its time made many appearances on the stage, some of them unrehearsed and exceedingly inopportune. She figured conspicuously in *The Queen of Hearts* in the kitchen scene, and always got a big laugh when she was "discovered" as George Robey lifted up the big dish cover.

One evening during the run her absence just before she ||

was due to make her entrance caused considerable consternation. Stage hands searched frantically for her high and low without success, and eventually a cat had to be borrowed from a little shop at the back of the theatre. Later the truant was found in an obscure corner of the property room, the delighted possessor of several baby cats! Obviously wishing to be the founder of a theatrical line, she was determined to start her family in the right environment.

* * *

Season 1907

The 1907 season had not been running long when the annual general meeting of shareholders in the Theatre Royal Birmingham Ltd. was held. Mr. Harry Lewis presided, and a doleful account he had to present.

Though a trading profit of £1,973 had been made on the year to December, 1906, the balance sheet still showed a debt of £729 to the bank, and £4,158 owing to creditors. The deficiency account stood at £8,267 after subtracting the year's profit. These figures, it is true, showed a considerable improvement on the first year, when there was a total loss of £6,006 (including £5,492 written off on the ill-starred *Babes in the Wood*), and a deficit of £9,477. The preliminary expenses, however, had also been written off, leaving a net deficit of £6,793.

What must have startled the shareholders was not so much this succession of figures as the chairman's considered statement that there was no reasonable expectation, "having regard to the risky nature of the theatrical business generally," of better results until the company was in a position to produce its own pantomimes.

"Speaking generally," said Mr. Lewis, "the greatest difficulties are the dearth of first-class touring companies and the impossibility of opening the theatre during three months in the summer except at a loss." He strongly advocated a reduction of capital, pointing out that an increased ground rent of £2,000 yearly would be due from January, 1909. The capital he wanted to write off was no longer covered by available assets, and consequently there was no reasonable prospect of dividends as the figure stood. By wiping off capital and writing down the shares to a fair value they might hope for a return of their remaining money.

One can imagine the shareholders saying to themselves, or to one another, "What about the prospectus? What about Mr. Tom B. Davis's conservatively-estimated annual profit of £13,200 a year, not counting raised prices, bars, advertisements, etc.? Where is the £5,000 which was to be available for dividend after paying the debenture interest and six per cent. on the deferred ordinaries?"

Well might they ask. It cannot be denied that Mr. Davis, in framing his report for the prospectus, had been transparently over-optimistic. Owing to ill-health he was not present at the meeting to answer questions on the hiatus between expectation and realisation, but Mr. Cobay, another director, read a letter from him in which the regrettable descent from airy fancy to unpalatable fact was beautifully explained away.

For the opening pantomime, it now appeared, the company had been unable to obtain any of the best-known artists, who were engaged years ahead by managements more firmly established. Consequently the show had not attracted the public in large numbers. The Board had therefore decided that until the stars were to be had they would hire their pantomimes on sharing terms. Hence the two already done by arrangement with Robert Arthur, and the *Cinderella* which Robert Courtneidge was to send to Birmingham at the approaching Christmas.

There was no mention of under-rehearsal, lack of technical knowledge, or any similar contributory to the great failure. Even Tom B.'s eminence as a manager had not enabled the Royal directors to clutch the stars from the firmament, all of which was regrettable, but "worse remains behind."

Having explained how the sharing system removed the risk
of a loss on pantomime, but removed also the chances of a
high profit, Mr. Davis went on to lament that the weeks not
covered by spring, autumn, and pantomime seasons could not
be employed on a profitable basis. "Some time ago," he
pleaded, "I put forward the idea of reproducing each summer
some favourite comic opera for three or four weeks, with the
cast and chorus recruited almost entirely locally, but I regret
that the scheme did not attract sufficient response to justify
my thinking it would prove popular or remunerative. I
thought such a scheme might serve to bring out local talent
in acting and singing, and perhaps later on we could have
produced some original comic opera written and composed
by local ladies and gentlemen."

Here Tom B. became almost lyrical:

"What a glorious result it would be if such an enterprise
ended in the formation of another partnership like that of
Gilbert and Sullivan!" he wrote, and with this idyllic
possibility to comfort them for the loss of their dividends, the
shareholders, having passed votes of thanks to the chairman
for presiding and to Philip Rodway for his year's work, took
their hats and their departure.

The first engagement of note was the visit of *Amasis*, which
was a welcome return to comic opera of the genuine kind. It
introduced to us Drury Lane's principal girl for the next
three years in the person of Madge Vincent, a sister of Ruth
Vincent. *The New Aladdin* was not so great an attraction as
most of George Edwardes' pieces, though so much had been
said about relighting the sacred lamp of burlesque.

April brought another welcome visit by Seymour Hicks and
Ellaline Terriss, this time in *The Beauty of Bath*. They paid
the theatre and the management a delightful compliment by
telling P.R. that when they had previously come to Birmingham they had been promised by people most learned in
theatrical circles that they would have a record week. As
they had already done wonderful business with *The Catch of*

the Season, they doubted this, but had been most happily surprised. They had beaten all records of the old Royal and the new, with receipts exceeding by more than £200 anything they had before played to.

"What a fine house this new Royal is," they said. "Beautiful dressing rooms, lovely decorations, stately lines, and a grand entrance! This and the King's at Glasgow are by far the best we have seen. They are the two show theatres of the English provinces, worthy of the towns to which they belong —but they show up the majority of places! It makes one wonder why so many managers delay reconstruction and modernising houses in other great cities, which are not in any way comparable with this lovely theatre."

"The visit of Mr. Martin Harvey the week following" (said P.R. in an interview) "is noteworthy from the fact that this actor is the one 'star' who can visit each big town in the country twice every year without showing the least falling off in popularity."

Oscar Asche and Lily Brayton, supported by Caleb Porter, H. R. Hignett, Alfred Brydone, etc., played Rudolf Besier's *The Virgin Goddess* for the first time in Birmingham this spring. *The Royal Divorce* filled Whit-week—its thirty-eighth visit to this city! The popularity of the play seemed absolutely inexhaustible. P.R. remembered well at the old theatre how some of the gallery boys used to clamber upon the umbrella-shaped dome from which the centre chandelier was suspended, and lying flat on their faces, and craning their necks round the edge of the dome, watch the play literally upside down!

The third season of the Proms followed for another three weeks. Philip Rodway, as usual, supervised all the internal arrangements, and this year he caused the stage, on which were grouped the orchestra, to be roofed in, so that the sound was made to travel all over the theatre. Sir (then Mr.) Whitworth Wallis and Dr. Russell had secured a still larger number of guarantors. Landon Ronald returned as conductor, while Max Mossel presented himself as solo violinist on the opening night. A very high tone was maintained throughout the season. The concerts had now turned the corner of financial success, and had, moreover, gone far to solve in an artistic way what was known to theatrical managers as "the summer difficulty."

P.R. had secured an admirable Autumn season, which included the second visit of Lewis Waller in *Robin Hood*, and the notable engagement of Beerbohm Tree, who appeared in seven of his best-known parts. The first performance in Birmingham of *Tom Jones* provided a noteworthy week, with Ruth Vincent, Dan Rolyat, Carrie Moore, Harry Welchman, and Jay Laurier in the cast.

Later came Weedon Grossmith, producing "for the first time on any stage" a new farce *Among the Brigands*, and playing his famous rôle in *The Night of the Party* for the two thousand and twenty-first time.

When Julia Neilson and Fred Terry brought *The Scarlet Pimpernel* they took more money during that week than they had ever done before during a similar period in London or out of it. It was originally intended that Charles Laughton (in 1934) should take the part in the film of the *Scarlet Pimpernel*, but for innumerable lovers of Baroness Orczy's famous story there will always be only one Sir Percy Blakeney in our hearts and memories—Fred Terry.

Another "First in Birmingham" was *Captain Brassbound's Conversion* in which the effervescent Ellen Terry, fresh from an American tour, was supported by her third husband, James Carew, and an interesting matinée was *The Earl of Pawtucket* with Mr. Cyril Maude in the title rôle.

P.R., in his *Review of the Theatrical Year* in the Press, observed that with pleasure he acknowledged a measure of public support which had been greater than at any time since the opening of the new theatre. Never in his recollection had a year brought so many prominent actors and actresses to Birmingham. . . .

"The conclusion I have formed . . . is that the public taste is gradually undergoing a change. The class of musical play which was so much in vogue a few years ago seems to be losing its hold upon the public. Local playgoers have been showing that they want a return to good drama, combined with an occasional genuine comic opera of the type of which *Tom Jones*, recently produced by Robert Courtneidge, is a good example.

"I believe that if another play of the class and quality of *The Silver King* were to come along to-day, it would make as much money in five years as the older play has done in twenty. The type of people to whom this would appeal is, I think, the one which used to support the musical comedies with so much enthusiasm, and which now for light entertainment goes to the music halls. . . .

"The past year has also shown that there is a rapidly increasing section of the Birmingham public who want the best that the stage of to-day has to offer, and I think the Theatre Royal may take some credit for having catered fairly well for this very welcome type of playgoer. . . ."

*　　*　　*

PANTOMIME 1907–08
CINDERELLA

Cinderella, the last hired pantomime during Philip Rodway's régime at the Royal, was produced by Robert Courtneidge on Boxing Day, 1907. Written by the producer in collaboration with "Dangle" (A. M. Thompson) it had already been seen in the north, and the principals were all well versed in their parts. The humour rose naturally out of the plot, and the characters were recognisable to playgoers from the nursery. Conrad Tritschler, R. McCleery, James Gordon, and W. R. Coleman were responsible for a series of spectacular scenes, the greatest triumphs appearing in the forest set with its lightning change from winter to summer; the Ballroom, and the Fairy Wedding. Alfred Haines, Herbert E. Haines, and Guy Jones composed the music for the pantomime.

Phyllis Dare, still a very young girl, was a charming Cinderella—her best song *Bonnie Jennie;* Carrie Moore was the gallant Prince, with *Put me among the Girls* for her greatest song success. The chief dancers were Gwennie Hasto and Rosie Begarnie.

The comedy was safe in the hands of Dan Rolyat as the Baron (Rolyat came from Birmingham, and had reversed his father's name of Taylor), John Humphries as the Baroness, Stephen Adeson as Choddles, and Fred Leslie as that *rara avis*, a male Dandini. The slimness of Mr. Rolyat's figure contrasted boldly with Mr. Humphries' massive build, and gave endless possibilities for frequent comical eposides. Poor Dan, a born comedian and a magnificent eccentric dancer, died relatively young as the result of an accident sustained while playing his greatest rôle, Simplicitas, in *The Arcadians*. The ugly sisters were not ugly, for once in a way, one being Marie Rignold, and the other (who sang *The German Band* and *The Smart Brigade*) Esta Stella.

P.R.'s night was celebrated on March 2nd, and was as happy an affair as ever, with many presentations and an excellent programme. The pantomime ended on March 7th, after a run of ten and a half weeks, and P.R.'s announcement on the last night was that the pantomime for the following year would be *Dick Whittington and his Cat*—a story beloved in every nursery.

* * *

Two outstanding years of particular joy and contentment for Mother and Daddy were those of 1907 and 1908. Fortune had been very kind, his position at the theatre was well-established, and he had less worries than ever in his life before. The story book ending "and they lived happily ever after" was indeed coming true.

"I will pass by and see their happiness." Had Browning's *Pippa* passed them by singing, as they stood knee deep in meadow-sweet on the banks of the Avon during their fishing week-ends, or as they were together in their small first home, her song would have seemed just simple truth to them, and in their hearts they would have echoed it . . .

"The year's at the spring,
The day's at the morn;
Morning's at seven;

JULIA NEILSON AND FRED TERRY
in
The Scarlet Pimpernel

PHYLLIS
Aged 2

LOIS AND PHYLLIS
Aged 2 and 5

> *The hill-side's dew-pearled;*
> *The lark's on the wing;*
> *The snail's on the thorn;*
> *God's in His heaven—*
> *All's right with the world!"*

Some periods in life remain as a kind of peaceful backwater in our minds, when Time stands still, and in recollection all is sunshine. Such were those two years.

Not long after Cinderella's silver slipper had been lost for the last time, on a Tuesday, March 23rd, 1908, their second daughter, Lois, was born. Mother recalls that she was just like a little pink and white doll, with yellow fluff for hair, and for days her dark-haired sister certainly regarded her as such. And ever anxious not to keep anyone waiting, the new baby, in her entry on to the stage of the world, anticipated the set date of her arrival by a full three weeks.

As it happened, therefore, on her birthday Daddy was away from home on business at Newcastle. Mother tells of a curious coincidence of that day; how Phyllis, aged two and a half, emulated her father's unconscious example of absence in the coalfields of the Tyne by vanishing herself, and being discovered by her Granny at 6 a.m. in the coal house, industriously helping the maid to get in the coal!

Telegrams of congratulation were hastily despatched to greet the too-previous visitor, while Daddy raced back post-haste from Newcastle. And the christening cups* this time were filled with snowdrops and violets instead of roses.

Baby Lois, less than four weeks old, was taken for a long summer holiday by the sea, mostly at Rhyl—that paradise for babies; after three months there they went on to The Grange at Knightwick-on-Teme for still another few weeks, Daddy joining his little family for week-ends.

---

*One of these from Julia Neilson and Fred Terry.

CHAPTER 11

(1908-10)

There is a Philip Rodway story that Tom H. Townson loves to tell. The incident occurred during a week when P.R. was rather concerned about the bookings.

Summoning an attendant to his office,

"Go and see how many boxes have been sold to-night," he told him.

Ten minutes passed. At last there was a knock at the door. The attendant presented himself with a beaming smile, saluted, and announced triumphantly,

"Twenty-three Cadburys and sixteen Kunzles, sir!"

Season 1908

The annual meeting for 1908, held early in March, was a more cheerful affair than its predecessor, though the theatre was by no means out of the wood into which *The Babes* of 1904 had led it. The chairman was able to tell the shareholders there had been a substantial improvement in trade for the year. The net profit, after providing for depreciation and sinking fund, debenture interest, and directors' fees, was £2,816, and the deficit, which a year earlier had been £8,267, now stood at £5,450. The company was slowly but surely gaining ground, thanks largely to the diligent and far-seeing work of Mr. Philip Rodway.

"Having regard to the risky nature of theatrical business," went on Mr. Lewis, "there is no reasonable expectation that the accounts will show much better results." (How greatly later dividends disproved this!) "While the theatre is becoming more firmly established, and more popular with the public, we have still to face the increase of £2,000 in our ground rent as from New Year's Day."

The point of chief interest in the chairman's speech was that at last, after three years on sharing terms, the management had completed arrangements to present its own pantomimes at the following Christmas. By this step it was hoped to make the money needed for the increased ground rent.

The old—and ever-present—difficulties of the dearth of first-class touring attractions, and the impossibility of playing through the summer at a profit, were again stressed by the chairman, who concluded with a reiteration of his regret that the Board's recommendation for reducing capital had fallen on deaf ears.

The dramatic season was ushered in by Forbes-Robertson and Gertrude Elliott and their company in *Hamlet*, *Othello*, *Mice and Men*, and *For the Crown*. *Mrs. Wiggs of the Cabbage Patch*, as popular a piece of simple sentimental comedy as *Daddy Long Legs* became years later, paid a successful visit, and a "first-timer" for Birmingham was *The Education of Elizabeth*. Lewis Waller gave a special matinée at which he recited; with him was Sybil Arundale, the Royal's next principal boy. The Martin Harveys, the Asches, the Moody Manners Company, and a "good strong dose of Hall Caine" (as P.R. expressed it) helped to fill the spring list.

About this time the whole country was shocked and saddened by news of a dreadful tragedy in a colliery at Hamstead, near Birmingham, involving the deaths of many miners and the consequent distress of widows, children, and other dependents. The Hamstead Colliery disaster is still recalled as one of the blackest in Midland mining history.

Praiseworthy efforts in several quarters were made to lessen the force of the blow, as it affected the women and children. Philip Rodway at the Royal, which was already noted for its activities in the cause of charity, took a prominent part in swelling one of the funds raised by rival newspapers. A special "Miners' Matinée" was held at the theatre, and a

profit accrued of £680, which the *Evening Despatch*, the
journal concerned, could claim as constituting a record for
a charity matinée in the provinces. (Actually, within ten
years the Royal was to eclipse the yield by many hundred
pounds, but it would be unfair to compare the war-time
"Mary Anderson" matinée, when over £6,000 was raised,
with the Hamstead effort, so different were the circumstances
and atmosphere.)

All things considered, the success of this Miners' Matinée
was as creditable to the members of a conspicuously generous
profession as it was gratifying to the promoters, and the record
result entitled it to a prominent place even in Birmingham's
great theatrical annals.

One of the earliest subscribers to the *Evening Despatch* fund
was Harry Lauder, who in his pre-stage days had himself
been a miner. Years earlier he had toiled in the dreary
darkness of a northern colliery, sensed the ominous threat of
death at every moment of his working life, and experienced
the desolation of a pit-head in the hour of disaster. In his
eight years on the stage he had not forgotten—and it was his
telegram, "Arrange a matinée and I will appear," which
prompted the effort at the Royal.

P.R. got together a monster programme lasting four hours,
with contributions from a host of stars; each artist was introduced by him to the audience. So far as quality and variety
are concerned, we suppose, nothing like it had been achieved
in the City:

> Vesta Tilley, José Collins, John E. Coyle, Syd May,
> Wilkie Bard, Ben Nathan, Harry Lauder, The Kel-
> linos, Daisy Jerome, Maude Mortimer, Joe Elvin,
> Barrett and Knowles, Eugene Stratton, Margaret
> Cooper, Fred Russell.

We give them in the order in which they appeared, without
attempting to arrange them in order of importance, for it is a
canon of the profession that all who serve in charity's cause
are equal.

But what a list; and what an entertainment they gave! It was likened to a "revue" (in the French sense) of famous pantomimes, recent and long past. Old melodies of a dozen years' oblivion were revived to haunt the ear, to set the vast audience humming and cheering, and to rouse the Theatre Royal to a scene of indescribable enthusiasm.

Vesta Tilley, blithe and debonair, changing from smart military tunic to swagger summer suit; from a song about the right girl to a song about the seaside smile; José Collins singing *My Cuban Girl:* Syd May burlesquing Robey to the life; Harry Lauder warbling *The Wedding Bells are Ringing*, recounting McNab's r-r-romance in Scottish accent rich as Golconda, then changing to the mood of pathos and telling his hearers, in simple language, just how nearly the Hamstead tragedy had affected an old, experienced miner.

Those who were there will never forget that speech.

"I worked for ten and a half years in the coal mines," he said, "and I know the position of those relatives to-day, because I know a miner only has what is due to him at the end of the week. He is not prepared for a reverse, or accident, or death; and when a calamity such as this occurs, we have got to come to his assistance. I do so because I feel in duty bound."

Nothing could have been more pathetically appropriate than his monologue *The Miner*, when, pointing to his pick and lantern at the conclusion, he said, "These are the tools with which I used to work. These are the boots I wore. I would not take £10,000 for them."

Let the kaleidoscope revolve again: Eugene Stratton raising the roof with *The Lily of Laguna*, dancing with that feathery lightness never surpassed: Margaret Cooper trilling quaint little "Songs at the Piano," with her inimitable air. The orchestra was conducted in turn by Guy Jones, of the Royal; W. Southworth, of the Prince of Wales; J. H. Whittaker, of the Grand; W. Crabtree, of the Hippodrome; and J. W. Clegg, of the Empire. The Lord Mayor, who was present, sent to the Editor of the *Evening Despatch* an expression of the Relief

Committee's heartfelt thanks for the services so willingly and generously given.

"Above all (said the *Despatch* next day) our acknowledgments are due to Philip Rodway and the management of the Theatre Royal. No more suitable building for the matinée could have been found; the theatre was placed at our disposal free of cost, and the whole staff unhesitatingly gave their services for nothing.

"We feel that a good deal of the success achieved is due to the manager of the Theatre Royal. As regards personal effort he was indefatigable, his professional experience was invaluable, and to him we offer our best thanks."

One point of particular interest is that the effort fell at a time when a sharp dispute was afoot between the Variety Artists' Federation and Mr. (now Sir) Oswald Stoll, controller of many music halls, over the very matter of charity matinées. Only for a very special occasion could the opposing viewpoints have been even temporarily reconciled, in order that a programme might be built up. Tact and goodwill, however, smoothed the way, and Mr. Stoll, no less than the Federation and other managers of local theatres and halls, did everything he could to crown the venture with triumph.

This year's Promenade Concerts, directed by Max Mossel and conducted by Landon Ronald, with a different vocalist and instrumentalist each night, went very well. Ernest Newman, who never flattered, found the orchestra distinctly the best that had appeared at these concerts. Mr. Mossel had recently been seriously ill, a fact which evoked from Mr. Newman the characteristic remark that if illness would make all violinists play as finely, the recipe might be recommended to others.

After the customary three weeks of "Proms," back came *A Royal Divorce*, with Beth Elliott playing Edith Cole's time-honoured rôle. Seymour Hicks, with Zena Dare as his leading lady, brought *Sweet and Twenty*. The month of June was further distinguished by a flying matinée at which Sarah Bernhardt presented *La Dame aux Camelias*.

The summer vacation terminated on August Bank Holiday,

when *The Silver King* filled the bill. P.R.'s bookings for the
Autumn were magnificent. The touring system was in its
glory. They included Fred Terry and Miriam Lewes in *The
Scarlet Pimpernel* and *Matt of Merrymount;* Lewis Waller in *The
Duke's Motto;* Seymour Hicks and Ellaline Terriss in *The Gay
Gordons;* Martin Harvey in *The Corsican Brothers* (which he
had just performed by Royal command at Windsor), and
other pieces, notably *Slander*, a brand-new play by F. Nird-
linger, from Echegaray's novel; the Bensons in Shakespeare;
Jimmy Welch in *When Knights were Bold;* The Moody Manners
Opera Company; Harry Pélissier and his Follies; Dan Rolyat
and Florence Smithson in *Tom Jones;* Phyllis Dare as Peggy
in *The Dairymaids;* and Marie Studholme in a new musical
comedy, *My Mimosa Maid*.

Thus a large proportion of the season was filled by artists
of world-wide repute. Nor were the remaining weeks greatly
inferior in point of attractiveness, for to the above list must be
added features such as a new version of *The Christian;* a return
of *The Prodigal Son;* the first production of Roy Horniman's
Idols, from W. J. Locke's book (with Evelyn Millard, Herbert
Waring, Alfred Brydone, and the late-lamented C. W. Somerset); Hayden Coffin and John Coates in *Dorothy;* Herbert
Sleath and Ellis Jeffries in *A White Man;* Cyril Maude in
Toddles, at a flying matinée; and standard items.

Not many provincial theatres, of course, could boast such
a schedule, for few could take the money needed to make the
bookings worth while. It must be emphasised that the great
stars of the period *liked* playing at the Birmingham Theatre
Royal. They liked the house, they liked the town, and they
appreciated Philip Rodway's calm efficiency.

So the period was one of heyday not only for the theatre,
but also for the young acting-manager, who at little over
thirty years of age was now recognised as one of the significant
figures in the scheme of things theatrical. As manager of
the Birmingham Royal he was already beginning to dominate
the touring system (of which the house was for so long the

K

keystone) and to be able to demand the best of the shows on the road. The fact that in this season the Royal was the only provincial theatre visited by Martin Harvey and Lewis Waller is, perhaps, the most striking proof of his influence.

* * *

PANTOMIME 1908-09
DICK WHITTINGTON AND HIS CAT

The first pantomime to be written by Philip Rodway— *Dick Whittington and his Cat*—was produced on Boxing Day, 1908. It both promised and performed great things. For the past three seasons, following the fiasco of *The Babes in the Wood* of 1904-05, the directors had played for safety by sharing with outside producers, who had provided star casts in established pantomimes. This policy, as explained at successive annual meetings, had been forced by the inability of the infant company to secure big names for their own productions, as the artists most likely to draw money to the box office were contracted several years ahead to Messrs. Courtneidge, Robert Arthur, and other elder brethren of the pantomime sphere.

Now, after three years of waiting, planning, angling, a new era was about to dawn. The Royal was ready to produce its own pantomime, stand all the risk, take all the profit. The subject chosen to mark this important departure was *Dick Whittington and his Cat*, a happy theme, and one associated with some of the greatest pantomime triumphs.

At the Royal *Dick Whittington* had often been played. It was the theme in 1870, 1880, 1884, 1888, 1897, and again in 1900, when it was the old theatre's last pantomime. Many brilliant artists had made or cemented their local fame therein: Charles Coborn (the Fitzwarren of 1884) and Vesta Tilley (the Dick of that year and of 1888), George Robey (Idle Jack in 1897, his first Birmingham pantomime), Marie Loftus and Whimsical Walker. Vesta Tilley had been Dick Whittington for the third time in 1900 (at a salary, according to one authority, of £500 a week), so the subject was glorified by many memories.

For 1908-09, the book was entrusted to Philip Rodway, whose knowledge of the methods of the old Royal, combined with his success in building up the reputation of the new house, made him amazingly valuable at this juncture. Associated with him was Douglas Buchanan, a Birmingham journalist, and on the production side Herbert Cottesmore. The costumes were designed by R. Crafter and Wilhelm, executed by Landolff and Co. (Paris), Obronski and Co., and Elkan and Co. (London); and W. R. Young and R. C. McCleery painted the scenes.

As to the cast, there was a very popular choice of hero in Sybil Arundale, already known in musical comedy (in which she had been seen in Birmingham in her brother's play *The Gipsy Girl*), and who had also played in pantomime at the Lyceum.

It was intended to bring back George Robey as Idle Jack, but another manager claimed his services under a prior contract, and a fight in the law-courts went against the Royal. Tom Foy, therefore, was engaged for the part. He was a "Yorkshire" comedian, though born in Manchester, familiar to music-hall patrons, with a record of versatility. He had made his name by the sketch which he produced some five years before—*A Yorkshire Lad in London*. Here it may be added that Mr. Foy earned high praise for his work as Idle Jack, but there is no doubt that the loss of George Robey's services cost the management a lot of money.

Fred Whittaker, perfection in animal parts, was the harmless, but in this case very necessary, cat; Lupino Lane the Bottles; Arthur Reynolds the Cook; Aimée Grey the Alice; John Power the Fitzwarren; Eric Campbell the Emperor of Morocco and Ethel Negretti the Princess; Drew and Alder, from Drury Lane, the captain and mate of the *Pitch and Toss;* Harry Lupino (Lupino Lane's father), the King Rat; and Wee Wallace Lupino something not very clearly defined.

The Lupinos, brilliant stage family as they are, never produced a more remarkable phenomenon than "Nipper" Lupino Lane. He was almost literally cradled in the business, for at four years old, when Vesta Tilley was taking a benefit in Birmingham at the Prince of Wales Theatre, he made his début. In subsequent years he similarly assisted Queenie Leighton, Bransby Williams, Mark Sheridan, Wilkie Bard, and other stars. When he was eight he showed signs of making a dancer, and so he was given a stage career.

We shall encounter "Nipper" Lane and others of his comprehensive family again as we go along. At the moment, all we need add is that when he played Bottles at the Royal that year, he was scarcely sixteen, yet he had already appeared before Her Majesty the Queen, played Boy Babe at Liverpool, and frisked about as the Dog at Manchester. His brother, Wee Wallace Lupino, was still younger (13), and a phenomenal dancer as well as a lovely child in appearance.

Despite George Robey's absence, then, this important production (for which Guy Jones composed and selected the music) had a strong team. Its reception was sufficiently warm to satisfy the management that policy was being judiciously shaped.

As to Philip Rodway's share, one critic said:

"The pantomime is exquisitely produced. We had been led to expect great things in the way of scenery, dresses, and general staging, but the actual production positively astounded us. It is supreme. . . . *Dick Whittington* is an artistic triumph, and one which in many respects will never be eclipsed. . . . The book is workmanlike, . . . and workmanlike in these days involves, *ipso facto*, not a little distinction. The authors have wisely borne in mind the paramount importance of the story. It is written clearly, with a sporadic touch of honest sentiment, and an abundance of clean, good, if occasionally homely, fun. The name of Mr. Philip Rodway, the discerning acting manager, appears as joint author, and this alone is a guarantee of freedom from all those doubtful features by which pantomime is all too frequently disfigured. There is happily little attempt to make capital out of topical inanity, for which we all thank Mr. Rodway's discriminating judgment."

The Press were unanimous in their praise. Already P.R. was stamping his pantomime work with that guarantee which for years was the hallmark of a Rodway pantomime.

Highgate Hill was a delightful scene: as the curtain rose on a darkened stage the trees to left and right were dimly disclosed. Gradually and delicately the dawn tinged the glimpse of sky seen through the foliage in the background. One by one the trees began to stand out, until the summer morning burst forth in sunlit splendour. The distant meadows, bathed in radiance, stretched to the far-away hills, the whole scene a blend of contrasted colouring, an example of the stagecraft for which P.R. and the Royal were to be world-famous.

Fitzwarren's Stores showed scenic art of the more conventional style. London Docks, with a panorama of quaint masonry, busy river, and old-time shipping, was strikingly conceived, and the effect, as the good ship *Pitch and Toss*, her lights twinkling, drew off on her voyage, never failed to bring down the house. Flamboyant charm imbued the Moroccan scenes, and for finale there was the gorgeous spectacle of London's ancient Guildhall, where a special feature was made of the trade guilds of the city.

Tom Foy's Idle Jack was one of the simplest and most natural impersonations imaginable, a study appealing to stalls for its cleverness and to gallery for its breadth, with a great asset in his Yorkshire accent, and a mastery of stolid stupidity. Sybil Arundale's Dick was a distinctive figure, with charm, pathos and comedy fairly proportioned, and the advantage of much technical skill in acting. Has she not since shown us that in serious drama she is as much at home as in pantomime?

Fred Whittaker gave a wonderful impersonation, almost uncanny in its realism, of Dick's Cat. His feline performance is always unforgettable, for he not only "gets into the skin of the part," but into the heart of it, and to see him catch a mouse and play with it is enough to rouse the envy of any ordinary, common cat.

This was not a good year for songs (highly as Guy Jones's musical setting was praised), and one of Lupino Lane's was the only number which ever threatened to become popular, until *Put me upon an Island* was added for Tom Foy. "Nipper" Lane's extraordinary agility in dancing was a special feature of the pantomime.

After the inevitable pruning and grafting the production settled down to a happy run. Students' Night came and went, with its concomitant invasion of auditorium and stalls by a crowd of students in costumes of picturesque gaiety or topical allusiveness. (Maud Allan, the Suffragettes, and Violet Charlesworth were the year's favourite inspirations. The last named was the notorious swindler who staged the dramatic suicide "exit" at Penmaenmawr.)

Philip Rodway's own night was a great success, with extra turns by Jay Laurier and Hetty King from the Prince of Wales Theatre, Nat Clifford and Frank Harwood from the Gaiety, and Ada Reeve.

The run ended on March 6th, ten weeks from the opening. Until the very last week there were excellent houses, but heavy snow ruined the business at the end. On the final night George Robey, who had been secured as Ada Reeve's co-star for the next year's *Jack and the Beanstalk*, joined P.R. on the stage and helped to bring to a fine conclusion the run of a fine pantomime.

*　　　*　　　*

Robert Courtneidge, manager and producer, discussing his own profession, writes: "Horse-racing apart, I question if there is any other business so full of hazards or lucky chances." How often Daddy used to emphasise this to us. A brilliant play may fail because it is produced at a time when the public are not ready for it, or are out of tune, temporarily, with its theme. An extremely bad play, he used to say, will make a great success for the opposite reason. It may have no other quality but its topical appeal. One of the greatest difficulties in management is the testing of the pulse of the public. When is the time ripe for action? *Journey's End* was hawked round the West End offices many times before it was accepted. "The people don't want to be reminded of the war." But, surprisingly enough, they did.

He used to tell us that *Peter Pan* was produced at psychologically the right time. When we insisted—"But *Peter Pan* would have been a success anyway," he replied, "One can't tell. Other Barrie plays, better written plays, have missed their mark. Once it was an established success (and mainly circumstances made it so) enough people saw it to love it, and to make its revival an institution. The difficulty is to keep a good play on long enough for people to learn to appreciate it."

Places of entertainment are affected by outside events, and by weather conditions, to an enormous extent. Drought can kill a play as effectually as the most damning notices. A manager may have backed it to the extent of many thousands, and it may be a "flop," for reasons which no foresight could avoid. A change in Government, General Election times, etc., affect receipts adversely.

These dangers possibly apply more to the provincial theatres than to London. After all, London has a floating public, for almost everyone who has money to spend gravitates to London to spend it. In the provinces, however, it is for the most part the same band of followers that go each week, and if they be depressed by conditions, financial or otherwise, there is no crowd of pleasure seekers to take their places.

Managers bless the "herd instinct" in their public when they meet it—only wishing they could spread the receipts over the bad weeks when the house is "papered" from gallery to stalls. For one or two weeks the house could be filled twice over at each performance; probably not because the play is surpassingly good, but because everyone has told everyone else he or she "must go": because at every club or tea-table for the next month one will be completely out of it if one cannot answer the inevitable "Have you seen?" in the affirmative. (This lucky fate will occur, sometimes without warning, to a play or film, and women in particular cannot resist.) When the tumult and the shouting has died, three-quarters of the public agree "it was not nearly as good as we expected," but in the meantime the houses have been packed and the manager's heart gladdened.

The health of Royalty is a most potent factor in the entertainment world. During the illness of His Majesty receipts dropped lower and lower. On his recovery, everyone joyfully started theatre-going again.

* * *

Season 1909

The season of 1909 opened with the first performance, outside London, of *An Englishman's Home*, a play written to encourage recruiting for the Territorial force. *Havana*, with Dorothy Ward, George Gregory, Veronica Brady, and Fred Allandale (later the central figure of a Theatre Royal Pantomime tragedy) came for the first time; and Ada Reeve, Louis Bradfield, Lauri de Frece (later Fay Compton's second husband), and Phyllis Monkman were seen in *Butterflies*.

At the annual meeting of shareholders, in March, a further slight improvement was recorded, a net profit of £3,153 being announced. This was £337 more than the year before. In the balance sheet the liabilities had increased by £3,448 and the assets by £6,777, mainly because of the outlay on pantomime productions at Birmingham and Liverpool.

Tom B. Davis explained that the Theatre Royal Company had not put all their eggs into the Birmingham basket. They had contracted an arrangement with their old friend W. W. Kelly, lessee and manager of the Shakespeare Theatre, Liverpool, whereby they obtained the use of that house without liability for rent or standard expenses, and were to produce pantomimes there, drawing a large share of the profits. *Dick Whittington* would be taken to Liverpool the following Christmas.

Mr. John Melvin (to-day probably the oldest of the company's original shareholders) complimented Philip Rodway on his work as manager for the year.

For the remainder of the Spring season, the most notable of the attractions were Oscar Asche and Lily Brayton in *Count Hannibal;* the first visit of *A Waltz Dream* (Amy Augarde, John Humphries, and May de Sousa); Martin Harvey and Nina de Silva in repertory; and Maud Allan in three dance recitals, her chief item being the famous *Vision of Salome.*

The Proms this year, with the same director (Mr. Mossel) and conductor (Mr. Ronald), opening to rather thin houses, finished up by playing to capacity. Summing up the season, Ernest Newman wrote:

> "As always happens on the last night, the audience was very large and enthusiastic. One could not help wondering where the majority of those delighted music lovers could have been during that depressing week of half-empty houses. The management might try the experiment next year of commencing with the last night and going through the season backwards."

The same critic observed a great improvement in Landon Ronald himself, who was "fast learning to achieve force and impressiveness without strain or exaggeration."

A Royal Divorce (with Edith Cole restored to royalty) closed the season, and *Charley's Aunt* re-opened the theatre in August. Roy Byford, nowadays the portly comic lead of Stratford Festivals, played Spettigue.

P.R. had booked a magnificent Autumn, with Lewis Waller paying two visits. He came in August with *Fires of Fate*, and in October played the name-part in the first stage presentation of William Devereux's *Sir Walter Raleigh*. Ideal in heroic rôles (such as Monsieur Beaucaire and Henry V), Waller naturally found himself congenially cast. He had with him Lilian Braithwaite, Winifred Emery, A. E. George, and C. W. Somerset.

George Alexander, in giving Birmingham its first sight of Sutro's *The Builder of Bridges*, was supported by Dorothy

Green (Stratford's unequalled Cleopatra, of the Bridges Adams régime), James Carew, and Godfrey Tearle.

The Marriage of Mayfair, the latest in melodrama from Drury Lane, was here for the first time; so was *The Dashing Little Duke*, Seymour Hicks' play, in which his wife, Ellaline Terriss, appeared as the Duke.

The name of William Devereux, Lewis Waller's latest author, appeared again in the same season, when Fred Terry and Julia Neilson formed a grand combination in his *Henry of Navarre*, an excellent piece of work ablaze with colour and full of movement, with many fine scenes and strong situations.

Ada Reeve came again, this time in *Butterflies;* Cyril Maude in *The Flag Lieutenant;* Walter Passmore in *Merrie England;* George Graves in *The Belle of Brittany* (there were many "belles" in those days); Marie Studholme in *Miss Hook of Holland*, and Jimmie Welch in *When Knights were Bold*. With Jimmie, by the way, was H. K. Ayliff as Sir Brian, a part which one somehow finds difficult of association with the Birmingham Repertory Theatre's eminent and somewhat austere post-war producer.

A pleasant event in theatrical circles fell at the end of this season. "Joe" (J. F. Graham) gave a re-union and supper at the Grand Hotel on December 18th, to commemorate his twelfth year as manager of the Prince of Wales Theatre, and Mr. and Mrs. Philip Rodway were among those present to congratulate one for whom P.R. had always a deep affection and respect. The menu card which Mother saved is signed by Chester Fox, Robert Courtneidge, Jay Laurier, G. H. Elliott, etc.

In September of last year (1933), when we first began to collect material for this book, Mr. Graham was one of those whose reminiscent aid we sought. From his home at Sanderstead, in Surrey, came this characteristically courteous reply:

"I am of course thoroughly in sympathy with your natural and laudable wish to preserve the memory of your dear father, and his many years' association with the theatrical life of Birmingham.

For the last two days I have been trying to remember if any circumstance of interest took place during the thirteen years I was running the Prince of Wales Theatre.

"You see, I first took up the management in 1898, and before that your father had left and gone to the Royal with Mr. Dornton, who never encouraged intimacy with any opposition theatres. I only used to meet your dear father casually—generally at the Villa or Birmingham football ground. I knew of him as a capital cricketer, a brilliant billiard player, and a most enthusiastic fisherman; but, though concerned with him in a little billiard tournament between the Birmingham theatrical managers, I was not drawn against your father—who, I'm sure, would have easily beaten me.

"After the P.O.W. was sold to Sir Alfred Butt, and then to the Royal—when your dear father began his long and very successful joint management of the two houses—I very seldom came down to Birmingham, but on looking in at the old house I was always most courteously received and cordially welcomed by him.

"Being now very nearly 83 years of age, I cannot make sure of a much longer lease, but I shall eagerly look forward—if spared—to the perusal of your book, which I am certain will be warmly welcomed by the many hundreds of Birmingham friends and admirers of your dear father. With every good wish,

"I remain, most sincerely yours,

"Joe Graham."

Alas! Within a month this fine gentleman of the old school had reached the end of his long lease. His death cost the English stage one of its most courteous, charming, picturesque, and versatile personalities, whose wonderful career as actor-manager in many parts of the world is described with a perfect blend of modesty and humour in his autobiography, *An old Stock Actor's Memories*.

The billiard contest to which he referred was held at the Woolpack Hotel early in 1910, so we may tell you about it here. It bore the dignified title of the Theatrical Managers' Billiard Handicap, and, being quite impromptu in its inception, turned out an unequivocal success. Mr. Maurice Bernstein, editor of a past publication called *Midland Amusements*, presented a souvenir, a spirit Tantalus, for competition, and the first heat was set down for February 1st, when "Mr. Philip Rodway, Theatre Royal, had to meet as his antagonist Mr. P. O. Elbourne, of Birmingham Hippodrome, and with the reputation attributed to Mr. Rodway as a cueist, fine play was anticipated."

Mr. Harold Wallis, mine host of the Woolpack (now of the Stork), did the handicapping, and "awarded to Philip Rodway the onerous task of conceding his opponents 120 each in a game of 250 up; and, as if this was not sufficient, he had further to owe them 100 points." "Rodway," says the reporter of fact, "in his heat with Elbourne put in some really brilliant work, knocking up fine breaks, and finally beating his opponent. Elbourne, in his fight, showed himself no mean player, executing several respectable breaks, but from the first it was evident he was over-weighted."

Next, Albert Bushell (Gaiety) and Alfred Matcham (Empire) played a heat, which the former won by 12 points. In the third heat, J. F. Graham (Prince of Wales Theatre), "playing with great deliberation and a style peculiarly his own," beat W. G. Woodward (Bordesley Palace) by 38 points. Lester Collingwood, the handsome, ill-fated manager of the Alexandra Theatre (he was killed in a motoring accident in 1913), displayed "dash and energy," and beat E. Foster (Grand Theatre) by 31 points.

The first semi-final: Rodway versus Collingwood. P.R. made a splendid fight (said the chronicler) against long odds —his opponent receiving 120 and being owed 100—but his "plucky and determined effort" failed by 85 points against Bushell. "Joe" Graham won, again playing the same steady, patient game. The affair culminated in a dinner at the Woolpack, where the prizes were presented and many toasts honoured.

Tom Webster, the talented cartoonist of the *Daily Mail*, then working in Birmingham, drew for *Midland Amusements* some sketches, in one of which a shirt-sleeved, moustached P.R. is represented as saying to Elbourne: "You'd better

THE THEATRICAL MANAGERS' BILLIARDS HANDICAP
TOM WEBSTER'S CARTOON
1910

THE RULING PASSION.

P.R. captains Speedwell Past v. Present
at Warwickshire County Cricket Ground

Tom Webster's cartoon, 1908

stick to music-halls." "Joe's" peculiarly deliberate style is hit off by a sketch in which he remarks: "Give me my compasses, marker!" while Lester Collingwood murmurs "My curtain goes up at 7.15."

One cannot help noticing that Mr. Graham's letter characteristically makes no mention of his victory; just "I was not drawn against your father, who, I'm sure, would have easily beaten me."

Mr. Graham's reference to billiards and cricket gives us the opportunity for which we have been waiting to mention P.R.'s affection for these games.

Cricket, which he regarded as a pursuit to be played and watched with a reverential attention to every detail of practice and artifice, filled another space in his leisure. He was captain of the Old Speedwell Club, when to bat against the fast bowling in which club cricket abounds was often a risky adventure. An old friend of his tells us that he would play to the last possible moment before going off to his work at the theatre. Every keen cricketer who reads these lines can imagine him slowly retreating across the grass and along the paths, casting a glance backwards over his shoulder every few steps in order not to miss an incident, and at last, when even the nearest outfielder was no longer visible, running like a hare so as to be punctual to the call of Duty! We ourselves know that in later years he would often go after tea to see the finish of a game at the County Ground at Edgbaston, and cut his departure just as fine. . . .

PANTOMIME 1909-10

JACK AND THE BEANSTALK

Jack and the Beanstalk was for Birmingham the first-fruits of the arrangement regarding pantomime with the Shakespeare Theatre, Liverpool. It was presented at the Royal on Boxing Day (December 27th), 1909. J. J. Hewson was the author, and Guy Jones the arranger and composer of the music. The book followed the familiar story, with the slight divergence that the Giant, instead of breaking his neck by falling down the beanstalk, was heroically slaughtered by Jack in single combat.

The prettiest scene, Dame Trot's Back Garden, was a sunlit landscape, with rose-clad cottages, a pump, a well, a lovely gateway, and a clothes line industriously employed by the comedians. The Fair was another effective setting. To close the first half there was a spectacular scene showing the rapid growth of the magic bean, where scarlet blossoms and scarlet-clad nymphs and gnomes made vivid splashes of colour.

George Robey, returning to the scene of his several triumphs, was an unqualified success as Dame Trot. His songs included the famous *Archibald, certainly not!* This year, as Mr. Crompton Rhodes has reminded us, was the last in which a Royal pantomime played upon political "follies of the year," and in *John Bull's Smoking Concert* Robey had, therefore, his last opportunity at the Royal of poking fun at the party leaders.

A scene which many readers will recall was the potted *Hamlet*, on the lines familiarised by the Follies, with Ethel Haydon (Mrs. Robey) as Ophelia.

Ada Reeve's performance helped to make this a great pantomime. As Jack, she played her part with infinite distinction, and her work in the scene where the cow was sold at the fair was a perfect example of comedy laced with pathos. It was in this pantomime that she sang the delightful *Somewhere the Sun is Shining;* she also had *Naughty Boys*, a number in which she guyed Mr. Lloyd George.

The Brothers Griffiths made the cow a perfectly amazing animal, and were equally successful when, having resumed human form, they indulged in their hilarious wrestling bout. Tom Shale added to his Birmingham popularity by his performance of King Stoneybrokish, in the course of which he sang *Has anyone here seen Kelly?* Barry Lupino capered with the family liveliness as Miffins, Ethel Haydon (Mrs. George Robey) sang sweetly as the fairy, and Sam Elton conjured cleverly in the Giant's Kitchen scenes. Others favourably noted in contemporary reports were Jessie Lonnen (Dulcie), Angela Hope (the Princess), Mark Daly, and E. Story-Gofton.

One of the big nights of the season was engineered by the Rocket Club, a famous convivial and benevolent organisation in Birmingham which was then about fifteen years old. The members, who included many men of musical and dramatic talent, visited a place of amusement every year during the pantomime season, wearing the familiar scarlet geranium, their club badge. On this occasion the Royal was bedecked correspondingly in scarlet, and all the artists received gifts. Will Gardner, a member long noted as a drawing-room entertainer, contributed a turn in reinforcement of the regular programme.

On March 7th, for P.R.'s night came George Formby, Harry Weldon, Sammy Shields, and other visiting artists.

By this time Philip Rodway had become general manager. That night his new dignity was warmly recognised by an overflowing audience, and many presentations were made.

"Mr. Rodway," says a contemporary report, "spoke gracefully and gratefully a few words of thanks from the stage. Had he taken the audience into his confidence and told them of one half of the successful pieces of work he has carried through during his thirteen years association with the Theatre Royal, he would, though speaking no more than the truth, have appeared immodest. As it was, he was modesty personified, and he received an extremely warm and friendly greeting."

Robey's benefit a few nights later was very successful, for few comedians enjoyed greater popularity. One of the extra turns was by pupils from the dancing school conducted by the late Miss Rose Tyrrell, a former ballerina who for many years carried on her academy locally, and trained numerous present day stars. Before her death at a great age a few months ago, she fell on hard times, and a subscription fund was raised to ease her last years.

The run ended on March 12th, 1910, ten and a half weeks after the opening.

In *Round the Theatres* we read that the Royal was entering on a new era—an epoch-making period of prosperity—"and Mr. Rodway's value to the theatre must be enormous, for he knows the public pulse, so far as Birmingham is concerned, better than any man among us. With that blend of knowledge and experience I rather think that Mr. Rodway believes in the leavening of the old with the new, as in his last year's *Dick Whittington*, which this year is going strong at Liverpool. . . "

CHAPTER 12

(1910-11)

Season 1910

Not long ago, Birmingham was solemnly assured by one of its papers that the Royal was going to be turned into a picture house. Actually this was not accurate, but in any case such an event would not have been the first time films had been shown at the Royal, for in Holy Week of 1910 (Good Friday excepted) P.R. arranged to be presented *The Royal Picture Programmes*. Some of the films shown were: Visiting in Japan; Fishing at Boulogne; Tritien to Vallerame; Crocodile Hunting; a Mohammedan Carnival; and "The famous children's picture, the Antwerp Zoo"—a cross-section, in fact, of a present-day News Cinema's programme, with all the exciting bits left out, and no audible accompaniment except the carefully adapted sequence of more or less appropriate airs. Films in those days were still thought of as "animated pictures," and certain tunes went inseparably with certain subjects.

Looking through the attractions for the Spring of 1910, the first interesting point we note is that Weedon Grossmith, who opened the season, was supported in *Mr. Preedy and the Countess* by a young actor named Ronald Squire, to-day's popular star of four-character comedy.

A Royal Divorce was followed by *Pinkie and the Fairies*, which W. Graham Robertson wrote and which Beerbohm Tree's Company toured. The Follies, on their return, included H. G. Pélissier, Effie Cook, Gwennie Mars, Douglas Maclaren, Ethel Annandale, Lewis Sydney and Morris Harvey.

Martin Harvey gave his first Birmingham performance of Gloucester in *Richard III*, and Beerbohm Tree himself appeared in repertory—one of his supporters being Nigel Playfair, later Sir Nigel of Lyric Theatre (Hammersmith)

L

fame, who died this year (1934). He played Lancelot Gobbo in *The Merchant of Venice*, and other parts. ,

On May 6th, 1910, the death of King Edward VII threw the British Empire into mourning. By general consent, public amusements of all kinds were abandoned, and next day P.R. announced that the Royal would remain closed until the end of the week. Mother's diary recalls the beauty of that late spring week-end at the Lower Lode, Tewkesbury, and how the mourning spread from the big towns to the little villages:

"Friday evening—to Chaceley Village; Saturday morning—up the Severn Bank to the lock, where the steam boats and barges go through. In the afternoon to Tewkesbury, over the Abbey, draped in black and purple for the death of King Edward. Sunday morning—through the meadows by the riverside to Deerhurst church; in the evening—to Forthampton village and church . . . the whole place a fairyland of pink and white blossom; the meadows a cloth of gold with cowslips; the banks all bluebells; and through all this Sunday, so full of life, and hope, and spring, and sunshine, the village bells are tolling for the death of King Edward."

The season at the Royal was resumed with the annual Promenade Concerts, directed by Max Mossel, with Landon Ronald as conductor. The series included Saint-Saëns' *Concerto, Number 3*, and at the end of the performance, Mr. Mossel, who had played the violin exquisitely, was presented by an admirer with what Ernest Newman described as a beautiful floral horse-collar. Thus "E.N.":

" 'Do you think I am a prima donna?' asked Richter, when one of these curious compliments was paid him in Dublin. 'Thank you,' said Bülow, when *he* received a huge wreath, 'but I am not a vegetarian!' Mr. Mossel's remarks have not so far been recorded. Surely some better way of signifying that you like a man's playing can be found than this. One was simply left wondering what Mr. Mossel would do with his collar—wear it or eat it?"

When the season had run its course, the usual three weeks, it was stated the concerts had been a decided financial success. "E.N." allowed that they were doing excellent work, though he found the programmes still too conventional, and the type used in printing them too small. One suspected, he said, that the theatre was in collusion with the Birmingham oculists!

On the last night Landon Ronald made one of the most grateful speeches ever heard in the Royal. A year earlier he had to beg; now he had only "thank you" to say. He had appeared before many audiences throughout Europe, and had always regarded the Birmingham audience as his favourite. His season with Mr. Philip Rodway had been a wonderful success, and its repetition next year was beyond question.

The shareholders' meeting was held in May, much later than hitherto, because the directors had decided to fall in line with other provincial managements by bringing the most recent pantomime season into the accounts. The report showed a trading profit of over £4,000, which reduced the deficiency to £1,700 as against £6,500 or so in December, 1905.

Additional revenue was being derived through producing pantomimes in other towns, and *Jack and the Beanstalk*, with George Robey in his "dame" part, was booked for Manchester next Christmas on terms which ensured a profit. In the period covered by the accounts the results from touring attractions were much the same as the previous year's, which was satisfactory, seeing that there were now seventeen picture houses and skating rinks, mostly with music licences, and all to be regarded as rivals to the theatres.

How little theatre managers of those days had to contend with, had they only known it! To-day the cinemas have grown to a hundred, and wireless, dog-racing, daylight saving, and even motoring have all ranged themselves in opposition.

The Heiress, postponed from the tragic month of May, was produced in June. It was a new comedy opera, written by Harold Weston and Follett Thorpe, with music by Guy Jones, who had long directed the Royal orchestra. The proceeds went to swell the fund, opened by the *Birmingham Daily Mail*, for building the magnificent Children's Hospital in Ladywood

Road. The amateur cast included the names of several who will be recognised for their later prominence in musical and dramatic circles—Lillie Aston, Leonard Brown (a staunch member of the Rocket Club), Blanche Freeman, George Worrall (so long a pillar of the amateur stage), Ada Price and Mrs. Guy Jones.

During the week, a complimentary matinée was given for Guy Jones. Daisy Dormer, Sybil Arundale, Frank Titterton, Walter Newman, John Waterhouse, Pichel and Scale, A. Mackelvin, the three Comedy Chanters and Daisy Taylor were among those who appeared.

A sign of the times may be read in the extension of the summer vacation to August 29th, when the autumn campaign began with the first public performance of *Bardelys the Magnificent*, a romantic drama by Henry Hamilton and Rafael Sabatini, with the following fine cast:

Marcel de St. Pol, Marquis de Bardelys ...	Lewis Waller
Louis XIII	Herbert Jarman
Philippe, Comte de Castelroux	William Haviland
Vicomte de Lavedan	Frank Woolfe
Réné de Lesperon	Cronin Wilson
Pierre Rodenard	Alec F. Thompson
Vicomtesse de Lavedan	Mrs. A. B. Tapping
Roxalanne de Lavedan	Madge Titheradge

This picturesque play had a great reception, and Lewis Waller a part after his own heart. The recent death of Cronin Wilson robbed us of one of our distinguished actors, who was always welcome in Birmingham.

September brought to the Royal for the first time the Cavaliere F. Castellano's Grand Opera Company, fresh from a remarkable triumph at Drury Lane. Mabel Russell (as Daisy in *The Dollar Princess*), the Bensons, James Welch, Tittell-Brune (as leading lady in Hall Caine's plays), Lewis Waller and Madge Titheradge (in *Monsieur Beaucaire*), Lyn Harding (first as *Sir Walter Raleigh*, later in *The Speckled Band*), the Martin Harveys and the beloved Terrys are some of the well-known names of the season.

Towards November we had two more first visits—*The Blue Bird* and *The Brass Bottle*, the latter with Holman Clark, Harry Paulton, and Mary Brough,* invaluable adjunct of post-war Aldwych farce.

*   *   *

PANTOMIME 1910-11
ALADDIN

The *Aladdin* of 1910-11, though not ranked by connoisseurs as one of the Royal's finest, fully justified its production in a run of normal length—ten and a half weeks. The Oriental nature of the subject allowed amply for spectacle.

Robert Courtneidge and A. M. Thompson wrote the book, Charles Taylor and Dudley Smith the lyrics, Guy Jones composed and arranged the music, and Tritschler and W. R. Young painted the scenery. The first performance, a matinée, was far too long, four hours being taken up even when a scene had been cut out wholesale, and P.R. immediately did some drastic pruning. The pantomime which emerged was full of life and movement, but still not epoch-making.

Carrie Moore, Mr. Crompton Rhodes felt, was hardly so successful an Aladdin as a Prince Charming, though she had some excellent songs, remembered even to-day, such as *Fall in and follow me, I wonder if you care* (a duet with Olive Moore), *Nobody Cares* (evidently a sequel!), and *Dreamland*.

Tom Foy was a popular Widow Twankey, and Harry Tate was as active as ever. It was never settled whether he was funnier in *Golfing*, with the ubiquitous scrap of paper, or in *Motoring*, with the precocious boy passenger and the trouble over the sprockets not running true to the differential gear; but in all he did he was inimitable.

Pekoe was played by Ethel Negretti; Ray Ford was opposite as "second girl." The comedy side was strengthened by the presence of Barrett and Knowles, then at the height of success in their long partnership as *The Green Lizard and his Friend*. Florence Phillips, in solo dances composed by Guy

---

*Died September 1934.

Jones, began a career as prima ballerina of Theatre Royal Pantomime which lasted for several years, and Eric Campbell was a fine Emperor.

Other favourite songs of the season were Olive Moore's *Sweet Kathleen* and Ethel Negretti's *Beautiful Garden of Roses.*

As to the settings, the tableaux in the magic cave were extraordinarily spectacular, and in the second half an ingeniously worked flying palace transported the Princess to Africa, the curtain finally coming down on a brilliantly colourful Chrysanthemum Fête.

The principals this year formed a society whose inaugural (and probably only) supper was held at the Imperial Hotel on January 27th—"covers raised at 11-59." To judge from the programme, to which everybody who was anybody contributed, they had an extremely jolly evening. Stars from other local theatres vied with our own in giving turns not usually regarded as within their province. Guy Jones was billed for his Great Acrobatic Act—and Philip Rodway for a recital *Shall we exercise the Option?*

Students' Night brought its customary merriment on and off the stage, and its customary gifts to the artists and P.R. The Rocket Club came in again, two members—Walter Newman and Allan Reid—supplementing the show.

Philip Rodway's own night, on Monday, March 6th, was as ever a great occasion; we read, "The popularity of the general manager is unique, inasmuch as it will be difficult to find room for all the turns promised." The friendliness of the profession was exemplified by artists from far away as well as those appearing locally, his extra list including John Humphries, who travelled from the North of England in order to assist, G. H. Elliott, Charles Whittle, Hetty King, Jay Laurier, Madge White, Harry Rogerson, the Arthur Gallimore Trio, and Walter Newman.

The curtain fell for the last time on *Aladdin* on March 10th, 1911.

*   *   *

Season 1911

A Message from Mars, which had been played close on 4,000 times, was an old friend to start the 1911 season's ball rolling. First visits in the Spring included *The Chocolate Soldier* and *The Quaker Girl*, while Isabel Jay made her farewell in *The Balkan Princess*. Martin Harvey introduced *The Lowland Wolf* into his repertory, and a curious show was *The Merry Magician*, a so-called musical comedy serving as a vehicle for the mystifying talents of Horace Goldin, "the Royal Illusionist," who claimed to have performed four times in eight days before the late King.

Local amateurs, emboldened by the success of *The Heiress*, took the theatre for a week in May to produce *The Belle of the Skies*, again in aid of the Children's Hospital. This musical play was composed by Guy Jones and written by Graham Squiers, creator since of "Aerbut Paerks" for the wireless, and author of numerous lyrics. Those taking chief parts were Ada Price, Alfred Butler, O. H. Russ, Frank H. Timings, Allan Reid, J. M. Holt, George Worrall, and Walter Newman.

And of this production Graham Squiers tells us a little story.

"One incident I remember," he says, "which is against myself! Mr. Philip Rodway was sitting next to me at the dress rehearsal of this play. I was very pleased with one of the gags which I had introduced, and I believed it to be my own—or else the wish was father to the thought. I know that Philip Rodway had not read the book, neither had he been to any of the other rehearsals, and when the cue came for the gag with which I was so pleased, he quickly repeated the whole of it before the comedian in the show could get his words out!"

At the annual meeting the chairman, explaining that the figures covered twelve months and one pantomime, instead of fifteen months and two pantomimes, as in 1910, added that the general financial position was much the same. The expenses on the administrative side had been reduced by £700, and general expenses had increased by £300.

In explaining the difficulties incidental to management of

a provincial theatre, he said that the type of play popular in London was too short, too after-dinnerish, to suit Birmingham, which wanted something longer and more substantial. Some London successes would not draw as much money here in a week as they took in one night in London.

The "Proms," under the established auspices, were given in the latter part of June this year, and passed without incident, Ernest Newman finding the solo vocalists rather disappointing, and the programme printing worse than ever!

A summer vacation lasting through July and August terminated with a visit by Lewis Waller (his last before a three years' absence in America and Australia) in *A Butterfly on the Wheel*, with Madge Titheradge as Mrs. Admaston, himself doubling Sir Robert Fyffe and Roger Collingwood.

The Autumn season, while possibly not rivalling its predecessors in magnificence, had one or two notable features. P.R.'s predilection for Shakespeare (to which extended notice is given elsewhere) was reflected in the presentation of *The Winter's Tale* by Richard Flanagan's Company from the Queen's Theatre, Manchester, where it had been the sixteenth of Flanagan's famous revivals. He had also the first visit of *Kismet*, a colossal spectacular attraction from the Garrick Theatre, London, with Arthur Holmes-Gore in the Oscar Asche part of Hajj, the beggar. This was a real Arabian Nights' Entertainment adapted to modern stage purposes, and paved the way for Mr. Asche's later and greater success with *Chu Chin Chow*.

The Birmingham Drama Society extended its patronage to an interesting venture when Iden Payne sent a company to play a week of Shaw (*Man and Superman*), Masefield (*The Tragedy of Nan*), and Bennett (*Cupid and Commonsense*); but the city did not rise to the occasion.

A flying matinée by the Playhouse company, *Dad*, including Cyril Maude, Alexandra Carlisle, Kenneth Douglas, J. D. Beveridge, and Sam Sothern, closed a season to which such eminent personalities as Guy Newall, Julia Neilson (in *The

Popinjay), Frank Benson, Athole Stewart, Madge Titheradge, Martin Harvey, and Robert Evett had contributed. "Flying Matinées" were immensely popular and profitable in those times, when Birmingham people thought less casually of a trip to London to see the latest West End success in its regular habitat.

CHAPTER 13

(1911-12)

PANTOMIME 1911-12
JACK AND JILL

The 1911-12 pantomime, *Jack and Jill*, has naturally an
especial sentimental and historic interest for us, because it is
the first described in the printed matter as "produced by
Philip Rodway." There is abundant evidence of his activities
in connection with previous productions since 1904, but this
Christmas sees him at last receiving formal recognition; sees
him launched on the tide which was to sweep him to inter-
national success as a producer of pantomime.

Here, then, we may perhaps aptly give one or two general
observations on his progress and achievements in this sphere.
Tradition, environment, and experience had by the Christmas
of 1911 combined to give him a flying start and to ensure him
a high standing among contemporary producers. Emphasis
has already been laid on the historical background which so
strongly influenced his managerial career, but it is even more
important when considered in relation to the creative side of
that career.

Other provincial theatres have splendid histories as play-
houses: none has a record equal to that of the Theatre Royal,
Birmingham, in the matter of pantomime. Producing his first
pantomime there was for Philip Rodway to add a chapter to
a history begun in 1840. Even before that year there had
been many pantomimes in Birmingham, but they were performed during the summer months and as after-pieces on odd
nights.

Since 1840, however, the line had lengthened in unbroken
progression, with what Mr. Crompton Rhodes aptly calls

"an evolution of form, as intriguing as the change from tadpole to frog, from the short after-pieces in dumb-show, through a species of variety entertainments, to the full-length piece which is growing nearer and nearer to a stage play." As with the drama in general, so with pantomime—a survey of "Royal" casts from 1840 commands the figures of all the most distinguished artists who adorned that line of the theatrical profession. Squire Bancroft, even, had been banged on the head with a bladder by Goosey-Gander while making his stage début as a masked courtier in *The Great Gosling* in 1869-61 (though it was not as a pantomimist that Sir Squire was destined to fame).

It is when one comes to 1873—*Beauty and the Beast*—that the roll begins to be studded with the names of the stars of the lighter stage. In that year the great G. H. Macdermott played his first Theatre Royal pantomime. He returned in 1876, to be followed by Chirgwin (the famous "white-eyed Kaffir"), Vesta Tilley, Charles Coborn (afterwards creator of *Two Lovely Black Eyes* and *The Man who broke the Bank at Monte Carlo*, and who still broadcasts occasionally), Letty Lind, Harry Randall, Arthur Rickets (the first American comedian in Birmingham pantomime), Jenny Hill ("the Vital Spark"), Peggy Pryde (her daughter), George Moore (the D'Oyly Carte favourite), Harriett Vernon, Billie Barlow, Fred Emney, George Robey, Marie Loftus, Whimsical Walker, Tom Murray, Maggie Duggan, George Mozart, and the many whose work in the new theatre we have already mentioned.

It was thus a splendid heritage and an impressive responsibility into which Philip Rodway entered. How he faced the responsibility and fostered that heritage is gracefully described by Mr. Crompton Rhodes, who calls him the Arthur Collins, the Augustus Harris, of Midland pantomime, and adds:

"His chief endeavours have been directed to bringing pantomime back from a mere disconnected series of vaudeville turns towards the fairy story, where comedy is never forgotten, nor romance utterly obscured. And the parts are all treated as dramatic

characters—'pantomime,' of course, but each taking its due share
in the action. Some of Mr. Rodway's plots are, indeed, delightful
and original fairy stories which would make admirable books for
children. Not, of course, that pantomime is merely a child's
entertainment: far from it."

The inimitable Mr. A. P. Herbert has summed up the
production side of theatrical work to perfection in his preface
to Mr. C. B. Cochran's autobiography:

"No one who has not been involved in the production of a
musical play can realise the number of things that have to be
fussed about and argued about, foreseen, arranged, or calculated,
not in the week of production only, but for many months ahead.
Military generals in the field are complimented and decorated if
they succeed in thinking only a single day ahead, and provide for
only one-tenth of the possible contingencies thereafter. I have
seen something of the preparations for a battle, and I swear that
they are child's play compared with the preparations for a musical
production. One important difference is that when a general tells
people what he wants them to do, they then have to do it. Like
the centurion he says to one 'Come,' and he cometh, 'Do this,' and
he doeth it. But say to a leading lady 'Come,' and as like as not
she disappears at once. Say to the dressmaker 'Do this,' and he
may do the exact opposite. The theatrical general has to perform
feats of more than military organisation without the support of
military discipline.

"Another difference is, that there are any number of colonels
or possible colonels, but as a rule there is only one possible leading
lady: and if she threatens to desert in the face of the enemy she
cannot be put in the guard room, but has to be restrained with
qualities of tact and patience which not every leader of men
possesses.

"Another difference is that the military gentleman is provided
with an army and an enemy and unlimited resources before he
has to think at all, and need not (in these days) worry much about
expense. The producer has to find everything *and* pay the bill.

"The modern producer's departments are manifold, and demand
from one man manifold qualities of brain and character . . . he has
to exercise the qualities of a shrewd financier, who inspires confidence; a man of the world, who commands the favour of the
Press; a sensitive showman, who knows what the public wants; a
bold man, who risks much money on his judgment; a careful man

of business, who has worked out exactly how much he can afford to spend if he is to get it back; a man of literary taste and appreciation . . . a man with second sight . . . a man of musical taste and appreciation, who chooses good music and will have it well performed; a man who understands colour and design; a man of vision who sees his production already as a whole, with the three arts mentioned above blended together in their due proportions.

"No mean achievement for a single man, you will agree. And he has not yet begun to people his stage . . . endless disappointments, worry, and patience. Then casting . . . judgment and knowledge are needed in this department of a kind quite different from what has been in use before . . . the last week brings a multitude of new troubles and new tests. Principal actors fall ill or fall out. Irreplaceable singers develop laryngitis. There are mechanical troubles, costume troubles . . . whole rows of dresses turn out wrong and have to be scrapped. When laymen read this sort of thing they conclude that theatrical folk are extremely complex and difficult; the true conclusion is that the production of a big musical play is the most difficult and complex form of corporate effort yet attempted by the human race. It is an active alliance of all the arts; and where it is controlled by a single mind that mind must be a big one. It is as if a military general had to find his own army, choose his own officers, arrange and finance his own war, do his own work and the War Office's as well, write operation orders with one hand and diplomatic notes with the other, be equally familiar with the principles of strategy and the arrangement of his soldiers' underclothes, control his army without an Army Act, and risk financial ruin on the result of every battle. All this, then, makes up a big theatrical production."

Jack and Jill, the first of the long line of authentic Rodway pantomimes, was produced on Boxing Day, 1911, the opening day from which he never deviated. The book was by Hickory Wood, with whom he was to enjoy a long and prosperous association. The principals were Wilkie Bard (the Widow Cobble), John Humphries (Baron Bounce), Lily Morris (Jack), Maidie Scott (Jill), Lillie Leslie (Prince Paragon), S. T. Poluski (Teddy), Florence Ray (the Good Fairy), Jocelyn Hope (the Demon), Florence Phillips (solo dancer), Norah Burke (Poppy Cobble), Bert Monks and a Tiller dancing troupe.

The old nursery rhyme of *Jack and Jill* had never before been used for a subject at the Royal. It does not sound a very solid basis for a four-hour entertainment, but there was woven into the skeleton plot a delightfully fantastic story. Jack and Jill climbed a magic hill to fetch a pail of magic water; a traditional Dame and Baron romance was written in for the chief comedians, and there was also a story for Prince Paragon and Poppy Cobble, the widow's daughter; but the main theme, as in every good pantomime, concerned the confounding of Vice by Virtue through the gallantry of the hero and the fidelity of the heroine.

Lily Morris is not nowadays thought of as a principal boy, her talents having developed in the line of comedy. In 1911, however, she was as dashing a Jack as one could wish, with a special appeal to the popular parts of the house. She started off right away with her song *I don't care if the ship goes down*, which carried a hornpipe chorus, though her biggest hit was *Wedding Bells are ringing for Sammy*.

Maidie Scott scored one of the biggest triumphs of her career, and captured Birmingham's heart with her roguishness and saucily-demure songs. Who can forget the droll dolefulness of *If the Managers only thought the same as Mother*, or the appealing jollity of *I've got a sweetheart now*, with Maidie surrounded by golliwogs and billikins and teddy bears? Another number which she handled with skill was the crinoline song and dance by Guy Jones, preserved from *The Belle of the Skies*.

Wilkie Bard, a Dame with a quiet, confidential expansiveness all his own, was well furnished with songs of the descriptive type, such as *I want to sing in opera*, and *You've got to sing in Ragtime*. With John Humphries, too, he caused great amusement with *The Waltz is the Popular Dance of the Day*, which they demonstrated, a long way after Lily Elsie, by dancing merrily up and down a diminutive staircase. John Humphries had a good topical number in *Lucky Mr. Green*.

In the first half of the pantomime was a memorable transformation scene, through dawn and daylight to sunset and moonlight. The Interior of the Marriage Mart gave great scope for a big comedy hit by the Baron-Dame combination; and the act-drop fell on a scene of frost and icicles, with charming lighting and a wonderful impression of softly falling snowflakes. Muddle Junction, in the second half, was a hilarious scene with many surprise effects, and the story ended in the Palace of Jewels, radiantly bright and picturesque.

All through the run it was a happy pantomime, despite several "circumstances beyond the management's control," which conspired to prevent the full reaping of the deserved financial harvest. Snowstorms interfered with the early business, and then Wilkie Bard went down with an illness which kept him out of the cast for a fortnight. For all these handicaps, however, it remained an excellent production, and a bright and jolly pantomime.

The seventh annual Students' Night went off with its customary flourish. On P.R.'s own night, Birmingham theatregoers flocked to the Royal to compliment him on the success attained by his production, and extra turns were given by Nella Webb, Elsie Robey, The Quaint Q's, the Masters Rich, etc. Wilkie Bard, as spokesman for the company, presented him with a case of cutlery, and there were also added a silver centrepiece, a bronze figure from one of the directors, and a set of silver brushes and mirrors "from an unknown admirer, for Mrs. Philip Rodway."

* * *

Season 1912

Harry Pélissier, Louis Laval, Audrey Hislop, Lena Hutchings, Ethel Annandale, Lewis Sydney, and Morris Harvey were prominent among *The Follies* when that incomparable concert party opened the next spring season. In recent years there have been many super-pierrot shows, from the Co-optimists onward, but they all take their inspiration from *The Follies*, whose black-and-white pattern of costume and stage decoration was for several years famous throughout the land.

This 1912 season had some bad luck to contend with, for a great coal strike raged from March well into April, and in the latter month the sinking of the "unsinkable" *Titanic* cast a gloom over the whole civilised world.

To the Royal came well-varied musical plays and drama. *The Glad Eye*, the most successful farce of the day, came on a flying matinée from the Apollo, and W. W. Kelly sent Juan Buonaparte, a great-grandson of the Little Corporal, to play Napoleon opposite Edith Cole's Josephine in *A Royal Divorce*. From Drury Lane, in succession to *The Whip*, came *The Hope*.

The great event of this season was Birmingham's first view of *Oedipus Rex*, Max Reinhardt's immense production of the Sophocles tragedy, in Professor Gilbert Murray's translation, staged by Martin Harvey. Those who saw Sir John's performance in the title rôle will never forget it. It was in every phase magnificent, perhaps most of all in that last poignant scene when, blind and broken, he groped his way into the unknown from the palace which had seen his triumphs. Mary Rorke was the Jocasta, Franklin Dyall the Creon.

Flanagan's *Twelfth Night* was followed by an amateur week in aid of the Women's Hospitals. The promoters, the Midland Musical and Dramatic Society Ltd., put on *The Democrats*, a new musical play in two acts by St. John Hamund, with music by Guy Jones and additional lyrics by Follett Thorpe and Graham Squiers. In the cast were Alfred Butler, Lillie Aston, J. Finnemore Retallack, Hugh S. Gibson, Oswald H. Russ, Ernest Wright, George B. Worrall, and Bonnie Phillips. May brought Marie George in *The Boy Scout*, for the first time on any stage, with Hayden Coffin—looking younger than ever.

The shareholders, at the annual meeting, had a more encouraging statement of affairs to consider, the net profit being shown at £1,103, though there was still a deficit of £1,958 to dispel hopes of a dividend. The gross profit (£3,050) was up by £2,759, and would have been still higher but for the hampering influences previously described. Harry Lewis, in the chair, once more explained that Birmingham would not patronise the light, short pieces favoured by London, and bewailed the springing up, mushroom-like, of the cheap, popular places of entertainment.

The "Proms" opened auspiciously with the first Birmingham hearing of what Ernest Newman called "the newly-discovered symphony that is supposed to be by Beethoven," and ended, after the usual three weeks, to a crowded house. Financially and artistically it was the best of all the eight seasons up to date. Landon Ronald had taken his place in the front rank of conductors, while the programmes had steadily improved in quality and now included items which would have been wasted only a very few years earlier.

We have a story of the "Proms," told us in an interesting letter from Mr. Joseph H. Riley—("Joe," to his innumerable friends and acquaintances), of the unfailing cheer and good spirits—at whose Paradise Street domain, "O.T.H.," the art of personality salesmanship is so successfully applied to everything in the musical line. As Mr. Riley tells us, it illustrates the fact that in Daddy's eyes the integrity of the Theatre Royal, Birmingham, was so much a fetish that the slightest hint against it was a direct and personal insult.

Max Mossel, who combined the artistic temperament with a keen business instinct, took it into his head one afternoon to carry out the precautionary operation, beloved by visiting managers, known as "checking the house." Persuading Mr. Riley to go with him, he climbed up to the gallery, and started his count of the patrons, with a view, of course, to making sure that the theatre management, in collusion with the box office and checktakers, was not falsifying its returns to his disadvantage.

As luck would have it, Daddy was also making one of his periodical tours at the time, and arrived in the gallery just as Mr. Mossel's count was in full swing.

"Your father," says Mr. Riley, "beckoned us outside on to the landing and said 'Now what exactly is all this? First of all, what are you doing here, Joe?'

M

"I replied 'Don't take any notice of me, Phil; I'm just having a stroll round with Max. I'm only a guest in this act.'

" 'Very well,' he said, 'Then my remarks don't apply to you. Now then, Max. It looks very much as if you were counting the house. I hope you weren't, because, if anything like that ever happens,—all is over between us!"

"Max worked for all he was worth to smooth matters over, and eventually your father said 'Well, just tell me one thing. Do you think we are trying to diddle you?'

" 'Good gracious, no,' exclaimed Max.

" 'Then that's lucky,' said Phil. 'Because if I thought you did,' —he paused impressively—'we shouldn't half diddle you—and neither you nor anybody else in the wide world would be able to catch us out!' "

It was to "Joe" Riley, by the way, that one of the biggest theatre magnates in the world remarked "If I were opening a new theatre, or taking over England's best house, there is one man I would like to have on the board with me, and that is Philip Rodway."

The summer closure, which covered most of July and all August, was broken by the flying matinée of Pinero's farcical romance *The Amazons*, from the Duke of York's Theatre, with a wonderful cast: Phyllis Neilson-Terry, Pauline Chase, Marie Lohr, Weedon Grossmith, Dion Boucicault and Godfrey Tearle.

The Boy Scout, renamed *Merry Miss Mischief*, came back in September. The Royal had a good autumn, the first high spot being George Dance's company in *Ben Hur*, which was so heavy a production that it could not open until Tuesday evening. It stayed a fortnight, and caused plenty of excitement with its chariot race, its galleys and so on.

Sarah Bernhardt gave a flying matinée of *Lucrece Borgia*, *Une Nuit de Noël sous la Terreur* and Act Five of *La Dame aux Camélias*. Film devotees will recognise one of their favourites in Lou Tellegen,* her chief supporter.

The Scots comedy, *Bunty Pulls the Strings*, was followed by the Quinlan Opera Company on a fortnight's visit, which opened with the first local performance of Charpentier's

---

*As we go to press we have just heard from Hollywood of the tragic death of Lou Tellegen.

Louise. And what a company! Robert Parker, Jeanne Brola, Maurice D'Oisly, Edna Thornton, Gladys Ancrum, Spencer Thomas, W. T. Samuel, Arthur Wynn, John Harrison, Sydney Russell, Enrichetta Onelli, Agnes Nicholls, John Coates, Norah D'Argel, Robert Veevers, Hilda Morris, Rosina Beynon, Mabel Dennis, Allen Hinckley; with Hubert Bath, Ernest Knoch and Tullio Voghera to conduct.

One of the biggest casts ever seen here came with *Autumn Manoeuvres.* It included Louie Pounds, Marie Dainton, Maud Harris, Robert Evett (a Birmingham man), Huntley Wright, Lionel Mackinder, and Leonard Mackey. One of the nights was given up for the benefit of the Hebrew Educational Aid Society.

Two special matinées came in before the pantomime. The first was given by Lilian Braithwaite and Aubrey Smith, playing in *Instinct,* and Irene Vanbrugh and Donald Calthrop in *Rosalind;* the second, by the United Kingdom Commercial Travellers' Association Dramatic Society (in aid of their schools and other institutions), was *Sweet Lavender,* the names of the performers being H. Timmins, Guy R. S. Tebbitt, C. L. Moore, A. Batchlor, W. C. Webster, L. A. Cronk, H. V. Currie, Nance E. Boulton, Nora Bind, Edith Hall, and Irene Marsden.

Before leaving this season, we should mention that in August, 1912, P.R.'s lengthening career was the subject of a gracious article written by "S.G." in *Edgbastonia,* a journal which had flourished for many years. After reviewing his progress from the Prince of Wales Theatre box office to the general manager's sanctum at the Royal, the writer went on:

"Mr. Rodway took managerial control of the new theatre (of which he considers the equipment perfect) with a very full sense of the responsibilities of the post. The manager of a large theatre to-day has to be an acute, far-seeing man. The contesting claimants for public support in the matter of amusements are innumerable. Where there were ten places of amusement in Birmingham fifteen years ago, now there are forty. The public taste, moreover,

is continually getting higher and higher, and the task of supplying
the new demand is not becoming any easier. The mass of work to
be done merely on the commercial side would surprise many
business men; and when to the ordinary control of the theatre are
added the extra responsibilities of similar interests that extend into
many other towns (the Birmingham Theatre Royal always having
been a centre, as it were, of diverse activity), the position held by
Mr. Rodway is seen to be one that makes him no sinecurist. He
is, indeed, general manager for the whole wide control summed
up in the term 'Theatre Royal'; and he stands in general as expert
adviser to the directors. One of Mr. Rodway's chief concerns is to
maintain the dignity of the Theatre Royal. To him it is not a
place where vulgarity can be permitted to enter. Despite the
pressure of counter-attractions, he is determined that it shall
maintain its truly enviable reputation. His own affection for it is
based on respect, and he feels that only by the same means can full
public regard be secured.

"As to the position of drama in Birmingham, Mr. Rodway considers that the city is comparatively well served. He deplores the
fact that there is not yet a big audience here for Shavian and
modern plays in general; but he feels the future prospects are
bright, if for no other reason than that the critical reputation of
Birmingham play-goers is held in high esteem by actors, managers,
authors, and, in fact, all who are qualified to speak on the matter.
The famous 'stars' who tour the provinces look with particular
respect upon the Theatre Royal audiences. The Theatre Royal
also is able to produce a pantomime unsurpassed by any provincial
theatre; and this point, though apparently unimportant in the
eyes of the student of serious modern drama, is very significant
when looked upon in conjunction with a year's working.

"Mr. Rodway does not allow the weight of his office to crush
him, and remains quiescent under stress of worrying conditions.
He has considerable sympathy with the fatalism of the Oriental,
feeling that what will be, will be; and that what may be, is a matter
to be distressed about only when it actually is. He gets no little
pleasure out of the endless constructive advice he receives from the
public. The theatre manager, like the editor of a paper, or the
organist of a church, holds one of those offices which every man
thinks he could fill, and so he has to hold himself out against a perpetual rain of recommendations, tips, suggestions, and criticisms.
As about one-half of the public feel that they themselves own the
theatre they visit, some of their interest becomes at times a little

embarrassing. But Mr. Rodway, both by nature and by experience, knows the course to pursue, and he has not yet displeased anyone by the way in which he has not acted upon their ideas. Whether he would have displeased them if he *had* done so, is another matter.

"With regard to theatre audiences of the present day, managers of Mr. Rodway's stamp have not yet lost the feeling of wonder at the vast and complete changes that have taken place within even the few years of his experience. Less than half a generation ago the queue system did not exist for us in Birmingham. The heavy fists, the cruel crushes, and the brutal walking over shoulders by pit and gallery people, is as remote to-day as the Danish piracies on the ancient coast of Britain; yet when Mr. Rodway first took office at the Royal, the state of the cheaper parts of the house was as hinted above. The gallery to-day on normal occasions is as comfortable, quiet, and (without much exaggeration) as exclusive as an ordinary concert room. The change has come about through a general public sense of the duties one man owes to another, and through a gradual realisation that ease and system are more profitable than crude disorder and irregularity. But whatever the cause, Mr. Rodway is grateful for the change, and obviously regards it as a symbol of the great improvement recently made, and of others still to be made, in the working control of places of public resort.

"In private life Mr. Rodway indulges more or less in most sports —cricket, fishing and the like. He is an excellent walker, and plays a good game of billiards, a break of a hundred being well within his powers. He married, in 1904, Miss Ethel Brown, of Edgbaston, and has two little daughters. As he is not yet half-way through his 'thirties,' one may believe that he has many years of active and useful work before him, and that Birmingham will be the place in which the greater part of them are to be spent. It is his native town. His life-long friends are here. The artistic position of the district is steadily improving. The next ten or fifteen years may well see Birmingham and the Midlands standing high in the eyes of the world of art and letters. If this should be so, the consummation will be effected not solely by the artists themselves, but in a great measure by those who alone make the practice of art a possibility—the directors, managers, agents and organisers, amongst whom will be placed in a foremost position the present manager of the old New Street playhouse."

CHAPTER 14

(1912-13)

The first car!—The 2.40 train to Hampton-in-Arden—*Goody Two Shoes*,
1912-13; George Robey, Nellie Wigley, Maie Ash, Fred Conquest—"The
Man Who Pulls The Strings"—Retrospect—An imaginary interview.

THE FIRST CAR

It was in the far-off days of 1912 that we had our first car.
It was a tiny Morgan of great personality, on three wheels,
and brightly painted. We remember that Morgan so well
because it is the only thing, animate or inanimate, that ever
got the better of Daddy. As such it deserves a definite place
in this book.

One day Daddy came home and announced: "This morning
I have bought a car."

Rapturous joy and pride flooded all our hearts, though
mingled with Mother's excitement there was the little feeling
at the back of her mind that their beautiful country walks had
gone for ever. (Twice a week they had caught the 2.40 train
to Hampton-in-Arden, and then walked to Barston village.)
However, as it turned out, she need not have worried. That
gay little car was to be hoist with her own petard, her pride of
race her downfall.

Two days of glorious power she wielded over our family,
and then she was resold. It was many years before we had
another car, and Daddy never drove again. But that is the
end of the story, and we are yet at the beginning.

After the applause following Daddy's stupendous announcement had died down, he followed it up with: "I will go
straight back to town and get it."

So back to the Midland Garage he went, while Mother sat
on the bottom step of the staircase and waited, in hope and
fear, for its arrival. Particularly as she had not been aware
till that day that Daddy could drive. . . .

It drew up an hour later than expected, as it appeared
there had been some difficulty: first, in getting it started,

second, in getting it out of the garage. The pride in our hearts was almost unbearable when we saw *our* car turn the corner, with Daddy at the helm. We two were so excited that we implored to be taken in it first, so once round Speedwell Road we went, feeling Lords of Creation. Then Mother went with Daddy alone, a foretaste of the country ride he was to take her the following afternoon.

The next day dawned bright and clear. All morning Mother pondered over a motoring outfit; she felt her ordinary clothes were not suitable for this Great Adventure. She must look SPORTING. Finally a very large hat with about six veils swathing it (and an extra one in her bag as a spare) was decided on as the very thing for her head; and a neat tussore suit, with a suspicion of a hobble, to go with it. At 2 o'clock they started, we two waving goodbye furiously from the front windows. Had we realised how nearly it was goodbye for ever we should have been even more energetic.

They turned the corner and very soon were covered with a fine white dust. Even Mother's Salome-like veils could not keep it out. There was, of course, no hood, and within half an hour a modern John and Mrs. Gilpin with apparently powdered wigs could have been seen bowling along the Alcester Road, very erect, in a tiny three-cornered car. For all the trouble it caused it might have been the incarnation of the Eternal Triangle itself.

They came into the country much quicker than they intended. They tore through Alcester, Wixford, and Bidford, and became aware that the Morgan wouldn't stop. They gathered speed, and tore through the remaining Warwickshire and Worcestershire villages without once being able to pull up. The pleasant, quiet country drive of their imagination had turned itself into a Marathon race by the time they reached Stratford-upon-Avon. However, coming down Sunrising Hill there were so many bumps it was obvious there were some screws loose. The car stopped. Mother, ever cautious, alighted and walked down the remainder of the hill, while the Morgan, gaining momentum from the incline, passed her at top speed.

In Stratford the loose and missing screws were replaced, but the Morgan was not the same after the operation. The first fine careless rapture, the old fire and verve, were gone. Daddy made his way cautiously along the Stratford Road in the direction of home. Towards the bottom of College Road, they saw, to their horror, road repairs were in progress. Not only was there the car to contend with, but fearsome notices:

"Beware of the Steam-Roller"

"Beware of the Ramp"

showed Daddy he had further dangers to tackle. He decided to brave both ramp and steam-roller, and had just passed the latter when the Morgan, exhausted with the effort, sat down in its path and crouched there, with the huge roller towering above it, and a terrible voice coming out of the giant's interior: "Get out of my way or I'll flatten you out."

Mother, for the second time that afternoon, hopped rapidly from her seat. Workmen had to push the car from almost underneath the steam-roller's wheels to a place of comparative safety. There Daddy tinkered away until the engine started, but again it failed them going up College Road. This time they both alighted and pushed it over the brow of the hill into Wake Green Road. From there the journey was mostly downhill, and with the wind behind her the Morgan sailed along as if she were a model car. Mother was deposited at home. She sank exhausted into a chair, and knew not whether to direct her prayers in gratitude for her safe return, or for help in the hour to come. For Daddy was on his hazardous way down Bristol Road back to the garage.

At Wellington Road he had his name taken by a policeman for having a completely obscured number plate. Surely nothing more could happen to him? But Puck, in the shape of a Madcap Morgan, had not yet finished with him. Weary and worn, he yet managed to take the entrance of the Midland Garage in a fine flourish, a grand sweep. It was not his fault

. . ."*and we caught the 2.40 train to Hampton-in-Arden and walked to Barston*"

MOTORING IN ITS INFANCY
Granny, Mother, Lois and Phyllis

GOODY TWO SHOES.

THE MAN WHO PULLS THE STRINGS.

Reproduced from "The Searchlight," January 2nd, 1913

but certainly his misfortune that a man was standing with his
back to him in the centre of the entrance, and that the horn
had long since ceased to blow. The car caught the man up
on its bonnet and, with him astride and cursing, sailed proudly
into the garage like some small Viking vessel with a figure on
the prow.

There is a limit to human endurance. Normally courageous,
after what he had been through Daddy could not stand up to
the showers of abuse that descended on him and his Morgan.
He escaped by the back way. And the following Tuesday we
all caught the 2.40 train to Hampton-in-Arden and walked
to Barston. . . .

*   *   *

PANTOMIME 1912-13
GOODY TWO SHOES

In this production of Philip Rodway's the irrepressible
George Robey came back to play the rôle of Mother Hubbard
in *Goody Two Shoes* (not done here since 1887), and to cement
the huge popularity established in his four previous panto-
mimes. With him were the McNaughtons, Alfred Clark, and
Harry Kisbey on the comedy side; Fred Conquest as the dog;
Charles Goff as the Red Dwarf; Nellie Gallafent as Susannah;
Alice Venning as the Fairy. Nellie Wigley played Robin
Goodfellow, the principal boy, and Maie Ash was Goody
Two Shoes. The book was by James J. Hewson.

Goody Two Shoes was at once greeted as likely to prove one
of the finest pantomimes ever put on at the Royal. It settled
even more firmly P.R.'s position among the leading producers. The inscription "O.K. 1912" on Mother Hubbard's
tri-car was fully applicable to the show in its entirety. While
the songs, dances, and dresses were well above standard, the
scenery was singularly effective, and the cast failure-proof.
George Robey, a host (or rather a hostess) in himself; Nellie
Wigley and Maie Ash, principals who could sing and act;
in fact *Goody Two Shoes* was more than a pantomime, having
in it comic opera, farce and musical comedy.

The story began in the village of Honeybloom, a lovely scene with a river in the background and, at the side, Mother Hubbard's "Stop and Step" Inn. Here it was that we saw Mother Hubbard bait her line and hook a fish at the first cast (wherein we recognised some of Daddy's own favourite fishing tricks).

The next scene saw the McNaughtons in some clever foolery, the Red Dwarf in malignant mood, and other characters in whatever the author required. Next we went inside the "Stop and Step" Inn, to hear Nellie Wigley sing *That Mysterious Rag*, a song which the gallery was whistling in no time—save ragtime. George Robey's *Footprints in the Snow* followed, after which came his love scene with the Baron (Alfred Clark), and Maie Ash triumphant with her big song-hit *Dixieland*, looking as pretty as the picture she conjured up in this catchy number.

Then came the memorable dress parade, illustrating the elaborate finery of the Elizabethan and Stuart periods, the fragile daintiness of the Dresden style, the charm of the crinoline, and finally, the most up-to-date confections of the year 1912. It was a boldly conceived spectacle, with a playful thrust at the colossal extinguishing hats of its own day. Here Florence Phillips showed the intricacies of the measure known as the Gaby Glide (after Mdlle. Gaby Deslys), and George Robey, as a type of rare English maidenhood, brought down the curtain on a striking first half finale.

After the interval came Maie Ash's second big song hit, *Oh, you beautiful doll*, sung and danced with Leonard Wallis; the McNaughtons' comic fight; and a very lovely daybreak scene. Clever lighting devices helped the effectiveness of Nellie Wigley's *My Heart is with you to-night*, one of the many ballad successes of the pantomime, and Harry Kisbey had a good coon number. Then came the arming of Robin for his fight with the Red Dwarf; a scene on the ramparts of Castle Mystical (with Mother Hubbard in an excruciating ordeal by haunting); and the brilliant closing scene in the Castle Gardens.

Goody Two Shoes played to excellent business throughout its run of nearly ten weeks. P.R. had been steadily encouraging local clubs, social associations, and industrial concerns to make up parties to visit the pantomime, and a growing number was welcomed each year. On his own night came (as extra turns) Phyllis Dare and George Gregory (then at the Prince of Wales Theatre in *The Sunshine Girl*); Moira Hammon and Bert Harrow from the Alexandra; Marriott Edgar from the Hippodrome, and Mike Whallen from the Empire. George Robey made an extra incursion into burlesque as the manager of the Splitz Hotel, but, according to the critics "There was no turn the audience liked better than Philip Rodway's short speech reviewing his association with the Theatre Royal, delivered to the accompaniment of *For he's a jolly good fellow*. It is remarkable what a hold this Night has upon the public; many people who know Mr. Rodway simply leave a standing order for seats, which could always be allotted over and over again."

Shoals of congratulatory telegrams poured in, as usual; we came upon a bundle of them only the other day. How many of the names are gone from the boards for ever—

"Handed in at Liverpool, Feb. 8th, 1913.
"Best of good luck—hope you will have a record benefit and one that we can just beat next year for you. . . .
"BOBBIE ALLANDALE."

There were others from Maie Ash, Quinlan, Rose Tyrrell, Forster, "to the best manager in the kingdom"—all who have since taken their last call.

Students' Night, coinciding with Robey's benefit, gave George an apt excuse for putting in a sketch *Ninepence for Fourpence*, in which he was abetted by a group of Medicals. The run ended on March 1st, 1913.

It was during this season that the *Searchlight*, a journal of the period, published a cartoon, showing P.R., top-hatted and debonair, as a marionettist manipulating the puppets (among them Mr. Robey). It was called *The Man Who Pulls The*

Strings, and with it went another of the many biographical notices accorded to him at this stage of his career. Observing that there was no more popular man in Birmingham "than the wonderfully astute general manager of the Theatre Royal," the writer went on . . .

"Wherever he goes he is liked; he is always the life and soul of any social circle of which he may be a member, temporarily or permanently. He is rightly regarded as one of the champion 'leg-pullers' of the country, and it would really be startling to many if they were to know what a multitudinous circle of acquaintances Mr. Rodway possesses. You have only to look into the theatre on the night of his annual benefit, and you see the professional and public life of Birmingham well represented. You see sport in all its phases represented; you see, in fact, an essentially composite audience. Mr. Rodway is something more than a successful theatrical manager; he is a genial companion and a loyal friend.

"When a youth he was a good cricketer, and at one period captained the redoubtable Speedwell Club, whose doings have had no counterpart in local cricket. Even now Mr. Rodway can wield the willow, for he plays in the annual match at the County Ground, Edgbaston, between Speedwell Past and Present, and generally manages to do his side useful service; in fact, the Past have rather more than held their own up to the present. Mr. Rodway is an ardent angler. Whenever he can snatch a little time from the heavy calls made upon him by his theatrical duties, he is whipping some stream—preferably the Teme at Knightwick, but he is most cosmopolitan in his angling tastes. Mr. Rodway is also a clever billiard player; indeed, he is one of the finest amateurs in the city.

"Tact is one of the essentials in connection with the life of a theatrical manager. Mr. Rodway is the embodiment of tact. No man knows what immensity of tact is required in this world until he comes to manage a pantomime company. The ordinary business man has no conception of the difficulties that fall to the lot of the man who essays that Herculean task. To satisfy this comedian and that comedian, to keep everything going smoothly, and eliminate the hideous element of jealousy—well, you scarcely know how it is done, and it is *only the man of the Philip Rodway temperament who can do it.*"

The same journal devoted a very amusing essay, on the *Imaginary Interview* lines, to P.R. about this time.

*　　　*　　　*

"IMAGINARY INTERVIEWS

"MR. PHILIP RODWAY

"General Manager of the Theatre Royal

" 'Oh, good evening, Mr. Rodway,' I said, as I advanced with my best smile towards the box office, through the window of which I espied the subject of this interview.

" 'Well,' Mr. Rodway replied, 'we're pretty full. Just see if there's anything left, Frank.'

" 'Pardon me,' I broke in, a little indignantly, 'I don't want a free seat. I've come to interview you on behalf of the *Searchlight*.'

" 'I'm sorry; but I mistook you for a deadhead. You know, whenever anybody comes up to me with a particularly expansive smile, and more especially when they are tenderly anxious about my health, I generally know what is coming. You happen to be the exception. The "free-seat look" is usually unmistakable. But about this interview, I really don't think I've anything to say.'

" 'Indeed. That's rather strange for a theatrical manager. Don't you even want to grumble? Don't you want to say there's no longer any money in the business? Don't you want to abuse the music-halls, the picture theatres, and the licensing magistrates?'

" 'No, I don't. I am the exception now, and you have made the mistake. The fact is, I'm too busy to grumble about anything. We only do that in the slack season.'

" 'Well, you've cut the ground from under my feet. You *must* talk about something. You wouldn't like me to go away and make this interview up, would you?'

" 'I don't know that I should mind. It has been known. It's much more fun to read done that way. A man never really knows what he thinks till he has been interviewed.'

" 'Quite an epigram, Mr. Rodway.'

" 'Oh, I can do better than that. We always have a few of those things ready. Frank keeps a list for me. It's known as *Rodway's Ready Reference Book of Repartee and Humour*. Some of its contents have become famous. For instance, I ask a person, "Why does a herring cross the sea?" '

" 'Quite so, and what is the answer?'

" 'Why, "Because Jack's the Boy for Work?" '

" 'But, I don't see the point. I'm afraid I'm a little dull.'

" 'Oh, you must see it. The emphasis is on the word *Jack*. "Because *Jack's* the Boy for Work." See?'

" 'Ha, ha, very good.' Here I smiled expansively, and felt very uncomfortable.

" 'You do see it, do you? Well, I don't! The point of that joke is that there isn't a point. The fun comes in when people pretend to see it, and laugh as you did.'

"Here there was an awkward pause. At least it was awkward for me. Mr. Rodway had scored, and I wasn't getting on with my interview a bit. However, *nil desperandum*. I returned to the attack.

" 'One to you,' I said. 'And now let us be serious. What do you do to fill up your spare time when you are not pulling people's legs?'

" 'Oh, in my odd moments I run this theatre. It's a very simple business. You just stand in front every evening, looking pleased and prosperous, and at the end of the week you count up the money you have taken.'

" 'Then, I may take it, the theatre manager's business is an easy one to learn?'

" 'No, no. I didn't say that. The difficult thing is to get that pleased and prosperous look. It takes years to acquire. And in the present state of things, with a picture theatre in every street, I have to practise to keep it up. My assistant, Mr. Frank Smith, is only just beginning to get it.'

" 'And what is the precise value of that pleased and prosperous look?'

" 'It is a decoy. It makes the public think we are doing well, when we are not. The public never support you unless they think you are prosperous.'

" 'But you do make money sometimes. The theatre is often full?'

" 'Yes, but that only pays the losses when it is not full.'

" 'Then how do you keep going at all?'

" 'Well, you see, we make a small profit on the programmes, and we have once been supported by the Drama Society. In the near future we may get some of the overflow from the Repertory Theatre.'

" 'And, have you any ideas as to what could be done to improve the theatrical business in Birmingham?'

" 'Oh, yes. It is quite simple. Picture houses and music-halls ought to be forbidden by law, and the existing number of regular theatres ought never to be added to.'

" 'What about the Art Gallery and Free Library?'

" 'Well, I am prepared to be generous as regards those places. There must be somewhere for people to shelter in wet weather.'

" 'Do you think there is any immediate prospect of your idea being carried out?'

" Not under the present Government; but if Sir George Alexander is really going in for Parliament, great things may happen.'

" 'Excuse the apparent irrelevance, but have you ever known a theatrical manager who admitted that he made money?'

" 'Oh, yes. Mr. Charles Manners.'

" 'You are pleased to trifle with me. But I will ask if you have any alternative to the monopolist policy? What do you think can be done to popularise the drama under existing conditions?'

" 'Well, prizes for regular attendance and full teas and suppers might help; but of course there is a third course, of throwing the Drama overboard altogether. Now the Repertory Theatre is about to open, the Drama is no longer on our conscience. We can just devote ourselves to entertaining the people. Pantomime all the year round, with different stars in the cast every week, is one of my projects. That would give the music-halls one to go on with. Pantomime is the only thing that pays nowadays, and it is an obvious commercial proposition to give only the thing that is profitable.'

" 'But what would Birmingham playgoers do without their Fred Terry and their Julia Neilson, and the stupendous Ben Hur?'

" 'They wouldn't have to do without them. We should work them all in. Some of them are often as good as a pantomime already.'

" 'Wouldn't the public get tired of always seeing more or less the same piece?'

" 'Oh, no. All the popular pieces are much the same now, only they have different names.'

" 'Quite true. And would you never have a specimen of the Higher Drama?'

" 'Well, yes, we might when we wanted the theatre clear for re-decoration.'

" 'That's excellent. The last question. Which would you rather do or go fishing?'

" 'Go fishing, of course. Who told you I was one of those? Have you heard how I caught the big pike with—'

"But I fled."

CHAPTER 15

(1913-14)

The spring was marked by another very important step in the romance of Philip Rodway's theatrical life. In May he was elected to the Board, and then appointed to the Managing Director's chair.

So in the brief space of about fifteen years the young box office clerk had risen to perhaps the most important executive position in the provincial theatre. In 1900 he had been the country's youngest acting manager, in 1909 probably the youngest general manager, and now he could have had few rivals for the title of youngest managing director.

Since the opening of the new theatre in 1904 he had grown increasingly accustomed to shouldering responsibilities heavier than those nominally attached to the positions he had held. He had piloted the good ship Royal through stormy weather and rough seas, and his latest promotion coincided aptly and happily with the prospect, vouchsafed for the first time, of fairer conditions ahead.

His managership had made a great change in the company's financial position. At the Annual Meeting in May it was announced that the deficit (£1,958 the year before) had at last been cleared off, even leaving a surplus of somewhere about £313 from the net profit of £2,272.

For the first time in the company's history, there was no deficit in the balance sheet. On the contrary, there was a very strong cash position, with a sinking fund which fully provided for all contingencies.

Considering that the competition of inexpensive entertainment was mounting year by year, this position was obviously one with which the shareholders could be very well satisfied.

P.R. received generous recognition from them for his work as manager since the opening, and equally generous congratulations on his new directorship. Walter Alldritt, the company's first (and while he lived, only) secretary, had been added to the Board, and his appointment gained warm approval.

We may be pardoned for thinking P.R.'s election the great feature of the spring of 1913—but Ernest Newman would probably give priority to the first Birmingham performance of Wagner's *Ring* cycle. This was achieved by the Quinlan Opera Company, and Robert Parker carried out a genuine *tour de force*, both artistically and physically, as Wotan.

In these months were also comprised the first visit of *Gipsy Love* (with Blanche Tomlin, Leonard Mackay, Daisy Burrell, Ian Colquhoun, and Billy Spray), the *n*th visit of *The Sign of the Cross*, and the annual call of *The Follies*, especially interesting this time in that Fay Compton, Harry Pélissier's girl-wife, made her local début. This wonderful actress, only seventeen years old, was not fated to enjoy long happiness with her genial first husband, for the burly leader of *The Follies*, one of the most likeable men in the profession, died a few months later in his fortieth year. It was a tragic ending to their romance. Since then Fay Compton has enhanced her reputation in every form of dramatic art, from Shakespeare and Barrie to pantomime and musical comedy.

A Royal Divorce scored its half-century of Birmingham weeks in May, and Cyril Maude brought the Playhouse company down for a flying matinée of *The Headmaster*. The Proms, popular as ever, ran their usual course, and then the theatre was closed for two months.

It re-opened for the first week with Cyril Maude and the Playhouse company, who were just off on an American tour. The even tenor of the autumn, with its well-ordered round of classic and modern drama, musical comedy, etc., was sharply disturbed on November 10th, 1913, by the first presentation of a revue in the Theatre Royal.

N

This new form of entertainment had already caught on in London, and had been seen at local music halls, but nothing on the scale of *Hullo, Ragtime!* (the name typifies the age) had yet appeared in the city. It came from the London Hippodrome, where, according to its statistically minded publicity agent, it had been played to 1,000,000 people.

Those who expected to see in it a piquant, lively commentary on the affairs of the day were sadly disappointed, for *Hullo, Ragtime!* was vaudeville undiluted, with the loud pedal down all the time. Nevertheless it was greatly enjoyed by many people. The principals included Teddie Gerrard, Maud Tiffany, Bonita, Lew Hearn, George Gregory, Morris Harvey, and a beauty chorus of sixty. One of the best remembered numbers will be *You're my Baby*, with a diminutive Lew Hearn striving manfully to suit the action to the word ("I'd like to bounce you up and down upon my knee") while singing the duet with Bonita.

Who were the legitimate touring stars of 1913, the last full season before the war? Those still with us include the Martin Harveys, the Bensons, Julia Neilson, Phyllis Neilson-Terry, Cyril Maude, and several others, but their ranks have been sadly depleted in the last twenty years. Leonard Boyne, the handsome hero of *General John Regan*, has gone. So have the two most glorious costume-romance actors of their day, Lewis Waller and Fred Terry. George Alexander, Mary Moore, Herbert Lomas, Edith Cole, Stanley Cooke, Laurence Irving, Mabel Hackney, Charles Wyndham (their names taken at random and with no attempt at gradation), have all answered their last call.

Of such was the season's quality: Sir Charles Wyndham and Mary Moore in a flying matinée of *David Garrick*, with which they had closed the old Royal; Fred Terry and Julia Neilson (though he always billed her first) together again after four years during which one or other had always been ill; Laurence Irving and his wife, Mabel Hackney (doomed to a watery grave only six months later in the sinking of the

LITTLE · MISS · MUFFET · SAT · ON · A · TUFFET · EATING · HER · CURDS · & · WHEY · THERE · CAME · A · GREAT · SPIDER · & · SAT · DOWN · BESIDE · HER · & · FRIGHTENED · MISS · MUFFET · AWAY ·

· LITTLE · MISS · MUFFET ·

Design for Nursery Stained Glass Window. Ethel Rodway.

THE PICTURE WHICH INSPIRED THE
PANTOMIME

Design for nursery stained-glass window
by Mother

Empress of Ireland off Quebec, but in 1913 playing together in *Typhoon*); the Martin Harveys in a simplified production of *The Taming of the Shrew*, and in Reinhardt's settings for *The Faun;* Phyllis Neilson-Terry opposite Allan Aynesworth in *The Real Thing;* Herbert Lomas in *Hindle Wakes;* Stanley Cooke in *Oh! I say!*

All was merry as a marriage bell for the theatres in this happy Autumn, the last England was to know for some six years.

* * *

PANTOMIME 1913-14
LITTLE MISS MUFFET

Little Miss Muffet, like *Jack and Jill*, had never figured in the Royal's long list of pantomime subjects until Philip Rodway saw and explored its possibilities in 1913. For principals he engaged Ernie Mayne (Simple Simon), Maidie Scott (Miss Muffet), Ella Retford (Boy Blue), The Brothers Griffiths (nominally Private Enquiry Agents), James A. Watts (Queen Peckapepper), Fred Allandale, Will Gardner, Cicely Eldon, Fred Goddard, Percy Mayne, and Leonard Wallis, with Florence Phillips as principal dancer, and a Tiller Troupe.

P.R. gave the book to James Hewson—a story built on the fragmentary basis of the single incident described in the nursery rhyme. Throughout he kept the fairy element well to the fore; he arranged for Miss Muffet to be carried off by the predatory spider, and rescued by her lover Boy Blue, with the aid of the Fairy Firefly. Boy Blue, of course, subsequently turned out to be the rightful heir to the throne, then occupied by the usurping Queen Peckapepper, with Simple Simon as her reluctant consort. This thread was strong enough to hold together a pantomime which gave great scope to the scene painters (W. R. Young, T. Dunn, R. C. McCleery, and James Hicks) and the costumiers.

W. R. Young was responsible for the Spider's Web, a truly wonderful stronghold hidden among the flowers, from which Miss Muffet was dramatically rescued, together with a kaleidoscopic collection of lepidoptera—brilliant beetles and lady-birds, bees and wasps, dragonflies, grasshoppers, butter-flies and moths. Here the dresses were striking to a degree, extraordinarily effective in colour and design. Another beau-tiful set of Young's was the scene in the little village. Dunn painted a splendid Bull Ring Market scene, which fulfilled P.R.'s fondness for a local touch whenever it could be applied without spoiling the illusion. McCleery was represented by a realistic "corner of the Casino at Monte Carlo," with a huge roulette wheel, where Simple Simon had a flutter with the proceeds of the crown jewels; and Hicks painted a striking picture of a terrace of the Palace of Beautiful Dreams, with a dim vista of lofty mountains over a shimmering moonlit lake. In it black, white, and gold were used in bold and effective combination. In the cleverly contrived ship scene, with its cabin interiors, a violent storm arose, wherein the Brothers Griffiths showed their great skill as acrobats, rocked to and fro, clinging to the luggage racks above their bunks, and finally making a complete circle with the ship. Humour, imagination, and ingenuity went hand in hand to furnish *Little Miss Muffet* with a worthy frame, and Birmingham's pantomime was dressed and mounted with a distinction never before approached.

It was while this pantomime was in process of construction that we two were allowed by Daddy to set foot for the first time upon the professional stage! The great theatre was empty and deserted, in semi-darkness and dustsheets, the act drop up and the stage clear, save for a huge spider's web pencilled in chalk upon the boards. Our feelings were a comical mix-ture of pride, excitement, and awe, for the vast stage stretched away to illimitable distance, far into the wings, high into the flies, and a dozen steps across the immensity of it made not the slightest impression on the space. Perhaps, after all, this was not so surprising, for in those days the Theatre Royal stage was the largest in the provinces!

Ernie Mayne, playing his first Birmingham pantomime,

JACK BUCHANAN

was a tower of strength in the comedy line. He soon established himself as a favourite with his irresistible blend of vacant foolishness and cunning canniness. *Puss in the Corner* was his best song, but his boy scout number ran it very close. Will Gardner, a local man who had not previously been in pantomime, also made a big success of a football monologue which was a model of homely wit. The comedy side was strengthened still further by the Brothers Griffiths as the performing horse, and by ill-fated Fred Allandale, mischief-maker by the author's command, but a most lovable one. We still remember him—dashing and debonair, with blue cloak aswing—in the gay number *All the Girls are lovely by the Sea Side* in the Monte Carlo scene.

On the other side we had a finely-contrasted boy and girl— Ella Retford with her clear cut gracefulness, and Maidie Scott bubbling over with high spirits. It was this year that she sang the cleverest and most effective song in her repertory, *The Saucy Little Bird on Nellie's Hat.*

Jack Buchanan! "How does England's best-loved musical comedy star of stage and screen come in here?" you ask. In this way. A handsome young aspirant to the stage, full of an eager enthusiasm and charm of manner difficult to resist, he called on Philip Rodway. As he himself modestly tells us, he was "looking for a job." P.R. gave him his chance, and marked him as a man to be watched. He made a great success of a comparatively small part, and his speciality tango with Maidie Scott on the steps of the Casino in the Monte Carlo scene was one of the big hits of the pantomime.

Jack Buchanan adds "I also had ambitions to understudy Mr. Ernie Mayne, but here Philip Rodway drew the line, one imagines wisely."

Mr. George M. Slater, Daddy's life-long friend and associate, has given us a valuable insight into P.R.'s work in the sphere of pantomime. May we at this stage find a convenient place to insert something of what he has written? It may hold up the action for a while, but it all has a direct bearing on the plot.

"In bygone years," says G.M.S., "it was my great pleasure to be associated with Philip Rodway in the production of many panto-mimes for the Theatre Royal, Birmingham. Philip was meticu-lous in his preparation of the plot, story, and construction for the annual Christmas Festival, and to his eternal honour, it may be stated, no *double entendre* or doubtful 'business' was ever per-mitted to blemish the pages of his manuscripts. I wrote several 'books' for him, and collaborated with him in others, also in the work of devising stage settings and in the literary labour of the dialogue and lyrics incidental.

"Many hours were passed in study, much ink flowed, and dawn succeeded night, during the strenuous period prior to Boxing Day; I recall many of his quaint and witty sayings, and his unfailingly kindly treatment of artists, who were often intolerant of restraint, and averse to receiving his good advice.

"'Lulled in the countless chambers of the brain,
    Our thoughts are linked by many a hidden chain;
    Awake but one, and lo! what myriads rise!
    Each stamps its image as the other flies.'

"We, the assistants and ushers in 'Dr. Rodway's Academy of Pantomime,' were tuned up for rehearsals, each bringing his latest ideas to submit for the Headmaster's approbation; he read every-thing submitted, listened to even the most humble members of his staff, and from *miscellanea* obtained the best results by process of selection and elimination.

"Frequently a touch of wit, applied by our chief, would change trivial dialogue into something which provoked applause. Surely no manager was ever a more efficient 'Play Doctor.'

"When I first met Mr. Rodway he was a very young man, occupying the position of acting manager to Mr. Dornton (then lessee of the Theatre Royal). As acting manager he was tactful and assiduous in the performance of all the thousand and one duties appertaining to his office. He saw everything, missed nothing, and was expert in the direction of every branch of adminis-tration. I believe he was at one time employed by a lawyer, and I feel certain that his forensic ability would have caused him to adorn the Bar, and possibly the Bench, in his later years, had he not forsaken the legal profession for the Thespian calling.

"This early training proved of remarkable utility when he became managing director of the theatre where he served his apprenticeship; his skill in drafting contracts and agreements was extraordinary, and recognised by many managers, who, though his senior in theatrical business, were rarely his equals in knowledge of these matters.

"In the construction of that special type of pantomime which obtained a vogue at the Theatre Royal, his talent was manifest; occasionally I disagreed with him, but he never failed to convince me that his was the correct view, and the great successes he achieved have earned for him an imperishable record on the scroll of Fame.

"At scenic, lighting, and dress rehearsals, when everything went wrong, when the *coryphée* wearing the costume of a grasshopper had to be changed into a bluebottle owing to hitherto unnoticed obesity, or when the moon appeared base over apex, he instantly remedied these imperfections, and remained imperturbable. Although his temperament was artistic, he displayed complete control of mind over matter.

"I remember at one of his pantomime rehearsals an eminent comedian (who now sleeps with his ancestors) objected to certain of his 'business' being cut out, and threatened to throw up his part. Mr. Rodway firmly but mildly remarked 'You are wrong, my dear fellow, that type of business would "get the bird" here. I want you to make a big hit—do as I tell you and you *will*, but if you think you are indispensable and that the pantomime cannot be produced without you, let me remind you that if you were dead we should *have* to do without you. If you refuse to be advised, *as far as I'm concerned you die this afternoon*, but the pantomime will be produced and the curtain will rise on Boxing Day.'

"The comedian departed in anger, but returned within half an hour, accepted the managerial edict, and ever after held his peace; he did as he was directed, and scored one of the greatest triumphs of his career, and our dear manager never afterwards referred to the incident at the rehearsal.

"The last night of the pantomime each year was followed by a reception of all the principal artists in the comfortable stalls saloon bar. After the fall of the curtain, every performer was called upon to make a speech. What fun we had, what sorrow that the run was ended, and what joy was felt by those re-engaged for the following year! The last oration was usually delivered by Mr. Rodway; it was always a model of a speech, conspicuous for brevity, wit, and kind expressions of mutual regard between the management and the 'mummers.' Oysters were eaten, champagne flowed freely, and the symposium terminated with the singing of *He's a jolly good fellow, Auld Lang Syne,* and the *National Anthem.*

"Eheu fugaces labuntur anni . . . never more shall we enjoy those merry parties.

" 'We have all dispersed and wandered
Far away, far away!'
"May the earth lie very lightly upon my honoured friend—we shall not look upon his like again."

Dear George Slater! His letters are instinct with the classic courtesy, kindliness, and loyalty which were his characteristics. Always a delightful exponent of the Grand Manner, he used to flatter us from the ages of 3 and 6 upwards—because one was fair and the other dark—with the lines from the play *The Two Roses* (by Mary Moore's husband, James Albery, produced in 1872), in which Irving first made his name:

"One like the rose when June and July kiss,
One like the sweet young bud that May discloses,
Sweetly unlike, and yet alike in this,
They are two roses."

Just as *Knightsbridge* heralds *In Town To-night*, so we always knew when George Slater and Daddy were approaching Box B.4. The door always opened on those words. And we are proud to be his "Two Roses" to this present day.

Mother well recalls his frequent appearances at the Royal, always dressed in the perfection of style, invariably wearing immaculate white kid gloves, or occasionally lavender, after a fashion set by His Majesty. Which reminds us of another pantomime story.

Robb Wilton, when he first turned up for rehearsals of *Babes in the Wood*, was rather afraid of P.R.'s methods with comedians. "I'm told they cut out all your best stuff here," he said to Wee Georgie Wood. "Yes," said Georgie encouragingly, "all your pet gags." Just then George Slater appeared in his famous white gloves, and also in a white coat. "My God," whispered Robb. "They're going to start cutting at once—here's the surgeon!"

It had become an axiom that, as *The Stage* aptly summed it up, "It would be almost easier to get a refund of your

Photos. by Harold Baker

LOIS AND PHYLLIS

Aged 3 and 6

GEORGE M. SLATER

income tax than to interpolate a gag into a Rodway pantomime." And the tact and diplomacy necessary to effect these
"cuts" without hurting any feelings can perhaps only be fully
realised by those who have had to deal with such situations.
As Robert Courtneidge reminds us in his reminiscences (*I was
an Actor Once*), " 'Rachel weeping for her children and would
not be comforted' is the image of a comedian shorn of a
favourite gag. If there is any doubt which is the comedian's
pet saying, it is only necessary to suggest cutting one; then,
though it may be the weakest of the *jeux d'esprit*, an excres-
cence upon the story, violating time and place, the comedian
exhibits an unreasoning affection, . . . increasing in fondness
with every slight that is offered to the little darling."

And this again is aptly capped by Albert Douglass, in his
Memories of Mummers, where he says that pantomime is so often
thrown completely out of focus by the interpolation of the
current popular songs, irrespective of sense or sequence:

> "Environment counts for nothing. Assuming that next Christ-
> mas the popular hit of the year is an imaginary ballad entitled
> *Here am I, back in Borneo*, it will probably be sung by Dick Whitting-
> ton on Highgate Hill, Robinson Crusoe on Wapping Old Stairs,
> Cinderella in the Palace Ball Room, and no doubt the ravenous
> wolf will conveniently postpone his lunch until Red Riding Hood
> has warbled the ditty in her grandma's cottage.

> "Fortunately whilst we have managers like Robert Courtneidge,
> Julian Wylie, Philip Rodway, Francis Laidler, and J. B. Mulholland
> . . . who not only approach the subject in a spirit of reverence,
> treating it artistically, but are enthusiasts in the cause—panto-
> mime cannot die, but what of the future? . . ."

Back again to the past. It was G.M.S. who introduced
Daddy to *Anzora* and flattened hair! And it is George Slater
who tells an excellent story about a manager (it may have
been Daddy) and an artist who insisted on bringing her pet
snake into her dressing room. It used to repose on her street
wearing apparel after she had changed into her stage costume, and for some time escaped the notice of her dressing
room partner. One evening shrieks were heard back stage,

and the other young lady, almost distracted, rushed up to the stage manager, loudly proclaiming that she was being frightened to death by a horrible reptile.

The snake had issued from its hiding place, and was wandering by the hot water pipes, when the actress found it in proximity to her shoeless feet. When the stage manager found the owner and explained the situation, she declared that she couldn't bear to be parted from her little friend, and that if she were not permitted to retain it she must give up her engagement. Upon reflection, however, she decided to dispense with her pet's company while in the theatre, but protested that there was no notice prohibiting pets upon the premises or in the dressing rooms, and she was as fond of the snake as she was of her own mother.

In consequence the management caused to be displayed upon the call board a notice which ran as follows:

"*No animals, reptiles, or relatives are permitted in dressing rooms during times of rehearsal or performance.*"

Daddy, it should be observed, had always been strongly against a crowd of visitors in dressing rooms. He used to say "It seems singular to me that people should expect to visit actors during their duties! If they were bank clerks no acquaintance would dream of calling on them in working hours." One of his main reasons for putting up the ban against visits during performances was that the animated chatter of the dressing room, usually accompanied by some kind of refreshment, as often as not made the artist miss his cue. He forbade this entertaining during the show, and found, as a rule, that the most important artists were the most amenable to reason, since they recognised the importance of keeping their work up to concert pitch.

"P.R. and the Pass Door" had become a tradition in the profession, so much so that one Anniversary Night, Billy Merson, presenting him with a gold watch, announced that the accompanying platinum and gold chain was "for the pass door!"

As we are so far from Miss Muffet and her tuffet, we may as well roam a little further, for the sake of adding Wee Georgie Wood's comment on the late soirées in the stalls saloon.

"How we used to look forward," says Georgie, "to those gatherings of artists on special nights—after the dress rehearsal, anniversary, or last nights. The late Ernest Edelsten and George Slater had a habit of making speeches against each other. Edelsten would hold forth in extremely humorous if Rabelaisian terms; Slater would use most beautifully-phrased periods of academic weight. They took it in turns to speak first. One night, I remember, Edelsten got up and gravely said that, having heard all about the great things Slater had done in pantomime, he assumed George's strange expression must be due to pantomime poisoning.

"Another time, Slater, taking first turn, and using his most dictionary-like manner, pulled Edelsten's leg in a harangue full of the longest words ever used in any theatre. Thereupon Edelsten replied: 'I'm very glad to think no one here has the slightest idea of the meaning of what George Slater has been saying. I have a shrewd suspicion that he was trying to insult me, but his long experience with actors ought to have taught him that the only really effective way of insulting anyone like me is to offer me a cigar and a drink at a time when I am getting them gratuitously from P.R., and there is not a hope of his paying for them or respecting the offer.'

"There was no malice in their exchanges, but P.R., sensing that the atmosphere was beginning to tighten up, smiled his whimsical smile and interjected 'Very good idea, Ernest. Time we had another round, and your turn to pay.' And so we were all able to relax again."

And now back to *Little Miss Muffet*. The critics found it the freshest, most truly humorous of the long series at the Royal, a children's pantomime, fine and beautiful, and declared that Drury Lane could not improve on the scenery.

On P.R.'s own special night Birmingham playgoers rallied round him as strongly as ever; "They owe much to Mr. Rodway, and they will not be behindhand when it is possible to make some little recognition of their indebtedness to him." Never during its happy run had *Little Miss Muffet* gone with a better swing. He was presented, among other things, with a travelling suit case from the company, and silver candelabra from the heads of departments, and, in his usual brief but telling speech, thanked everyone who had helped to make the night a success, mentioning the many sectional interests, and instancing especially the Conservative Club, the Central Club, and the various railway companies—as well as the all-conquering Aston Villa team, who were there in force.

Never, he said, had a better tempered or more genial cast been brought together; they had needed no management, they had been completely happy and united. In some quarters there had been predictions of failure because several of the principals had not before been known to Birmingham, but, as he had confidently expected, the pantomime had been a triumph.

The run ended on February 28th. The charm of the production was generously praised by Charles S. Adcock, who, in a local *Society Journal*, said:

"It must be generally conceded that the Royal pantomime is second only to the wonderful productions of Drury Lane in the matter of beauty of scenic effect and dresses.

"Mr. Rodway is exceedingly jealous of the dignity and good name of his theatre; it is a place where vulgarity and disorder cannot be permitted. He may well regard the Royal with affectionate pride, and feel himself honoured in association with it, but the Theatre Royal is also fortunate in possessing the services of Mr. Rodway, for although it has only been our privilege to come into direct personal contact with him on a few occasions, each has served to impress upon us his courtesy and tact.

"Like master, like man. A word for the front-of-the-house staff. The necessary contact between them and the public is always most pleasant, and the quiet, decorous aura of friendliness which seems to pervade every one of them adds in no small degree to the pleasure of an evening at the Royal. The excellence of the performance bears indisputable evidence of the adequacy of the stage arrangements, staff, and stage-hands."

For all that the maintaining of his beloved theatre on its pedestal was his first care and his abiding preoccupation, Daddy was not altogether an anchorite. He enjoyed being

AN EARLY VICTORIAN PHILIP RODWAY

Flashlight photo by Whitlock at the Lord Mayor's Fancy Dress Ball, **1914**

with congenial friends, and though distinctly *not* fond of making public appearances, he recognised that his position as the head of his profession in Birmingham carried its social responsibilities. So we find that in February, 1914, when the Lord Mayor (Alderman Ernest Martineau) gave a magnificent fancy-dress ball at the Council House, Mr. and Mrs. Philip Rodway were among the guests present.

Mother, having achieved a great triumph in persuading Daddy to accept the invitation, set her heart on going in a crinoline, and endeavoured to inveigle him into the costume of an 1840 dandy, so that they should be a pair. Daddy, however, probably feeling a vague chagrin that he had given way at all, refused to be further induced, and announced his intention of going as a banana! He actually had the sketches made for a wonderful creation in yellow swallow tails, so Mother, disappointed at the difference between her dream escort and a "property" banana who could not even sit down, cancelled her crinoline and ordered a picturesque Norwegian bridal dress, a beautiful affair of hand embroidery and characteristically striking head-dress.

At the last moment Daddy relented, renounced his fruitarian disguise, and adopted that of the *Early Victorian dandy* which Mother had originally sketched and suggested. It was generally complimented as being one of the most effective and accurate among the hundreds of fine costumes displayed. But his distaste for fancy dress and dressing up remained proverbial, and as Mr. Crompton Rhodes actually said to us when we showed him the accompanying picture, "*That's the Philip Rodway none of us knew.*"

His colleague, Barry Jackson (not yet knighted), whose Repertory Theatre was in the cradle stage, looked remarkably dignified and handsome as a Moor, so the Theatre may be said to have held its own.

CHAPTER 16

(1914-15)

About this time a new influence, that of "R.C.R.," was beginning to make itself felt in Birmingham's theatre world. The year before, in 1913, the genial, companionable, and erudite Raymond Crompton Rhodes had succeeded Besant Rice as dramatic critic of the *Birmingham Post*, beginning a career of distinction rarely surpassed in the provincial sphere, or, indeed, among the most highly-regarded critics of the national Press. His brightly discursive comments on first nights in Birmingham, London, Stratford, Oxford, and other points within his wide ambit are eagerly read by patrons of his famous paper, while his Saturday articles on contemporary or past stage history, literature, and personalities are in the highest degree authoritative.

The Birmingham theatres have for many years been fortunate, generally speaking, in their press, and we know that Daddy would wish us here to take the opportunity of acknowledging the debt. As a good manager should be, he was himself on friendly terms with most of the journalists in the city, but beyond this conventional friendship he had a warm regard for many of them—a mutual regard unqualified by considerations of other relations between manager and critics. Some visiting impresarios have formed the impression (and perhaps with good reason, so far as they are personally concerned) that the Birmingham Press is "hard," but resident managements have never shared this opinion.

Certainly P.R. did not. He regarded the critics as collaborators in the work of keeping the Birmingham stage up to concert pitch, and he never had the slightest doubt that their help would be forthcoming for any worthy venture. Like all managers, of course he preferred a good notice to a bad notice—but even when he felt that some writer had been unduly severe on a show he would say "Well, maybe it will have its value."

One who later became a close friend of his writes:

Once we quarrelled over my use of a word; we were both right, and both too strong-minded, or pig-headed, to abandon the position.

Philip wanted an apology for what I had written. I felt he owed *me* one for the terms in which he had expressed his annoyance. For months we didn't speak, though I was still regularly visiting his theatres and writing notices. Then one evening I was wandering along the corridor past his sanctum, when he opened the door and popped his head out.

"Thought it might be you," he said, as though there had been no breach. "How about a whiskey-and-soda?"

"Don't mind," I answered, and went in.

"Take your old place," he said, pouring out the pegs, "and here's a quotation for you. 'In this I bury all unkindness, Cassius.'"

So what could I answer but "My heart is thirsty for that noble pledge"? We took up our friendship from the point where it had broken months earlier, and I am sure we liked one another better for the incident.

But this happened a long time after the period of which we were talking, the period a year or so before the war, when "R.C.R." first began to adorn the *Birmingham Post* (*Daily Post*, as it used to be titled) with his knowledge, his wit, and his descriptive flair. He was Daddy's close friend and associate for nearly twenty years, their artistic tastes running much in common. It was "R.C.R." who in 1924, when the 150th birthday of the Royal was celebrated, acted as general secretary to the organising committee, and it was through P.R. that he wrote the "short history" issued as a souvenir.

* * *

Season 1914

The 1914 spring season opened well with a visit from *Peter Pan*, with Pauline Chase as Peter, and Mary Glynne as

Wendy. *The Marriage Market*, on its first appearance here, had Nellie Taylor as Mariposa, and Mark Lester, Peter Gawthorne, and Leonard Mackay in the cast. *Where the Rainbow Ends*, the lovely play for children by Mrs. Clifford Mills, also came, with Roland Pertwee (now better known for his writings) as Saint George. Other "first-timers" were *Mr. Wu* and *Who's the Lady?* the latter with Millie Sim in a small part.

The "Proms" ran for their customary fortnight in June, with a fine orchestra and programmes of a very high order. Each successive year had seen a raising of public taste, exemplified not merely by the inclusion of unfamiliar works but also by the rapt attention paid to them. It was unfortunately becoming more and more expensive, however, to run them. The instrumentalists demanded and received higher and higher salaries, while heavy fees were exacted for most of the modern works performed. The public were warned that the Proms might have to cease, after ten years of progressive development, just as Landon Ronald had reached the height of his powers as a conductor. Ernest Newman declared that it would be a ghastly irony if they did.

* * *

At the annual meeting in June the cash position was such that the company could pay all its trade liabilities and have a surplus of about £3,500. Again Mr. Lewis was pessimistic about the fate of the theatre in Birmingham, remarking that it was fighting for its very existence. On the one hand it was threatened by the music-hall, which had both a dramatic and a music-hall licence, on the other by the picture house. The licensing magistrates had come to the assistance of the dramatic stage with some regulations to protect it from unfair competition, but the position remained very unsatisfactory. It was only the personal star attractions that drew people in from the districts, and the improved train services, with weekly excursions, encouraged many potential patrons of Birmingham theatres to see the plays in London.

Tom B. Davis observed that in town as well as in the

country things were getting worse. All the London suburbs had their local entertainment houses. Most of the West End theatres were relying on the "nine o'clock" type of play, which was no use for the provinces.

The licensing regulations to which we have referred represented Philip Rodway's most statesmanlike service to the legitimate theatre in Birmingham. They were the result of a long campaign, with protracted negotiations, during which he filled the van of the battle on the theatres' side, and bore the brunt of virulent opposition.

Some years earlier the local music-hall managements had made strenuous efforts to secure unrestricted Free Trade in entertainment. They wanted to be at liberty to present every type of show from the single turn up to the full stage play. P.R., seeing the danger which such unrestricted competition would represent to the "legitimate" theatres, fought against it with all the vehemence at his command.

Meeting after meeting was held, volumes of correspondence were produced, and eventually it was agreed that the music-halls should have their stage-play licences, but that a clause should be inserted preventing them from putting on a dramatic piece lasting more than forty-five minutes, intervals included. The purpose for which P.R. strove was that the halls should keep to their proper business, which was the presentation of vaudeville, with occasional one-act plays, short sketches, etc., capable of being given in three-quarters of an hour. His contention was that full-length plays belonged to the theatre, variety items and sketches to the hall, and that each, by keeping to its province, would benefit by attracting a regular following for its recognised system.

When revues began to establish their hold, the music-hall managements returned to the fray. They urged that a revue was not a stage-play, and reiterated their demand for Free Trade. The matter was once more thrashed out at great length before the Justices. The Variety Artistes' Federation gave its vote in favour of the time-limit, and P.R. told the

o

Justices flatly that if the regulations were relaxed there could be no pantomime in the Royal at Christmas.

The upshot of it all was an understanding by which the music-halls, while given freedom to stage revues, were debarred from presenting stage-plays with a connected plot extending beyond the accepted limits of a sketch or one-act play. Most important, they were not to put on anything except variety during a period of several weeks from the usual time of opening the pantomime run at the theatres.

During P.R.'s lifetime the agreement, for which he had worked so hard, was scrupulously observed, and was obviously of the greatest benefit to the "legitimate" theatres, while it could not be said to do the other houses any harm. Latterly, under changed conditions of ownership and control, it has sometimes been ignored, but officially it still operates on a year-to-year basis.

*   *   *

The summer of 1914 was one of the loveliest on record. Daddy had taken the cottage on the river at Welford-on-Avon as usual for us to stay at, and for him to visit at welcome week-ends. June was a quiet month, England was basking in a heat wave. But abroad, peace was broken by an event that occurred in the far-off Balkan territory of Austria—the murder of the heir to the Austrian throne, the Archduke Francis Ferdinand, at Serajevo. July in England was still normal, however, and the Kaiser, apart from replying that Austria could count on Germany's full support, made preparations for leaving on July 7th for his annual holiday in the North Sea. The German and English fleets were reviewed off the Isle of Wight. Admittedly there was a tension in the air, but of course it could not have any connection between England and Germany, for there were the two flags intertwined at the head of the programme of naval manoeuvres. (Grannie had been at this Royal review, and had brought back with her from Southampton the elaborately printed souvenir of events in the Solent, for Mother, who still cherishes it.) The tension still grew—and on July 28th the British Cabinet ordered the fleet, which was about to disperse, to remain concentrated.

Even the little post-office at Welford-on-Avon was buzzing with news and rumours of news. Everyone in the village, as everyone in the world, seemed to be waiting for something. And on Monday, August 4th, the bombshell burst. War was declared!

Within an hour the quiet sleepy village was transformed. All the horses were commandeered, and the first one to go was the old white mare which drew the station trap. No longer would she jog along the country lanes. Instead—?

Daddy hurried back into Birmingham. Mother went to the little landing stage on the river, and wondered how many weeks it would be before the war was over.

As she sat there, a very young officer, about nineteen years old, white and breathless, ran down to the river bank and looked up and down the stream. He saluted, and asked,

"Have you seen a boatload of four row down the river?" When she said no, he looked terribly disappointed, and added,

"I am so sorry, I did want to say good-bye to them—I'm crossing to France to-night. Shall you be here just a little while longer? Could you say good-bye to them for me?— they'll know who it was."

Mother had a lump in her throat when she answered,

"I'll stay, of course. How soon will it be over? Not long?"

"Unless we can get the Expeditionary Forces over at once, they *could* be here in a fortnight. But as it is, it may not be many months."

He saluted, turned on his heel, and ran. Mother sat all afternoon to give his message of good-bye, but she never saw his friends. In after years she has often wondered whether he survived even the first year of the war. The little incident brought home to her the tragedy of war perhaps as much as anything that happened later; the "good-bye" of the youth of England to the happy, halcyon hours of river days, of normal life in summer weather and fair country fields. Much has been written of the gay and gallant answer the boys of England made in the first days of the war. It was true that many of them went out as to a Glorious Adventure. But in that one boy's white, strained face there was the poignancy, no less brave, of the knowledge of all they were giving up. It was to come to all before many months were out. It looked out of his eyes on that first summer afternoon.

Our cottage was of course immediately given up, and we all returned to The Woodlands. Daddy was as yet well over the military age, and Mother thanked God for it.

The war! How unimportant seems a single life and a single theatre by comparison with the vast consequences involved! But this is a biography of Philip Rodway and a history of his theatres, so we are bound to concentrate on the issue. So far as the Theatre Royal was concerned, the first effect of the outbreak was to leave everyone in doubt whether stage illusion, imaginative beauty, dramatic artificiality, could use- fully be granted a place in a world of stark, tragic realism. Could footlights continue to shine in England while Verey lights were flickering over No Man's Land? Was it not every man's duty to be fighting, or to be serving in some capacity, however humble, behind the fighting men? Could Life go on, with Death all-powerful?

Fortunately for the national sanity, a lead of unmistakable clarity was given by the highest authority. It was impressed upon the public that Life must go on at home: that every man in the trench or the gun-pit was dependent for his efficiency on the many men and women in factories, work- shops, hospitals, camps, laboratories, offices, farms, and bakeries of England. This home army, again, needed services to keep it vigorous and cheerful. It needed amenities, relax- ations, distractions which would refresh it mentally and physically, renew its determination, strengthen its courage. Thus were marked out the channels through which individual effort could most usefully be applied to the common objective, the winning of the war.

Sorrow and disturbance and tragedy do not mean that theatre-going stops. England had all that in the maelstrom of the great war. The cry was soon—Let us get away from this horror for a few hours; let us forget. Above all, let those home on leave forget, and let us give them gaiety and a certain happiness, even if it be only superficial. And so the plays of the war years, *The Bing Boys*, *Kiki*, and *The Glad Eye*, cheered and heartened, and the men went back to the front singing *If you were the only girl in the world* . . .

In the category of amenities likely to be most helpful to, and appreciated by, the army in the field, no less than the army of those at home, theatrical entertainment therefore was given a high value. "Business as usual," which became a catch phrase as soon as the national reaction to the mood of exalted self-sacrifice set in, was not merely permitted to the theatres, but demanded of them. They were urged to supply bright, cheerful entertainment for the troops on leave and for the war-workers, while their potentialities as centres for the generation of patriotic enthusiasm were immediately recognised.

So the theatres settled down to do their best. P.R., with depleted staff, adapted the Royal to the changed conditions and uncertain future, one point being the immediate reduction of prices. The summer vacation of 1914 lasted until the end of that fateful August, and then Lewis Waller made his farewell visit in *Monsieur Beaucaire*, and also produced a new play, *The Other Side of Life*, by Harold Bourne and Dion Clayton Calthrop. Waller perfectly gauged the public taste by adding to the evening's bill an impassioned rendering of Henry V's speech to the troops before Harfleur, bringing the audience back from the realms of fancy to the thought of those gallant gentlemen who were giving their lives for England over in France. After Waller's visit came in succession *The Whip*, *Oh, I Say! Diplomacy* (with Charles Macdona as Henry Beauclerc), Horace Hodges in *Grumpy*, the Terrys in *Sweet Nell* and *The Scarlet Pimpernel*.

It had been intended that the Quinlan Opera Company should give a fortnight of grand opera in October, but this strong booking was knocked on the head, for obvious reasons, by events. P.R. substituted for it a fortnight of Promenade Concerts, with an all-British orchestra of forty, under Harry Rushworth, who had not long succeeded Guy Jones as musical director. Ernest Newman, writing after the first night, said:

"The programme for the coming fortnight will be wisely made up from the lighter orchestral repertory, of which there is an abundance. One may suggest that it is as well not to overdo the patriotic and nautical element, for there is extremely little good music of this kind, and there are limits to the times even the most ardent patriot can bear the repetition of the same sentiment. With the newspapers naturally becoming obsessed with the war, it is a mistake for public entertainers to keep harping too much on the same string. It will really be doing the nation a service to help it for an hour or two a day to forget its griefs and cares."

Mr. Newman was one of the millions who could not foresee that years of obsession with the war, years of unforgettable griefs and cares, were in store.

In the theatre world now came P.R.'s biggest and most timely innovation—the twice-nightly system. It occurred to him that in those days of crowded and strenuous hours there would be an instant response by all types of theatre patrons to the offer of entertainment in a more or less concentrated form. He asked himself whether the ascendancy of the Music-hall over the Theatre was not in a large measure due to its reliance on this concentration, and decided that it was so.

He began by arranging with Louis Meyer for *Mr. Wu* to be played twice-nightly for a week from October 26th; it was a good choice, for the play could be run through quite comfortably in ninety minutes, excluding intervals. The experiment was successful, and was repeated before Christmas with *Hindle Wakes*, which proved not quite so suitable for the system. From these tentative overtures came the impetus for the master-stroke which a few months later set up the bridge of twice-nightly presentations across the summer gap.

Other features of the Autumn were Louis N. Parker's flamboyant *Joseph and his Brethren* (the censor having at last withdrawn his veto on plays with Biblical themes), a return of Lewis Waller, with Evelyn D'Alroy, in *The Three Musketeers*, and the first visit of that shrewd Jewish-American work, *Potash and Perlmutter*.

* * *

PANTOMIME 1914-15
SINBAD THE SAILOR

Sinbad the Sailor was the Royal's first war-time pantomime, and it may well go down to history as Birmingham's funniest. It was produced under Philip Rodway's personal supervision and direction, by George M. Slater, who wrote the book, and it played to wonderful business for nine weeks.

The subject had been used at the Royal several times (though not since 1891, when Vesta Tilley, who should have been principal boy, fell ill and was replaced by Jenny Hill). Always it had been found that the only one of Sinbad's many voyages amenable to stage representation was the journey to the Cave of Diamonds in the Valley of the Roc, and this was again made the main theme, though parts of other voyages found their way in too.

In *Sinbad the Sailor* was first emphasised a characteristic of P.R.'s pantomimes, that of pursuing the *via media* between slavish adherence to a set story, and surrender to the whims of the comedians. He struck what most people regarded as a happy medium, by giving the story its head in the first half, and the specialists their fling in the second. Thus the first half of *Sinbad* pursued a carefully arranged and coherent course, while the second was more loosely devised. Up to the half-way point the fanciful main story, with its supernatural element, was lightened by comic relief, but the comedy characters, even to Jacko the Baboon, had a definite share in the plot.

And what a comedy team it was! If ever Philip Rodway exhibited genius in casting a pantomime, it was when he

engaged George Robey for Tinbad and Fred Emney for Mrs.
Tinbad. The former, though he had been Idle Jack in 1897
and a Babe in 1899, was known to the generation of 1914 as
a Dame. P.R. took him out of "skirts," and played him as a
man opposite Fred Emney, who was entirely new to pantomime in Birmingham. Fred's fame rested on his classic sketch
A sister to assist 'er, in which he presented a wonderful study
of garrulous femininity. It was a bold experiment to match
these two in these particular rôles, and it reaped the fullest
possible reward of inspiration. Mother, we must add, claims
the credit of having finally persuaded Daddy, who had not
quite made up his mind, that Emney was his Dame.

The two, cast as Sinbad's parents, revealed a magnificent
effectiveness in combination and in contrast.

Each in his own way was a master of comedy, each gained
by the contrast, where pessimists had predicted loss. Emney
gave a consistent study of an old woman from the mean
streets of London, preserving her peculiarities, racial and personal, in a strange land. It was a portrait of common life
executed with exactness, clearness, and fine humour. One
could not call it low comedy because it was too genteel:
because Mrs. Tinbad was so circumspect and respectable a
person, even when her bonnet was at its most rakish tilt.

George Robey's Tinbad was a near kinsman of his happy-
go-lucky Idle Jack, the Jack-of-all-trades, "everything by
turns and nothing long." First he was a tailor, then a sub-
urban photographer, then a dowdy professional witness of
register-office marriages, then a bearded denizen of Baghdad
speaking in a strange Oriental tongue, then a 'bus conductor,
and so on.

Where Emney painted one faithful portrait, Robey opened
the pages of a family album in rapid sequence. Where Mrs.
Tinbad kept herself *to* herself, never addressing the audience
directly, Tinbad ignored the "fourth wall," and incorporated
the audience in his company. Robey's every entrance was
marked by a *leit-motif*, a curious gesture of protest, to assure

GEORGE ROBEY

us that the unrecognisable individual just arrived was really
George Robey.

The happiest combination of these two actors was in the
never-to-be-forgotten domestic scene, devised by P.R., in
which Mrs. Tinbad nagged, nagged, nagged, while Tinbad
sat perfectly still, saying never a word, just biting his lip and
staring at his nails. Both Robey and Emney needed a great
deal of careful argument before they could be persuaded
to play the scene—which was to become historic—on those
lines. It is a fact that Robey, when the idea was first put to
him, simply could not "see" himself at all. It needed all
P.R.'s tact and diplomacy to convince him of its novel
possibilities, and at last it "came"; but few people knew
how nearly the pantomime failed to include its greatest
scene.

To him the simplest jokes were the best. So, later on in
this famous kitchen scene, when Tinbad and Mrs. Tinbad
were "making it up," he persuaded George Robey to push
the dame off his knee with an agonised expression and the
words "You're sitting on my keys." Robey wasn't sure, but
at the first performance it brought the house down.

From this famous episode we move swiftly to the hilarious
"Paperhanging," with its inimitable sing-song of the plank,
"Turn it round the other way." Gallons of paste were used
every night, and the audience literally rocked in their seats
with laughter. (So great was the success of this sketch that
ever afterwards Emney kept it as his stock speciality, and it is
a tragic coincidence that, years later, he was to meet his
death in a similar whitewashing scene, at the London Opera
House, now the Stoll Picture Theatre, in Kingsway, when he
fell and injured his spine.)

Next followed Robey singing *Heigh-ho, what might have been!*
and presenting a hat to an embarrassed young man "on
behalf of the working staff."

We still remember the great finale of the first half, where
the giant roc, bearing Sinbad on his outstretched wings,

took off for his flight—the voices of the chorus following as he rose in the air:

"Sinbad, farewell, fortune favours your flight, Threading your way thro' the stars and the night. Sail away, sail away, up in the air, Speed thro' the clouds to Zobeide the fair...."

And that wonderful transformation scene in The Valley of Diamonds, where from the distance, to the swing of slow, rhythmic music, came "The Jewels," marching in ceaseless single file, with a strangely effective, swaying step. . . .

"The March of the Giants." Hermann Finck.

Tinbad had another hilarious episode—fishing from an island which proved to be the back of a whale; and Mrs. Tinbad a marvellously funny encounter with a stile, where, after unlimited efforts and entanglements, she finished up on the wrong side! In both of these one recognised Daddy's personal touch again; how many times on his fishing expeditions had he watched Mother tackle just such a stile!

The principal comedians owed a good deal to the tactful support rendered by Fred J. Little, as the comfortable Caliph. He formed a link between them, and kept a perfect balance in numbers such as the nigger minstrel burlesque. His laughing song was among the big hits of the production. Edward Sillward, who played the almost human baboon Jacko, was a universal favourite in his Simian *pas-de-seul*, and also in an "Androcles" incident with a splinter in his paw.

Nora Delaney, as Sinbad, endowed the hero with presence

and grace. Her two best songs, *When Irish Eyes are Smiling* and *We sang God Save The King*, were excellently rendered. The second, the one outburst of patriotic feeling in the show, had choruses which neatly embodied the refrains of British national songs, and at once took the ear of the town. Princess Zobeide was played by Margot Kelly, Florence Phillips returned as principal dancer, and Florence Sweetman was the Prince Hassarac.

One widely applauded feature of the production was its freedom from reference, direct or indirect, to the war, except for the stirring song already mentioned. It was during rehearsals for the pantomime that Scarborough was bombarded, and P.R. decided that the war was not a topic for improvised wit or crude music-hall jokes.

But if the war was not brought into the theatre the theatre was undoubtedly carried into the trenches. In Hannen Swaffer's entertaining *Who's Who*, we read "It is almost true that an old lady, seeing a special constable with G.R. on his hat, thought it stood for George Robey; it is quite true that, when his name was used as a password by troops in France, a soldier was nearly shot one night for replying 'George Formby' by mistake!"

Sinbad needed no revision during its run, it was a thoroughly good all-round show, and carried people away from the cares of wartime life to a realm of laughter, where grey skies and everyday drabness were forgotten in warmth and colour.

When P.R.'s own night came on February 23rd, he gave the proceeds to the war funds. The artists from other theatres on that occasion included Clifford Morgan (Prince of Wales), Mona Magnet (Alexandra), the Anartos, Farr and Farland, and Cruikshank, and acknowledging the presentations P.R. spoke with pardonable pride of the great success of the pantomime.

Of course the Royal, throughout the war, was constantly at the disposal of organisers of entertainments for soldiers and similar special affairs. One such invitation matinée of *Sinbad*, organised by the *Weekly Dispatch*, was given for the

children of men on active service, P.R. and his directors
lending the theatre for the occasion.

*   *   *

Season 1915

The war was already taking away many of the best young
actors (the Benson Company, for instance, went to a man of
those eligible), but in the spring of 1915 it was still possible
to book an attractive season, opening with *The Man Who
Stayed at Home* (the first definitely "war play" presented at
the Royal), with George Tully and Mary Merrall in the leads.
Then followed the first English production of *Seven Days*, by
the Americans Mary Roberts Rinehart and Avery Hopwood.
A fine cast included Lottie Venne, Lennox Pawle, Marie
Hemingway, Auriol Lee, and Athene Seyler.

Lewis Waller, who must have regarded the Theatre Royal
as a home from home, returned with Evelyn D'Alroy in
The Three Musketeers, after which the Midland Musical and
Dramatic Society revived *Véronique*, in aid of the Red Cross
and Blue Cross Funds. J. Randall Cook was the musical
director, and the leading players were Edith Ryland (Agatha),
Alfred Butler (Florestan), Beth Costello (Comtesse de Champ
Azur), George Worrall (Coquenard), Harry Preedy and
Tom Hudson.

Easter brought back *A Royal Divorce*, with Agnes Verity
as Josephine, Barbara Gott as Marie Louise, and Tripp Edgar
as Napoleon.

The season was further distinguished by the first English
production of *Wild Thyme*, adapted from the French by
George Egerton. In this dainty light comedy Ellaline Terriss
was an exquisite heroine, and Seymour Hicks showed how
capable he could be in serious vein. Sam Sothern and Mary
Rorke were with them.

April 19th, 1915, was a red-letter day in Theatre Royal
history, for it saw the twice-nightly system adopted as part
of Philip Rodway's regular policy. He inaugurated his first
long season on these lines with *The Land of Promise* (Evelyn

Ormonde as Nora), which was played without a single cut. Prices were brought within the most modest reach, and the system of booking the pit stalls on the day of performance was launched.

The results fully justified his boldness in being a pioneer of the twice-nightly scheme among first-class provincial theatre managers. In the 1915 list we find such varied plays as: *Diplomacy*, *Brewster's Millions* (in which Percy Hutchison played Brewster), *Oh, I Say!* (with dapper Frederic Bentley, Ida Stratham, and Ian Fleming), *The Younger Generation* (with the uncle's habitat tactfully moved from Hamburg to Amsterdam, and that since-regular visitor, William Daunt, cropping up for probably the first time), *Broadway Jones* (with Seymour Hicks and Rita Jolivet), *Officer 666* (another starring rôle for Percy Hutchison), *The Speckled Band*, and *The Marriage of Kitty* (with Norman V. Norman and Beatrice Wilson).

The fruits of wise control were exhibited at the annual meeting in June, when the accounts again showed a profit. Weeks had naturally had to be filled at short notice, but the results achieved, in these circumstances, were admirable.

P.R. was congratulated by the Board for what had been accomplished in emergencies, when they compared the sound position of the Royal with the state of all the London theatres.

In the longest oration he had yet delivered on such an occasion, P.R. expressed his conviction that twice-nightly attractions were what the public wanted. Brevity and inexpensive prices were the key-notes of the method, and the attendances had proved that the step was sound. In the past there had been only small support for what was known as the West End after-dinner play, when given once nightly, whereas plays of exactly similar calibre had seen excellent business under the new system.

"As a result," he declared, "I believe we shall be able to present many plays which it would not have paid us to book under the old conditions. Without losing any of its regular patrons, the theatre is tapping an entirely new source. I believe, moreover, that our step may cause dramatists to write plays from the definite viewpoint of their performance twice-nightly. Of course, many of the plays written for stars are not capable of compression into the shortened time, and such plays we shall present once-nightly.

"Other first-class theatres are following our lead, which will naturally make it easier to arrange twice-nightly seasons. I see in the innovation the possibility of abolishing, or at least reducing, the summer vacation when normal times return."

This was an important point, for at all times the question that inevitably confronted local theatrical management was "the great summer difficulty." Close the theatre for the summer months, and "dead charges" were eating its head off; keep it open, and there would be poor houses, with a full staff *plus* dead charges still to be reckoned with. Lawrence Levy observed in his book of Theatrical Reminiscences that

"the adoption of the summer time two shows a night, by the 'Alexander' of the Theatre Royal, that is to say, Mr. Philip Rodway, was the turn of the tide in the fortunes of the theatre, to lead on to prosperity. The new departure was justified by the success which crowned it. Money was made with the production of two representations nightly, before which the one turn was a monetary molehill to a mountain! If you want to see the monument erected to Mr. Rodway's triumph in this direction, it is to be found in the balance-sheets of the theatre since the duplicate turns were initiated."

A start in this desirable direction was made at once, by closing only for the month of July. On re-opening, twice-nightly remained the order, with *Mr. Wu, A Chinese Honeymoon, Baby Mine*, and return visits of *The Land of Promise* and *A Pair of Silk Stockings* occupying the August.

And of *The Chinese Honeymoon* of 1915 there is a little story. It reached us, through a Speedwell Road postman, in the February of 1932:

"'Was that the Mr. Rodway of the Theatre Royal?' he had asked one of the gardeners. 'I shall never forget a good turn he did me seventeen years ago. I was invalided home from the front, and me and the wife had decided to go to the theatre and see *A*

Chinese Honeymoon—we'd only been married that very morning! Well, we got there, and there wasn't a seat left in the place. I know I was standing leaning against the wall, feeling thoroughly down, when Mr. Rodway happened to pass by. Recognising one of 'the boys in blue' he came over and spoke.

" 'You're looking very despondent, old man,' he said; 'what's wrong, eh?'

"I explained that it was our wedding night, probably all we should have for a honeymoon, and the theatre was full.

" 'Come along with me,' he said, 'and we'll see what we can find.' And he took us both along a corridor, put us into a box next the stage, gave us a box of chocolates, and then with a quiet smile and 'Now settle down and enjoy yourselves,' he went out and left us. Seventeen years ago it was, but we've never forgotten."

In the same season there was also a flying matinée of *The Angel in the House*, in which H. B. Irving, Lady Tree, Holman Clark, Vera Coburn, Mary Glynne, and Langhorne Burton appeared.

Some of the plays given twice-nightly were so successful that they were quickly repeated. Examples are *Brewster's Millions*, *Broadway Jones*, and *Oh, I Say!*. Regarding the return of *Brewster's Millions* there is a little story. Percy Hutchison and his company had come from Ireland over the week-end. Missing a connection, they actually arrived in Birmingham (with their scenery) at 6.35 p.m., five minutes before the curtain should have risen. P.R. and his staff created a record of celerity by getting the scenery in and set in time for the show to commence only ten minutes late!

In *The Flag Lieutenant*, one of the season's successes, Henry Hallatt played the hero. This very cultured actor, who has since achieved great local popularity both as a touring star and as the leading man of resident seasons under P.R.'s old friend Leon Salberg at the Alexandra Theatre, had a specially warm place in his heart for the Royal, where his father, the late W. W. Hallatt, had been a notable figure in the old "stock" days.

"Your father and I," he writes, "were of course old friends, and we had many chats on the theatre. I shall always remember how he urged me to go into actor-management. . . . He told me I could have a date any time—but most of the other managers either wanted to see the play I proposed presenting, or had no dates! So I remained an actor.

"All my visits to Birmingham were made particularly happy; your father was always the perfect host."

New shows were given fair representation as compared with revivals. Thus Maltby's *The Laughter of Fools*, not previously seen at the Royal, preceded a revival of *Florodora*, with Evie Green and Edward Lewis in their long-familiar rôles. Martin Harvey revived *The Breed of the Treshams*, but he also put on *Armageddon*, a war-time morality play.

The twice-nightly season continued until the end of October. A month of full-length attractions followed, the outstanding item being *The Spanish Main*, with Oscar Asche, Lily Brayton, Caleb Porter, and Randle Ayrton (now stage director of the Stratford Memorial Theatre, where Caleb's son Neil was a leading man this year) combining to make a huge success.

Before the pantomime opened there was an amateur performance of *Liberty Hall* in aid of the Commercial Travellers' Schools and Benevolent Institution. Parts were taken by Nora Bind, Alfred Batchlor, G. F. Ostins, Doris Rushworth, Guy St. Clair, H. V. Currie, Mrs. G. Fisher, C. L. Moore, Gertrude Rees, C. Andrews, and Master B. H. Batchlor. The autumn season proper had closed on Charles Macdona's revival of *Niobe*, with Peter Amos played by Macdona himself.

CHAPTER 17

(1915-16)

The House that Jack Built; Billy Merson and Clarice Mayne—*Jingle Johnnie* —a Graham Squiers' story—"Blossomland," "The Waterfall," and "The Snow-clad Hills"—Special entertainments to wounded soldiers—"The Tale of a Timepiece"—Mr. Howard Jaques—Zeppelins over Birmingham— 1916 Season—Parties at the Botanical Gardens—Mr. Neville Chamberlain.

PANTOMIME 1915-16
THE HOUSE THAT JACK BUILT

Here was another typical example of the pantomimes which made Philip Rodway famous. Not since 1859 had this subject been tackled at the Royal, and one can easily understand why, for the nursery rhyme, which is believed to owe its origin to a Chaldee hymn, is a mere cumulative jingle leading nowhere. However, P.R. saw possibilities of a coherent first half, with scope for specialities in the second, and George M. Slater's book fulfilled his wishes to perfection.

A special point of interest is that this pantomime saw the first of the series of dress rehearsals thrown open by P.R.'s invitation to an audience of wounded soldiers and sailors.

Speaking figuratively, *The House that Jack Built* was a large well-furnished structure, commanding lovely prospects, heated and lit by humour and wit, sheltered from any possible dullness by eminences of attractive songs, dances, and pageants, and inhabited by a very happy family.

"Mr. Philip Rodway and his coadjutors" (said a critic) "must be envied in every other provincial theatre for their knack of satisfying the public taste in pantomime. The one now presented avoids overstressing any one feature at the expense of others. All the units of pantomime have been mobilised and consolidated, and the result is a beautiful, compact, amusing, and thoroughly enjoyable entertainment."

As in 1914, so in 1915, there was a complete exclusion of war jokes. Had it not been for an imposing scene in which ambassadors in colourful and picturesque uniforms, with their attendant suites, represented the allied and friendly nations, there would not have been a hint of the troubled

P

state of the world. This was the scene for which Philip Rodway and George Slater, under the name of Phil George, wrote the great song hit, *The Right Shall Prevail* (sung by Leonard Mackay, the handsome, dignified Prince Edgar of Pleasantia). A copy of this was accepted by her Majesty the Queen.

Great triumphs were scored in the production by Clarice Mayne and Billy Merson, both new to pantomime in Birmingham. Clarice Mayne, "charming, biddable, and essentially ladylike" (says Mr. Slater), had hitherto been known as a vocalist of essentially feminine charm; now, as Jack, she was a delightful boy, whose confidence, clear singing, and infectious sense of mimicry made her an instant success. Her accomplished husband, the late J. W. Tate ("That" of their double turn), the composer of many ear-haunting melodies, wrote several fine numbers for her: *Blossom Time*, for that wonderful first act finale; *Come and Cuddle Me*, for the Farm Scene, accompanied by all the animals and fowls; and— *Jingle Johnnie!*

This last song took her straight into the hearts of her audience, grown-ups and kiddies alike. She sang it in a multi-coloured costume, half Harlequin, half Touchstone. A mammoth Jingle Johnnie, second cousin to a Billikin, was lowered from the auditorium ceiling, and sang the song with her by a clever arrangement of synchronised telephone and microphone amplification. On the stage was a troupe of Jingle Johnnies, and at every performance you would hear the audience, caught up by the swing of the chorus, singing:

"Jingle Johnnie, Jingle Johnnie, Jolly Jingle John!
Though you've got a funny face,
In my heart you've found a place;
Rings on every funny finger,
Bells on every toe.
You'll have music, Jingle Johnnie,
Everywhere you go!"

Jingle Johnnie souvenirs, one of Daddy's happiest inspirations, were thrown out into the house each night. Theoretically, they were for the children, but many found their way into the front line trenches over in Flanders.

Clarice Mayne's fourth song hit was *I do like living in England*, a topical song in which her gift of caricature was brilliantly displayed in mimicry of fellow-stars. As her Princess Suzetta she had the roguish Winifred Delevanti, who was as happy sentimentalising with Jack as burlesquing with Sammy, and helped to make a big success of the duet *Underneath the Honey Moon*.

Of "topical" songs, by the way, Graham Squiers has another story:

"One characteristic of Philip Rodway's which always impressed me," he says, "was his power of persuasion. At one time I did a fair amount of work for him in connection with topical songs and local lyrics for his pantomimes. Of course, all the local touches had to be put in at the last hour, sometimes even at the last minute. I would get a 'phone message to go and see him, and keen as I was to be associated with his shows, I often protested that I could not do it in the time. Yet it was always done, and I was, and am, proud to say that he never turned down any of my work.

"On this occasion he rang me up and asked me to do some verses for *I do like living in England*. It had been written by Valentine, and many will recall it. It was one of those songs which in those days was advertised as 'an eleventh hour success,' and consequently went into several pantomimes at 'the eleventh hour.' I firmly refused to write any verses for another man's song: told him if he wanted a song I could write him one of my own, and so forth.

"This was at 9 p.m., and he wanted the verses by 10 o'clock the next morning. He got them. But he was the only man in the world who would have had me sitting up into the small hours, writing verses against time to another lyric writer's song!"

Clarice Mayne tells us that this, her first pantomime in this city, was actually the second one of her career, and she was therefore correspondingly unsure of her reception by the Birmingham audiences, who "are not enthusiastic to an artist at first, until they make up their minds to like her, and then they are wonderfully loyal."

On the second night of the production she asked:

"What do you think of it, Mr. Rodway? Are we a success or not?"

"I'm so sure, I'm off to London in the morning on other business!" was the reply.

Billy Merson, also new to Birmingham pantomime and not yet a familiar figure on the local halls, proved anew Philip Rodway's genius for finding the right comedian at the right time. He came back in the 1917 *Cinderella*, the 1919 *Dick Whittington*, and the 1922 *Puss in Boots*, each time with complete success. (It was a pleasure to see him last winter in yet another Birmingham pantomime, Leon Salberg's *Babes in the Wood* at the Alexandra, and to observe how quickly he resumed his sway.)

As Sammy, in *The House that Jack Built*, he not only looked amusing with his mop of auburn hair, but he was amusing— not in any slapstick way, but with a neatness, a finish, which few comedians have surpassed. During the sequence of scenes he played a dozen parts—a farm hand, the enterprising manager of the Universal Agency, an unheroic duellist, a Spanish serenader, an ambitious operatic singer, an obstreperous spectator at a stone-laying ceremony, a relic of ancient Rome—but he never forgot which of his many rôles he was "in" at any moment.

Leonard Mackay's excellent singing was matched by that of Klit Gaarde as the Demon Discontent, and the general success was also helped by John E. Conan (Dame Barleycorn), E. J. Langford (Farmer Barleycorn), William Fullbrook (Constable Crackpot), Doris Thomas (Fairy Flora), Sylvia Bassano and Sidney Black (chief dancers), and Jackson's Eight Australian Girls.

The most beautiful of all the sets was the ethereally lovely "Blossomland," which remained Daddy's favourite among all his scenes. On it he spent many happy hours of thought and care, and he always considered the set to be one of the finest W. R. Young ever painted. The whole stage was transformed into a bower of apple-blossom, with delicately

"BLOSSOMLAND"

The Transformation Scene

Devised by Philip Rodway
for his pantomime
"The House that Jack Built,"
1915-16

Painted by W. R. Young,
scenic artist of
the Theatre Royal

interwoven boughs and exquisitely tinted flowers. Almost the scent of an orchard in full bloom drifted across the footlights, and the slow curtain at the end came down to the soft fall of petals.

In striking contrast was the wind scene in the market place (when, during the first rehearsals, so much dust was created that it gave George Slater bronchitis for six weeks!). A terrific storm arose, which blew away the goods from the stalls, and carried off the statue of Nelson (at the top of Digbeth—the local touch). It was an extremely difficult effect, and most troublesome to synchronise properly. Rehearsals were unlimited, with endless repetitions of:

"Oh hasten quick, the sun is clouding" ("Check your lights" from P.R.),
"Let us all to Church be gone." ("Thunder.")

The thunder box usually worked in the wrong place, and it was P.R.'s idea to get George Slater singing the words of the chorus, for the wind and the rain to be properly synchronised. After a dozen or so times George became extremely fatigued, and turned on the wind too soon, with the result that immediately the balloons and silken "props" were thrown up at full pressure into the grid, and the wind pressure had to be shut off until they could be retrieved and placed on the market stalls, before beginning all over again! Incidentally, it was then that dislodging the props also dislodged several hundredweights of dust, but finally the cylinders of compressed air worked on their correct cue, and the storm proceeded, to the delight of the audience at subsequent performances.

In this scene, where complete co-operation was essential, we may find a fitting place to mention four who for many years gave fine and loyal service to Philip Rodway: S. Stevens, who supplied the mechanical effects; J. S. Riches, the property master; W. Stackhouse and J. W. E. Childs, who were responsible for so many brilliant electrical effects.

Two more of the scenes from that memorable pantomime

stand out in one's memory: "The Waterfall," with a full moon rising beyond the pine trees to the sound of cascading water; and "The Snow-clad Hills," with changing colours glowing and fading on the fir-clad slopes, and a beautiful Snowflake Ballet.

"The Gardens of the Palace" made a fine setting for the arrival of the Ambassadors and their reception on the long flight of steps, and "The Ballroom in the House that Jack Built," a symphony in Wedgwood blue and white, brought down the last curtain.

One of the "Theatre Royal Special Entertainments to Sick and Wounded Sailors and Soldiers, and Nurses," was given on Wednesday, February 23rd, to an enthusiastic house that testified to the success of the move. It was by now a recognised fact that amusing and interesting entertainment was absolutely imperative for the treatment of certain cases; it was not merely a question of giving the soldiers a few hours of pleasure, but of helping in a cause which had definitely beneficial effect on their health.

"Theatre-goers and the public generally," said a writer, "are indebted to a very considerable extent to Mr. Rodway, for while he spends his working hours in searching for the best possible attractions to place before his patrons, and having secured them sees that they are presented in first-class style, most of his 'leisure' hours are devoted to the noble cause of charity. I have watched his work upon the general and executive committee of The Birmingham Theatrical Charity Sports—one of the best charity organisations Birmingham has ever known—and know that the splendid successes achieved by that body were largely due to his never tiring efforts (even as I write he is superintending the entertainment of nearly two thousand wounded soldiers at a special free matinée at the theatre), and I am not surprised to see that upon his Benefit night next week charity claims his first thought, for the proceeds are to be devoted to the funds, among other objects, of the Blue Cross. That his services are appreciated is proved by the splendid way in which tickets have been taken up; a capacity house is certain, and if the theatre were ten times as big, and thoroughly packed, it would be no more than Mr. Rodway deserves."

There were many soldiers present at his night the following Thursday, when a packed house enjoyed the special turns given by the principals, with the addition of Dorothy Ward and Shaun Glenville (who were to star in the following year's pantomime), Walter Newman, Coram the ventriloquist, and others.

These nights, of course, were never the stock complimentary affairs taken as a matter of routine, but occasions when the Profession and the City combined to pay tribute to P.R. for another fine year's work. This time there was special cause for congratulation, for not only had he kept the Royal on a prosperous course in conditions of the utmost difficulty, but in his speech acknowledging the gifts and the enthusiastic reception, he was able to make the announcement that the pantomime would be reproduced the following Christmas in two capitals, London and Melbourne, which went to show how far *The House that Jack Built* had realised the best traditions of the Royal.

Billy Merson, with a little speech of warmest tribute, made various presentations to P.R., which included a set of silver table candelabra and a spirit kettle from the principals, and a cheque from the Board asking him to make choice of his own gift.

This wide choice left him by the Board is the subject of a playful commentary which Daddy wrote for Mother afterwards, when she was on holiday with us at Rhyl. It was a little half-humorous essay which we came across enclosed in a letter to her. . . .

The Tale of a Timepiece

"The man met the woman and after a long period, in which they grew to learn and respect the other's qualities, they dallied, which they did at the house of the woman's mother. It was in those days that the woman did revile the habit which her mother had of locking up rooms and things, and the woman spake thus unto the man:

"'Behold when we are one I will not be like unto others in this respect but will use all that we have for our comfort and use.' To which the man nodded his head and looked forward with much joy of heart to the great day when all the habits of foolish forebears should be put right.

"And lo the years sped.

"And it came to pass that when the man and woman had been made one a house was taken near unto the domicile of the woman's mother. The man became afflicted with a disordered mind because forsooth he thought he had a right to expect more freedom in the home than with his bedroom and a small room which was called his study but which was filled with boxes and where the ink was chained up. And he marvelled because of what had happened in past years.

"And lo the years sped.

"And it came to pass that step by step barriers were slowly removed, fire-irons being restored to their lawful and proper use and stripped of their brown paper coverings—the four legged harp had its white teeth struck, and one year the man took his breakfast *for four mornings* in the east chamber, whereat the man did rejoice, for it had been the command that he should remain locked in his room lest the woman should have had to put his egg and his slice of pig on the dresser overnight.

"And lo the years sped.

"And in this parchment must be told a story as it were an Arabian Night.

"And it shall be set down as the tale of the watch, and in it there is much instruction, and so:

"The man who had gathered in his harvest—which with him was in the winter months—was greeted by the harvesters who said, 'What can we greet thee with withal—jackal? We would fain purchase for thee something as a memory of the trying time just past.'

"And the man spake to the woman on the matter as had always been his wont, for as was said at the commencement he was suffering from a disordered mind.

"And the woman said, 'Lo, I will buy me a present for thee. Thou may'st rely on my purchasing things of great use, for what boots it to make store of things save to use?' And the man said, 'Yea.'

"And it came to pass that the woman, not being sufficiently disturbed as to what to purchase with the pieces of gold, arranged with her mother to complete her perturbation and purchase. And she did bargain for and obtain a piece of glass whereat the man was much pleased, for it could not be hidden. And then a strange thing came to pass—for on leaving the mart of one Davis, a Jew, the woman espied a lovely little timepiece cunningly devised for attachment to the wrist, so that it might be worn at all times, and the owner being thereby always assured of the sun's altitude.

"And the woman did make it her own, and said to the man when next she espied him, 'Lo, see what I have bought me for thee. It was just begging for me to buy it—dost thou mind?' And the man, whose mind by this time was not only disordered but diseased, after laughing many times and making funny noises with his throat, said, 'The present that thou hast bought thee for me, keep, and so long as thou wearest it I am content, for as thou sayest, it will always be useful and near at all times, and as thou hast felt the need of such for many moons or would'st not have purchased it, wear it now and be happy.'

"And lo the weeks passed.

"And it came to pass that the woman did write to her husband a letter to London saying that she would not lock up her present that she had bought to make him glad.

"And lo, five days later the woman with her children did depart for the land of Wales—and the man unto her spake thus as she left: 'Thou hast forgotten thy timepiece,' whereupon she did revile him and fetched him the loose silver timepiece which she never kept with her, and because of which she had purchased the wrist one, and spake unto him saying, 'Look, fool, I will lock up the new watch and take the other with me.' Whereat he being now by this time in stupefaction, owing doubtless to his putrid brain, was told that the watch would be kept in close confinement in a certain dark hermitage in the next chamber for his little girl for when she should become a woman!!!

"And the minutes passed.

"And in the end the woman on starting for her journey found she had no timepiece with her *at all*, which was clearly the fault of the man.

"And the man with the braincase with no brains in it, having for long appreciated in secret the care and skill with which the woman had been thrifty and ministered to her children, yet failed to understand the watch and similar things, for in that hermitage were many things like unto the timepiece.

"And the man whose brain he hereby admits is completely addled is a fool, because he will not understand that to use a thing for the purpose for which it is made is wrong and unwise, whereas if a thing is locked up it is at least doing as much good as if it were in the window or shop of one Davis, a Jew, from which it was purchased.

"Here endeth the Chronicles."

* * *

We two, as children, were more than fortunate during the war years. We were too young to realise the full meaning of the tragedies that were happening abroad, and at home our only personal contact with actual warfare was the air raids. Mother had determined we should not be harrowed, and so had evolved a plan. She promised Lois that if there was a raid we would all wake up and have cocoa and biscuits in the middle of the night. Consequently Lois looked forward enormously to the possibility. Phyllis, a little older and therefore more sensible to the fact that it might not be merely a nocturnal picnic, she quietened in a different way.

"Will the Zepps come to-night, Mummie?"

"No, dear, it's moonlight, and they wouldn't dare to, because our anti-aircraft guns would easily find them."

And the next time,

"The Zepps aren't coming to-night, are they, Mummie?"

"Of course not, dear, it's much too dark, they wouldn't be able to see their way."

Somehow this consoling theory always seemed to ring true. Such is the complete faith of childhood; such the re-assuring power of a parent. This is leading up to an incident in 1915-16 during the run of the pantomime *The House that Jack Built*. Mr. Howard Jaques, of Water Orton, had for many years made a hobby of marionettes, creating wonderful little figures, miracles of mechanical perfection, for whose miniature performances he also designed and painted his own scenery. He and Daddy—old friends—had discussed together certain lighting effects for the transformation scene at the end of the first act, "The Snow-clad Hills"—for which he had made some very helpful suggestions; and he and Mrs. Jaques were sitting with Mother in her box watching the show.

The curtain came down to a burst of applause, the interval took its course, and the curtain rose on the second half. Almost immediately there was a tap on the door. It opened for a second, and Daddy appeared, beckoning Mr. Jaques out of the box. After five minutes he returned, looking rather strained, and so Mother left her chair and hurried to the inner room at the back of B.4 to ask if anything was wrong.

"Now it's all right; you're not to worry," began Mr. Jaques.

Mother, infinitely more worried, "Is it the children?"

"No; you are just to sit quietly until Philip returns."

"Is The Woodlands on fire?"

"No, no. Philip specially told me not to alarm you, but . . . *there's a Zeppelin over Smethwick.*"

That meant, of course, that the lives of everyone in Birmingham and its suburbs were in danger. Daddy went round the theatre giving instructions to the staff and to the orchestra and principals to carry on. Everyone responded. Every spare man was put at the emergency exits, with the doors unbarred ready for opening. Orders were flashed all over Birmingham for every light (already screened) to be put out, and for every train, tram, and car to come to a standstill no matter where it was.

As soon as instructions for the prevention of any panic in the theatre were given, Daddy came back to the box. Mother had by now determined to get home somehow to look after us, and as he himself could not leave the theatre, nor spare any man from his duties, she set out on her dangerous journey alone. She and Daddy said goodbye, quite expecting it to be their last, and she plunged into the blackness that was Colonnade Passage.

She soon began to run, and kept it up as best she could the whole way home, weighed down by her fur coat, and feeling her way round the stationary vehicles. She was nearly knocked senseless by colliding with a taxi which was standing in the middle of John Bright Street. Every minute she kept looking up at the sky, expecting to see balls of fire dropping in the vicinity of Speedwell Road. The night was alive with searchlights and the noise of anti-aircraft guns. Somehow she reached home, to find us safely asleep, as usual.

The Zeppelins were looking for Kynoch's Munition Works —but they never got them. Thanks to the complete plans for safeguarding the town, and the absolute obedience of the city in carrying them out, Birmingham, lying silently in the safety of complete darkness, was passed over unnoticed, and instead the Zeppelins made straight for the lights of the Black Country, where the glow of the blast furnaces could not be put out, and their fiery blaze made irremediable target, so that a trail of desolation and death was left along their track.

* * *

Season 1916

Air raids scares—and air raids themselves—were beginning to make people nervous about being out late at night, so P.R., ever on the look-out for new ways whereby the methods of management might be suited to the exigencies of the times, introduced another innovation. After a couple of weeks or so (two filled by *To-night's the Night*, with Jack Buchanan playing his first speaking part in the theatre) he arranged with the Wylie-Tate management, controllers on tour of that fine revue *The Passing Show*, to present it *twice daily*, the evening performance being guaranteed to close not later than a quarter to ten. Thus he gave night workers and children a chance of going to the theatre in the afternoon, while those who braved the risks of the night were able to get home at a comfortably early hour.

In this production, the music of which was played on the gramophone of well-nigh every mess in the British war-zone, Ella Retford scored a considerable triumph, and Fred Duprez, Tom Hearn (the lazy juggler), Paul England, Deane Tribune and Christine Roy all enhanced their reputations.

The twice-daily experiment, proving a success, was continued for some weeks. Seymour Hicks and Ellaline Terriss came in *Broadway Jones* and *Wild Thyme*—Mr. Hicks, in the latter, switching from André to Valentin in order to let Rupert Stutfield, just invalided out of the West Surreys, play André.

Easter week was filled in time-honoured style by *A Royal Divorce*, with Edith Cole in the part which by now must have become second nature to her. On May 2nd Birmingham received with delight the news that Frank Benson had been knighted by His Majesty, after assisting in the Shakespeare Tercentenary performance at Drury Lane.

The annual meeting, on June 1st, was an occasion for great congratulation for Philip Rodway, who was able to inform the shareholders that a net profit of £3,400 had been made on the year. The Board complimented P.R. in generous terms on the outcome of his various experiments, which were being generally copied elsewhere.

Comments were also made on the recent introduction of an amusement tax (a feature of the 1916 Budget). The tax was going to yield an enormous revenue, *but no one could foresee that an impost laid on purely as a wartime measure would be allowed to continue, crippling the business long after the war had ended.*

*   *   *

In the August of 1916 a novel matinée was given at the Royal, when some 2,200 convalescent warriors from local hospitals were entertained by fellow-soldiers and airmen who had as yet escaped the attentions of the enemy. This function was a wonderful success. It lasted over three hours, and a large sum of money was raised by the sale of the dress circle (the only part not reserved for convalescents and nurses) at a guinea and half a guinea a seat, for the purchase of a motor-coach, named the Royal Alexandra (after the two theatres), for the conveyance of wounded men to places of amusement.

The programme included any number of chorus songs for the audience to join in, while solo items were given by Sapper

Gerrard (Royal Engineers), Air-Mechanics Butt, Bone, and Milburn (R.F.C. as it then was), Sergeant-Major Barlow (Royal Warwickshire Regiment), and Piper Daniel Laidlaw, V.C. (9th King's Own Scottish Borderers), the spectacular hero of Loos. There was sword-dancing by Sergeant-Instructor D. T. Cooper, and the Birmingham Athletic Club—of which Daddy's old friend the late Lawrence Levy was so long a pillar—furnished a display of boxing, weight-lifting, singlestick, and quarter-staff fighting. The only professional on the bill was Jay Laurier.

Half way through, the thanks of the audience to P.R. and his co-directors, plus all others who had helped to provide this pleasant novelty, were voiced by Professor Bostock Hill, seconded by Alderman W. E. Lovsey, and supported by Colonel Hart, C.B., and Colonel Sturges.

August saw the continuation of twice-nightly fare, light attractions like *Are You a Mason? Mice and Men, Baby Mine, A Little Bit of Fluff*, and *To-night's the Night*, alternating with the more serious *Fanny's First Play, Dying to Live* (with Georgie Wood's sketch partner, Dolly Harmer, in a Lancashire character part), etc.

Julia Neilson and Fred Terry, in the favourite *Scarlet Pimpernel* and *Sweet Nell*, launched the once-nightly season in early October. *Toto* came next, and a year of well-maintained standard closed with Arthur Bourchier and Kyrle Bellew in *Find the Woman*.

Stars visiting us during the autumn also included Hilda Trevelyan and Martin Harvey. Managers whose companies were often seen at the Royal were Percy Hutchison and T. C. ("Tommy") Dagnall (husband of Evelyn Ormonde, who played lead in many of his shows).

Once more the Commercial Travellers' Dramatic Society took the theatre for a night in December, presenting *Caste*, with Alfred Batchlor as Eccles, Guy St. Clair as Captain Hawtrey, Charles L. Moore as Sam Gerridge, and also G. F. Ostins, Mrs. Geoffrey H. Gay, Kate Watson, and Marie Rice.

1916

GARDEN PARTIES FOR THE WOUNDED

Mrs. Philip Rodway judges the Hat Trimming Competition
Botanical Gardens

1932

V.A.D. Birmingham 2 Detachment
British Red Cross Society

Phyllis

This was always a fine company, guaranteed to give an excellent show.

A notable series of the functions which Philip Rodway helped to organise for war charities was given in the Botanical Gardens, Edgbaston, every week. They were immensely enjoyable affairs, under the auspices of the Navy League and the British Red Cross Society, together with the Birmingham Jewellers' and Silversmiths' Association. These garden parties, given all through the spring, summer, and autumn of the war years, became social gatherings where one was sure of meeting, with the "men in blue," every one who was in any way helping the cause of the soldiers wounded or on leave. A military band played on the lawns, and tea was beautifully served in the conservatories against a background of flowers and uniforms. Each week P.R. arranged original games and competitions for the men and nurses, supplying innumerable baskets of dresses for the "Theatrical Costume Race," and hats for the "Hat Trimming Competition" (for which Mother often acted as judge). All these the men tackled with unquenchable optimism and good spirits, till the gardens rang with their gallant and happy laughter. The accompanying picture is a *Daily Mirror* photograph showing Mother with two of the prize-winners.

At the Royal a great many special performances were given, one of the first being a matinée of *Wild Thyme*—for wounded soldiers and V.A.D. nurses—in April, 1915, with the co-operation of Seymour Hicks, Ellaline Terriss, and their company. For the part he took in the proceedings P.R. was presented with a photograph of the blue-clad audience, taken from the stage, and Seymour Hicks and his wife received similar mementoes.

A dear old friend of Daddy's and Mother's and a moving spirit in everything done in Birmingham for our heroes, was the late Major John Hall-Edwards, the famous martyr-radiologist whose fearless and ceaseless experiments with the applied Röntgen Rays theory ultimately cost him his life.

He was the first X-ray specialist to go abroad with a fighting force.

Another very important step taken in the fighting men's interests about this time was the establishment of the Birmingham and District Professions and General Trades Fund for their entertainment. It was launched at a meeting presided over by Mr. Neville Chamberlain, then Lord Mayor and an Alderman of the city. Its special purpose was to continue and expand the kindly work done by the Jewellers' Association and other bodies.

In his speech from the chair Mr. Chamberlain spoke highly of Philip Rodway's services to the wounded, observing that more than 30,000 had been guests of the Theatre Royal since the war began. Now it was time that the entertainment of these heroes was made a town's matter. In order to provide adequately for all the men, a lot of money would be needed, and the best way of raising it was by combined effort among all the trades of Birmingham.

The officers then appointed were: chairman, Mr. J. H. Francis (whose death in January, 1932, robbed the ex-service men of a noble friend); vice-chairman, Mr. Arthur L. Lowe (chairman, British Red Cross Society, Birmingham Branch); hon. treasurer, Mr. H. A. N. Smith; hon. secretary, Mr. Ernest C. Thomas (now so widely known by his work for the Alexandra Musical Society and Disabled Men's Handicrafts Ltd.).

Soon afterwards Philip Rodway was appointed chairman of the Entertainment Committee.

CHAPTER 18

(1916-17)

PANTOMIME 1916-17

BOY BLUE

One of Philip Rodway's own favourite stories arose out of the tradition of the formal—almost State—opening of the Theatre Royal Pantomime on Boxing Night. Under his régime, the Royal made a point of having the box office available for pantomime bookings several weeks before Christmas. Half Birmingham wanted to be there that night, and the house could always have been sold out a dozen times over.

Scene. The Theatre Royal Foyer.

Time. Boxing Night. A few minutes before the rise of the curtain.

P.R. is standing near the box office window, watching the audience flock in. Since nearly all have their tickets there is little going on at the window.

Enter a flustered gentleman who makes for the box office. He raps on the ledge, and receives immediate attention.

"I want four seats, front row dress circle please," he announces.

"I'm sorry, sir," replies the box office clerk, "the circle is completely sold out."

"Sold out? Sold out? Most annoying. I always sit in the circle. Well, never mind, four good stalls will do this time, then."

"Very sorry, sir, but there's not a seat left in the stalls."

"Confound it all; what a place! Then I suppose we must put up with a box for once."

Here P.R. thinks it time to intervene. Quietly and tactfully he explains that every bookable seat has been sold weeks ago, and that the queues for the unreserved seats had begun to form twenty-four hours earlier.

"Do you mean to stand there," fumes the would-be visitant, "and tell me that I've brought my party all the way from Solihull,

Q

after ruining our dinner, and now you haven't got a seat left in
your confounded theatre?"

P.R. agrees that this is exactly the position.

"Then, sir," bellows the irate gentleman, by now positively
seething with temper, "allow me to tell you that I call it *damned
bad management!*"

*   *   *

In *Boy Blue* Philip Rodway again introduced principals
new to the Royal in a pantomime of which the theme also was
new. The title had long attracted him as having possibilities,
and now, having decided that the time was propitious, he
went all out for success, with George Slater enthusiastically
working with him.

The principals were Dorothy Ward, Shaun Glenville,
and Jay Laurier. Dorothy Ward especially had a claim on
Birmingham's affections, for she was born in the city, had
appeared for the first time on any stage in a pantomime at the
Alexandra Theatre (under Lester Collingwood), when a girl
of fifteen, and had already won golden opinions for her work
in pantomime and musical comedy at the Prince of Wales
Theatre.

Then there was Shaun Glenville, her husband, a jovial
Irish comedian with an almost ferocious energy in all his
stage work. Their long and happy association in professional
and private life was emphasised only a few months ago when
their son, Peter Glenville, president of the Oxford University
Dramatic Society in its Jubilee year, gave his brilliant study
of Gloucester in the society's production of *King Richard the
Third*, in Christ Church Cloisters.

"Jimmy" Laurier had played himself to local fame on the
music-hall stage and in several pantomimes at the Prince of
Wales Theatre, so there was never any doubt that the principals would maintain the Royal-Rodway tradition of triumph,
and *Boy Blue* worked out into one of P.R.'s biggest successes.

It continued the movement towards the reconstitution of
pantomime standards which he had begun a few years earlier.
It was a theatrical entertainment in which the dramatic

action was linked up by music, spectacle, and dancing—not the customary procession of vaudeville items strung together without coherence or sequence, but an agreeable compromise—a play of fantasy.

Boy Blue opened with an original prologue in the Observatory of Father Time, where, from his pot-pourri of old pantomimes, he summoned the fragrance of "rose leaves when the rose is dead." At his bidding there came two friends long absent, Harlequin and Columbine, whose recall instead of the usual modern Demon King and Fairy Queen stamped the production with immediate distinction and delicacy. In the past they had been the gay serving man and the captivating maid of Italian extemporal comedy;* now they were awakened from their sleep, lasting since Victorian days, to be Father Time's servants. So little known to modern audiences were the dancing and dumb-show of the two that the revival of a tradition centuries old struck most people as a veritable innovation.

The parts were wonderfully well assumed by Sidney Black and Isla Raine, a very accomplished dancer. They gave both charm and continuity to the whole fable. Their *pas bouquet* had a seductive fragrance, and little wonder, for it had been one of the most celebrated dances in the old pantomimes.

P.R. gave the part of Father Time to Henry Baynton, a young "old boy" of the famous King Edward's School, Birmingham, of imposing presence and fine, declamatory voice, in whom he saw possibilities. (His connection with the Prince of Wales Theatre after the war will be dealt with later.)

By the immortal servitors of Time we were transported to the Village of Nursery Rhymia, realm of the fantastic and grotesque, whence Boy Blue traced his way, through strange adventures and beautiful places, in search of Little Bo-Peep's strayed flock, assisted or hindered by Patsy O'Crummles,

*Appendix.

showman, his dog Toby, Johnny Stout, Jack Horner, Contrary Mary, and all the other nursery favourites.

From the village we were directed past an old Georgian
wayside tavern, and then through the "Bunville Bakeries,"
an ingenious place of living cakes and tartlets—beautifully
constructed "props"—wherein children supplied the motive
power. And so, after more adventures, into the Realm of
Riches—a wonderful transformation scene with processions
of the coins, copper, silver and gold, banknotes and diamonds,
with the final revelation of Fortune in her chariot. On this
eloquent note ended the quest for Wealth.

Then followed Boy Blue's quest for Love; through noble
halls, along autumnal country lanes, on the margin of lovely
lakes, at last attaining the beautiful palace of ivory and ebony,
where black and white costumes made a scene of astounding
simplicity but equally astounding effectiveness.

As Boy Blue, Dorothy Ward's dashing presence aptly
matched her full voice and determined methods of attack,
and carried her straight to success. The chief comedians
could never have been better contrasted. Shaun Glenville
literally flung himself into his part, with Irish indefatigability
and a jollity which streams of greasepaint could not quench.
When he spoke his whole body supported and supplemented
his words; his mimicry of a puppet on a string was really a
caricature of his invariable methods! In one scene he imitated
a baby, gigantic, grotesque—a perfect example of panto-
mimic comedy.

On the other hand we had the quietly confidential, bash-
fully ingratiating style of Jay Laurier, as rotund and rich in
gurgling humour as in appearance.

Alice Russon was a sweet Bo-Peep, and George Green's dog
Toby captivated everyone by its discerning sense of character.
Aimée Bebb, the first female Dame during P.R.'s régime, was
the eccentric Duchess, and Harry Rushworth's music, composed or selected, was always in the right vein.

The production preserved Philip Rodway's record for excellent taste, and bore generous evidence of the personal supervision, free enterprise, and careful study of the theatre-going public which distinguish active management from that of deputised syndicates.

The song successes of the season will be remembered by many—Dorothy Ward's *Tennessee*, Jay Laurier's *Glass of Ginger Wine*, Shaun Glenville's *Birmingham*, and Alice Russon's *Broken Doll*. Again all mention of the war was strictly banned.

Boy Blue, running into March, beat all provincial pantomimes—except Leon Salberg's at the Alexandra—for longevity that year. Like its predecessor, it remained practically unaltered to the end, thanks to the care and wisdom of its inception.

P.R.'s Anniversary Night, on February 28th, was unique. He was approaching his majority in management at the Royal, and had preserved it, almost alone among first-class provincial theatres, from the tentacles of ring, syndicate, or combine. He had made thousands of friends in the city and district, who would in any event have packed the house to pay him their annual tribute, but beyond all these factors there was one cause that raised the occasion above any other in his long series of "nights." Probably never before on such an occasion had the presentation been made by a Bishop!

This signal honour, received at the hands of the Right Rev. the Lord Bishop of Birmingham—Dr. Russell Wakefield, that wonderfully genial and many-sided prelate (now passed on, alas! like so many of those who figure in this record)—was a specific mark of the city's gratitude to Philip Rodway for his services to the fighting men. He had been foremost among England's managers in the entertainment of our wounded heroes, and he now received recognition from leading public and military men, who openly declared that what he had done had been invaluable in helping to restore the convalescents to full bodily and mental health.

There could have been nothing more appropriate nor more acceptable to Philip Rodway than the form of the chief gift of the evening, the album prepared at the instance of the Committee of the Professions and General Trades Fund, and containing the signatures of many hundreds of the grateful men. Not all of them, of course, for their numbers had now mounted to over 40,000 (and were to be doubled before the forces were demobilised), but still a finely representative set of signatures.

The album, bound in royal purple leather, is inscribed in gold "Presented to Philip Rodway, Esq., managing director of the Theatre Royal, by the Birmingham Professions, etc., Committee as a small token of esteem and regard in connection with valuable services rendered in organising entertainments for wounded sailors and soldiers during the war."

Ypres, The Somme, Armentières, Neuve Chapelle, Arras, "German East," Messines, The Dardanelles, Macedonia, Palestine, Egypt—wherever England fought, that place is immortalised in this volume.

The first signature in it is "W. Powell, 2nd Batt. Worcestershire Reg., wounded on the 1st November, 1914, Battle of Ypres." There follows name after name, representative of innumerable units in the navy and the army, the colonial contingents, the flying corps.

The University of Birmingham, Highbury, Uffculme, Moseley, Moor Green Hall, Lordswood House, Lightwoods Hall, The Norlands (Erdington), Marston Green, Harborne Hall, the Naval Convalescent Home (311 Hagley Road), Sutton Coldfield, and other war-time hospitals and institutions are all represented.

On the illuminated fly-leaf are the signatures, on behalf of the committee, of A. D. Brooks, Lord Mayor of Birmingham, president; John H. Francis, chairman; Arthur L. Lowe, vice-chairman, and chairman of the British Red Cross Society, Birmingham Branch; Arthur J. Leeson, hon. secretary, and vice-chairman of the Navy League, Birmingham Branch;

A. Bostock Hill, chairman of the Navy League, Birmingham Branch, and member of committee; and Ernest C. Thomas, organising secretary.

Scattered among its pages appear the names of "John Hall-Edwards, Major, R.A.M.C., Senior Medical Officer"; "Andrew L. Bicker, Brigadier-General Commanding Command Depot, Sutton Coldfield," and other high officers, among the careful signatures of privates, corporals, and sergeants. Some of the writing is neat and legible, some of it is uncertain and struggling, but every word, every letter, was treasured by Daddy for the writer's gallantry and friendship.

In asking Philip Rodway's acceptance of the album, Bishop Russell Wakefield described him as one of the warmest-hearted leaders of a warm-hearted profession. As a mark of personal appreciation he also gave him a gold cigarette case. Those on the stage included Colonel W. E. Sturges, who commanded the Birmingham recruiting area, Mr. Francis, and Professor Bostock Hill.

*　　*　　*

Before leaving *Boy Blue*, we would add that Sidney Black, the Harlequin, was practically blind, yet he gave each night a perfect exposition of an intricate sword-dance. His part demanded regular appearances through "table traps," and for twelve performances he was absent from the cast. His understudy was too large to get through the traps!—so for those twelve shows George Slater deputised, traps and all, in the dress in which he had himself played Harlequin twenty-five years earlier!

And again, "Jimmy" Laurier conjures up a vision of P.R. being always able to persuade an artist to see reason, except in the most extreme cases, by gripping him firmly under the elbow and murmuring "As a personal favour to me, old man."

Season 1917

Events of great importance to the theatre, both nationally and locally, took place in the year 1917. Early in March Mr. Neville Chamberlain, who had become a leader of the war-time government, convened at the St. James's Theatre, London, a great meeting of theatre and music-hall managers, artists, musicians, and people engaged in the cinema industry, with Sir George Alexander in the chair.

Mr. Neville Chamberlain delivered a profoundly considered oration, in which he described amusements and recreations as essentials of the times. They took people out of themselves for an hour or so, and sent them back to work refreshed and invigorated.

"I do consider," he declared, "that the amusement of the people is as essential to the national success as is the feeding of the people. Yet, just as we are warned to eat and drink in moderation, as regards both quantity and quality, so I think in war time our amusements should be taken in moderation. I am not sure that the sight of long queues of pleasure seekers during the daytime is calculated to conduce to that seriousness of spirit and appreciation of the necessity to put all our strength into the struggle that we so want to impress upon the great mass of the populace."

Thus praised and admonished, the managers went back to their various theatres with no very clear idea of where they stood! Another pointer, however, was soon forthcoming, for the Budget of 1917 raised the Amusement Tax to a considerably higher level, with effects which we shall describe in a moment.

As to the Royal, the chief interest early in 1917 centred on the success of the Board in at last persuading the shareholders to sanction a reorganisation of the financial position. Under this scheme, which had been advocated ten years earlier, the capital was reduced to £24,349 in just twice that number of 10/- shares.

It was the one step needed to give Philip Rodway and his co-directors a chance of demonstrating the company's prosperity to the world at large by declaring the long-awaited dividend. This was done at the annual meeting in July, when 10 per cent. (less tax) was paid on the new share capital. The preferred shares received 6 per cent. in discharge of accumulated dividend, and the surplus balance of £5,594 was carried forward.

On the year P.R. had produced a net profit of well over £5,000. The Royal had never stood higher in the affections of Birmingham, and in the opinion of London managers it now took rank as the premier theatre in the provinces.

The chairman told the shareholders that now the capital had been reduced they might look forward in normal times to unbroken success. The year had been a harassing one for the management, and rendered doubly difficult by rules and regulations which were more or less necessary adjuncts of a state at war. They had been told that amusements were vitally necessary, yet the Government, for the sake of a small, problematical increase in revenue, were going to increase the amusement tax by an amount which would work out at 200 per cent. on the scale for some parts of the house.

"In my opinion," he said, "the increase will defeat its object. The improved position of our company is not due to exceptional profits made through the war. That has adversely affected us, because while all our expenses have advanced, we have not advanced our prices. The improvement is mainly due to the able carrying out of a progressive policy by Mr. Rodway and his staff."

Tom B. Davis, too, hailed the coming of the era of regular dividends. All the estimated receipts contained in the prospectus were being obtained, and in many cases exceeded, and the reason the enterprise had not yet fulfilled its greatest promise was solely that expenses had increased in a manner which could never have been anticipated. When the company was formed, £100 a week was an exceptional salary, even for the greatest star artist in pantomime time. Now, the extraordinary multiplicity of amusement houses, especially music-halls, had created such a demand for artists at Christmas time that those whose value had been from £80 to £100 now asked £200 to £250 a week. Thus the weekly cost of a pantomime

was £130 to £200 more than was ever anticipated, and on a
ten weeks' season there was a difference of as much as £1,500
to £2,000. But for this unprecedented rise there would have
been no arrears in the preference dividend, nor any need to
reduce the capital.

In addition, all other expenses had gone up, and it spoke
volumes for Mr. Rodway's efficiency that it had been possible
to do so well on the year, in face of many exceptional difficulties. Among them were Daylight Saving (this device had
been introduced since the last meeting), the curtailment of
local transport services, which had much affected the evening
attendances, and the difficulty of getting touring shows owing
to the inconveniences of travelling from town to town. Many
strong attractions booked for the coming Autumn had been
cancelled solely for this reason, yet the list completed by Mr.
Rodway would be found one of which any first class theatre
could be proud.

The new amusement tax was definitely calculated to de-
crease support. It had been demonstrated by many theatres
that since the tax, which meant simply an increased charge
for admission, had been instituted, the takings had gone down
by just about the amount paid to the State. The Government
said they had no desire to tax the Theatre, but merely to tax
the play-going public, but in fact, although the tax might
appear to be put upon the patrons direct, the result was to hit
the Theatre.

Going back once more to the season itself, we note it began
in March with the production of an entirely new piece,
General Post, presented prior to its long run in London at the
Haymarket, by Percy Hutchison and Herbert Jay, who had
Madge Titheradge, George Tully, Lilian Braithwaite, and
Norman McKinnel in the fine cast of Harold Terry's fine
play. There was never a more excellent comedy-drama of
wartime upheaval, though Daddy told us that there was
considerable doubt, before the production, as to whether the
title was the best that could be devised—whether the general

public would tumble to the connection between the children's game of *General Post* and the reversal of social values which the war occasioned.

First visits included *The Bing Boys are Here*, the revue which George Robey, Alfred Lester, and Violet Loraine had raised to great success at the Alhambra.

An April feature was a special matinée promoted by Lady (then Mrs.) Brooks, the Lady Mayoress, for the fund out of which Miss Lena Ashwell was supplying concerts at the front. Martin Harvey, Dorothy Silk, Constantin Stroesco, Sydney Brooks, John Goss, Arthur Cooke, and Richard Wassell (now director of the Birmingham City Police Band) appeared, and Miss Ashwell made a speech. There was an augmented orchestra, which, according to Ernest Newman, did not seriously impede the conversation of the audience.

The twice-nightly system, restored in April, ran right through to mid-September with only a short break in July. How well the average play of the day was suited to that speeding-up process may be seen from the inclusion of such varied items as *Potash and Perlmutter*, *The Little Minister*, *Tiger's Cub*, *The Cinema Star*, *The Rotters*, *Quinney's*, *The Catch of the Season* (with Seymour Hicks and Ellaline Terriss), *A Butterfly on the Wheel*, *The Headmaster*, *Baby Mine*, and *The Land of Promise*. In September we had the first production of *The Enemy Within*, a topical spy play with Julian Royce and Kenneth Kent in the cast. When the once-nightly régime was restored, with Monckton Hoffe's fantastic comedy *Anthony in Wonderland*, we saw a charming performance of Aloney, the cow-girl heroine, by Alice Russon, the Bo-Peep of the previous pantomime.

The increased amusement tax came into force on October 1st. It meant ninepence on a 5/- seat, and just as much on a 3/6 seat. The first show to experience its effect was *Under Cover*, in which Matheson Lang reappeared after an absence of some years from Birmingham.

The following week saw the first of the two great "Mary Anderson" matinées at the Royal. This was on October 6th, in aid of the Roman Catholic Huts on the various battle fronts, and yielded the handsome profit of £1,000—more than had ever been raised before by a charity matinée at the Royal.

The result was both a tribute to the value of the huts and a proof of the delight with which people hailed Mary Anderson's return. She had been in retirement since 1890, the year of her marriage to Count de Navarro, but the long rest at Broadway had not stolen her charming presence nor her histrionic ability.

Emerging from private life in order to help the fund, she received a rapturous welcome wherever she played, and nowhere was she more cordially greeted than in Birmingham. When she came here, her performances had already raised £23,000.

Her appearances were made in *Pygmalion and Galatea*, and the Balcony Scene from *Romeo and Juliet*. Galatea, of course, had been one of the most successful rôles in her repertory when at the height of her fame. Her natural grace and dignity gave distinction to the movements of the statue endowed with life. There was rich humour in her simple reaction to the marvels of the world into which Galatea was cast, and strong emotional force in the last scene with the blind Pygmalion, a part well played by Henry Baynton. Others assisting were Beatrice Wilson, Ben (now Sir Ben) Greet, Norman V. Norman, Susan Richmond (long a valued member of the Birmingham Repertory Theatre Company), Arthur Vezin, J. Anderson, and Miss Pauncefort.

As Juliet, the rôle in which at seventeen Mary Anderson had made her début, her presence was poetry itself. The Romeo to whom she played was Matheson Lang.

In announcing that £1,000 had been cleared, P.R. revealed that Mary Anderson had herself given a hundred guineas.

Two days after the matinée, in a letter to him from her beautiful home at Broadway, she wrote:

"Dear Mr. Rodway,
"I want to thank you very much for your extreme kindness over our performance at your theatre on Saturday. You made everything quite delightful, and I shall always have happy memories of

you and of your theatre. I think the stage looked very pretty, and everyone else thought so too. Things seemed to go without a hitch.

"I sent a letter this morning to your theatre for Mr. Lang, and shall be much obliged if you will kindly forward it to him. He also was very courteous, and I want him to have my word of appreciation.

"I hope you were not too tired or worried over all the extra work. When such a satisfactory sum is got together for the help of our poor boys at the front, I always feel my own fatigue to be a very small sacrifice, and I am sure that you, with your kind-heartedness, feel the same.

"Yours, with renewed thanks,
"Most gratefully,
"MARY ANDERSON DE NAVARRO."

Mr. (now Sir) Martin Melvin, always to the fore in good works, was chairman of the organising committee. In his letter of thanks to P.R. he said:

"I cannot tell you how very grateful I am to you for all you did to make our performance the wonderful and magnificent success it was, and we can never be sufficiently thankful to you. Believe me, Madame de Navarro feels very delighted with everything that was done for her. I myself am pleased to have given a little help in making it a record for the Theatre Royal. We have also broken another record of which you may not have heard, *viz.* it is the highest result which Mary Anderson has ever had outside London.

"I am sending you a little souvenir which I hope you will be good enough to accept."

*   *   *

The season ran on smoothly, with variations between twice-nightly, twice-daily, and once-nightly systems, as suited to each particular type of attraction.

A special matinée on behalf of the War Distress Fund of the National Union of Journalists, given on November 22nd, drew a fine house, and we saw the Lord Mayor and Lady Mayoress (Alderman and Mrs. David Brooks), Sir William and Lady Bowater, and Mr. and Mrs. Neville Chamberlain in the audience. The Birmingham Repertory Theatre Company, including Joseph Dodds, Frank Clewlow, Frank Moore,

Cathleen Orford, Margaret Chatwin, Isabel Thornton, Alfred Brooks, and Sydney Leon, presented an act from *Trelawney of the Wells*. John Drinkwater read his poem *In Lady Street*. Martin Harvey, Nina de Silva, Alfred Ibbetson, and Marie Linden gave *Rougêt de L'Isle*, the stirring interpretation of the legend of the Marseillaise. Rutland Barrington and Mary Grey gave a sketch *Not a Bad Judge*, and Martin Harvey recited a *Hymn of Love for England*.

As usual during the free fortnight prior to the pantomime, the Birmingham Branch of the United Kingdom Commercial Travellers' Dramatic Society had a night for their benevolent institutions. The play was *A Pair of Spectacles*, and in the cast were Alfred Batchlor (Benjamin Goldfinch), G. F. Ostins (Uncle Gregory), Guy St. Clair (Percy), Horace Wentworth (Dick), Charles L. Moore (Lorimer), H. V. Currie and George Sparrow (Shoemakers), Ernest Cross (Butler), Kate Watson (Mrs. Goldfinch), Dorothy Ostins (Miss Lorimer), and Gertrude Rees (Maid).

*   *   *

PANTOMIME 1917-18
CINDERELLA

Cinderella is every mother's story to every child, therefore the most engaging, the most enduring of all themes for pantomime. At least once every ten years since 1886 it had been done at regular intervals at the Royal; presenting a new version in 1917, Philip Rodway was about to challenge established tradition. Continuing in the style which he had been developing for several years, he was determined to make it a coherent fairy story, yet so constructed as to suit the talents of his carefully chosen artists. He went back to Perrault's *Cendrillon, ou la petite pantoufle de verre* in his search for original treatment, and eventually evolved an adroit plot which, without disillusioning any childish mind, yet contrived to give a new note of distinction. His production, since it ran until March 9th (a week longer than usual), may be allowed to have satisfied the sternest critics.

Most of the principals were on familiar ground in Birmingham. Clarice Mayne revived her great local popularity. Always effective in a scene with children, she had a good plantation song *Black Eyed Susan*, with the Tiller Troup of Tinitots, though nothing could excel her *Jingle Johnnie* number in the *House that Jack Built*.

Billy Merson, also here in pantomime for the second time (and for the second time sharing honours with Clarice Mayne), was the heroine's faithful, hopeless, humble admirer Buttons—a performance instinct with his genius for comedy characterisation. Of his new songs, the best was *The Good Ship Yacka-Hicky-Doola*, the rollicking ballad still in demand whenever and wherever Billy Merson appears.

The Cinderella of the season, Daisy Burrell, had been hitherto unassociated with such a part, as her latest appearance in Birmingham had been that of a midshipman in *The Marriage Market*. Nevertheless she revealed just the air and the appeal of personality needed. Dandini was played by Kitty Empson.

Aimée Bebb and Bert Byrne provided an excellent contrast as the Ugly Sisters, and the robust comedian, Charles Penrose, was the Baron. Bart and Bart, "knockabouts" who never tired, played the Brokers' Men, and there were the Lawrence Tiller dancers.

The action of the characters was no longer directed by Harlequin and Columbine, who had been brought from their long retirement the previous year, but by a traditional Fairy Sunshine and Demon Killjoy. The latter gave the cue for an ingenious continuation of the story (which invariably finishes all too abruptly after the discovery of the shoe). The second half opened up on a picturesque and what proved to be a most puzzling scene—"The Enchanted Lake," where on the real water of a large pool real ducks sported with surprised but evident enjoyment, and gondolas glided beneath the arches of an ornamental bridge, whereon stood the Prince, dreaming of his unknown Princess, and holding in his hand the only hope for her recovery—the crystal slipper. It was here that Clarice Mayne sang the wistfully appealing *Every Little While*, composed by J. W. Tate.

Now the Demon Killjoy makes his appearance, announcing:

> You fondly hope to recover your love,
> A hope that I soon will frustrate,
> A novel departure from pantomime lore
> By a means I will soon illustrate.
> Your courage I'll test
> By a means I know best
> And your hopes shall be drowned in the lake.

Prince. I fear not any threat from you.
> On one thing I am set,
> While I retain this crystal shoe
> I'll find my princess yet.

Demon. Your hopes of happiness I soon will sever
> You and the slipper shall part—*for ever!*

On the last words he seizes the shoe and hurls it far out into the lake.

We still have these verses as part of "the original manuscript" for this scene, scribbled in pencil on an odd sheet of paper just as Daddy thought of them one Sunday lunch time, and written straight off exactly as the lines were afterwards spoken.

Now comes a greater mystery than that of the water itself (which, by the way, was quite complicated enough, for one evening during rehearsal the huge tarpaulins burst under the strain, and the orchestra was submerged in four feet of water!). The Fairy Sunshine, coming to the Prince's aid, summons a troupe of water nymphs, who are bidden to descend into the pool and recover the crystal slipper. Eight or ten green clad maidens go gracefully down the steps into the lake—and disappear! The audience holds its breath. There is a swirl in the water; one of the nymphs reappears triumphantly bearing the slipper, gives it to the Prince, and vanishes once more. And none of them is ever seen again.

Perhaps we should relieve your minds by telling you that P.R. had engaged the finest local swimmers to carry out this particular trick (Doris Molesworth, the Olympic champion, being one of them).

The settings in general were of a distinctly unusual type, following the "new art" styles in colouring and design. There were dark, cone-like trees, and narrow winding pathways or flights of steps, which had a marked influence on the processions and ensembles.

Philip Rodway and George Slater wrote lyrics additional to those provided by Clifford Harris and "Valentine." The music was composed and selected by Harry Rushworth and the talented Jimmy Tate.

The first week of 1918 saw the great Tank Bank Race, in which the chief cities vied for the credit of subscribing the highest amount in war savings certificates over a given period. Birmingham went all out to win the race. Victoria Square was turned into a huge counting house, and a large tank took up its position there, from which various influential people, including P.R., made speeches. Crowds thronged the square at all hours, fervently watching the progress made by rival cities, as shown by a great chart on the Town Hall wall. The theatres gave valuable aid in publicity for the campaign, and also sent their principal artists to entertain the waiting crowds— a task in which Billy Merson, for one, revelled. Birmingham won the race with consummate ease, contributing £6,585,439 in the week, and the theatres were included in the Lord Mayor's message of thanks to all who had helped the cause.

P.R.'s own pantomime night, on March 6th, at which the Lord Mayor and Lady Mayoress were present, was of special interest. It was, indeed, a coming of age celebration, for he had just completed twenty-one years of service in the Theatre Royal, during eighteen of which he had been manager, and an agreement had just been made with the Board for a further five years' contract. He set apart one-third of the proceeds of the performance for the Professions and General Trades Fund, of which he was chairman of committee, for the entertainment of wounded soldiers and sailors.

R

CHAPTER 19

(1918)

The 1918 drama season, destined to be among the most significant in the theatrical history of Birmingham, opened with a return visit of Matheson Lang in *Under Cover*. *Carminetta* came for the first time, with Klit Gaarde and Maria Minetti (who were afterwards married); *Theodore and Co.*; and *The Little Brother*, Benedict James's moving plea for religious tolerance, in which Lyn Harding, Fisher White, and Ben Nathan headed a magnificent cast, and the young lovers were played by Cecily Byrne and a handsome dark youth named Ronald Colman, whose name to-day is famous wherever the films are known.

Philip Rodway began to extend further his already extensive system of entertaining sailors and soldiers in the theatre. He was especially keen on finding occupation and amusement for the convalescents, who, allowed out of hospital on Sunday afternoons, had nothing to do but walk up and down the streets. He came to the rescue by organising a regular series of weekly Sunday concert matinées which went on until the end of the war, open to all wounded men, convalescents, nurses, and wearers of the silver badge. The Bishop of Birmingham (Dr. Russell Wakefield) was a frequent visitor at these matinées, and paid eloquent tribute to the excellent work which P.R. had accomplished.

The first programme, on April 21st, included a lantern lecture by Major Hall-Edwards on *The Wonders of Photography;* the season was one of varied interest, including performances by the favourite Robins-Piercy Entertainers and others, together with selections by an augmented orchestra under Harry Rushworth. Sometimes P.R. himself delivered a brief informal lecture on a topic of theatrical interest. Smoking was allowed, there was of course no charge for admission, and the concerts were followed by tea in the rest rooms at Queen's College and Daimler House.

One lecture in particular was such a success that P.R. had to give it again in the course of the season. He called it *Producing a Play*, and in it he demonstrated, by means of a cleverly worked out story, all the "tricks of the trade," to the great delight of the audience. He not only made them understand what a complicated undertaking a large theatre is, and the immense amount of labour which a production entails, but caused great amusement with his "burlesque drama," which introduced not characters but stage-effects.

By means of a miniature stage he showed the planning of big scenes, and explained how the lighting effects were worked, while on the screen were shown views of the property- and other rooms behind the footlights. The large audience thoroughly enjoyed hearing "the horses clattering into the courtyard of the village inn," followed by the parade of those same horses and that courtyard—a couple of empty cocoa-nut shells on a flat stone! The "thunder" (a zinc sheet well shaken), the "rain" (a box of dried peas on the egg-timer principle), the "wind" (very like a mangle with linen rollers), made a great appeal to them, but perhaps the biggest "hit" was made by the snowstorm which, by an ingenious electrical device (a reversed film), descended on the whole of the auditorium. And, however paradoxical it sounded, P.R. explained, each separate stage snowflake had to be fireproofed, even if the fireproofing spray turned the flakes brown and the result was a convincing shower of autumn leaves!

* * *

The "twice-nightly" season set in with a revival of *La Poupée*, in which Stella Gastelle once more played the doll, and we recall with pleasure the appearance in *Sweet Lavender* of Cora Goffin, the charming star of musical comedy and pantomime (who is now Mrs. Emile Littler).

Largely by force of Philip Rodway's example, managers of first-class houses everywhere had adopted the twice-nightly system for a considerable portion of the year, and there was now no difficulty—apart from those created by the national crisis—in obtaining standard plays under this system. *Bella Donna*, *The Melting Pot*, plays old and plays new were all fish for the twice-nightly net which he had first cast.

* * *

In June P.R. brought to its consummation a bold scheme for uniting under one direction the two principal theatres of Birmingham, up to 1918 rivals—very definitely rivals, with little attempt at mutual assistance or fraternisation between managers and staffs. He had for some time cherished this notion and had successfully impressed his co-directors with its soundness. Now the time was ripe for the decisive step.

We have told you how twenty-one years earlier, as a quiet yet determined boy with the will to get on in the world, he had entered the Prince of Wales Theatre in Broad Street as box office clerk; how, after a few months in that post, he had gone to join Dornton at the other house; and how the Prince of Wales Theatre had passed from the personal control of the Rodgers family into that of a syndicate. In those twenty-one years the Broad Street house (the earlier history of which we have already summarised) had known several managers, from the courtly J. F. Graham to William Joseph Andrews, and various syndicates had held it on lease. In April, 1911, the Prince of Wales Theatre (Birmingham) Ltd. was registered as a company, with John Hart as chairman, Robert Arthur, Milton Bode, Edward Compton, F. W. Wyndham, and J. Macready Chute as directors, and J. M. Sharp as secretary.

The directors, in June, 1918, at the time of the take-over were John Hart (still chairman), J. F. Graham, Robert Courtneidge, F. W. Wyndham, and Edward Compton. The Prince of Wales had vied with the Royal at every turn, and in one way or another there had been a good deal of duelling between the two.

P.R.'s scheme was to end all this Montague-Capulet enmity
and make Birmingham indisputably the keystone of the touring system, by amalgamating the two sets of interests. Protracted and delicate negotiations were involved, but on July
24th, 1918, when the annual meeting of the Theatre Royal
(Birmingham) Ltd. was held, he was in a position to ask for
the shareholders' approval of the purchase of all the shares in
the Prince of Wales Theatre (Birmingham) Ltd.

The chairman stressed the directors' view that the Theatre
Royal's position would be immensely strengthened. The
fusion, long desired, was on the lines prevailing in other towns
where similar conditions existed—Manchester and Glasgow,
for example. The management of both theatres would
thenceforth be in the hands of Mr. Philip Rodway, and the
Board was confident that the methods which had served so
well in making the Royal a success would have equally good
results in Broad Street. The town would definitely benefit,
because it would be possible to give a better selection of
theatrical attractions and to allot each show to the house best
suited to it.

P.R. was very definite that the acquisition of the Prince of
Wales Theatre was a good thing for the Royal. Working
the two together would, as he pointed out, have many ad-
vantages. After a few months he hoped to arrange for a
number of new shows to be produced in Birmingham with
West End casts before they went to London—a distinction
hitherto reserved for other cities. At Christmas the D'Oyly
Carte Opera Company would open a five weeks' season at the
Prince of Wales Theatre, and Sir Alfred Butt would follow
with a new musical play, so that pantomime at the Royal
would be distinctly contrasted at the other house.

The directors' recommendations were unanimously adopted
and a dividend of 15 per cent. less tax was declared. The
year's net profit was shown as £7,712, more than £2,000 up
on the previous year.

And so it was that on August Bank Holiday, 1918, when the

Prince of Wales Theatre re-opened after a six weeks' closing, Philip Rodway returned as general manager to the theatre where, in 1897, he had first begun in the box office.

His ascent to the summit of influence and distinction in the life of the provincial theatre had been achieved, and his own life had become "*A Tale of Two Theatres.*"

Yet we always knew (and he never really tried to conceal it) that the Royal was his first, last, and only love among theatres. The Broad Street house he recognised as a fine property in its own right, and a tremendous asset when conjoined with the Royal, but it was never the home from home that he found in New Street. While the two theatres were running tandem, in the halcyon days of their abundant prosperity, one might have summed it up by saying that he "frequented" the Royal, "visited" the Prince of Wales. Ten years later, when he had effected the brilliant stroke of business which resulted in the changeover of the Royal, his heart still remained in the old theatre . . . but this is yet to come.

With the first-class theatres of Birmingham under his control, P.R. made Birmingham an essential link in every important tour. He was now able to pick and choose among the best attractions on the road. For the next ten years Birmingham saw every touring production worth seeing, always subject to the proviso that it came up to P.R.'s definite standard of suitability for his audiences. As Mr. Michie Fraser wrote last year in the *Birmingham Weekly Post*:

> "When he booked a show for either of his theatres the success of the tour was usually assured; when he refused a booking the reverse was very often the case, owing to the long jump that had to be made from London to a good starting point. His refusals were frequently actuated by his strong personal predilections, and no power on earth would change his mind. Either a show was fit for Birmingham or it wasn't. It didn't matter to 'P.R.' what any other manager felt about the production, or what the Press said about it. There was no argument and no appeal."

The setting off of one attraction against another was resolved by P.R. into a fine art when the return to normal

conditions gave him a completely free hand. In that first fortnight of unified control we find *A Butterfly on the Wheel* at the
Royal, *The Belle of New York* at the Prince of Wales, where
splendid audiences gave the new management a propitious
opening; *Love in a Cottage* at the Royal (still running twice-
nightly shows), with the musical success *Bubbly* at the erstwhile opposition house. So it continued: musical comedy at
the one theatre, strong drama at the other; farce at the one,
crook play at the other—the best of all types carefully chosen
and placed where it would do most good.

In August the Royal also had a flying matinée of Barrie's
Seven Women and *The Twelve Pound Look*, with Irene Vanbrugh
playing the lead. Rita John, the heroine of surely the most
"equitable" argument in recent theatrical annals, took a
small part in *Be Careful, Baby*. Fred Terry and Julia Neilson,
in September, brought *Henry of Navarre*, with Meggie Albanesi
(whose early death cut short a career of brilliant promise)
playing Marie. In October Klit Gaarde, the fine actor-
vocalist who nowadays sings and sails his way round the
world, came with Maria Minetti and Edward Lauri in a return
of *Carminetta*.

Meanwhile the Broad Street audiences were seeing Bromley
Challenor, the new Sir Guy in the old *When Knights were Bold;*
a first production in Birmingham of *Dear Brutus;* Mrs. Patrick
Campbell in *The Thirteenth Chair* (with George S. Wray, a
star this season of drama at the Alexandra, as the Inspector);
the Carl Rosa Opera Company; and Dorothy Dix with Jerrold
Robertshaw in that powerful drama *The Yellow Ticket*.

October 23rd, 1918, is a great day—one of the greatest—in
the annals of the Theatre Royal. It is the date of the second
Mary Anderson charity matinée, when the fine sum of £6,200
was raised for the Lady Mayoress's Prisoners of War fund.
Never in the history of the English stage had a theatre performance yielded so vast a sum for benevolent purposes. Never,
we think it may be said, has the figure been since exceeded.

Philip Rodway announced "An unprecedented programme,

which will include Miss Mary Anderson, supported by Mr. Lyn Harding, in scenes from *Macbeth*, etc., etc. For this unique matinée the prices will range from 2/6 for the gallery and 5/- and 10/- for the pit, to 100 guineas for a private box. The upper circle will be 15/- to three guineas, the stalls three to five guineas, and the dress circle five guineas."

A fortnight before the event there was already an enormous list of applicants. All seats were reserved, and a ballot for places was conducted at noon on October 16th by Mr. H. F. Harvey, Editor of the *Birmingham Mail*, with P.R. allocating the seats as the fortunate names came out of the hat.

We remember the curtain rising on a house completely sold out in every part, so eager were Birmingham citizens to support a fund which had done so much to help men of the Royal Warwickshire Regiment in enemy hands. Mary Anderson once more received an extraordinary ovation, and liberal indeed was the measure of dramatic art she gave in acknowledgment. First she repeated her classic portrayal of the Balcony Scene from *Romeo and Juliet*, rendering the exquisite poetry with a tremulous passion and ecstasy which convinced her audience she had discovered the secret of perpetual youth. Basil Gill's Romeo was a fitting complement to such a Juliet.

Then came four extracts from *Macbeth:* The Letter Scene, the Plotting of the Murder, the Murder Scene, and the Sleepwalking. As Lady Macbeth, Mary Anderson achieved a contrast which was a tribute both to her versatility and to her powers of rising to the heights of tragic intensity. From the reading of the letter announcing Macbeth's immediate return, in which one became aware of the sinister purpose in her ambitious mind: through the scene in which she taunted her husband for letting "I dare not" wait upon "I would," she triumphed ceaselessly by the power and sincerity of her acting. Lyn Harding was a tower of strength as Macbeth, and the minor parts were played by Ben (now Sir Ben) Greet as the Doctor, Estelle Stead as the Gentlewoman, and Lieutenant de Navarro (Mary Anderson's son) as a Messenger.

The programme further included songs by Nellie Carlyle, items by the Belgian Quartette (Desirée Defau, violin; Lionel Tertis, viola; Emily Doehaerd, 'cello; Harold Samuel, piano) and selections by the theatre orchestra. During the interval the Lord Mayor (who had become Sir David Brooks) took turns with the Lady Mayoress, Viscountess Fielding and Sir William Bowater in holding an auction from the stage, by which means £570 was added to the total of about £5,500 raised by the sale of seats.

One of the lots was an autographed letter from the Prime Minister to Mr. (now Sir) Martin Melvin, Chairman of the Executive Committee, in which Mr. Lloyd George wrote:

> "10 Downing Street.
> "October 22, 1918.

"Dear Mr. Martin Melvin,

"I have learned with the greatest satisfaction of Birmingham's efforts since the earliest months of the war on behalf of her brave sons and the men of Warwickshire who had the misfortune to be taken prisoners by the enemy. Our hearts go out to these men, but sympathy is not enough. We must reach our hands to them, that they may receive the food and clothing necessary to sustain them until the day of their deliverance. That glorious day is drawing nigh. The armies of the Allies are marching to the victory which will fling aside the gates of their prisons and call them back to life, freedom and home. They are looking to the people of Birmingham and Warwickshire to stand by them to the end, confident that they will not look in vain.

> "Yours sincerely,
> "D. LLOYD GEORGE."

Autographed letters from Field Marshal Haig, General Pershing, and President Wilson were sold for £25, £30, and £85 respectively. The final proof of the matinée programme, altered and corrected by Mary Anderson, drew a bid of £50, which was raised to £75 when she autographed the proof. Sixty pounds were forthcoming for an autographed photograph of Marshal Foch. A touching contribution to the sale was a gold watch given by a woman who could not afford to buy a seat. It was sold four times, realising altogether £80.

When Philip Rodway announced the approximate result of the matinée there was a storm of cheering, and at the end of the programme Lady Brooks expressed her heartfelt thanks to him, his colleagues, and the staff for their services. At this time her fund was regularly sending parcels of food, etc., to more than 1,500 prisoners in enemy countries, at a cost of £1,300 a week, a total of 115,768 parcels having been forwarded.

When Madame de Navarro learned that we were engaged on this biography, she wrote to us from Court Farm, Broadway:

> "Good news to hear you are writing your father's life. I vividly remember what a courteous gentleman (in the right sense of the word) he was, and how he went to the greatest trouble to make the performances in his theatre as perfect as possible.
>
> "He left a charming impression on all who came in touch with him.
>
> "When you are this way I shall be glad to see you. Every success to your work of love.
>
> "Yours sincerely,
>
> "MARY ANDERSON DE NAVARRO."

This notable matinée completed, the theatres resumed their normal activities, with the shadow of war continually lightening. To the Royal came *The Boy*, to the Prince of Wales *The Maid of the Mountains*. Martin Harvey brought *The Burgomaster of Stilemonde* to the Royal, with *General Post* as the friendly opposition "up the street."

And then—that wonderful, poignant, Eleventh of November, 1918. Armistice Day! The day for which civilisation had yearned through the four dreadful years. The "war to end war" was itself ended—the day of peace had dawned. Birmingham joined in the national paean of thanksgiving which broke out, and memorable indeed was the atmosphere which pervaded the theatres that evening.

As a matter of record, the Royal had George Gregory in musical comedy, and Frances Doble was playing Cavallini in *Romance* at the Prince of Wales Theatre.

Among P.R.'s most treasured souvenirs was a silken miniature of the red ensign, autographed by Admiral Lord Charles
Beresford, as a token of appreciation by the Navy League of
his work for sailors. Later he received the special Navy League
decoration for the same cause.

A fortnight of opera by Sir Thomas Beecham's Company,
who gave Birmingham its first rendering of *Coq D'Or*, and a
visit by Seymour Hicks and Ellaline Terriss in *Sleeping Partners*,
distinguished the last month of the season at the Prince of
Wales Theatre. The Royal had the customary visit by the
Commercial Travellers' Dramatic Association, in whose presentation of *David Garrick* the principal parts were played by
G. F. Ostins (Garrick), H. Lewis (Gresham), Gertrude Timmins (Violet), F. H. Lawlay, H. Lupe, C. Read, H. Timmins,
Eve Connel, and Miss F. Tabberner. Alfred Batchlor, a
stalwart of the society since its formation, was absent from the
cast itself for the first time, acting instead as stage manager.

On November 13th of that year, 1918, Tom B. Davis
resigned his position as joint managing director, and Philip
Rodway became sole managing director of the Theatres
Royal and Prince of Wales.

CHAPTER 20

Characteristics—His bookshelf; Dickens, Conan Doyle, George Borrow, Edgar Allan Poe—Sense of humour—Generosity—Simplicity—Religion— Some comparisons—P.R. and his pipe—His friends speak; Sir Charles Grant Robertson.

This is a chapter of small things. But whatever reveals the central figure more clearly, be it anecdote, direct description, or comparison, must not be omitted, for who knows just what quality, what characteristic it may be that will turn a lay figure of the written page into a living man? We remember Dr. Johnson more for his habit of burning orange peel and his inseparable pot of tea, than for his Dictionary. (Did not he himself say: "Nobody can write the life of a man but those who have eat and drunk and lived in social intercourse with him. They only who live with a man can write his life with any genuine exactness"?) We know not if there is a modern school of biographers, which believes only the broad outline; but we know no better in certain instances than to go straight back to that same James Boswell, of whom Carlyle wrote, "if he had never been a great fool he would never have been a great writer," and emulate his folly in our detail.

Comparisons, too, must needs be dearly loved by the biographer, for they help to conjure up before the mind's eye of the reader a vivid mental picture; and they are in themselves a delight to the writer, who has instantly recognised the kinship in the comparison, and now cannot refrain from writing it down for fear of keeping back one tithe of one revealing quality. And so there is something of every-thing in this chapter, collected with fidelity, if not art, in the hope that somewhere in it there is some trace of that philo-sopher's stone that will turn the dross description into the gold of a new life in your memories.

*　　　*　　　*

If we go to his bookshelves and look along his favourite books we can discover much of the man himself, hidden between their much-worn covers. (These bindings, so well thumbed, were a great distress to Mother's well-ordered mind. The more worn they became the happier was he—for it showed, he said, that they were used and appreciated.) Daddy kept certain immutable favourites on his bookshelves, and these he read again and again whenever he had a spare half hour. He did not seem to have the inclination to make friends with many new books, instead being content to renew acquaintance with his old ones times without number. One of the few recent novels he read and enjoyed was Priestley's *Good Companions* which Mother gave him as a 26th Wedding Anniversary present. He loved every page, and later he was full of enthusiasm when Julian Wylie produced the play, based on the book, at the Prince of Wales Theatre.

First we shall see a green edition of Izaak Walton. We are not surprised, for all true fishermen love the *Compleat Angler*. Next to it are more well-tried books of the river: Viscount Grey's *Fly Fishing*, *Rod and Stream*, *The Way of a Trout with a Fly*, and half a dozen others, whose pages have carried him many a time in imagination to the rivers he loved.

Then come several of Dickens. His favourites were *Nicholas Nickleby*, with the Vincent Crummles theatrical pages well turned, and *The Pickwick Papers*. How often on a Sunday afternoon have they beguiled him, with Nip, our fox terrier, to keep him company.

Next is a slim black and gold edition of Edgar Allan Poe, fit covering for the sombre genius that broods and flashes within. These tales of the Grotesque and Arabesque had always fascinated him, and many an evening when we were very young has he thrilled us with *The Fall of the House of Usher* or the *Masque of the Red Death*. Next to it are the poems, and then a small book of Burns.

Conan Doyle's *Adventures of Sherlock Holmes* follow on. With every fibre of his being Daddy approved of and appreciated Holmes' deductive powers, and so was enormously attracted by Doyle's brilliantly-thought-out plots. He believed in applying the "reconstructive theory" to ordinary life, and it was surprising how often the end justified it. If anything was lost in the house he would start us with "Where did you last see it?" and trace on until we invariably found the missing article. He prided himself on his excellent memory, and rightly so. He never seemed to forget a name or a face, even after thirty years, and, most difficult, never failed to attach the right name to the right face. He hated the idea that memory might get rusty, and constantly made tests of his own and of ours. Nothing worried him more than forgetting temporarily a word or joke on which we had previously commented. The flattering unction that most of us lay to our souls—"we shall remember it presently"—was never employed by him. The missing word or phrase must be recollected there and then or it troubled him exceedingly. In an active brain such as his any word forgotten proved an intolerable irritant.

Next on the most-read shelf are Shakespeare's Plays. He had an exceptionally good knowledge of these, and was as exceptionally attached to them. Many of them he knew from cover to cover, and he could quote by the hour the speeches of his favourite characters. By them, widely differing, stand Thomas Hood's poems, and then come half a dozen of O. Henry's books of short stories, and *Lorna Doone*.

Lavengro next. George Borrow's love of the countryside was his also, and the book opens readily at the page: "There's night and day, brother, both sweet things; sun, moon, and stars, brother, all sweet things; there's likewise a wind on the heath. Life is very sweet, brother; who would wish to die!" *Wild Wales* also, which Daddy particularly loved because of its references to one of his favourite fishing villages—Ffestiniog, on the Bala moors. H. V. Morton's *In Search of England* stands near Longfellow's *Hiawatha*, then come several volumes of theatrical reminiscences, with *The Green Room Book*.

And now, in a place of honour on his shelves, a collection of nursery rhymes, their stories and origins, *Perrault* and *The Arabian Nights*. Daddy never wavered from his belief that

Pantomime should be based on a coherent story, and if it was possible he liked to follow the original version. Sometimes, as in the case of *Old King Cole*, nothing rewarded his research, and then he would enjoy building up a story of his own. But if there was an original plot he thought it right to stick to it.

Such were his best loved books. They reflect his favourite interests, his fishing and his pantomimes, the countryside and the theatre. In Conan Doyle we find his love of detail and deduction; in Poe his own imaginative powers could have full flight.

Perhaps the volume of Edgar Allan Poe on his shelf is more of a revelation than any other, for although their lives were so diverse there was an affinity between the characters of the two men which makes comparison inevitable. There was a strange duality in their tempers and their minds. Just as the wide divergence of contemporary judgments on Poe points to the "co-existence in him of two persons," so anecdotes in this biography may appear to be contradictory unless we solve the mystery in the same way.

Both men were gentle and affectionate at some times, sombre to a degree at others: swept at one time by a light-hearted gaiety, at others by an impenetrable gloom. The following passage is a quotation on the art and character of Poe. It might well be a contemporary portrait of Philip Rodway:

"On one side he was an idealist and a visionary. His yearning for the ideal was both of the heart and the imagination. His imagination carried him away from the earth and the material world into fairyland or dreamland, or into the empyrean where souls dwell in immortality. Another mode of evasion from the universe of common experience was through haunting thoughts that belong to an eerie world of dreams.

"On the other side he is conspicuous for a close observation of minute details which characterise the realist. He resorts to this gift of precise Defoe-like apprehension in the narrative. Closely allied with this accurate scanning of actual or imagined things is his power of ratiocination. He prided himself on his faultless logic. . . . "

Poe's escape from the material world, his Dreamland, was in Israfel. P.R.'s Fairyland was in the setting of *Beyond the Snow-capped Hills*. Poe's idealism found expression in Eleanore and Helen; P.R.'s idealism was not expressed in actual writing, but in his life. Both knew the eerie, haunted places of the imagination where were conceived Poe's *Premature Burial* and *The Pit and the Pendulum*, for to P.R. too *claustrophobia* had ever been a dread, since the day of the secret Hide-hole of Aston Hall. He was both attracted and repelled by these two excursions into the grotesque, as he was by his own dread. Both were possessed by the same passion for detail and for logical measured argument. This they carried into their work and their everyday life.

"The double contents of his temper, of his mind, and of his art are fused into a oneness of tone, structure, and movement, the more effective, perhaps, as it is compounded of various elements that give depth and intensity to the dismal glow or total sheen." Sombre, gay, brooding or flashing, gleam the many-sided facets. Here is at least the very stuff of which genius is fashioned.

*   *   *

Well might Daddy have said, with Elia, "I am naturally, beforehand, shy of novelties, new books, new faces, new years." This affection for the old, dislike of the new, was of course most apparent in his attitude towards his home. All he asked was the peace and quiet of the garden, and for it to remain (with the house) completely unaltered from year to year.

Although passionately devoted to The Woodlands garden, he was never at any time a gardener. Possibly this was due to lack of opportunity, but we think not; we never saw him pick off a dead flower head or pull up a weed. The flowers

Photo by Harold Baker

MRS. PHILIP RODWAY

we gathered for his table would be greeted with "Yes, they're very lovely, but I like to see them growing—it's a pity to pick them."

Everyone has his favourite hobby or sport, and while Daddy's were fishing and an occasional game of billiards, Mother (never athletic) had hers—house decoration, and lawns! Nothing could have been better calculated on her part to arouse contradiction on his. His motto "Let The Woodlands remain unchanged!" hers (fired with a passion for paint and pastures new) "Let me improve The Woodlands." Hence an annual tug-of-war, until at last a little more of the vegetable garden was won over, reclaimed, and triumphantly sown with grass seed, and now most of the lower garden could be called a series of lawns, interlaced with paths and flower borders. Incidentally the green and cream stonework of the house has always had an enviable lustre usually associated with new paint. . . .

There is no doubt all this appealed to his sense of humour, which manifested itself in a hundred ways: in the little fancy costumes he devised for Nip; in his quaint way of giving us presents; in the practical jokes he loved to play upon the fishermen of Pontrobert, settled cosily into the bar parlour at nights. He possessed a keen sense of comedy. But he had more than humour—he had wit. He was always the quickest man in the party to turn a phrase, and not my Lord Buckingham himself could have given more point to a joke when he was in the mood.

Like Lamb, in his early days he was an inveterate punster. But whereas poor dear Charles was notorious for his "shower of bad puns," Daddy was famous for his good ones. He once took part in a punning competition, and was winning easily. The other entrants, determined to outwit this magician who could twist any word to his use, held a consultation and finally said: "We've got you this time, old man—we bet you can't pun on 'Japanese'!" Like lightning came the answer: "You couldn't give a Chap-an-easier one than that!"

s

After that they gave it up!

He loved practical jokes, but these were never of an unkind or dangerous variety. When our first telephone was installed at The Woodlands many years ago, Mother and we two were all agog to use it, but for several days the instrument and cords were there with no connection. Daddy knew that Mother's first call would be to Mrs. Jaques at the other "Woodlands"; so on the Sunday he waited until she was upstairs, and letting us into the secret, started an animated conversation with an imaginary Mrs. Jaques. Well primed, we pranced round and told Mother the 'phone was working at last. This was kept up for about five minutes, while Mother became almost hysterical in her desire to speak; and so at long last Daddy handed over the 'phone to her. It took her another five minutes to realise she was not cut off, and that it was all simply vivid play-acting on his part.

Another of his favourite tricks, at Sunday lunch, was to read out imaginary paragraphs concerning us or our friends, from the newspapers. He read so convincingly in "journalese," with controlled voice, and face well hidden between the news-sheets, that we were almost invariably taken in. If we caught but a glimpse of his expression, though, the game was up, for his face, when he was perpetrating this joke, was humour incarnate. Incidentally, we often beguiled half an hour of the Sunday lunchtime with making up verses and lyrics, and even reams of blank verse.

Robert Courtneidge writes: "I am convinced from my own observation that many of what are regarded as the most up-to-date stage jokes, gags, wheezes, wisecracks, or whatever name they may be called by, are really of astounding age, for many of these that we used in my youthful days, and which I yet hear, were then regarded by my elder comrades as 'ancients of the earth.' If I am to credit a learned friend, there are some that may be traced back to the cuneiform inscriptions of Assyria. . . . Apparently nothing in Nature is more indestructible than a gag."

In these words we can almost hear Daddy speaking again.
One of his favourite hobby-horses was this very subject—
perhaps it is one of all managers. We remember him sitting
down at Lois's writing desk and dashing off a pet Gilbertian
quotation of his from the *Bab Ballads:*

"Quixotic is his enterprise and hopeless his endeavour is
Who seeks for jocularities which haven't yet been said:
The world has joked incessantly for over twenty centuries
And every joke that's possible has long ago been med."

* * *

Daddy was the most generous of men, but it gave him
little real pleasure to make gifts on orthodox occasions. In
fact he was quite capable of forgetting all about a birthday
or Christmas. Instead, he enjoyed giving "unbirthday"
presents, and making a gift when it was least expected of
him. It appealed to his sense of humour, too, to make his
presents in an unusual way.

One glorious night, on his return home from the theatre,
he came along to our respective rooms, sat on the bed, and
presented us with a £1 note each. We were naturally delighted, thanked him, and he said good night. Re-entering
quickly, "You might as well have another," he said with a
twinkle. Again good night and a rapid exit. This performance
was repeated another eight times, and he had disposed of £30
in half as many minutes! Then he went to bed, well satisfied,
leaving us almost inarticulate.

In the same way, many years ago, when we were very small
children staying at Babbacombe, near Torquay, I (Lois)
found a brooch on the beach. Going a little further, I actually
came across a sixpenny piece. From now Daddy decided to
assist the element of chance, and by the end of the walk I'd
picked up half a dozen other coins, with the grand finale of
a ten shilling note. Later in the morning the joke was explained to me—but he made me a present of my winnings!

Whenever he was lucky himself on the Stock Exchange,
he let us share his luck. In cases where he had been given

leather notebooks, silver pencils, or even gold fountain pens, he invariably brought them home and distributed them among the three of us, round about the midnight hour.

His own needs were of the simplest and most frugal. He never used a fountain pen, and instead always carried a two-inch stump of old pencil in his waistcoat pocket. This stump never seemed to diminish in size. It went on year after year, always handy, and apparently always the same pencil. We used to wonder how a man with so much business to transact could manage with such inadequate writing material, but he seemed to do it very well. Desk models by the score were presented to him, and Eversharps of every shape and size, but he still stuck faithfully to his pencil stump, and any old penny pen that was near.

All his needs were simple, it seemed. No man could have been less extravagant about his own personal belongings. He was uninterested in clothes, and occasionally, when absolutely necessary, ordered himself, in a detached way, two or three new suits. Questioned about them, he rarely knew the colour or the style. There was not a particle of vanity in him about his personal appearance. He threw his clothes on any way for the most part, and was happiest in his fishing kit, so covered with contraptions that he might have been the White Knight out of *Alice* himself. But unlike that unfortunate knight's impossible inventions, these contraptions were invariably useful, first making the fish bite, and then netting them. But his success as a fisherman is another story.

The only time Mother insisted that he took trouble with his clothes was in evening dress. Sometimes it seemed incredible that the muddy fisherman of the morning could become the infinitely distinguished figure of the evening. Impatient at all times of fal-lals in dress or behaviour, he made one concession on his anniversary nights, or whenever he was wearing evening dress. From the first day of their marriage Mother had always given him, from her flowers, a tiny spray of lilies of the valley to wear in the lapel of his coat, and this he continued to do all his life. It became a tradition. Up to the very last he came to her in our box for this little finishing touch, the two lilies of the valley—never more, never less.

He regarded this flower from Mother as a talisman—as much of a talisman as the buttonhole which George Arliss (not unlike a more elderly P.R.) as Nathan Rothschild loses in that most moving film, *The House of Rothschild*. Failure stares Nathan in the face, but while he fingers his empty buttonhole, and the cry goes round "You've lost your luck, Rothschild," a small packet is delivered to him. It is another buttonhole, sent by special messenger from his wife. Radiant, he pins it in, and is again ready to face the world, secure in the knowledge that success will never fail him while he is wearing her flower.

Of this bond of sympathy and understanding the late Chaplain of the Queen's Hospital, the Rev. G. H. Moore, writes:

"May I reverently add a word on Phil Rodway's home life? His wife, whose father and mother honoured me with their friendship, was a source of great inspiration. She has maintained, and she yearns to keep up, the high ideals of her husband. . . ."

P.R.'s ideals really made up his religion. A few years ago Hannen Swaffer was writing in the *Daily Express:* "I have two revelations to make which will rather upset your established ideas about life behind the scenes. One of them concerns Philip Rodway, who in Birmingham has for over twenty years produced Christmas Pantomimes. When the talk moved towards religion the other night, I found him championing . . . the teachings of Unitarianism. People who produce pantomimes are conventionally supposed to indulge in all the frivolities and follies of life. This veteran producer was as serious as a judge. He offered to lend me books on Unitarianism which he quoted as though he knew them by heart."

In reality it is doubtful whether he thought much of the actual form of his creed, and it is certainly true he was bound by no ritual or conventional observances of the church. He was not a churchgoer in the normal sense, but on the other hand no man had a greater reverence in church, or found more comfort from moments of personal prayer there.

His devotion to the memory of his father was a beautiful thing. Every June 5th (the day on which his father died), every Christmas, New Year's Day, and birthday, he went up to the little churchyard at Northfield. For over forty years he never missed these anniversaries, unless he was actually absent from Birmingham.

Yet perhaps it may be said that as he did not conform to the outward observances, and only very rarely attended a Sunday service, he was not a religious man. Nothing could be a greater mistake. He lived his religion. "Do the right thing" was his creed; to do your best in all honesty was, he believed, the most important theory in life. To prove that he lived up to his ideal seems hardly necessary, for every day one meets another friend who, unasked, testifies to his loyalty, his good-fellowship, his courage, and his idealism.

Perhaps as good an example as any is the remark, made in his lifetime on many occasions, "Philip runs the Royal like a cathedral." If a man is strong enough to run a theatre like a church, how might he not have "run" a church? It is a great subject for speculation as to where he might not have ended had he been able to choose his profession, with no outside considerations of finances to affect his decision.

A fine lawyer or barrister, with his passion for logic and truth, and his unique powers of memory and public speaking? A brilliant preacher, with the courage of a Bishop Barnes, and a great appeal to the average man? It seems strange that he made good in the one profession which has among its component parts "glamour" and greasepaint—both heartily detested by P.R. He succeeded in it for two reasons. The first is really all-sufficient—because we can say sincerely that he

ad the will to succeed in anything he attempted. He had
blossal drive and will power, and there is nothing on earth
hat can keep such a man from rising to the top. The second
eason is that there is great Art, as well as Artifice, in stage-
raft, and this made a tremendous appeal to him. He had a
enius for the management of men and things, coupled with
keen perception of artistic beauty.

There was more than a trace of Pantheism in him, for he
vas deeply moved by the sense of an all-pervading purpose
n Nature. How often, in the Avon-washed orchards of the
Vale of Evesham, he would watch as "blossom by blossom
he spring begins"; or, lost in the heart of Wales, see the cycle
ound and Autumn come to the woods.

* * *

"Clearness and singleness of purpose; brevity, simplicity,
and directness, sympathy with his audience or with his
friend, perfect natural tact and good taste; all these he had
and each to a rare degree. But all these combined made
only part of his charm. He had an indescribable quality of
quickness. . . ."

Lord Kelvin is writing of the great scientist Michael Faraday; yet these words expressly describe Philip Rodway.
And strangely enough (or perhaps, after all, it is quite natural)
the faces of Michael Faraday and Philip Rodway are in
certain phases identical; the same far-seeing, quizzical eyes
under the heavy black brows; the same determined nose; the
same firm, sweet lines of the mouth; the strong chin—almost
we are tempted to reproduce them side by side. . . .

The purposeful square set of the head, and the strength of
countenance, have led many of his friends to point out to us
also the likeness between him and Stanley Baldwin, and the
comparison would hold were it only in their devotion to their
respective pipes.

Daddy and his beloved pipe! Rarely, if ever, was he
without it—it became almost a part of him; and rarely, if
ever, did he even change his tobacco—it was "Westward Ho!"

as far back as we can remember. He must have had sco
of beautiful pipes presented to him, yet he remained faithf
to one or two.

Perhaps his favourite was a little cherrywood which
friend lent him, to tide over an unfortunate hour when I
had mislaid his own. So attached did he become to it th
his own pipe remained mislaid for several days, and whe
he did return the cherrywood, his friend, sensing his affectio
for it, insisted on him keeping it. From that time onwards
was his constant companion; in fact, so much a part of hir
was his pipe that one could almost read his opinions from th
way he smoked it. Do you remember Washington Irving'
Nicholas Vedder in *Rip Van Winkle?*

"When anything that was read or related displeased him, he wa
observed to smoke his pipe vehemently, and to send forth shor
frequent, and angry puffs; but when pleased, he would inhale th
smoke slowly and tranquilly, and emit it in light and placid clouds
and sometimes, taking the pipe from his mouth, and letting th
fragrant vapour curl about his nose, would gravely nod his head ir
token of perfect approbation."

* * *

Sir Charles Grant Robertson, Vice-Chancellor of the
University of Birmingham, writes to Mother:

"I was impressed particularly by two characteristics—his own
independent sincerity, and his instinctive but firm aversion from
anything that was not clean, wholesome, and elevating. No one
liked more—I should say—fun and the truly comic; no one loathed
more—it is not too strong a word—the 'fun' that was at best
sheer vulgarity and at its worst indecency. He had strong views and
even stronger principles; and he felt that the public did not want
vulgarity and worse, and that if it did, it was the duty of a theatre
to teach the public what it ought to want. It is not surprising that
Philip Rodway was a powerful personality not merely in Birmingham but in Great Britain. He had a fine position in his profession,
and everyone admired his devotion to the theatre, his integrity, high
principles, and artistry. He did much to keep our theatres clean,
efficient, and on a high level, and he had a real love of the best
drama. He will be sorely missed. But he leaves the kind of tradition behind him of which his daughters can be proud. And you

who shared his life can feel that his life has done much for thousands who never knew him."

Let others of his friends speak for us. Mr. Gerald Forty says:

"My main impression of him, throughout my acquaintance, was of a man who was absolutely straight, consistent, and uncompromising, as one could see from his brave, challenging eyes. You always knew how you stood with Philip Rodway—whether you liked it or not; and taking it all in all I think that quality of absolute reliability is the attribute one honours most in a man, as it is one of the most rare."

And Mr. Charles Ferrier adds:

"It was always delightful to transact business with him: his word was his bond. An honourable, courteous, and kindly gentleman."

CHAPTER 21

Hobbies; Billiards; Mr. H. F. Harvey's recollections—The Midland Club—
The Press Club—A Gerald Lawrence story—Our own billiards room—
Cricket; County Ground and home—Fishing; Harvington—Mr. J. J.
Noble's angle.

"When all else failed, 'Sir Philip' could always take the
shine out of a comedian by playing him a hundred up at
billiards."

This maxim, coined recently by Wee Georgie Wood,
makes a text for a chapter on Daddy's hobbies. Already in
this book we have spoken of his love of fishing and cricket,
the two outdoor recreations which meant more to him than
any other, but we have only glanced at his fondness for
billiards.

Daddy was a natural billiards player, endowed with the
keen eye, the facile touch, the suppleness of wrist, the ability
to co-ordinate brain and hand, the patience and the self-
control essential to the billiard player's make-up. He did not
allow himself the time for the practice, which, had he cared,
would have made him a champion, but there is not the
slightest doubt that if he had been able to apply himself
seriously to the game, he would have been one of the best
amateur players in the country. As it was, he had a reputation
throughout the profession, and in the best Birmingham clubs.
After all, it was only natural that billiards should appeal to
him, for no game is more definitely an exact science, and his
analytical mind rejoiced in the problems presented of angle,
side, strength, and all the other factors involved in break-
building. His old friend Mr. H. F. Harvey, editor for nearly
thirty years of the *Birmingham Mail*, and himself a good
billiards player, writes to us:

"Philip Rodway's life was bound up first and last—but not all
the time—with the theatre. He never evaded the demands which
his work made upon his time and energies, and never resented
them, so far as one could see, but he did find time for less exacting
pursuits, and of these, as I knew him, the chief were billiards—for
the odd hours in town when he could slip away from the cares of

office for a while, or lengthen out the lunch interval—and fishing, when the desk was clear, or the pantomime running smoothly, and he could take a day or half-day off. He was keenly interested in his garden (as is every real nature lover), without ever being a gardener, and one would often spot him at a football match, or at the County Ground watching the cricket, of which he was a knowledgeable critic. But at the billiard table, or by a stream with a rod in his hand, he was in his element.

"There is no truer saying than that games exhibit a man's real attributes of character more clearly even than his business activities. Watch him on the golf course, the cricket field, or at the billiard table, and by his reactions to the run of the ball, to the luck or ill-luck of the game, you shall know him. Philip's ruling passion for the theatre came out in his pastimes. At billiards he was apt to play for effect, as if the box office and the gallery appeal were in his sub-conscious mind; but there was always the quality of cheerful doggedness to reinforce his genuine skill and knowledge of the game, and to confound spectator or opponent who presumed on the spectacular aspects of his performance.

"For a good many years Philip ranked among the best amateur billiards and snooker players in Birmingham—that select little company of 'hundred break' men; and while, so far as I remember, he never actually played for the Midland Amateur Championship, he was the equal of many of the men who achieved that honour. In the Midland Club or the Press Club he was recognised as in the first flight of players, and was always worth watching. When he set himself to it he could run up a score more rapidly than most men, but he had a penchant for preferring the difficult shot—the all-round-the-table-off-four-cushions-cannon—to the easy and obvious winning or losing hazard. Very often it came off, and secured the round of applause which one had a feeling that the Philip of the stage or box office might be laying himself out for, and only occasionally did it narrowly fail, and thus put an end to a promising break.

"If, however, he was out to win, there were among amateurs few who were such masters of tactics. He could be the dour fighter, giving nothing away, leaving the balls safe if there was little chance of scoring, wearing down his opponent, and then stepping in with brilliant effort to close the game in his own favour.

"Other characteristics which came out in his billiards were his scrupulous fairness, his unfailing cheerfulness, and his love of a jest. Members of the Midland Club still recall an occasion on which he was playing an old opponent, and, when the latter's back was turned, substituted a rubber facsimile ball for the red; and another on which he attached a slip of chewing gum to his opponent's cue tip. The comical result of the subsequent shot, in each case, equally amazed the player and amused the spectators who were in the joke."

P.R. did not have a great deal of time or inclination for club life. In fact, we cannot help recalling the epitaph on The Hon. Thomas Wentworth, which we came across lately in York Minster:

"By abilities he was formed for publick,
By inclination determined for private life."

However, as Mr. Harvey indicates, he was a member of several clubs—the Conservative, the Eccentric, the Press, the Midland, and others, and was on the Committee of the latter club. Mr. E. Marston Rudland, the honorary secretary, writes appreciatively of the active interest he took in the club's welfare:

" . . . frequently arranging billiard tournaments; affording the members a yearly opportunity of seeing his pantomime under favourable conditions; and arranging that the 'gags' should refer to the club or some of its members, to the general delight. . . . He threw himself into everything with the utmost vitality and charm. His knowledge of dramatic and literary matters was profound, and his conversation frequently brilliant. I have been astonished more than once by his learning. He was a many-sided man, equally interesting when joining in club chatter or when discussing more weighty matters."

At the Birmingham Press Club, of which he was a member for many years, P.R. achieved a spectacular performance when, not long after the war, the move to the Club's present premises was effected. As part of the house-warming, a billiards-match was arranged between him and Captain Walter Thornton. In pre-war days they had been stern antagonists, but they had not played one another for some years, and there was a good deal of speculation as to the outcome of this meeting.

Captain Thornton, one of the best-known amateur players in England, was then at the height of the form on which he won (and held for some time) the Midland Amateur Championship. P.R., on the other hand, was in no special practice, and in the circumstances it seemed reasonable for the match-makers to offer him a start. Actually, he rather deprecated this concession, and made up his mind to win—which he did by a most remarkable display of tactics and strategy. His inspired stroke play in that memorable match is still recalled at the club; he was ahead all the way through, and ran out a winner by many more than the points allotted to him in the handicap!

While on the topic of billiards, we should like to quote a letter we have recently received from the distinguished actor Gerald Lawrence:

"When I was in Birmingham we were always so busy that I saw far less of your father than I should have liked, but I well remember lunching with him at his club. After lunch he suggested that he and I should take on two very good billiards players and give them 150 start in a game of 500 up. Ignorant of what a magnificent game he played (he was by far the best amateur I have ever seen), and being myself a most indifferent performer, I said 'We can't do it.' 'Let's try,' said he.

"On his first visit to the table he made just under 100. 'Put them on another 80,' he remarked; and this was done three times in the course of the game, which we won—in spite of me!

"What a loss to the stage, to his many friends, and most of all, to you, his wife and his children."

How Daddy loved the rare occasions on which he had half an hour to spend in our own billiards room at home, where he would instil into us the intricacies of the game, explaining the how and why, the necessity for following through, for playing for the next shot, for looking ahead. Just as in his theatrical business, so when he was playing billiards, one could not help but marvel at the extraordinary foresight he displayed. Just as he always knew the position or situation likely to arise in the future, so he always knew exactly where the balls would be four or five shots ahead. He showed us all his own particular little tricks and turns and twists, explaining to us the value of developing delicacy of touch with "nursery cannons"—while we were hankering after the thrill of "long jennies" and all-round-the-table shots. To make it more exciting for us, when we first began to learn he treated it as a proper little match, but even when he handicapped himself by playing with only one hand (and that one the left) he always found it very difficult to lose! How often, when we really knew what we were doing, have we seen him deliberately try impossible shots towards the end of the game, just to give us the pleasure of winning. And he would sometimes break up one of his best positions by a swift "in off" at the top of the table, solely for the benefit of Nip, who, an interested spectator, was sitting expectantly beside one of the pockets, and making frantic dabs at the ball as it shot in.

Often Daddy talked to us of the great age of the game of billiards. He would remind us of Shakespeare's *Antony and Cleopatra*, where, after having asked for music, Cleopatra changes her mind and says "Let it alone; let's to billiards." (And curiously enough, within half a dozen lines she has veered again, this time to the still more ancient art of fishing, for she announces: "I'll no more now:

Give me mine angle; I'll to the river.")

How many an evening, after the show has finished, have we heard the car pulling up outside, the sound of the latchkey in the door, the fox terrier's excited scurrying among the bushes in the front garden after he had hurled himself out to greet his master; the door shutting, and then Daddy's voice as he came through, "Come along, Nip, old man; we'll go up and see if they're awake, shall we?" And if we were still up, perhaps he'd say, "Let's go and sit in the billiard room window, and I'll smoke a pipe for half an hour. . . ."

So many such nights we remember; often beautiful, still nights of full moon and stars, when we switched out the lights and opened wide the window over the garden. In the darkness of the room we could just see each other's silhouettes, and on the lawns below the shadows of the apple trees were dark and clear-cut. Garden scents began to drift up; fleecy clouds passed across the moon; and imperceptibly the peace and enchantment of it all would surround us. At such times would be set free the poetic and philosophic side of Daddy's nature, and he would speak of Life, and Death. . . . We remember once he said, quite quietly and naturally, "I wonder if you realise that some day one of us will not be here? ——And that there is one of the four of us who will have to see the other three go. . . ."

And had we known it, it was to be in this same billiards room that so much of the book of his life would be written; but on the table where the balls had rolled there would be piles of manuscript, files and letters, cuttings books and snapshots, boxes with treasured mementoes. And in the window overlooking the garden there would be the three who were left, writing, and remembering. . . .

But back again on that moon-lit night, Nip, who had long since lost all interest in the conversation, fell sound asleep and slid off the wide arm of Daddy's chair, bringing us all to earth once more, and "the great C major of this Life."

* * *

On many an afternoon in the summer Daddy would slip away from the electric light of his office to the sunshine of the green pitch at the Warwickshire County Cricket Ground, within a quarter of a mile of our home in Edgbaston.

He was completely content there, in some quiet corner, and the cricket, however slow, was never dull to him. He knew so well from his own cricketing experiences the charm of a quick turn of the bat, or a cunningly bowled ball, and he was never bored by apparently slow scoring. Naturally, he was most pleased when he chanced to be there for an hour of brilliant play, and when there were matches in progress too good to be missed he would take us over to lunch with him, and explain the details of the game.

But one of the things he never could stand (unless he

happened to be in the mood for it, when there was no one jollier) was the unsolicited chatter of other people who liked to keep up a running commentary just for the sake of talking, when he wanted to smoke his pipe and watch in quietness. A great friend of his tells how well he remembers an afternoon in July, when they had been sitting there for a couple of hours without exchanging a single word, enjoying the game, silently content.

Another man came and sat down on the next seat. After a minute or two,

"Nice day," he remarked.

P.R. took his pipe out of his mouth and shot a glance at him.

"Very," he observed.

A long pause, then the newcomer exclaimed, "Good shot, wasn't it?"

Daddy got up and turned to his companion. "Come on, old man, I think it's about time we went and had a cup of tea. Too talkative here."

Sometimes, when he had come home for tea in the garden, a burst of applause from the County Ground would swell and die away among the trees, and he would say, "Is that a catch— or someone made his fifty, I wonder?" And so, when tea was over, we would be a small County to ourselves. He would fix up a wicket with a couple of tennis rackets, tell one of us to use a third as bat, and he would take the bowling. Mother and Nip were the fielders. Right up to the time of his last illness he loved these games on the lower lawn. There was a round game of catching with a tennis ball, into which he loved to inveigle Mother to take an active part. (Her fielding in the cricket was purely a courtesy title, though more than balanced by the excessive zeal of the fox terrier. For Nip fielding meant "Whenever you can get the ball, get it, and for as long as possible prevent anyone else getting it from you!")

It was a code of honour to send an easy one to Mother,

THATCHOLM

Our country cottage at Harvington

but however carefully it was placed the result was always the same. She gave a scared little squeal, waved her arms about wildly, and usually turned her back on the ball. On rare occasions she would keep a firm hold on her courage, face the ball bravely, and bring both hands together in the spot where it had been five seconds before. On really Great Occasions she might even accidentally catch it once in an afternoon. Daddy's pride when this happened was immense.

* * *

The third, and undoubtedly best-beloved of his hobbies, was fishing. In the very early days of 1902-04, during the time when the old theatre was demolished and the new Royal not yet built, his main solace lay in fishing on the Avon at Harvington, where he could pit his brains against the cunning of the chub, and work off some of his surplus energy in mighty battles with the pike.

Among these river-pirates he wrought notable slaughter, as we read in contemporary press notices, and one fish, which scaled 18¾ lb. (November 2nd, 1902), and which Mother herself actually helped to gaff, he allowed to be set up. Many of his finest catches since have vanished without record, for Mother had visions of a home completely overhung with stuffed specimens. This one, however, in the capture of which she herself had a definite share, still hangs above the staircase at The Woodlands. Below it is a large and very beautiful water colour of the actual hole beside the weir which, thirty-two years ago, that pike had left at the end of Philip Rodway's line. This picture, which was specially painted for Mother in 1933 by Mr. Sam Towers, R.C.A. (who lives at Harvington in a charming thatched cottage opposite our own), was hung at the Spring Exhibition of the Royal Birmingham Society of Artists, and a colour reproduction is on another page.

Our old friend W. R. Young, the scenic artist, recalls a fishing expedition at Harvington with Daddy, on which occasion they landed over twenty pounds of roach. "We

T

carried them down to the station," he adds, "but when we were on the platform your father looked at me, smiled, and said, 'Well, W.R., what are we going to do with them?' Then he had some newspapers laid out on the platform, arranged the fish on them, and divided the whole catch among the station staff!"

On fishing days, one of Daddy's frequent companions was Mr. J. J. Noble, the assistant editor of the *Birmingham Mail*, who sends us the following observant commentary.

We should point out, however, that this amusing account is of Daddy's fishing in his last years; he was no *de luxe* angler in the natural way, revelling in the weeds, the dampness, the very discomfort of it all. We have seen him times without number, as happy as a sandboy, perched precariously on a slippery river bank, surrounded by nettles and overhung with willows. There he would sit the hours away, a crust of bread and cheese in his pocket for his lunch.

We are very grateful to Mr. Noble for this delightful angle:

"Phil's characteristic combination of skill, knowledge, individuality, and thoroughness was equally well displayed in his fishing, for he was a great angler, who could catch fish by methods of his own perfecting where other followers of the craft often failed. Moreover, a day's fishing with him was all pleasure and no pain.

"Unlike so many anglers who cannot bear anyone with them, he welcomed a companion on these excursions. So it came about that, once or twice in a season, he would ask me to go with him for a day. I always jumped at the invitation, for it was an experience to be enjoyed.

"Just as I was finishing breakfast, (for Philip believed in setting off in a comfortable frame of mind and body—no cold, hungry, dawn-breaking trips for him,) his roomy saloon, driven by his dependable chauffeur Wilfred, would draw up outside, and I would pack myself and my impedimenta in amongst the piles of gear which already loaded the back. Off we would start down the Alcester Road for one of the mills on the Avon where Philip was ever a welcome visitor, and where a nice bit of carefully preserved fishing was to be had. We would bowl along merrily, but never too fast, in the morning sunshine, enjoying the delights of the ride as we went. For Phil, though a townsman, had a deep knowledge of the rural scene. His quick eye detected things of interest which I had to have pointed out. Trees, birds, buildings, he knew them all, and could find something quaint and interesting to say about each as it came. He was a great lover of Dickens, and often made the point that the novelist must have known our district inside out, as his use of such typical names as Upton Snodsbury proved.

"Driving in comfort practically to the bank of the stream or river, where the car was finally parked, the well-trained chauffeur got busy, whilst we stretched our legs and inspected the pitches. I have said Philip was always welcome to these generally exclusively reserved spots. Not merely the greeting of the miller showed that. We would find that an awkward bank of nettles had been cleared, a still more awkward wasp's nest attended to with cyanide, and, most important of all, a nice head of water accumulated in the backwater and the mill sluice, adjusted to give just the even flow, at a gentle pace, so desired.

"We selected our spots, with due warnings from Phil not to show myself over the edge of the bank or stamp upon it. Then Wilfred appeared heavily laden. A couple of canvas stools with backs were placed in position; the rods put up and equipped with reels, lines, floats, casts and everything but the bait; bait, landing net, and all the other items placed ready at hand. What more could the most exacting of fishermen want? We took our seats and began operations, with Wilfred (having from long experience and tuition absorbed the necessary order of things) ready to net the fish, unhook it, supply bait, and perform every other essential service without the necessity of a word. And at lunch time, there it was spread out ready for us, whilst at four o'clock a tea-tray, with the compliments of the mill, appeared. It was fishing *de luxe*.

"Phil, as I have said, had his own methods of angling for coarse fish. There was no plumbing the depths, flogging the water, or any other nonsense. His style was really legering with wheat. A fair load of shot, a quill float with a cork ball as top guide, some 10 or 12 feet above, and a medium hook, was the usual tackle. Casting well out, he relied on the current to take the shotted end down to the deepest point in the water, where the bait would be gently carried out. Then the float was drawn almost to the bank and the rod put down. With a rod on each side of him within quick reach of his ready hands, he would wait for the slightest motion of the float. Then a lightning twist, a tight line, and a few minutes later a fish in the net.

"I always envied his quickness, for I never could strike fast enough, and my tackle was very different from his, a circumstance which always led to a friendly discussion, and the gift of one of his special floats and hooks.

"Though these were his general and favourite methods, he could adapt them to all the varying conditions to be met with. I have seen him spot a shoal of fish in a shallow, attract them with a few grains of wheat, drop his own bait amongst them, and hook a fish straight away. Or we would ramble over to the mill sluice itself for a change, chase the fish to some hiding place under a patch of bushes, or try a hundred and one ruses which he knew when sport flagged.

"And throughout he was always imperturbable, patient, and cheery. Even when Wilfred, the net being for the moment left behind, tried to land the best fish of the day by hand—and lost it—his temper was never ruffled. He was too good a sportsman not to know that such things were all in the day's fishing.

"He had another virtue in my eyes—he always knew when we had had enough. There was no staying on, weary and bad-tempered, till all hours of the night. The claims of business, for one thing, and commonsense for another, prevented him being tempted to overdo it. So when we were satisfied, and evening arrived, we packed up whilst the daylight was good, and set off home in reasonable time.

"There was always a call at some quaint hostelry which he knew, where he had his one whisky and I my beer; Wilfred, like a good driver, being content with lemonade. Then, instead of hastening straight back, we would slip aside through the Lenches or some other beauty spot off the main road on our way home. A halcyon day, indeed, by the time we pulled up at my gate again.

"Though he had plenty of invitation fishing available, Philip, like most anglers, hankered for a stretch of his own. And I was not surprised when one recent winter he told me he had at last got a mill stretch out Stafford way. We arranged that I should go and sample it when the season opened. Alas! when it did, Philip was in no condition to take me, and I never had that last day's outing with him.

"Nor, for some reason or other, did I ever manage to get away when he took to trout fishing, going off into the wilds of Wales and elsewhere after the game fish.

"There he joined the ranks of the angling aristocrats, the expert fly fishermen. It was his ruling passion, and his last holiday was a week among the trout."

CHAPTER 22

(1918-20)

Babes in the Wood, 1918-19; Wee Georgie Wood, Ella Retford, Robb Wilton, Fred Allandale—"Meccanoland"—Some letters and stories—Reminiscences—1919 Season—Messager's *Monsieur Beaucaire*—Annual meeting—*Dick Whittington and his Cat*, 1919-20; Billy Merson and Clarice Mayne.

PANTOMIME 1918-19
THE BABES IN THE WOOD

"'Father,' whispered a little boy who sat among the elect at the dress rehearsal of *The Babes in the Wood*, 'where is the Fairy King? Is that him?' and he pointed to a figure silhouetted in black against a corner of the stage. 'Yes, it is, in a way, sonny, though they don't call him that on the programme—that's Mr. Philip Rodway.'

"The answer was wise, for Mr. Rodway has been for many years the Fairy Godfather—*le compère invisible*—of Birmingham pantomime. Not by supernatural powers, but by patient and adroit experiments, he has at length turned pantomime from the disconnected succession of music-hall performances into what may be called a play of fantasy." So said the *Birmingham Post* of December 27th, 1918.

Since that unpropitious production of 1904, *Babes in the Wood* had perhaps naturally been avoided as a theme for pantomime at the Royal. Now that fourteen years had passed, Philip Rodway felt justified in rescuing it from the lost limbo of the past. Actually it was a theme which appealed to him through its essentially English nature and the scope it afforded for creating scenes of fragrant, old-world beauty in the heart of his beloved country. The deciding factor of his decision to revive *Babes in the Wood*, however, was probably Wee Georgie Wood.

P.R. did not make many really close friends among actors and actresses. As Clarkson Rose writes:

"Mr. Rodway was noted for his polite but rather cursory treatment of the ladies of our profession; he really much preferred the men always, and was at no great pains to conceal the fact."

Even of the men very few were allowed into the inner sanctum of his friendship; the cases in which manager and actor merged that relationship into one closer, warmer, were rare. We call to mind possibly less than half a dozen, and high on the list is Wee Georgie Wood.

P.R., always responsive to intelligence, capacity for deep thinking or creative genius, found all these qualities in this artist (comedian is too limited a word) who has long been recognised as incomparable in his own branch of the profession. To know Georgie Wood intimately is to fall under the sway of a peculiar attractiveness; when he exerts himself to charm he is irresistible. When he talks he is a mine of knowledge, information, and worldly wisdom. When he makes a speech (so his Masonic friends have told us) he exhibits the power of the spell-binder to an extraordinary degree. To him we are indebted for many intimate sidelights on Daddy's career, and our gratitude cannot be too warmly expressed.

As an actor he had just the gifts of creative interpretation calculated to please and attract P.R. In 1918 he was already a well-known figure on the music-hall stage, but, as he has told us, Philip Rodway was the first manager to put him in the "star" class, at a "star" salary, of pantomime artists. P.R. had been watching him for some little time, and the choice of *The Babes in the Wood* as the subject for the first post-war pantomime at the Royal was considerably influenced by the conviction that he could play Georgie to great advantage as the Boy Babe Reggie (a part presented on burlesque lines in 1899 by George Robey, and by a girl—Phyllis Dare—in 1904).

The war over, pantomime came into its own again throughout the country. At the Royal, of course, it had never lost popularity or prestige, and the success of the new *Babes in the Wood* merely emphasised P.R.'s wisdom in maintaining standards at a time when temptation to lower them was strong. The book and lyrics were commissioned from Lauri Wylie, George Slater, Clifford Harris, and Valentine. James W. Tate and Harry Rushworth composed and arranged the music; W. R. Young, John Bull, and P. Howden painted the scenery. George Slater produced, and the entire pantomime, which was to be one of the most elaborate and entrancing ever presented anywhere, was under Philip Rodway's personal supervision and direction.

"Littery gents," as Thackeray playfully called the men of letters, are never tired of recalling Addison's saying that *The Children in the Wood* was one of the "darling songs of the people, and the delight of most Englishmen at some part of their age." A century before, as a *melodrame* by Thomas Morton, it made its first appearance at the old playhouse in New Street, where it had since been staged in version after version. This latest edition had something in common with the first, since both presented, as the title page of the old chapbooks said, "the two innocent children, the barbarous villainy of their unkle, and the duel between the two murdering ruffians," whilst both ended with their miraculous preservation instead of "their unhappy and dolorable death." By a pretty fancy the story of the babes was told by the aid of the legendary hero, Robin Hood, who took the name of Robin Goodfellow, the woodland sprite.

The play opened at Nottingham Fair, where we met all the principal people—the children, the baron their "unkle," their nurse, the ruffians, Robin Hood and Maid Marian, Will Scarlett, the Merry Men of Sherwood and the Fairy Morning Star. A peep into the babes' nursery at bedtime, and then away, *via* the Outlaw's Oak, to the inn called "The Half-way House," where Greedy Gorgibuster, with a gigantic and realistic head, exhibited amazing and comical voracity. Then to the Home of the Fairy Goose, for the clever and curious speciality of Les Klicks, an electrical novelty set against a pitch black background.

Then the Road to Pixieville with a real touch of poetic fantasy; and so by a bypath, which would naturally be taken by any twentieth century babes on their way to the wood, to the memorable Meccanoland—a child's dream-town, built from a giant box of Meccano parts, where little boys played to their hearts' content at making their own toys. No scene so perfectly combining deceptive simplicity with profound ingenuity had previously been staged at the Royal, and the climax of the Babes' flight in a Meccano aeroplane invariably "brought the house down."

Dame Tibble's Schoolroom, where children of the Allied nations came from a huge map of Europe, opened the second half. In The Heart of the Forest we had the traditional duel and a very beautiful bird-ballet, with the robins covering the forlorn babes with leaves, to the Brocken music from Gounod's *Faust*. Then, to the unfailing delight of the little folk in front, came the rescue by gallant Master Goodfellow, and so on to the wedding reception of Robin and Marian.

Perhaps the most notable feature of *The Babes in the Wood* was that the personages of the play were not merely names, but vivid personalities carefully characterised by members of a notable cast. Ella Retford, who in *Little Miss Muffet* five years earlier had won golden opinions, confirmed them by her portrayal of Robin Goodfellow; neat and trim, she radiated vitality, and easily "put over" her various songs, such as *My Girl and Me* and the favourite *K-K-K-Katie*.

And Georgie Wood. How to convey adequately in so brief a space the amazing genius which inspired his study of the Boy Babe, Reggie? It is a truism to say that he not only acted in the child's manner, but he penetrated the child's mind. That is the secret of his unchallenged supremacy among impersonators of childhood. The most microscopic observance, the most faithful reproduction of a boy's thoughts, actions, and characteristics are inspired and sublimated by his controlling brain. Wee Georgie Wood is a paradox, boyish in appearance and manner, his gravely-humorous characterisations directed by the keen intellect, and never so truly the mature artist as when apparently lost in the mischievous pranks, or the shy, reflective ponderings of childhood.

Robb Wilton and Fred Allandale made a pair of robbers as totally unlike each other as could be imagined; Wilton, with his slow, confidential air of half-asleepness, his readiness to oblige, coupled with a desire to drop the whole boring business and go home, and his innate goodness of heart beneath a vain pretence of sternness; Allandale, who swash-buckled gloriously, and painted Marmaduke with the broad romantic touches of a Brangwyn. Their scene in the sky, where we heard their lively conversation, was a sheer delight.

Minnie Rayner as Dame Tibble reproduced the merry, muddle-headed, Malaprop manner germane to her part in *The Rotters*. Cecil du Gue played the Baron with forceful comedy; Vanwy Chard, whose mother, Madame Nellie Pritchard, was well known in Birmingham, was the Maid Marian; Florence Sweetman and Ethel Ward played second boy and girl, Emmelyn Walter the good fairy Morning Star; while Nora Bentley, as the Girl Babe Gracie, was a valuable foil to Georgie Wood's Reggie. It was a great pantomime for specialities, and next to the mysteries of Les Klicks, Jack Harvey's Midget Cart-horse Teddy was firm favourite with the children.

The pantomime production was preceded, as was now usual, by a full dress rehearsal on Christmas Eve, to which Philip Rodway invited 2,000 wounded sailors and soldiers. Mr. A. J. Leeson, honorary secretary of the Birmingham and District Professions and General Trades Fund, wrote:

"I know I am only one, and a small voice at that, but I feel I must write a line of thanks for the delightful time you gave our wounded boys this afternoon. . . . You seem as keen on pleasing them now as when you started your most admirable work, and if anybody deserves recognition in an order of the British Empire it is yourself, for you are easily first of the theatre managers of the country in entertainments for our wounded."

From Mrs. H. F. Currall, M.B.E., Commandant of the Bir-mingham 2 Detachment, V.A.D. British Red Cross Society (to which detachment Phyllis now belongs), comes a note bridging the years:

"The citizens of Birmingham, of whom I am one, owe a debt of gratitude to the late Mr. Philip Rodway for his kindness and generosity to our wounded during the great war. He gave many thousands of tickets to the various hospitals, enabling the men who had been, and were, suffering, to enjoy themselves, and for a time forget their infirmities.

"These men will always remember with gratitude the good times he gave them, and the kindly interest he took in all and sundry at a time when they most needed the helping hand of good fellowship.

"This, Philip Rodway gave unstintingly. And yet, when a small souvenir was presented to him at the theatre, he was overcome to think that others so deeply appreciated his efforts on their behalf."

On his own special night, when extra turns were given by Wilson Hallett, Will Gardner, Scotch Kelly, and Josey Layton, P.R. himself contributed the evening's chief novelty. This was the burlesque *Producing a Play*, which he had given for the soldiers' matinées during the war. In fifteen minutes he presented a three-act drama, reversing his stage, as it were, and showing how each and every one of the different effects were contrived. Jack Riches, the property master, who was supposed to be "assisting," tells us the following little anecdote:

"I remember the house was packed," he says, "and when Mr. Rodway gave the cue 'Hark, is it the lark or the nightingale?' I ought to have walked across the stage with a glass of water, blowing into it down a pipe, and making a warbling noise like a bird, but instead I put my head round the wing and whistled *I'm for ever blowing bubbles*. The audience yelled, but Mr. Rodway, though he enjoyed the joke, told me I must never do anything like that again."

Robb Wilton tenders some happy memories of this *Babes in the Wood*. In a charming letter, in which he recalls Daddy as "the most conscientious producer of pantomime of his time," he says:

"I have just written as I feel, and if I have done no more than remind you of one or two items of interest connected with the earnest work of your dear father, I shall have the satisfaction of knowing that I have been privileged to be of some, if ever so little, assistance.

"There was one special night each week of the run of the pantomime to which I always looked forward, and so, I have every reason to believe, did all the men of the company,—and that was Friday. No, not because it was 'treasury night,' but because it was the night which the Guv'nor set aside for a little friendly gathering in his office after the show, when each of us vied with the other for the best story. I have very fond memories of our Friday nights with the Guv'nor—they were indeed a feature, and a wonderful relaxation after the day's work. Mr. Rodway's quiet, delightful personality seemed to make it a specially joyful interlude.

"One hears much about the toilsome rehearsals of pantomime—the poor tired chorus, the small part people, and the principals all dragging their weary way home, not having had time to snatch a bite of food all day. I am afraid I must disappoint those who look upon this as the usual unfortunate lot of pantomime artists. It never befell them where Philip Rodway was concerned. The luncheon hour was always a fixture from the first day of rehearsals to the last, no matter how important each particular day's work became. You could always bank on having your lunch at the right time and in peace, an important amenity so much neglected by the majority of producers, and invaluable for preventing frayed tempers all round, let alone avoiding the awful fatigue entailed by hanging about all day and most of the night.

"His rehearsals were the most pleasant affairs imaginable. No losing of temper, no raising of the voice, no shouting at electricians, stage hands, or call boys; always the quiet encouragement of

" 'All right. Take your time. It'll all come. No need for anyone to get excited.'

"On one occasion (and there are many such during the production of a pantomime on the enormous scale to which Philip Rodway was accustomed) he was sitting in the stalls during the rehearsal of a particularly heavy scene, when something happened to one of the 'cloths' as it was being hauled up. A beautiful and most essential bit of the show, it caught on a piece of woodwork and was practically torn to shreds—and we were within twenty-four hours of opening! Most producers would have torn their hair, sacked about six flymen, and chased everybody out of the theatre.

Not so Mr. Rodway. He merely got up, turning to Tom Townson who was sitting next him, with a quiet 'Well, that's that!'

" One of the two annual occasions which I really believe he enjoyed the most was the full dress rehearsal. The house was filled with wounded soldiers (his guests, of course), and the show went straight through with the Guv'nor strolling on and off at intervals, and making everyone in front feel that each had a personal share in the construction of another wonderful Rodway pantomime.

"The other was the very last performance, when, as a fitting finale to a most happy engagement, each artist was called upon by Mr. Rodway to make a little speech to the friendly audience. Then, at his special invitation, the full company foregathered 'behind' for a little farewell party, at which each member of the company was supposed to say a few words, preceded, to the general delight, by a few dance steps, whether you could dance or not. It was the cause of much amusement, and relieved the sadness inseparable from the breaking up and parting of a happy band of players, and once again illustrates another kind thought cleverly displayed by Mr. Rodway."

And now to sum up: Georgie Wood has found time, despite the pain and worry caused by his serious motor accident at Newcastle last Autumn, to set down his personal memories, instinct with observant humour, of Daddy as manager and man. Thus he writes of their first season's work together:

"Whenever I think of him, and that is often, I look straight into those twinkling eyes and feel, as I used to feel from the first moment of meeting him, that he is looking right into my innermost thoughts, with a mental message which carries the conviction that whatever I say to him, or whatever I think I am conveying to him, he is aware of that 'something' deep down, and I might just as well discard the mask of polite conversation and get down to brass tacks.

"In the days when I first acted for him, that is 1918-19, his musical director and others of his staff used to call him 'the Guv'nor,' but to my mind he was so essentially Mr. Rodway because of his dignified gentility, his humanity towards those he cared for, that I felt the need for something less formal, yet quite respectful. He supplied it himself one day by addressing me as 'Sir George,' to which I replied 'Yes, Sir Philip'—and between our two selves only we accepted the titles we had bestowed upon each other, and eventually, quite secretly, gave our acquaintances and friends 'distinctions' in a private 'Honours List.'

"What an experience that first pantomime was for me! It is a coincidence worthy of note that I am giving Phyllis and Lois these recollections of their father at a time when I ought to be playing the Alexandra Theatre, Birmingham, in *Babes in the Wood*—which would have been my first appearance as a Babe since my original Theatre Royal pantomime; and it is especially curious when I recall sitting in 'the little office' on the O.P. side of the stage on the auditorium side of the almost sacred Pass Door: P.R. pouring me my lemonade or ginger ale (that was another nice point about him—his consideration and toleration) and with his whimsical smile saying 'Well, Sir George, being a Babe will make a man of you.' He then confided to me his plans for me, whereby while still playing parts that called for the little boy characterisation, I should have scope, as part of the story, really to act, and develop on comedy lines without the usual limitations. I said with relief:

" 'Well, I'm awfully glad you're going to let me play the Boy Babe in that way, for really I hate the part, and wouldn't take it for anyone in the world but you. In fact, after your Pantomime, I hope I never play it again.'

"He warned me that most statements we make we have to prove, and that it doesn't do to say what we are going to do or not going to do. This is brought home to me by the fact that owing to a broken knee, caused by a motor accident seven weeks before I was due to be kidnapped by comic robbers, I am forbidden by my surgeon to play in the pantomime, and this time I honestly believe and hope I shall never again have to be covered with leaves by robins whose flying terrifies me with visions of a broken wire.

"After P.R.'s *Babes* I was at Kennington Theatre in pantomime for another management, but happy in the knowledge that I was to return to my beloved Theatre Royal, Birmingham, and Sir Philip's direction and management, the following year in *Mother Goose*.

"When I say 'direction and management' I do so advisedly, because very few managers can actually direct and produce (the playbills would have you believe otherwise, but I'm telling you!), and very few producers can direct. George Slater 'directed' *Babes*, but under the 'direct' supervision of Philip Rodway.

"I hope that one day I may in some way collaborate with Phyllis Philip Rodway and her sister Lois in writing a pantomime on the Philip Rodway lines, and producing it in the Rodway tradition."

Season 1919

While *Babes in the Wood* was still running happily at the Royal, the Prince of Wales Theatre—where the D'Oyly Carte Company had been booked for a Christmas season of Gilbert and Sullivan Opera—went back at the end of January to a sequence of touring attractions. *Going Up*, on its first visit to Birmingham, with Madge Saunders and Cora Goffin, stayed for a fortnight of excellent business. Stanley Cooke and Edna Best, appearing in *Fair and Warmer*, were supported by Clive Brook, another of the British actors who have found universal fame in American films. Arthur Riscoe, now a most popular comedian, was seen in *The Lilac Domino*.

The Prince of Wales scored the first spectacular success in their friendly rivalry by staging, on April 7th, the first performance anywhere of Messager's romantic opera *Monsieur Beaucaire*, based on the play in which Lewis Waller had made one of his biggest trumphs.

The choice of Birmingham by Gilbert Miller for this important launching was a tribute to the city's freedom from entanglement with theatrical syndicates, its accessibility from London, and its discriminating audience. The following cast appeared:

Monsieur Beaucaire	Marion Green
Philip Molyneux	John Clarke
Frederick Bantison	Lennox Pawle
Rakell	Spencer Trevor
François	Yvan Servais
Duke of Winterset	Robert Parker
Beau Nash	Robert Cunningham
Townbrake	Dennis King
Captain Badger	Percy Carr
Bickset	Leigh Ellis
Lucy	Alice Moffat
Lady Mary	Maggie Teyte

Marion Green, making his first appearance on the English stage, proved something of a discovery. Dennis King, a young aspirant who had been call-boy at the Repertory Theatre, is the same Dennis King who a few years ago stormed London with the charm of his personality at Drury Lane.

Incidentally, it was during this production that P.R. arranged for the old Prince of Wales act-drop, bestrewn with advertisements, to be replaced by a picturesque portrayal of Warwick Castle, by W. R. Young.

The Royal restored the theatrical balance a few weeks later, for on May 5th it introduced to the English stage Matheson Lang's famous adaptation (in which he collaborated with H. C. M. Hardinge) of Signor Pordes-Milo's *Scirocco*. Under the title of *Carnival*, this warm-blooded drama of love and jealousy in Venice at carnival time caused a terrific sensation by reason of the extremely scanty Bacchanté costume worn by Hilda Bayley, the modern Desdemona to Matheson Lang's modern Othello. Poor Dennis Neilson Terry, whose recent death was sadly mourned, made a handsome, insidious third in the passionate adventure.

While *Carnival* was filling the Royal, Sir Thomas Beecham and his Grand Opera Company were providing for music lovers at the Prince of Wales Theatre, where his fifth season lasted for three weeks. In June the Carl Rosa company gave a fortnight's opera on less elaborate lines, so Birmingham might congratulate itself that the aesthetic angle of entertainment was well maintained under the new joint régime.

At the annual meeting on July 2nd, 1919, Philip Rodway delighted Theatre Royal shareholders with the announcement of a net profit of £8,380. The shareholders voted themselves a 15 per cent. dividend and the directors an additional £1,500, in recognition of the fact that no fees had been paid in connection with the management of the Prince of Wales Theatre.

The chairman, reviewing the position in the light of various

financial factors, such as the amusement tax and the high
cost of everything, pointed out that a high water mark in
profits had been reached. Mr. Tom B. Davis, seconding,
referred to the value to the company of "the enthusiasm and
unerring judgment of Mr. Philip Rodway, their managing
director."

The Royal closed for only one week this summer, the
Prince of Wales for less than a month. A feature of August
at the Broad Street house was the visit, in *Roxana*, of Farren
Soutar, the fifth generation of his family to act in Birmingham,
where his great ancestor William Farren had played Romeo
to Sarah Siddons' Juliet in 1776.

The Royal had another first production in September, when
The Whirl of To-Day was produced. Old friends in George
Green (a wonderful dog) and John Harcourt were in the cast.

The same week saw Henry Ainley, Marion Terry, Athene
Seyler, Meggie Albanesi, Ion Swinley, and Otho Stuart—a
combination hardly surpassable—in *Reparation* at the Prince
of Wales Theatre.

The railway strike in September gave P.R. some anxious
moments. Owing to the immobilisation of touring companies
he had to make emergency arrangements, under which *The
Land of Promise* played an extra week at the Royal, and *The
Belle of New York* did a three-night stand (the only one in our
records) at the other house.

Fred Terry and Violet Farebrother, who reopened the
once-nightly season at the Royal, were supported by James
Carter Edwards, then the oldest Birmingham-born actor on
the stage. He had been a leading man in the theatre's stock
company half-a-century earlier! The scenery for this presentation of *The Scarlet Pimpernel*, by the way, was put up, with
great success, from the Royal store, as transport was still a
problem.

Both the theatres were now at the flood-tide of success, and
some exceptionally strong casts were secured in the chief
attractions of the day. In *Lord Richard in the Pantry*, for

example, Cyril Maude's company at the Prince of Wales Theatre included Connie Ediss, Lydia Bilbrooke, George Shelton, and Elizabeth Pollock. The outstanding note of the season, however, was provided by two special matinées of *Othello*, in which Arthur Bourchier played Iago to the Moor of Matheson Lang, and Murray Carrington, Hilda Bayley, and Hutin Britton were also in the cast.

For their annual night at the Royal the Commercial Travellers' Dramatic Society put on *The Squire*.

* * *

PANTOMIME 1919-20
DICK WHITTINGTON AND HIS CAT

The History of Sir Richard Whittington, thrice Lord Mayor of London, has always been second only to *Cinderella* in favour as a pantomime subject, and *Dick Whittington* was the theme chosen by Philip Rodway in 1919-20 for the renewal of the pantomime partnership between Clarice Mayne and Billy Merson. Lauri Wylie, Clifford Harris, Valentine, and G. M. Slater collaborated over the book and lyrics. James W. Tate and Harry Rushworth saw to the music and Reginald Highley to the dances and ensembles, with a singularly efficient stage director in Walter Wichelow. The scenery was painted by W. R. Young, Philip Howden, Marc Henri, John Bull, and J. M. Barrett and Sons—"the entire pantomime under the personal supervision of Mr. Philip Rodway."

Once more coherence and continuity were the characteristic features, and despite the disconcerting and dazzling list of names on the playbill, the same guiding hand had touched everything deftly, so that while presenting a faithful story, it was embellished with a series of modern developments which kept the audience on the *qui vive* and evoked constant outbursts of admiration. The production also marked a further advance in the history of the theatre in what might be termed the new art, which obtained its effect by skill in the handling of colour rather than by garish extravagance.

U

The prologue was set in the Belfry of Old Saint Paul's, where King Rat and Fairy Sunshine introduced the story, as modern compère and commère. The first and last scenes were laid in Old Cheapside, and Dick's fortunes were followed from tattered boyhood to Lord Mayoral dignity, when, mounted on a fine white horse, he received the greetings of the people. From Fitzwarren's Emporium we went to Highgate Hill, with its flock of real sheep and its floral ballet; so to the Quay Side at Wapping Old Stairs, with the ship of effectively futuristic design lying alongside, and then aboard the *Hicky-Doola*. The first half finished with a beautiful scene in the Gardens of the Palace in Morocco, where a simple setting (intricate on examination) and simple costumes in white and silver made an unusually striking effect aided by the clever lighting. It has been called "the most engaging scene ever presented in a Birmingham pantomime." The inspiration was derived from the Taj Mahal, the world's eighth wonder, and the scene caught a good deal of the beauty of that lovely memorial.

The Emperor's Palace which opened the second half was almost as great a triumph, vividly contrasted, yet catching the same spirit. To England again and the Old Hostel, with the big spectacular effect The Turning World, which was a graceful and extraordinarily successful conception. So to Fleet Street, another example of really masterly scene painting, and the last finale, with its procession of trading companies in the *Mastersingers* style.

Clarice Mayne, on her third appearance as the Royal's principal boy, was a Dick with just the air of romance and reality to convince and charm. She had some big song successes, notably *Bubbles*, with its striking costumes and elaborate effects, and some happy duets with Billy. They made an ideal couple, working together in complete harmony.

Captain Billy, of the *Hicky-Doola*, was of course Billy Merson, the life and soul of the piece from the moment of his first appearance with a budget of seafaring yarns. The burlesque which ended in his sinking his own ship was perfect foolery, while in his many curious disguises, and with his irresistible *Senora*, he was a constant joy to the audience.

Fred Whittaker's brilliant impersonation of Thomas the Cat revived memories of his fine performance in the 1908 *Whittington*. Luna Love as Martha the cook was a certain success. Susie Belmore (Alice) sang and danced delightfully and played with an unusual sense of characterisation, especially in the vision scene on Highgate Hill. William Fullbrook (Idle Jack) did well in the effective sailor scenes. Also in the cast were Dorothy West (Princess Mameena), Edwin Brett (Fitzwarren), Tom Redmond (the Emperor of Morocco), Little La Coupe (Fairy Sunshine), Katarina Renoff, and an agile Tiller Troupe.

The general impression that this was one of the best of the Rodway pantomimes was confirmed by its length of run, which extended to eleven weeks, and ended on March 13th.

CHAPTER 23

The arrival of Nip—The soul of The Woodlands—Silver.

On Saturday, January 17th, 1920, there arrived at The Woodlands a black and white fox-terrier puppy, a long-promised gift from Daddy for us (and for himself).

From that day Nip ensnared all our hearts and became an integral part of The Woodlands. Never was the day too hot for him to enter into a game with us; never the hour too late for him to shake himself out of his midnight sleep and follow his master, oh, so willingly, up the stairs for half an hour's conversation. Never was a dog more loved or loving. He and his master were mutually devoted to one another; Daddy would tell all his troubles and worries to Nip and swear that he understood. Sometimes he could be heard telling him:

"We're the only two men here, Nip, and we've got to stick together, you and I."

Daddy was indeed very fond of all animals. In every hotel and fishing inn, wherever we stayed, he at once made friends with all the dogs and kittens of the village. He was infinitely tender with any animal injured or in pain. A month after Nip took up residence with us, the fox-terrier cocked his head out of the upstairs breakfast-room window and surveyed his world below. Daddy was on the lawn beneath, and, thinking only to attract his attention, gave a whistle. To our horror the sporting dog, evidently under the impression "My master wants me," took a flying leap of some thirty feet and rolled down the grassy slope to where Daddy stood. We shall never forget Daddy's face as he picked him up and carried him indoors. He sat quite still with him, and quite hopeless, for we were sure all Nip's bones were broken, since he had landed on his back. He lapped up the warm milk we had brought him—then wriggled and asked to be put on the floor. A final shake, and a perfectly sound puppy was wagging his tail

NIP AND HIS MASTER

On the Lower Lawn

NIP

Patience on a monument

waiting for his master to devise some new test of skill for him. (Needless to say, great precautions were taken to prevent the repetition of this particular feat.)

It was Daddy who taught the puppy his repertoire of tricks, and it is difficult to say which enjoyed them most, Nip or his audience. Some of the well-chosen few were "Shake" (offering alternate paws for so long that it seemed he had discovered the secret of perpetual motion); "Playing the Piano" (in this he mounted the piano stool and proceeded to walk along the keys, making a discordant melody very dear to his ears); "Jumping the Tennis Net" (he sailed over the fully raised net in what even unbiased opinion must admit to be a magnificent leap); and last, "Find the Ball," when his tennis ball would be hidden by Daddy in various parts of the room while Nip was kept waiting, like a child at a party, outside. Finally allowed to enter, he would hurry round the room, with loud sniffings, in his search. He invariably went first to the place where it was last hidden, and then proceeded on his way. He was never beaten, and always found it in the end.

Every year Daddy presented Nip with a pantomime souvenir, cat, dog, or cow, as the case might be. It never lasted long, but Daddy would have considered it rank treachery not to have given him one.

Daddy was at his most natural, at his best, with animals. He would relax with them, and his worries would slip from his shoulders. After a gruelling day at the theatre he would come in very tired at perhaps 11 or 12 o'clock at night; but however late it was, Nip must accompany him upstairs and have the accustomed talk by the bedroom fire. Titbits from the supper tray found their way into a very willing fox-terrier, and usually a short exhibition of Nip's tricks was given, while Daddy told of the events of the day. Much later a well-fed, well-spoiled dog trundled down the staircase for his good-night biscuit, usually presented to him in great state on arrival at his box.

From that January day when he arrived Nip was, in a way, part of the soul of The Woodlands.

It was a house which gripped your senses and your memory, and it had little ways of not letting you forget it when away from it. In the spring, on holiday, we should find ourselves saying "But wouldn't the daffodils in the lower garden be looking beautiful!" In the early summer we should wish we were waking in our own bedrooms to see the wistaria sweeping its mauve sweet-scented festoons in at the windows, and to watch the apple-blossom blowing in the wind.

Mother and Daddy had loved The Woodlands long before they bought it, and it often seemed to us we had never lived anywhere else. For many years we hoped to find family treasure or the Rodewaye's Secret Cipher in the apple-loft among the dark recesses. Certainly whenever we did venture to climb the narrow step-ladder we found something unexpected or strange. It was a wonderland up there, with Pantomime annuals, a ghostly model of "Blossomland," one box full of fancy dresses, another of assorted animals—stuffed relics of pantomimes long since gone, all dreaming of the day when in a shower of lights they were tossed high in the air to a delighted audience. What a jostling up there in the loft there must have been at nights! Cinderella in her one red shoe went a-walking with Whittington's cat, while Jessie the Cow had mournful conversation with Cowslip, the huge teddy bear from *Little Miss Muffet*. Perhaps it was the rustling of pantomime characters in the low room over his head that kept the Spirit of Pantomime alive in Daddy's mind. Often in the morning he would come down and say "A new idea for Christmas came into my head in the night. I dreamed . . ."

The staircase at The Woodlands is one of exceptional beauty, dark oak, carved by the man who built the Wycliffe Chapel. Half-way up is a very long and very high stained glass window. Though of lovely colourings, this hid the view into the garden beyond, and many times Mother wished the centre pane could be of plain glass. This would certainly

The First Garden

The Lower Garden

THE WOODLANDS

never have been allowed in Daddy's lifetime, had not the decorators, removing their ladders one day with a flourish at the finish of their work, sent the end of one of them crashing through this middle pane, the design of which it was impossible to replace, and so the change was made. Daddy was ever doubtful as to whether Mother had not instigated that ladder!

Mother chose the name "*The Woodlands*" partly because of its beautiful trees, and partly after the house of one of her greatest friends, Mrs. Howard Jaques, of Water Orton.

In after years Charles said, "*There's something so safe about The Woodlands*," and we realised that this quality of protection had been at the back of our minds all the while we were thinking of it as home. It seemed as if nothing could ever break up our happy family life there. For how many years was our faith justified. Fate was kind, and the house seemed to keep us safe from any injurious change. But even a loving house cannot protect its inmates indefinitely from harm, and on February 2nd, 1932, it knew its greatest loss.

And Nip? For various reasons he could not accompany us on holidays, and when on our return our car swung round the corner of Speedwell Road and stopped at the green gates, the first sound we used to hear was his vociferous bark of welcome. But one day in November, 1932, as their car drew up, Mother and Phyllis listened for that welcoming bark in vain. Even as they entered The Woodlands they knew. Nip had died in his sleep, in his fourteenth year, only a few months after his beloved master.

Dear house, the Spirit of Sadness stalked through your rooms that year, and left you powerless to resist or protect. Since then you have taken Time on your side, and together done your best to heal the scars. You tell us to remember the happy times we spent under your roof and in your garden, when the master and the dog were with us; you tell us to forget the pain and think only of earlier joy. You are a wise consoler—believe it that we are very grateful. We realise too that it is fitting the dog should pass away in the same year as his master; and, old house, we thank you for being wise in the order of events. Hard though it is to write, it is better for Nip to have been the last. It would have broken Daddy's heart to be told of his death.

Sometimes there arrives on a visit to The Woodlands a mad wag of a black and white dog, a certain very gay spaniel named Domino. He careers round the garden haunts once sacred to a white fox-terrier, with never a thought that he is on hallowed ground. He is the answer to the promise I* gave Daddy before I was married—"Promise me you will always keep a little dog."

* * *

And of "Silver," what shall we say now? For when we think of faithful friends and servants of The Woodlands, we must always think of those two together—the loyal little houseman and the loyal little dog. Silver reminds one of Lamb's favourite in the Inner Temple, Lovel. "I know this Lovel. He was a man of incorrigible honesty."

Silverthorne, to give him his full and charming surname, has been with us now for nearly twenty-five years. His father, as he likes to tell us, was butler to Lord William Somerset, brother of the Duke of Beaufort, at Tormarton, Badminton, and his mother was lady's maid to Lady Somerset, so he has the tradition of faithful service born and bred in him. He himself can cook excellently, he can clean his own namesake, silver, superlatively, and, best of all, he has never once in all the twenty-five years given of anything but his very best for us in his work and in his loyalty.

He has a Heath Robinson touch of inventiveness about him, and once invented either a blacklead composed chiefly of marmalade (to help it to stick?), or a marmalade chiefly of blacklead; we can't remember which, but we are afraid in either case it was a failure. Once, too, he invented a way of

*Lois.

preventing a milk pudding boiling over by putting a glass marble in it; this nearly led to Mother's early demise, as the invention never said anything about it coming out again, or about its cracking into splinters, and she nearly swallowed the bits because no one but Silver knew of its presence.

Like Barrie's Mr. Morland, Silver has a *flair*. His is for antidotes. As an antidote to the savour of fish frying he will burn feathers; to remove the odour of the feathers he puts his trust in burnt mint; and to do away with burnt mint he has great faith in the effect of vinegar. Personally, we are all in favour of the savour of fish frying.

He is sincerely sorry for any mistakes, but they are such lovable ones, and all invented for the express purpose of the smoother running of The Woodlands, that we would not be without a single one of them. He has the driest of slow, unconscious humours, and he can raise a laugh and join in it at his own expense more cheerfully than any man we know. He has seen, and approved, the anecdotes which follow.

Silver's manners are perfection, his voice most pleasing, though he has a habit, beloved by all who know him, of inserting unnecessary aspirates. The rest of his speech is cultured, quiet, and correct, but he seems to feel that H's have been harshly used in the alphabet, and, ever kind of heart, he is determined to make up to them for their pathetic case. He never omits one in its right place, nor refuses admission to an interloper, and he delights in the result. When he becomes excited, moreover, they rush upon him as upon their prey, and he becomes smothered in them. They almost turn into concrete things; aspirates enter into possession. The result is so quaintly appealing that one would not wish to deprive a single H of its honorary position.

As when Daddy discovered under the billiard table a collection of window-leathers, dusters, and polishing cloths. Silver is asked what they are.

At first he can't see them. Then he regards them lovingly with his head on one side. As always in moments of stress extra aspirates come crowding upon him, and he remarks sorrowfully:

"Ho! H'is they a h'eyesore?"

"Yes," says Daddy. "They is. What is it, anyhow?"

"Ho!" he observes illuminatingly and conclusively. "H'it's me what's-it."

Tableau.

Or again, an imperious ring at the front door. Long conversation with Silver, apparently unending. Voice from within, "What is it, Silver?" Voice from the door, "Ho, it's a gentleman." Then, as an afterthought, "selling h'onions."

Or, on our return from a holiday:

Mother: "Any more letters? Any 'phone calls?"

Silver: "No! Oh no, ma'am."

Mother: "Sure?"

Silver: "Ho! Miss—her—her—Nicolson."

Mother: "Well?"

Silver: "Rang h'up for Miss Phyllis."

Mother: "When?"

Silver (dazed completely): "Beg pardon?"

Mother: "*When?*"

Silver (absolutely addled): "When—her—what?"

Mother: "*What time* did she ring up?"

Silver (brightly): "Ho! H'on the h'evening."

Mother: "*Which* evening?"

Silver: "H'of the same day."

Mother (beginning to despair): "*Which* day?"

Silver: "H'as you went." *Collapse of Mother.*

Or with his *Alice in Wonderland* watch (which, however, always keeps perfect time):

One of us, in a hurry: "Silver, what's the right time?"

Silver: "Beg pardon, Miss?"

Us: "The right time, please."

Silver, taking out his watch and consulting it long and with great care.

Silver: "Just a minute, miss, it's—let me see—yes, it's just two minutes."

Us: "Two minutes what?"

Silver (calculating carefully): "Oh, two minutes to."

Us: "Yes, but to what?"

Silver (triumphantly): "Ho, the Hour, miss."

Or more often, after several of these "two minute gags" the last attempt is:

"Two minutes what?"

"Ho! slow, miss."

Third alternative:

"What's the time, Silver?"

"It's just five minutes past two."

"What! Surely not!"

"Ho no, it's nine minutes to one, I mean past."

"Oh, Silver, *do* make up your mind!"

"Ho, it's the hands, miss, they do get so mixed."

Sometimes he seems to be the victim of Puck or Robin Goodfellow; names given over the 'phone transform themselves into something quite different and untranslatable under his pencil at our end. As a matter of fact, answering the 'phone has always been one of the few things he prefers to be "excused him." Likewise, if he is left to whitewash the coach house while we are on holiday, twenty to one Puck gives the ladder and bucket a push and poor old Silver has to spend the rest of the week cleaning the whitewash off himself rather than putting it on the walls. But whatever happens, Silver is never put out of temper. He never sulks with man or Fate. Given a chance, he will be wreathed in smiles again in one minute.

He is an excellent shopper, if naturally slower nowadays than formerly. I believe the almost legendary beginning of Silver's faithful service was the purchase of some lemons for Mother when he brought Daddy's letters and papers up from the theatre one day. He bought those lemons so extraordinarily well that Mother decided then and there that he must be the one always to buy us fruit. His duties have increased since then, and sometimes it seems as if there is nothing about the house that Silver cannot do.

Silver is the stuff of whom proverbs are made. Our friends have coined phrases on him, for example, "Silver is worth his weight in gold"; and even "Gardeners may come and go, but Silver goes on for ever." In fact we have secret papers that prove indisputably that Silver is the origin of that time-honoured phrase "A treasure."

All through our childhood days he and Nip were there to welcome us on our arrival home from school or holidays, and never were there better friends to each other, to The Woodlands, or to us. Silver has never been known to say a harsh word to animal or man, nor of animal or man. He is scrupulously honest; a lie has never, nor will ever, pass his lips; he is very gentle, but we know he would, like Lovel, defend the weak if necessary.

When Daddy was so dangerously ill it was Silver who said, and meant it, that he only wished it could be he and not the master, and that he would willingly have given his life to save him. It is not too high praise to say that we know no one who comes nearer to the definition of a true gentleman than this same Silverthorne.

And curiously enough, just as we wrote these last lines, he came to us shyly proffering a page from the little notebook which he always carries. "It isn't much," he said apologetically, "but I would have liked it to go in the Book. I'm not much good at finding words, and nobody knows I've written it, but it is from my heart—you'll understand." And the pencilled words hold a lifetime of loyalty:

"I would like to add a word to the memory of my dear master Mr. Philip Rodway, as an old servant of his of over twenty years. I never met with a better master, with his kindly cheer in times of trouble. His greatest ambition was going about doing good. Tom Silverthorne."

THE ARCHWAY TO THE LOWER
GARDEN

The Woodlands

(*Lois, Mother, Phyllis.* 1916)

CHAPTER 24

. . . ."*It still matters nothing to me that the earth and the solar system are whirling through space at the rate of sixty miles a second, from no one knows where to no one knows whither, if I may sit in my garden and listen to the bees on a summer afternoon.*"

So wrote Bagshot. His fascinating *Comments* were first pointed out to us as being appropriate to Daddy by our friend Mr. J. M. Nicolson, of Winterbourne, Edgbaston, himself the possessor and lover of beautiful gardens.

How Daddy loved the garden of The Woodlands! His days were passed in the electric light of the theatre, and time and again in spring and summer he would long for the peace and quiet, the fresh sweet air, the very daylight of his garden; and whenever he could, he would slip away from the glare and come home for an hour in the afternoon. It was for him a haven of rest, which by

> "*Annihilating all that's made*
> *To a green thought in a green shade*"

would send him back refreshed in mind and body to his business life.

Country gardens are loved by their owners, but they can hardly be so cherished, so looked to as an oasis, as the city garden. When one lives in a town, and only a quarter of an hour away is the roar of the city, it is little short of a miracle to be able to pass through a green gate, with never so much as an open sesame, and find oneself in a pleasant solitude enclosed by high walls and old trees, against which the outside world may beat and flurry as much as it will and yet never gain entrance. It still remains as peaceful as a dream.

At The Woodlands there are two gardens, an upper and a lower, and it is the lower one which lends the charm and unusual quality to this city garden. It doesn't quite know why it's there at all! A long quaint length, set at right angles to the garden proper, it has attached itself as it were by

affection to The Woodlands, which welcomed the lost garden
to its heart, and has made it its especial darling. The prosaic
explanation is that these old Edgbaston houses were placed
in the form of a huge square, each with its spacious pleas-
aunce; and in the centre, when each had been served, was
found another garden left on its own. The original house,
now named The Woodlands, acquired the ancient "pepper-
corn" lease, and through generations of tending and tree
planting it has become a favourite child and no orphan.

There are lawns of the richest green and softest velvet
grass in both the upper and lower stretches. It is the lovely
quality of these smooth expanses of finely cut turf that gives
the garden its chief claim to critical appreciation; for as a
whole it is a pleasant rambling old place, with no particular
pretentions to meticulous display of bedding out. This garden enjoys itself! One solitary hop, first brought from the hop
fields of Harvington, has been allowed to run riot over
an arbour, and its descendants reach their sticky fingers to
stop you as you pass. Willow herb, beloved from its associations with the river, is assiduously cultivated here, and
is no outcast. Valerian or Venus's Looking Glass has reproduced itself in huge clumps, and we should never dream of
uprooting it to replace it by a more modern-sounding flower.
It takes its place in a lovely old perennial border, where
delphiniums and lupins rear their blue spikes to try and reach
the lower boughs of the fruit trees, bordering the gravel path.

There is here the pleasant medley beloved by Addison,
of orchard, vegetable, and formal gardens. At one corner,
if you wish, you can pluck raspberries and gooseberries with
one hand and sweet peas with the other, and gather thyme
while you are picking your lilies of the valley. The lilies,
by the way, are our especial pride, as they have made their
beds and lain on them most comfortably in the most unexpected places, and flourish exceedingly, making sweet the
garden with their scent in season.

There are several greenhouses, and one, the vinery,

separates the real and adopted gardens. (You dive under a thick archway of ivy and through a heavy gate, if you wish, as you will, to pass to the lower garden.) There are, then, in the largest greenhouse, eight old vines which yield each year their hundred bunches of black grapes. At one time there ran along the length of the wall a fine aquarium, purchased by Daddy for our delight. There goldfish disported themselves, but they and the aquarium are long since passed away. Let us hope they now frolic as happily in that Heaven of Fishes, where

> "Under that Almighty Fin
> The littlest fish may enter in.
> And more than mundane weeds are there,
> And mud, celestially fair;
> Fat caterpillars drift around,
> And Paradisal grubs are found,
> And in that Heaven of all their wish
> There shall be no more land, say fish."

How rambling are these pages, but it is surely the fault of the old rambling garden itself, which draws you one moment to marvel at the neatness of the beautifully clipped edges to the paths and lawns, and the next entices you to a pleasant wilderness in a secluded corner of the lower garden: on one hand asks you to admire its arches of rambler roses, and on the other intrigues you with its quaint basket of ivy, and its weeping ash with the shadowed arbour within its branches. What is one to do with such a garden?

Two of the winding paths lead to what was an enchanted playground for us as children—the old stables and hayloft. There "twilight dwells at noonday" and its secret recesses seemed as full of mystery as the apple loft at the top of the house. A private pathway, now but seldom used, leads from the stables into the high road, and through it the horses were led in the more spacious days of carriage and pair. And there, too, is the little wicket gate through which we passed to our kindergarten at Parkfield, as children.

The swing, which came originally from Cottesmore Priory, hangs under the curiously ornate porch of the stables, which we used to pretend, with only a little trial of the imagination,

was either a Swiss chalet or an enchanted cottage. There
are so many magical changes possible in an old-world
garden. For example, that towering, ancient laburnum tree,
with trunk and boughs as thick as any oak, has in fact
become King Charles' oak on many occasions for a Cavalier
in wide-brimmed hat, caped coat, and (alas for the ana-
chronism) Wellington boots. And when Lord Calthorpe's
foresters came to hew down the old willow whose branches
had been cracked by the gale, what more natural than to
pretend they were Robin Hood and his merry men?

Thus the garden gave each one of us what we wanted:
solitude and peace for tiredness, consolation in weariness,
and magic to foster our dreams and imagination; beauty at
all times. It formed the background to all our lives, and is
the paper on which our home life is written.

* * *

We seemed to crowd all the concentrated domesticity of
the week into one day—Sunday. For there is of necessity
something unusual about the weekday home life of a theatrical
director. Never once, all the week round, all the year round,
can he return from his office with the majority of the world
at 6 o'clock, and be with his family in the evening. Hence
when we were small children it was only on Sunday that
we saw him in home surroundings at all. We had started
off to school before his letters were taken in at 9 o'clock in
the morning; and we were in bed and asleep long before he
would return, wearied, at night. As we grew older we stayed
up or awake in order to see him when he came in after the
performance, and so he was not the stranger to us of our
early years.

Each day of the week is said to have, in different people's
minds, a different appearance, form and colour. We mentally regarded our one day, with its ritual and unwavering
formula, under the title of that quaint, precise old periodical
called *Sunday at Home*. Yet, though we borrowed the title
in our minds, the actual contents we knew were widely

THE WOODLANDS

From a water colour by W. R. Young, scenic artist to the Theatre Royal. Painted in 1916

different; for on Sunday with us strictness became leniency, and relaxation was the order of the day.

It began, of course, with Nip. He would take in his master's papers, and with a bound be on the bed, proclaiming by ecstatic rollings on the eiderdown, and by every quiver of his tail, that he too knew it was Sunday. Looking back on those days, it is borne in on us that Nip was certainly the most privileged member of the family—for who but he would have been allowed to pull the Head of the House out of his room by the cord of his dressing gown? (which he did every Sunday, barring holidays, for roughly thirteen years).

On the journey from the upper landing to the hall we were given the canine interpretation of the staircase waltz, for Daddy usually bounced a tennis ball between the high walls, the balustrade, and the fox-terrier. The blue and white tiles of the hall once safely reached, we would all make our way through the jasmine hung porch into the garden. In a stately procession we walked the paths till we came to the lower lawn; then, hey presto, the procession turned by magic into a skilled troupe of jugglers for the benefit of the appreciative audience of Mother and Nip. The morning promenade over, we returned to lunch.

The Sunday mid-day repast has always made its mark in the week, from the legendary day when Henry VIII knighted the baron of beef and called it Sir-Loin, right through the Victorian era, when to depart from roast beef to any other joint on a Sunday was unthinkable heresy. We did not hesitate, unlike the Victorians, to vary the dishes, but if the repast had been set for the jovial eighth Henry himself it could not have been more Gargantuan, and this for a certain reason. It was like a birthday party once a week to celebrate that domestic rarity, the four of us together! The proceedings were invariably festive, and toasts were drunk. Other families assembled often, we but seldom, and therefore we made it an occasion.

One ritual, which had its place in the luncheon hour, we

x

can claim was probably counterparted by no other family in England. This was a friendly jousting between us of memory against memory, with lightning thrusts from Daddy of Shakespeare quotations, parried on our part, if possible, by the context, speaker's name, and play. Dear Mother, when in doubt, which she often was, invariably replied *King John* to every question! We two, however, had to keep well in training, and were not allowed out of the lists by so laggard an expedient.

"Once more the lists were dight in Camelot, and all was gay with the shimmer of silk and gold; the earth shook with thunder of hooves, ash staves flew in splinters, and the firmament rang to the clash of sword on helm. The varying fortune of the day swung doubtful—now on this side, now on that." No knights of Camelot enjoyed their jousting more than we did our imaginary tournaments; although our ash staves were only words, and the firmament was bounded by the walls of the dining room; the earth shook with no thunder of hooves, only the gnarled ropes and blossoms of the wistaria outside the window shook instead with our laughter.

In this wise did Daddy bring Shakespeare most truly home to us! and never can we read the plays, and light on one of his favourite quotations without the old well loved scene, now never to be re-enacted, rising before our eyes. He believed, above all things, that one's faculties should not be allowed to rust. He hated to find a word or a name slipping from his memory. How often are we tempted so to let names slide away, but mental laziness had no part in his make-up, and by reconstruction and applied thought, the fugitive word was recaptured, never to escape again.

On Sunday afternoons another Woodlands ritual was observed. After lunch, two hours were put aside for Daddy's well-earned rest; with the Sunday papers, opened at the theatrical page, and perhaps a Conan Doyle or Dickens, we used to tuck him up with a rug on the couch under the big window, which was his favourite spot.

By this time Nip would be showing unbounded interest, waiting for us to draw up his armchair alongside, and for his own cushion to be put upon it. When everything was arranged, up he would jump and settle down immediately to his Sunday rest. If we were especially indulgent and tucked him up with a small rug too, he was by that so much the happier. He always knew the exact moment, and began to look expectant, and if his chair were not at once forthcoming, would fuss round and begin to look for a place for himself on the couch. Many a time has he jumped into the chair in the actual moment of its transit, and been pushed into position in triumphal state.

There until tea-time they would rest and talk together. The quiet relaxation of his "Sundays at Home" were, so Daddy always said, the means of his carrying on during the rest of the week. Without them he swore he would have been lost; and so never from their earliest married years were invitations accepted for that day. Then, however difficult the turn of events might be, he knew there was always a twelve hour space of serenity to look forward to in the seven days.

In the early evening, however, he could rarely resist walking down to his beloved Royal for an hour; he would make sure that the next week's advertising had gone correctly to press, and that the scenery had arrived safely and was in its place in the scene dock; he might interview the advance manager, glance at the advance booking, and prowl quietly round the building and have a word or two with the fireman. At 8 o'clock at The Woodlands we should hear the 'phone ring, and that same fireman's voice say "Mr. Rodway is on his way home."

For an hour previously the terrier would have been watching the door, and when the latch key turned in the lock, he was ecstasy incarnate. Supper was waiting, and as we four sat down at the round table, mysterious parcels were set in the centre. Occasionally this procedure was varied by the time-honoured "If you look in my overcoat pocke you may find . . ." These packets contained toffees and sweets, a most attractive assortment, the crinkle of whose paper wrappings alone sent a dog already ecstatic quite beyond the bounds of control. Never once did Daddy fai to remember to buy us these packets on the way home, and never did he fail to give Nip, with much by-play, his quota of a good quarter of a pound.

Later, Daddy would either stroll over to the piano or up to the billiard room. He had an amazingly good ear for music and could pick out any melody on the piano in a moment. He had never actually had lessons, but he loved harmonies, and if we would call out the names of songs to him he would play them instantly. Each family has its catch-phrases, and we were no exception; how many years ago this one began we can't remember, but Daddy would half-turn on the piano stool and say "Any tune from the works of Charles Dickens?" From the beginning of time at The Woodlands we have this mental picture of him, half-turned, repeating it with a quizzical smile. Very occasionally he would be in a singing mood, and we would all gather round the piano, Mother or Phyllis playing, and sing the old songs of their engagement days: *The Troubadour, In Old Madrid, Nita Gitana, Love's Old Sweet Song, The Valley by the Sea* and *By the Fountain*. Somehow these songs, old fashioned as they are, have a quality but rarely found to-day, and a sweet sadness hung about them even on our gayest nights. When Daddy could be persuaded to sing, he had a most charming baritone, and these evenings were the more treasured by us because the ordinary "home" evenings of an average family were denied us. It was the one night we were together round the fire.

Daddy used to tell us of his plans for next year's panto-mime, of beautiful transformation scenes he visualised. And best of all, sometimes he would tell us of his early childhood and the secret hide and the haunted room. After the midnight

1our the air grows chill, however high the fire, and doubly
o when in it hang the ghostly legends of old Aston Hall.
How often have we listened enthralled far into the night, and
at up with a jerk to realise the lateness of the hour; how
often have we dreamed the centuries away, until it would
1ave seemed the most natural thing in the world to write in
ur diaries, as dear Samuel Pepys did in his: "I stayed up
ill the bellman came by with his bell just under my window,
s I was writing of this very line, and cried 'Past one of the
lock, and a cold, frosty, windy morning.' And so to bed."

* * *

Each year when we were children we used to have a
garden party in June. At first Daddy always made an
ttempt to evade the question, but before many days had
assed his innate love of producing would assert itself, and
ve should have a marvellous programme of events carelessly
ut before us. Such a one was this:

"THE WOODLANDS," Thursday, June 27th, 1918.
EVENTS.
1. *Neidel Threddin Rase.*
2. *At Trimming Raiz.*
3. *Berloon Raze.*
4. *Hegg Hand Spoone Rais.*
5. *Komicle Kostoom Kompettishun.*
6. *Sak Rays.*
7. *Into the Lyon's Mouth.*

Sillekshuns by Mr. Grammerfoan.

PRIZES ....*PERRAPPS*
TEA.................*SURTIN*

KERFEW AT KNINE
Keep this programme until April 1st, 1919, when nothing will happen.

No collection.

Tempus Fugit.   Nux Vomica.
Brimstone and Treacle.

Glossary or explanation of terms.
Aurora Borealis .... *Northern Lights*
Hippopotamus .... *Never found in England*
Fruit .... *Often eaten in hot countries*
&c., &c., &c., &c.
For further particulars see small bills.

Daddy was generous to a degree once interested in an idea and the "Prizes perrapps" would come rolling in, followed on the actual day by the "Tea surtin"; basket after basket of huge strawberries, all to be set out in the conservatories half-way between the upper and lower lawns.

Then on the afternoon of the party would arrive back from the theatre Daddy himself, with an aloof air and baskets of millinery for the "At Trimming Raiz"; one year a pink ballet skirt for Nip, the fox-terrier; the next a toy-monkey jockey on a saddle for the back of the same delighted animal.

At 3 o'clock, thirty or more children, in spotless frocks and flannels, trooped in. For six hours we raced round and over-ate, and at 9 o'clock thirty not so spotless children trooped out again. Allan, Leslie, and Norman Carlyle, Nora Wheatley, Harold and Phyllis Wall, Gwen Maitland, Harry Swift, Molly Rider, Marjorie Bland, Phil Cheatle, Gwen Simmonds, and Hilda Deeley. . . . Men and women now, yet even to-day when we meet, one of them is sure to say "Do you remember those wonderful garden parties—and the straw-berries? And is the branch of the pear-tree still bound up where our swinging broke it down?"

Everyone of them had the greatest admiration for Daddy and looked on him with awed eyes, somewhat as we did our-selves, as a magician who could evoke spirits far removed from the workaday world in which we dwell. That he could so unbend that day did not remove the aura of aloofness, but rather seemed a charming condescension on his part. Every one of us was the more excited for his being there. Even on that one day his distinction and dignity were apparent to them through his charm and gaiety. We need quote only two lines from a letter of February 3rd, 1932, to reveal the respect he inspired in the younger generation. Allan Carlyle writes ". . . *The noble and useful life he lived sets us young people a fine example.*"

But we have sounded a serious note too soon, and must go back once more to the major key.

For one afternoon Daddy gave us the freedom of his Woodlands, with the exception of his own room, which was to be entered on penalty of extreme torture. Judge, then, of his expression at the door of that holy of holies during the course of the 1920 garden party. A small band, headed by Phyllis, was using his private telephone, and Lois was creeping round to borrow his own particular scissors to complete the mending of a large gash in a small boy's flannel knee (result of one of the more strenuous games with Nip). Looking back on these disgraceful episodes we can only suppose that the general excitement must have gone to our heads. Deservedly, it was a very long time before scissors or telephones were easy topics of conversation in our house.

The "pink ballet skirt" year was the year of the best race inspiration. Suddenly, after Nip had galloped round the lower lawn twice in his best Bertram Mills manner, Daddy cried "A prize to whoever catches him!" and off we went. It sounds incredible that thirty agile children should be unable to stop the progress of one fox-terrier, but Nip was as great a showman as his master in his way. He played up to his audience, and gave us a fifteen-minute show of expert side-stepping and double-tracking. We converged on him from all sides, only to find ourselves clutching thin air and falling over each other. Nip was such a happy dog, and they were such happy days. To both Daddy and the fox-terrier the lower garden was very nearly heaven.

Both Nip and his master are gone from those lawns now, but for certain, if spirits ever do revisit loved places, there walks under the apple trees in June a thoughtful man, with a small white dog beside him.

CHAPTER 25

(1920-21)

Mother has often told us the story of "The Removal of Daddy's Moustache."

It was about the time when it became fashionable for men to be clean shaven. To Mother's delight Daddy began to make tentative remarks about removing his moustache. (She had tried to effect this change for twenty-five years without success.) But one night he came home with rather less on his mind than usual, and said to her as he got to the dressing gown stage, "What would you say if I took off my moustache?"

Mother, positively shaking with excitement, exclaimed that it would be just marvellous.

Daddy: "Right! No, we can't; my scissors have gone!"

Mother: "Have mine?" (hopping out of bed and flying for her workbasket).

Daddy: (Beginning to repent.) "No, I can't; I've no hot water to shave it off with and it's too late to get any."

Mother: (Realising it is now or never.) "Here—have my hot water bottle!"

One slice of the scissors over the one side of the upper lip.

Mother: (Aghast, and with a wan smile.) "Yes, oh yes! very nice, very nice indeed."

Daddy, with slightly heightened colour, removes the other side.

Scenes. Next day. At the Royal he is greeted with frank horror, at the Prince of Wales almost with despair. At the Midland Club he is told that his moustache was an institution, as much a part of the Royal as its front hall or portico, and

PHILIP RODWAY

Photo by Whitlock

AS HE USED TO BE

To Philip Rodway
from his old friend

Geo: Gale:

Fred Terry 1920

as such didn't belong to him at all, but to the Public. Telegrams begin to arrive, on the lines of

"*Just heard the sad news about your face, can strongly recommend my Tatcho.* George R. Sims.*"

The Press declared there would be an outcry against such wilful destruction, and threatened to have leaders in the paper about it. But it grew on one, and it was never regrown.

At the time, however, the world seemed dark to his two little daughters. We took one look at him next day, burst into tears, and retired weeping to our rooms. Lois's diary records, under the ominous date of May 13th, 1920, in huge letters and underlined, "Daddy has had his moustache off." Underneath is added:

"Of course he looks very different, but I s'pose I shall have to get used to it, but I feel as though I had lost him."

Of all the treasures cherished by our sentimental family, none is more closely guarded than the remains of this very black moustache, safely gathered into a matchbox then and there by Mother, and now reposing in a drawer of her bureau. Mrs. Disraeli evidently felt the same way about Disraeli's hair.*

* * *

The Kiss Call, the latest musical comedy from the Gaiety, was booked by P.R. as the Christmas (1919-20) attraction at the Prince of Wales. This translation by Fred Thompson of a French play, *Le Coup de Téléphone*, had not before been outside London. A gay, tuneful, amusing affair, it filled the house to the end of January, leading parts being played by Cora Goffin, Tom Shelford, Stephanie Stephens, H. V. Surrey, John Hagan, Eric Vivian, Doreen Montgomery, and Mabel Heath. The last scene, in the Botanical Gardens, was particularly attractive.

The subsequent bookings for the Prince of Wales Theatre included several shows which ran for a fortnight. The D'Oyly Carte Company (headed by Henry Lytton, Leo

---

*Every fortnight when Mrs. Disraeli cut "her Dizzy's" hair, she sealed it up in little packets. Hundreds of these envelopes were found in her bureau after her death.

Sheffield, Sydney Granville, Sylvia Cecil, Elsie Griffin, Derek Oldham, and ill-fated Bertha Lewis) gave place to *Who's Hooper?*, a farce with Peggy Fishwick, a daughter of the Warwickshire amateur batsman, in the cast. Another fortnight was allotted to *Our Peg* (with Bert Coote as Triplet), and three weeks to *Chu Chin Chow*. *Peter Pan* brought Lila Maravan in the title-rôle; and in *The Bird of Paradise* the Beachcomber was played by Henry Wolston, and the part of Captain Hatch taken by Victor Fairley, later P.R.'s stage manager for some years at the Royal. The D'Oyly Carte Opera Company made a quick return for three weeks in May.

The "twice-nightly" season having started at the Royal, the balance of importance lay with the Prince of Wales for some weeks. On June 28th, when Sidney Bransgrove presented Henry Baynton in a series of Shakespeare and other classical plays, there was launched one of Philip Rodway's most interesting ventures.

P.R. was a fervent devotee of Shakespeare. During his management of the Royal, up to the outbreak of the war, he had assiduously sponsored Shakespeare in Birmingham, but since the war there had been no touring company with the strength and reputation of the great Benson troupe—almost the last company, it will be recalled, to play in the old Royal.

The lack of a successor to the Benson company exercised P.R. considerably, not only because he himself loved to see the works of the master dramatist performed, but because he felt that the management of the city's principal theatres was in duty bound to keep the Shakespeare flag flying, however lukewarm the interest of the public might be. "We don't make money on Shakespeare," he often said, "but we'll stick to him as long as other shows make enough to justify the luxury." It was this same attitude of mind that insisted on the annual seasons of the Macdona Company in Bernard Shaw's plays, though the returns were usually disappointing.

From every viewpoint, therefore, Philip Rodway was full of enthusiasm over the possibility of the Bensonian mantle descending on Henry Baynton, whose career he had been watching keenly since the young Birmingham born actor had declaimed the part of Father Time in *Boy Blue* at the Royal in 1916-17. Here, it seemed, might be the man the country was awaiting to restore the grand traditions of Shakespearean acting!

Everything was propitious for the venture. Theatrical business generally was at its peak. The public had had a rest from an entire season of Shakespeare. The schools were clamouring for it. The principal critics were pledged to be more than ordinarily kind and helpful. Henry Baynton had a big local following, a picturesque personality, the energy of youth, the spur of ambition. The Bransgrove Company, moreover, was studded with experienced Shakespearean actors and actresses—Lilian Braithwaite, Basil Rathbone, Stanley Howlett, B. A. Pittar, Gertrude Gilbert, Edward Dunstan and others.

Philip Rodway took the plunge. He booked Shakespeare for a four weeks' season, and the Prince of Wales Theatre curtain went up on *The Merchant of Venice*, the opening play, before a highly distinguished house, which included the Lord Mayor (Alderman W. A. Cadbury). It was P.R.'s firm intention to persevere with Henry Baynton, and so he did for five years, until circumstances overcame his resolve. Things went with delightful ease, and the support, if not tremendous, was at any rate encouraging.

With Shakespeare at the Prince of Wales, the Royal was catering for lighter tastes, with well-varied fare such as *Our Mr. Hepplewhite*, *The Passing Show of 1920* (in which Mona Vivian, principal boy in prospect for the next pantomime, appeared), and *The Younger Generation*. So good was the business that both houses were able to dispense with a summer vacation.

At the annual meeting in July, 1920, Philip Rodway disclosed a trading profit of £13,147, and a dividend of 20 per cent. was declared. Receipts had reached high-water mark.

Tom B. Davis spoke of some of the mounting difficulties, for costs must continue to rise, whereas receipts were liable to decline. He particularly mentioned the application of the Shop Hours Act, with its restrictions on the sale of chocolates in theatres. He made the amazing statement that the income from such "by-products" represented a dividend of something like 10 per cent. on capital.

* * *

P.R. launched another series of Sunday concerts at the Royal on September 5th, when the newly formed City of Birmingham Orchestra, under Appleby Matthews' direction, gave their first performance, with Alex. Cohen as leader. Among the outstanding personalities associated with the sequence were Gustav Holst, who conducted four of his own works; Arthur Cranmer, the Birmingham vocalist (whose son Peter has within the last year figured for England at Rugger and for Warwickshire at cricket); Holst again, conducting the first Birmingham rendering of *The Planets;* Sir Granville Bantock, conducting his Hebridean Symphony; Sir Dan Godfrey, the Bournemouth idol; Sibelius; and Eric Fogg, then famous as the Manchester boy composer of the idyll *Sea Sheen.*

Features of the Royal's dramatic season were a special matinée by Anna Pavlova (this on August 18th); *Trilby*, with Phyllis Neilson-Terry's wonderful rendering of the name-part, in which she sang "G above high C"; *Mr. Pim Passes By*, with Irene Vanbrugh, Ben Webster, May Whitty, and Sebastian Smith; a brilliant *Much Ado*, with Julia Neilson as Beatrice and Fred Terry as Benedick; *Ned Kean of Old Drury*, with H. A. Saintsbury and William Farren, a great-grandson of *the* William Farren; and three matinées by Diaghileff's Russian Ballet.

The Prince of Wales Theatre, *per contra*, had Henry Ainley and Claude Rains in *The Jest*, a month of Beecham Opera, a fortnight by Carl Rosa's Company, and a visit of *Trimmed in Scarlet*, with Violet Vanbrugh.

PANTOMIME 1920-21
MOTHER GOOSE

In the long roll of Christmas pantomimes there had been no *Mother Goose* until P.R.'s production of 1920, this with the sole exception of the year when Edmund Kean the younger played Harlequin in a summer production.

For more than two hundred years *Mother Goose* has been a term especially associated with nursery literature, less for its intrinsic value as a story, than because it was the title given by the Frenchman Perrault to his famous book of fairy tales—*Stories of Mother Goose*. In 1810 *Gammer Gurton's Garland* added considerably to the English collection of nursery rhymes which followed, and in 1817 we find the chap-book couplet:

"Here Mother Goose on winter nights
The old and young she both delights."

There is of course Grimm's Golden Goose, as well as the little-known nursery rhyme, but so vague and shadowy have the outlines become that the story needs considerable strengthening and amplification.

There is no doubt that Philip Rodway, having found the highroad to a fascinating pantomime story, rode his own particular hobby horse hard into the bargain. The condemnation of the search for artificial beauty, as opposed to natural beauty, runs throughout the pantomime, under the aegis of Discontent versus Content. It is significant of his theme that artificiality comes to a sad end. Yet what more amazing theme for any spectacular theatrical production?

It was as nearly as possible a morality play in the guise of pantomime! The poor lyric writers for that production came to grief time and again, in their understandable but misguided efforts to praise the extraneous attributes of beauty, which was the very reverse of what P.R. wanted. Of this Tom H. Townson, a clever young Birmingham lyric-writer who became Daddy's lieutenant from this pantomime onwards, writes:

"Your father always knew exactly what he wanted, and would never accept anything that fell the least bit below the standard at which he aimed. An example of this is furnished in the fact that

I had to make seventeen attempts before I finally succeeded in supplying the exact lyric he required for the end of his *Dream of Beauty* scene in *Mother Goose!*

"The test lyric which I wrote for him after my first interview luckily struck the right note. He accordingly engaged me, and that was the start of a business association and friendship that lasted until his death.

Here is the *Dream of Beauty* lyric which sounds the keynote to the plot:

> "Temptation very soon will sound its call,
> And if into its clutching hand she fall,
> Lured by the lust for beauty, she will find
> That fairies can be cruel to be kind.
> 'Tempt her with beauty,' that's the Demon's plan,
> Not beauty *real*, but beauty made by man;
> Not Nature's gift, pure, wholesome, free from taint,
> But beauty made by powder, cream, and paint.
> Be thankful, Mother Goose, for all you've got.
> Be discontented, and you lose the lot!"

Philip Rodway, having decided on his theme, took into collaboration Hickory Wood and George Slater, unfolding a story of the struggle between Content (the Fairy Heartsease) and Discontent (the Demon Discord), for the immortal soul of Mother Goose, the homely yet frolicsome owner of the ingenious bird Priscilla, layer of the golden eggs which raised the old lady from poverty to affluence, from a cottage (a lovely cottage, portrayed by W. R. Young, near the old bridge at Pershore on-Avon) to a palace; from simple Mother Goose to elaborate Madame de Guise.

Thus metamorphosed, the adventurous dame soon became a prey to Discontent. She had gained wealth; she wanted beauty (if only so that the squire might be able to say to himself, "I can now propose to her and look at her at the same time!"). An easy mark for the machinations of the Demon Discord, she gazed entranced while he showed her a vision of what she might be, in that still-remembered spectacle *The Dream of Beauty, or the Temptation of Mother Goose*. As the procession of powder-puffs, ribbons, fans, and other requisites of the fashionable toilette passed before her, she reached eagerly towards them—and when the magic mirror reflected the image of radiant beauty, her fall from grace was complete. Nothing would satisfy her but an instant journey to the Magic Pool in the Orchard, where Beauty was to be had for the asking; but Priscilla, the feathered emblem of Content, perforce flew sadly away from her discontented owner's side.

Robin, the hero, set off on his search for Gooseland, and we followed through the Wishing Gate to the Home of the Old Woman who lived in a Shoe. Meanwhile Mother Goose began to see the error of her ways, and long for contentment, even if accompanied by her homely face. The Good Fairy was appeased, Priscilla allowed to return, and the stage set for the grand finale on the Great Stairway to Gooseland.

We are tempted to linger over the plot, because of its intrinsic merit and human appeal; over the scenery, because some of the sets have never been surpassed for charm and splendour; over the dresses. . . . But we must pass on to the cast, which has been described as ideal.

Horace Mills, a newcomer to Birmingham in pantomime, created in Mother Goose a remarkable figure of eccentric comedy, in contrast to the old fashioned "dame." His quaint, quiet style was very effective, and the old lady became a lovable and appealing person.

A new principal boy, Mona Vivian, made an instant and decisive hit. One sound critic said she was the best since Ada Reeve, whose vivacity and versatility she certainly captured. Her sense of character and of comedy was strongly developed, while she could sing, dance, and infuse welcome little touches of individuality into her work. *Wyoming*, *Swanee*, and other songs are still associated with her name.

John Humphries played the Squire in his usual genial way, battling bravely against illness. Barbara Babington was Jill, and also in the cast were Mabelle George, Maggie Fraser, and St. John Medley.

Fred Whittaker made his appearance as the Goose. We cannot imagine anything more difficult than the endowment of a bird of such limited movement with personality and charm, yet that is just what Whittaker achieved. Priscilla became as lovable as her mistress.

And then, Georgie Wood. The Peter Pan of comedians made his way, as ever, straight into the hearts of his audience —grown-ups and children alike. The completely natural charm of his childish ways are the finest examples one could have of that art which conceals art. One of his best numbers this year, as Jack, Mother Goose's little boy, was *Do I want to see my mother any more? Do I? Yes I do!* which he soon had the whole house singing with him.

Georgie has an excellent story of P.R. and this year's pantomime. Let him tell it in his own words:

"We assembled for the first rehearsal. After introductions had been effected, Sir Philip, as was his wont, made it clear in his diplomatic manner that there were certain rules which possibly were observed in the breach at other places, but which were rigidly observed here. One in particular was that friends and relations of artists were not permitted on the stage in any circumstances, and in the dressing room only on a pass signed by Mr. Rodway or the stage director. When he made this announcement I ventured to say,

" 'Yes, Mr. Rodway, but my mother was allowed in my dressing room all the time when I was here before. I'd like her to be able to come in without a pass.'

" 'All right, Mr. Wood,' he replied. 'Your mother may have unrestricted entry to your dressing room.'

"After this Horace Mills, in his confidential manner, said:

" 'But-er—my wife—Mrs. Mills is my dresser—er-surely——?'

" 'Very well, Horace,' interjected P.R. 'Your wife can go in your room without a pass—now let's get on with the rehearsal.'

"Mona Vivian had, however, been waiting to explain that her mother dressed her, and without Mrs. Vivian she would be lost, at which Mr. Rodway felt sorry I'd started all this, and said:

" 'All right—now this must stop. It's understood the rule is relaxed for your mother, Mr. Wood; your wife, Mr. Mills; your mother, Miss Vivian; and now, ladies and gentlemen, we'll start with the first scene. Fairy and Demon, please.'

"Demon starts: '*The world is breathing moans and sighs,*
     'Tis well, I would not have it otherwise——'

"As this point was reached, P.R. noticed big, fat unctuous John Humphries (who must have been over sixty then) ambling towards the stage door.

" 'Jack,' he called, 'we're rehearsing—where are you going?'

"He smiled that shy smile of his, and quietly answered:

" 'I'm just going to wire for my grandfather to dress me!'

"The rehearsal thus started the show on a big laugh, and a happy family spirit which continued throughout the run."

John Humphries could not help joking, even at a time when, as we have said, he was in considerable pain. Neuritis had him in its clutch, and before the curtain went up on *Mother Goose* Daddy was doubtful whether the burly comedian would be fit to open. He struggled courageously through the run, and even found strength to appear at a big charity show in the Town Hall. He was a pathetic sight for those near the platform, as he laboriously mounted the steps, his face twisted with suffering, but once on the boards he gave the song *I do like an egg for my tea*, with all the little gestures and inflections which had made it one of the hits of the pantomime. This fine comedian and good-hearted friend died in 1927.

In those days, as Georgie Wood and a few other privileged stars recall, the greatest compliment Daddy could pay an artist was to invite him into his little office at the stage end of the stalls corridor. His favourite gambit was somewhat to this effect:

"I *think* I shall have some work to do on Sunday evening. If you *happen* to be passing the theatre, and *care* to look in to the little office, I *may* possibly be there."

The late Ernest Edelsten, the theatrical agent, who was a forceful personality and a great friend of Daddy's both in and out of business, was frequently in the precincts of the theatre at pantomime time. He had a habit of starting every sentence with "Listen"—so strong a habit that P.R.

Y

once said to him "Ernest, I'd like to build a special palace scene, with ten thousand 'Listens' painted all over it, and dedicate it to you!"

Which reminds one of the tremendous amount of attention that Daddy always paid to detail:

"In one of his pantomimes," says Tom Townson, "there was a Chinese wedding, and I had to spend hours looking up points connected with these Oriental celebrations. On other occasions I had to check the distances, on maps, between certain places, to ensure that if a principal boy, for instance, exclaimed 'I have come all the way from so-and-so, a distance of 5,680 miles,' the distance quoted would be quite correct.

"He was most particular that nothing of a doubtful nature should be introduced into his pantomimes, nor would he tolerate any political gags. Once I gave him one which would have drawn loud applause from the Conservative members of the audience. I shall always remember his reply as he turned it down. 'Birmingham may be a Conservative city,' he said, 'but don't forget that some of our best friends belong to the Labour party.'

"Always prepared to listen to suggestions, even when they came from some of his most insignificant assistants, he was very appreciative of work which pleased him. At the end of my first engagement he paid me double the amount I had expected, and the next year gave me another 100 per cent. increase."

Incidentally, P.R. and he together wrote two songs, *The Coal-scuttle Bonnet* and *Love's Barometer*, which were set to music by Harry Rushworth and sung in a later Royal pantomime.

Remembering that pantomime of *Mother Goose*, one may readily appreciate the special joy P.R. had in the first scene, a country village with an old bridge over the river. Georgie Wood still recalls how, during an early rehearsal, Daddy had said to him mysteriously "Come with me for a minute, George; I'm going to let you into a secret." Together they went through the darkened auditorium, and from the back of the stalls Daddy showed him the stage half set. "There," he announced with great satisfaction, "that's the little village where I fish!"

And this is how it actually happened. On one of our summer holidays at Pershore-on-Avon W. R. Young had

From a water colour by Ethel Rodway

THE OLD BRIDGE, PERSHORE-ON-AVON

come over for a day's fishing, and we were in the meadows
near the old bridge, when Daddy suddenly stopped and said
"Why, that's the very thing for a setting for my village scene
in *Mother Goose!*" Originally he had planned to bring a
donkey cart, complete with donkey, over the bridge, but at
rehearsal it stuck halfway, so the idea did not reach production stage.

On P.R.'s anniversary night, among the contributors to
the programme were Cicely Courtneidge, Billy Bennett, Ray
Wallace, Victoria Carmen, and Willie Cave. As a climax to
a jolly evening Wee Georgie Wood, Horace Mills, and John
Humphries escorted P.R. on to the stage, and Georgie explained that "in testimony to the most popular and considerate of managers," the company had subscribed for a roll-top
desk and a silver inkstand, which they wanted him to accept
as a memento of a pantomime stamped by the utmost smoothness and goodwill. Congratulatory messages were read, and
cases of pipes and more gifts having crossed the footlights,
P.R. in turn made presentations and a speech.

*   *   *

Each February, as far back as we can remember, Daddy
gave us the dress circle boxes for a "Pantomime Party."
Each February he was confounded to hear the repetition of
the time-honoured request. As year succeeded year till we
were in our late teens, he vowed:

"The boys will be doddering down the stairs with long
white beards if you carry these parties on much longer."

However, he contrived to render these occasions—which
in the end he always allowed us—very happy affairs. Sometimes he even gave the comedians a couple of our names with
which to conjure, and our boxes would be thrown into a
state of pleasurable excitement and collapse by a reference
from the stage to Edgbaston College, or Georgie Wood's
comment, when we had changed places after the interval:

"You've shuffled yourselves, haven't you?"

The Theatre!

What child living is there who is not enthralled by the colour and pageantry which pass, brilliant and melodious magic, across the stage? What mattered it that under the box ledge we were trying to solve an equation, if over the top of that ledge we could watch the gay Co-optimists? What mattered a Latin unseen compared with the Russian Ballet seen? We well remember trying to solve trigonometry problems in bed at 11.45 with the strains of *Mary Rose* or *Rose Marie* still running in our heads. Yet, as a matter of fact, the Theatre is an education in itself!

The last night of the pantomime on March 12th was perhaps more hilarious than any we remember; and yet charged with a deep and genuine regret at the finish of such a happy run. As Georgie Wood confessed, he had to laugh—or he would have cried. He was a wonderful ringleader in the many and varied tricks played by the principals, wherein he appeared as the Fairy Queen, and John Humphries was discovered as the Queen of Beauty in the finale of the Temptation Scene! Finally Georgie took everyone in with a tale of the heroics of St. John Medley, who had apparently made a dramatic rescue from drowning, and was just about to receive a presentation watch amid the applause of a duly impressed audience, when Horace Mills came on and announced that the stage manager wanted his watch back!

Auld Lang Syne brought the curtain down on a pantomime which had reached its hundred and eighth performance. And this, considering that a wave of economic hardship was steadily flooding England, was undoubtedly a splendid record.

"At the end of *Mother Goose*," says Georgie Wood," it was understood that I would be back at the Royal in about two years, but such were those pantomimes that, having created the part, it was possible to retain it when the production was sublet by Philip Rodway to other managements, and I again played the part of Jack at Manchester, for Julian Wylie, followed by Glasgow and the London Hippodrome, and returned to my favourite theatre for the season of 1925-26 to create *Humpty Dumpty*."

Season 1921

For a Christmas and New Year attraction P.R. arranged at the Prince of Wales Theatre a season of the gay musical comedy *Irene*. It was a new version of the old *Cinderella* theme —a shop-girl transported to the heights of social success— modernised by James Montgomery, with music by Harry Tierney and lyrics by Joseph McCarthy. Alfred Butt brought it from the London Empire by arrangement with "Joe" Sacks.

Billie Browne (Adrienne Brune to-day), the Irene, had a very popular song in *Alice Blue Gown*. Harry Ray played Madame Lucy, the costumier, and Bibi Delabere and Hilda Harris were a bright pair of mannequins.

After the end of January, when the run of *Irene* finished while still at the height of its popularity, came a week of *Tarzan of the Apes*, a fortnight of D'Oyly Carte, a fortnight of *A Little Dutch Girl*, and a week of *Mary Rose*, with Lila Maravan an appealing heroine.

Mother Goose over at the Royal, Philip Rodway, Sir Barry Jackson, and Bache Matthews (Sir Barry's manager at the Repertory Theatre) joined in a whole-hearted effort to make a success of Warriors' Day on April 2, 1921. Their purpose was to raise funds for ex-service men's charities; various trades and professional organisations, besides many individual well-wishers, did their best to help the cause. Unfortunately, the effort hung fire; by this time there were more than 55,000 unemployed in Birmingham.

The joint contribution of the three theatres was a matinée of *Arms and the Man*, by the Repertory Theatre Company, at the Royal, with the help of the orchestras, stage-staffs, and house-staffs of the Royal and the Prince of Wales Theatres.

The year 1921 was not an easy one for touring attractions, and few new works of importance were being sent out to fight the depression. Things were made more difficult by the devastating coal-strike, which lasted several months, made transport problematical, and eventually led to the introduction of such drastic economies by public lighting authorities that for a time the matinées at both theatres had to be cancelled.

Still the two houses held their own, and actually made money, though the year's trading profit of £5,700, compared with £13,000 on the previous year, was an ominous sign of the times. P.R. was able to recommend a dividend of 20 per cent., less tax, thanks largely to the strong reserves already built up, mainly by the success of his pantomimes, but the warning that the peak of prosperity had been passed was beginning to find fulfilment.

Five weeks of the summer at the Prince of Wales Theatre were allotted to Henry Baynton and his Shakespeare company, now under the aegis of Robert Courtneidge. A promising young actor named Robert Donat received good notices for his work in secondary parts; to-day he is a noted star. Actually the best production of the season was not Shakespeare, but Sheridan—*The School for Scandal*, in which "Joe" Graham, returning to the theatre he had so long managed, gave a fine performance of Sir Peter Teazle.

Albert Chevalier, the creator of Cockney characters, came to the P.O.W. in *My Old Dutch*, a play based on the song by which, long after his death, he is still remembered. The D'Oyly Carte Opera Company came back for a fortnight, and that brilliant actress Constance Collier was seen in *The Fulfilling of the Law*.

Tom Walls (later triply famous as racehorse owner, film star, and genius of Aldwych farce), played at the P.O.W. in *Brown Sugar*, Eileen Beldon appearing as the heroine, and Colin Clive (with his *Journey's End* furore still ahead of him) as the young man.

An all-star cast came in *The Charm School*—Owen Nares, Joyce Carey, Sidney Fairbrother, and Kenneth Kent. Mr. Nares, in his *Myself and Others*, tells how on this (or a later) visit to Birmingham, when leaving by the Prince of Wales stage-door, he was so hemmed in by autograph hunters that a policeman shouted to the crowd: "*Now* then! This won't do—just let the gentleman get to his car." Having struggled into the driver's seat, Mr. Nares was letting in the clutch when a large hand gently inserted an autograph album under his nose, and a large voice said: "Just one more signature, if you *don't* mind, sir." It was the helpful bobby.

Other distinguished visitors to the younger house were Maurice Moscovitch, the Russian actor, in *The Great Lover;* Irene Vanbrugh and Dion Boucicault in *Miss Nell o' New Orleans,* a colourful romance of the Creole community in the States; Murray Carrington and Margot Drake in *Carnival;* Renée Kelly and Sybil Arundale in *The Heart of a Child;* Peggy O'Neil in *Paddy the Next Best Thing;* Bransby Williams in *David Copperfield;* and Matheson Lang with Lillah McCarthy, Florence Saunders, Nancy Price, and Hubert Harben in *Blood and Sand.*

P.R. had a profound admiration for Matheson Lang, both as man and as actor manager. For several years he was a regular visitor and a certain attraction; it seems a great pity that the films have taken him from us. He never had finer support than in *Blood and Sand,* his bull-fighting play. Lillah McCarthy (Lady Keable) has retired; Florence Saunders, who not long afterwards married a Stratford colleague, John Laurie, died after an all-too-brief period of stardom; and Nancy Price nowadays tempts Providence by running a People's Theatre in London.

Finally, no summary of the 1921 season at the Prince of Wales Theatre would be complete without reference to Sir Nigel Playfair's production of *The Beggar's Opera,* in which Pitt Chatham, as Captain Macheath, played the part last assumed in Birmingham forty years earlier by Sims Reeves.

P.R.'s plan for the Royal was to rely not so much on personality attractions as on musical comedies, straight dramas and comedies, and a few spectacular pieces such as *The Garden of Allah* (in which Henry Hallatt and Nell Carter came for a fortnight), *The Bird of Paradise, The Voice from the Minaret,* and *Peri, the Slave of Love.*

Plays presented under this plan included *Sweet Nell of Old Drury*, with Julia Neilson and Fred Terry in their time-honoured parts; *The Right to Strike*, which hit a topical note in May; *Kiki*, with Joan Clarkson, a musical version of *The Glad Eye; The Naughty Wife; Toto; Baby Mine; Remnant; The Skin Game; La Poupée; Three Wise Fools; Hindle Wakes; French Leave; A Safety Match* (which, since *Tilly of Bloomsbury* was at the Prince of Wales, made two Ian Hay plays in town simultaneously); *Bulldog Drummond*, most desperate of modern dramas; and *Romance*, with Tittell-Brune as La Cavallini.

MATHESON LANG

My love to Phyllis
& Louis
Bobbie Allandale

FRED ALLANDALE

CHAPTER 26

(1921-22)

The Queen of Hearts; Fred Allandale, G. S. Melvin, Harry Weldon—"Cardland Castle," "The Pageant of the Seasons," "The Tournament"—The
Tragedy of Allandale—1922 Season—The "commercial" theatre—Lawrence Levy's book—Royal pantomime reminiscences.

PANTOMIME 1921-22
THE QUEEN OF HEARTS

The fateful pantomime *The Queen of Hearts* was produced
by Philip Rodway on Boxing Day, 1921; the first presentation since 1883, nearly forty years before, when Charles
(Monte Carlo) Coborn and Letty Lind were the stars. P.R.
had only the nursery rhyme jingle on which to work, but he
saw therein the germ of a dramatic story, and from this he
cultivated a pantomime which for its ingenuity, its blend of
the novel with the traditional, its brilliance of scene and
costume, and above all its profusion of actable parts, has
never been surpassed.

For the Queen he engaged Fred Allandale, already known
locally through his performances in *Little Miss Muffet* and *The
Babes in the Wood.* With him in mind, P.R. created a wonderful part, writing a book which revolved round such a "dame"
as had never before been played—charming, cultured, and
debonair—an entirely new departure, unique in the annals
of pantomime. There was only one man who could play it
as he meant it to be played, and that was "Bobbie" Allandale.

P.R. conceived the idea that the Joker, who is always
getting left out of the case when the pack is put away, should
retaliate upon his fifty-two card companions, whom he blames
for the carelessness of ordinary mortals. For fifty weeks and
two his magical powers shall transform them into mortals.
"Then, when they've learned to like the joke too well, I'll
bring them back; and so—I cast the spell!"

Straightway there rise the enchanted battlements of Cardland Castle; music sounds dimly in the distance, nearer now,
and clearer; the great door swings open, the drawbridge is

lowered, and in brilliant array there marches forth the entire
pack of gloriously coloured cards.

Entry of the Boyards, Johan Halvorsen

"Shuffle; cut; deal; play;" and the King and Queen of
Hearts, establishing their court in mediaeval splendour, themselves play an intriguing and perfectly accurate game with
their living subjects—a pageant in itself.

And now the Queen of Hearts hands round her celebrated
tarts, which to-day—May Day—have the power of causing
love at first sight. A visiting prince from the land of mortals
falls in love with Maid Margery, the village Queen of the
May—but so does the Knave of Hearts, and the latter, as
the rejected suitor, does his best to get rid of his rival, first
by making magical tarts (but his incantations go wrong), and
next by fighting him in a tournament, where he again fails.

No demon, no fairy, as you see, but a Joker to start the
action moving, and a Gipsy Queen to keep the influence at
work. (Here Pershore-on-Avon again supplied a motif, for
we remember watching with Daddy a gipsy encampment by
the side of the river, and his saying "That's given me an
idea! I'm going to try a new kind of fairy queen for the next
pantomime.") She takes the side of the Knave, and leads
him on, but he must win his lady within the fifty-two weeks
of his mortal existence, and to enable him to realise what
this means there is a lovely ballet of the seasons as the finale
to the first half.

"Three of the scenes," said "R.C.R." "are as fine as

anything that has ever been seen in Birmingham—certainly in the two chief London pantomimes of this year there is only one scene to compare with any one of the three, let alone the others."

The first of these was the decorative Cardland Castle, designed by Paul Shelving, who has since become famous in the world of theatrical art, and who was at that time (1921) the scenic designer at the Birmingham Repertory Theatre.

The second was the exquisite Pageant of the Seasons, painted by W. R. Young. Spring dawned with the witchery of the woodlands in lilac-time; then it was summer, with the rising sun, and roses in bloom; next an autumn sunset, with dull red poppies and sheaves of golden corn; and lastly winter, with its ice and snow, and scarlet-coated children at their invigorating play. Movement and lighting effects were exactly synchronised, working up to the last brilliance, when the sparkles of frost on the branches glowed more and more brightly into a blaze of light.

The third was the great Tournament Scene by Bruce Smith which opened the second half. Here was a fascinating set, true to period down to the minutest detail, most intricate in its actual working, and most ingenious in design. Every bit of scenery, cloths, flats, and borders, was painted on both sides, so that in the twinkling of an eye, during the storm which the Curse invoked, the stately castle was reduced to complete ruin, and crumbling stonework and broken walls showed where before had been ramparts and towers. It all took place before the eyes of the audience, at such a speed and with such perfect timing, that they actually *saw* the scene crashing into chaos before them.

And when the fury of the storm had passed, into the quiet which succeeded it came the final touch of artistry . . . against the evening sky a little flag was fluttering bravely from the ruined tower, the only moving thing in the stillness of the scene.

The Road by the Sea, with the ruins of the castle on the distant hillside, led to The Bewitched House (J. S. Riches),

both novel and amusing; over The Common, with its delightful background; to the finale at the Carnival revels, a scene
reminiscent of Watteau or Fragonard. Such was the setting
of the pantomime which, great though it undoubtedly was,
would have been finer still but for the tragedy which befell.

On the night of December 22nd, after a splendid rehearsal,
on his way home in the car, Daddy dropped Allandale at
his flat in Edgbaston. Almost the eve of Christmas, it was a
brilliant night, crisp and clear, the sky full of stars, and they
enthusiastically talked over the opening scene with its first
song, *Silver Star*.

*   *   *

The next morning the company assembled for rehearsal.
"Everyone here?" asked Daddy.

A little murmur ran round.

"Allandale's not come yet. . . ."

"He's sure to be here soon; we'll start without him."
Another five minutes passed. Daddy looked at his watch.
It was the first time he had ever known "Bobbie" Allandale
late. The old stage door keeper, Hall, appeared, and spoke
a word or two to Daddy in an undertone. Very quietly
P.R. turned to the company. "Go on without me," he told
them, and he and Hall left the stage together.

Later he rang through to home. We two heard Mother
answer, and gathered that something dreadful had happened;
imagined scenery collapsed, someone injured—perhaps Daddy
himself? Then, her face very white, she came in and told
us. *Bobbie Allandale had died in his sleep.*

We two cried hopelessly all morning. There on our bedside
table was the box of chocolates he had sent us only the day
before, with the photograph (which we reproduce), a little
note in pencil on the back: "A few chocs, with Uncle
Bobbie's love."

Daddy himself rang off from speaking to Mother and went
back to the waiting company on the stage. When he broke
the news to them he was almost the only one there to keep

his head; but amid his grief at the tragedy, which meant the loss of a close personal friend, and at the same time the removal of the key figure of his pantomime at the last moment, he could not neglect his duty to the public.

It is an axiom of the profession that whatever happens the curtain must go up. For a good many producers it would have been too much, and perhaps no one outside his own family knew what the effort cost him, but immediately he set humming the telephone wires between Birmingham and London, in pursuance of the quest for that most elusive entity, a dame comedian of good standing who was disengaged, or could anyhow be secured, on the eve of pantomime. At the dress rehearsal the part of the Queen was sketched by Sidney Russell, who was cast for the Joker, and P.R. (who for one desperate moment had contemplated playing Allandale's part himself, whose every line he had written and knew so well) spoke the Joker's lines. His quest was successful, for the theatre must never fail to accomplish these apparent miracles. Eddie Garr, an Old Edwardian, was found by telephone, brought to Birmingham post haste, acquired a nodding acquaintance with the lines, and on the opening night took the stage as the Queen of Hearts.

"On with the show!"

Without any attempt to force the note, Eddie Garr's quiet restraint was a good foil for the mercurial humour of G. S. Melvin as the King of Hearts. That amusing monarch was played on individual lines, and his dancing, "like an inspired puppet," was at once droll and graceful—a masterpiece of lightfooted agility. One of his biggest song-hits was the irresistible *I said, "Cheerio!"*

Harry Weldon, as the Knave of Hearts, became an appealing fellow, far from knavish at heart, but with an infinite capacity for making blunders. Yet nothing was overdone, not even his catchwords "S'no use," or "S'long, boys, see you soon," with their quaint whistling sibilants. His attempts to make his own tarts from the Gipsy's magical recipe, where he entangled himself and everything on the stage with real dough, were diverting in the extreme, as was his "grate fite" in the Tournament scene, aided by the unwilling horse, Milk-o.

What a shock must artists have had who came with a penchant for one particular form of dress, when directed by Philip Rodway! If the scene was mediaeval, with a tournament in progress, as in *The Queen of Hearts*, then the chorus dresses were copies of old pictures, and Harry Weldon must be in jerkin and hose. One may have said all this precise attention to detail was unnecessary and unheeded, but to P.R. it was the most essential part of production. If genius is an infinite capacity for taking pains, he had it. One evening at home he told us with tremendous pleasure that he had had property falcons made, so that one of the pages could carry them while mingling with the throng, and give the authentic touch.

Only an artist would have conceived such an idea, only a mind akin to Oliver Messel's would have troubled to see it carried out. They both blended the three things: the fantastic, the period, the topical touch. (For example, Evelyn Laye, in Oliver Messel's London production of *Helen*, was beautifully gowned in a Greek period dress, with a Mercury cap and a little suitcase in white and blue with her initials emblazoned on it.) Harry Weldon perhaps wishes to retain his bowler with his jerkin and hosen? Well, he may, as long as he sticks a fifteenth-century feather in it, so that he may look a kind of Henry VII* buffoon; but as for letting the Prince enter the lists in a particularly attractive suit of even 1600, no!

Partly it was P.R.'s own well-ordered mind that refused to allow glaring irrelevancies of attire or plot to creep into his pantomimes, and partly a sense that, pantomimes being primarily for children, a child's mind asks "Why?" Never was anything approaching revue sequence allowed. If the Knave and the Prince were to have a back-chat number in

---

*Cards were introduced into England in the reign of Henry VII, and the court cards wear the dress of that period.

a front-cloth scene, well, there were a few lines to lead away from the plot, explain their presence there, and lead them back into the story when their interlude was over.

Billie Browne (nowadays Adrienne Brune), in mediaeval robes, was a distinctly unusual type of principal girl, fresh from her musical comedy triumphs in *Betty* and *Irene*. Christine Roy played the Prince, with a handsome presence and a fine voice, her *Silver Star* and *Avalon* songs two of the best numbers in the pantomime.

The Brothers Griffiths, as Dilly and Dally, were always hilariously amusing, and they have never excelled their caricature of the horse Milk-o, an animal with sagacious eyes, who "pranced and danced and caracoled and curvetted" till one was literally limp with laughter.

Nina Lynn made an impressive Gipsy Queen; the Dainty Danes danced like silent clockwork, and there was also some beautiful dancing by Mdlle. Listakova, of the Russian Ballet.

P.R.'s Anniversary night proved something more than the usual tribute. Besides the principals, visiting artists who appeared included Malcolm Scott, Dick Tubb, J. H. Scotland, and Harry Barrett. As P.R. explained in his speech, the pantomime had been produced under exceptionally difficult circumstances, for the tragedy two days before production had pulled down a structure to the making of which had gone nine months' hard work. By the loyal co-operation of everyone concerned, he said, the difficulties had been overcome, and the pantomime had run with the utmost smoothness and success. The members of the company are always before the public; the essential work for which the staff "behind" are responsible finds but impersonal recognition, and so here he created a precedent by introducing to the audience the scene-painter, the property master, the carpenter, and other functionaries who had never previously faced the footlights. Jack Riches, the "props" in question, recalls with evident delight that when his turn came P.R. announced, "Ladies and gentlemen, it gives me great pleasure to introduce to you my property master, Mr. Riches. He has made all the properties out of his own head, and has enough wood left to make a wheelbarrow."

* * *

That pantomime season of 1921-22 was a tragic one for Daddy and Mother, who lost several of their oldest friends within a few weeks. Fred Allandale's death was of course deeply felt by all the pantomime people, and indeed by most of Birmingham's theatre-going public. Then Mrs. Captain Rodgers died, the widow of the Captain Rodgers who had been proprietor and manager of the Prince of Wales Theatre until 1897. (Oscar Pollack, the distinguished critic, in *The Playgoer* of twenty years earlier, wrote "Captain Rodgers had in Mrs. Rodgers a valuable adviser, who by her excellent taste and judgment materially helped to make the panto-mimes a success.") We still see her daughter in her box at the Prince of Wales Theatre—sometimes accompanied by her son, Godfrey Winn, one of the brilliant coterie of young writers of to-day; and we still meet her stately little white-haired sister, Mrs. Cassera,* at the theatre or at her home in Harborne Road. The Rodgers family still own the lease of the Prince of Wales Theatre.

Another well-known stage figure who took his last call about this date was Sir John Hare. James W. Tate, the fine pianist and composer of most of his wife's (Clarice Mayne's) songs, died on February 5th; he was the celebrated "That" of their double music-hall turn, in which, at the piano, he accompanied her singing. He caught a chill, insisted on travelling to Stoke-on-Trent on business, developed pneumonia and died there within the week, aged only 46.

Season 1922

Again the Prince of Wales Theatre carried its Christmas attraction well into the New Year. This time the musical comedy was *Mary*, a piece liberally endowed with melodious

Since died, autumn, 1934.

songs by Louis A. Hirsch, and presented by Alfred Butt in conjunction with Macdonald and Young. The principals were Sally Thomas, George Vollaire, May Marton, Stephanie Stephens, Fred Leslie, Percy le Fre, Bert Evremonde, Decima and Eddie McLean, and Percy Parsons, the last-named making the hit of the show with his song *Deeper*.

Mary ran to the end of January, and was followed by Percy Hutchison and Marie Hemingway in a new piece *In Nelson's Days*. Next came Bransby Williams, doubling Peggotty and Micawber in *David Copperfield*, and giving a fine study of Fagin in *Oliver Twist*. It was now that he and P.R. got together over Bransby's long-cherished ambition to play *Hamlet*, an ambition which, as we shall chronicle, was fulfilled a year later.

The Royal, where *The Queen of Hearts* closed its run on March 4th, launched its spring season with a return of *The Maid of the Mountains*, in which José Collins played her original part, Teresa, with a magnificent supporting cast, including Bertram Wallis, Peter Gawthorne, Faith Bevan, Edward D'Arcy, Alfred Wellesley, and Mabel Sealby.

A Royal Divorce, then in its thirty-first year of tour, came for Easter. Violet Vanbrugh appeared in *The Knave of Diamonds*, and Cyril Maude brought a young actress of great promise, named Binnie Hale, in Ben Travers' *The Dippers*. Other stars seen during the once-nightly season at the Royal were Ethel Irving in *Renovating Eve*, and Gerald Lawrence (his first visit for several years) with Madge Compton and Roy Byford in Louis N. Parker's *Mr. Garrick*. Probably the best play of the season was Clemence Dane's *A Bill of Divorcement*.

During the same period the Prince of Wales Theatre concentrated mainly on musical shows—*Gabrielle*, *The Lady of the Rose*, C. B. Cochran's *League of Notions* revue, *The Gipsy Princess*, *Sally*, and *The Lilac Domino* (with Jamieson Dodds, Clara Butterworth, and Arthur Riscoe). Straight fare, nevertheless, was not neglected, for Henry Ainley appeared in *Uncle Ned*, Ruby Miller in *The Edge o' Beyond*, Diana

z

Bourbon and Henry Hallatt in *Woman to Woman*, and Edmund Gwenn in *Old Bill, M.P.* The author, Captain Bruce Bairnsfather, famous for his war-time cartoons in *The Bystander*, made a personal appearance each night in the *Old Bill* fortnight.

Then there was a three-weeks' Shakespeare season by Henry Baynton. The leading lady this time was Robert Courtneidge's daughter Rosaline (who a few years later married Peter Haddon, and died just after the birth of her baby).

The Macdona Players, in a series of plays by George Bernard Shaw, were installed by P.R. for three weeks, and gave Birmingham its first view of *Pygmalion*. They were an excellent combination, headed by Florence Jackson and George S. Wray—but audiences, though enthusiastic, were distressingly small as a rule.

At the annual meeting in July, when a profit of £3,954 was disclosed and a dividend of 15 per cent. paid, Philip Rodway was congratulated by the Board, particularly on the success achieved by the pantomime under great initial difficulties.

P.R., after reviewing the seasons at the two theatres, made one of his most widely-quoted speeches. He justifiably claimed that every section of playgoers had been borne in mind, with the pantomime, the Shakespeare season, Dickens, Grand Opera, Gilbert and Sullivan, and, most recently, the Shaw season.

"A great deal of nonsense," he went on, "is talked and written from time to time about the 'commercial' theatre. It is a little amusing at times to hear of certain 'high-brows' talking about Art and the Drama as if they had just invented them. Without the much-derided 'commercial' theatre the public would have no chance of seeing some of our greatest actors, plays, and a multitude of operatic and other performances, which, by reason of the great expense involved in creating them, could only be played in such theatres.

"The commercial theatre, I suppose, may be said to be a theatre which expects to get a fair return in exchange, as in our case, for the expenditure involved. The first Theatre Royal opened its doors in 1774, and I imagine it was a commercial theatre in the same sense as the present theatre in 1922. I do feel that the commercial theatre should at least be free from the criticism of people to whom it has been a source of use and profit."

This outspoken declaration, coming from one who so rarely plunged publicly into controversy, was warmly applauded by many theatre-lovers who had grown tired of hearing eminent performers, dramatists, critics, and others denouncing the institution from which they derived a handsome sustenance.

"When we consider the relevant facts," wrote one of Birmingham's soundest observers, "we can sympathise heartily with Mr. Rodway's spirited little defence of the much-derided commercial theatre. Personally, I think he might have pitched it a little more defiantly and taken even higher ground. . . .

"The danger throughout the history of the Theatre Royal has not been the lack of capital to establish the theatre, but the possibility that it might not pay its way. There have been periods, I believe, in the history of the old house, when successive managers found themselves in parlous straits, and the only thing that kept it alive was the ability to 'make the ghost walk' at the end of the week. When this was happily the case, it has always been done by skilful management, both in the actual economy of the house and in studying the public taste in order to obtain the necessary support.

"It is chiefly due to this, rather than to Birmingham's overpowering desire to support the drama, that the Theatre Royal Ltd. is now in such a sound position. By the skilful choice of a programme to suit all classes of playgoers; by the exploitation of the twice-nightly system, which has enabled the theatre to carry on during the dead season, and so keep the theatre-going habit alive; and by the success of the Christmas pantomime, the Theatre Royal has become one of the soundest concerns of its kind, and its results this year are in consequence a pleasant contrast to those of most other provincial theatres.

"This is a matter for congratulation to all playgoers, since the stability, success, and good management of the company have a decided influence on the fare we receive. The best actors, managers, and entrepreneurs are not prepared to leave London to

visit ill-attended, badly-managed, insecure establishments; but
under the present conditions they are always anxious to come to
Birmingham. That they do so because they make a profit here is a
matter of course, but why should we object to that if we get our
money's worth in return? They would not come if it did not pay
them, and even a great artist must live, which means he must
make money by his art. So let us not talk too much nonsense
about the 'commercial' theatre. After all, the Globe in which
Shakespeare was so largely interested and where he made a
handsome fortune, was a 'commercial' theatre, which owed its
success to the poet's skill in giving the public what it liked."

*   *   *

The chief event of the summer of 1922 at the Royal was
the world première, on August 28th, of *The Return*, a comedy
turned into English by Arthur Wimperis, from the French of
Robert de Flers and François de Croisset. Here we saw
English acting at its very best, as was only to be expected
from a team comprising Marie Lohr, George Tully, Dion
Boucicault, Alfred Bishop, Lottie Venne, and Jack Hobbs.

The Royal this year also had Iris Hoey in *Clothes and the
Woman;* José Collins, Billy Leonard, Bertram Wallis, Amy
Augarde, Vesta Sylva, and Kingsley Lark in *The Last Waltz;*
Julia Neilson as Mary Queen of Scots and Fred Terry as
Bothwell in their new play, *The Borderer;* Harry Welchman
(in Birmingham for the first time in fifteen years) in *The Lady
of the Rose;* Martin Harvey in a round of old favourites; and
a week of Carl Rosa operas.

The same six months at the Prince of Wales Theatre saw
Dennis Neilson-Terry and his wife, Mary Glynne, in the first
Birmingham performances of *Down and Out;* Harry Green in
Welcome Stranger; Owen Nares, Marie Polini (Mrs. Nares), and
Grace Lane in *If Winter Comes;* a return of *The Beggar's Opera*
(then in its third year at the Lyric, Hammersmith), with Gordon
Sherry as Macheath, Rose Hignell as Polly Peachum, and
Dorothy Gill (later to succeed Bertha Lewis with the D'Oyly
Carte organisation) as Lucy Locket. The first season locally
of the British National Opera Company, Joyce Barbour in

Sally, Phyllis Neilson-Terry and Ion Swinley in James Bernard Fagan's *The Wheel* (her first venture in management), Vernon Sylvaine (in recent years the Repertory Theatre's popular leading man) in *The Naughty Wife*, and Jack Hulbert, Cicely Courtneidge, and—smaller type in those days—Bobby Howes in *Pot Luck*.

Times were becoming very hard throughout England, and not least in Birmingham, and one night in December saw a big combined effort by the Birmingham theatres to help the Lord Mayor's Unemployment Relief Fund. The Town Hall was taken for an all-star concert, for which the orchestras of P.R.'s two theatres were amalgamated, and the Royal contributed turns by Billy Merson, Susie Belmore, May Carpenter, and the Hanlon Brothers.

*   *   *

In 1922 a book of Birmingham Theatrical Reminiscences, 1870-1920, by the late Lawrence Levy, was published, and in Daddy's presentation copy was inscribed:

> "To Philip Rodway, with E. Lawrence Levy's kindest regards, along with the hearty recognition of the fact that it was entirely due to his—Mr. Rodway's—generous co-operation that the publication of the book was possible.   May, 1922."

Under the heading "Pantomime at the Theatre Royal," he gives some of "R.C.R.'s" reminiscences, as contained in the following letter, which, since it refers so often and so directly to P.R., we beg leave to include as a valuable addition:

"My dear Lawrence Levy,

"Why will people always ask us which is the best pantomime we have seen, instead of which is the worst? I think I know. Memory is like 'a sundial that counts alone the happy hours': we remember our entertainments by their pleasures, and forget their *longueurs*, while the

> Silver bells and cockle shells
> And pretty maids all a-row

at most hover in the shy and soft twilight that is between remembrance and oblivion.

"I am glad you have narrowed me to the pantomimes of this century at the Theatre Royal. *Dick Whittington*, the last Christmas pantomime of an unbroken line of sixty to be performed in the old playhouse, whose walls had stood since 1774, was the last in many ways—the last in the building, the last of the nineteenth century, the last of the Victorian era, the last in which Vesta Tilley played.

"So I am to consider a new theatre, a new century, a new era, and (I think) a new man, Philip Rodway. He was not, of course, a novice even then, but he took chance by the forelock in reshaping a disorderly pantomime, *The Babes in the Wood*, of 1904, with Bert Gilbert, Phyllis Dare, and Maidie Andrews, and this first piece in the new theatre established him as a producer.

"The New Royal pantomimes fall into two periods, the out-break of war showing a definite cleavage. Taking your cue of 'the best,' I find that the principal boys whom I liked best in the first period were Ada Reeve, Carrie Moore, and Sybil Arundale; in the second Clarice Mayne, I think, was incomparable and inimitable, in pantomime, as in musical comedy, where I should place her level with Evie Greene, and ahead of the rest of their time. Her personality amounted to genius, both in *Aladdin* (1905) and in *Jack and the Beanstalk* (1909). Carrie Moore, bright and bustling, was more delightful as Prince Charming in *Cinderella* (1907) than in *Aladdin* (1910). The Cinderella to whom she played was the seventeen-year-old Phyllis Dare, but the colours, never bright, have faded from my memory, and I remember only the jovial comedy of John Humphries and Dan Rolyat. Sybil Arundale gave a definite impersonation of Dick Whittington (1908) as the poor neglected 'prentice of the old tale—an impersonation which was full of dramatic force, and at times very touching, yet Tom Foy's Idle Jack was not a good contrast.

"After Dan Rolyat and Humphries (how funnily they clowned on the steps 'after the ball'), the best pair of comedians in the first period were John Humphries and Wilkie Bard, in *Jack and Jill* (1911). The best boy and girl combination, with vivacity contrasted with demureness, were Nelly Wigley and Maie Ash, in *Goody Two Shoes* (1912), and Ella Retford and Maidie Scott in *Miss Muffet* (1913). But if I am to avoid a catalogue of names, though these will set tongues a-wagging round a winter fire, I must mention the name I have deliberately avoided, our illustrious comedian, George Robey. Was he in Birmingham in the winter 'when Aston Villa won the League and the Cup?'—that Hegira of local chronology. I am not sure, but it was about that time when he became one of the three Gods of Birmingham—Joseph Chamberlain, Aston Villa, and George Robey—and George was never a jealous god, but always assiduously and felicitously joked about *ses frères aînés*. . . .

"And then again in *Sinbad!* George Robey as Mr. Tinbad, and Fred Emney as Mrs. Tinbad! I think the best tribute I can pay to this couple is that I wished Sir Herbert Tree would have had the courage to stage *Romeo and Juliet* with Emney as the Nurse and Robey as Peter. For both of them had the Elizabethan spirit, and could have found the Elizabethan manner, and they could have been, had they wished, great comedians instead of great comics. I am a sworn enemy to the male Dame (and Philip Rodway has more recently given the parts to actresses like Minnie Rayner), but Fred Emney was beyond the reach of prejudice. . . .

"Philip Rodway is almost the last of the local producers who stand apart from any syndicate. He aims, not pedantically, at a coherent story, treating a pantomime as a play with a fable and characters. The change is slow and the way is hard, but even where, by the exigence of conditions, he had to rebuild on another foundation (as I think in the 'Merson and Mayne' pantomimes, *Dick Whittington*, *The House that Jack Built*, and *Cinderella*), he has really rebuilt, and not merely patched. Of Billy Merson I am a great admirer, for his talent of touching a mock-heroic or mock-sympathetic sentiment is rare, and he wears costumes with an innate sense of caricature second only to Robey's. I hope one day Philip Rodway will complete his emancipation from tradition —or, rather, return to the pre-Victorian tradition of melodrame— by producing *Dick Whittington* with Billy Merson as Dick.

"You will see that the cloven hoof of the dramatic critic will keep pushing out under the chronicler's robe, because I think, after all, the best pantomime I have seen has not been with these mortal eyes, but in my own fancy. And I daresay Philip Rodway would say the same thing, for he takes pantomime seriously.

"Yours very truly,

"R. CROMPTON RHODES."

CHAPTER 27

(1922-24)

Puss in Boots, 1922-23; Billy Merson and Dick Tubb—"The Old-world Garden"—1923 Season—Sybil Thorndike's *Medea*—Bransby Williams' *Hamlet*—The annual meeting—P.R. and the "Highbrows"—An insight into the cash takings—*Aladdin*, 1923-24; Lupino Lane, G. S. Melvin, Elsie Prince—Special matinée—1924 Season—The Astaires in *Stop Flirting*—First visit of "The Co-optimists"—The Zeitlin Story.

PANTOMIME 1922-23
PUSS IN BOOTS

Puss in Boots, which Philip Rodway chose for this year's subject, had not been done since 1862. The long interval is a little surprising, in view of the fact that the Perrault story of the Marquis de Carabas and his intelligent feline friend is a relatively complete one, with much more incident on which to frame a pantomime plot than is found in most nursery rhyme themes.

In repairing the omission after sixty years, P.R. commissioned from F. Maxwell-Stewart a book which paid exemplary attention to the original narrative of *Le maistre chat ou le chat botté*, yet succeeded in capturing the true spirit of pantomime. Clifford Harris wrote the lyrics, and the music, as had become almost a tradition, was "composed, selected, and arranged" by James W. Tate and Harry Rushworth. Dances and ensembles were by John Roker, with Martin Adeson as stage-manager, while Dolly Tree designed the costumes, and Oswald Williams, the famous illusionist, invented special magical effects for the scene in the dungeons. A platoon of scenic artists was composed of W. R. Young, Marc Henri, Philip Howden, George Harris, and Ernest Howard.

Billy Merson, on his third visit, proved himself one of the first comedians of his day. It was a surprise to most people to hear that P.R. was going to play him as the cat, but the outcome fully justified the choice. No one who saw that pantomime will forget Billy's extraordinary evolution from completely feline, through the floundering stage of half-human, half-feline, to full human form, as the magic boots worked their wonders upon him. He was not the first leading comedian to play Puss, for (as "R.C.R." reminds us) Charles Matthews himself had set a fashion often followed; but no star of past pantomimes could have managed more adroitly and more funnily this extremely difficult rôle.

Once humanised, of course, Billy had full licence to indulge his penchant for adopting quaint and varied disguises. He was a dashing Hussar, singing about *The Portrait of the Girl I left behind me;* an ancient Roman smiting his lyre in honour of a Persian charmer somewhat inconsequentially named *"Desdemonia";* next a Russian dancer, Madame Anita in her dignified moments, Annie from Brierley Hill to her friends. In these and other characterisations he surpassed even his earlier successes, and *Desdemonia,* with its catchy, swinging tune, became the song of the year.

Colin, the hero, was brightly played by Susie Belmore, in what was her first attempt at a principal boy's part. She did well with three songs of American type, *Off to Carolina in the Morning, Shufflin' Along,* and *The Midnight Choo-choo,* in which the chorus assisted to original effect. May Carpenter was a graceful principal girl, experienced in musical comedy. To her fell the inevitable song of the season, this time *Hiawatha's Melody of Love,* and she contrived to make it sound unhackneyed.

A new dame, so far as the Royal was concerned, was Dick Tubb, a tall fellow with a humorous, "elastic" face, a wonderfully mobile mouth, a rich fund of comic invention, and an undoubted talent for acting. He presented a pantomime queen which was a really clever study.

Another good performance was that of Eddie Jaye as King Sollum, the monarch who could not laugh. Here was quite a new sort of pantomime baron, with lugubrious humour in every stolid feature as he moped his way through the show, steadfastly refusing to yield the glimmer of a laugh until the joyful moment when the ogre's bogeymen carried off his oppressive spouse. We shall always remember with appreciation the picture of quaint little King Sollum at his knitting.

The Hanlon Brothers, well-named Silence and Shadow, were pantomimists in the almost forgotten sense of the term, dumb-show actors such as Birmingham had not seen for years. All that they did was enhanced by their identical make-up, their striking scarlet suits, and the marvellous precision of their simultaneous step-dancing.

Reginald Crompton (the Ogre), Zelinda Davis (a fairy Queen who could speak lines), and Yvonne Winifred (a graceful dancer) were others who did well in this pantomime.

Some of the scenic effects were exceptionally beautiful, particularly the country sets, dear to Daddy's heart as reminiscent of his beloved villages. But it was the Old-world Garden, at the end of the first half, which was his special favourite. Quietly, with the sound of a song of eventide, the words drifted across the footlights:

"*Not far away there stands an old-world garden,*
Sweet-scented flowers beside its pathways grow,
There in the shade, a lady old and weary
Sits all alone, and dreams of long ago. . . ."

We know that Daddy had enshrined there, against a visionary background of our Woodlands garden, a picture of his own mother, then in her 83rd year, and a memory of mother's mother, who had died that September. The whole scene, round the central figure of a white-haired old lady seated in a garden chair, was a tribute to age, and the serene beauty of the after-glow of life.

The setting for this exquisite series of garden transformation scenes was one of the most delightful things that Daddy ever devised or W. R. Young painted. As the children danced their way through among the living roses and lilies, they might have found their flowers for Granny's posy on the canvas itself, for they almost literally blossomed there.

In quite a different key, appealing essentially to the youngest there, was the finale of the second half—The Candy Cave, where every possible kind of lollipop and chocolate came to life, to the delight of all the little boys and girls in the audience.

For P.R.'s Anniversary celebrations on March 7th there was a fine list of extra turns. Georgie Wood came specially from Manchester, Lupino Lane from London, and among others there were G. H. Elliott, Arthur Prince, Jack Lane, Teddy Stream, and the Dominion Singers.

Greeted by audience and company alike with the singing of *For he's a jolly good fellow*, he received various presentations; this was the opportunity for Billy Merson, handing him a gold watch with a platinum and gold chain, to announce that the latter was for the pass door! (the door dividing the stage from the front of the house, about which, as you may recall, Daddy had a very firm rule).

Puss pulled on his magic boots for the last time on March 10th, and the pantomime was then completing its 109th performance.

*   *   *

On February 23rd Philip Rodway arranged a matinée performance of the *Medea* of Euripides, in Professor Gilbert Murray's translation, which furnished a profound contrast to the jollities of pantomime. Sybil Thorndike, the greatest tragic actress of the day, played Medea, with Frank Cellier as Creon, Lawrence Anderson as Jason, and Lewis Casson (Sybil Thorndike's husband and producer) as the messenger. P.R., as may be imagined, was delighted to have so distinguished a matinée at the Royal, but he did not expect to make a financial success of it. To him it was one of those luxuries which a profitable pantomime justified.

For probably the only time on record, his assessment of box office value was slightly out. Almost always he could foretell how much was going to be in the house on any given occasion. Once, as a test, he wrote down beforehand the figures he estimated for every individual performance of a twice-nightly week of thirteen shows—and on the entire week he was only out by a matter of shillings. On this occasion, however, Tom Kealey, Dame Thorndike's manager at the time, recalls how he secured percentage terms which gave him practically all the takings above a figure which Daddy assured him could never be approached, let alone passed. In the result, the house was packed to suffocation, the players were recalled fourteen times at the close, and Mr. Kealey walked off with a cheque for an unbelievable sum!

Here is another little percentage story on a rather different basis. We heard it in this way. When Seymour Hicks was playing at the Prince of Wales Theatre in *It's You I Want* last November (1933), on the night that we were there he sent his manager, Harry Hardy, round to the box with a charming message to say how glad he was to see us at the theatre again. In the few remaining minutes of the interval Mr. Hardy began to speak of Daddy, and though he did not then know of this memoir, in that short conversation he told us feelingly and appreciatively how much his name had stood for in the profession. He related how, some years before, Seymour Hicks had been appearing at one of P.R.'s theatres, on a basis which gave Mr. Hicks an extra percentage if a certain figure were passed. At the end of the week the accounts were made up, and the margin of attainment was in the balance.

"Many another manager," said Mr. Hardy, "would have simply said 'Bad luck—pity you didn't quite manage it,' but not so P.R. He went straight round to Seymour Hicks, shook hands with him, and said 'Congratulations, old man! Very glad you've done it!'"

Season 1923

At the Prince of Wales Theatre the old year was seen out, the new year in, with a new type of musical comedy, *The Cousin from Nowhere*, which on Boxing Day, 1922, had its first presentation in England. It was adapted by Fred Thompson, with lyrics by Adrian Ross, from a book by Herman Haller and "Rideamus," the music being by Edward Kunneke. Its novelty lay in the fact that it was a musical comedy without a chorus!

Helen Gilliland's glorious voice made her one of the best musical comedy heroines in recent years, and Walter Williams, cool and debonair, was a capital hero. Jimmy Godden, handicapped by a not very funny part, was the chief comedian, and Cicely Debenham was a great addition to the comedy side.

The D'Oyly Carte Opera Company followed for a three weeks' season. Then came John Drinkwater's *Oliver Cromwell*, with Henry Ainley, Irene Rooke, the veteran Hayden Coffin, the late William J. Rea, and Milton Rosmer, Murray Kinnell, Harcourt Williams, Mary O'Farrell, and Algernon Blackwood in the fine cast.

In March came Bransby Williams' short-lived but none the less famous excursion into Shakespeare, planned with P.R. a year earlier. For the first week of his fortnight he provided two spectacular *tours de force*, the doubling of Peggotty and Micawber in *David Copperfield*, and of Dubosc and Lesurques in *The Lyons Mail*. The second week he played *Hamlet*.

In the course of twelve months' preparation for this gallant venture he had worked out a boldly original version, in which Hamlet's first speech was the soliloquy "To be or not to be"—for, as he argued, a fellow simply couldn't talk about "the undiscovered country from whose bourn no traveller returns" *after* he had seen a ghost. He made various other striking alterations in the arrangement of the text, besides bringing forward the colloquy between Hamlet and Ophelia from the third to the second act, as in the first existing print of the play.

That this *Hamlet* was ever staged was entirely due to Daddy's encouraging attitude towards the famous expert in characterisations classical and modern. He "saw" Bransby Williams as Hamlet. He was, we believe, the only manager who did.

A week before the eventful first night Bransby undertook (*via* the *Birmingham Mail*) "to give the critics something to think about, and the public a new conception of the Prince of Denmark."

He went on:

"I am putting up a production sufficiently opulent for a twelve months' run in the West End, though actually it will be played, so far as I know at present, nowhere save in Birmingham for six nights and in Leicester for two.

"I have no other dates for it; the managers tell me I am too late; that so-and-so or such-a-one is before me with Shakespeare.

"Only in Birmingham, one of the last remaining dramatic centres outside London, have I received such encouragement as is necessary before one dare even begin to fit oneself for saying the lines of Hamlet, let alone producing the play.

Birmingham asked me for a *Hamlet*, and after twelve months' continuous preparation I am ready to obey. In passing, it is twenty-three years, I fancy, since this play was last done by one man for six consecutive nights."

For Birmingham read Philip Rodway.

He was predisposed towards any Shakespeare venture, always alert for any opportunity of helping a touring management to put up a production. He was a great admirer of Bransby's studies of Dickensian and other characters, and fully expected that the brilliance of these individual cameos would be transferred to the larger canvas.

On the Monday of production, all the principal newspapers were represented. On the Tuesday they nearly all fell on Bransby Williams. They dealt with him after their kind, some gently, some wittily, some brutally, some scornfully, but there was no ambiguity about the verdict.

Bransby will forgive our saying (because the critical verdict leaves us no option) that his special gifts could not be turned to advantage in such a performance, and the character of Hamlet became disproportionate to the production as a whole, so much larger than life-size did he play the part.

The show certainly went on and on. By the time it was over, most of the audience had gone home. Daddy stood with a friend near the orchestra rail towards the end, wondering what was going to happen to his licence, and how many taxis he would have to provide for his staff. As the curtain finally fell for the last time he regretfully murmured "It won't do, Bransby."

Doubtless it was the Birmingham notices which persuaded the Leicester management that Bransby would be better received in his indisputably brilliant characterisations of Mr. Micawber and Bill Sykes—so that his Shakespearean venture only existed under the aegis of Philip Rodway.

In *Peter Pan*, which visited the Prince of Wales Theatre as usual in the spring, Lionel Gadsden played Captain Hook. In our view the Old Etonian pirate has never been better represented than by Mr. Gadsden, who has played the part many hundreds, probably thousands, of times.

Derek Oldham and Winnie Melville came next in *Whirled into Happiness* (in which they were playing when their engagement to be married was announced); Henry Baynton (with Esmé Beringer, Rosaline Courtneidge, Kenneth Wicksteed, Basil Howes, etc.) in Shakespeare; the Macdona Players in Shaw; and another visit by the D'Oyly Carte Company helped to speed the coming of June.

Meanwhile the Royal's most interesting item, judged from this distance, was *The Merry Widow*, in which one Carl Brisson "a Danish gentleman who a few months ago spoke no word of English," was the Danilo to the Sonia of Evelyn Laye, "a beautiful young successor to Lily Elsie."

Another revival at the Royal was *Magda*, with Mrs. Patrick Campbell in the rôle she had played thirty years earlier. Two Charlot revues, *Snap* and *Pot Luck*, were given in June, with the inseparable song-writing duo, R. P. Weston and Bert Lee, supporting Jack Hulbert and Cicely Courtneidge in *Pot Luck*.

* * *

So we come to the annual meeting, with a net profit of £4,118, a dividend of 20 per cent., and a warning from Harry Lewis that things had begun to go badly! Tom B. Davis suggested that the latest competitor, wireless, would prove the most formidable, because it would keep people at home at night. He congratulated Philip Rodway on the resourcefulness which had resulted in the current balance sheet, adding that there was a dearth of new plays in London, and that P.R. had done wonders in keeping the theatres open all the year round.

Up rose Daddy, and delivered another of his rare assaults. It was a development of his theme at the previous annual meeting, when he expressed his opinion of those who were continually running down the "commercial" theatre, but this time he dealt particularly with the so-called *cognoscenti*—the highbrows—who, while paying lip-service to Art with a capital A, were conspicuous by their absence when the most worthy plays were presented.

"One of the greatest problems of the big provincial theatre is how profitably and creditably to carry on during the spring and summer seasons. We have endeavoured for some years to solve this annual difficulty by the creation of separate and regular seasons of Shakespeare, Dickens, and Shaw repertory. It is with very much regret that I am forced to the conclusion that for certain attractions Birmingham is as hopeless as ever. Shakespeare and Bernard Shaw do not meet in this city with anything approaching the response one would reasonably expect, and one of the most irritating features of this lack of support is the fact that such plays are not attended by the very section of the community to whom one would imagine they would most appeal.

"The highbrow student of the drama who affects to turn up his nose at the popular plays of the people—musical or otherwise—is the first to show his appreciation of our efforts in his direction by staying away. I think I am right in saying that Birmingham is the only provincial city with two first-class theatres open the entire year round. I have always said the theatre habit must be encouraged, in competition with other forms of amusement, and I have always endeavoured to see that the fare was worthy of the city. It is, however, heart-breaking, even with trade in its present state, to find the lack of interest, as evinced in the attendances during, for example, the Bernard Shaw season just concluded at the Prince of Wales Theatre. My difficulties in regard to arrangements with companies like the one mentioned are greatly increased when I endeavour to persuade them to play a similar season next year. They can rightly point out that this was the second Shaw season in two years. The excellent nature of the performances is admitted, but the Birmingham public will not support them, and therefore they must go to some other city whose public will do so. Nothing would please me better than to be able to give more of this class of fare, and I hope it will not be necessary to substitute other and less worthy bookings."

Again P.R. had an excellent press in response to his protest, though what he had said did not meet with entirely unreserved support. The *Birmingham Post* devoted half a leader to a discussion of "What is a highbrow?" and arrived at this conclusion:

"Broadly, we should say, the highbrow is the rather too consciously superior person who takes pride in being in the van of progress, and would find need to revise his ideas if he discovered they were being shared by the public at large.

"Such, then, is the class which (Mr. Rodway explains) absents itself from the theatre just when it really ought to muster in full force with shell-rimmed glasses complete. Why has it thus failed to appreciate separate and special seasons of Shakespeare, Dickens, and Shaw repertory? We should say, because the Shaw play which particularly interests your true highbrow at any given moment is the very newest play and none other; because Dickens was never a highbrow author, and also because Dickens's novels are altogether beyond the possibility of conversion into satisfactory plays of any class; and because the appeal of Shakespeare is an appeal to humanity at large, your highbrow recognising no special obligation to become enthusiastic over plain, straightforward Shakespearean productions, more or less upon traditional lines. (*Macbeth* played in modern dress, or *The Tempest* in a futurist setting, he may perhaps approve; but that is quite another thing.)

The theatrical correspondent of the *Birmingham Mail* observed that the obvious answer to P.R.'s protest against non-support was the twenty per cent. dividend, but that against this was to be set the fact that the money had been earned by the popular, rather than the artistic, portion of the year's programme.

"The success of such an enterprise," he went on, "should not be estimated on any particular week, but on the year. The Birmingham Theatre Royal, Limited, is not primarily a money-making affair; it was established at considerable expense and sacrifice on

AI

the part of the shareholders, to provide the city with a theatre worthy of its standing and tradition. To do this it is necessary that the enterprise should pay its way, and it is equally right that it should give its shareholders a fair return for their money. But that is not to say that every week should be a paying week. On the contrary it is part of the duty of a public-spirited management deliberately to play for a loss some weeks by the production of attractions which, by reason of their cost or limited appeal or both, cannot hope to recoup the management except in *kudos*. These things form that intangible thing, the 'goodwill' of the undertaking, since that rests largely on its reputation for giving the Birmingham public the best that is going, both from the popular and the artistic points of view.

"This, I am happy to think, is realised by the Theatre Royal management to the full. It is proved by the mere fact of the provision of special fare for such a limited section, and a glance at the fine list of attractions promised for the autumn shows that this policy is to be maintained—the 'best sellers' of the theatrical market being freely interspersed by pieces whose claims are on a higher artistic plane. The point I am trying to make, however, is that it is not recognised by the 'highbrow' critics of our commercial stage. If the management they are so constantly deriding were to be guided purely by the box office test, then it would no doubt be possible to make every week a paying week and pay a 40 per cent. dividend. But, to the credit of the Theatre Royal directorate, this policy is not followed, and this might well be remembered by the reformers the next time they voice their fulminations. Let them acknowledge what is done before they ask for more, or at any rate abstain from what is a flagrant misrepresentation of the 'commercial' theatre when applied locally.

"If they are not satisfied with the share of the annual programme they are given, it is their own fault, for I agree heartily with Mr. Rodway in his complaint that the 'highbrows' do not do their duty by the Birmingham managements.

"I am afraid the truth of the matter is that the 'highbrow' is a fraud as far as theatre-going is concerned. He or she is willing to talk, but not to act. The intellectuals of Birmingham do not even fill the tiny Repertory, let alone the mighty Royal. They stop away from Shakespeare and Shaw with one accord—but I bet they'll roll up in their thousands like the rest of us when Miss José Collins brings the new Gaiety piece next month."

So concluded the *Birmingham Mail* correspondent.

Philip Rodway, when invited by the *Mail* to wind up the general discussion, departed from his usual rule of refraining from expressing his views publicly because, as he wrote:

"I feel there is a certain, if small, section of the public who frequently misunderstand the position of the two Birmingham theatres in relation to the provision of theatrical fare. With your permission, therefore, I propose to state a few facts, which, when absorbed, will, I think, convince the most ardent playgoer, whether 'highbrow' or not, that my lament over the Shaw season this year, for example, was a justifiable one.

"I am in entire agreement with you when you state that the success of an enterprise like ours should not be estimated on any particular week or attraction, but on the year. Naturally, like every other concern, one has to take the rough with the smooth, and we have always been imbued with the desire to give the best possible theatrical fare in the theatres we control. The Shaw plays fall within the definition of the 'best possible,' and no real theatrical season can be deemed complete without the inclusion of some of this author's works.

"It was in dealing with the prospects for the current year that I made special reference to the Shaw season, and I feel perfectly certain in my own mind that the public have no idea of the terrible lack of support evinced in this great city of ours during that season. The receipts for the *entire first week* of seven performances by the Bernard Shaw Company at the Prince of Wales Theatre were £50 below the receipts of the D'Oyly Carte Opera Company for their *opening night*.

"When the Shaw Company, at the end of their season in Birmingham, went to Oxford, the receipts from the six perform-ances given there were easily more than the receipts for the first fortnight of fourteen performances in Birmingham. The Birming-ham record of the number of persons paying for admission for the first week was: Monday, 278; Tuesday 229; Wednesday 242; Thursday matinée 120; Thursday evening 310; Friday 340; Saturday 442. The press were unanimous in their praise of the performances.

"Some correspondents attempt to show that this is due to the prices charged, for no weather conditions have ever been more favourable to the theatre than this spring. Now with regard to prices, there is a range in operation from 1/- to 7/- (tax included), but to take one Shaw performance at random—the average being much the same the week through—out of the total of 229 persons present on the first Tuesday, 41 persons paid for the upper circle 2/-, plus tax 4d., and 24 persons for the dress circle and stalls 6/- (tax 1/-), but in the 5/- (tax 9d.) dress circle (the intermediate price that so many people seem to forget) there were only 2 seats taken, and in the balcony at 4/- (9d. tax) there were only 3 seats taken. In the pit stalls (of which there are 156) 15 seats only were taken. Of the 5/- (9d. tax) and 4/- (9d. tax) reserved seats, the week's record shows that the largest number of 5/- (tax 9d.) seats sold at any performance was 18; at one performance one was sold, and at another performance not one. Of the 4/- (tax 9d.) reserved seats 42 were sold during the entire week. I think these figures will show to any reasonable person that the non-success of the Shaw season was not due to the prices.

"May I add just a word or two about theatre prices? It is not my purpose or intention to enter into the question as to whether the amusement tax is a just or an unjust one, but I do wish gently to point out that we do not *retain* the tax, we merely *collect* it. In the days before the war it was a usual and customary thing, when certain big star attractions came round, for the prices to be raised, instead of our present custom of having a fixed scale of prices for every attraction throughout the year (with the single exception, of course, of the National Opera Company's visit). These prices for star attractions (it will probably surprise a great many people to know) were greater in the past than we receive for our star attractions now. It was not possible to book a seat for certain of these attractions under 6/-, and frequently some of the other prices were raised. This, I always felt, was a bad system, and it is no longer in operation. The scale of charges which we have allows the public (which has this autumn, for example, a London season to look forward to) an opportunity of going to the part of the house which they feel they can afford at certainly less than half the London prices."

We shall find this topic of the Highbrow and the Theatre arising again. Here, for the moment, we must leave it, with the additional note that this statement in July, 1923, was probably the only occasion on which P.R. gave the public an insight into the cash takings of any show.

A welcome visitor to the Prince of Wales Theatre in July was Murray Carrington, a brilliant actor and very courteous gentleman who had just launched himself as a manager. His début in this capacity was made, appropriately enough, at Stratford-upon-Avon, where he had been a star of the Festivals.

Philip Rodway's faith in him was expressed by a booking for three weeks, during which he presented picturesque old favourites such as *The Three Musketeers*, *Charles I*, *If I were King*, and *The Judgment of Pilate*. It was a most enjoyable, if not remunerative, season, and culminated with a great production of *Julius Caesar*, in which Murray Carrington played Cassius, Ion Swinley Marcus Antonius, Basil Gill Brutus, and Oswald Roberts Caesar—the best Caesar of the day. The company also included Neil Porter (a Stratford lead this year), Margot Drake, Joan Clement Scott, Madge Burbage, and Arthur Seaton.

A few weeks later the Prince of Wales Theatre saw the first production on any stage of *Catherine*, directed by Matheson Lang, with music by Tschaikowsky. José Collins, tranquil and tempestuous by turns, played the famous Empress of Russia, with Robert Michaelis as Menshikoff, Bertram Wallis as Peter the Great, and Mark Lester, Billy Leonard, Amy Augarde, Faith Bevan, and Cressie Leonard.

The year's casts at both houses were liberally sprinkled with stars. Looking through our Theatre Royal programmes we note Richard Cooper in *Double or Quit*, Joe Coyne, Helen Gilliland, Binnie Hale, Evelyn Drewe, George Bishop, and Peter Gawthorne in the pre-London try-out of *Katinka* (with music by Rudolf Friml), Martin Harvey in his repertory, Arthur Bourchier, Graham Browne, and J. R. Tozer (a member of Birmingham's distinguished fire-fighting family) in *Treasure Island*, Phyllis Neilson-Terry in *A Roof and Four Walls*, her ever-welcome parents in costume dramas, Violet Vanbrugh in *The Flame*, Harry Welchman and Huntley Wright in *The Lady of the Rose*, Frederick Blamey and Horace Mills in *Lilac Time* (the first of many visits of this lovely light opera, with music by Schubert), Norman Griffin in *The Cabaret Girl*,

Lilian Davies in *Polly*—a sequel to *The Beggar's Opera*, but nothing like so successful—Mrs. Patrick Campbell in *The Second Mrs. Tanqueray* and *Magda*, and Peggy O'Neil and Rosaline Courtneidge in *Paddy the Next Best Thing*.

When Marie Lohr returned with *The Laughing Lady*, her leading man was Herbert Marshall, who is another of the many who have since become film favourites. Of the plays which had to depend on their own merits, without the benefit of star names, the best this season was unquestionably *R.U.R.*, the unforgettable Robot play by the Brothers Carel and Carl Capek.

The Prince of Wales Theatre, meantime, had its full share of all the best attractions that were going. Iris Hoey in *Jill the Giant Killer*, and Marie Tempest in *The Marriage of Kitty*, preceded Sybil Thorndike, who had Robert Farquharson as Iachimo and Lawrence Anderson as Cloten to her Imogen in *Cymbeline*. During the week she also played in *Jane Clegg*, *Medea*, and Act V of *King Henry the Eighth*.

In *Toni* we saw Jack Buchanan, now an established ruler of musical comedy. The show was intended for immediate production in London, but it was still on tour when seven months later it paid a return visit, with Jack Buchanan and this time a leading lady called "June."

November brought a remarkable "first on any stage" in *Lord Adrian*, a problem play in which Lord Dunsany visualised the alarming consequences to posterity resulting from an experiment in rejuvenation. Arthur Bourchier was the ancient peer who regained his youth by monkey-gland treatment, and Frederick Peisley the tragic heir who developed Mowgli-like propensities and had to be shot lest he should lead his animal friends against mankind. A curious, compelling improbability, which made one shudder.

We recall Arthur Riscoe's excellent performance in *Battling Butler*, and Murray Carrington's return with *Marigold o' the Garden*, written by Basil Gill's son David, who was also in the cast.

Matheson Lang chose the Prince of Wales Theatre, in December, for the launching of *The Phantom Ship*, Temple Thurston's drama on the Flying Dutchman theme. This was an exciting production, with some excellent examples of stagecraft, and a new leading lady of much charm in Muriel Alexander. It was a fitting climax to one of the best seasons enjoyed by Birmingham since the war.

*   *   *

PANTOMIME 1923-24
ALADDIN

The story of *Aladdin and his Wonderful Lamp*, so strong in plot, so generous in the scope it offers for brilliant scenery, lighting, and dressing, has not been done as often as one would expect at the Royal. In 1923, when P.R. revived it, thirteen years had passed since Carrie Moore's appearance in the title-rôle, and eighteen years since Ada Reeve's memorable performance. We have already mentioned the Aladdin of Jenny Hill in 1889, and the only other record of the subject being chosen is in 1866. For 1923 the book was by Lauri Wylie and F. Maxwell-Stewart, and the lyrics by Clifford Harris and Valentine. There were special pictorial blocks designed for one of the scenes by the humorous artist, H. M. Bateman.

While splendour is legitimately the keynote of an Oriental production, here it was never allowed to become mere garishness; on the contrary the eye was soothed by the skill with which each item of elaborate detail or brilliant colouring sank into its proper place as part of a harmonious whole. The first big scene, where the grandeur of Pekin was unfolded; the instantaneous change from Abanazar's abode to the city's restless heart; the brilliance of the Garden of Jewels; the amazing materialisation of Aladdin's Palace and its equally mystifying disappearance; the exquisite finale in Plum-blossom Time, were all examples of scenic art and manipulative skill in their highest degree.

Elsie Prince, the hero, caused some of the most loyal to Ada Reeve's memory to revise their choice of the Royal's best Aladdin. One doubts whether Ada Reeve herself could have given a more vivid impression of the idle, good-for-nothing, good-for-anything young scamp than Elsie Prince conveyed. Here was an Aladdin with a natural quality which pervaded all she did. Her principal songs, *Running Wild* and *The Blue Danube Blues*, had the jazzy, jolly, tip-tapping stuff in them that exactly suited her personality, and in *Wonderful One* her voice was heard to advantage.

Dorothy Viggars was the Princess, singing her two songs, *Little Johnnie Chinaman* and *Singapore*, with Chinese charm.

It is a far cry from 1908 to 1923. In the fifteen years Lupino Lane, the sixteen-year-old prodigy of *Dick Whittington*, had grown up into a star of the first magnitude. Here we met him again (we promised you we would), and with him was his young brother Wallace, who was also in the 1908 pantomime. Lupino, playing Pekoe, son to the Vizier, was the same round-faced, wide-eyed, alert, confident "Nipper" Lane of fifteen years ago, but he had become widely famed as a comedian, an acrobatic dancer and a "trap" artist. In comedy his method was quietness itself, with a curious sense of reserve, but when he became acrobatic he was like an electric eel, and when he got to his beloved trap act he was a darting, hurtling, bouncing ball of mercurial vitality.

G. S. Melvin (King of Hearts of 1921) rejoined us in 1923 as Widow Twankey, Aladdin's surprising mother. This was his first appearance as a pantomime dame. Many people, when they first heard of the idea, wondered "what made Phil Rodway think of putting George Melvin into 'skirts'?" The answer, definitely conclusive, was soon forthcoming. G. S. Melvin established himself as a dame of dames, and ever since has been in demand among the leading producers for similar rôles. Never was such a quaint mixture of dignity, impudence, coyness, and comic inventiveness as this sharp-featured Chinese laundress, who ran a bar as a sideline and practised the art of girl guidery in her spare time. Madame Twankey might be a person in reduced circumstances, but she was always one of distinction. Her costume was always the very latest fashion, and her coiffure, like her complexion, owed as much to art as that of the proudest mandarin's lady in the land! In all her vicissitudes her cheerfulness inspired good cheer in others. *Do Shrimps make Good Mothers?* the duet she sang with Pekoe, was a clever nonsense-song, and her brilliant skit, in which she appeared as the head of her girl guides, was sheerly uproarious.

Due credit for their share in a great success must be allotted to Stanley Turnbull (the Emperor), Wallace Lupino (the Vizier), Albert Darnley (Abanazar), Richard Norton, Victor Fairley, Hilda Dick, and Lena King, who danced so well in the big scenes.

The difficulties incidental to the economic depression were heightened by the railway strike of January, 1924, yet *Aladdin* ran merrily on until March 8th, winning laurels all the way. On January 29th, Philip Rodway arranged an all-star matinée in the theatre, one of a series promoted by the various managers in aid of the Lord Mayor's unemployment distress fund. All the principal artists appearing in the town gave their services, as did everyone else concerned behind the scenes or "in front," and the Lord Mayor (Alderman T. O. Williams) waxed warm in his expressions of gratitude when he spoke from the stage.

A special feature of the matinée was the auctioning of Bonzo replicas by Lupino Lane. Bonzo was the comical "Studdy" dog (the creation of G. E. Studdy), which "assisted" Nipper in the show—and during the run of the pantomime whole families of these lovable toys, beautifully made of the softest cream-coloured velvet, had been thrown out into the audience at every performance. For this matinée they were of all sizes, from baby Bonzos to their biggest brothers, and when it came to the sale of the largest of them all, the most eager bidder was Lupino Lane's little son, who ran the lot up to £13 before going proudly forward to claim his purchase. The chairman of the organising committee was Harry

Raymond, then (and now) the manager of the Birmingham Empire Theatre.

P.R.'s Anniversary night on March 5th was enhanced as usual by the interpolation of special items by the principals and by other leading artists. The funniest turn of a joyous evening was a burlesque of the Astaires' famous dance by Lupino Lane and Wallace Lupino. When the moment came for P.R. to address the audience, he made the announcement that this year the Theatre Royal would celebrate its hundred and fiftieth birthday. Such an anniversary called for special commemoration; he had not definitely decided what form it should take, but most probably it would be a performance on elaborate lines, from which the whole of the proceeds would be given to the Birmingham hospitals.

* * *

Season 1924

For the Christmas and New Year season at the Prince of Wales Theatre P.R. had booked a joyously inconsequential show called *Stop Flirting*, which had run a long time in three London theatres, and now came along to introduce to Birmingham those delightfully original personalities, the Astaires. Adèle Astaire (now Lady Charles Cavendish) and her brother Fred took the town by storm with their ultra-American liveliness and their grotesque dancing, most of which conformed to no standard, but simply made its own rules. Who can forget the magnetic rhythm of *The Oom-Pah Trot*, or the infectious lilt of their duet *Oh Gee, oh Gosh, oh Golly, I love you?* With them were Jack Melford, E. Louis Bradfield, George de Warfaz, Dorothy Waring and Mimi Crawford.

After five weeks of this pleasant nonsense, the house settled down to its spring season. An early attraction of note was the first production on any stage of *The Street Singer*, written by Frederick Lonsdale, with music by Fraser Simson. It brought back to Birmingham Phyllis Dare, last here when little more than a child, and now the quintessence of gaiety in a highly congenial rôle. She gave a charming performance as Yvette, a part which offered plenty of scope for her sweet singing voice and graceful dancing.

Arthur Pusey played Bonni, and Henry Caine was Armand. A hit on the first night was scored by Sam Wilkinson, deputising at twenty-four hours' notice for Hugh E. Wright as François, the woman-hater. Phoebe Hodgson, Hector Abbas, and Dorothy Fane were also in the cast.

Robert Courtneidge followed with *The Bohemians*, another new piece, though based on an old novel, Henri Murger's *La Vie de Bohème*. The play, written by Mr. Courtneidge in collaboration with Alexander M. Thompson ("Dangle" of the old *Sunday Chronicle*) was in four acts and innumerable scenes. Henry Baynton played the hero, Dorothy Turner the heroine, and the trio was completed by Fedora Rozelli.

The outstanding items during the first half of the year at the Royal were *Outward Bound*, *Stigmata* (Phyllis Neilson-Terry), *What Every Woman Knows* (Hilda Trevelyan as Maggie, her original rôle), *Good Luck* (a Drury Lane drama with Claire Romaine and Leslie Perrins), *The Bad Man* and *Carnival* (Matheson Lang), and—the first visit of The Co-optimists.

These noted entertainers, so reminiscent of and yet so different from *The Follies* of happy memory, provided one of the romances of the English theatre. Fabulous profits have been attributed to the three men who conceived the idea of revising the pierrot super-party on "common-wealth" lines. No doubt the figures have been liberally exaggerated, but it is equally certain that the first small investments were repaid many times over. The troupe which came to the Royal in the June of 1924 comprised Phyllis Monkman, Babs Valerie, Doris Bentley, Gwendoline Brogden, Davy Burnaby, Gilbert Childs, Stanley Holloway, Austin Melford, Wolseley Charles, and the late Melville Gideon, whose lilting, appealing music was so great a feature.

In the same period some of the noteworthy attractions at the Prince of Wales Theatre were *Partners Again*, a new *Potash and Perlmutter* comedy, *Sir Jackanapes* (a romantic play with Harry Welchman), *The Rat* (in which Ivor Novello, on the Birmingham stage for the first time, had the support of Madeleine Seymour, Dorothy Batley and the late Norman Leyland), *The Return of Sherlock Holmes* (with Eille Norwood as Holmes), and seasons by the Macdona Players and Henry Baynton's Shakespeare Company.

The month of June finished at the Wales with a curious oriental fantasy called *Omar Khayyam*, an attempt to express the Rubaiyat in terms of dance, mime, and song. It proved much too short and slight for a full-length show, and the one act play which preceded it served merely to extend the programme.

At the annual meeting in June Philip Rodway was able to announce a net profit of £3,858, and a dividend of 15 per cent. was declared, the chairman explaining that if the world remained peaceful and the country avoided industrial upheavals there was hope of better times in store. P.R. outlined the arrangements for the forthcoming observance of the Royal's hundred and fiftieth birthday, for which he had been planning since he first brought forward the idea on his anniversary night three months earlier.

* * *

In September Arthur Bourchier, supported by Kyrle Bellew and James Carew, brought a new production of *The Thief* to the Royal. Next came an excellent musical comedy *Katja the Dancer*, in which Gene Gerrard made his local début in this type of entertainment, and Carl Brisson, Joan Clarkson, Bobbie Comber and Dolly King were in the cast.

Madame Pompadour, the latest production from Daly's Theatre, came in October, with Edith Cecil in the title-rôle, while Julia Neilson and Fred Terry brought *The Marlboroughs* when they came for their annual visit, and Reginald Purdell, to-day so popular on the films and wireless, was seen in *Little Nellie Kelly*. George Melvin played the Jack Buchanan part in *Toni*, and Lynne Overman, the American comedian, provided a fine finish to the Royal's season with his brilliant performance in *Just Married*.

Henry Baynton, of whom P.R. still had the highest hopes for the restoration of the brave days of actor-management, came to the Prince of Wales Theatre in August for the third time this year (1924), and achieved an outstanding success in *The Melting Pot*. A new farce, *The Other Mr. Gibbs*, found Will Evans in the dual rôle of part-author and leading player. He was very amusing as Mr. Gibbs, though the work itself was negligible.

Matheson Lang's new play this season was *The Hour and the Man*. The British National Opera Company, following him on September 15th, gave the city its first hearing of *Hugh the Drover*, by Vaughan Williams.

The visit of *Patricia*, a new musical comedy, to the Prince of Wales Theatre in October was interesting from the fact that a few months later, on its return (to the Royal) it involved P.R. in a little controversy. Turning a few leaves ahead in our cuttings-book, we find that in May, 1925, he threatened to cancel its booking because portions of it had been broadcast, an admitted breach of contract with provincial managements. Numerous listeners-in wrote to the local papers saying that as a consequence of what they had heard they were anxious to see the complete show. So he gave way—but he could not repress a little satirical smile when *Patricia* on its return played to half-empty houses.

In November, 1924, Dennis Neilson-Terry and his wife, Mary Glynne, then venturing into management for the first time, came to the Prince of Wales with Jeffery Farnol's *The Honourable Mr. Tawnish*. José Collins played Nell Gwynne in *Our Nell*, with Robert Michaelis as King Charles, and Owen Nares brought his revival of *Diplomacy*, with Ben Webster, Frances Doble, and Marie Polini (Mrs. Owen Nares) among his distinguished colleagues.

A very fine revue, *Brighter London*, is remembered for the dancing of Ruth French and the comedy of Jack Edge, Hal Bryan, and Elsie Prince. The last production of the season at the Prince of Wales Theatre in 1924 was by The Commercial Travellers' Society, who gave *Uncle Sam*, and *Pygmalion and Galatea*. The farce was played by Charles L. Moore and Eve Connell, while in the main piece Pygmalion was G. F. Ostins, Galatea Dorothy Ostins, Minos L. Habberley, and Chrysos H. T. Tandy. Other parts were taken by H. Lewis, Edith Brunner and Miss F. Tabberner.

*   *   *

Philip Rodway used to tell a good story of Alfred Zeitlin, an important London theatrical agent. He arrived in Birmingham unexpectedly one evening, called at the Theatre Royal box office during the performance, and asked to see Mr. Rodway.

"Tell him I'm Zeitlin from London, and would like to have a word with him," he said.

After five minutes or so no answer appeared to be forthcoming, and he repeated his request. Still no reply from P.R.

"Have you told him I'm Zeitlin; Zeitlin from London?" he demanded.

"Yes, oh yes, sir!"

Impatiently he turned on his heel and marched straight off through the doors and down the stairs to P.R.'s sanctum.

"Look here, Phil, what's the meaning of this? I've been kept waiting outside that box office of yours till I'm tired. Didn't you get my message?"

"Good gracious, I didn't even know you were here, old man. The only news I've had"—suddenly he broke off. "So that was it! For the last ten minutes the call-boy has been bobbing in and out and apparently doing his best to tell me something, but all I could get out of him was 'There's a gentleman cycling from London to see you, sir!'"

Quick curtain.

* * *

Georgie Wood gives us an equally amusing variation. In this version it was not only Alfred Zeitlin, but P.R.'s old friend the late Ernest Edelsten, the theatrical agent, who had come up from town together especially to see him.

This time the message came in as:

"Mr. Edelsten's cycling from London to see you, sir."

P.R. looked up in amazement; then, shaking his head sorrowfully,

"He'll never do it," was all he said.

CHAPTER 28

(1924-25)

The 150th Anniversary of the Theatre Royal—Celebration performance
on Christmas Eve, 1924, in aid of the Birmingham Hospitals: Dress
Rehearsal of *Jack and the Beanstalk:* Sir Frank Benson speaks the Prologue—
Theatre Royal Bed dedicated at the General Hospital, May 1st, 1925; and
at the Queen's Hospital on October 20th.

On June 20th, 1924, the Theatre Royal, Birmingham,
reached its 150th Birthday.

1774-1924! "For a century and a half," wrote Mr. Crompton Rhodes, "the history of the Theatre Royal, under its
managers from Richard Yates to Philip Rodway, has been
the history of the English stage in epitome." And this
memoir, having given an outline of that history from its
beginning in 1774 would, while attempting a pen picture of
the life and work of Philip Rodway, also afford a record of
Theatre Royal history for the past thirty years.

For some time before the 150th anniversary, P.R. had given
much thought to the means whereby so rare an occasion
might be fittingly celebrated. He was of course desirous that
whatever was done should be calculated to focus attention
on the historic theatre itself, but beyond this aim was a
sincere wish to benefit Birmingham's most deserving institutions, her far-famed hospitals.

It could not be done on the actual birthday, for various
reasons, and in any case it was appropriate that pantomime,
which had so largely contributed to the theatre's fame, should
have an integral part in the scheme. If a further cue was
needed, it was found in the war-time memory of Philip Rodway's pantomime dress rehearsals thrown open to wounded
and invalid soldiers. The public were used to the idea of the
dress rehearsal being a more or less "set" performance, so
that from every viewpoint it seemed sound to make the
birthday celebrations coincide with it.

The Theatre Royal, be it noted, had held throughout its

history a reputation for helping the Birmingham hospitals. Actually, the association had begun, like the troubles of Tristram Shandy, before either of them was born. The theatre in New Street was opened in 1774, the General Hospital in 1779, yet it was in 1770 that this series of associated charitable performances was initiated. The first meeting to establish a general hospital had been held at the Swan Inn in 1765. The building was begun the following year, but the benefactions were insufficient, and for nearly twelve years the hospital remained untenanted. From 1770 onwards, then, the connection went on, from the first musical concert to the triennial musical festivals of 1782-1834. The Mercer Simpsons, managers of the Theatre Royal for so long in the nineteenth century, gave hospital benefits for many years, the younger Mercer Simpson closing the series in 1887 with performances on three successive nights to commemorate the jubilee of the family control.

So the directors of 1924 had abundant inspiration in the theatre's annals for their benevolent endeavour, and Birmingham, as a city, had a record of generous support to sustain. This became triumphantly apparent on the day of the performance, when P.R. was able to announce from the stage that the receipts were at least £2,500.

It was an elaborate and highly distinguished occasion, this formal celebration of a longevity which no other provincial theatre could boast. As patrons it had H.R.H. Princess Beatrice, the Lord Mayor of Birmingham (Alderman, now Sir, Percival Bower, J.P., O.B.E.), the Bishop of Birmingham (Right Rev. E. W. Barnes, D.D., D.Sc., F.R.S.), the late Sir Squire Bancroft (with memories, no doubt, of his début in a Royal pantomime sixty-three years earlier), Viscount Cecil, P.C., K.C., M.A., LL.D. (Chancellor of the University of Birmingham), Colonel Sir Gilbert Barling, Bart., C.B., C.B.E., F.R.C.S. (then pro-Chancellor of the University), Mr. (now Sir) Charles Grant Robertson, M.A., C.V.O. (Principal of the University), the late Sir Charles Starmer, Lord Leigh,

BI

J.P. (Lord-Lieutenant of Warwickshire), Mr. (now Sir) Austen Chamberlain, M.P., Mr. Neville Chamberlain, M.P., Sir Evelyn Cecil, G.B.E., M.P., Colonel L. S. Amery, M.P., Mr. P. J. Hannon, M.P., and the late Sir Francis Lowe, J.P., M.P.

Seats were sold at special prices ranging from 100 guineas and 50 guineas for the boxes, 5 guineas for the stalls and dress circle, down to 2/6 for the gallery, and many had to be balloted, at P.R.'s suggestion, in order to ensure absolute fairness in allocation. Mr. R. Crompton Rhodes' handsomely produced Souvenir of the occasion was on sale at 2/6, with an edition de luxe at 1 guinea.

At the Celebration performance on Christmas Eve, in the magnificent audience were countless leaders of Birmingham's civic, industrial, and social life. Philip Rodway had invited Sir Frank Benson, as representing the stage of the day (and whose Shakespearean Company had been the last but one to play in the old theatre twenty-two years earlier), to speak the Prologue, and he came specially from London for the occasion. These historic lines, written by Samuel Foote for the opening of the original "New Theatre at Birmingham" on June 20th, 1774, had first been delivered by the first manager, Richard Yates:

> "From fiddling, fretting, Monsieur and Signior,
> And all the Dangers of the Italian Shore:
> From squeaking Monarchs and chromatic Queens,
> And Metastatio's mixed and mangled Scenes,
> Where Fashion, and not Feeling, bears the Sway,
> Whilst Sense and Nature coyly keep away,
> I come. All hail the consecrated Earth
> Whose bounteous Bosom gave our Shakespeare birth,
> Gave that great Master of the Scenic Art,
> To Feed the Fancy and correct the Heart,
> To check th' unruly Passions' wild Career,
> And draw from Pity's Eye the tender Tear;
> Of Folly's Sons t' explore the ample Train,
> The Sot, the Fop, the Vicious, and the Vain;

Hypocrisy to drag from her Disguise,
And Affectation hunt thro' all her Lies.
Such was your Bard; Who then can deem the Stage
The worthless Fav'rite of an idle Age;
Or judge that Pleasure with Instruction join'd
Can taint the Manners, or corrupt the Mind?
Far other Thoughts your generous Breast inspire,
Touch'd with a Spark of True Promethean Fire;
Sure that the Arts with Commerce came to Earth,
That the same Parents gave those Sisters Birth,
Cold creeping Prejudice you dar'd despise,
And bade this Temple to the muses rise,
Oh, that my Tongue could utter all I feel,
Or that my Powers were equal to my Zeal,
Plac'd by your Favour, not by Right Divine,
Th' unworthy High Priest of the sacred Nine,
No tainted Incense should pollute their Shrine,
Nor ought be offered to the Public View,
But what was worthy Them and worthy You."

SAMUEL FOOTE.

From *The London Magazine,*
August, 1774.

"It means nothing to me that the boards are not the same, the bricks are changed," declared Sir Frank. "The main thing is that the tradition has been kept up, the spirit is the same. That spirit has pervaded the work of many eminent men, of whom the last in the line, though not the least, is Mr. Philip Rodway. Those who know anything of the British stage know that in this direction, as in so many others, the life of the great metropolis of the midlands is the life of the country and of the Empire."

P.R. then took charge, and the curtain rose on the first scene of *Jack and the Beanstalk*. The Lord Mayor, introduced by Sir Charles Hyde, in the interval expressed the hospitals' thanks for the various activities undertaken on their behalf in connection with the commemoration. While the hospitals were ostensibly to benefit, the advantage would really accrue to the citizens destined to occupy the beds.

The late Sir John Barnsley, speaking for the General and

the Queen's Hospitals, endorsed the Lord Mayor's words. He emphasised how much was owed to the directors of the theatre, and to Philip Rodway in particular. There was, he said, an appropriateness in applying the sweet art of Thespis to the sacred cause of charity as represented by the hospitals, because human life was a strange, ceaseless intermingling of joy and sorrow. What was true of individuals was true of communities, and it was fitting that the great playhouse which had for so long been a centre of Birmingham life should hold out a hand to help the hospitals. From the abode of laughter, pleasure, recreation, education, was stretched the hand of sympathy to the abode of pain, where suffering and weariness prevailed, yet where men and women broken by Life were mended, and where, in the course of years, many thousands had been restored.

Philip Rodway replied for the theatre. He said it had given genuine pleasure to all those connected with the effort. They counted it a privilege to carry on the traditional association between the Birmingham stage and the Birmingham hospitals.

Four months later, when all the detailed matters connected with the matinée had been cleared up, April 21st "saw the consummation of the effort in the handing over by Mr. Philip Rodway of cheques for £1,250 each to the representatives of the General and Queen's Hospitals." The ceremony took place at the final meeting of the executive committee, when the late Sir John Barnsley presided. Sir Charles Hyde, though unable to attend, wrote congratulating the organisers on what had been done to produce an occasion worthy of the traditions of the theatre.

P.R.'s balance sheet was submitted and approved, wherein he showed the interesting fact that the house receipts for the matinée totalled £1,634, and the advertisement revenue amounted to £787.

The thanks of the hospitals were moved by Mr. C. H. Saunders (representing the General), seconded by Mr. John

TO-DAY. 1934

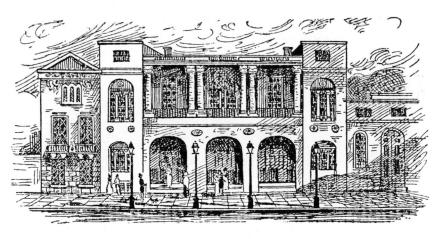

YESTERDAY. 1774

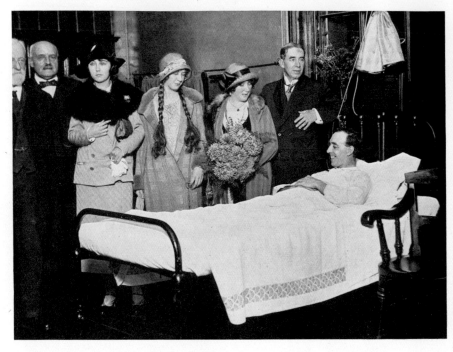

THE "THEATRE ROYAL 150TH ANNIVERSARY BED"

Dedicated by Philip Rodway at the Queen's Hospital

October 21st, 1925

Alderman Clayton, Sir John Barnsley, Phyllis, Lois, Mrs. Philip Rodway, Mr. Philip Rodway

Glaisyer (Queen's), and supported by that wonderful Birmingham sportsman philanthropist, the late Mr. Harry Butler. Mr. R. Crompton Rhodes, the hon. secretary, paid special tribute to the services of Mr. Philip Rodway and the entire staff. P.R. replied that the Theatre Royal was wrapped up with the life of the city, and that the directors were actuated by no other motive than to take their place in the city's activities. Votes of thanks were also accorded to the advertisement committee (chairman, Mr. H. D. English; hon. secretary, Mr. R. I. Scorer, M.C.), the various sub-committees, Mr. Crompton Rhodes, and Sir John Barnsley.

The first bed thus endowed was dedicated at the General Hospital on May 1st, 1925, and stands in Ward I of the Surgical Block, inscribed "*The Theatre Royal Hundred and Fiftieth Anniversary Bed.*" On October 20th the same year we attended the formal ceremony at the Queen's Hospital. In the Jordan Lloyd ward, Mother was presented with a beautiful bouquet by the matron on behalf of the Queen's and General Hospitals, and Daddy unveiled the commemorative tablet.

It may be interesting to record his speech:

"Sir John Barnsley, Ladies and Gentlemen,

"You have asked me to unveil this Tablet, and thereby dedicate this bed in the Queen's Hospital for the use and benefit of the sufferers of Birmingham for ever.

"I do so with great pleasure and a certain amount of pride. The pleasure is derived from the feeling that the act marks the consummation of a good deed well done. In saying that, I am of course speaking not merely for myself, but as the representative of all the many thousands who have had some share in the movement which has led to the endowment of this bed. There is, as we all know, a very precious satisfaction to be derived from a good deed well done, and I feel that the endowment of a bed in one of our great voluntary hospitals is such an occasion, beyond a doubt; for we are all very proud of and deeply attached to our voluntary hospitals. I do not suppose I am right in thinking they are a peculiarly British Institution—I fancy in truth they date back to the two coins of the Good Samaritan on the road to Jericho—but in this country we like to consider them pre-eminently British in their conception and functioning, without casting any aspersion or reflection on the admirable institutions provided by the State or the Municipal authorities. We like to think that there is something superior in the combination of generous donors and self-sacrificing officials who make up our voluntary hospitals—something so precious that we view with alarm any suggestion that they should become merely State Institutions. But *alarm* is not enough to prevent that fate. If we are to preserve the voluntary system it can only be done by doing our duty as did our forefathers, who built up these grand institutions, and by seeing to it that they are supplied with a constant relay of devoted workers and the necessary funds. We cannot all take part in hospital administration, but we can all do our share in the raising of money to make their work possible. It is one such effort we are consummating to-day in the best possible way by the permanent endowment of a bed, and the fact that we have, by a united effort, been able to ensure that this bed shall be available for the amelioration of a long succession of sufferers in the future, must give the greatest pleasure to us all.

"So much for my representative character to-day, as voicing the feelings of all who have played a part in this affair. Will you permit me to say just a few words more to record my personal pride in being asked to perform this ceremony, for I take it, Sir John, that when you and your committee insisted on my accepting this office, you intended it as a compliment to the profession to which I have the honour to belong, and as a recognition of the part the profession has always been happy to play in affairs of this sort. I venture to think that apart from the medical profession no section of the community has shown a greater readiness to assist worthy causes of this kind than my own. From the managers of all branches of the entertainment industry, down to the humblest employee, there is always shown the greatest readiness to give their services in the cause of charity. This is not a new development, and you will remember, Sir, that we are here to-day as the result of the commemoration of the 150th Anniversary of the theatre now committed to my charge, and that throughout the 150 years the connection between the Theatre Royal and the hospitals of the city has been continuous and close. It was this fact that led my directors and myself to the decision that a proper commemoration of a notable event—for it was a notable event in many ways—would be a performance in aid of the hospitals. Thanks to the enthusiastic collaboration of many friends, the performance was so successful financially that we are to-day inaugurating this bed as a permanent memento of the 150 years of the Theatre Royal, and the connection between the theatre and the hospitals. During these 150 years, both institutions have developed greatly, and I am hopeful that to-day they are both considered as essential parts of the life of the great community in which they are situated. You minister to the bodily ills of the citizens, and I trust that we do something to lighten their mental afflictions. The stage is often attacked on many grounds, but, without introducing unduly controversial subjects, I believe that with the passing of the years it is becoming recognised that a theatre is as essential in a civilised community as an art gallery or public library. I trust also, in spite of the sneers of the reformers, it is becoming apparent that the commercial theatre (as it is often dubbed by many who ought to know better) is not quite so self-interested as is sometimes represented.

"Speaking for my colleagues and myself, I can assure you that the management of the Theatre Royal is not considered mainly from the box office angle. We realise that we are in a position of trust, and that we owe certain duties to the public, and within our lights we endeavour to carry these out and to run the Theatre Royal as one of the institutions of the city. That you recognise this is, I venture to think, proved by your invitation to me to perform this function. It is therefore with considerable pride that I now ask you to take over this bed and use it as part of the beneficent work of the Queen's Hospital, and that I unveil this commemorative tablet.

"Sir John Barnsley, ladies and gentlemen, I thank you for your patience in listening to these remarks, and for the honour you have done me, and I assure you once more on behalf of all associated with me that it has been a great pleasure for us to make the work of this bed possible, and so assist the Queen's Hospital in its great and noble work."

CHAPTER 29

(1924-26)

Jack and the Beanstalk, 1924-25; Jay Laurier, Clarice Mayne, and Dick Tubb
—Foreman of the fairy works—1925 Season—Philip Rodway and Shake-
speare—The Stratford-upon-Avon Company—W. H. Savery's recollections
—Subterfuge!—1925 Season—*Charlot's Revue of 1926;* Jack Buchanan,
Gertrude Lawrence, Beatrice Lillie—Sybil Thorndike in *Saint Joan*—Canon
Stuart Blofeld—P.R. vice-president of the Birmingham Amateur Dramatic
Federation—British Drama League Festival—B.U.D.S.—The Crescent
Theatre.

PANTOMIME 1924-25

JACK AND THE BEANSTALK

Jack and the Beanstalk, memorable as the pantomime of the
150th anniversary year, opened in The Village of Arcadee,
a village of gabled houses and quaint cottages, smothered in
roses and foliage. Here lived Dame Trot and her son, with
Jessie the Cow, soon to be sold to pay the rent, so that before
long we saw the Cattle Market. Dawn was breaking and as
day came there was disclosed—not the prosaic mart one
might expect, but a place snatched by the imagination
straight from Toyland. A whimsical toy soldier ballet struck
the right note, and nothing was allowed to disturb the harmony. Even the toy train was well in the picture, built on
the stage, and then steaming away laden with happy children.

Jack having parted with his beloved cow for a bag of beans,
his mother, in despair, threw them over the garden wall.
"Where the Beans were thrown" depicted the growth of the
wonderful ladder to the skies, a fine example of artistic
ingenuity and intricate mechanical skill. Amid ever-changing
surroundings Jack clambered on and on, catching fleeting
glimpses of the Giant's Castle, until at last the solid gates of
the stronghold appeared, and he stood before them, a glittering figure in armour with a gleaming sword, while all around
him rhythmically swayed the scarlet and green-clad figures.
As the gates clanged open at his command, a shower of gold
descended, completing the brilliant picture.

The second half opened in the Giant Fee-Fo-Fum's Library, where everything was on a gigantic scale—writing desk, pipes, telephone, etc.; and where in the huge volumes ranged round the walls were held captive the heroes and heroines of all the fairy tales of the realms of pantomime. Jack's first task was to set free these charming little people, Bo-Peep, Red Riding Hood, Sinbad, and the rest. Each one who emerged carried a little mascot, a tiny replica of Jessie the Cow, which was the symbol of their escape, since only by the sale of that intelligent animal had Jack obtained the beans and come to liberate them. And so at every performance a little herd of cows went hurtling over the footlights to gladden the hearts of the children (and, we must add, the grown-ups too, for many a Jessie became the much-travelled mascot of many a motor-car).

Jack's biggest task, of course, was to rescue the Princess, for whom he fought the giant in single combat. The duel took place in the huge kitchen, and Jack's final thrust sent the giant backwards into the fire. Immediately the entire scene became the great face of Fee-Fo-Fum, a mechanical "close-up," weirdly effective.

The final scene was the Palace, set for a great Christmas festival, with a living Christmas tree surrounded by an ever-growing medley of living dolls and golliwogs, chocolate boxes and bon-bons, crackers and flowers—a bright and happy background for the assembly of the whole company.

As Jack the hero, Clarice Mayne was at the Royal for the fourth time, and many will always think of her as the ideal principal boy for a Royal pantomime. "I look back on those four pantomimes," says Miss Mayne, "as some of the happiest in my career." She filled the rôle with her wonted grace and charm, and her fine singing voice, distinctive personality, and quiet confidence established her more firmly than ever. Besides her own big song hits, she had several jolly duets, and her imitations and burlesques were as usual warmly appreciated.

As Miffins, Jay Laurier wended his way through the

pantomime with a light heart and airy tread. Always he seems to have the guileless smile and trusting disposition of the most innocent child, and here he meandered happily about, helping or getting in the way as occasion demanded. His humour was entirely natural and unforced, as spontaneous and inevitably a part of him as were his songs, *Oh, you don't know nobody what don't want to buy no nine-inch nails?*, sung with a disarmingly hopeful expression and a confusing chorus of multiplied negatives; *Get upon a Puff-puff*, a duet with Jack; and *The Boy with the Bye-bye Blues*, where his little bed came up to him through the floor, his nightie fell over him from the ceiling, and then the bed, with him in it, vanished serenely down through the floor again.

(This, by the way, was accounted for, as everything always was in Daddy's pantomimes; in this case by the fact that though Miffins began as the King's major domo, he very soon fell under the spell of the fairy, and became what he declared to be "foreman of the fairy works." From that moment he attached himself completely and whole-heartedly to Jack, as a kind of counterpart of Sancho Panza, and refused to leave him, so that when Jack, in despair, gave him a push to escape this continuous care, Miffins announced reproachfully: "You can't mess us fairies about like this. Now look what you've done, you've torn my fairy blouse!")

Dick Tubb as Dame Trot introduced a conception of the part which was as fresh as it was acceptable. An unconventional dame comedian, he was vivacious and youthful to a degree, and possessed a wardrobe of the most astonishing dimensions, perfectly up-to-date and yet sheerly ludicrous (especially a certain extremely modern red knitted costume worn with a rakish red beret!). The expansive smile, the engaging glance, the droll speech were ever in evidence, whether she was masquerading as the Kodak girl, the giant's cook, or the society lady. Two of the song successes of the pantomime were her *Has anybody seen my pom?* and her skit on the patriotic ballad *Drake is going to sea*.

Arthur Conquest, playing the King, had little to do, but contrived to make him a quaint if ineffectual figure. The princess, his daughter, was Molly Milne, who looked the part and sang sweetly the season's inevitable song *What'll I do?*, though here, appropriately enough, as a prisoner in the Giant's Castle. Emmelyn Walter proved herself a fairy with an exceptionally fine voice; Margot St. Leger was an original and accomplished dancer, and Raymond Wood made an almost benevolent Fee-Fo-Fum, whose only fault seemed to be his extraordinary appetite.

And finally there was the real heroine of the pantomime— Jessie the Cow. As portrayed by the Brooks Brothers she was a most intelligent, lovable, loving, if ungainly creature. The pathos of her parting with Jack brought many a little handkerchief out in the audience. (This pathetic touch was a favourite one of P.R.'s—the disconsolate dog, having been "spoken to severely" by an indignant Dame; the Goose reproached by Mother Goose for not laying her a Beauty Egg; and the sentiment was so genuine that it was not only the children who were touched.) So firm a favourite was this cow that one could not help regretting her untimely departure so early in the first half, and one wondered if it would not be possible to teach such an intelligent animal to climb the beanstalk too, and so stay in the story!

On P.R.'s Anniversary night, March 4th, he announced that for the first time in the history of the theatre *Humpty Dumpty* would be the next year's pantomime, with Wee Georgie Wood playing the name part. And here Georgie Wood, who had come specially to join in this festive night, seized the opportunity to give an amusing parody of "Mr. Rodway's speech as it will be delivered on the 200th Anniversary."

*　　*　　*

Season 1925

Boodle, a musical comedy presented by Alfred Butt, was the Prince of Wales Theatre's Christmas attraction. It was based by Sydney Blow and Douglas Hoare on *The New Clown*, lyrics by Douglas Furber, music by Max Darewski and Philip Braham. Jack Buchanan and June played the leading parts, and Elsie Randolph, now Mr. Buchanan's partner in most of his plays and films, made a great success, as also did Veronica Brady as "the tattoo'd lady."

The D'Oyly Carte Company were succeeded by *The Letter of the Law*, in which Violet Vanbrugh and her daughter Prudence (leading lady a year or two later in Leon Salberg's first repertory company at the Alexandra Theatre) were associated with Leslie Perrins. Prudence Vanbrugh had not long before this made her stage début as a member of the Festival Company at Stratford.

Robert Evett brought his new musical comedy, *Frasquita*, in March, but José Collins was unable to play owing to an accident. Marie Dix, her understudy, made a big hit, and Edmund Gwenn, Spencer Trevor, Amy Augarde, Ethel Baird and Pop Cory were also in the cast of this charming piece, with music by Franz Lehar.

The Royal had the first production on any stage of *The Tyrant*, Rafael Sabatini's play in which Matheson Lang gave his superb rendering of Cesare Borgia, and Isobel Elsom was so good as Madonna Panthasilea, the girl who gave her life for love of the treacherous hero-villain. Also at the Royal, Birmingham saw *White Cargo* for the first time, with Kathleen Boutall as Tondeleyo, Murray Carrington as Weston, and Fred Wright as the doctor.

The Merry Widow came to the Royal for what was described as, but was far from, its farewell visit, Adrienne Brune in the title rôle. Another strong booking was St. John Ervine's *Mary, Mary, Quite Contrary*, with Eva Moore. The Co-optimists this year had the same men in the cast, with Anita Elson, Doris Bentley, Polly Ward and Cicely James.

At the Prince of Wales, meanwhile, the British National Opera Company and a sequence of widely-varied dramatic attractions led up to the annual Shakespeare season in May. Shakespeare was the passion of Philip Rodway's theatrical life, so far as a manager whose business was to exercise a catholic taste may be said to have had a ruling passion. He once said "I have been presenting Shakespeare for thirty years without making it pay—but *I shall go on presenting it so long as other attractions can be persuaded to balance the books.*"

We do not think he meant to imply that isolated examples of a paying Shakespearean season could not be cited. He was more probably speaking in terms of decade to decade; setting off the many profitless weeks against the few profitable. In later years, moreover, he conceded that the loss on a Shakespeare week was at least assessable and limited, whereas with some of the stop-gap productions touring in the bad years of the great depression it was impossible to foretell the worst.

His interest kept him in close touch for many years with the principal exponents of Shakespearean acting in England. He had a particularly warm friendship with Mr. W. H. Savery, then and now the general manager of the Stratford-upon-Avon Festival Company—an acquaintance dating back to 1907.

"I was managing the Benson 'North' Company" (writes Mr. Savery to us); "and at the same time that Mr. and Mrs. Benson were playing at the Theatre Royal we were in possession of a theatre not far away. Through illness Mrs. Benson was unable to appear one evening as Lady Macbeth, and we lent our leading lady, Dorothy Green, to fill the breach. I met Philip Rodway in connection with the emergency, and at once I felt I had made a very warm friend, how warm was amply proved in later years.

"Young to the work of touring management, I conceived a great admiration for his strong character and firm outlook. If ever there was a man whose example one might wisely follow, here, I felt, was that man. Our meetings for some years were infrequent, through the exigencies of tour, but we never lost touch, and from 1912, when I first visited the Theatre Royal as general manager of the Benson Companies, our friendship strengthened apace.

"That visit was largely supported by school parties, always the backbone of the patronage for Shakespeare in Birmingham. P.R. hated this fact, and for a long time set his face against giving special inducements to the schools.

" 'Savery,' he said, 'when Education enters the door, the public fly out of the window.'

"Here was a man of fixed ideas, and here was a touring manager for whom returns, however composed, were important. Of course we had frequent discussions on the pros and cons of school support, but it was some time before he would allow that it was inevitable.

"In 1913 we came again to the Royal, after the Stratford Festival and in advance of our first American tour. P.R. and I met daily for our argumentative discussions, and I grew daily more aware of his enthusiasm. He took a deep interest in the projected trip overseas, which he assured us was not only a big venture but a right venture."

The story is taken up again by Mr. Savery during the Stratford season of 1914. "Rodway wanted a full account," he says, "of conditions on the American circuit, and I told him it was largely because I thought it would give him pleasure that while we were playing in Birmingham, Alabama, we had inspired the town to send greetings to Birmingham, England. It may well be that our long talks at this time set his mind planning the scheme which resulted, years later, in his taking out his pantomimes to Canada.

"During the war period P.R. and I met often enough to keep our friendship warm. In 1919, when the New Shakespeare Company was formed, under the direction of W. Bridges Adams, to continue the Stratford Festivals, his interest at once awakened. In 1925 we got together over the Birmingham question, with the eight annual seasons as the result.

"While the preliminary negotiations were in hand I found that his views on school patronage had entirely changed. He asked me to frame a comprehensive scheme for organising this support, and threw himself whole-heartedly into its fulfilment. With the help of the Birmingham Amateur Dramatic Federation, we obtained the highest civic countenance for meetings of Birmingham and surrounding educational chiefs, teachers and others. At these meetings he spoke with keen enthusiasm on the importance of their help, declaring that he had banked on it in booking our company.

"Again he showed that nothing was too much trouble for the sake of the cause he upheld. He did everything a man could do for the success of those seasons, always, I think, with the conviction that one day they might be expanded beyond the bounds of a mere fortnight or so.

"It was the postponement of his greater vision, I am sure, which distressed him much more than the thin houses to which we sometimes played. Throughout this period of our closest association he never grumbled about business, never failed to place all the lavish resources of his fine theatre at our disposal. We could not feel that we were dealing on the ordinary lines as between touring and local management, for reinforcing our business relations was the consciousness of the tremendous goodwill he displayed to us at every turn.

"Financial loss, as such, meant nothing to Philip Rodway, though of course he did not neglect his duty to his shareholders. He held to the determination of presenting the best in all classes of stage entertainment, and his judgment of shows as a whole was so good that the cost of his adherence to Shakespeare was adequately set off every year. This being so, he could regard momentary losses with true philosophic calm, content with the compensating gain of credit for his theatre and experience for himself. I think we may claim, moreover, that over the eight years we did not do so badly as other enterprises with which comparison is possible, and we certainly helped to maintain the status of the house."

The 1925 Stratford Company, which stayed at the Prince of Wales Theatre for a fortnight, included Florence Saunders, James Dale, Randle Ayrton, Richard Goolden, Maurice Colbourne, Kenneth Wicksteed, Rosa Burgess and Frank Darch— a brilliant combination superbly directed by "Bridges."

As usual, Shakespeare, in the familiar phrase, "failed to attract." Despite the zealous efforts of local societies and individuals to whip up support, the first performances were shockingly neglected.

"Our civic heads," says Mr. M. F. K. Fraser in a note to us on this post-war period, "have again and again co-operated with Philip Rodway in his efforts to make the Birmingham public Shakespeare-minded. In May, 1925, Alderman (Sir Percival) Bower lent himself whole-heartedly to a little device we exploited in a despairing effort to buck things up for the Festival Company's season.

"Business was at its lowest, or so I should imagine, though I never conceived it my business to study cash returns. One evening, when a noble play was being finely rendered to an almost empty house, the Lord Mayor went on the stage and spoke seriously as to the danger of such apathy. Birmingham, he was sure, would regret it, too late, if Mr. Philip Rodway at last gained the natural impression that Shakespeare was not wanted, and decided not to book him again for several years, until a new and more discerning generation had arisen.

"Next day, in the *Birmingham Mail*, appeared a long interview with P.R., solemnly discussing what the Lord Mayor had said, and hinting that in justice to his shareholders and the Stratford Governors both he and Mr. Savery would have to consider discontinuing the season unless things improved.

" 'I have had experience of Shakespeare seasons,' said Philip Rodway, 'by all sorts of companies and in all sorts of methods, for nearly thirty years in Birmingham, and not more than once or twice have I known the city to give even moderate support.

" 'This is not a question of relative enthusiasm,' he added, 'it is not that we expect to play Shakespeare to crowded houses, but that we can get absolutely no house at all for it here, except so far as our own faithful supporters, the school-children, help us out.

" 'Time of year, weather, prices, personalities, all the factors which would apply if it were merely a question of relatively poor business, can be left entirely out of account. Right through the theatre, from the most expensive to the cheapest parts, the position is the same. If it is suggested that Birmingham is following its old habit of hanging back until the end of the week, I can inform you that up to noon to-day only thirty-one seats have been booked for *Macbeth* on Saturday night.

" 'I have booked these seasons of Shakespeare, Shaw, etc.,

for many years, not hoping to make a profit, but hoping that the credit and goodwill gained among a substantial minority of playgoers would balance a loss. If no such substantial minority exists in Birmingham, how can I justly continue this type of booking? In fact, unless by the end of the Stratford Company's fortnight there is definite indication that we have a general public here for classical plays, there is little doubt that I shall have to cut Shakespeare and Shaw out of my consideration.

"'If once we come to the conclusion that there is no general public here for Shakespeare, I may conceivably decide to try a season exclusively for the benefit of our special public, the school-children. That is to say, it might be possible to run a series of Shakespeare matinées, in co-operation with the educational authorities, but it would be a most humiliating thing for Birmingham if we did so.'

"P.R. said he felt most keenly the neglect of those who were most assiduous in their lip-service to the great authors, and in their readiness to condemn the 'commercial theatre' for its soullessness.

"'This,' he concluded, 'is not going to become an annual grumble from me. It will be the last time I shall attempt to put the position frankly to the public. If we cannot please the people with such a programme as we are now offering, including a strong comedy element and four rare plays, and with perfect production and acting, it's no use going on. The very fact that *The Winter's Tale*, played last night *for the first time in Birmingham this century*, made no appeal to the general public, is sufficient justification for the conclusions to which one is being forced.'"

All this sounded highly alarmist, and it had some bettering effect on the subsequent business. The public, you see, did not know that the whole affair, from speech to interview, had been "arranged" well in advance, and that P.R. had not the slightest intention of abandoning his beloved author!

Nevertheless, the failure of Birmingham to support the

CI

classic drama was a serious fact, and the following day the *Birmingham Mail* ran a leader on it, together with an amusing cartoon produced by Tom Ellison for the occasion. The leading article was headed "Low-Brow Birmingham," and here are some extracts:

"The good name of Birmingham is once more in jeopardy. This time it is accused of neglecting Shakespeare. A little while ago it was the city's disdain of opera, as proved by the attendances at the season of the B.N.O.C., which was under reproof. Just about the same time it was the artistic ideals of the community which came under the lash of a vigorous critic. A short time before, a wail arose over the threatened closing of the Repertory Theatre. In between there was the perennial discussion over the failure of the City Orchestra to become self-supporting. Birmingham is, therefore, evidently in a bad way, intellectually, artistically, and as a centre of taste or culture. 'Where there is no vision the people perish,' so it behoveth us to take warning while there is yet time. . . .

"The worst of it is that we have really no excuse to offer. It is no good saying the times are hard and money scarce, when the critics can point to crowded houses for some light farce or musical show of a kind calculated to make the judicious grieve. It is no good saying theatre-going is too dear when good, comfortable seats can be had at prices to meet every pocket. It is no good urging the weather, the 'pictures,' the wireless, tennis, motoring, the band in the park, or any of the stock excuses which have been put forward in the past, for these only emphasise the accusation that we neglect the things we ought to support and favour those which should come second. . . .

"How comes it that these cities (Manchester, Edinburgh, Dublin, London) have such an exalted reputation and Birmingham such a low one? The cause, we believe, lies in one point of difference between the intelligentsia of Birmingham and of other centres. In every city the vast majority of the people are Philistines and glory in the fact. But amongst the mass there is in every city, including Birmingham, a leaven of cultured, earnest folk who believe it their mission in life to 'love the highest when they see it.' Unfortunately, whereas in other places these people do rally to the support of intellectual and artistic movements of all kinds in a practical way—'I sympathise two dollars, what do you sympathise?' as the miner said—in Birmingham they content themselves with talking about the necessity for doing so.

"They are very fond of condemning the 'commercial theatre,' which in their exalted opinion is the acme of all that is puerile and bad, but they never go near anything that is specially provided to meet their exacting taste. On the contrary, it is whispered that when they do seek relaxation it is by booking seats for the lightest of dramatic fare, the things they have just denounced so vigorously as an insult to the intelligence of any reasonable person. . . .

"It is no good abusing the parvenues for not doing their duty if our intellectual leaders do not do theirs. If the people who really count lead the way, the parvenu will follow. But our intelligentsia find talk cheaper. So it is left to our Labour Lord Mayor, to his credit be it said, to set an example by taking a personal interest in the intellectual and artistic life of the city. That life is much richer and fuller than our critics give Birmingham credit for. But it is undoubtedly endangered by the apathy to which attention has been called on so many occasions recently."

Mr. Bridges Adams, addressing the Birmingham Rotary Club at the Queen's Hotel the following week, had a word to say concerning the support his company was receiving at the Prince of Wales Theatre.

"Thanks largely to the efforts of your most sporting Lord Mayor, and partly to the loyal support of the Press, our prospects are very much improving.

"Don't blame Philip Rodway because he happens to do better business with his revues than with Shaw and Shakespeare. Rather let us all be thankful for his high civic purpose in giving us Shaw and Shakespeare at all. The rest, it seems to me, is clearly up to you."

            *   *   *

At the annual meeting in June a net profit of £4,941 was disclosed, and a dividend of 20 per cent. (less tax) declared. The profit was an increase of about £1,000 on the previous year, and Tom B. Davis, complimenting the shareholders on this progress, emphasised how much it was due to the "personal unerring judgment and indefatigable work of Mr. Rodway."

A landmark in the history of 1925 was the first production in England, at the Prince of Wales Theatre, of *Mrs. Warren's Profession*—our most distinguished contemporary author's sincere, reasoned attempt to handle a social problem. To the

Macdona Players, in July, Birmingham owed its introduction to George Bernard Shaw's drama, banned by the censor for nearly thirty years. It is curious to reflect that when the veto was removed, England was a week or two behind Scotland in regard to this play—for Mr. Macdona's company had presented it a week or two earlier in the North. The principals were Florence Jackson, Valerie Richards, George E. Bancroft, Oliver Johnston, Charles Sewell and Arthur Claremont.

Dear Little Billie, which visited the Prince of Wales for a fortnight, had a wonderful cast—Laddie Cliff, Phyllis Monkman, Adrienne Brune, Robert Michaelis, etc. In the second week Laddie was taken seriously ill (he had to stand out of the London presentation). Teddy Fox stepped straight out of the chorus and deputised with such success that he afterwards took most of Laddie Cliff's parts on tour.

This season also gave us our first view of Arnold Ridley's remarkably fascinating thriller, *The Ghost Train* (with fine performances by Hugh E. Wright as Saul Hodgkin, and Tony Holles as the detective), while the same theatre scored again with the presentation of *Rose Marie*, the outstanding and most spectacular musical comedy seen for many years. The cast included Virginia Perry, George Gregory, Jamieson Dodds and Leonard Mackay.

The English début of *De Luxe Annie*, an American crook drama with a psychological basis, by Edward Clark (based on a story by Scammon Lockwood) was also secured by P.R. for the Prince of Wales Theatre. It was presented by Violet Melnotte, doyenne of manageresses, who has been very much in the news lately, and Mary Servos played the heroine, with Frank E. Petley as the sleuth and Arthur Finn as the hero.

Gerald Lawrence, reviving *Monsieur Beaucaire* as a straight play, with Madge Compton as Lady Mary to his own Beaucaire, was yet another *coup de théâtre* for the Prince of Wales. The rise of that youthful genius among authors, Noel Coward, is hinted at by the first visit of his *Hay Fever*, with Eva Moore as Judith Bliss.

Photo by Guttenberg

SYBIL THORNDIKE AS "SAINT JOAN"

In December the Commercial Travellers' Dramatic Society finished the year with a performance of *The Serious Family*, leading rôles falling to G. F. Ostins, H. Lewis, Gertrude Timmins, Eve Connel, Clifford Read, and Dorothy Ostins.

The Royal, meantime, had completed its twice-nightly season, and during the autumn it had a full share of the best attractions. One was Baroness von Hutten's *The Halo*, with Arthur Bourchier, Rosina Filippi (magnificent as an old French woman), Frances Doble, and Jack Hobbs in the cast. Julia Neilson and Fred Terry appeared once more in *Sweet Nell*, then in its twenty-fifth year of touring, and Sir Frank Benson, playing a week of Shakespeare, had Robert Donat among his youthful leads.

At the Royal, moreover, P.R. arranged for André Charlot to give his *Revue of 1926* a try-out prior to taking it to America; Jack Buchanan, Gertrude Lawrence, Beatrice Lillie, Herbert Mundin, and Betty Stockfield were the brightest stars. Basil Gill was seen in an impressive modern morality, *The Fool*, by Channing Pollock, and on November 16th came the production for which Birmingham had eagerly been waiting, Bernard Shaw's *Saint Joan*, with Sybil Thorndike as the Maid of Orleans. Her supporters included Lewis Casson, Lyall Swete, O. B. Clarence and Lawrence Anderson.

Dame Thorndike must have happy recollections of Birmingham, for it was here that Lewis Casson wooed and won her over the coffee-cups in the Kardomah Café in New Street. She paid many visits to the principal theatres while they were under P.R.'s control, and we have just received (August, 1934) with profound appreciation, a very charming letter signed by her and Mr. Casson:

". . . . It is with great pleasure that I write these few words about your father. My husband and I played many times under his management in Birmingham, and always had such consideration and kindness shown to us. He was an example of the best type of 'personal manager.' In these days the theatres have become more and more part of a big machine, and it was always a delight to find in his theatres that care and sympathy, that real love of the artist and his work which the 'machine' type does not produce, and without which there can be no growth.

"Co-operation between the commercial side of the business and the artistic side is a necessity for the life of the theatre, and he was a real proof of this. His loss as a personal friend of actors is a very big one; we miss him a great deal."

*   *   *

Canon Stuart Blofeld writes from The Vicarage, Edgbaston:

"It is eminently right that Philip Rodway's work for the theatre, and his high ideals, should be perpetuated in any possible way, and I am glad to know of the proposed biography.

"When the Birmingham Amateur Dramatic Federation was founded eight or nine years ago it was unanimously felt that Mr. Rodway should be a Vice-President. That Federation is concerned, not only with good dramatic art and production, but with the preservation of the best ideals. Every human being is a potential actor, and responds to the portrayal of life on the stage. The theatre is therefore an essential part of the life of the community, and the work of such men as Philip Rodway is extraordinarily valuable. His productions at the Theatre Royal including, notably, the Christmas Pantomime, were, to my own personal knowledge, always of the highest standard, and reflected his good influence. I was impressed too by his active share in the belief that the theatre could be a valuable asset in contributing to, and raising, the spiritual welfare of the individual. He was an impressive and helpful friend to many, in this and other ways, and we pray that his work for the stage shall have lasting good."

Philip Rodway was always a warm friend of the amateurs, whose help in providing enthusiastic "walkers-on" for Shaw and Shakespeare productions he much valued.

In 1925, when the Birmingham Amateur Dramatic Federation was formed, and Sir Barry Jackson, himself a distinguished amateur in pre-war days, was made president, P.R. was one of the two vice-presidents elected. The other was Sir Gilbert Barling.

P.R. retained his vice-presidency to the last. He retained also a close and interested touch with the organisation, whose help in arousing the support of the schools for the Shakespeare seasons at the Prince of Wales has been elsewhere mentioned.

The Federation has for several years been responsible for organising the British Drama League Festival in the Midlands. Various methods of adjudication have been tried, and nowadays the matter is simplified by the appointment of professional adjudicators. In 1926-27, however, funds were not plenteous, so P.R. was asked to formulate a scheme. He suggested a panel of amateur judges, four of whom were to view each performance in the area, and finally meet under his supervision to compare notes and arrive at a communal choice of teams for promotion to the next stage.

This scheme, though unavoidably elaborate, was accepted by all concerned as the most practical in the circumstances. P.R. was not content merely to give it his blessing; he went to great pains in seeing that it was carried out to the letter, and at the selection meeting held in due course at the Theatre Royal he showed the utmost patience and sagacity in reconciling mutually opposed opinions.

It was in part due to him that the Federation became the recognised agent for supplying amateur players to help out the professional repertory companies, such as the Macdona Players and the Stratford Festival Company, on their visits to the Birmingham theatres. While he would not encourage blacklegging by amateurs, he felt that they could bring to certain supernumerary parts an enthusiasm and a style which the disciples of the professional "supermaster" could not command.

Such was his attitude to amateurs—outside his own home! But inside! At The Woodlands he wished, as far as possible, to make "theatrical" synonymous with "taboo." Lois once tried to evade this restriction in what she thought a perfectly legitimate way. When the Shakespeare Company came round to his theatre in Birmingham, not wanting to carry too large a cast, they sent out invitations to the various dramatic societies to send members to swell the crowd scenes. One such invitation arrived at the B.U.D.S. (Birmingham University

Dramatic Society). All Lois's friends in it were delighted, and planned to go to the Prince of Wales and be the crowd at the next performance of *Julius Caesar*. Now, thought she, at last I shall be allowed on the stage; he can't deny me the privilege that all the other B.U.D.S. are having.

Can't he? . . . Little did she know Daddy even then. She felt she ought just to mention the Society's pleasure, and how they were all going to do their very best to be the most Roman crowd possible.

"But, of course, Lois, you are not going?"

"Well, yes, please, Daddy, all my friends are."

"That's as it may be, but you know I've never allowed you to go on the stage, and I'm certainly not going to alter my rule now."

And he meant it! All her friends donned togas and shouted "Peace, ho! let us hear him," and "Revenge!" at appropriate moments, but she sat alone in the deserted common room, and reflected on the strange fate that prevents a theatrical director's daughter from stepping on the stage, while the daughter of any other profession may do so at her will.

How many times have we heard Daddy say "Rather than either of my daughters should go on the stage, I'd take them down the garden and shoot them!" And even here he managed to bring in his beloved garden. Dear Daddy! How consistently he lived up to his principles; like Julius Caesar in the play in question, he was "constant as the Northern star, than whose true-fix'd and resting quality there is no fellow in the firmament."

Of dancing classes he disapproved; he saw no reason for the lessons or for the parties they led to. He never really approved of the small school plays, though he was quite kindly about them, and usually helped with the dresses (at his own personal expense, for he would never upon any consideration make use of the theatre wardrobe). In 1921 a rare thing was effected: he was enticed to see the play at Edgbaston College. This may have been partly because it was *The*

Court of Hearts, with Lois playing the Knave and Phyllis the Queen, and the title was reminiscent of pantomime. Whatever the reason, they determined to astonish him with their dramatic powers. Alas for any hopes they might have had of a stage career—the obvious love of acting of Knave and Queen had the exactly opposite result, for it only made him more afraid than ever that they might want to take it up professionally.

He was asked many times by the Birmingham University Dramatic Society to come and lecture to them, as he had done at the Rotary Club and elsewhere, but he always declined. The secretary of the society used to say it was impossible to get through his bodyguard for a personal interview, whatever devices were employed. Polite and evasive replies were returned from his sanctum, culminating presently in a direct refusal, till his methods became known in the B.U.D.S. as "the iron hand in the velvet glove."

One of the amateurs in this society whose name to-day is internationally famous was Madeleine Carroll. She took the title rôle in *Salma*, the 1926 university play—a fantasy in which the students taking part, Lois among them, spent some very happy weeks. It was in *Salma* (composed by Cranmer Byng, with incidental music by Sir Granville Bantock, and under the production of Stuart Vinden) that Madeleine Carroll first came into the public eye. Lois was her contemporary in the Arts Faculty, taking her degree in English and Madeleine taking hers in French.

Nowadays the Crescent Theatre (of which Mrs. Philip Rodway is a vice-president) is doing excellent work in the presenting of new plays and the bringing out of amateur talent. Birmingham's first Little Theatre is not primarily conducted for profit, but for the production of plays of quality, and there are many who see in it the development of a theatre on the lines of the famous Repertory.

CHAPTER 30

"Ye who love the haunts of Nature,
Love the sunshine of the meadow,
Love the shadow of the forest,
Love the wind among the branches,
And the rain-shower and the snow-storm,
And the rushing of great rivers . . .
Listen to this simple story."

"God grant me always the key of the fields." The far-off Huguenot in exile who first breathed that prayer could have wished it no more fervently than Philip Rodway. For him the meadowlands held peace, and in the green of the country-side he could forget, if only for a few hours, the stress and strain of theatrical worries. For him the flicker of a float meant infinitely more than the flicker of the footlights, and the rush of the weir made sweeter music than the biggest round of applause.

And so, on his brief little holidays—an afternoon here, a week-end there, which few and far between he allowed him-self—one would always find him somewhere by the river. From those early days when he had watched the new Royal rising from the ashes of the old, Harvington and the little Avon villages had called him; quiet spots, which seem to have belonged to another and more lovable age than our own, and which even to-day serenely dream away the hours, undis-turbed by the rush of the modern world. We may still eat cherries in the garden of "The Cottage of Content," Barton's sleepy wayside inn, and still spend days in summer meadows where the silence is unbroken, save when

"Some little village church bell far away
Slowly and dreamily strikes the hour of noon."

There were happy days at the Lower Lode, Tewkesbury, where the Severn and the Avon meet in one wide stretch of waters. There from the floating ferry we two have watched with Daddy and Mother the netting of the salmon, and there we played, as children, in the old orchard behind the riverside hotel. Our memories of the Lower Lode are less of fishing than of flowers, for we were just at the age when an armful of wild flowers held a very heaven of delight, and certainly never since have we found moon-daisies so large and white, ladysmocks so lilac, or dog-roses so deeply pink. The orchard seemed endless to us, with its crooked old apple trees, and the grass so high and thick that if we knelt down we were quite hidden. It was like being in a wood, and always a great adventure to explore our way from one corner to another. Fifteen years later we stayed for tea at the Lower Lode Hotel on our way home from a fishing expedition, and we saw again the same old three-cornered field with the apple trees. Alas! our great orchard was so small that the eye travelled over it and beyond in one glance. . . .

The first thrill of fishing came to us at Welford-on-Avon, with a peeled willow, bent pin, black cotton and bread paste —the paste itself usually black, from too zealous kneading. Daddy soon substituted a No. 9 hook for the bent pin, and installed us by the mill pool, where we gaily hauled out minnow after minnow, which were taken home to spend the next week swimming in patient misery round a bowl on the cottage table. If, by the end of that time, any of them had survived the ceaseless attention they received, they were taken pity on and returned to the mill pool.

But the lure of angling was upon us; Daddy was soon showing us how to make up a cast, and before long we each had our own rod. Shall we ever forget the thrill of catching our first fish! That sudden little dip, dip, of the float; "Oh, Daddy, is it a bite, or only the wind, or the current?" "It's a bite, but don't be in a hurry; give him another chance. There —he's at it again; wait, now—strike!" We struck with a will, the line tightened, the reel screamed joyously, and in our excitement, so did we "I've got him! Oh Daddy, I've got him!"

How many a day at Pershore-on-Avon have we all started off with Daddy, laden with tackle and creels and camp stools and thermos flasks, and a collection of cameras and cushions "which we might want." Sometimes we took the field path to the meadows by the lock, and there we would unpack— well away from the bank, lest our shadows disturb the fish— and having ensconced Mother with her sketch book and paint-box, make up the rods, and settle down quietly beside Daddy.

Sometimes we set off by boat, and rowed upstream three miles or more to Wyre Mill and the weirs beside the lock. There we would tie up under the willows of a tiny islet, our "*Mary Rose*" island, as Daddy used to call it.

What is the strange fascination of islands? Why does the very sound of the word set the spell working? Compton Mackenzie, with his *Fairy Gold*, in exquisite imagery pictures for us the islands that he loves . . . "small green islands in blue seas . . . misted blue islands in grey seas . . . tawny islands in green seas . . . pearly islands in dove grey seas"; and though we too have felt the magic of Sark at sunrise, of Herm and Jethou dark against the sky, yet this little wooded island on the Avon had a witchery of its own. It was so small that in less than a minute you could make your way through the trees and the tangle of wild roses, and be on the other side. Yet the saplings had planted themselves so thickly, with branches so closely intertwined, that the middle of the island lived in perpetual twilight, and even from there the boat tied up on the tiny beach was quite out of sight. And all the while the air was full of the roar of the two weirs, one on either side, thundering down from the upper to the lower reaches of the river. . . .

After a long day's fishing there, we packed up reluctantly and rowed slowly back in the evening light, the swifts circling and screaming high in the deepening blue; a little breeze beginning to ruffle the surface of the river. Or perhaps we waited for "the evening rise," and the bats would be wheeling before we cast off from the island. By then the afterglow had

FISHING DAYS

On the Avon at Pershore

(Lois's 6½ lb. pike)

vanished from the Bredon Hills, and the golden disc of the full moon was rising, rising, swiftly and gloriously; no sound save the swirl of the water, the drip of the oars, or the occasional "plop" of a water-rat, until we neared the darkening landing stage, and then the sound of the Abbey bells came drifting across the fields.

Many a time Daddy asked W. R. Young, his scenic artist, or another of the theatre staff, to come over to the Three Tuns Hotel at Pershore for a day or two's fishing. Jack Riches, his property master, loves to recall one of these occasions, when as they were walking through the fields Daddy said to him, "I think we're going to have some luck to-day, Jack"; to which he facetiously replied "Yes, if someone hasn't gone off with the river!" Lo and behold, when they reached the bank, the river *had* completely disappeared. Luckily we can account for this, since an early diary says "*They've started to draw the river to put a new turbine in at the mill, so we can't have the boat out, because there's nothing to row on!*" Corroborative evidence is also forthcoming of another of Jack's stories, where he tells how in one day Daddy "caught nearly a hundred of the finest perch I ever saw."

If only Daddy had kept a diary! With the exception of one early fishing story and his letters to Mother, we have no record of any kind which he himself made. So often our own attempts (ranging from the time when "*Ate an apple*" comprised the complete record for the day, through the stages of "*Daddy says it is a* BLIZZHARD," to the period of "*Went to school and lost my knitting. Went to school and found my knitting*") have resolved themselves into pages of "*Forget what did. Forget what did.*"

Vivid pictures flash across our minds; of the market day at Tenbury when Daddy pointed out to our delighted gaze an old Ford car, the front full of baskets and vegetables, and a cow and a bicycle in the back—the cow sitting comfortably on the back seat; of a quiet country road with the tempting notice "*Beware of cattle on the bend*," and the wood with the equally surprising sign-board "*Anyone found shooting trespassers will be prosecuted*"; of a day at Knightwick-on-Teme, when we helped to carry up Daddy's morning catch—half-a-dozen pike strung from the forked branches of trees; of walking home through the hopfields in the twilight, improvising softly on a favourite old song *Sweet chiming bells of long ago.* . . .

In such surroundings were the early fishing days, but now we must cast further ahead, and let a "Wickham's Fancy" or a "Coch-y-Bondhu" carry us to the trout streams of Wales.

First to Llanbrynmair, in Merionethshire, where the tiny village is little more than the Wynnstay Arms Hotel, and the boulder-strewn river gurgles below the old bridge,

> "*Where the pools are bright and deep,*
> *Where the grey trout lies asleep.*"

There, too, we found the fascination of the Welsh lakes. High up in the hills, unutterably lonely and remote, it almost seemed that until Daddy discovered them no human being had set foot there, for we never saw another soul, or heard a sound of the world below. Only the solitary curlew called, his plaintive note echoing weirdly across the water, and from far away came the bleat of a wandering sheep.

And next Ffestiniog, and the Pengwern Hotel across the Bala moors, standing at the head of the lovely estuary of the Dee, and looking down to Maentwrog. There the river broke into waterfalls, and the lakes were lonelier and lovelier still; Dubach, Tysani, and the Cymerau Falls, and Lake Morwynion, lost among the hills. . . .

And then—Pontrobert! Happy though Daddy had been in the haunts of his earlier years, no village in Wales could compare with this, no rivers ever hold the spell of that great pool where the Vyrnwy and the Banwy meet, and no fishing hotel ever possess the indescribable charm of "The Royal Oak." And where could we find the counterpart of the jovial keeper —that good-hearted Falstaff of a man—George Hayes? or of his wife, who has a way with a trout in a frying-pan which has surely never been excelled?

THE PENGWERN HOTEL, FFESTINIOG

Mother, Daddy, Phyllis, Lois and friends

Shall we ever forget those trout breakfasts; the setting off afterwards with light hearts and our fly-rods, and a whole long glorious day before us; the sight of the waters of the Vyrnwy sparkling in the sunshine below the arch of the old stone bridge, racing down the shallows in a series of little waves; working upstream, trying fresh water for a few minutes, and then on again for two or three miles; the *zppp* . . . as the line sings out, then "Got him," and the exultant note in Daddy's voice and the light in his blue eyes, as the little 9 ft. greenheart bends nearly double and he is in to a good fish. . . .

Sometimes Daddy invited a friend to join us for a few days; often when we started out in the morning George Hayes would set off the same way with his gun; and Wilfred Nunn, our chauffeur of many years, always accompanied us on these expeditions, loaded with paraphernalia and hung about with fishing tackle. Besides knowing everything there was to know about cars, there were few subjects, even to the most abstruse, upon which Wilfred could not discourse with complete ease and a wealth of learned argument. Moreover, he was a good judge of character, and he pictures Daddy clearly and simply when he says "He was a man of very small pleasures, with two main objects in life: his work and his family."

He recalls many of Daddy's characteristics, and one especially struck us as a very true point. "In forgiveness he was complete," writes our erstwhile chauffeur, "and he never raked up old scores. An incident in this way I recall which happened by the lakes at Llanbrynmair. I was about twenty-one at the time, and the inaction of fishing by the lake was boring me badly, so I set off to climb the nearest hill. Approaching the top the ground became very much broken and rough, and in my climb I started a few stones rolling. The hills were steep, the fall of the stones was rapid, and they echoed considerably. After listening for a few seconds, without any actual thought of what I was doing, I started off a couple of good sized boulders. Just a pause to let them go, and I started to descend. Mr. Rodway was waiting for me on

the other side of the lake, waiting with a real rating for me.
Those boulders had started an avalanche of rocks and stones
which had come down with terrific speed; some had bounced
from the bank very nearly to the middle of the lake. How near
Mr. Rodway had been to them was not among the things he
told me, but finally he wound up with 'And now let's forget
all about it.' He did, and never referred to it afterwards."

A story of the type which all fisherman love to tell happened
on the Banwy at Pontrobert. Wilfred had just caught a half-
pound trout, only to have the line break when it was within
a foot of the bank. A few minutes later Daddy, about twenty
yards further on, called to him to bring the net. They landed
the fish, and there, hanging from its jaws, was a length of gut.
It was the same trout, caught for the second time.

Daddy and George Hayes usually had some trick or other
in progress. The keeper thoroughly enjoyed a joke, whether
it was played by him or on him. They once made a bet with
each other as to who would catch the best trout of the day;
both landed a fish of about 2 lb. weight, and it looked as if
the result would be a draw. George, suspicious that there
might be a catch in it, kept a close watch on Daddy, but not
close enough to prevent him stuffing his trout with a quantity
of small stones, the effect of which definitely decided the
issue! When they returned to the Oak and the fish were
weighed, Hayes took his defeat with a good grace, though he
vowed revenge next morning when Mrs. Hayes opened the
fish to cook for breakfast.

Another time, knowing that he had spent the whole morning lying in wait for a stoat which had been causing havoc
among the chickens, we decided that he must not be disappointed, and set off on a search of the surrounding fields.
At tea-time we dashed into the Royal Oak with the news that
we could actually see the stoat in the hedge just opposite.
George was on his feet in a flash. "Quick, Lizzie," in a loud
whisper to Mrs. Hayes, "my gun, let me get at my gun!"
Breathlessly we all tiptoed through the door. "There he is—

can you see him?" Yes, he saw him, and two shots rang out in quick succession. George crossed over to pick up his prize. "Why, it's—it's—!" he exploded. Here we fled. After all, no keeper likes to discover that he has shot an already dead stoat, carefully extracted from one of his own traps that very afternoon.

George himself was equally well versed in the art of make-believe, and if you want to see his face become wreathed in smiles you have only to ask "How's John Watt?" This episode was undoubtedly his greatest triumph. Aided and abetted by Daddy—who provided a false beard and moustache, and worked up the necessary atmosphere—he came up to the Royal Oak, and for a full half-hour so completely carried the illusion of a stranger on his travels, that not a soul there doubted his authenticity.

An event which always brought keepers and farmers for miles around was that of "digging a fox," when, accompanied by earnest little terriers, half a dozen of us would set forth, and as we passed the different farms the men would come out and join us with their guns and spades, until there were twenty or more. One such hunt we had when the whole countryside was deep in snow, and that most amazing walk, silently tracking a fox along the timber track below Lletty Derryn, was an experience which we shall never forget. We came striding back through fields of snow straight into the sunset, and the colours and reflections of the sunset on the snow were almost unbelievable—white hills glowing with pink, shadows a clear blue, and the sky beyond blue with pink clouds.

On a bitterly cold day in March we remember walking back from Goblin Wood, and as we turned into the last lane we met Ivor Williams of Hen Dafarn, with two little lambs staggering along in front of him. We were astonished to see such tiny creatures walking, and Daddy, always interested in animals, stopped and asked how old they were. Ivor told him two hours. "Surely you mean two days?" No, they had only been born that afternoon, and had already walked more than

DI

half a mile. Every morning Daddy went down to the little post office to put through his daily trunk call to the theatres. Every morning Ivor's black dog Jet would meet him and accompany him across the bridge, and always before he went through the little shop to telephone, "A bun for Jet, please, Mrs. Jervis."

One of the first things Daddy always bought from the village shop (wherever we were) was a little ball, which usually accompanied us in one of his pockets whenever we were not actually on a fishing expedition. Many a time have we tossed it between us as we walked back to the inn, and often, lingering by the bridge on the way, has there collected a wistful and admiring group of little boys, who to their great joy were quite naturally allowed to join in, by the simple expedient of putting an accidental catch within their reach. Once the number grew till there were nine little boys and two small girls, and we had a hectic and glorious half-hour together outside the old inn before dinner.

The next evening, coming up laden from the river, thinking of the roast ducks awaiting us, we were astonished to see a crowd of children standing about outside the Royal Oak. Signs of excitement manifested themselves at our approach.

"I do believe it's those youngsters turned up for their game!" exclaimed Daddy. "Come along, we can't disappoint them"; and along we came, disentangling ourselves from the creels and haversacks and rods with which we were slung. Down they went on the bench outside, the ball was fetched, and once more we were in the midst of the game, making new and ridiculous rules as we went on. Daddy christened them "The Team," and every evening after that they were observed assembling in hopeful twos and threes for their nightly match.

Dinner in the low, lamplit room was always a cheery affair, discussing the day's catch and plans for the next morning—should it be Ty Mawr? or Dolanog? or the stretch below the Frieth Woods? After dinner we often slipped across the tiny hall into the cosy little parlour, where George Hayes and his wife would greet us with enthusiasm, and we should all have a couple of hours talking or playing Derry down Derry before we lit our candles and said good-night.

This game, otherwise known as nap, was a hilarious affair as played there, as whenever occasion demanded Daddy delighted in calling out "Derry down Derry, Derry down Day," and we would all join in and sing it together. Strangely enough, though he never played cards in the ordinary way, his luck whenever he did was phenomenal. Time out of count he was dealt a complete nap hand, till it began to get beyond a joke, and the cards were shuffled and dealt in every conceivable way to try and prevent it—all without avail.

But in whatever way we began the evening, we should generally finish up with one of George's fishing tales. He was, and is, an inspired teller of stories. As he related them, even the simplest incidents were always worth hearing; he had such a rare sense of humour, and withal took such an obvious delight in the telling, that Daddy invariably led him on.

We can see them now, settled comfortably after dinner on the wooden bench in the little parlour, with the shadows of firelight and lamplight falling between them. . . . Daddy takes his pipe out of his mouth, and with a twinkle across the room at us, says, "Come on, George, let's hear that story of yours I like so much."

"Now which one would that be, sir?" asks George innocently.

Daddy reminds him, and he begins to chuckle:

"Well, sir, it was like this," he says. "It's a true story, you will remember, and it happened on this very river, the Vyrnwy. One evening a Mr. Griffiths came down asking me if I could catch a fish for his mother who was very ill. I told him to come down the next evening. I made up two casts for the morning, and started by lower Glanafon. When I got to the river, fish were rising well to the fly, and I caught eight fish very quickly, so I thought I would carry on. While going upstream I saw a gentleman wading and fishing; when I saw him I got out of the river not to disturb the water, and walked on the bank. He said 'Good morning, keeper, have you had any luck to-day?'

"I said 'Yes sir, I have had a few, I only started in the pool just down below.'

" 'That's funny,' he remarked, 'I haven't moved a fish to-day! What have you caught them with?'

"I answered and said 'A little Cock Wing.'

" 'Wait a minute,' and he waded across to me. 'May I have a look at that fly?'

"I showed him the fly, then he asked me if I had any to sell? I said I was sorry that I had only seven, but if he would care to accept three he was more than welcome.

"He wanted to pay me for them, but I refused, saying that I might be short of a fly some day and would be glad for him to return the compliment.

" 'Well,' he said, 'It's jolly kind of you,' and gave me two cigars and a drink of whisky.

"He then asked me if he might see my fish.

"I said 'Certainly, sir,' and showed them for him.

" 'By Jove, you have got a nice lot,' and indeed they were a very even lot of trout.

" 'Look here, keeper, would you mind selling me these fish?' I said 'No sir, I never sold a fish in my life, but if you care to accept them you are quite welcome. I have come out to catch one or two for a sick person. I dare say I can get higher up what I want.'

" 'Well, it's jolly good of you; I quite understand you're not selling the fish, but you have a drink when you go down to the village,' and he put a coin in my hand, which I thanked him for and put in my pocket and said good morning.

" 'Oh,' he said, 'look here, keeper, I have a gentleman friend fishing upstream, and we have got a bet on who catches the most fish; you won't tell him, will you, that I have had these fish off you?'

" 'Certainly not, sir.'

"After going round the corner I went to see what my friend had so kindly given me; to my surprise it was half a sovereign! Thinks I to myself, Where is this other gent? and I started fishing very careful and had twelve fish before I saw the other gent, and he was in to a good fish I could see from the way his rod was bending.

"I knew he hadn't seen me, and I wanted him to see me, so I asked him if he would care for me to help him to land his fish. He said 'Thank you.' I was very quickly behind that fish, and had him in my landing net.

" 'It's the first I have had to-day; what sport have you been having?' I told him not too bad.

" 'What flies?'

" 'A little Cock Wing was taking well this morning, but they have come on to the Red Spinner.'

" 'Cock Wing? I have never heard of that fly,' so I gave him three. . . .

" 'Did you see a gent fishing down below?'

"I said 'Yes sir.'

" 'You don't know what sport he has had?'

"I answered and said 'No, I don't.'

" 'Will you have a drink, keeper?'

" 'Thank you, sir.' I had two cigars and a drop of whisky.

"I was about taking my leave, when he asked me if he could see my fish.

"I said yes and showed them for him.

" 'By Jove, you have got a nice lot. Will you sell me those fish, keeper? Because I have got a bet on with that gent down below who catches the most fish.'

" 'Well, I won't sell them, but if you care to accept them you can have them. I want two or three for a sick person.'

" 'It's awfully kind of you.' . . . I had another ten shillings and was jolly sorry there were no more gents.

"Before parting he said, 'Now look, keeper, you won't tell that gent that I have had these fish?'

" 'No sir,' I said.

"I have wondered many a time who won the bet."

Here George's eyes would seek the ceiling, and come to rest on one of the smoked hams hanging there. This was a pre-arranged signal between him and Daddy that he was ready for a drink, and every evening, whenever he was asked "Have a drink, George?" and his eyes rolled heavenwards, Mrs. Hayes or Gladys would disappear into a dark little room adjoining, and return bearing the refreshment on a tray. Even here Hayes was not always safe—it's extraordinary what a resemblance there can be between whisky and cold tea! Never shall we forget his face when he swallowed that first mouthful, nor his expression one night, when, looking up, his eyes roved the rafters in vain—the last ham had been taken down to cut for Evan Arthur!

Not long ago we heard again from Pontrobert, and George, writing about Daddy, recalled once more "the many miles we tramped together on our fishing expeditions, and the feverish battles we related to each other after a hard day's fishing. Mr. Rodway was indeed a very keen angler, and he was far from being a selfish one. Kind and thoughtful to everyone, I noticed many a time he would put his friend or his chauffeur on the best stretch of water; for all that, as a rule he would have the best catch of trout."

It may have been purely intuition, though more probably it was the result of his extraordinarily keen powers of observa-tion, but the fact remains that Daddy always knew exactly what a fish was likely to do under any given circumstances; he knew just *why* a trout would rise in a different way in the same spot an hour earlier or later. One of the things which he and Hayes often discussed together was the curious phe-nomenon that, for a short period at a certain time of the year, the last "rise" was definitely somewhere about four o'clock in the afternoon. His old friend James Hewson, whose name was associated with some of his early pantomimes, wrote a little story on this early-closing theme while staying at

Pontrobert, and Daddy so loved to turn it up in the visitors' book that we have been tempted to give it here.

FISHING—TEN TO FOUR

Hayes said to me, "It's no use you going down to the river, sir, the fish won't rise now."

"What's the matter with them?" I asked him.

"There's nothing the matter with them, but you'll catch no fish after four o'clock at this time of the season."

I looked hard at him, and he returned my look unflinchingly. He had told me so many weird fish stories that—however, let that pass. I have myself related tales of feverish battles with trout, that my friends have given way to drink and disbelief, so I forgive Hayes freely. But this four o'clock closing movement for trout was a new idea, and required faith.

"Well, Hayes, I'm going down," I said stubbornly.

"Very good, sir." And he washed his hands of me, as one full of unreasoning and ignorant obstinacy, who would come to a bad end someday. And I went down and flung flies about the weir with a recklessness that boded much profit to the tackle manufacturer.

I had made my way down the river about a hundred yards from my base, without a rise, when I heard a voice near me say:

"They've all left for the day, sir."

I looked around, and seeing no one, and having belief in but one kind of spirits, I concluded I was mistaken. I was preparing a most elaborate and scientific throw, when I heard the voice again, saying:

"We close here at four o'clock, sir, week-days, and one on Saturdays."

Again I swept the landscape with a searching look, and found no one. It was uncanny. I had heard of wood nymphs, and water babies, but I did not believe in them. Though there is nothing of the wood-nymph or water baby about Hayes, I thought that he was playing me a trick from some place of concealment.

"It's all right, Hayes, I see you," I called out, sadly perjuring myself.

"It isn't Mr. Hayes, sir, it's me," replied a voice, with regrettably bad grammar. And then to my amazement, I saw, standing on her tail, on one of the stones, an old chub, looking up at me.

"I'm the caretaker, sir, and everybody else has gone for the day."

Pulling myself together to grapple with this astounding phenomenon, I said:

"What do you mean?"

"Well, sir, our hours down here are ten to four at this time of the year, and there's no one on the premises but me, and I don't suppose you've called for me?" And the old dear looked up archly at me, remembering moments of tenderness in her youth.

"What nonsense is all this? Hayes told me something about this early closing, but . . ."

"Oh!" she interrupted, "I don't hold with anything what he says as a rule, but for once he's right, if he said that. I've heard of some of the things what he says to gentlemen what comes here, and they fair make my fins stand on end!" and a tremor of scorn and indignation shook her from head to tail. "Why! He is telling everybody that he once shot two pike with one barrel, up at the bridge yonder, and they must be ninnies what'll believe that. Not but what I wish he could shoot the whole lot of them with a penny whistle—nasty, greedy, blood-thirsty things, them pike be."

"But that story's quite true, for I was with him at the time he shot them."

"Was you, sir?" still dubiously. "Oh, well, I'll take your word for it, sir."

She ogled up at me in quite an embarrassing manner.

"I don't want you to go, sir, but it's no use you staying here if you're expecting to catch anyone. My Word! Who's that?"

And in her excitement she slipped and fell back into the water, but was up and out again in a jiffy. Something had sharply seized upon one of my flies, which I had left trailing down the river while I was holding this extraordinary conversation. I struck, and pulled up a fish about the size of my finger.

"Well, I declare, it's that little Billy Samlet. He's stopped after the others, larking about, instead of going straight home. You'll put him back again, won't you?" she pleaded.

"I would if it would be any good to him, but I'm afraid the shock has killed him."

"Dear, dear, this'll be a sad blow to his mother. She lives just behind that big boulder in the pool yonder. These young imps do give us old uns a lot of trouble and no end of anxiety. His Mother'll break her heart over this."

"Oh, she has so many youngsters that she'll never miss this one. They give us a lot of trouble and anxiety, too, confound them," I added, with a touch of irritation. "We don't want them."

But she didn't heed me, for with tears streaming down her motherly old cheeks, she had laid the little chap out on a stone, and was tenderly wiping him dry with a fin.

"Well, it's no use me waiting here any longer, I suppose?"

"No sir, it isn't," she replied, stifling a sob and drying her eyes. "You'd better come to-morrow, about ten o'clock. Some of them is sure to be here then."

"I'll come," I replied very decidedly. I handed the old lady a tip of a choice bit of cheese. She looked at it with manifest misgiving.

"It ain't got any hook in it, has it, sir?"

"No, no, I wouldn't play that dirty trick on you after the pleasant little chat we've had together."

"Thank you, sir," and she brightened up and took the tip which she at once swallowed with gusto.

"Mr. Hayes has had me before with cheese on a hook, and I was hard put to to get away, so I have to be careful. He doesn't go straight with the likes of us, and ain't to be trusted."

"I'll talk to him about it when I get back."

"Thank you, sir, I wish you would. It would be such a relief to us to feel that we could enjoy a bit of a meal without being suddenly jerked into the air in the middle of it."

"I'll see to it. Good evening."

"Good evening, sir, and thank you for a real gentleman. You'll not forget, sir, ten to four is our hours down here, at this time of the year." And she slipped off the stone and flopped into the river, leaving me to tie up and return to the Royal Oak, fishless, to the unconcealed triumph of Hayes.

Looking through this same old book, which we have borrowed from the Royal Oak, we find an entry by Hayes:

> "March 18th, 1927. Mr. Rodway killed 8 good trout in 30 minutes while staying at the Royal Oak."

The eye travels on; we come upon our own names on almost every page. Against the last note but one, July, 1931, in Mother's writing (though inspired by Daddy) is a favourite catchphrase of hers, "*I'll be back in a minute.*" Her next—and last—entry (in September, 1931), reads, in unconscious tragic irony, "*The minute's up.*"

*   *   *

Never again shall we come up from the river with our fly-rods, when the owlet light is come, and along the darkening lanes dim hedges glow with the pale stars of dog-roses. And we can only seek for "consolation in the fact that though things change, they pass in a perpetuity of beauty. The stream remains though it does not stand still—the stream of lovely things that change, watched by loving eyes that change."

"Where the pools are bright and deep,
Where the grey trout lies asleep"

Snapshots by Phyllis

THE LAST HOLIDAY, PONTROBERT, SEPTEMBER, 1931
Daddy and Mother. The Royal Oak

CHAPTER 31

THE BIRMINGHAM BAN

(From 1925 onwards)

As far back as 1925 there was aroused general interest in what came to be known throughout the country as the "Birmingham Ban." As P.R. was closely concerned in the circumstances leading up to and surrounding the notorious "Pavlova incident" and the "Robey song controversy," it may be as well to give the history, so far as we can trace it, of happenings which caused Birmingham's name to be a jest among newspaper readers everywhere.

It must be premised that few people ever knew "the truth, the whole truth, and nothing but the truth" about these matters. One, at least, is dead. Another is a police official who cannot well be asked to tell all he knows. Others most closely concerned have their own reasons for maintaining a discreet reticence. What we are about to write, however, has been compiled and tested very carefully by enquiry from every possible source, and by reference to statements published under credible authority from time to time.

In November, 1925, Anna Pavlova and her company of Russian dancers were engaged to give two "flying" matinées at the Grand Theatre, Birmingham, then, as for years previously, one of the principal music halls in the country.

That same week the evening attraction at the Grand was a revue presented by Francis Laidler (the Bradford producer), whose wife, Gwladys Stanley, played the leading rôle therein.

The first intimation that the public had of the so-called "trouble" was a report published in a Birmingham paper to the effect that Pavlova had been refused permission to dance without tights at the Grand. Refused by whom? Presumably by the Public Entertainments Committee of the Licensing Justices . . . though later, when the "Birmingham Ban Joke" was in full cry, imaginative newspaper correspondents fell into the habit of putting it on the Watch Committee.

References to the Birmingham Watch Committee became a "sure laugh" for comedians everywhere, whereas in truth whatever regulations were involved in the matter were dictated by the Public Entertainments Committee. The Watch Committee, as the body responsible for the control of the police, merely lent to the other committee an officer whose duty it was to visit theatres and music-halls, and see whether the regulations were being obeyed.

To revert to Pavlova, the newspaper report was entirely erroneous, and whoever inspired it must have known it was so. She was never refused permission to dance bare-legged in Birmingham. She *never applied for permission* to dance bare-legged in Birmingham, and we doubt whether it was ever her habit to dance bare-legged anywhere. Our own recollection is that some of the men in her company used to do so when it was artistically necessary, but that Pavlova and her women colleagues invariably wore fleshings (except, perhaps, the girl who performed Anitra's dance, in long flowing draperies; and no one ever heard of official objection being raised against her costume!).

In point of fact, there is the strongest ground for believing that the whole Pavlova affair was a publicity stunt engineered, strangely enough, not by any one associated with Pavlova, but by Mr. Laidler's publicity agents. Certain it is that Miss Stanley had been accustomed to play bare-legged in revue elsewhere in England, that she wanted to do so in Birmingham, and that, to quote an official communiqué from the Public Entertainments Committee a short while later, "objection *was* made to the costume of a woman who appeared at the same house in a revue presented during the same week, but this woman did *not* appear in Madame Pavlova's entertainment." The italics, which are ours, stress the point that if all this was a coincidence it was a very timely one.

On this shaky foundation was built the famous "Birmingham Joke," which was to become current coin of comedians' patter in a short time, and is not yet out of circulation. It required one more spectacular incident to attract national attention.

That incident was soon forthcoming.

A fortnight later George Robey appeared at the same hall—the Grand. He duly "worked" (in vaudeville you "work," whereas in drama you "play") two houses on the Monday night. On the Tuesday certain newspapers, not only local, came out with the statement, boldly written up as a sensation, that one verse of one song sung by him at the first house had been banned by Superintendent May . . . for there is no point in withholding the name of the experienced, efficient, courteous, and tactful officer whose duty it was to visit the theatres and music-halls on behalf of the committee.

The affair was screamed from newspaper housetops throughout the country, found its way to foreign parts, and completed the spectacular launching of the Birmingham Joke. A minor "incident" on the same Monday night involved a sketch by Robey, which he withdrew from his programme after it had been pointed out to him that the "tag," or closing line, did not appear in the script as licensed by the Lord Chamberlain. From these two "bans" George Robey naturally drew a tremendous bulk of advertisement and no doubt profited therefrom in other places on his tour.

All who know the snowball-like propensities of such a story in the hands of certain newspaper correspondents will realise that "G.R." was probably not responsible for all the embellishments which this particular story soon acquired. He may not have sponsored the statement, for instance, that the verses objected to in his song, *I stopped, I looked, and I listened*, had been sung by him before the King and Queen. Whoever it was, received the lie direct in the *Daily Express* on November 19th, 1926, from Mr. Hannen Swaffer, who wrote: "That was not true. The King and Queen never heard this verse, which was interpolated. Besides, since I objected to this song when Mr. Robey sang it at the Alhambra, in London, years ago, I am surprised that no other city took objection to it before it was submitted to the calm sense of Birmingham's judgment."

On November 30th, 1925, a private meeting between the Public Entertainments Committee and representatives of the Watch Committee was held for consideration of "the two recent incidents arising out of the local censorship of the stage performances in Birmingham." The communiqué above quoted was issued to the press. It contained the following terse statement on the second incident: "With regard to the comments as to Mr. Robey's song, it should be known that one verse only formed part of the particular performance in question, and that verse was considered to be prurient. At the conclusion of the first house a note was handed to the manager of the Grand Theatre, in which it was pointed out that the verse in question 'was cut out when sung at the Empire on September 26th, 1921, *and is still objected to.*' "

There can be no doubt at all that the jovial and astute George Robey was deliberately "trying it on." He knew the verse had been cut four years earlier, and that the same authority could not fail to object to it again. If the Entertainments Committee, through Supt. May, did the logical thing, he was going to make a big stunt out of it—as he did: it was perhaps the finest free publicity stunt of his career. *If they had passed in 1925 what they had excised in 1921*, who would have been more disappointed than Mr. Robey? The only point in which the stunt may have failed was that no newspaper, so far as we can trace, was bold enough to publish the words of the verse!

Philip Rodway's interest in these affairs was mainly indirect, but none the less vital. As the senior and principal theatrical manager in Birmingham he was, of course, deeply concerned over anything affecting, or likely to affect, the relations between the licensees, the licensers, and the police. Beyond that, he was one whose attitude to such a question would be bound to emerge from motives higher than self-interest. His whole professional, public, and private life was the life of one intensely proud of Birmingham as the theatrical centre of provincial England, intensely jealous of its high reputation as a leading city. For all his far-flung interests he was truly "of Birmingham," fierce in his local patriotism, and no pen-portrait of him is authentic which does not delineate this quality.

Judge, then, how his anger mounted as the great Birmingham Joke went round the halls and through the newspapers. Not that he could not be a severe critic of local conditions or proceedings when they offended his brain or his heart: not that he was one to bow before an official decree, however weightily backed, if he felt resistance to be necessary and feasible . . . but here he *knew* the inner history, *knew* that the house of anti-Birmingham humour was founded on sand. He was pained beyond expression by the things he read and heard, indescribably hurt that anyone, owing Birmingham gratitude, could yet heap ridicule upon so hospitable a city. As for the imaginative correspondents who fledged their wit at Birmingham's expense—his opinion of them was, like Mr. Robey's verse, unprintable!

Often he stated his intention of telling the public the whole truth about the Pavlova and Robey incidents, but he always added "Not until I've retired." We know it was a genuine intention, which would one day have been fulfilled had he lived to enter on a period when disclosure was unhampered by business considerations. As it is, we can give no more of the inner history than we have collated from other sources, though in due course we shall quote various utterances of P.R.'s which indicate his mind on this most interesting matter.

First, though, it is desirable to explain exactly what constituted the "notorious" Birmingham Censorship. In contrast to a welter of public misunderstanding and confused thinking, here are the simple facts.

As in every other English city, town, or district, it is the duty of the Licensing Justices to make regulations for the conduct of public entertainment, and of the police authorities to ensure that these regulations are observed. There is nothing unique so far, in Birmingham's procedure, is there?

Is there, then, anything in Birmingham's actual regulations calculated so to distinguish the city from other centres as to render it abnormally conspicuous or ludicrous? Anything to justify the accusations of priggishness, unco'guidness and so forth which were so freely levelled against us a few years ago? Anything to make it irksomely difficult for the performer to follow his or her legitimate calling, or for the citizen to derive pleasure and profit from attendance at theatre or music hall? That compendium, surely, contains all the relevant considerations.

The answer must be both general and particular: general, for the regulations as a whole; particular, for those specially involved in the Birmingham Joke.

Birmingham, be it admitted, has a great many regulations for the conduct of theatres, music-halls, cinemas, etc. They govern every conceivable detail on construction and management. They are designed to guard against every possible risk which may threaten the safety, comfort, or health of man, woman, or child while in a place of public entertainment. To the lay mind they may seem meticulous and finicky . . . but a whole volume of justification is summed up in the statement that within living memory Birmingham has had no tragedy, no panic, no serious fire in a playhouse or similar place.

When one reads, as one does periodically, of dreadful happenings in other places (some of comparable importance) one is inclined to forgive the over-cautiousness, if it be a fact, of the Birmingham authorities. Besides, there is ever a ready and constant disposition to hear the managers when they think it worth while putting forward a case for the modification or relaxation of any clause, though it is natural that a definite wish expressed by, say, the head of the Fire Brigade, should out-balance a weighty volume of managerial argument. The proved value of this, we repeat, is Birmingham's long immunity from disaster . . . or as P.R. put it once to Hannen Swaffer, "The licensing people of Birmingham have made certain regulations for controlling entertainments and, unlike many other cities, they see that they are carried out. They are not content with merely printing them and leaving it at that. Good luck to them!"

Now for Baptista's "special thing," the governance of stage performances. . . . Many years ago a rule was made that the licensee of a theatre or music-hall should maintain and keep good order and decent behaviour on the premises during the hours of public performance. Nothing should be done, acted, recited, sung, or exhibited which was profane or improper.

On those half-hundred words hung—and hang—all the law and the prophets, all the arguments, recriminations, and "wisecracks," yea, the great Birmingham Joke itself. But surely (you will say) an extremely ordinary and reasonable regulation? Surely no self-respecting city would expect its licensers to content themselves with narrower powers? And surely no self-respecting licensee would cavil at signing to such a bond? Dear readers, we hoped you would say just that, and we quite agree with you.

But there is more to a regulation than its *wording*. There is its *interpretation* and, most important, there is its *administration*. If we are to deputise efficiently for Daddy in exposing the Birmingham Joke, we must try to explain exactly how far Interpretation has expanded Wording, and how far Administration has ruled Interpretation.

About the time of the Pavlova and Robey incidents, Interpretation had undoubtedly accepted as a general principle for some time that tights would be worn on the Birmingham stage. This reading had become authoritative fourteen or fifteen years earlier, when revue began to sweep England.

We must qualify what we have written. While the magistrates were against the general principle of bare legs, the

EI

door of artistic necessity was never completely closed. If it was considered necessary to the artistic verity of a performance, it was always open to the presenter to ask for a departure from the general rule. No such application, as we have shown, was made by or for Pavlova, but before that incident arose there had been relaxations in several cases. Mr. Leon Salberg, we know, resisted the rule during the previous winter, when the Cinderella of his pantomime at the Alexandra played for three months without tights; here it would have been grotesque to make her wear them.

At the time Pavlova was at the Grand, P.R. had Karsavina and a Russian ballet at the Royal, and certainly some of the girls danced bare-legged in items which demanded it. Can there be the least doubt that if an artist of Pavlova's eminence had wanted a concession she would have got it?

For the moment, so much for the Pavlova incident.

*   *   *

Now for the Robey incident, and all that arose from the two.

For nearly twenty years Supt. May had been the officer supplied by the Watch Committee to the Public Entertainments Committee for the purpose of supervising theatrical and music-hall performances. It was his habit, when he saw or heard anything to which he felt objection should be taken, to give the management a friendly hint. One can imagine that this system of friendly hinting was generally acceptable to the managers, who had to live in the city week in and week out, if not to those performers who could pack up and move on at the week-end.

Occasionally Supt. May and one of the managements would be at variance over a point, but in the vast majority of cases there was provided an avenue of amicable agreement, which must have been of direct advantage and assistance to the managers, who might otherwise have become liable for conduct on the stage by performers outside their effective control. Imagine, for example, some local manager, employed by a syndicate, trying to prevent a star comedian, drawing £250 a week, from interpolating risqué lines. Compare how much easier it would be for that same manager to go to the same comedian after the first house on Monday and say "Sorry, old man, but the magistrates' inspector says that line must come out."

The system, like all long-standing systems, was open to criticism in operation if not in theory. In theory, the management could fight the inspector before his employing committee, but in practice, plainly, the committee would be prone to rely on his judgment. In other words, the opinion of the inspector was apt to become the opinion of the committee, and thus something like a dictatorship was created. At worst, however, it was a benevolent dictatorship, and if Supt. May's judgment had ever been frequently or flagrantly at fault there must have been ways and means of revealing his fallibility to the justices. In fact, he was on excellent terms with the managers as a group, and P.R., while deprecating the necessity for any supervision which implied that he was not capable of preserving propriety in his own theatres, said more than once that nobody could have made a better job of it than did Supt. May.

What the committee thought of their officer may be gauged from the preamble to the statement issued to the press just after the Robey incident. They had passed a resolution entirely approving the action taken by Supt. May, and accepting responsibility for it, and were of the opinion that he "had been the means for many years of preventing a very large amount of undesirable incidents which would have discredited the good name of Birmingham."

That was exactly what P.R. felt, too. "While our so called censorship and bans are being guyed up and down the country by every low comedian," he once said quite bitterly, "the fact remains that as a rule any citizen can safely take his wife and his children into any Birmingham theatre or hall without the danger of a string of questionable jokes. There are not many towns of which the same can be

said, and there are not many towns which the really tip-top
artists are so anxious to keep on their date books. Even the
comedians who get laughs at Bolton by gagging about the
Birmingham Watch Committee would be down on their
hands and knees begging for a return date if they thought
there was any danger of being really banned in Birmingham."

The frank and full statement of fact issued by the justices
after the Pavlova and Robey incidents naturally did not
stifle the great Birmingham Joke.

It is axiomatic that you can never catch up with a libel,
and this particular libel was far too good fun for its perpe-
trators to let go.

It was both a libel and a slander, for it proceeded by word
of mouth as well as in writing. Additions to it were deliberately engineered by various publicity agents, who would
arrange for something to be done or said on the stage which
no licensing authority could possibly allow . . . and then
they would enlist the aid of the local correspondents of
certain London papers, always eager for "copy" of this sort,
to get the story of another "Birmingham Ban" broadcast.

On one occasion, during a minor heat-wave, a comedian
whose revue was not doing at all well at a local music-hall,
wrote to Supt. May calmly demanding that all his girls
should be allowed to appear without tights in scenes in which
they wore little else. He sent copies of his letter to the Press,
and another Birmingham Ban was announced.

P.R. was dead against the publicity use made of Birmingham's so-called "ban," because he recognised the harm it
was doing to the city's entertainment houses by constant
reiteration. He foresaw, too, that the magistrates would in
time be goaded into altering their system, and that any
change might well be for the worse so far as licenses were
concerned.

Which is exactly what happened.

In February, 1929, following an upset between Supt. May
and a couple of music-hall artists over some lines in their

act, an important change of procedure was instituted. It was explained in a statement published in the following terms:

"For the public information, it may be pointed out that, while stage plays and revues have to be submitted to the Lord Chamberlain for license, this does not apply to the smaller acts which constitute a variety performance. In Birmingham these minor performances (minor in the matter of length) have been subjected to 'cuts,' and Police Supt. May, who acts for the Police and the Public Entertainments Committee, has been in the habit of issuing 'chits,' giving particulars of lines which he regards as breaches of Rule 6 of the justices' regulations.

"These 'chits' will in future not be issued, for according to a letter sent by the Chief Constable, Sir Charles Rafter, to managers of places of entertainment, Supt. May, who will continue to visit the shows, will no longer make his requests direct to the manager, but will report to the Chief Constable. The latter, it is to be inferred, will then bring the complaint before the Public Entertainments Committee.

"In his letter the Chief Constable states that for some time past certain difficulties have been raised in connection with the procedure followed, and misrepresentations of the action of the 'police censor' have appeared in the Press. The notice by Supt. May, it is added, 'was intended entirely as a friendly action on the part of the authorities to assist the managers in the administration of their very difficult duties; but the matter seems not to have been accepted in that light.' "

Thus the managers were deprived of the benefit of the Superintendent's support in bringing pressure to bear upon recalcitrant performers, and were in the position that, if official objection were taken to anything said or done, the first intimation they might receive would be by summons. By which time the performer concerned would be miles away from Birmingham, but the manager would have a black mark against him when the time came for renewal of licence.

It was not long before some of them were sighing for a return to the old system of friendly hints: but, as Philip Rodway remarked when one of them was complaining to him, "You can't have it both ways. You've made May and the Justices a laughing stock throughout the country, and now you've got to put up with the consequences."

Before this change, we must explain, the position in regard to bare legs on Birmingham stages had been clarified beyond cavil by the Public Entertainments Committee, who, in July, 1928, decided to remove all restrictions beyond those imposed by the common law as to ordinary propriety. Here follows the *Birmingham Mail* report (July 17th, 1928) on the decisive meeting:

"Yesterday the question as to whether the policy of compelling artists to wear tights should be continued any longer was considered by the Public Entertainments Committee, and the magistrates came to the conclusion that the regulation, which has been so irksome, particularly to dancing girls, might well be dispensed with, provided, of course, that the entertainment was conducted in a perfectly proper way."

Officially, it was emphasised by the chairman (Mr. S. E. Short) there had never been any such rule in force. Everything depended on the type of the entertainment, and the decision rested on the police superintendent.

A good deal seems to have rested on the police superintendent, who emerged from the affair with more distinction than most others concerned. Certainly the performers who plugged the Birmingham Joke so unscrupulously had nothing to boast about. Neither had the newspaper correspondents who went about exploiting it for the sake of copy. We must admit that the Public Entertainments Committee let their officer continue for years to enforce a non-existent embargo, and then at last made a climb-down which, if it had to be made at all, could with advantage to everybody's dignity—not least Birmingham's—have been made years earlier.

We have said that Philip Rodway's interest in the Birmingham Ban was mainly indirect. But not completely, for, much against his will and to his annoyance, he was dragged in on a side-issue while the Joke was in full cry.

It must be understood that during his management of the Royal and the Prince of Wales Theatres he exercised an unfettered discretion as to what plays should be presented there. Naturally he would compare notes with trusted colleagues and professional friends, but when it came to filling the date book his hand alone dictated the entries.

It was his fixed habit to *see* a piece before he booked it, or, at least, to *read* it. He had the firmest possible determination not to admit any play "not suitable for his patrons." In that tactful yet unequivocal phrase is summed up his whole theory of management. He simply would not have a play which was not fit for the family audience to see (both from personal and managerial predilections). He didn't care in the least that a play had been a riot in Glasgow or the talk of London: if it wasn't suitable for his patrons he would have none of it.

Now this unwavering attitude was a source of grievous offence to many authors, touring managements, and actors, who resented the determination which prevented their visiting Birmingham with certain plays calculated to draw a lot of money on their "notoriety value." When the Birmingham Joke was at its height these people were quick to seize on the possibility of publicity afforded, and thus it came about that play after play was stated to have been "banned in Birmingham," when the plain truth was that Philip Rodway, exercising the responsibility vested in him, had declined to book it.

We have already quoted from Mr. Hannen Swaffer's *Daily Express* article of November 19th, 1926. It was headed "Birmingham not prudish: City that keeps a clean stage," and here is further quotation to show what he thought about the Joke as a whole, and P.R.'s attitude in particular:

> "When I was a young man people said Birmingham was the best governed city in the world. Now, to my surprise, I find the great Midland capital jeered at and insulted, merely because a so-called 'Watch Committee' is lampooned for things it never does, and because a most conscientious policeman called Supt. May is the laughing stock of many revue comedians. Newspapers all over the world reprint stories of theatre censorship which make Birmingham look ridiculous, when the truth is that Birmingham,

so far as I know, is the only city in the country that is doing its duty in keeping the stage clean.

"I wish some of these critics of Birmingham would visit the city's theatres. One of the theatres, because of its repertory system, is famous all over the world. As for the Theatre Royal and the Prince of Wales Theatre, they are in structure, modernness, comfort, and general efficiency superior to all the theatres of London, with the exception of four.

"You would think, to read some of the criticisms I have seen, that there was a standing war between the Licensing Committee and the theatre managers. This is absolutely untrue. So far as I can see, the committee and the managers are on the same side.

Having dealt with the Pavlova and Robey matters, Hannen Swaffer goes on:

"Then the story went round that *The Love Game* had been banned in Birmingham. This was a play by Mrs. Cecil Chesterton in which Marie Lohr appeared. The truth is that Philip Rodway would not book this because he did not think it suitable for his theatres. When it reached Manchester it was called 'the play that was banned in Birmingham': which it was not. . . .

"Every time a manager, acting on his own, makes a necessary alteration, or refuses to allow a comedian to interpolate a doubtful word, the poor old Birmingham Watch Committee are attacked, although in Birmingham the Watch Committee have nothing to do with the theatres in any way at all. . . .

" 'What's the matter with Birmingham?' said a citizen one day to Philip Rodway. 'People of other towns are calling it the Holy City. We are being laughed at in public speeches and lampooned everywhere. All I know is that I can get here for 7/- as good an entertainment as I can see in London for 16/-, and from a better seat in a better theatre.' "

Or read Mr. James Pearson in the *Birmingham Gazette*, December 29th, 1927:

"From London we have heard a great deal this year about Sex plays . . ., and we have seen one or two specimens there which made us rather more thankful than usual to see on our return to Birmingham the burly figure of Birmingham's Guardian of stage morals, Supt. May; though no one who knows Mr. Philip Rodway will imagine for a moment that any official censorship is needed to keep unpleasant plays out of Birmingham.

"The Birmingham theatres have seen nothing of them, though

Mr. Rodway confessed at the beginning of the year that it was a matter of considerable difficulty to find dramatic attractions of the right class and standing 'without having recourse to unpleasant plays and booking attractions which would tend to lower the theatre in popular esteem.' "

Popular Esteem! That, even more than popular support, was what Philip Rodway coveted for his theatres. It was for that, and that alone, that he exercised the discretion which, when he refused to book questionable plays, was translated by imaginative journalists, press-agent inspired, into "Another Birmingham Ban."

It is hard to believe, but *five years after* Philip Rodway had refused *The Love Game*, and when the piece was presented in London, the expression "Banned in Birmingham" was assiduously used as publicity for it.

"The expression," said the *Birmingham Mail*, "goes beyond being another example of the exaggerations applied to what has become known as the 'Birmingham Censorship,' for in this case the play never reached the stage of being submitted to, or seen by, let alone banned by, any local authority.

"All that happened was that in 1926, while Mr. Philip Rodway had control of the two principal Birmingham theatres, he was asked to provide a date for *The Love Game*. Having read the script, he decided that it was not a play which would be acceptable to his audiences, and declined to book it."

Without straying too far, we hope, from the point, (one thing does lead to another in a discussion of this sort,) let us remind you that at the "Royal" shareholders' meeting on June 15th, 1926, P.R. said "I have been particularly careful that in the programmes for the two theatres there should be no place for some of the very unpleasant plays which have given rise to so much controversy, and I think Birmingham's record in this respect is one of which we all have every reason to be proud."

Incidentally the question of the Lord Chamberlain's license was the only one over which P.R. came into conflict —and then not very seriously—with the local authority. Nowadays it is accepted that the Lord Chamberlain's stamp on a script is the play's passport wherever it goes, so long as lines are not interpolated, but up to fairly recent times there is no denying that the local justices felt they had a title to an over-riding jurisdiction. Many people may think they ought to have, judging from what the Lord Chamberlain sometimes passes. Others will argue that any censorship is illogical in a free State, and that if we must have one, the only way to avoid chaos is for that censorship to be national. However that may be, the fact remains that no such over-riding power actually attaches to any local authority, with special exceptions which do not affect the issue.

P.R. came up against the problem back in 1925, when *White Cargo* was first played at the Theatre Royal. In the script licensed by the Lord Chamberlain appeared the "sanguinary word" used by Mr. Shaw in *Pygmalion*. Though P.R. knew his legal position, he felt it only courteous, in view of the existent understanding, to approach the local authorities for their views. He was told by Supt. May that the Entertainments Committee wanted the word deleted. He did delete it, but took an early opportunity of formally taking exception to the committee's action in over-riding the Lord Chamberlain, and told them frankly that if they persisted in such a course a number of desirable plays would be prevented from visiting Birmingham.

In due course, and in conjunction with the *White Cargo* management, he carried the issue to the Lord Chamberlain (Lord Cromer) himself, and Lord Cromer, having consulted his legal adviser, replied to this effect: that he was aware of a certain over-lapping in the administration of the censorship, and that he was arranging to ensure, should the necessity arise, that no action in similar circumstances should be taken by local authorities until he had been consulted.

The reply, though not conclusive, went some way towards establishing the now generally accepted principle that the Lord Chamberlain's license is sufficient passport for any play in any theatre. We need hardly add that P.R. was no supporter of bad language on the stage. After, as well as before, the *White Cargo* incident, he made a point of seeing that no performer spoke lines likely to be unacceptable.

It was always his habit to be his own censor in his own theatre.

CHAPTER 32
(1925-26)

Humpty Dumpty: Wee Georgie Wood, Mona Vivian, Barry Lupino, Arthur Conquest—"Under the Sea" and "The Scotch Moors"—Anniversary Night; George Lupino, last of the clowns—The silver salver story—Hal Bryan's reminiscences—1926 Season—Annual meeting—*Betty in Mayfair.*

PANTOMIME 1925-26
HUMPTY DUMPTY

Humpty Dumpty will go down to history as one of the most enthralling productions for which Philip Rodway was ever responsible. Throughout that long and unique pantomime record of the Theatre Royal, there had never before been one on this subject, so that when P.R. chose it as his theme he was attempting a hazardous experiment, for there was practically no material on which to work.

All that was known was contained in the four lines of an old rhyme of the Plantagenets, offering the frailest of foundations on which to build the elaborate structure of pantomime. For that reason *Humpty Dumpty* had remained almost unknown in any pantomime history. But in what appeared to be an insuperable difficulty, P.R. saw his opportunity, and he set to work to *create* the character of Humpty.

For his central figure he took Wee Georgie Wood, the ideal Humpty Dumpty of a child's imagination, and round him and for him he devised the plot and wrote the part. He explored a wide literary field, including an unfinished manuscript of Hickory Wood, and with the thread of his own imagination wove a web which was to catch and hold the interest of all with whom it came in contact. His theme was new, but in it he united daring with discretion. Like Montaigne's old lady who was found before the shrine of St. George burning two tapers, one for the Saint and the other for the Dragon, he took no unnecessary risks, for while he burned his taper to novelty, he did not forget to burn one to convention. Thus he had no traditional Demon or Fairy Queen (unless the little queen of the mermaids be counted a

WEE GEORGIE WOOD

fairy), but the "influence" throughout was provided by a strolling troubadour. The lyrics were written by Tom H. Townson, the music composed or arranged by Harry Rushworth, and the scenery painted by those two fine artists, W. R. Young and Bruce Smith.

The first scene opens outside the castle wall, on which is precariously poised the Egg, silhouetted in the cold light of a waning moon. The troubadour passes by, and from his song we hear a hint of the theme to come, for he sings of the legend of the Egg, and of what its fall will portend. Dawn breaks, and gradually is revealed the magnificence of the court of King Half-a-Crown—a brilliant crowd in mediaeval costume, with soldiers in chain armour. The skies begin to darken, lightning flashes and thunder rolls, the court depart, and the Egg, left unguarded, topples from its place. And out of the broken shell emerges—a mystified little boy, who looks about 7, but who computes his age at 2,407. Besides all the unnatural wisdom which that age implies, he is endowed with the power to have four wishes instantly fulfilled.

By a very human touch Humpty's first wish is for a mother, who duly appears. Certainly an odd sort of mother, who turns somersaults and cartwheels, a lady who never walks, but skips and hops and jumps instead! We meet the daughter of the king, Princess Elaine, and Prince Robert of Scotland, who has come to seek her in marriage, and then we catch another glimpse of the castle, this time the Long Gallery. Next we find ourselves on the Royal Yacht, for the King having lost his crown in the sea, the Prince and Humpty must set out to find it, with the princess's hand as the reward for success.

Humpty, still feeling forlorn in a strange world, asks the aid of all the children in the audience in finding him a friend. To their great delight, lo! a friend materialises in the form of an amiable penguin called Squeak. An amusing scene in the Diving Bell follows, and then we are Under the Sea—a marvellous series of transformation scenes of delicate beauty, giving an impression of great, misty, mysterious depths, where mermaids float amid living corals and seaweeds, where sea-horses prance and sea-urchins play, and lobsters and crabs disport themselves among other denizens of the deep. Here the Prince fights the Sea serpent; victorious, he makes for the crown, only to see it soar from his very grasp at Humpty's second wish. And in this P.R. again played a novel card, for surely this was the first pantomime in which a principal boy had been allowed to go through his perilous adventures—and fail!

The curtain is rising on the second half. A Scottish moorland, veiled in mist; the morning gradually clears and one has a vista of heatherclad hills and glens, with a stream in the foreground. A shepherd pauses to light his pipe; his dog rounds up the flock of sheep; the troubadour passes through. And now in the distance comes the skirl of bagpipes, faintly at first, but drawing nearer, nearer. The sound of marching is heard, and from the top of the hill there comes filing down the winding pathway a procession of the Highland clans, kilts and sporrans a-swing, to mass on the stage for the impressive Gathering of the Clans.

Now the king calls upon the competitors to produce the crown, and it is not the Prince, but Humpty, who does so! The promised reward withheld, Humpty wishes that he were king, and in the twinkling of an eye the solid mountains down which the Highlanders have marched, the clans themselves, and every one else have vanished, and in their place is the fantastic white-and-gold City of Topsy Turveydom, with Humpty as king and the king as his lowliest subject. Into this scene of whimsical beauty strolls the troubadour, and the words of his song so touch the little boy-king that he relents, and even goes so far as to make his last wish—"that the princess may marry the prince and live happily ever after." And so the last scene of all brings us to the Hall of Lace, and the display of the living wedding presents.

Wee Georgie Wood, as Humpty Dumpty, made what was

probably the greatest triumph of his career. The part demanded more maturity of style than the rôles he usually filled, and he surprised even his most enthusiastic admirers by the skill with which he rose to the occasion. One could hardly have imagined so much dramatic force could be concealed within that small frame. With consummate genius he suggested the dual nature of Humpty. To begin with, when he emerged from the egg, he was a bewildered little mortal, rather afraid of the power he knew to be bestowed upon him; at one moment he was joyously juvenile, a thoroughly human boy; the next, in a fit of boyish pique, mortified and indignant, he became an agent of magical vengeance; and then, in a trice, as the occupant of a throne, he was the embodiment of regal dignity. And gradually, but in a manner that perfectly accorded with the character, he discarded his sceptre and crown, renounced his love, sacrificed his ambitions, and became once again a free and happy boy. His performance was a memorable piece of acting.

One of his greatest gifts is his perfectly natural style; there was nothing impossible in the diverting questions he put to Dame Martha when she attempted to tell him the story of William Tell, and the scene in the little portable house of the Diving Bell, with his mother and Squeak, had an irresistibly human appeal. Humpty's biggest song hit was, appropriately enough, *Chick chick, chick chick, chicken, Lay a little egg for me!*

As Prince Robert of Scotland there was Mona Vivian, whose wide experience of revue work fully equipped her for whatever the occasion demanded. She imparted the right note to everything she did, acting seriously or farcically, dancing lightly or singing catchy songs. One still recalls her *Ukelele Lady* success. Incidentally, she was heard to remark plaintively at rehearsal,

"It's the first time I've ever had to be a principal boy without being a hero! To all intents and purposes George is the hero of this show; I only get the girl in the end because he gives her up!"

Humpty's mother was a thoroughly quaint and lovable character as portrayed by Barry Lupino. Though he had played Dame parts in Australia, this was the first time he had done so in England, and his Martha was one of the big successes of the pantomime. He shares the talent which is common to all the Lupino family in his unbelievably skilful acrobatic dancing, and yet his Dame was notable for the way in which it combined restraint with agility. "She" regularly brought down the house by a brilliant if wicked parody of *The Swan Dance*, when as a ballerina, anxiously awaiting the familiar strains of Saint-Saëns, she was compelled by an obstinate band to execute hornpipes, reels, and every conceivable dance except the one she wanted. We can still hear her beseeching *sotto-voce* "Swan, SWAN." As Humpty's wished-for mother she was the essence of loving, if erratic, care, and her decorous little flirtation with the king, where they reminisced over the little wicket gate—"that wicket little gate"—was another clever bit of comedy.

King Half-a-Crown was a cheerfully flippant soul, light-heartedly played by Hal Bryan. Especially noteworthy were his excellent diction and charming speaking voice. Every syllable could be clearly heard, and this, together with his genial manner, made him at once a favourite. His performance brought him to the front rank of pantomime comedians.

The Princess Elaine of Florence Hunter held easy sway from the first moment of her appearance. She had charm of manner and a sweet and cultured voice, heard to full advantage in her big song scena *Bouquet*, where the flower-laden chorus converged to make a huge floral bouquet.

Arthur Conquest's Squeak was immensely popular with the children, of whom many a lucky one went home hugging a little black and white penguin replica, which this year was the throwaway toy. Bernard Dudley's fine singing as the picturesque troubadour made him a notable figure, Leonie Conradi gracefully played Undina the Mermaid, and Barry Russell was the quaint Prime Minister.

There were several distinguishing features about the programme for P.R.'s Anniversary Night on Wednesday, March 3rd. The event of the evening was the appearance, at his own special request, of George Lupino, one of the last of the great Clowns. Actually, P.R. was very worried and anxious as to how the old man would stand the strain. In a short Harlequinade, signifying the last occasion on which he would ever tread the boards, the old clown played Joey, with Barry Lupino, his eldest son, as Harlequin, Mona Vivian as Columbine, Arthur Conquest as Butcher, and Bernard Dudley as Policeman. This farewell to the stage was one of the memorable events of the Royal's long history. Seventy-three years before, George Lupino had been born in one of the dressing rooms of this very theatre, where his father, Signor Guarrino, and his mother, known as Mlle. Rose, were performing. It was at the Royal that when only three years old he had played the cat in *Mother Hubbard*.

"Take it; I've finished," and as the last of the Clowns uttered the words the merry comedy of the harlequinade was turned to drama.

With touching dignity he resigned his red-hot poker, bringing a hush to the crowded theatre; tears were in his eyes and it was in a broken voice that he addressed the audience. As he removed his wig he spoke of past and present; of his son standing beside him, his grandson sitting in front. "May the greatest Producer of all shower His best blessings upon you," he concluded.

He collapsed as he retired from the stage. . . .

The customary ceremonies of the Anniversary were observed in special items by the principals, and by visiting artists including Randolph Sutton, G. S. Melvin, Rona Ray, George Hirste, and the Brothers Egbert. P.R. made his usual brief but entertaining little speech, and was presented, on behalf of the company, with a rosewood revolving bookcase. Various other presentations were made, and here comes what might be called "The Saga of the Silver Salver." Georgie

FI

Wood, Barry Lupino, Mona Vivian, and Hal Bryan had bought presents for certain people, but suddenly discovered they had forgotten one important functionary. It was too late to buy anything, and in a great state they went to Daddy and asked his advice. He suggested that they tide over the difficulty by presenting a silver salver *already presented to some-one else!* This they did, and had to explain later that it had gone back . . . to be engraved. The recipient spent the next day searching jewellers' shops for it; eventually he came back and asked Georgie and Barry where they had bought it. An explanation followed on "George Washington gag" lines, so the deluded one departed no wiser than before. Finally he saw a similar salver being carefully packed away by a member of the company. To this day he believes it was his!

Of *Humpty Dumpty* Hal Bryan has sent us some happy reminiscences:

"Pantomime recollections. . . .Philip Rodway. . . . Which of us who had the great good fortune to play under the late Philip Rodway's management in pantomime at the Theatre Royal, Birmingham, can help but have pleasant recollections?

"I look back on my engagements with the Guv'nor, as he was affectionately called by us all, as the two most important and satisfying engagements I have ever had. *Important*, because one knew that to be in pantomime at the 'Royal' for Philip Rodway meant that one had 'arrived,' and much was expected of one; *satisfying*, because Philip Rodway had the uncanny knack of producing a pantomime in which all his characters really meant something, consequently each artist had that happy feeling of being satisfied with his part.

"What an understanding man the Guv'nor was, too; one could always be sure of the kindly and shrewd advice he gave, and how extraordinarily right he nearly always was! Always so perfectly calm and dignified—I never once saw him ruffled or excited, as one can recall having seen so many producers. I recollect the opening night of the first pantomime I played at the Royal, *Humpty Dumpty*, in which I played King Half-a-Crown.

"We opened to a full house, and the show was going splendidly. I had just come off from a comedy scene with Georgie Wood and

Barry Lupino. In the excitement I dashed along to my dressing room and my dresser changed me into the next scene costume, when suddenly I remembered I had still another entrance to make in the scene which I had just left! As I tore back to the stage the call-boy was yelling for me, and by the time I did eventually get on there had been quite a stage wait, which is an unpardonable occurrence.

"I was so distressed it quite upset me, but I shall never forget how splendid the Guv'nor was about it when I apologised and explained the reason, nor shall I forget the merry twinkle in his eye as he congratulated me after the show and said:

" 'I think probably the cause of your being off in that scene was that your comedy song went so well there. Perhaps we ought to change it, eh?'

"Needless to say he never did.

"What a fine sense of humour the Guv'nor had, too. Each night after the show Georgie Wood, Barry Lupino and I went round to the Guv'nor's office. I shall always remember those nights—the jokes we had and the discussions of pantomimes past and to come, and I shall always remember the Guv'nor as I knew him then, sitting in his armchair, smoking his beloved pipe, without which we very seldom saw him!

"One recollects, too, the wonderful parties he gave us during the run, when the whole company was invited and each one of us had to make a speech. Grand fun, and a lasting memory to those who had the honour and pleasure of participating.

"There were so many sides to Philip Rodway, and to an engagement in pantomime with him. He was a charming and lovable Guv'nor, though frightfully strict. He was generous to a degree, but above all he was a man who *helped one to achieve things*, and who would go out of his way to help an artist to get on.

"I remember an instance of this during the run of *Humpty Dumpty*. Florence Hunter had been seen, while playing there, by a big Australian management, who wanted her for musical comedy in Australia. It was a great chance for her, and I remember how very excited she was, but alas, the Australian contract demanded that she must sail three weeks before the pantomime ended.

"In nine cases out of ten that would have been the end of the story, but not so with Philip Rodway! Although I know definitely that he disliked the idea of upsetting what was one of his most successful pantomime runs by changing the cast, he generously gave his permission for the Australian contract to be accepted, and the understudy finished the run of the pantomime."

A trait of P.R.'s, which Georgie Wood emphasises, was his insistence on faithful adherence to the text. All good producers have it, whereas very few artists, even the best, seem to understand that when an author writes a word he wants that word spoken! "Much virtue," quoth Touchstone, "in '*if*'." He would have sympathised with Daddy's determination to *make* his artists utter the "ifs," "ands," and "buts" which, at rehearsal, they were so curiously prone to omit.

Georgie goes on:

"A Royal pantomime was not a matter of a scrappy 'book' supplemented by 'star' (or unknown) comedians putting in their regular turns irrespective of anything and everything. If artists such as Clarkson Rose, Barry Lupino, Robb Wilton, G. S. Melvin, and myself had specially suitable comedy scenes, they were woven into the Rodway tapestry to become part of the pattern. The only occasions upon which any deviation from the book was permitted were when the entire theatre had been taken by some firm such as the Austin Motor Company, Mitchells and Butlers, or another party, when the stage manager would bring to the comedians a list of alleged jokes, having no meaning whatever to the actors, but certain to send the 'initiated' into wild laughter."

Daddy and Georgie Wood, both devotees of football, often went to see a match together. One of Georgie's favourite stories is of an occasion when Aston Villa were playing a team from the North East. His sympathies that way inclined, he was zealously cheering the visitors. Eventually a total stranger (evidently a firm supporter of the Villa), who was sitting near them on the stand, leaned across and exclaimed: "You can shout, but let me tell you, Albert Burdon and Frank E. Franks are both better comics than you."

On March 6th, *Humpty Dumpty* came to the end of its long run. One of those most impressed with the pantomime was Mr. Hugh Ward, the Australian impresario (who had taken

Philip Rodway's *Jack and the Beanstalk* of the previous year over to Melbourne, where it was now playing to packed houses). After seeing every moment of *Humpty Dumpty* he had averred solemnly "There cannot be a finer pantomime in England!"

Season 1926

Difficult as the times were growing, there was no hint of it at either theatre over the 1925-26 holiday season. While *Humpty Dumpty* was packing the Royal, the Prince of Wales was doing equally well throughout January with *Mercenary Mary*, a delightful and tuneful new production. Renée Reel played Mary, with Cecile Maule-Cole as June. Syd Howard (he had not yet adopted the more formal Sydney) was Christopher, in which rôle he scored the first of his numerous Birmingham triumphs, and paved the way for the subsequent productions there of *It's a Boy*, *It's a Girl*, *Ladies' Night* and other long-running farces.

In February, after a three weeks' season by the D'Oyly Carte Company, The Prince of Wales Theatre enjoyed a distinctive fixture in the visit of *La Chauve Souris*, that indescribably quaint, beautiful, and intelligent Russian cabaret revue in which Nikita Balieff appeared as *compère*. The town took him to its heart, this beaming benevolent man with the moon-like face and the flow of unusual English, this Grock in evening dress, who ambled down to the footlights before each item and "explained" its charms with a disarming smile, in a speech that left one dazed, if delighted.

Henry Hallatt and Christine Silver came next in *Tess of the D'Urbervilles*, while soon afterwards *The Last of Mrs. Cheyney* provided a vehicle for Zena Dare's return to the stage. Carl Brisson, with one of the best parts of his career, visited the Prince of Wales in *Yvonne*, and the ever-green *Peter Pan* gave us a new Peter in Kathleen Vaughan.

While the Prince of Wales had *Mercenary Mary* for the first time in Birmingham, the Royal could claim *No, No, Nanette*, the other big musical comedy hit of early 1926. The first Nanette we saw was Cora Goffin, and others in the cast were

Arthur Riscoe and Charles Heslop. The New Street theatre also welcomed Jay Laurier, Annie (nowadays Anne) Croft, Reginald Sharland, and Mona Magnet in *Riquette;* Gerald Ames, Edgar Norfolk, and Eleanor Stuart in that delightful play *The Man with a Load of Mischief*, and the Co-optimists, with Betty Chester and Gilly Flower added to their ranks.

The General Strike of May, 1926, played havoc with theatrical business, as with everything else, for two or three weeks. When it had run its disastrous course, the Prince of Wales Theatre received the Stratford Festival Company again, this time with Roy Byford, Randle Ayrton, George Skillan, Rosaline Courtneidge and Ethel Carrington in the principal parts.

The annual meeting was held on June 15th, when P.R. was again able to recommend a dividend of 20 per cent., less tax. Speaking from the chair, he said that having regard to the fact that theatrical receipts were influenced immediately by the least sign of industrial unrest, political crisis, or fluctuating trade, the directors were very satisfied with the results of the year's trading.

Tom B. Davis, congratulating him on his work, observed that the entertainment tax burden was still with them. (An illuminating sidelight on the question of profits is that this entertainment tax amounted to no less than four times the amount received by the shareholders.)

Betty in Mayfair was the next attraction at the Prince of Wales Theatre. Evelyn Laye and Mary Leigh were the twins whose 21st birthday provided the starting point for this delightful musical play (adapted from John Hastings Turner's *The Lilies of the Field*). Happily enough, it coincided with Phyllis's 21st birthday, and Daddy agreed to her having a theatre party that night. Ever punctilious where his theatres were concerned, he gravely went to the box office and chose and paid for the block of seats as simply as any member of the public. The play, with its grace and charm, and the two birthday parties, will always be associated in our memories.*

---

*With the bouquet of pink carnations, presented to Phyllis by Mr. J. W. E. Child "on behalf of the Prince of Wales Staff."

The Macdona Players followed at the Prince of Wales; the Royal had just turned to its customary twice-nightly season, during which Tom Arnold presented a new musical comedy, *Oh! Patsy*, with Mona Vivian as lead. George Lacy, also in the cast, was described as "a nimble-footed dancer"; but he had not then made his name by that mastery of characterisation which was to carry him to such success in *Mother Goose* at the same theatre a few years later.

At the Prince of Wales, in September, Harry Welchman played Carl Franz to the Kathie of Rose Hignell in *The Student Prince*. This was our first view of a beautiful musical play (based on *Old Heidelberg*) which has since vied with *Lilac Time* for popularity. The following week at the Royal, Godfrey Tearle made his first local appearance as a star of musical comedy in *Merely Molly* with Evelyn Laye.

The Apache was produced by Julian Wylie at the Prince of Wales Theatre in September. Carl Brisson was at his picturesque best as Romain Tierce, while Dorothy Ward, as Lallage, gave a bright and forceful performance, and Shaun Glenville worked with his usual vigour as Redingote. There were also Adrienne Brune, Blake Adams, A. H. Majilton, and Mark Turner in the fine cast.

For the rest of the season standards were finely maintained. To the Royal came Henry Ainley and Jane Wood in *Prince Fazil*, Julia Neilson and Fred Terry in *Henry of Navarre*, Sir Frank Benson and Arthur Phillips in Shakespeare, Irene Vanbrugh and Allan Aynesworth in *All the King's Horses*, and a notable Anglo-American cast (Billy Taylor, Marion Saki, Roy Royston, Rita Page, Clifford Heatherley, Tom Shale) in *Happy-Go-Lucky;* while at the Prince of Wales the outstanding personalities were the Irish Players—Sara Allgood, Maire O'Neill, Arthur Sinclair, Fred Morgan, etc.—in Sean O'Casey's *Juno and the Paycock*; Violet Vanbrugh and her daughter Prudence, with Ben Webster, in *The Duchess Decides;* Anne Penn in *Little Miss Danger*, and the British National Opera Company.

CHAPTER 33
(1926-27)

During his managing directorship the letters Daddy used
to receive from people he had neither seen nor heard of
must have run into hundreds. Letters quaint or pathetic,
amusing, extraordinary, or absolutely unintelligible. Yet,
however busy he was, he always made a point, whenever
possible, of answering them. He hated to disappoint or hurt
anyone, even though their requests might be as strange and
impossible as the mythical tasks of Hercules.

Many of the letters, of course, were from would-be stage
stars, very full of aspirations, very short of aspirates, yet
withal breathing such a hopeless fervour that Daddy had
not the heart to disregard them altogether, and usually sent
a courteous reply. Here are some actual letters with which
he had to deal:

"To the manager,
"The Threater Royal, New Stroet, Birmigham.

"Dear Sir. Please could I beg. of you to give me a. Job. on your
stage. I can do lots. of cleaver things I can sing also. my height
being 5ft. have fair hair. Blue eyes. nanonality English I coald
send you my phatograph showing my talant. Please sir I would
do my best for you I enclose stamped encolus for. reply. Yours
faithfully. . . . "

Or this (in an envelope with no address other than: "Please
Be So Kind As To See That This Letter Goes To One Of
The Large Theatres Birmingham To The Manager):

"My dear sir I am writing to ask you if you will permit me I
beg please to sing for one night on the stage as I can sing well and
am awfully eager to sing for once on the stage dear sir I hope you
will understand it may get me on in the world as I have tried lots
of times and have not succeeded but with your kind permission I
may be able to succeed and get a bit of money to start me in some

theatrical work which I have tried to get in and could not and which I have honestly got my heart and soul in a hundred times over and always have had it dear sir therefore I beg and pray you will please help me if you can do please Dear Sir and I shall be fearfully obliged to help you in anything I possibly can in theatrical work as I have honestly dearly longed for all my life. Oh my Dearest Sir I hope you will forgive me writing to you like this a perfect stranger but dear sir I have got it in me to get on in the world if I had got someone to give me a bit of a start so thats why I am writing to you like this dear sir I would go down on my knees willingly Sir to you to help me and I think your kind heart will so I beg of you to please let me know soon if you will please help me and let me sing."

We remember another letter which came to him in 1917, addressed, in pencil, to the Prince of Wales, Birmingham Palace, England. It was evidently intended for His Royal Highness, but somehow or other it found its way to the Prince of Wales Theatre and to Daddy. It was from Washington, U.S.A., and it ran:

"Dear Prince of Wales,

"I am a little sick boy in the Seattle City Hospital. I heard you and King George collects postage stamps, I do too, about how have you got? If I'm not asking to much would you please send me a few of your duplicates and ask King George to send me a few too please for I am a poor boy with one brother and Mother, and I have no father.

"I would like very much if you would answer my letter for it would be nice to get a letter from the Prince of England and if you send any stamps I'll keep them separate for a keep sake because you sent them to me.

"I bet you like to be Prince don't you? I read in a paper about you and it says you don't care for wild life like the princes in storys does so I guess your the right kind of a Prince for England to have to Rule over them next. Please answer my letter if it isn't asking too much of you for it is nice to have Princes write to you. Write very soon please. Goodbye, Ralph Reynolds, City Emergency Hospital, Seattle, Washington, U.S.A. P.S. Write soon please."

Daddy was genuinely touched, and pondered as to how he could in some way fulfil the childish hopes. And so to a little boy in America a letter went out which seemed to come from a fairy prince. . . .

And here is another little story which was sent to us:

" 'Harfleur,'

"Maney Hill Road, Sutton Coldfield.

"June 21st, 1933.

"Seeing from the *Birmingham Mail* that you are engaged upon a biography of your father, and would be glad of fresh details, I wondered whether the enclosed letter might interest you.

"Several years ago, at the age of fourteen or thereabouts, I wrote a long and highly-coloured pantomime, and optimistically posted it off to Mr. Rodway, no doubt expecting that he would receive it with open arms and offer me a fabulous sum for the copyright by return of post. Incidentally, it was scrawled out in about five exercise books, slightly the worse for wear. Mr. Rodway acknowledged receipt of this strange bundle, which was more than I deserved; however, as no further criticism was forthcoming in three weeks' time, I thought something had better be done about it. So I wrote to Mr. Godfrey Tearle, who was playing at the Theatre Royal, and asked him if he would mind 'reminding' Mr. Rodway about my valuable manuscript. He replied, 'I spoke to Mr. Rodway about your play, and he promised me he would attend to it at once.' That designation, *your play*, appealed to me immensely; and the result was the return of the great work by registered post—another unlooked-for honour—with the accompanying letter from Mr. Rodway. I was soothed by his very kind criticism, but was actually base enough to listen carefully at the next season's pantomime, to see whether he had incorporated any of my jokes!

"Naturally I have since realized how extremely good it was of him to take the thing up at all, and on that account I thought you might like to hear of the incident, trivial though it seems. I should be glad if you would return his letter at your convenience, as I have kept it as a sort of talisman, and hope before very long to justify his encouragement. I recently completed a novel, and am working on a play at present.

"Wishing you every success with your book, which I for one shall read with great interest.

"I remain,

"Yours truly,

"VERA N. WYLDE."

Here is a copy of his letter:

"Miss Vera N. Wylde,
 "Arley Castle, Near Bewdley.

"Dear Madam,

"I have now had time to read the pantomime you sent me, and in my opinion it is very brightly put together and contains much originality. There are a great many technicalities of the stage which would entail alteration before it could be produced, but the story is told in a fanciful way which is very pleasing.

"I cannot suggest anything personal which will be helpful, as we should not be doing *Puss in Boots* in the ordinary way for some years to come, and the houses producing Pantomime are getting less and less, but it might encourage you to write something one of the London managers might accept one of these days.

"I am returning the MSS. by registered post, and remain,

"with compliments,

"yours faithfully,

"Signed—PHILIP RODWAY."

* * *

PANTOMIME 1926-27
CINDERELLA

This Christmas brought the seventh *Cinderella* in the great series of Theatre Royal pantomimes. It is curious that in that long list, unequalled even by Drury Lane, we may search in vain for a *Cinderella* during the first forty-six years, among quaint subjects such as *Harlequin and the Knight of the Silver Shield*, *Baron Munchausen*, *Princess Battledore*, and *The Dragon of Wantley*.

Philip Rodway, in his versatile capacity as deviser, writer, and supervisor of every detail associated with the production of a pantomime, set himself many a difficult task to perform in maintaining his own ideal that each one should be better than the last. Probably none could have been greater than his *Humpty Dumpty* of twelve months before, yet this *Cinderella* was generally acclaimed by the Press as one of the "most charming, amusing, melodious, and certainly most brilliantly spectacular pantomimes in the country."

The story opened up picturesquely in the Foxglove Inn, where the Prince (Evelyn Drewe) and his friends arrived at dawn for the meet of the hounds. While the M.F.H. (Herbert Cave, the well-known tenor) was leading a rousing hunting chorus, the Inn room faded away, and dissolved into Daffodil Wood, a sylvan setting with the ripple of real water over mossy stepping stones. This scene was in itself an exquisite creation of W. R. Young's brush; one could see the movement of the river as it swirled among the reeds, and feel the peace from the distant hills held in the leafy stillness of the trees. . . . It was a little wooded island on the Avon, beneath the Bredon Hills, within sound of the rush of the weir, which Philip Rodway had known and loved on many a fishing holiday. And so to Pershore he took his old friend the scenic artist, and together they planned and devised and conferred, and with much loving care the actual pantomime scene came into being.

Here were the huntsmen in their pink coats, accompanied by real hounds, and here Cinderella (Greta Fayne) made her appearance across the stepping stones in the stream. By degrees all the principals were introduced—the Baron (W. S. Percy); his Ugly Daughters (Dan Leno, jun., and Lola Hunt); the Sheriff's Officers (Naughton and Gold) who were shadowing him when they were not executing funny dances or indulging in amusing backchat; his quaint page (Archie Glen); the Fairy Godmother (Lily Vining); and the Cow (Shanks Brothers) which interrupted the picnic.

And so to the Baron's Music Room, where the diminutive elder step-sister (Leno) regularly reduced the audience almost to hysterics by her comical attempts to sing a song to her own harp accompaniment. Here was another example of P.R.'s adherence to coherence. In how many other pantomimes would this harp struggle have been introduced without the least regard to the story! Now, occurring in the sisters' music room, he made it into an intelligible development of the play.

Thence to the traditional kitchen, where impressive simplicity gave plenty of room for hilarious interludes or

Cinderella's solitary dancing. An incident which always aroused great speculation occurred on the arrival of Buttons with a very large and very real steak and kidney pudding, from which the steam rose invitingly. We watched the hungry Cinderella actually eat the entire pudding, and so well was it done that the fact of a trick table and a plate sectionally-hinged never occurred to the audience, who turned to one another with "How *can* she get through it all?" To which the knowing answer usually came back, "Oh, of course, you know, she never has anything to eat during the day!"

At the Fairy Godmother's behest the Kitchen was transformed into the Fairy Boudoir, where attendant sprites robed Cinderella for the ball, and sent her off rejoicing, seated in the heart of a rose—the latest thing in fairy-land coaches. Dolly Tree, who was again responsible for the dresses and décor, had designed with great success, and the brilliant colours, with the unfailing spell which the incident always casts over our minds, made the conclusion of the first half of the pantomime a really moving scene.

But it was "At the Ball," where the staircase was set with the significant clock, that P.R. as deviser rose to his greatest heights. When the gaiety was at its zenith—and there were some very droll as well as beautiful incidents in the festivities —our attention was cunningly focussed on the clock, which began to strike the fatal hour, and hey presto! when the chimes ceased, the ballroom with all its splendours had vanished, and we were in the Royal Gardens, with lights ablaze from the Palace windows, fountains playing, and masses of lovely flowers.

While one was marvelling at this miracle of organised stage-craft, carried out in the twinkling of an eye, Cinderella herself —not a double—who a moment before had fled up the ballroom stairs a Princess, came running down the garden steps in her kitchen dress once more, to find instead of the wonderful coach a pumpkin, rats, mice, and lizards awaiting her!

There was an even worse equipage for the baron and the sisters, a genuine hansom of the pre-motor era with an amazing horse, and it was no wonder that Cinderella had been home for hours and sobbed herself to sleep long before the rest of the family arrived! But the scene in the Baronial Hall set everything right, and so to the last transformation, "The Wedding Cake," a beautiful and original idea, a cake of living and wonderfully designed ingredients, o'er-hung by a fairy Cupid.

In selecting his principals P.R. had been bold enough to arrange a cast which, as far as pantomime was concerned, was almost entirely new to Birmingham, though most of them were well-known in other productions. He was universally congratulated on the experiment, for it brought together artists who could sing, act, dance, and generally work as a fine team.

Evelyn Drewe, the principal boy, had had considerable experience in musical comedy, and played with princely dignity and a gracious presence. Her cultured soprano voice had plenty of opportunity for expression, notably in the numbers *Red Red Robin*, *Talking to the Moon*, *The Two of Us*, and the great ballroom song *Let to-night be a Night of Delight*. As Cinderella there was Greta Fayne, with a demure wistfulness and simple naturalness which enlisted our sympathy throughout. She had a haunting melody to introduce herself, an appealing song *Lonesome*, and a *Sleepytime Girl* duet with Buttons.

Among the comedians an interesting appearance was that of Dan Leno, jun., son of a famous father, who soon proved that heredity counts. His arch manner, his freakish dancing—featherlight of foot—and his quiet sense of the grotesque carried him easily to success. With him, as the other sister, was Lola Hunt, a clever comedienne who made an excellent foil.

Their father, the baron, became a delightful character sketch in the hands of W. S. Percy; he might have stepped straight from the pages of Goldsmith.

Naughton and Gold were inimitable sheriff's officers; whimsical in themselves, their backchat was pointedly humorous, and whether propounding bewildering gags, or in their burlesque boxing, slow-motion dancing, or hilarious Lancers with the sisters, there was laughter every minute they were on the stage.

These two are incorrigible humorists in every day life. When they arrived at the Royal, the first thing they did was to go round the stalls corridor, take down the historic old playbills hanging there in frames, and replace them with their own posters. P.R. came down before this sacrilege could be rectified, and the entire staff were aghast with apprehension —but, having called the two boys into his office, what he actually said was "Well, that's a good start. I only hope you'll be as funny on the stage as you are off."

They thought a great deal of P.R., and accepted the strict discipline of the Theatre Royal in what was, for them, a remarkably submissive manner; people wondered how they would ever fit into the Rodway scheme of things, but they did it very well.

Archie Glen was a new type of Buttons; a comedian of solemn demeanour, quietly avoiding any exaggeration or straining for effect. His restraint in the traditional fooling was almost welcome, for the part is liable to be so overdone as to imperil the main outlines of the story proper. Possibly his best number was the dance with the dummy, as a reveller at the ball.

Connie Browning endowed Dandini not only with the dash and liveliness which the part demands, but also with an excellent voice and enunciation, most effective in the song-successes *That Certain Party*, and *Who'd be Blue*. Herbert Cave's fine voice increased the musical strength of the cast; Lily Vining was a Fairy Godmother true to tradition; and Ernest A. Plumpton the picturesque landlord of the Foxglove Inn.

There was some excellent and amusing work by the Shanks Brothers, whose horse and cow were creatures of lovable if quaint proclivities. Finally, there was the well-trained chorus, singing the lyrics of Tom H. Townson, set to music by Harry Rushworth, or in dances arranged by John Roker; and the orchestra, as usual, played their important part.

And perhaps among the "characters" we may mention the charming little replicas of Cinderella, in silk and velvet, with golden curls and a minute bundle of sticks, which were thrown out into the audience at every performance. Here again, as in previous years, was an example of P.R.'s fore-thought, for not only were they distributed from the stage, but, knowing that even herculean hurling could hardly reach the gallery and parts of the upper circle and pit, he arranged for a separate set to be given out in those sections of the house. These little models went beyond their toylike character, and became mascots, even talismans to the lucky recipients.

Philip Rodway's anniversary night on March 9th was a more than usually notable event. He decided to devote the entire proceeds to the founding of a Theatre Royal Staff Benevolent Fund. "To those who do not understand the theatre" said the *Birmingham Post*, "this may mean nothing in particular; to those who do, it is a gracious and unpreced-ented act." While theatre staffs all over the world are eager to give their services to any charity, their own affairs are seldom regarded, and P.R.'s lead in establishing this fund indicated that the Theatre Royal, the oldest playhouse in the country with the exception of Drury Lane, was still pre-pared to take the initiative in all that concerned the welfare of the stage. It was thirty years since Philip Rodway made his first appearance at the Theatre Royal, and in com-memoration of the event he was presented by the principals with a portrait of himself, painted in oils by Fleetwood Walker, R.B.S.A.

As usual, there were the customary diverting interruptions of the orderly progress of the show. The visitors included Tex McLeod, Nellie Wigley, Herschel Henlere, Ilene Evelyn, Keeley and Aldous, and Gilbert Payne.

Cinderella went to the Ball for the last time on March 12th, having been present there regularly for eleven weeks instead of the customary ten; proof, if any were needed, of the universal popularity of the 1926-27 pantomime.

In February, P.R. was asked to address the Birmingham Y.M.C.A., and in "Pantomime; Then and Now," he gave an interesting and entertaining account of the development of this form of dramatic art, tracing it through the days of Jingo songs and transformation scenes, war-time references and patriotic scenes to its present elaborate condition. As a reason why old theatre-goers are prone to compare modern pantomime unfavourably with the pantomime of their youth, he suggested that in the old days the Christmas annual was the one big scenic show of the year, whereas to-day, while still the biggest, it was merely one of many. Entertainments of all kinds had multiplied enormously, and the average young man had a choice of so many that only the very outstanding could give him cause for remembrance.

*　　*　　*

There was probably only one occasion on which P.R. was ever at a complete loss for words. It happened one evening at the Theatre Royal.

The advertising man had made a series of mistakes on the day in question. He had done almost everything wrong that he possibly could do, and P.R. had found it necessary to call him to his office with a view to dismissing him, or at the least, severely reprimanding him. Having detailed the list of offences, P.R. asked him what he had to say for himself.

The man clenched his fists, and in what appeared to be a perfect paroxysm of anger, red in the face, and shaking with suppressed excitement, made straight for the table at which Daddy was sitting. If ever the light of murder was in a man's eyes, it surely shone from his.

"Guv'nor," he exploded, crashing his fist down on the table, "*I entirely agree with you!*"

GI

P.R. was so completely taken by surprise that he could not think of a single thing to say, and the offender was allowed to return to duty.

* * *

Philip Rodway took a leading part in the local efforts for the rebuilding fund launched immediately after the Stratford Memorial Theatre was burned down in the early spring of 1926. After the first flush of enthusiasm had subsided, the governors, through their secretary (Mr. Henry Tossell), asked P.R. and Mr. M. F. K. Fraser to form a committee for the purpose of raising an auxiliary contribution from Birmingham. A strong committee was formed, with representation of the theatres, music-halls, amateur movement, and other interested parties.

The task of gleaning where the *Birmingham Post* and the *Daily Telegraph* had reaped was difficult and thankless, but it was vigorously tackled. The then Lord Mayor (Alderman A. H. James, C.B.E.) acted as chairman, and gave the committee his personal and unstinted support. P.R. and his co-directors of the theatre started the list with a cheque for £100, and other amounts were received.

A benefit performance was naturally in every one's mind. It was decided to hold it at the Grand Theatre, by generous permission of Moss Empires Ltd., and to make it representative of the stage in all its branches. Frank Jolly, then manager of the Grand, was helpful in every possible way.

The date was fixed for February 25th, 1927, towards the end of the pantomime season. In pursuance of their catholic idea, the committee arranged a programme of monster proportions, with principal boys, principal girls, knockabout comedians, troupes of chorus dancers and music-hall stars jumbled together in a glorious medley. There was not the least difficulty in getting the co-operation of artists resident in Birmingham or paying a week's visit to the town. They were all willing, even eager, to come on the bill. From the first, however, the committee realised that a few stars of high magnitude were needed to sell the steeply-priced stalls and dress-circle seats.

P.R., remembering the triumphant appearances for charity of Miss Mary Anderson (Madame de Navarro) at the Royal during the war, secured her promise to appear on this occasion. Many of the biggest people in London were approached by letter, with disappointing results. Like the men in the parable, they put forward diverse reasons why they could not come.

A fortnight before the event, therefore, the organisers found themselves committed to run a matinée at a top price of a guinea a seat, but with no outstanding star except Miss Anderson (and she only pledged to utter a few words) to justify the extortion. The cause, besides, was not particularly popular in Birmingham—there had been no frenzied rush to buy seats in advance, though the Rotary Club and other movements had done their best.

At a meeting one afternoon when time was growing perilously short, several members expressed the view that the venture was sunk before launching.

"Look here," said Daddy suddenly, "we *must* have some visiting talent, and we can't get it by writing. Why not push the secretary off to London to-night, and let him try personal approach?"

Within half an hour Mr. Fraser, the unfortunate secretary in question, was aboard a London train, armed with numerous suggestions from Daddy as to folk who might succumb to flattery or other treatment. He spent the whole evening, until well after midnight, cruising from theatre to theatre, from music-hall to actors' club. He came back next morning with a reasonable bag—Lyn Harding, Ion Swinley, Ernest Truex, Dorothy Green, Alfred Harris—and the programme was completed.

The matinée, though nowhere near full, raised £222, which in the difficult times and circumstances could be called satisfactory. Miss Anderson was unable to appear, sending a cheque as forfeit. Mr. Harding and Mr. Swinley played a scene from *Julius Caesar*—and nearly missed their return train through sportingly waiting on to do another. Miss Green and Mr. Harris gave a passage from *Richard III*. Mr. Truex talked amiably to the audience about whatever came into his mind.

Principal boys, principal girls, and other pantomime leaders did after their kind. Gerald Ames (a great friend who did not long survive Daddy) came in with a scene from *Escape*, in which he was playing at the Prince of Wales Theatre.

It was all very comprehensive, very jolly, very practical, if only in parts Shakespearean. . . .

And when it was all over, Daddy said it was the "stickiest" effort he had ever helped to handle. The total raised by the committee from all sources was £623 2s. 6d.

The complete programme is here set out:

Overture: Nicolai's *The Merry Wives of Windsor*. (Grand Theatre Orchestra: Conductor, Mr. Gilbert Smith)

The National Anthem ... (Miss Doris Tompkins)

Mr. Skeets Martin ... ... (Birmingham Hippodrome)

Mr. Herbert Cave ... ... (Theatre Royal)

A Few Minutes with Mr. Ernest Truex ... ... (from the Apollo Theatre, London)

Miss Connie Browning ... (Theatre Royal)

Messrs. Naughton and Gold ... (Theatre Royal)

Miss Nellie Wigley ... ... (Alexandra Theatre)

Mr. George Carney ... ... (Grand Theatre), in *The Mess Orderly*, assisted by Miss Annie Donoghue and Messrs. Arthur Blossom, Charles Stephens, and Dennis McKernan.

Mr. Ion Swinley and Mr. Lyn Harding in scenes from *Julius Caesar*.

Orchestral Interlude: Incidental music to Rosse's *The Merchant of Venice*.

Escape (Episode 3) by John Galsworthy:
>> Scene: The bedroom of an inn on the moor:
>>> Matt Denant: Mr. Gerald Ames
>>> The Shingled Lady: Miss Elinor Palmer
>>> A Maid: Miss Edith Purser

Miss Doris Tompkins ("Polly" of *The Beggar's Opera*)
>> (*a*) *Can Love be Controlled by Advice*
>> (*b*) *O Ponder Well*

Mr. Dan Leno ... ... (Theatre Royal)
Miss Greta Fayne ... ... (Theatre Royal)
Mr. Archie Glen ... ... (Theatre Royal)
Miss Evelyn Drewe ... ... (Theatre Royal)
Miss Florence Desmond ... (Grand Theatre)

King Richard the Third, Act I, Scene II:
>> King Richard: Mr. Alfred Harris
>> Lady Anne: Miss Dorothy Green

Such a gesture as was represented by this benefit performance and the auxiliary committee's general activities, naturally strengthened the bonds between Birmingham and Stratford. P.R.'s interest in the rebuilding scheme grew daily deeper, and he became a regular guest at the annual Birthday celebrations in Stratford.

To quote Mr. W. H. Savery:

"He was now paying a more particular attention to the question of overseas tours, which we had successfully resumed. Our talks revived his old ambition to take out his own company, which at length, as is told elsewhere in this memoir, he did in the autumn of 1929.

"We were touring Canada at the same time, and I know that no man could have more amply earned the respect and gratitude of the Canadian managers, in the short time he could spare from business duties at home for a personal visit.

"Following him from town to town, I found that all the managers he had met were full of his praises. His forthright personality and strongmindedness had made a deep impression wherever he went. When they knew I was his friend they urged me to use all possible influence towards persuading him to return every year. 'He is just the sort of manager we want out here,' they said; 'How is it he has never been over until now?'

"Looking back over many chats during our long friendship, I realise clearly that his concern was never confined to his own theatrical doorstep. He had the widest imaginable desire to better his profession as a whole, and to further the cause of every member of the body theatrical.

"It will probably have been said elsewhere in this memoir that he was a man of few friendships, strong prejudices, and rigid determination. Because his friendship was so carefully bestowed, one was infinitely proud to have it. And for a friend there was nothing he would not do. I never heard him say an ill word of anyone. He was not a gossip—talking for talking's sake did not interest him; he liked to have a practical subject and to keep to the point, and he never said anything unless it was worth while saying.

"*The personal touch* in theatre management was a fetish with him. To have the whole thing, so far as it concerned him, under his own eye; to know what was happening at any given moment in every department of the theatres for which he was responsible; to give personal attention to every detail affecting his patrons, his company, or his staff—those were his guiding principles. Many of the changes introduced into theatrical life and management during and after the war met with his disapproval, because he was such a stickler for style and dignity.

"Tradition he respected profoundly, yet he was not bound by old-fashioned ideas for their own sakes. While he would not scrap a method just because it was old, neither did he retain the traditional just because it was traditional. When one put a new idea to him, he might be against it at the moment, but often one found a week, a month, or a year later that he had been turning it over in his mind, testing it by every standard. And if he decided it was good he made no bones about admitting it.

"To a keen eye for beauty of scene and language he added tremendous enthusiasm for the work of the new theatre. He visualised great possibilities, and had great ideals for the theatre of the future and the ultimate value of its work.

"Despite his keenness he worked quietly and methodically, without rush or fuss, getting through in a short space of time what would have taken others many hours. His kind advice, assistance, and cheery smile I shall never forget.

"All in all, a man who stood by his word and made it good; a man and a friend most difficult to describe in words, but who leaves a lasting memory of enthusiasm, friendliness, and goodness of heart."

*　　　　*　　　　*

Season 1927

No, No, Nanette, which had already been seen at the Royal, came to the Prince of Wales as the Christmas and New Year attraction, its six-weeks' run finishing on January 29th. Cora Goffin was again the Nanette, and the show rivalled *Mercenary Mary* in popularity as a holiday attraction.

Lily Elsie, another of the stars who, like Zena Dare, returned to the stage about this time, came to the Royal in *The Blue Train* in March, with a strong cast including Bobbie Howes, Cicely Debenham, Peter Haddon, and Arthur Margetson. In April *Dawn* was produced for the first time on any stage, Godfrey Tearle and Grace Lane being the stars. Sybil Thorndike and Basil Gill in *The Greater Love*, and The Co-optimists in their thirteenth programme (with a newcomer in Mary Leigh) helped to complete the spring season, after which the twice-nightly system was resumed.

A big new production at the Prince of Wales in March was *Mr. What's His Name?* in which Seymour Hicks figured with exquisite drollery as the barber who lost his memory. He had fine support from Mary Merrall, Frances Doble, Madeleine Seymour, Margaret Yarde, C. M. Hallard, Benita Hume, C. W. Somerset, and Tristan Rawson—while Ellaline Terriss watched the show from a box, to the great delight of the house.

In J. B. Fagan's much-discussed play, *And So to Bed*, Lawrence Baskcomb played Pepys and Gyles Isham was King Charles II. Soon after, the Prince of Wales had *Lady Luck*, the latest big musical comedy, with Leslie Henson, Laddie Cliff, Phyllis Monkman, Cyril Ritchard, and Madge Elliott in a wonderful cast. The Birmingham Grand Opera Society played *Carmen* for a week.

C. B. Cochran's immense production *Castles in the Air* was the chief attraction in May at the Prince of Wales, where it played for a fortnight, with Allan Kearns, Genevieve McCormick, Helen Gilliland, John Steel, and George Howe heading the company. When the Stratford company came for their annual Shakespeare fortnight, the leaders were Dorothy Green, Wilfrid Walter, Stanley Lathbury, Kenneth Wicksteed, George Skillan, John Laurie and Lydia Sherwood.

In his review, "R.C.R." wrote:

"For the last three years, except for Sir Barry Jackson's experiments with Shakespeare in modern clothes, Shakespeare would not have been acted in Birmingham at all if it had not been for the resolution of Mr. Philip Rodway in engaging what is by far the best of the few, the very few, Shakespeare companies.

"Birmingham has always recognised, more than any other town, its duty and privilege of assisting Shakespeare. The managers of the Theatre Royal, from Richard Yates to Philip Rodway, have never wavered in their allegiance. One immediate way in which Birmingham can help to save the Memorial Theatre is by encouraging the annual seasons, for unless they are a success it may mean that great calamity, the disbanding of the company between the spring and summer festivals."

(Nowadays, of course, the Stratford Festival runs continuously from April to September, but at the time under review there was an interval of about six weeks, during which the Festival company visited a certain few Midland theatres.)

We recall R.C.R. again, saying not long afterwards:

"If it were not for the great success of the pantomimes at the Theatre Royal, we should never see Shakespeare at all. As the convict said to the warder, so pantomime says to Shakespeare: 'If it wasn't for blokes like me there'd be no jobs for blokes like you.' Shall we ever remove this reproach on Birmingham's attitude to Shakespeare?"

At the annual meeting on June 15th a dividend of 20 per cent. was once again recommended, and P.R., making his speech to the shareholders in his joint capacity as chairman and managing director, touched on a theatrical phenomenon; "Why is it that the Birmingham public are so shy of attendance at the opening of the week?"

The "malady of Monday night," as the *Birmingham Post* aptly described it, was as a result the subject of several columns in the Press during the next few days. "As a matter of fact, the Birmingham Monday night audience, though sometimes small, is an audience that means something, receptive, intelligent, and discriminating. But it is often not till Thursday that the big battalions roll up, so that people who really meant to go, suddenly find that all the seats are booked, and all the queues of formidable dimensions, when on Tuesday or Wednesday they might have walked into good seats with ease.

"The Saturday night habit is deeply implanted in this city, so that always at the end of the week the house could be sold two or three times over, but if those patrons with the money and the leisure could only be persuaded to show public spirit by going on Monday night, the problem of tempting the big London shows to come to Birmingham would be solved."

Vast audiences flocked to the Prince of Wales in August to see Pauline Frederick, the screen star, in *Madame X*, whereas *Abie's Irish Rose*, a Jewish-Irish comedy which had run for years in America, was much less sought after. *The Desert Song*, still popular to-day for its rousing music and glamorous setting, was new to the town when it arrived in September, with Howett Worster (the Red Shadow), Daisy Elliston (Margot), Herbert Cave, John E. Coyle, Phoebe Hodgson, and Lola Waring. Towards the end of the year Seymour Hicks returned with *Mr. What's His Name?* Ellaline Terriss this time playing opposite him.

At the Royal in September we saw *Mary Rose*, Barrie's exquisite play, with Norman O'Neil's ethereally lovely music, and Fay Compton as the heroine. Doris Keane came in *Romance*, while Julia Neilson and Fred Terry brought *The Wooing of Katherine Parr*. In October, Sir Frank Benson and Gerald Lawrence, who had formed a company called The Bensonians, played a Shakespeare week. We saw Gerald Lawrence for the first time as Hamlet—and Sir Frank for the first time as the Ghost! The visit is memorable for brilliant performances by Robert Donat and Nigel Clarke in *Julius Caesar*.

Edgar Wallace, increasingly popular since the success of

The Ringer, was represented at the Royal in November by a dramatic musical play *The Yellow Mask*, a huge and interesting production in which Bobby Howes, Phyllis Dare, and Cronin Wilson took the honours. Here the revolving stage was employed with spectacular effect for "The Changing of the Guard" scenes in the Tower, and we remember the terrific amount of work which had to be gone through in the very short time for rehearsal before the actual production. *Lord Babs* followed, in which Billy Merson was supported by Hermione Baddeley, Lawrence Anderson, Charles Garry, and Stephanie Stephens.

CHAPTER 34

The booking of seats—Sir John Martin Harvey's opinion—The ritual of
booking for Boxing Night, and for grand opera—Booking by telephone—
Case before Judge Dyer, K.C.—Hannen Swaffer's comment—Theatre
starting times.

BOOKING OF SEATS

Was Philip Rodway too firm an upholder of tradition and
custom? The question will arise again and again, since his
whole career as a manager was influenced by his attitude
towards change of practice. Various observers of his character
will answer the question in various terms, according to their
own prejudices on the numerous changes in local or national
theatrical practice which P.R. opposed. We hope to have
shown in this book that he was not tradition's slave, but that
his objection to certain departures from custom was based on
carefully-considered grounds. We do not claim infallibility
for him, but there can be no gainsaying that he never adopted
a stand without being firmly convinced of its logical security.

An outstanding case in point was his resistance against the
modern habit of booking all seats in advance. To this he was
emphatically opposed. He would have none of it in any
theatre under his control. If you asked him "Why?" he
would argue the case with as much earnestness and wealth
of supporting data as a K.C. before the High Court.

Firstly, from the patron's viewpoint. P.R. had a deep-
seated respect and affection for his less opulent patrons, the
genuine thick-and-thin supporters, as he called them, who
loved their theatre so well that they would brave for it the
long hours of waiting in a queue, clamber up innumerable
steps to the gallery, and wait another long spell for the curtain
to rise.

"They don't want to book in advance," he declared. "To begin
with, there is a comradeship of the queue which makes watching a
play a much more congenial, happy-family experience than those
who take the easier way of booking can ever understand. My pit
and gallery are my true supporters, my most loyal friends, my
most judicious critics. They pay the least money, but they make

or mar the actor's reputation. What they pay is a real sacrifice, and they enjoy the fruits of it in proportionate measure, but if you don't give them their hard-earned money's worth—look out for squalls.

"If I book my pit and gallery, what happens? I satisfy a small percentage of them, mainly folk who could well afford to pay for better seats, but prefer economy to comfort. My concern is not for them. It is for the majority of genuine, poor enthusiasts, to whom theatre-going is a rare, hard-won treat. How many of them can be sure, days ahead, that on such a night they will be able to go to the theatre? How many can afford to lay out their money in advance? Most of them come when they have a shilling to spare out of the week's housekeeping, or when, by weeks of saving, they have put by enough for a family night out at the play or the pantomime.

"Suppose a big attraction is coming, a piece that is likely to pack the house. Allow booking throughout, and those who want to be sure of getting in on a particular night must be prepared to lay down their money a long way ahead. If the night chosen is booked out, they have to make their arrangements over again, or give up the idea.

"Under the queue system, those who are keenest get the best places, and that's as it should be. My regular pit and gallery people soon learn to estimate the relative attractiveness of various productions, and to know roughly what time they ought to turn up in order to be sure of getting in. For a big attraction they arrive hours ahead, for a moderate one they stroll along a few minutes before the curtain rises. It is a perfectly fair system, understood by and convenient to all genuine theatre-goers of restricted means.

"Those who can afford just a little extra join the early door queue, but the proportion is very small. Under the all-seats-booked plan, *everyone* is charged that early-door price, however it is camouflaged. What happens? The patron who has not been able to book in advance comes along and is asked eighteenpence for his old shilling seat. He mounts to the gallery, and finds it three parts empty.

" 'Nice thing,' he observes, 'why the extra sixpence?'

" 'Oh, but you could have booked in advance,' he is told.

" 'And why should I want to book in advance with three hundred seats waiting empty for me?' he demands.

"Or, he finds the gallery packed out, and has to stand. Again:

" 'Nice thing,' he grumbles. 'Eighteenpence for standing at the back of the shillings!'

" 'Oh, but you could have booked in advance,' they tell him.

" 'How could I do that?' he asks, 'I didn't know till to-night that we could get someone to mind the baby!' "

"He is left with a feeling that somehow it has been 'done across him.' He can't define it, but it annoys him, especially as he feels that the best end of the deal has gone to people who only visit the theatre when there is a big attraction. Result: a disgruntled 'regular,' easily receptive of the information that for ninepence he can get a nice seat on the ground floor of a cosy cinema, and go in and come out when he likes."

Then, from the theatre's viewpoint. On the economic side P.R. was satisfied that eventually the theatre must lose by booking throughout, unless it could be ensured an unfailing stream of 100 per cent. attractions.

"In that case," he argued, "we should obviously be on velvet from the cash standpoint, though even then I think we should be letting down our thick-and-thinners. But we have to think in terms of few hundred per cent. attractions and many moderate successes, with a proportion of certain losers.

"Why, then, make it easier for the house to be booked from the back instead of the front? At present, generally speaking, people go into the seats they can afford, because naturally those who can afford to book don't stand in queues. Besides, there are some who go in seats a little dearer than they like, because they don't want to be seen standing in queues.

"Now, if we book all parts for the moderate attractions, what must happen? People who at present pay, say, 6/- will find they can book a seat just as comfortable and not much further from the stage for half the price. So we shall fill up from the back, and the thick-and-thinners will be elbowed from their legitimate places by people who will all of them represent a loss of so much a head to us.

"Moreover, we must often reach the position when in order to avoid gaps in the various blocks, and to save turning money away, we shall have to put late comers into better seats at the same price as early bookers have paid. The result must be further dissatisfaction, since people are already very willing to believe that theatre managements wangle things to suit their friends.

"The pit and gallery are the backbone of the first-class English theatre. They always have been and they always will be. The decent homely people who have to make a few shillings cover a night's amusement; the intelligent patrons of modest means whose theatre-going is a regular mental stimulation; the boys and girls whom the cinema is taking from us, but who ought to be our adult support of to-morrow; all these are the folk for whom the queue caters and must continue to cater if the theatre is to survive."

Apropos this question, it is interesting to compare the following quotation from Sir John Martin Harvey's *Autobiography*.

He is speaking of a return to the Lyceum in May, '85, which, he says, "was memorable for Irving's effort to book the pit. Pittites were at once cleft in two parties: those who wished to book their seats and those who wished to stand in queues and take their chance. There was a violent uproar when Irving opened his theatre under these new conditions: ultimately the old order gained the day, and within a couple of weeks he went back to the long-established custom."

"Since Irving's day," writes Sir John, "the custom of booking the pit has very largely extended; always I think to the detriment of the theatre. . . . It is a curious fact that, as Irving himself pointed out, people who have booked a seat seldom applaud—hence one misses the expression of approval and the enthusiasm which are so great an encouragement to us in our work. A prominent member of the D'Oyly Carte Opera Company, after their last season in London, expressed the chagrin of the company in having lost the enthusiastic applause of the old-fashioned pit, and said that, whenever they came to town again, it would be to a theatre where there was a large unbookable pit.

"People who can well afford to go to the stalls or dress-circle will certainly save their money if they can be sure of a seat by booking it—even in the pit. Irving spoke of ladies arriving in their broughams to book their pit seats.

"My friend Rodway, of the Prince of Wales Theatre, Birmingham, endorsed this evidence, and told me the following tale of an experience when he tried booking the pit at his own theatre. One evening an urgent query was made from the stage as to whether a certain doctor was in the house. The doctor rose and answered in the affirmative from the pit! where he had booked a seat for 3/-. This was a man who hitherto had always patronised the stalls. Again, a house where the cheaper parts are booked has a forlorn and neglected appearance at night. In place of a line of people waiting for the doors to open—which in itself is a most useful advertisement for the popularity of a theatre—one sees what is apparently a deserted building, where even lights have been economised because no one stands waiting for admission. Lastly, the booking of seats necessitates use of the post, the telephone, or else a personal visit to the box office, all of which are sources of expense in time, cash, or trouble for those who go to the cheaper parts.

"It is my deliberate opinion that—as Irving predicted when he tried it at the Lyceum in '85—to book a pit is to break the backbone of the Theatre."

Another question on which Philip Rodway had strong views was that of preference in booking as between personal and postal applicants. Except for grand opera, for which he had an elaborate and complex system (of which more later), he laid it down that the preference must go to the patron who brought his money to the window.

He felt it could not be too often emphasised that theatrical management was a personal business, dependent for success upon the good feeling between the manager and every individual patron. Further, that the patron who deserved most consideration was the one who took the trouble to bring his order instead of sending it by post or telephone.

This conviction reached its highest expression at pantomime time. For many years the opening of the box office, some few weeks before the first night, was attended with a quite impressive ceremonial—which, incidentally, obtained for the Royal a further measure of that dignified publicity so valued by P.R.

Until he relinquished control of the Royal, it may truly be said that Boxing Night at that theatre was an outstanding point in Birmingham's social year. Leaders in every walk of Birmingham's life made it their business to be present at the launching of the pantomime, and thousands of less distinguished but equally determined citizens cherished the same ambition.

Thus it became a matter of keen competition, this booking for pantomime. In practice probably 90 per cent. of those in the first muster were there to book Boxing Night seats—and they knew there was going to be trouble at home, a Christmas deprived of a highly-prized amenity, if they failed to do so!

As the years rolled on, therefore, competition became fiercer and fiercer. Hours before the opening of the box-plans at 10 a.m. a queue would begin to form outside the theatre. Each year the first arrival got there earlier, because each year someone else had been fired with ambition to be photographed and paragraphed in the local papers!

"Mr. Blank, of 'The Gap,' Hiatus Road, Hall Green, told a *Mail* reporter (or a *Despatch* reporter, or both, if he could catch both) that he had taken up his position at 9.53 p.m. last night, armed with a thermos flask, a packet of sandwiches, the *Mail* and/ or the *Despatch*. Last year Mr. Blank was third in the queue, but this time he took good care to win the Waiting Stakes, and duly received the prize of four seats in the centre of the front row of the dress circle.

"Our picture shows Mr. Blank, who is a tailor's cutter and fond of pigeons, receiving the tickets from Mr. Philip Rodway (left) while a long line of 'also rans' eagerly await their turn at the window."

All this meant that the best Birmingham people had to bestir themselves in order to maintain their representation on Boxing Night. They could no longer roll down during the morning in their cars and pick up their dozen seats, or ring through when business duties allowed them a moment. They had either to be in the queue themselves, send the butler, the chauffeur, the maid, or pay a casual employé to wait in their stead. In this way and that, success begat success. The queue became longer and longer, more and more unemployed men were able to earn an honest half-sovereign for doing nothing throughout the small hours, and the Boxing Night occasion became increasingly a rallying point for local rank, fashion, and determination.

But we must not leave the box office until we have described the ritual and emphasised P.R.'s preference towards personal applications. At perhaps 5 a.m. or 6 a.m. (according to the weather, the numbers, and so forth) he would have the doors opened, and the sleepy-eyed queuesters would be admitted to the stalls. There they would be regaled with light refreshments and lighter music until a few minutes before 10 a.m. Then in strict order of admission they were marched round the long passage to the box office, and the real ritual began.

At ten precisely P.R. and his lieutenants would parade in front of the queuesters, solemnly bearing the untouched books of tickets for Boxing Night. Eight tickets alone had gone in four sets of two (for the critics of the four daily papers). The rest were complete—and anyone who doubted that fact was entitled to see for himself.

One by one the watchers approached the window. The first person had the whole plan from which to choose, the second a slightly restricted monarchy to survey, and so on down the queue. As the plan filled up, P.R. would begin to count up the number of seats still unbooked; at a convenient moment he would send an attendant round the corridor to ask people how many seats they wanted, and thus ascertain a point in the queue beyond which, even allowing for returns, it was not much use hoping for Boxing Night luck. By half-past eleven, as a rule, the house for the opening performance was sold out, a few seats had gone for other performances, and the routine of booking for the run had set in.

Meanwhile the exchange had had strict orders to ignore all calls for the Theatre Royal. The morning's postal delivery had been opened, and orders for seats dumped in a corner of the office. At length, the queue having entirely vanished, orders by post would receive attention, and the odd seats always remaining after a house, colloquially speaking, has been sold out, would be allocated.

"That's the only way you can give your keenest customers a

HI

fair deal and convince them that you're doing it," P.R. used to say. "It's not enough to *tell* them personal applicants receive preference. You've got to *show* them—show them the full books of tickets, show them the plan, show them the number of people ahead of them, and let them follow the working of the whole business with their own eyes.

"Seeing's believing—but in our trade only just! Ninety-nine patrons out of a hundred suspect you of favouring the next man; or of refusing to part with unsold seats because you think you'll get a higher price later, or something equally base.

"And many things conspire to excuse their suspicions. A man comes to the window on Tuesday and is told the house for Wednesday is booked out. His neighbour drops in casually on Wednesday evening, learns that two seats have just been returned for sale if possible, walks into the best stalls. Neighbour goes home and, being human, brags about it over the garden wall. Result: a letter to the editor and an enemy whom no reasoning, no demonstration, will soften. All we can do is to 'bite the bullet,' and retreat on our axiom that the Public is always right."

The ethics and practicalities of booking the whole house were to be raised on the notable occasion of the second visit of *The Desert Song* to the Theatre Royal, in March, 1928. Queues assembled in the small hours, and one day a newspaper reporter (probably sent as a consequence of a letter to his editor by some champion of booking) went along to see what people thought about it. He conversed with people who had stood for many hours, and he derived the impression that they had found their vigil quite pleasant.

"They appeared perfectly satisfied with the system," he stated. "A few frankly declared that they could not afford to put down the money for seats days in advance; others said they would have booked dearer seats had they been in time, but were not going to miss the show, however long the wait."

Then the reporter tackled the management with the suggestion that a general booking system would have more conveniently served the public. The management (P.R. in fact) replied that the experiment had already been partially tried, and that results had shown the system of a non-bookable pit, gallery, and upper circle to be suited to the majority of

Musical and other "notes" taken down in the Midland capital by "Matt," our famous caricaturist, a day or two ago. "Matt" spent part of a day and much cogitation over his subjects. His time for drawing each was a matter of minutes. And for once he shyly puts himself into the middle of his design. A favour to the Midlands!

Reproduced from the "Sunday Graphic"

BIRMINGHAM CELEBRITIES
AS "MATT" SEES THEM
November, 1929

Mr. Kaines Smith   *Mr. Philip Rodway*
Lord Ilkeston   *Mr. Sam Short*
Mr. Percy Edgar   *Mr. Stuart Vinden*
Sir Granville Bantock *Dr. Adrian Boult*

patrons. The cheaper seats, it was insisted, were primarily intended for patrons who could not afford to book in advance.

"At the time when partial general booking was tried," went on "the management," "well to-do people diverted their patronage to the cheaper seats, so that people of moderate means were crowded out when we had a really strong attraction, while the expensive parts were relatively thin. Visitors have come this week from distant parts of the Midlands, and taken their chance in the queues of seats which would otherwise have been denied them.

"It is a fallacy to suppose that universal booking will dispense with queues; one has only to remember what happens every year at pantomime time when the plans are opened for the season, and our all-night queue forms itself. When the time comes that the seven-shilling customer will still take a seven-shilling seat, even though he can book a three-shilling seat, it will be economically possible to book every seat."

We have promised to say something about P.R.'s system of booking for grand opera, a system which, in contrast to the one already described, gave absolute preference to postal applicants for several days.

On a stated day all letters were opened and dealt with in rotation; a week later the box office was at the disposal of personal applicants. It was, as we have said, an elaborate and admittedly rather complicated way of booking. The big rehearsal room at the Prince of Wales Theatre was turned into a temporary office, where on zero day the whole available clerical staff assembled under P.R.'s superintendence. Postal applicants had been required to send in a printed form, stating what seats they wanted for which opera, and enclosing the requisite money, together with a stamped envelope.

What made it complicated was that there was always a run on certain operas, and some applicants had to be informed, in writing, that they could not have all or any of the seats they wanted. Would another part of the house do? Or another night? Or another opera? It might be that a party had been specially arranged, in which case further correspondence can be imagined between various individuals. By the time a new date had been agreed, seats might no longer be available for it, and so forth.

P.R.'s argument for his system was that grand opera lay outside the range of theatrical attractions in the ordinary sense. It was a special line, and had its special patrons who probably did not go to a theatre at any other time. Those regular supporters, he said, knew all about the system and expected it to be put in force. They deserved consideration before the general public. In addition, grand opera was placed on a pedestal as something worth extra trouble to attain, and there was good publicity in the system.

Again it is not to be doubted that P.R. had argued the thing out exhaustively in his own mind. He was sure he was right. Some of his best friends were equally sure he was wrong. They said the system prevented the man in the street from becoming an opera supporter, frightened him by its elaborate details, and made him think that if so much palaver were necessary to get seats, he, as an outsider, was not likely to stand much chance. While some operas were packed out, others were not, and disgruntled observers were apt to say: "No wonder, when they make you go down on your hands and knees to get seats."

These considerations may lead one to wonder whether, after all, his arguments in support of his pantomime booking system were not as strongly in favour of the same method for grand opera booking, but the fact remains unaltered that P.R. had reason enough, for P.R., for what he did.

* * *

BOOKING BY TELEPHONE

Like all wise managers, Philip Rodway held firmly to the maxim that the public is always right. Whatever the ethical implications of any dispute between a theatre and a patron, the tactful manager will go to almost any lengths of accommodation rather than stand on his legal or common-sense rights, because he knows that one offended patron invariably makes

many. Has a patron taken away seats for the wrong performance? Very likely she (it is usually she) has received exactly
what she asked for. Never mind; it is the box office's business
to change the tickets without demur, and to accept the blame
for the mistake. Did Mr. So-and-so particularly desire his
seats to be kept for him long after the time at which he knew
perfectly well he should have taken them up and paid for
them? And did he fail to come after all, because the night
was foggy, or the car wouldn't start, or his wife had a few
friends in for bridge? Never mind; the theatre may have had
to stand the loss on seats which could have been sold if Mr.
So-and-so had telephoned his intentions ten minutes earlier,
but that is all in the game of public service.

Managers are continually coming up against such difficulties. P.R. had his share of them, and his theatres were
models of long-sufferance. There was one occasion, however,
on which he felt impelled to stand up for managerial rights,
even though his determination involved a lawsuit.

The case in point arose towards the end of the run of
Cinderella at the Theatre Royal, in the pantomime season of
1926-27. The sequel was a hearing before Judge Dyer, K.C.,
in the Birmingham County Court on October 17th, 1927.
The circumstances may more easily be understood by extracts from the report published by the *Birmingham Post* next
day:

> "An application for special costs arising out of an action that
> had been entered for the recovery of £3 17s. in respect of seats
> booked at the Theatre Royal, Birmingham, was made at the
> Birmingham County Court yesterday. The application ... was on
> the ground that the matter was of general and public interest,
> and Judge Dyer, K.C., awarded costs on Scale B.
>
> "Nineteen seats in the orchestral stalls were booked by telephone
> in the name of ——— and ———, for the pantomime performance
> that took place on the evening of February 12th last. Those seats
> were not taken up by the defendants, but fortunately at the last
> moment the theatre were able to sell some of the seats, and the
> claim was for the value of those which were not sold. The theatre

management felt they were bound to bring the case to court for
the protection of the public, who were in the habit of using the
very excellent system of booking seats by telephone.

"On January 18th a telephone message was received from someone giving the name of ——— and ———, booking nineteen seats
for the pantomime performance on February 12th. When told the
seats would have to be taken up before the day of the performance,
the answer given was 'We know that, and it shall be done.' Subsequently it was found that the seats had not been taken up.

"A clerk telephoned to them, and the answer was that they
wanted the seats. No one came for them on the Saturday night,
and on the following Monday a further telephonic communication
was made. After the theatre clerk had reminded them that the
seats had not been taken up, Mr. Rodway, the managing director
of the theatre, took the receiver, and when he asked to whom
he was speaking, the answer was 'I am the proprietor of this
show' (meaning ——— and ———). Mr. Rodway said the seats
had not been taken up, and the answer was that they were booked
for customers. Mr. Rodway replied that he knew nothing about
that, that the seats were booked in their name, and they were
responsible.

" 'You cannot prove that we sent the telephone message,' was
the reply given.

"Mr. Philip Rodway, managing director of the Theatre Royal
(Ltd.), said it was the universal practice to book seats by telephone
or letter, but in Birmingham more facilities were provided than in
many towns because of the suburbs. The number of seats booked
varied with the attraction.

"The Judge: 'Do the public largely avail themselves of the
practice?'—'Yes.'

" 'In what way does this affect the rights of the public?' . . .
'If we are not to treat a telephone message as a contract for seats
we should have to stop the practice of booking by telephone, for
if people, after booking the seats, do not turn up, there is a dead
loss to us.'

" 'Unless this is enforced you would have to alter the whole
system for the public's own sake?' . . . 'Yes.'

"The Judge said this was not a vindictive attempt to penalise a
wrong doer. After hearing Mr. Rodway's explanation of the
practice, and his view of what would follow if the practice was

abused with impunity, he considered the matter was of general and public interest. The application was legitimate, and he would grant costs on Scale B."

The action attracted much attention in theatrical and general circles. Most of the papers had long paragraphs about it, and we give herewith the leading article from the *Birmingham Mail* of the following day, which also published another of T. W. Ellison's cartoons, this time with a political twist, in which the artist cleverly linked the County Court case to the pending Municipal Elections.

The *Mail* leader ran as follows:

"The general public will note with satisfaction that the Theatre Royal has won all along the line in its action over the liability for seats booked by telephone, for this is a matter in which theatre-goers are even more interested than the theatre management. The system by which seats can be reserved in advance by means of a telephone call, and the tickets taken up on arrival at the theatre on the chosen night, was instituted for the convenience of patrons, and it has proved a real boon to many busy folk, whilst to suburbanites and country cousins it is an absolute necessity. But for this facility many a dweller a few miles out could never risk a journey into the city to see some attraction, because the odds would be in favour of its being wasted effort, all the seats having gone by the time the visitor arrived.

"Anything which endangers this convenience, therefore, is patently against the public interest, and it is equally obvious that the system could not be continued if seats so booked and reserved were to be left, not merely empty, but unpaid for, without any responsibility on the persons involved. It is not necessary to go into the question of liability for a transaction over the telephone, because that is pretty well established nowadays. If it were not so, then a great deal of modern business could not be transacted. Orders of all kinds are now given over the 'phone, and to wait for confirmatory letters would in most cases be impossible. There can be no question that an order for theatre seats is valid over the 'phone and must be honoured like any other business transaction. As a matter of fact, that issue was not raised in the present action, for the sum due was discreetly paid into court.

"Everyone knows also that the Theatre Royal was not claiming from mercenary motives the few pounds due. The money involved in these cases is not what a management is concerned with; it is the sight of empty seats in an otherwise crowded house. Such a thing gives rise to suspicion, malicious gossip, and public annoyance which is far more injurious than the loss of the seat money. There is never an important attraction put on in Birmingham, for which advance booking is essential to secure a seat, but someone has a grievance, and generally vents it by imputing 'favouritism' to the management in the allotment of seats. As a matter of fact, nothing is more jealously guarded against by all our theatre managements. They do their best to give the public a square deal in this respect, and they expect a square deal in return. When persons do not take up the seats after insisting on their being reserved for them, the management not merely loses the money, but an opening is given for suggestions of favouritism which are totally unfounded, though perhaps understandable, for one can sympathise with folks who have had to take a back seat and then find plenty apparently available in front.

"This is the real gravamen of the abuse of the telephone system, and unless such practices are put a stop to, it is plain that theatre managements in their own defence must drastically curtail the existing privilege. At present the seats can be taken up as late as fifteen minutes before the rise of the curtain. This does not give much opportunity for the sale of seats not claimed, but the management is prepared to take the risk, and generally it is justified.

"If the practice of not honouring the obligation were to spread, then it is clear that the fifteen minutes would have to be extended, probably to the day previous, which would destroy at a blow the chief value of the system, especially to those living out of town.

"That is why it is important to us all that any attempt to abuse the privilege should be checked, and why the action by the management was brought and pressed to the extent of asking for the special costs, which the Judge granted. Let us hope that such a vindication will not again be necessary."

Hannen Swaffer, whose picturesque services were then at the disposal of the *Sunday Express*, said the same thing in a characteristic paragraph, headed "Bogus Seat Buyers":

"Philip Rodway, of the Theatre Royal, Birmingham, has served all the theatre managers of England by obtaining a judgment, with special costs, against someone who ordered seats on the telephone and then did not claim them. 'Some people call up and order stalls,' he told me, 'and then, when they arrive at the theatre and find room in the pit, do not claim the stalls, which we might have sold.' I know of cases where successes have been harmed by people ringing up and ordering a whole row of seats and then not claiming them. The telephone is of use to the public. Where it is abused it hurts everybody!"

We need not stress that P.R. took legal action only on the greatest provocation and in the interests of the public. Had it been a case of mere thoughtlessness or carelessness he would never have done so. Incidentally, he had a suspicion that there was something behind it—that, in fact, the booking had been made with the deliberate intention of leaving his otherwise crowded theatre with a gaping row of empty seats. We know he was rather disappointed that a defence was not attempted on the facts, because he had hoped for an opportunity to show, through counsel's cross-examination, that this express attempt had been made.

The *Mail* leader pleased him very much. He told the author of it that it exactly covered all the pertinent considerations, and that the presence of empty seats on the night in question had already raised comment among patrons who had been compelled to sit farther back.

*   *   *

THEATRE STARTING TIMES

Another local change which Philip Rodway opposed with all the force he could command was the change of starting time from 7.15 to 7.30 p.m.

Soon after his official handing over of the Royal, in 1929, to Moss Empires Ltd. it was suggested to him that the new Royal management was anxious to institute a later starting time.

The arguments put forward were: firstly, that Birmingham's theatre starting time was earlier than that of other important provincial cities, and far ahead of London; secondly, that the better class public was having its dinner spoiled by the early start; thirdly, that the short West End diversions touring in increasing numbers needed a later start to disguise their brevity.

P.R. thought nothing of the third point as an argument. Still, he gave it his usual close attention, and dismissed it in these words (we quote from a note to a newspaper friend):

"If we have to put up short shows, it's a pity, but not to be avoided while things are as they are. There's not the slightest use in trying to fool the public. As Abraham Lincoln once remarked, 'You can fool some of the people all the time, and all the people some of the time, but you can't fool all the people all of the time.' I don't think anyone would be deceived into thinking that a show beginning at half-past seven and ending at ten is longer than one beginning at a quarter past seven and ending at a quarter to ten. If the short show is a good show, the public will get quality-value for money; if it's a bad show they won't forgive you however you camouflage it—but the best camouflage, in my view, is a curtain-raiser, not a delayed start."

As to the other two considerations, which were in reality one, P.R. fought them on the simple weapon of local conditions. It was at all times his view that Birmingham, by reason both of its traditions and its wide area, was theatrically unlike any other city, and required handling suited to its special features. Behind these convictions, no doubt, was his other firm belief that no syndicate with its seat in London could teach the local, personal managers in Birmingham their business—but he had much beside prejudice to support his cause.

Cartographers prepared for him scale maps of Birmingham, Liverpool, Manchester, Edinburgh, and other great provincial cities. These formed his brief for early opening, a brief he had at his finger tips.

Birmingham, he demonstrated, when discussing the matter with friend or adversary, was equal in area to Liverpool, plus

Manchester, plus a bit over. Yet Birmingham's population was only about that of Manchester alone, or Liverpool alone. Therefore Birmingham's population was spread over twice the area of either of these Lancashire cities. At its greatest width Birmingham was seventeen miles between boundary and boundary, so that patrons drawn from the city alone might have an eight- or nine-mile journey home after the show.

Nor was that the sum of his premises. Birmingham lived in its suburbs, so far as first-class theatres were concerned; on every side—except Edgbaston—the suburbs were far from the centre, and tending to become farther-flung. He had statistics to show how the central wards were losing their inhabitants, and how the process would be expedited as the Corporation and private housing schemes progressed.

Then again, Birmingham theatres drew a considerable patronage from towns and townlets within a twenty- to twenty-five-mile radius: Wolverhampton, Lichfield, Walsall, Dudley, the Black Country generally, Worcester, Kidderminster, Stratford, Evesham, Warwick, Leamington, intervening and outlying places of varying importance, but all of definite significance.

His maps, then, were charts built up in concentric circles. They showed how many miles Birmingham theatres had to reach out to tap a million, two million, five million of the population: how many miles were similarly involved for Manchester, Liverpool, Glasgow theatres: how widely the Royal and the Prince of Wales, in contrast to those other theatres, must spread their appeal.

Tapping chart with pencil, and pulling at his pipe, he would say:

"There's the answer to it. Seven to ten miles before we get an audience. Twenty to twenty-five miles before we can fill up for a week, let alone a run. We depend absolutely on our trams, 'buses, and trains to get our folk home. Already lots of theatre-goers have to leave before the end of a full-length show to catch the last train for Stratford or the last 'bus to Shirley. Are the Corporation going to alter all their schedules to suit us? And the railway companies, and the Midland Red? If we get a short show this week, we get a three-hour musical show next week. What about it?"

He contended, further, that years of habit-forming tradition had made Birmingham an early-to-bed city. Its inhabitants, generally speaking, didn't *want* to be out late. They were not addicted to after-theatre suppers at the hotels, or other forms of "night howling." Ours was a city of workers, who rose early, started work early, wanted to get to bed early. An extra quarter of an hour between 7.15 and 7.30 would still not allow the suburbs to get home much more conveniently for a meal, but it would mean many people being out of bed until midnight, and inclined to regard theatre-going as a labour instead of a pleasure.

CHAPTER 35

(1927-28)

PANTOMIME 1927-28
ROBINSON CRUSOE

"It is *Robinson Crusoe* at the Theatre Royal. Far below (my place is in the flies, behind the footlights, on the level of the gallery) the sea-captain and his men are singing their chanty on a sunlit jetty in the Port of Hull. Swiftly the darkness falls, like a suddenly drifting mist; and the only gleams of light come from a ship's lantern that swings in the captain's hand. Behind him black shapes are moving about quickly, silently, like those that worked at the behest of Ariel. The houses are crumbling to pieces before my eyes; they turn into long slabs of black shadow and are carried away to disappear into the outer darkness. Hull has vanished in a few seconds like the vision that Prospero conjured:

" 'The cloud-capp'd towers, the gorgeous palaces,
 The solemn temples, the great globe itself,
 Yea, all which it inherit, shall dissolve
 And, like this insubstantial pageant faded,
 Leave not a rack behind.'

"Still the lantern swings its yellow rays; still the jolly song rings out. Again black shadows move from the outer darkness, now shapeless, now taking shape. They pile themselves around, upward; the moving figures steal silently away. 'With one stride comes the *light*,' like a sudden tropical dawn, and down below, in the clear sunlight, the Captain and his men are still singing their chanty on board their ship. The miracle of dissolution has been followed by a miracle of creation.

"In the full light I look round me. Before me there are

dozens of ropes, hundreds of pieces of scenery suspended in
the air. Below, by craning forward, I can just see the drum-
mer on the far side of the orchestra. The stage is filled with
gay and brightly coloured figures. All these the audience can
see. But they cannot see the dozens of stage-hands moving
about quietly, surely, purposefully,—that group turning a
windlass, those three lowering a steel cable which bears on the
end a heavy sandbag, some others carrying a piece of framework which presently will take its place in the ordered scheme.
Silently, unrestingly, the work of demolition and preparation
goes on. Those cables will not be used for half an hour, when
the sandbags will be replaced by a living freight, yet to the
very second each night they are moved. At one time, though
the audience sees none of them, hears nothing of them, there
are ninety-odd stage-hands engaged in simultaneous activity
on one of the changes, every man of them a living cog in an
intricate piece of mechanism, which works as noiselessly as
some marvellous watch. There are dozens of ropes, hundreds
of them; and every man knows that by a moment's carelessness
or inattention, by pulling a wrong rope, or a right rope too
soon or too late, too short or too far, he could bring the entire
production to a standstill. But everything moves 'like clockwork'; the simile is ancient, but here it is literally true, for
every movement is timed to the second.

"At one moment all the flymen are standing by, silent and
alert; a red light glows for half a second, and at once the first
three men haul swiftly and steadily at the ropes which control
one of the pieces of scenery till it takes its position to the very
inch. As it reaches a certain point in its progress, another trio
takes to the ropes, and so it goes on through the entire 'transformation.' Not a word is spoken, unless some key-man
whispers to his mate: 'Now it's us, Bill.' Far away below, as
I peer between the ropes, I see the stage-hands moving noiselessly in their felt slippers—those two carrying some part of a
dismantled setting, these three swaying rhythmically as if
they were one man, at a steel cable which rocks the ship.

"There are no idlers; nobody wanders about. As the performers leave the stage they pass swiftly to their places. Chorus-girls are, of course, quite human, and naturally talkative, but at the first buzz of conversation the producer lifts a warning finger, or the stage-manager puts out his head, with a dark frown on the already darkened face that he assumes as the King of the Cannibal Islands. For two or three minutes during the 'big change' the stage seen from above looks as busy as an ant-hill that has been disturbed by some marauding foot, yet all the movements are as highly disciplined as a regimental parade, as responsive as an orchestra to some inspired *maestro*.

"It is not for me to give away secrets. I could, indeed, tell you why a dozen men crawl across the stage, one after another, in single file. I could reveal what happens to the ship that founders, and seems to be swallowed up by the waves. I could disclose the secret of the tossing waves—which is, of course, almost a *secret de Polichinelle*, for it is almost as old as the theatre, since a century and a half ago the seas swept about the barque that foundered in *The Tempest* when it was played in the old Theatre Royal. Perhaps William Shakespeare used the same trick at the old Globe on the Bankside more than three hundred years ago. Anyhow, you may be sure that the man who wrote *The Tempest*, where in the Masque of Shapes, 'to a strange, hollow and confused noise, they heavily vanish,' would be cordial, fraternally cordial, in his admiration for these great scenes that vanish lightly, in silence and darkness. If you see a pantomime elsewhere, the chances are ten to one that all the changes will be worked, perhaps with a deal of hammering and clamouring, behind a front-cloth, with lights full on, while the comedians vainly strive to make themselves heard.

"It is the superb mechanical efficiency of Mr. Philip Rodway's pantomime productions which has gained the admiration of his colleagues, the London producers and managers. No doubt it has been your pleasure to see, as it were, the clock face; it has been my privilege to see the works. But I do not propose to reveal any of the secrets except one—and that is, why the pantomime is recognised all over the country as a triumph of efficiency.

"And that is because the production is the result of two weeks' rehearsal, a year's thought, and a lifetime's experience. This efficiency could not be assured unless the mechanism was mixed, as the great artist said he mixed his colours, 'with brains, sir.' You see a beautiful Spanish galleon. So did Mr. Bruce Smith before he began to paint it. So, before Mr. Bruce Smith began it, did Mr. Philip Rodway in his mind's eye. But he also saw it as a structure of wood and canvas and gauze that could be taken to pieces and put together like a jig-saw puzzle—slabs that could be stacked in their appointed places along the wall.

"He saw not only Robinson Crusoe's ship, but the Port that came before, and the Island that came after. Continuous action can only be produced by a vast amount of scenic ingenuity and contrivance and resource. It is no doubt the very perfection of its mechanical side which makes the Birmingham audiences take these beautiful 'changes' as a matter of course." We quote R. Crompton Rhodes on that memorable production of 1927-28—a pantomime entirely written and devised by Philip Rodway.

It was his first production of *Robinson Crusoe* (Defoe's story of the shipwrecked mariner had, in fact, not been seen at the Theatre Royal since 1894). Actually this twentieth century edition was far truer than that strange caricature which appeared, dramatised by Sheridan, for the first time on the English stage in 1781.

One of the noteworthy features of this pantomime of 1927 was its almost miraculous continuity. For some years P.R. had been working towards this ideal, with the gradual elimination of "front cloths" and the evolution of one scene into another. This year he achieved his purpose—he managed to make the whole of the first half a progressive unity, by a

CLARKSON ROSE

series of carefully-thought-out stage devices, so that it was unanimously hailed as "the finest pantomime first half within living memory."

And then—Clarkson Rose as Mrs. Crusoe!

Here P.R. brought off another of his brilliant surprise hits. He had been the first to put G. S. Melvin into "skirts" (who was as one result playing the queen in Julian Wylie's *Sleeping Beauty*), and here was another *coup de théâtre* which added the worthy name of Clarkson Rose to that all too small list of successors to the famous dames of yore. And as if to set the seal upon his selection, Clarkson Rose was one of those chosen to play before Their Majesties the King and Queen at the Royal Command performance on March 1st that year.

In Mrs. Crusoe he created a new type of dame, cultured and clear-spoken, calm, polished, and composed; delightfully funny without the slightest trace of vulgarity; his work an object lesson in those two directions. Of his first engagement with P.R. he has written from Melbourne, Australia:

"I have to-day seen the paragraph in the *Stage* in which I read you are writing a Life of your father, and although I am thirteen thousand miles away, I hope I am not too late to give you some reminiscences.

"I am so delighted to hear of it; your book will be looked forward to by countless numbers of us who loved him as a man and respected him as 'The Guv'nor.'

"I cannot tell you how grateful I am to have known your father and worked with him. He placed me on the pantomime map by the way he handled me, and when I left him I was able, through having been with him, to obtain the best pantomime work available.

"You do not need me to tell you that he stood alone as a manager and a pantomime producer. His standard was high, and he kept his artists up to it; he was strict but just; he had definite ideas of how his pantomime should be played, and no-one could alter him. He proved himself very right at Birmingham, where his régime became world famous, and has so far been unapproached in this direction.

"I was first engaged by him in 1923, but, wishing to stay with the revue in which I was then playing, I 'phoned him and asked

II

if he would release me. He said he would postpone the engagement, but would expect me to be ready for him when I was free, and to notify him of the fact. He asked for nothing in writing.

"It was four years later that I notified him I was free, and he at once cast me for Mrs. Crusoe. I told him I had never been in skirts in a pantomime, but he quietly observed 'You speak the King's English, you know how to characterise, and how to sing a comic song. I have every confidence in you, and I know you will suit the Theatre Royal.' At the rehearsals which followed he gave me every assistance. . . ."

Robb Wilton, that excellent comedian, was inimitable as Will Atkins, the would-be villain of the piece. His genial inconsequential humour, his comical hesitation, his half-hearted attempts at bluff and boldness were sources of abundant laughter, and he ended, as ever, by winning everyone's sympathy instead of calling forth fear!

Clarkson Rose tells us of Daddy's pride in making Will Atkins and Mrs. Crusoe into the perfect pantomime combination. He used to watch them from all sorts of odd corners, sometimes when they were unaware of it, during rehearsals for the show, and if he saw them stealing out to have a drink (as they sometimes did), he always contrived to be on hand to stop them and divert their course instead to his own office, where he would dispense hospitality, saying:

"I don't want you two boys to go out and catch cold. Let me hear what you have been doing."

Irene Lister played Crusoe with all the dash necessary to carry her through his perilous adventures. Man Friday became a happy-go-lucky and irrepressibly cheerful figure as portrayed by Billy Rutherford, with a nonsense song (which he made into a big addition to the Stockade scene), *I left ma sugar in the rain*, and a catchword "Friday g'wine to be very useful," which was a favourite phrase, in our family at least, for several months.

Another clever comedian was Neil McKay, whose greatest skill was displayed in his agile and intricate dancing. He and Muriel Montrose had an amusing eccentric number together on board the ship. Elsie Bower was a vivacious Polly Perkins, at her best in a speciality duet with Rutherford. John Harcourt and Olive Prosser were two fine singers, Phyllis Strickland the principal dancer, and Josh Dixon a most engaging parrot. Victor Fairley was King of the Savages.

From the Port of Hull, a picturesque setting by Bruce Smith, the good ship *Saucy Puss* set sail, with everybody on board whose presence was imperative to the success of the pantomime. Here Clarkson Rose sang his irresistible ballad *Wave to me;* Robb Wilton plotted most divertingly to scuttle the ship; and in due course, in the midst of a terrific storm, it actually sank before our eyes. Crusoe was discovered on a raft, alone on a tossing sea, until we saw him sail into the safety of a sheltered creek, and so to the Heart of the Island.

Here, in a tropical scene of great beauty (painted by W. R. Young), was a brilliant assembly of living flowers and fruit, birds and insects, and to finish, a spectacular flying ballet.

The second half opened in Another Part of the Island (again W. R. Young), with the blue sea in the background. Here the savages landed from their war canoes, dragging with them the unfortunate Friday, and then performing elaborate sacrificial rites and tribal dances—terrifying indeed, had one not remembered that the preservation of Friday was essential to the story! True to tradition, the situation was saved, and one by one the other characters who had survived the wreck, appeared upon the island.

The high light of this particular scene was undoubtedly Clarkson Rose's brilliant satirical skit *The Girls of the Old Brigade*. Here was another instance of P.R.'s attention to detail, and scrupulous ruling to allow only what was right in the right place. He had taken infinite trouble to preserve the period of the pantomime, and he was not going to have Victorian and Elizabethan styles commingled unless with some perfectly sound reason. As Clarkson Rose recalls:

"His rigidity when he had made up his mind was unshakable.

People who did not know him might have called it 'pig-headed-
ness,' but I always found that if 'the Guv'nor' liked you sufficiently,
he would give you a definite reason for the attitudes he adopted,
and he was always right in whatever applied to his own theatre.

"Right up to the dress rehearsal he was not going to let me sing
The Girls of the Old Brigade—my biggest song success. In vain
did I plead that it was the song that he had heard me sing which
had appealed to him and influenced my booking.

"'That may be so, but Mrs. Crusoe doesn't belong to the period
when they wore bustles, and I'm afraid you will have to do something else, Clarkson.'

"Day after day I went to him, naturally very perturbed that
my cast-iron personal song was going to be cut, and each day he
gently but firmly said he was sorry, he knew it was a good song,
but unless I had a brainwave or he did, he wasn't going to allow
me to get laughs outside the picture of the pantomime. At the
last moment he conceived the idea that, having been shipwrecked
on the Island, I was left with very tattered clothing, and that Will
Atkins should have found a trunk washed up on the shore, wherein
I discovered the bombazine, and thus explained my subsequent
entry. The song now fitted in perfectly, and proved a great success.
Incidentally, he always came out of his office to watch it."

The Stockade scene which followed showed Crusoe in
historic setting with goat, dog, and parrot, and the realistic
attack of the savages, defeated with the highly diverting
assistance of Will Atkins and Mrs. Crusoe. These two had
a great number in their mock-sentimental duet, *Side by Side*,
when Atkins, after a long series of attempts to evade the wiles
of Mrs. Crusoe, finally surrendered.

And so to the memorable finale, The Spanish Galleon
(Bruce Smith). Here was an unusually beautiful and striking
setting, the interior of the galleon, picturesque, and true
to the minutest detail. Massive staircases swept down on
either side, and in the middle was a hatchway, through
which the whole company *ascended*—another original note—
to the swinging lilt of an old Spanish march, which John
Harcourt's fine voice made doubly impressive. Haunting
and strangely wistful was this last processional march, as if
it vaguely foreshadowed the still greater finale yet to come;

as it would say "This is the last but one—only one more."

For no reason that we then knew, we ourselves could never hear those opening bars without tears in our eyes. So must Barrie's Mary Rose have felt before she heard The Call of the Island.

* * *

Robinson Crusoe, which had an enthusiastic send-off on Christmas Eve—when Daddy filled the entire house with wounded soldiers and crippled children—ran through to the beginning of March.

On his own Anniversary Night he gave the entire proceeds, as previously, to his Theatre Royal Benevolent Fund, an institution unique in this country. Besides the principals, others who contributed numbers in honour of the occasion were Olive Fox (Mrs. Clarkson Rose), the Houston Sisters, Shaun Glenville, Billy Danvers, Violet Field and Frank Victor. A whimsical and gracious touch was given by one of the presentations which P.R. himself made. He summoned from the wings a small boy who had laboured in modest obscurity during the run of the pantomime in the wreck scene, and formally and with due ceremony he presented a watch to—"The Chief Wave."

There were enthusiastic scenes on the last night, enlivened by various unrehearsed incidents, chief among which was the exchange of parts by Robb and Clarkson in the *Side by Side* interlude. Before *Auld Lang Syne* brought the curtain down for the last time, each of the principals said a few words in time-honoured fashion first set up by P.R., who in his own speech made announcements for the following year. And of these there was one, relating to his next pantomime

---

*Spanish March, *El Puñao de Rosas*, by R. Chapi.

production, which calls forth the following reminiscence from Clarkson Rose:

"During the run of *Robinson Crusoe*," he writes, "I had a comedy photograph of an old-time comedian, one Cliff Ryland, on my dressing table. Every night when P.R. came in to see me, he used to point to this photograph on his way out and say:

" 'Take a good look at that face, Clarkson; you'll find it useful.'

"He would greet my puzzled 'What for, Guv'nor?' with a quiet chuckle, and a 'Wait and see—but don't lose that photograph.' It was not till the end of the run that he told me he was going to engage me for the following year to play 'King Cole,' and, pointing to the picture, he smiled and said 'And that's the type of make-up I want you to put on.' He thus conferred a great honour on me by making me the only principal who has played at the Theatre Royal for two years in succession.

"When I received my Royal Command to appear at the London Coliseum, I showed the letter to Mr. Rodway, and he humorously remarked:

" 'Well, I'll try and let you off that night, but I won't promise.'

"Georgie Wood sent a wire on hearing of my inclusion, which read '*Congratulations on being chosen for Royal Command Show, but your Theatre Royal Birmingham Command is greater still.*'"

CHAPTER 36

(1928)

A journey to Scotland—The Ten-o'clock Rule—Principles and predilections
—Lois's engagement—The dual personality—The Three of Us.

Like all men of temperament, Daddy was naturally not at
all times an equable companion. Some days, of course, he
was worried at a turn in events, and although his mind always
grappled skilfully with a difficulty and devised a way out,
on those occasions he liked complete quiet and no disturbing
irrelevancies. But if he could sink to depths of depression,
he had his heights of charm and gaiety, moments more
infectious and more endearing than those of an average temperament, both on account of their quality and their rarity.
And when the mood was on him he could be superlatively
charming.

If only his work had not taken up so much of his time,
these glimpses might well have become the whole man, and
the sombre gloom the glimpses. He was like a man who had
not the *time* to let his working self be submerged. In the
pleasant half-retirement he had planned for his old age he
was to have had time to "get to know us all better, and do
more fishing and reading." But Fate did not let those happy
days come to pass, and the plan that "some day he would
take Mother to Madeira" disappeared into the limbo of lost
hopes, together with the spare time which would have given
his geniality the latitude it lacked. As Dr. Healey Willan,
the Canadian composer, said to us, "He is a man with a
great capacity for enjoyment, if he would but allow it full
play."

At the end of September, 1928, he made a trip to Scotland
in order to meet Mr. Alec Cruickshanks and Mr. R. H.
Gillespie on important business. He invited me* to go with
him "as long as I sat quietly and amused myself," but all
the charm which was his to exert at will came into play once

*Lois.

we had fairly started. There was no need to amuse myself. He did it for me.

From the moment we stepped into the carriage at New Street he was the personification of the Holiday Spirit (an expression beloved of Mother, but too light a thing in the general way for a man who put in such a tremendous amount of hard work). He bought half a dozen books from the stall, chocolates, and was immeasurably gay with the dining staff. For the next four days he kept my eyes perpetually widening in wonder as this note of gaiety was sustained, not dropped. It was as if he had said, with one of his pantomime fairies, "Gloom, avaunt!"

His was the strength of personality which pervades the atmosphere with whatever note is sounded in himself. Let him be depressed: we were all depressed. (As a child I remember looking out of the windows to blazing June days and praying for rain because Daddy had said, "If this fine weather doesn't break we shall all be ruined!") And now here was a holiday of perpetual sunshine! Lift boys, waiters, whosoever came in contact with him, were all enlivened by its rays.

We walked along Princes Street and up to the Castle on the Sunday morning, with a soft grey mist hanging between. The silhouette of the ramparts looked like a fairy castle in the clouds, and he exclaimed "Doesn't that look like my castle in *Humpty Dumpty?*" He was passionately anxious that I should think Princes Street, as he did, "the most beautiful street in the world." Seen that keen September morning, it was indeed the very heart of romance. He showed me the tartans in the shops, and their different patterns, and explained the care and interest he'd taken in his different clans in the Scotch scene in *Humpty Dumpty*.

And as we looked at the shimmering grey Scotch mist still half veiling the Castle walls he said, "That's why I had to have the grey gauze curtains to open the Highland scene. It wouldn't have been quite Scotland to me without the mist." (Three soft, transparent curtains were raised in turn to reveal an old shepherd and his dog at the foot of the hill slope. It was an artist's touch, and so beautiful it brought a lump into one's throat.)

As we climbed to the Castle Daddy kept stopping small boys and asking them the way, just for our pleasure in hearing their accent. After a time he grew bolder. He now asked the way in broad Scotch himself! We laughed our way up to the Castle, only to find it was not open on a Sunday. So instead he continued asking the way back to the hotel in dialect. The formula varied, but on the whole it was a copy of Georgie Wood, with "Can ye no tell me the way to the Nor-r-rth British?" and many actions. I think the natives must have thought us a couple of mild lunatics with our pseudo Scotch, but we enjoyed it all the more.

We met Mr. Cruickshanks that afternoon, and in the evening there was an important business conference.

Next morning we set off early on a tour of the city. Straight to the Castle, and first of all into the Shrine. Daddy thought this War memorial the most perfect in Britain, and we stayed for a long time examining the beautiful figures in relief. Then to the Castle itself. We explored the Crown room, and while we were there he explained the exactitude with which Edgar Wallace had planned the Tower jewel robbery scenes in *The Yellow Mask*. He was always tremendously appreciative of attention to detail in others, it being a passion with himself.

The Argyll Tower, Queen Mary's room, and the dungeons left behind, we walked down from Old Edinburgh into the New. We called at the New Empire Theatre, which was being redecorated in rose-du-barry, and Mr. Gillespie showed us round. Carpenters were everywhere, but at night, when we went for the big opening of *Showboat*, everything was in perfect order. Daddy was charmed with the performance; it was of the type he himself delighted in presenting: colour, imagination, lilting music, old-world settings. . . .

After the show we returned to the North British Hotel for a

big dinner party. It was a sumptuously appointed affair, with everyone in the best possible humour. Mr. Gillespie was charming, receiving congratulations from right and left, helping us all to champagne, and throwing rolls across the tables to attract friends' attention. Speeches started early; Owen Nares spoke cleverly, and "Philip" was called on. His speech was, as nearly always with him, very short and excellent.

Earlier that evening, when we had finished dressing for the theatre, Daddy came into my room to inspect me, as was his wont, when we were going out with him. His "Yes, you look very nice," was the highest compliment possible, and would make us extremely proud. More often, alas, it might be qualified with "*But* isn't that skirt a little short, or those sleeves, or isn't that a rather fashionable hat?" Dear Daddy! Those were the days of knee-length and sleeveless dresses, and no healing balm could be laid to his soul that it was the height of fashion. (How often have we wished since that he could have seen the ankle length, puff-sleeved frocks of only four years later; they would have pleased him so much. But it was well-nigh impossible in those days for us to get such things, let alone wear them, and yet we knew that not until we did could our evening dress earn his unqualified approval. One hesitates to think what his opinion of backless frocks would have been!)

His ideal for us for day wear was the quietest of colours and most inconspicuous of cut. An extra half-inch on a Louis heel was noticed at once, or a slight wave in the hair that hadn't been there yesterday. For fair hair this attention was fatal! For days after a simple Lux shampoo at home I would go about in a hat, because otherwise the extra fluffiness and lightness would be certain to call down on my head "I much prefer your hair as it was." So we would always try and wait till our hair, or heels, or new frock had toned down to an accustomed level. Then would he be satisfied with us.

I think this was mostly due to his dislike of change in any

form, but added to this dislike was a positive hatred of make-up off the stage. In earlier days I believe he burned five of Mother's powder puffs (our only form of make-up) one month after another. Waves in the hair or fluffiness he was afraid were caused by unnatural means and so were taboo. He liked hair smoothed down quietly (except Mother's, and his own Mother's, whose curls he took for granted). His own hair, *when he let it alone*, was always very curly, and the first thing in the morning, when we took in his papers, waved all over his head. We tried to explain to him that it was more unnatural to flatten it all down as he did, than to leave it curly, but his only reply was, "Oh, you ladies, you won't be *logical*." We had felt this to be the essence of logic, but in Daddy's eyes women as a class had no reasoning ability, and so this little stock phrase of his often clinched any argument.

In the evening, then, he came to inspect me. He was standing by the dressing table, and suddenly I saw his eyes rooted to one spot. My eyes followed his and I became rooted too. It was the tiniest powder compact imaginable! I kept it for taking the shine off the very end of my nose, but I knew I oughtn't to have had it, and I was as afraid of his displeasure as if he had been Jove himself. I was crimson and numb, and my heart almost stopped beating.

This may sound ridiculous or impossible to other modern girls, but then they hadn't Philip Rodway as a father. He had as strong a personality as a Napoleon and just such a power of awe over others.

After what seemed to me a long silence he asked "What is that?" My predicament was terrible. I couldn't lie—even had I tried to. My guilt was self-evident. How to extenuate it? "It's just a little talc" burst from me in an inspiration. A twinkle, the last light in the world I expected to see at that moment, came into his eye as he said: "Well, don't let me find you ever using a little 'talc' again." And so, for the rest of that holiday at least, I went shiny-nosed. Let the east wind blow as it would, I had an easy conscience.

On the Tuesday morning we made plans for the return home. We walked down Princes Street choosing plaids and Edinburgh rock to take back to The Woodlands with us. All his life, on his periodical visits to Scotland, he had brought these home with him. He always liked to see us in Tartans— the only exception he ever made to his rule of conformity and inconspicuousness in dress.

On the train coming home we met Felix Edwardes in the dining car, and he and Daddy never stopped talking all the way. Daddy taught him geography and gave him fishing hints before they got on to stage personalities. They talked particularly of *Showboat*, then Carl Brisson's name came up, and Phyllis Neilson-Terry's, and finally the Astaires, whom Edwardes had produced in *Funny Face*.

There seemed no end to Daddy's gaiety, and they arranged between them that, for the benefit of the porters, I should say "Good-bye, Henson," and he should reply "Good-bye, Adèle," at Crewe where we separated.

In the train for Birmingham we had the carriage to ourselves, and Daddy became reminiscent about the old days when he was engaged to Mother. He started playing violently on an imaginary keyboard, observing, with the little humorous twitch at the corner of his mouth, "I can see your Mother now, in a very trim shirt waist, playing the piano, and singing *I'll stick to the ship, lads!!* Or for a change, *When I'm MARCHING with the Seventh Royal Fusiliers!* . . ."

So, in the happiest spirits, we drew into Birmingham.

* * *

So much for his charm when the enchantment of the holiday spirit was upon him. At home about this time, and for several years previously, there was in our family a fearsome edict invented by Daddy. It was known as "*The Ten-o'clock Rule*." It worked very much on the principle of the Curfew, only instead of everybody having to be *in* by a certain time, everybody had to be *out* by a certain time. The underlying

purpose was that we should have an hour and a half to prepare for his arrival. In effect we often had about two minutes,
but the strain was hardly worth it and we not seldom found
ourselves reluctantly showing visitors over the front doorstep as it chimed the hour.

By the time Daddy came in we were all supposed to be
safely in bed, and Charles used to say that if the prophet
Elijah had been going to pay us a visit we could never have
had a more wholesome respect and awe for the moment of
his Arrival. We were taught that a properly run home had
all its lights out and its correct quota of occupants safely
housed in bed from ten o'clock onwards. If either of us
were out, then the home certainly wasn't as well run that
night.

Part of the idea was his quite understandable desire that
when he came home—tired and often worried—from the
theatre, he should not have to meet people, when he wanted
to have a quiet hour with his pipe, and a chat with which-
ever of us was still awake.

But at the root of everything still lay his dislike of change.
All through our childhood days he had come in to find the
house asleep, and it was difficult for him to realise his household was growing up. We have said how any alteration in
the garden made him unhappy for days, as the change in the
position of a single piece of furniture in the house. That was
probably why he repeatedly remarked that no woman should
give a thought to marriage before she was thirty, and even
then it was too soon! We were part of The Woodlands, and
marriage would have made a change in the old-established
customs, the Sunday afternoons and Sunday night talks, and
broken up the old familiar ties. They were truly very dear
familiar ties, but if marriage is indeed a severing of them,
his own mother was married at sixteen, and he himself had
spent the years between fourteen and twenty-five in trying
to persuade Mother to follow her example. But Daddy,
withal the most logical of men, refused to see any analogy,

and, with all his acute hearing, became seriously deaf when any such allusion was made.

It was a homelife interwoven with typical P.R. rules and predilections, some stern, some humorous, but all of them essentially the man. He was strict, but looking back on his rules to-day, we feel we would not have been without a single one of them. A biography should attempt to give a true picture of the mental make-up of its subject, and we should be giving the light without the value of the shade if we superimposed leniency on his sometime sternness, and gaiety for his sometime seriousness. We could, by giving you only his sense of humour and omitting his scrupulous sense of the fitness of things, build you up a most robust picture of a manager, rich in practical jokes. In his home life we could paint him—by giving only the one side of his disposition— as the most carefree of fathers, continually romping in the garden with us and his dog, and ready for all and sundry. But would that suffice? Such a man would no doubt be loved. So was Daddy. But he would never have been the man of strict principles for which all Birmingham, and all his family, respected him.

Principles in a man are uncomfortable things, and so are Ideals. Men have been prepared to stake their all for them, and such a man was Philip Rodway. We have wandered far from the half-humorous sallies of home life, when possibly nothing more than an extra half-hour's grace was at stake. In the outside world there were bigger prejudices, more rigid principles.

A portrait painter fails in his duty as a realist if he omits the lines on the face and the shadows under the eyes, just as much as if he stresses them. Of the two perhaps the latter is preferable, for surely it is the lines on face or character that give it its value. What a flat, expressionless, pink and white thing is left without them! With a family biography there is less likelihood of the pitfall of stressing the lines, and rather the reverse. We must be forgiven if we do what we feel to be right, and faithfully give the often uncompromising attitude of our none the less beloved subject. Those lines that are there we may be proud of, in all conscience. There are few men who have only stern rigidity of principle, and a certain severity of manner and mental outlook, to offset a thousand purely "good" qualities. And who shall say that these principles in themselves were not "good"? We all may have strained at restrictions in the home and the theatre life, but one is bound to respect a character which admits of no frivolous elements in itself before forbidding them in others. Rarely could one meet a man with fewer "frills" or extravagances.

We often used to say that his principles and prejudices were Victorian, and they were so completely at one with his whole mental make-up that often they were not formulated as rules at all. One knew them instinctively: no smoking for ladies; no make-up; no theatrical proclivities; no careers for women; preferably no dancing—each and every predisposition so different from all one imagines in a visionary picture of a theatrical director. Never could there have been a stranger, more lovable blend of the centuries in the predilections of one man: he was at once Victorian and Mediaeval, Puritan and Romantic.

One can imagine him walking in a straight road, an Oliver Cromwell, Roundhead in a world of Cavaliers; a stern, fine character, impatient of the trimmings of civilisation, metaphorically saying "Take away that bauble" to the lighter, gayer elements of life. Perhaps the difficulty was that, in any case, the feminine portion of the world are for the most part Cavalier at heart, with an inherent affection for curling hair, airs and graces, and a dance.

Mr. Michie Fraser understood him when he wrote "His refusals were frequently actuated by his strong personal predilections, and no power on earth would change his mind."

And now to return to our home life, and the Christmas of 1928. Daddy, as we have said, did not approve of early marriages, and so when finally I was twenty and he sanctioned my engagement to Charles Slingsby, it may well be understood that a two-years' unofficial engagement had preceded it, and that he indeed liked Charles. A captain in The Royal Warwickshire Regiment (T.A.), in Daddy's eyes his chief claims to approval were that he was a pipe smoker and a lawyer. The legal profession had always attracted Daddy, from his own early days of training with Herd and Nutt, and the pipe and no cigarette probably clinched the matter. But the subject had been broached at least once a week for twenty-four months before he at last consented to an official interview. Then mystic letters passed between them, and a meeting was arranged in the private office of the Theatre Royal. Still we were all kept in complete darkness as to the probable result, and in no wise would he consent to discuss the probable result at all. Only once did he momentarily relax (a very ray of light in the darkness) on the day of the interview, December 4th. I remember him saying in the morning, "Had I better put my thick boots on to-day?" and I was sufficiently dull I never saw it at once. But apparently they were not needed, for the "Theatre Royal meeting" was from 7 to 8 p.m., and at 8.5 we were officially engaged. Charles assured us that no one could have been more charming and less like the Man of Granite we had depicted.

It was then the full dawning broke! We had always had an inkling of it, and now we were certain. He was a different man at home and in the office!

At The Woodlands he was sometimes delightful with us, sometimes stern, sometimes a very tired business man of whom we only caught glimpses. He was a man of an infinite number of moods, except with visitors, when his manner was invariable. To them he was very polite—and always in a hurry! He but rarely asked any of his own friends home, for he liked it to be a little oasis where he could always find what he most longed for in the desert of city and theatre life—complete quietness.

CHARLES

Capt. C. H. Slingsby

All these characteristics made up what we knew was a definite "personality," sometimes forbidding, often fascinating, but it didn't fit in with the good "clubman" and good fellow of whom we got the impression when his men friends talked to us of him. There was still another P.R. hidden away from us, and perhaps he hid his "home" aspect from others. One of the few people privileged to see him in both settings said, "When he gets to the top of Speedwell Road he becomes a different man." This dual personality did not involve essentials at all. He was always the essence of honour, and loyalty, and humour too. The change was solely in manner, and possibly the reason was that his family consisted of three women (and of course the dog). He believed in the absolute autocracy of the master of the house. Added to that we always knew that he was definitely *a man's man*. He could not have been anything else, for he never thought another woman existed except Mother! If we ever introduced a woman into the conversation it was twenty to one he would hurry her out of it as fast as possible.

Every year, as we have told, he allowed us to give children's parties, one in the summer and one in the Christmas pantomime season. Every year, therefore, he was introduced to our girl friends, nearly always the same ones. But had our parties gone on to 2000 A.D. (as he often said they would), with our girl friends the same every year, he would still have had to be introduced, for he never remembered one of them. One of their most frequent plaints, which we used to hear between parties, was "I passed Mr. Rodway in New Street to-day and smiled at him, but he never saw me." Occasionally this was varied by "But he looked through me." But he always remembered the boys!

Knowing his attitude to women—either they were illogical, or they just didn't exist—it is perhaps too much to have expected him to be natural in a home life composed solely of these strange creatures. We three existed, sure enough, but we were certainly illogical. Mother, Daddy felt, was

KI

inconsistent in the extreme, and one of his favourite phrases was "I shall never understand your Mother." We often felt it a little hard that with three totally different types of mind to choose from, not one of us was entirely satisfactory, compared with the male mind. Mother was too fluctuating; Phyllis too pliable altogether, and asked too many questions; and Lois asked too few and made up her mind far too definitely. Phyllis was never sure enough of anything, and far too over-analytical; Lois was too decisive, and should try and make her motto "I'll never be positive about anything." Or we might employ his own favourite metaphor which was always accompanied by expressive gesticulation: Mother went round in circles, Phyllis wavered to and fro, Lois got there far too quickly. Dear Daddy, not one of us was the ideal! Sometimes we wondered if he was not at his happiest with something to combat. After all, when he had moulded and modelled the recalcitrant clay into what he wanted, was he satisfied? No. When he first met Mother she was as gaily dressed a young lady as any in the nineties, with as thorough an interest in pretty dresses and hats. Though there is no doubt he completely admired her attractive attire, he felt that her interest in it was frivolous and giddy, and his ideal must be made complete—she must *not* be interested in fashionable wear. Their early walks were often taken up by lectures on the vanity of such things.

Eventually Mother actually began to agree with him. Her pleasure in pretty clothes gradually waned; her interest in dress shops was entirely transferred to furniture shops. Hats were as nothing compared to gardens and lawns, and a new coat of paint for the house pleased her infinitely more than the newest tailor-made for herself—so much so that Daddy used to say that if she were to die she ought to have a little paint brush and pot buried with her.

And so, about fifteen years after their marriage, the change was complete. The model woman stood before him—a pretty woman with no interest in clothes!

But was Daddy satisfied? From the age of thirteen or so we can remember hearing him say "Your Mother isn't doing herself at all justice in that hat, and can't you make her get herself a different pair of shoes? She's got the prettiest little feet, and who in the world would guess it?"

For many years it was useless—the metamorphosis was too complete, and could not be revoked as easily as all that! In fact, her flair for clothes has never fully recovered. That spontaneous quickening of the heartbeats as she passed a dress shop was killed somewhere about 1913. However, she pulled back a little, and by 1930 her interest in such purely surface things as hats was already beginning to give Daddy a little worry again.

CHAPTER 37

(1928-29)

Theatre Royal Change-over—"The feast is good, until the reckoning comes"—1928 Season—*Lumber Love*—Edgar Wallace—Sir Edward Elgar conducts—*Old King Cole*, 1928-29; Clarkson Rose, Tom D. Newell, Fred Conquest—"Over the Hills and Far Away"—The last dress rehearsal—Australia's idea of Pantomime—Some last reminiscences from Clarkson Rose—Anniversary—"Never more"—The end of a great régime—Iona.

On May 29th, 1928, Philip Rodway threw a bombshell into the social and artistic life of Birmingham by announcing that an advantageous offer for the lease and goodwill of the Theatre Royal (Birmingham) Ltd. had been received from Moss Empires Ltd., and that an extraordinary general meeting of the shareholders would be held the next month to consider the situation.

In a statement to the Press, in which he described the circumstances leading up to the provisional agreement, P.R. said:

"Moss Empires have for some time been anxious to own and control an up-to-date dramatic theatre in Birmingham, in addition to their local variety houses, to add to their chain of once-nightly theatres in the country. Having regard to the high building costs in these days, and the question of suitability of site, taken in conjunction with the unwisdom of adding to places of entertainment in view of the distinct shortage of first class dramatic attractions, the Theatre Royal with its complete equipment and its exceptional site has appealed to them very strongly."

The announcement naturally caused tremendous interest everywhere—the newspapers gave it much attention in London as well as Birmingham. The prospect of the Royal ceasing to be an independently-conducted house, and becoming a unit in a great entertainment combine, said the *Birmingham Mail* in a leader on it, would come as a great shock to many others than the shareholders.

"For the Theatre Royal " (added that journal) "is a Birmingham institution of which the city is justly proud, and one of the grounds

From a painting by Bernard Munns

PHILIP RODWAY

Exhibited at the Royal Birmingham Society of Artists, 1933

of this pride is that the theatre is one of very few leading houses in the provinces which are locally managed.

"Whereas the principal theatres in the other great provincial cities have either passed out of being altogether as dramatic houses, or come under the management of some entertainment syndicate, the Birmingham Theatre Royal has remained untied to any 'circuit,' and managed on strictly individual lines. Moreover, it has a history going back over 150 years, and indissolubly linked with the best traditions of the English stage, and it may fairly be said that never, during that long period, has it been managed with greater ability and success than during recent years.

"Many provincial dramatic centres have fallen on parlous times, but the Theatre Royal has more than held its own against the competition of other forms of amusement, and, whilst catering for almost all tastes, has kept the flag of legitimate drama, given under dignified conditions, flying gallantly.

"A long succession of our most notable actors and actresses has felt it a privilege to appear on its boards, and there have been few productions of outstanding merit but have been seen there.

"The management, besides being enterprising, has ever maintained a high standard of decorum, so that the average citizen has felt safe in taking his family there.

"All these things, and many more, have united to make the Theatre Royal a civic institution in the best sense of the word, and it has been an added source of satisfaction that the continued existence of the house was due to local effort. The present fine building, one of the best-appointed of its kind in the kingdom, was erected by a company of Birmingham shareholders whose chief concern was, not the reaping of extravagant dividends, but that the city should possess as one of its amenities what it had boasted for so long—a first-class theatre.

"It will doubtless be asked why, if the theatre be so successful and prosperous on its present lines, those responsible for its fortunes should be prepared to give up the fight and sell out. That is a fair question, and it is also a fair inference that in all probability, had the management decided otherwise, it could have carried on with success on much the same lines for many years to come.

"But those intimately acquainted with the changes which have come over the theatrical business in recent times know that the task of Mr. Philip Rodway has become increasingly difficult in late years, and promised to be much more so in the immediate future. The truth is that the old touring system, which used to provide a plethora of attractions amongst which a local management could pick and choose, has almost broken down. There is, in fact, scarcely enough first-class fare available to fill out the season, and at least half these attractions, and the best paying half at that, are syndicate productions.

"If the Theatre Royal and its subsidiary, the Prince of Wales, were faced with the competition of a new syndicate theatre—as they will be if the present proposal does not go through—plus the deprivation of such items in their repertoire as *The Desert Song*, *Hit the Deck*, and similar pieces which are controlled by the syndicates—then a very critical position for the local management would undoubtedly arise. . . .

"The increasing difficulties of filling the programme successfully, and the still more formidable ones likely to accrue in the future, with the extra competition thrown in, have influenced Mr. Rodway and his confrères to listen, though with natural reluctance, to the tempting offer of Moss Empires Ltd. Many of us will wish that the latter could have been induced to take the Prince of Wales and leave us the Theatre Royal, instead of the other way round, though this is perhaps expecting too much of such shrewd business men.

"And as a last resource, we could wish that a majority of the Theatre Royal shareholders would be content to forgo the temptation to take their well-deserved increment, and vote for continuing the fight under the present flag, with the same generous measure of public spirit as at the outset led the promoters of the Theatre Royal company to sink their money in the preservation of the city's chief theatrical asset."

This closing paragraph, with its suggestion of bold defiance, was counsel which would have struck a responsive chord in Philip Rodway—had he been merely a shareholder, and not managing director! In the latter capacity, unfortunately for his ease of mind, he was charged with the responsibility of advising his Board and the shareholders as to what was best for them to do at this most critical stage in the company's history; and after months of almost unrelieved consideration he had no doubt.

At least a year earlier Daddy had seen the writing on the

wall for the Royal as an independent house. Extraordinarily sensitive to indications of coming events, he had realised that the break-up of the old touring system, and the extension of syndicate ownership of, or interest in, the provincial theatre, must have a certain upshot.

The syndicate had to have a theatre in Birmingham, the key-town of the provinces, since otherwise their own touring system was like a chain with the middle link missing. What would be their logical recourse? Plainly, to build a "Number One" theatre in the city, or adapt one of their existing music-hall properties. Either expedient would spell disaster for the Royal, which, instead of having its choice of the touring attractions—syndicate or independently controlled—would thereafter have to take what it could get: in frank terms, what was left; the second visits, the second-rate replicas of London shows, etc.

Philip Rodway saw it all with heartbreaking clarity. If he sat passively waiting for the opposition to be established, his shareholders' property would become valueless, or nearly so.

How could he turn the crisis to their practical advantage? Only by persuading the syndicate that it was cheaper to buy than to build! So, with ruthless disregard for his own feelings: in the knowledge that what he was doing meant a dreadful severance from all he held dear in business life, he took steps to create the atmosphere best calculated to prove fruitful. He acted as executioner to his own ambitions, deliberately plunging the knife into a vital spot.

So it came about that the spokesmen of Moss Empires Ltd. were able to open negotiations with the shareholders of the Theatre Royal Birmingham Ltd. in the confidence that their advance would be met more than half-way.

For months before the formal approach came, Daddy was expecting it. He was haunted by its shadow, he brooded over its consequences, but his mind did not falter. At home, on sunny afternoons in the garden, or late at night when he ought to have been asleep, he would tentatively broach the possibility to Mother of one day selling the Royal. She, realising that something ominous was on his mind, but little knowing how definite was the shape of the calamity, would try to persuade him that everything would be all right, and to put the idea out of his head.

He never did, nor could. With Macbeth he might cry "Glamis hath murdered sleep . . . therefore Cawdor shall sleep no more" . . . but the mischief had been done as surely as though the contract of sale had been signed.

His mind dwelt on the pain of it—the torture of one who cannot help but jag an aching tooth. In the June of 1928 he would often wander in and out of his room to the billiard room, from there to Lois's study, where she was reading for the finals of her degree, and we would all talk of this problematical change-over.

Looking back, we are sure that from this dire period we can trace his physical decline. It can hardly be imagination, and that he brooded and fretted from the middle of 1927, or thereabouts, no question exists.

It was a curious position, commercially speaking. Here was Philip Rodway, controller of an excellent business proposition, with which he was practically forced to part on what were intrinsically very favourable terms. Whether the would-be purchasers could continue its success was problematical, but they could not afford not to make the attempt, and he, for his shareholders' sake, could not afford not to support their bid.

The vital elements of the proposed deal, as it affected both parties, were lucidly set forth in the *Birmingham Mail* leader above quoted. P.R., developing the theme in an interview, said:

> "Moss Empires attach great importance to the fact that Birmingham is the nearest to London of the big provincial towns, and there is little doubt that the Theatre Royal will see the first production of a good many musical comedies which will ultimately go to the Hippodrome or other London houses. . . .

MRS. PHILIP RODWAY
(Mother)
1934

Miniature painted on ivory by Mabel Delmé-Radcliffe

"The chief asset of the Theatre Royal lies in the valuable lease of the premises in New Street (the value of which has appreciated greatly in late years), and the great goodwill created by the presentation of first-class fare throughout the theatre's long history."

At the same time he gave the public an insight into the uphill struggle which had been involved in creating that valuable goodwill. For many years the way of the new theatre had been hard, and it was not until fifteen years had elapsed that it had commenced to be a commercial success. Since then, in 1918, the Prince of Wales Theatre had been acquired, and by a careful balancing of attractions, and playing musical comedies at that theatre against the big Pantomime productions at the Theatre Royal, the position had been greatly improved.

Then followed a suggestion—the strongest his reserved nature would let him give the public—of what the severance would mean to him:

"One would be less than human if one did not feel the wrench that a break after thirty years' association must mean, and the news must come as a shock to the staff, who have rendered loyal and whole-hearted service," he said. "I hope and believe that a change of control—if the deal goes through—will find many of the staff retained in their present positions. For those who may be displaced, no effort will be wanting on my part to consider their future—for some perhaps, by transfer to the Prince of Wales Theatre, and for others by some other means, agreeable to them, and acceptable to the shareholders."

Among the numerous comments on the deal was a striking tribute to Daddy by his old friend Harry C. Lomax, of the *Sunday Chronicle*, who wrote therein:

"I own to a tinge of regret at the passing of so admirable an instance of successful personal management. Under Philip Rodway's guidance this, one of the country's most historic theatres, has been brought to a fine pitch of prosperity.

"Rodway and efficiency are synonymous. His pantomimes especially have set a standard to the whole country. . . . I hope, if the transfer takes place, the new owners will maintain the high traditions of their predecessors."

A fortnight later the die was cast. The shareholders, meeting in private on June 13th, 1928, confirmed the provisional contract for the sale of the Theatre Royal lease and equipment to Moss Empires Ltd., for the impressive sum of £140,000. For them it was a splendid deal. The price yielded a cash distribution of not less than £2 5s. per original £1 share, and there was also a *pro rata* distribution of shares in the Prince of Wales Theatre (Birmingham) Ltd.

P.R.'s earlier hint that inevitable hardships upon employees would be alleviated by means "agreeable to them and acceptable to the shareholders" was fulfilled in generous measure, for the meeting authorised the Board to earmark £1,500 to be distributed, at their discretion, among any members of the staff whose positions might be endangered when the transaction was completed.

On this same June 13th the Board sang their directorial swan-song at the final ordinary general meeting of shareholders. And an ironically golden song it was. Philip Rodway, who presided, explained that over a period of 51 weeks they had made £8,012 profit—nearly £2,000 more than in the preceding 53 weeks. (Once again this profit would not have been possible but for the success of the pantomime.)

They declared a dividend, consequently, of 20 per cent. less tax, and laid down their charge with a just pride of achievement. Never had times been more difficult. Never had the Royal made more money. Could anything have been more calculated to evoke sardonic laughter from the high gods of Olympus?

"It is not competent" (ran the leading article in the next day's *Birmingham Post*) "for an outsider to criticise or applaud the transaction. If, all possibilities considered, shareholders who got a 20 per cent. dividend last year are ready to sell at the price offered, then one must assume that the price offered, all possibilities considered, is not a bad price.

"But the Theatre Royal is not merely a money-making concern. It is a Birmingham institution. It is the oldest of all provincial theatres, with a history going back over 150 years. It is a house that has made special efforts—and successful efforts—to give a great city the theatrical fare it needed. Moss Empires, in fact, buy something more than a valuable lease in New Street; they buy a goodwill to which many managers, more actors, and a multiplicity of playgoers have contributed. And we may be allowed to express the hope that the goodwill may be treated not less seriously than the lease—that Moss Empires, despite their general attachment to 'musical enterprises,' will pay some regard to Theatre Royal traditions.

"For the rest, it is reasonably to be expected that the soul of the Theatre Royal will live on at the Prince of Wales—which is intimately associated, in the financial sense, with the Theatre Royal (Birmingham) Ltd. Mr. Rodway has already told us that the Prince of Wales 'will be more the home of the non-musical or serious play.' That does not mean, we hope, that Mr. Rodway will cease to give the public his admirable Christmas panto-mime. . . ."

The hope that the new management would preserve the Royal tradition, while that tradition flourished in a new environment, inspired the *Post* to think Birmingham might lose nothing by a sale "which on sentimental grounds, is certainly to be regretted."

Had Philip Rodway, even at the eleventh hour, made up his mind to a spectacular resistance of syndicated encroach-ment, there is no doubt his hardihood would have been unreservedly backed by the powerful Birmingham Press, whose principal figures never disguised their bias towards independent and against multiple control. Many of the older generation among the citizens, too, would have stood by him, and would have sacrificed much to preserve what was to them a treasured local possession.

Daddy knew this, and the knowledge must have tempted him up to the last moment of possible withdrawal, but always overshadowing the hope of successful resistance was the vir-tual certainty of defeat by economic pressure.

*   *   *

So to the night of March 9th, 1929—the most doleful night in P.R.'s life, for all that his heart, had it not been charged with sorrow, must have swelled with pride at the splendour which over-rode the pathos of the occasion.

It was the final performance of *Old King Cole*, and the close of an epoch in the Theatre Royal's history. P.R. went on the stage before a crowded house, and with formal briefness thanked the Birmingham public for their support during his years of management. He introduced Mr. R. H. Gillespie, the managing director of Moss Empires Ltd., and Mr. Lloyd Davidson, the newly-appointed manager, with a warm appeal for a continuance of public favour on their behalf. Mr. Gillespie paid graceful tribute to P.R., thanking him for facilitating the transfer, and presenting him with a gold watch.

The act-drop falls on the last scene of the last entertainment produced by Philip Rodway in the Birmingham Theatre Royal. It rises, falls, rises and falls again and again, as though loth to speak the final word of the tragic drama. . . .

The principals take their farewells of the audience, as principals have done at the end of twenty-five Rodway pantomimes. . . . Audience and players join heart and hand in *Auld Lang Syne*, in *God Save the King*. . . . P.R. gives the peculiar sign which the stage-manager recognises as meaning "This time for good." . . . Two thousand people stream out into the street, chattering animatedly—not a few with sober headshaking—of the chapter they have just helped to close . . . and for Philip Rodway his life's work is over.

* * *

Do you believe in portents?

The sale of the Royal was confirmed on June 13th. In Daddy's bedroom hung a calendar from which each night he used to tear off a slip. On the night of June 12th, he crossed the room to the calendar, tore off the leaf, and stood transfixed before the quotation for the following day. Finally, he tore off the 13th too, and handed it to Mother.

"Look here. *The writing on the wall* . . . what do you make of this?" he asked.

She read the quotation.

A feeling of presentiment chilled her, and she wished she could have prevented herself from saying, "Extraordinary—most extraordinary!" The words were *"The feast is good, until the reckoning comes."*

The feast *had* been good, but the reckoning was heavy. "My luck will change with the change-over of the Royal." How often since have we recalled his tragic words, for we ourselves know that it all but broke his heart. In vain did he take to his new theatre the well-remembered Royal act-drop of Ann Hathaway's Cottage; in the year or two left to him he would often, when walking to the Prince of Wales, go past the Royal, pathetically pretending to himself that it was on his way, just for a sight of the beloved building. . . .* "My luck will go with the Royal." First, the passing of the theatre; and then . . .

"Until the reckoning comes!"

The operative directors of the company at the date of the sale were Philip Rodway, Tom B. Davis, and W. E. Alldritt. The day we landed in Canada, September 6th, 1929, Daddy was handed a cable telling him of the sudden death of Mr. Alldritt—heart failure unquestionably accounted for by the strain of the negotiations. On December 14th, 1931, news came of the death of Mr. Davis, whose life had been bound up with the Theatre Royal since its rebuilding in 1904. And less than seven weeks later, on February 2nd, 1932 . . .

---

* *The Royal fireman, Andy Gavin, said to us only a few weeks ago, "I'll never forget seeing the Guv'nor, one evening months after the old theatre had changed hands. He came in and had a chat with Mr. Lloyd Davidson, and then he came across the stage, his old way, to the telephone—to ring you up at home, ma'am, like he used to do just as he was starting—and if ever a man's eyes were full of tears, and him nearly crying, that man was Mr. Rodway. He loved the old place—it was home to him."*

Season 1928

Up with the Lark, the musical comedy which filled the holiday season at the Prince of Wales Theatre, was inspired by the pre-war farce *The Glad Eye*. With Stanley Lupino, Anita Elson, and Austin Melford, it ran from Boxing Day, 1927, to nearly the end of January, 1928.

This was followed by *Lumber Love*, which, according to Hannen Swaffer, was to establish a new British prestige in musical comedy. The book was by Leslie Stiles, the music by Emmett Adams. No new production ever had a more generous measure of praise in advance, but it worked out as a not very impressive reminiscence of *Rose Marie*. Fred Kitchen, Basil Howes, Jamieson Dodds, Joan Lockton, Mai Bacon, Frederick Leister, and a troupe of Plaza Tiller Girls were in the cast.

The Birmingham Grand Opera Society presented *Dido and Aeneas* and *Pagliacci*. John Bierman, their producer, had cast Florence Higgitt as Dido, Alec Shanks as Aeneas, Doris Harmer as Belinda, Eva Tollworthy as the Sorceress, and Gordon Redfern, Isabel Dampier, and Dora Fairey for the Purcell piece. In *Pagliacci* the Tonio was Paul Vacher (widely known as the manager of the Queen's Hotel, Birmingham), the Nedda, Vera Gilman, the Beppe, Charles Gellion, the Silvio, Oswald Rogers. John Ford sang Canio at most of the performances, but Parry Jones and Frank Mullings each appeared as "guest" performers. Appleby Matthews conducted the orchestra, with Paul Beard as leader.

George Clarke made what was probably his first appearance at the Royal, in March, with Ella Retford and Madge Saunders in *Lido Lady*. Godfrey Tearle and Mary Malone in *The Acquittal* and Gladys Cooper in *The Letter* were other personalities to visit the theatre before June.

Edgar Wallace, now at the height of his fame, saw his play *The Terror* at the Prince of Wales in March, with Dennis Neilson Terry and Mary Glynne. Matheson Lang brought Robert Farquharson and Winifred Izard in Ashley Dukes' *Such Men are Dangerous*. Arnold Ridley's *The Wrecker*, of the same type as *The Ghost Train*, though not so effective, gave us a fine performance by Ian O. Will.

In *The Barker*, an American backstage play, Claudette Colbert (to-day the Cleopatra of the latest epoch-making talkie) was seen as Lou, the snake-charmer, with James Kirkwood playing opposite her. Next came the first performance on any stage of *The House with the Purple Stairs*, quite a good thriller, with the curious feature that the author's identity was not known even to the producer or the players up to and including the first night. Even when Renée Kelly, the leading lady, appealed to him at the end to come forward and receive the congratulations of the audience, there was no response!

Marie Tempest, Graham Browne, Horace Hodges, and Stella Freeman led the fine cast in *Mr. Pim Passes By* at the Prince of Wales in May. More Edgar Wallace, in the shape of *The Flying Squad*, followed, with Peggy O'Neil, Henry Hewitt, Cronin Wilson, and C. W. Somerset. Heather Thatcher and Hugh Wakefield played the leads in *Quest*.

The Stratford Festival Company had new principals in Dorothy Massingham, Mary Holder, and George Hayes, besides such familiar figures as Wilfred Walter, Roy Byford, Kenneth Wicksteed, and Eric Maxon. The tragic death of Dorothy Massingham, a former member of the Birmingham Repertory Theatre Company, and authoress of *The Lake*, is a recent sad memory.

For the Macdona Players' annual season of Shaw, the experiment of a fortnight each by the "north" and the "south" companies was tried. A feature of the week beginning July 29th, 1928, was that Edgar Wallace had two theatres in Birmingham to himself, with *The Ringer* at the Royal and *The Man who Changed His Name* at the Prince of Wales Theatre. A little later (in September) Mr. Wallace's *The Squeaker* was at the Prince of Wales.

Philip Rodway had every reason to be proud of his autumn seasons this year. At the Royal, when the once-nightly system was resumed, he had Cora Goffin and Henry Lytton (jun.) in *The Girl Friend;* the Duncan Sisters in *Topsy and Eva;* Julia Neilson and Fred Terry in *The Scarlet Pimpernel;* Adèle and Fred Astaire, Leslie Henson, Rita Page, and Vera Bryer in *Funny Face;* Martin Harvey in *The Lyons Mail;* Gerald Lawrence in *Beau Brummel* (of which more in a moment); Binnie Hale and Bobby Howes in *Mister Cinders;* and George Grossmith, Mamie Watson, Lester Matthews, and Clifford Heatherly in *Lady Mary.*

Beau Brummel, written by Bertram P. Matthews, was produced at the Royal for the first time on any stage on November 5th, 1928. It just missed being a great success, because the dreariness of its plot distracted attention from its many fine qualities. Gerald Lawrence, as the immaculate Brummel, had a part with too little "command," too much self-sacrifice in it, and when, at the end, he died in exile, one felt the author had lost a chance of giving him a rôle worthy to maintain the Beaucaire tradition. Admirable performances were given by H. Worrall Thompson (Lord Harding), Gwen Llewellyn (Lila Dawn), J. J. Bartlett (Mortimer), Frederick Tomlin (Lord Mayne), and Madge Compton (Mary). H. A. Saintsbury was the producer. The late Sir Edward Elgar, composer of the incidental music, honoured the theatre and the players by personally conducting the orchestra.

The end of the 1928 season at the Prince of Wales saw Bransby Williams in *The Soul of Nicholas Snyder*, Russell Thorndike in his own play, *Dr. Syn*, Serge de Kazarin in *Alibi*, Murray Carrington in *The Fourth Wall* (one of the most intelligent mystery plays we recall), Billy Merson in *The Lad* (another Edgar Wallace!), George Clarke and Madge Saunders in *Vogues and Vanities,* Harry Welchman, Dorothy Brunton, and Klit Gaarde in *The White Camellia,* Owen Nares, Sidney Fairbrother, and Henry Wolston in *Two White Arms,* Nelson Keys and Claire Luce in *Burlesque,* Dennis Neilson Terry and Mary Glynne in *No other Tiger,* and *Her Past,* with Alice Delysia, Violet Vanburgh, and Paul Cavanagh.

One incident in the home side of that summer of 1928. On June 30th, Daddy and Mother went up to the Degree Ceremony at Edgbaston, when Lois took her degree of Bachelor of Arts (Hons. English), after three happy years at the University.

PANTOMIME 1928-29
OLD KING COLE

Old King Cole, 1928-29—and the last of the great Theatre Royal pantomimes of the Philip Rodway régime.

"In his capacity as deviser, author, and producer," said Mr. Crompton Rhodes, "he may be proud of his latest contribution to Theatre Royal records; *Old King Cole* is unquestionably destined to leave a name that will long be remembered in the history of the theatre's productions.

"Following a long line of pantomimes notable especially for their spectacular charm, this pantomime surpasses all previous ones in its appeal to the sense of beauty. Artistry and inventiveness have gone hand in hand in the creation of scenes that still glow in the mind's eye long after the descent of the curtain. . . . Ingenuity and wit have been expended on the building up of a story that gives King Cole something more than a habitation and a name. . . ."

Only once before in the history of the theatre had the subject been chosen, and that was sixty-eight years earlier. The adventures of "the merry old soul" as revealed by the nursery rhyme would not appear to offer much scope for pantomime, but Philip Rodway bethought him of another kindly soul of nursery folk-lore, of whom little was known save that she had a dog and an empty cupboard. And so he worked in the story of Mother Hubbard, thereby rescuing two worthy personages from the obscurity in which the old verses had left them.

The central idea for the pantomime came from an incident

LI

at home—the loss of P.R.'s pipe; and the loss of King Cole's pipe thus provided the starting point.

Tapestry curtains depicting the droll monarch and his court (painted by W. R. Young from a design by Rudolf Haybrook) parted for the opening scene. "The Winning Post on the Riverside" (Bruce Smith) was a charming set, with a broad river flowing through, upon which proudly sailed into view the royal barge, whereon the King received the loyal greeting of the courtiers. We saw the Watermen's race, in which Roland, Mother Hubbard's son, competed, and when his oarsmanship earned for him the title of king's chief waterman, what more natural than that he should fall in love with the king's daughter who presented him with coat and badge of office?

The Farmyard Ballet which followed illustrated Mother Hubbard's Dream, and was meant specially for the children, but so cleverly and quaintly was it done, carried through in genuine pantomime, that it had just as much appeal to the grown-ups.

The third scene was laid inside the palace—the magnificent Court of Old King Cole (Bruce Smith), where the king discovered the loss of his beloved pipe. The royal records disclosed an old legend foretelling the misery that would befall him until it should be recovered by a brave youth of humble origin, and so Roland departed on his quest.

The finale of the first act, the "transformation" scene revealing the hero's journey "Over the Hills and Far Away," was one of the most impressively beautiful stage pictures imaginable. The gallant Roland, piloted by a pixie, emerged from the castle ramparts, and we saw him, aided by the elves, cleaving a pathway through tangled wood, climbing amidst a storm a snow-clad mountain pass, and eventually reaching the magical lily pond. There, assembled to meet him, was every variety of lily known to horticulture, a magnificent congregation of gorgeously coloured blooms, and there the Fairy Flora told him, in cryptic fairy language, where the lost pipe was to be found.

The second half of the pantomime opened on the Royal
Golf Links, with the castle silhouetted in the distance, and
then came two hilarious scenes—"The New Bungalow" and
"The Kitchen of the Palace." Next the brilliant pageantry
of "The Chess Tournament," where a complete game was
played, with every move carefully planned, and carried out
by the living pieces. And so to the discovery of the pipe in the
lining of the king's dressing gown pocket, and the great finale,
"The Carnival in the Hall of Mirrors," in which the mass-
ing and mingling of colours, with the rhythmically moving
fairy lights of the lantern-bearers, made an unforgettable
picture.

Much depended on King Cole being true to type, and in
Clarkson Rose the merry monarch had an ideal representative. He was at the Royal for the second year running, so
that he had the distinction of being an "old favourite," but
he increased his prestige by the clever way in which he played
the name-part. Master of all the arts of the comedian, he
inspired good humour as soon as he stepped on the stage;
he was a soul of merriness incomparable, full of quips and
cranks and jests—until he lost his pipe! And there his
experience of repertory work proved valuable, for he found
opportunities for some really dramatic acting.

One of his most popular numbers was the brilliant broadcasting burlesque with the dame, with whom he had another
diverting duet *I can't give you anything but love*. Then there was
the song in which he persuaded the audience to join him in
inquiring *What did the village blacksmith say when the hard, heavy,
hammer hit his hand?* And yet two more, one a clever ditty
full of local and topical allusions (written by himself, for he
is an adept at that kind of thing), and the other a parody of
many well-known melodies welded into an account of a golf
match—and all these in his admirably articulate voice.

Mother Hubbard, a lovable old lady, was played by Tom
D. Newell. An experienced exponent of dame parts, he
invested "Winifred" Hubbard with an ingratiating manner

such as one would expect to find in a lady who could capture the heart of a king almost without effort. This confidential little soul found herself in full accord with "Kingey," as she called him, and the two together were irresistible. One of the best things she did on her own was a laughable skit on a "Spring Song" dance, but when she and Kingey were not together, she was generally to be found with her dog. Fido, played by the inimitable Fred Conquest, was a dog we should all love to possess, so intelligent, so amusing, so endearing! A wag of his tail or a roll of his eyes could convey whole volumes of meaning.

Still on the humorous side were the Hanlon Brothers as the king's clowns, two pantomimists in the real sense of the word, whose perfectly synchronised movements and shadow dancing were infinitely attractive.

Roland was the jolly young waterman played by Byrl Walkley, whose excellent voice had plenty of opportunity in her songs *Forty-seven ginger-headed sailors* and *Get out and get under the moon*, and in the duet *Heaven for two*. Florence Hunter was a charming Princess Amaryllis, who sang sweetly and wistfully *Just like a melody out of the sky*.

Olive Fox (Mrs. Clarkson Rose) made a dashing figure as Quilini, the King's efficient secretary, and sang the song *You can feel it doing you good* with great spirit. The Fiddlers Three were Mareski, Massona, and Boy Ronald, the first a talented violinist and the other two eccentric jugglers; and there was Ethel Alderson, a dancing pixie who might have come straight from fairyland instead of Australia; Leonie Proctor as the Fairy Flora; and Victor Fairley, who, in addition to being stage manager, found time to appear as Colonel Bogey in the golf scene. And the work of the Kitty Denton troupe of dancers was in every way worthy of the elaborate production. *   *   *

Since perhaps never again will there be a dress rehearsal at the Theatre Royal on the same lines as those first laid down by Philip Rodway, may we be allowed one final glimpse? . . . It is Christmas Eve, and for the last hour ambulances and private cars have been drawing up at the theatre, unloading their passengers and moving off again. Nearly two thousand guests have been specially invited to the matinée by P.R., and of these some 1,200 are war sufferers from St. Dunstan's, Highbury, The Royal Naval Club, The Navy League, The British Legion—and there are besides 575 children from the Royal Cripples Hospital—all assisted to their places by Red Cross nurses and orderlies. The greater number of these wounded men have been in hospital ten years and longer; the luckier ones are sitting in seats, but thirty or forty lie on stretchers placed over two or three rows of seats. To many of these stretcher cases the pantomime is the one day out in the year—a thing to look forward to for months ahead, and they enjoy the show with a wholehearted delight that only the very unfortunate can ever experience.

Among other guests present we see the Bishop of Birmingham (Dr. E. W. Barnes), the Lord Mayor (Alderman Byng Kenrick), the Deputy Mayor (Alderman James), Sir Percival Bower, Mr. Neville Chamberlain. . . . The house is astir with animated chatter and expectancy. Great interest is shown in the wooden platform which runs from the stage to the level of the first box on the "prompt" side.

The orchestra are in, awaiting their cue to strike up. Now Philip Rodway appears before the act-drop, watch in hand; with a few cheery words he welcomes the audience, adding, as he gives the signal for the overture to begin, "Don't forget this is a dress rehearsal." (Delighted applause, for everyone knows that, except for the novelty of the occasion, the show they are about to see is to all intents and purposes the finished article.) There will be many an alteration and addition though, of which they know nothing, for in the box behind P.R.'s platform are two men with notebooks, and all the time they are writing, writing, taking note of his final instructions:

> "Lower out No. 3 cloth Chess scene.
> O.P. perch cut out amber for blue first chorus.
> Battens dimmed and spot lime on cue 'forty-seven.'
> Capt. to enter R.U.E. not L.U.E.
> Bring helm of ship further right. . . ."

Little things like that, hundreds of them. The pantomime may seem finished and complete, but P.R.'s eagle eye is on the look-out for the slightest flaw, to ensure that on Boxing Night perfection will be attained so far as ever human limitations permit.

On occasion he will mount the stage, sometimes to put right a little difficulty as it occurs, sometimes simply to give the unsophisticated section of his audience the pleasurable feeling that they are really getting a peep behind the scenes. We vividly recall one rehearsal in which the transformation scene had been reached; cloths and borders were swiftly ascending, flats vanishing into the wings, traps opening in the floor, the edge of a huge golden sun beginning to rise. Something went wrong; the fifty odd men all working at top speed were not synchronised to the absolute pitch of perfection; the flower chorus began to dance on—and the traps were still open! Just in time P.R.'s command rapped out, "Stop. Stop everything!" Immediately all sound and movement ceased. A dark figure stepped swiftly on to the stage, a few quick, decisive orders were given, and what might have been complete chaos was restored to order. . . .

The performance of *Old King Cole* runs smoothly on. Every half-hour or so the door at the back of our box opens quietly and Daddy puts his head in to say "What do you think of it?" or "How did that go?" usually preceded by "*Don't* get up, now."

In the interval B.4 becomes a reception room for our many friends, who, while the teacups circulate, enthusiastically offer their congratulations on yet another success. The orchestra strikes up for the second half, our box gradually empties, and the curtain rises on "The Royal Golf Links."

And so to the finale. This year is undoubtedly a special occasion, for at the conclusion P.R. is given an oak tea-wagon, bearing the inscription:

"Presented to Philip Rodway, Esq., by the Birmingham County Joint Committee of the Order of St. John and the British Red Cross Society, a token of gratitude for, and appreciation of, his kind and generous entertainment of Wounded and Disabled Soldiers* of the Great War, during the past 15 years."

P.R. starts to express his thanks, but, for perhaps the first time, we can see that his feelings are overcoming him; he can hardly speak. . . .

*   *   *

Clarkson Rose, writing to us from R.M.S. *Strathaird* (*en route* for England), says:

"I keep thinking of things which may interest you for your book, and one is contained in a letter I have written to Australia's greatest dramatic critic in reply to an article he has written on Pantomime.

"It would have interested your father to have known that I have refused a three-figure salary to play in the pantomime here simply because they did not decide to do pantomime until December 8th, and then merely did so for the amazing reason that the big stores were not doing their usual toy grotto panto-mimes this year, and that the Christmas holidays would naturally bring a certain amount of children to matinées. They have thus 15 days to prepare the pantomime in the third city of the Empire. Can one wonder the public goes to the 'talkies'?"

In the letter to which he refers Clarkson Rose writes to the famous critic:

"Your doubt that the scenic glories of the past can be repro-duced is unfortunately well founded, in fact, I do not think it is too much to say that some of the present-day methods cannot produce any of the glories of the pantomime past. It is not merely a question of economics. The reason is contained in your trenchant query 'Maybe pantomime might have prospered to this day had the original story been retained to a greater extent.' The leading pantomime managements in England who still find the annual Christmas production a handsome source of profit are those who have retained the 'story' to its fullest extent.

---

*Over 80,000.

"It has been my good fortune to play under such pantomime experts as John Hart, J. F. Graham, Julian Wylie, and the late Philip Rodway. These men and their various departments spent a whole year in the preparation of the pantomime. Theirs was no haphazard affair thrown on because round about the holidays people must go somewhere, wherever it is.

"Mr. Rodway, who was recognised as the greatest of them all, took the most meticulous care in the selection of his cast and all arrangements. He would make long journeys to visit a comedian during the summer months, carefully going through the well-written book with him and getting him right into the atmosphere of the whole thing. On one occasion when I was playing 'King Cole' for him I wanted to sing a golfing song. It was a very good song, but Mr. Rodway would not agree to its inclusion until he had devised a scheme for having both myself and my pantomime courtiers dressed in medieval plus fours with a full set golf course scene specially built.

"These details may strike one at first sight as 'pernickety,' but they characterise the whole of his and of other right-thinking managers' treatment of Pantomime in the true sense of the word. The result was, and is, to-day in England, that fidelity to these details and to the story presented a faithful picture, and the runs of these pantomimes were always longer than the 'slap-dash' conglomeration of revue and 'talkie' theme songs offered to the public by some managers in England and elsewhere to-day."

Fred Conquest, the "Fido" of the *Old King Cole* pantomime, writes to us from his delightful Beach Cottage, almost at the edge of Bembridge Harbour, Isle of Wight:

"My happiest pantomime work has been under the management of your father. It seemed to me that he was always pleased when another pantomime season came round, and especially so when the first rehearsal assembled. Ever kind and considerate, he will be sadly missed. I only wish I could put into writing what I feel concerning him. . . ."

And Clarkson Rose, in *The Stage*, paints a pen-picture of his old friend, Fred, "for pantomime lovers who recall his wonderful Goose, or his equally famous Fido, or that quaint and lovable Penguin of his."

"He has truly earned this pleasant retirement, and he will be able to look from his large windows out into his paddock, and see through his mind's eye Priscilla the Goose ambling about by the little brook picking up stray worms and things, and then the Penguin will waddle through the rustic gate and have a chat with Priscilla, until finally the artful Fido will bound through the long grass, and cause Priscilla to flutter away in high dudgeon and the Penguin to skedaddle, leaving Fido in sole possession of the scene as he often was in pantomime."

"Another very characteristic chat I recall having with your father," Clarkson goes on in the reminiscences he sends us:

"Mr. Rodway had been up to London on business, and came back after two days, rather tired and weary. Sitting over a whisky and soda with him in his office, I said 'You look tired, Mr. Rodway.' He said, 'I am tired, and yet I wouldn't mind being twice as tired to be back in Birmingham.'

"It's only a fragment, but it was little snatches of conversation like this that brought us into such close contact. We got to know each other so intimately through exchanges of views, and I think one of the proudest moments of many I had with him was when he used to hand me his own beloved scripts in front of the other members of the company with a phrase like 'Clarkson, So-and-So hasn't got a very comfortable phrase there, and So-and-So could do with some of his dialogue polishing up. I would like you to see to it because I know you will do it as I like it.'

"The Guv'nor was a very far-seeing man, and never overlooked any possibility. In one of his pantomimes an unkind remark, essential to the book, had to be made. The line was originally given to a principal, but Mr. Rodway had it transferred.

" 'If Quilini speaks that line,' he said, 'the children in the audience will take a dislike to the part. I will give the line to one of the chorus.'

"Philip Rodway was never out for popularity. As he used to tell me, popularity of a temporal kind can be so easily bought, and the rigid stand for personal conviction is a much lonelier furrow to plough.

"The Friday night gatherings in his little office were always jolly and illuminating affairs, but promptly at ten minutes to twelve he would say:

" 'Well, boys, I think we'll have an early night.'

"I never remember him omitting this remark.

"I was privileged to be admitted to the intimacies of his club, and his favourite restaurant, the Exchange, and here we used to talk of things, and his wide knowledge has been of invaluable

help to me. One more thing I shared with him—an enthusiasm
for the Aston Villa Football Club, and this bound us together on
the sport side of friendship.

"The Birmingham Royal was a wonderful place and atmosphere in which to work. One hundred per cent. efficiency in all
departments was what the Guv'nor demanded, and got. The public
know now how great were his pantomimes, and we artists, who
at times may have chafed under his rigid exclusion of our own
pet jokes if he didn't like them, and his iron rule that everything
must appertain to the story, realise that he knew his business
better than we, and his theatre, and his public, for whom he
always gave his utmost."

Philip Rodway's last anniversary night was on Wednesday, March 6th—the last of a long series begun in 1901.
Again this year the entire proceeds went to the Theatre Royal
Benevolent Fund, of which he had been the founder; again
the customary features were observed, the speeches, the presentations. One of the gifts which touched him deeply was the
very beautiful silver loving cup from Sir William Waters and
Lady Butler, " . . . on leaving the Theatre Royal, with our
best wishes for the future."

Yet there was one very significant omission, for this time P.R.
did not announce the title of the next year's pantomime. Actually he had been invited by the new management to produce
it for them, but his forthcoming Canadian venture, together
with certain other factors, made this impracticable. His speech
did not dwell too heavily on the past, nor had it any touch
of self-pity or self-glorification. In one phrase it modestly
summed up the Rodway record at the Royal. "I have tried,"
he said, "to be straight with the public . . . and to live up to
the great tradition of our theatre."

The evening was a great one, but throughout ran the under-
current of sadness, the melancholy message of the Raven—
"*Never more.*"

And so to the last night, when a notable era in the history
of the Theatre Royal came to an end. Let King Cole speak for
us:

"OVER THE HILLS AND FAR AWAY"

Transformation Scene

Devised by Philip Rodway
for his pantomime
"Old King Cole,"
1928-29

Painted by W. R. Young,
scenic artist of
the Theatre Royal

"I was privileged to hand over the theatre officially to Moss Empires on Mr. Rodway's behalf—he was too miserable to do it himself—and to speak the last lines (a specially written verse) in the theatre under the Rodway régime. Though he did his utmost to conceal it from us all, I shall never forget his sad and resigned manner at the time. . . ."

Of the official take over you have heard already earlier in this chapter, but even now, in imagination, we seem to hear again the swinging lilt of music heralding in the last scene of the pantomime; we see once more, with all the strange bitter-sweet sadness of The Last Night, the unfolding of the great transformation scene "Over the Hills and Far Away," beyond the storms of "The Snow-clad Hills."

Où sont les neiges d'antan? . . . Such was the passing of *Old King Cole*, the last of the Philip Rodway pantomimes.

*   *   *

On the sacred Island of Iona, in the Inner Hebrides, lies the original Old King Cole, king of the islands of Coll and Colonsay in the far-off days of the fifth century. Centuries ago it was foretold that "Columba's happy isle" should be honoured and revered far into the future, when much that was less worthy had passed away. And so it became the burial-place not only of the princes of Scotland, but of the rulers of many a distant land.

And in the September of 1934, as we stood silently beside the Graves of the Kings, looking away over the hayfields and the little lanes of that tranquil island to the sea, thoughts of that last great pantomime came surging back, and we knew that still, in some Iona of the heart, Old King Cole and all that it stood for is enshrined as long as memory lasts.

THEATRE ROYAL PANTOMIMES

1840-41. *Harlequin and the Knight of the Silver Shield.*

1841-42. *Harlequin Sinbad.*

1842-43. *Baron Munchausen.*

1843-44. *Princess Battledore.*

1844-45. *The Dragon of Wantley.*

1845-46. *Guy, Earl of Warwick.*

1846-47. *Lady Godiva and Peeping Tom of Coventry.*

1847-48. *Harlequin in England, Ireland, Scotland.*

1848-49. *The Golden Regions of California.*

1849-50. *Baron Munchausen.*

1850-51. *Queen Mab.*

1851-52. *Jack in the Box.*

1852-53. *Don Quixote.*

1853-54. *Jack the Giant Killer.*

1854-55. *Robin Hood.*

1855-56. *Babes in the Wood.*

1856-57. *Old Mother Hubbard.*

1857-58. *King Blusterbubble.*

1858-59. *Little Red Riding Hood.*

1859-60. *The House that Jack Built.*

1860-61. *The Great Gosling.*

1861-62. *The Sleeping Beauty.*

1862-63. *Puss In Boots.*

1863-64. *Queen of Hearts and Her Wonderful Tarts.*

1864-65. *Old King Cole.*

1865-66. *Sinbad the Sailor.*

1866-67. *Aladdin.*

1867-68. *Robinson Crusoe.*

1868-69. *Forty Thieves.*

1869-70. *Bluebeard.*

1870-71. *Dick Whittington and His Cat.*

1871-72. *Fair One with the Golden Locks.*

1872-73. *The Fairy Fawn.*

1873-74. *Beauty and the Beast.*

1874-75. *Ride a Cock Horse.*

1875-76. *Puss in Boots.*

1876-77. *Sinbad the Sailor.*

1877-78. *The Forty Thieves.*

1878-79. *Robinson Crusoe.*

1879-80. *The Fair One with the Golden Locks.*

1880-81. *Dick Whittington.*

1881-82. *Beauty and the Beast.*

1882-83. *Sinbad the Sailor.*

1883-84. *Queen of Hearts.*

1884-85. *Dick Whittington and His Cat.*

1885-86. *Robinson Crusoe.*

1886-87. *Cinderella.*

1887-88. *Goody Two Shoes.*

1888-89. *Dick Whittington and His Cat.*

1889-90. *Aladdin.*

1890-91. *Forty Thieves.*

1891-92. *Sinbad the Sailor.*

1892-93. *Cinderella.*

1893-94. *Little Red Riding Hood.*

1894-95. *Robinson Crusoe.*

1895-96. *Santa Claus* and *Cinderella.*

1896-97. *Dick Whittington and His Cat.*

1897-98. *Forty Thieves.*

1898-99. *Cinderella.*

1899-00. *Babes in the Wood.*

1900-01. *Dick Whittington and His Cat.*

THEATRE DEMOLISHED AND REBUILT

1904-05. *Babes in the Wood.*

1905-06. *Aladdin.*

1906-07. *Queen of Hearts.*

1907-08. *Cinderella.*

1908-09. *Dick Whittington.*

1909-10. *Jack and the Beanstalk.*

1910-11. *Aladdin.*

1911-12. *Jack and Jill.*

1912-13. *Goody Two Shoes.*

1913-14. *Little Miss Muffet.*

1914-15. *Sinbad the Sailor.*

1915-16. *The House that Jack Built.*

1916-17. *Boy Blue.*

1917-18. *Cinderella.*

1918-19. *Babes in the Wood.*

1919-20. *Dick Whittington.*

1920-21. *Mother Goose.*

1921-22. *Queen of Hearts.*

1922-23. *Puss in Boots.*

1923-24. *Aladdin.*

1924-25. *Jack and the Beanstalk.*

1925-26. *Humpty Dumpty.*

1926-27. *Cinderella.*

1927-28. *Robinson Crusoe.*

1928-29. *Old King Cole.*

R. W. ELLISTON
1813

ALFRED BUNN
1819

MERCER H. SIMPSON
1837

PHILIP RODWAY
1897–1929

SOME MANAGERS OF THE THEATRE ROYAL
BIRMINGHAM

CHAPTER 38

THE CANADIAN TOUR OF THE PANTOMIMES
HUMPTY DUMPTY AND *MOTHER GOOSE*

August, 1929—January, 1930

PROLOGUE

It was early in 1929 that the first mention of the projected
Canadian tour was made, when the announcement appeared
that Philip Rodway had been approached to take over two
of his most successful pantomimes. So extensive was the venture, and so many were the important considerations involved,
that it was several months before the arrangements were concluded. Then the definite plans were made known. We
quote from the *Birmingham Mail* of June 20th:

> "Mr. Rodway could hardly say so himself, but I happen to
> know that this huge venture—no bigger combination, probably,
> has ever gone to Canada from England—has been conceived as
> a great compliment to him in his capacity of pantomime producer.
> The Canadian managements and the Canadian public have long
> been calling for a Philip Rodway pantomime: that is to say, for
> one of the real old English variety for which he has been noted
> during his control of the Theatre Royal."

The company of about sixty artists, headed by Wee
Georgie Wood, Dan Leno, jun., Fred Conquest, Hal Bryan,
Florence Hunter and Maisie Weldon, with John Harcourt
and Ethel Alderson, were to sail at the end of August, and
open in Montreal on September 9th. From there they would
blaze a trail of enjoyment right across Canada from East
to West, through the big cities like Toronto and Winnipeg,
and the little townships like Medicine Hat and Moose Jaw—
outward to Vancouver. There *Humpty Dumpty* would fall
from his wall for the last time, and be replaced on the boards
by *Mother Goose*, which would bring the company back again,
West to East, to Toronto. Afterwards they would complete
their adventure by a trip to the Maritimes of Nova Scotia.
The tour was to last six months, and during that time something like seventeen thousand miles would have been covered.

"We have often been told," continued the *Mail*, "that next

year's pantomime is begun while this year's pantomime is still running. I began to believe there was something in the statement when I met Wee Georgie Wood in Mr. Rodway's office at the Prince of Wales Theatre earlier this week. He had just been going through his parts for the tour—though the sun was shining outside from a cloudless sky and the Africans were batting at Edgbaston."

"It sounds a trifle odd," admitted Daddy, "to be rehearsing pantomime in June. Odder still to talk of opening the show in September, but remember this is a tour of thousands of miles, twice across a continent. If we want to give the shows in as many places as possible at the most seasonable period, we simply must get off the mark in September."

It was generally recognised that when Philip Rodway left for Canada with two of his most successful pantomimes, he would prove one of the most desirable ambassadorial representatives this country had ever sent to the Dominion.

"In his journey across Canada," said the Press, "he will be forging links between the Mother Country and the Dominion every mile of the way. Every night, in modern city or backwoods village, he will be arousing memories. To modern, go-ahead Canada, inevitably affected, no doubt, by American influences, he will bring the touch of the Mother Country. And the contact can do Canada, and her relations with ourselves, nothing but good.

"Nowhere in all Britain has the purity of pantomime as a distinct art form been better preserved than in Birmingham. Why? The reason is to be found in the genius, the artistic obstinacy, the intelligence—call it what you will—of Philip Rodway. Always has he held the view that a pantomime should consist of the presentation, with ingenuity, humour, spectacle, richness of colouring, music, and song, of a fairy story as a child would see it. And always he has attained his ideal.

"As a consequence, the Rodway pantomimes are known and appreciated throughout Great Britain. During the first year of their careers they delight Birmingham; during the second they usually find a home in London; the third year sees them at, say, Glasgow; during the fourth year they are in Manchester, the fifth in Sheffield, the sixth in Newcastle, the seventh in Liverpool, and so on.

THE "DUCHESS OF ATHOLL"

ON BOARD

Dr. Healey Willan, Philip Rodway and a friend

"The Philip Rodway pantomimes permeate all England, Scotland, and Wales. They go on, pretty well, for ever. For Birmingham is the Temple of Pantomime, and Philip Rodway the High Priest."

Said Georgie Wood:

"I feel that in presenting two of them to Canada we shall be giving the real home touch that Canada will welcome. You see, the Rodway pantomimes are the real thing. They are not only fine pantomimes; they are also essentially British.

"If anything is true, it is true that the mantle of the Drury Lane tradition has fallen on Birmingham. Some pantomimes one sees are simply fairy stories interrupted by ordinary music-hall turns. That's wrong. A Rodway pantomime is written as a play is written. It is all story—continuity of the story is all-important.

"Mr. Rodway has always realised that although a comedian may have a fine bit of business of which he is inordinately fond, it may not necessarily fit in with the story. He doesn't see why a comedian should not be able to act a part in pantomime as an ordinary actor on the legitimate stage acts a part in a play.

"In other words, a Rodway pantomime is not a re-hash of music-hall turns; it's a fairy-story-play, with the humour—everything—having relation to the story. And it's an illuminating fact that the part Mr. Rodway wrote for me in *Humpty Dumpty* provided me with some of the best comedy scenes I have ever had in my life.

"And the humour for Canadian audiences? Not a line will be changed. Because the humour in the Rodway pantomimes depends upon the human touch. . . ."

And so, in the workrooms at the Prince of Wales Theatre, W. R. Young, the veteran scenic artist, was busily engaged with his assistants in cutting up and hingeing the scenery for the enterprise, while Mrs. Florence Shelton, the wardrobe mistress, was putting the finishing touches to the dresses on which she and her staff of assistants had been working for months past. (Of course, as Georgie reminds us, her name would appear on the programme—together with Messrs. This, That, and Co.—as Madame Shelton. Why is it, he asks, that all wardrobe mistresses are designated Madame on the bills and programmes, and yet called Missus in the theatre, even when they happen to be Miss?)

M I

The last rehearsal story that he tells us is of the principals
trying over a song for *Mother Goose*, in the dress circle saloon
at the Prince of Wales Theatre in Broad Street, which is, of
course, opposite the studios of the British Broadcasting Corporation. An urchin's voice from outside floats up to the
window:

"Wot's that, Bill?"

Without the slightest hesitation comes Bill's rejoinder:
"Choir practice at the B.B.C.!"

*   *   *

OUTWARD BOUND

Liverpool landing-stage—The *Duchess of Atholl*—Across the Atlantic—
The Ice Track—Newfoundland—A thousand miles up the St. Lawrence—
Quebec—The *Château Frontenac*.

The "great adventure" actually started for us from the
moment we knew Daddy was taking Mother, Lois, and myself*
with him. A fortnight before we sailed he sent off the entire
pantomime production—company, staff, wardrobe, scenery,
on the Cunard liner *Alaunia*.

"Sent them off? But surely you all went together?" you
will ask. Oh, no, Philip Rodway with his family party
followed on the next boat out. . . .

Probably if he had been alone, exactly the same procedure
would have been followed, for never was there a less "theatrical" manager. With the three of us accompanying him, the
two boats were a *sine qua non*. The sky would have fallen before
Victorian Daddy would have allowed us behind the scenes
to meet the company on dry land, so why should the order
be reversed on water? Why, indeed? We couldn't have been
happier than on the *Duchess of Atholl*, but we permitted
ourselves a little smile at the idea of the Rodway Pantomimes
making their stately and decorous procession across the ocean.
And we imagined the improbability of it happening with any
other producer in the world.

And so the last day of August, 1929, finds us *en route* for
Liverpool, full of excitement and snowed under with white

---

*Phyllis.

heather and telegrams of good wishes. A farewell luncheon party at the North Western Hotel, and we set off for the docks, and there, with a strange thrill of ownership, we see, towering alongside, the *Duchess of Atholl*, the great Canadian Pacific liner which is to take us across the Atlantic and another thousand miles up the St. Lawrence river. We make for the gangway, hurry aboard with all possible speed, and we are on board our floating hotel.

From this moment everything is full of new interest: the rows of white-coated stewards lined up on a spotless deck, the endless white corridors (in which for the first hour or so one gets inextricably lost), the attractive cabins, and the excitement of finding one's own way back, either by the wide staircases or—more surely—by the lift; and so into the luxurious entrance hall, from which we catch a glimpse of spacious lounges as we pass through the revolving glass doors and on to the deck once more.

The last passenger has come aboard, the last cabin trunk (Lois's!) comes bumping up the incline (as usual, we were early, and our luggage therefore thoroughly buried beneath all the rest). Among the watching crowds on the quay waving handkerchiefs are appearing, faster than swirling snowflakes, and before we are aware of it we are moving— already there is a wide channel between us and the landing stage. We watch until the last roof has become a blur, then begins the first eager patrol of the deck.

The sound of a distant orchestra calls us into a luxurious lounge for tea, and then the putting back of the ship's clock gives us an extra and unexpected hour in which to explore, before the notes of a bugle ring out *The Roast Beef of old England* and suggest we should descend for dinner in the flower-decked saloon of ivory and satin-grey sycamore, where the music of the orchestra floats down from an old-world minstrels' gallery.

We are already finding friends among the passengers. Ernest Truex and his wife and two sons are on board; also the *Bird in Hand* company from the Repertory Theatre, Birmingham, England (which incidentally is billed to follow the pantomimes at the respective theatres); and Dr. Healey Willan, the distinguished Canadian composer, of the Toronto Conservatory of Music.

Dancing in the ballroom after dinner that night, it was hard to imagine we were on the open sea, and several times we had to cross over to the wide windows to convince ourselves we were really moving. At such times we might catch sight of Mother and Daddy quietly pacing the promenade deck; we could never get *him* to come anywhere near the ballroom, except when occasionally he would look in through the windows to make comical faces at us out of the darkness. It reminded us of those lines of Rupert Brooke:

"I strayed about the deck, an hour, to-night
Under a cloudy moonless sky; and peeped
In at the windows, watched my friends at table,
Or playing cards, or standing in the doorway,
Or coming out into the darkness. Still
No one could see me."

Mother spent most of her time hovering backwards and forwards between us, but at no time during the entire voyage, either going or coming, morning, afternoon, or evening, would he even set foot on that polished floor.

There were times when we ourselves realised that dancing was very nearly sacrilege "on such a night as this" . . . but that first evening it was all so new and thrilling, and when eventually we climbed into our bunks, still feeling extremely well and wide-awake, we felt we must indeed be sailors born. (Extracts from our log-book of the following day would seem to show that Daddy was the only born sailor of the four, for he alone had no need to "seek the seclusion that a cabin grants.")

We woke next morning to a slow, rhythmic roll—curtains swinging inward from door and porthole; frocks and coats on hook and hanger slowly standing out at right angles from the wall and as deliberately swinging back, in time with the

lurching ship; an occasional thud as book or shoes slid gracefully from a table or dropped off a couch; the vague but
persistent vibration of the engines and, with maddening
regularity at the end of each roll, the answering creak of
straining woodwork.

An hour or two later we staggered along after the stewardess
to find that even the bath water was swinging majestically
from side to side, three feet one second and three inches the
next. Everything on board seemed to have developed the
same disconcerting habit of sliding away, and though one
usually slid after it, it was a relief when the tables turned up
their edges and the chairs were firmly chained in their
places.

Each new day from now onwards was perfect summer
weather, and every morning we came on deck to find it
swaying gently to the wash of long blue rollers, under a blue
unclouded sky.

Further exploration discovered the perfectly equipped
gymnasium, where for the first day or two we enthusiastically
practised fencing, riding, rowing and everything else available; the library, the up-to-date little shop, the miniature
nursery, the white austerity of the little hospital. There were
so many things to do, from exciting games of deck-tennis,
shuffleboard or quoits, to the more restful lounging in deck
chairs in the sunshine, talking to friends. The hours passed
all too quickly, lost in a haze of tournaments and "movies,"
concerts, and fancy dress dances.

And all this time Daddy was sending out and receiving
wireless messages. Every day brought some new situation for
him to tackle. When one thinks of the difficulties entailed in
dealing with people over three thousand miles of water, of
making arrangements, of seeing that they are put into effect,
it is hardly surprising that he had a great deal on his mind.
He said little about it, but we knew how much he was pre-
occupied, planning, thinking—always thinking. Even after
thoroughly enjoying half an hour's deck tennis, he would

suddenly throw the ring across to us and say "Go on without me for a bit—I'll see you later," and off he went to deal with some new problem or other.

Before long came the morning when the temperature began to fall lower and lower, and for twenty-four hours we were in the danger zone of the Ice Track. Daddy, searching the skyline with his binoculars, sighted the first iceberg, "an errant princess of the north," glittering white and shadowy blue; soon after another appeared on the distant horizon, with gleaming peaks like some fairy castle; then a third, shaped like a gigantic hat-box, some two miles in circumference, passed quite close on the port side—and so on all that day. After the eleventh we began to lose interest. But not so a cutter, just discernible, on duty in the far distance. It was the Ice Patrol. The captain explained to Daddy and Mother that this patrol was inaugurated as a direct result of the *Titanic* disaster. Movements of bergs are plotted on a large chart and the findings broadcast several times a day to all ships, and often icebergs are dispersed with gunfire. All American-bound shipping keeps sixty miles south of the nearest ice, so that it is now extremely rare to sight a berg from a ship bound for New York. But the Canadian-bound ships cannot detour to such an extent, and must perforce go through the ice region.

There was the thrill of life-boat drill, when at the warning signal of klaxon sirens we dashed to our cabins and emerged at our respective muster stations, encased—with difficulty—in life jackets, and watched the lifeboats swing down the davits to the promenade deck level. The night before, Daddy had decided that he and Mother ought to have a dress rehearsal of this life-belt performance; if there were any question of striking a berg, it might be just as well to know how to do it! It took some clever acrobatics on the top bunk to get at the cork-jackets, which were stowed tidily out of reach high on the wardrobe. When they were finally secured, more acrobatics were necessary to get into them, and when

OUTWARD BOUND

On board the "Duchess of Atholl"

LIFEBOAT DRILL

(Lois and Phyllis)

Snapshot by Daddy

this was successfully accomplished the result was a perfect imitation of a strait-jacket. "How on earth is one expected to swim in them?" he asked, in conversation with the captain the next day. "It's practically impossible even to move your arms or head." The reply was that they are not intended to allow swimming; the sole idea is to keep afloat, head above water, until picked up.

There was the night of the fancy dress dance, when an engaging if unorthodox young American, garbed in seaweed and sponges, declared himself to be the Duke of Atholl, and spent the rest of the evening looking for his Duchess; when a Canadian composer became a *fascisti*nating Italian; and when we could not help but notice once again that Daddy, outside theatre precincts, was the least theatrical of men. The pageantry and scenic effects of the stage appealed to him, but never the "dressing up" element. Everyone else might put on false noses and enjoy changing his identity for the night, but not so Daddy. He was as austere and aloof as ever.

From 6 o'clock we two were preparing for the Ball. Daddy came into our cabin when we were ready, raised his expressive eyebrows, and said:

"But I thought you weren't bringing fancy dresses on board?"

Secure in our righteousness we explained that we hadn't. Lois had on her black velvet evening frock, with the only addition tulle frills at neck and wrist, as Pierrette, and I was wearing my Japanese *happi* dressing gown, with a couple of chrysanthemums, as one of the Three Little Maids out of *The Mikado!*

Poor Daddy looked more than a little dubious. We had obeyed him in the letter but not the spirit; somehow we had evaded the restriction, and yet quite legally. Making the best of a bad job, he collected Mother and solemnly took us down to dinner.

There was the night when, from the quiet sun deck, we

watched the wonder of the Northern Lights, like the unfurling of some giant fan, flashing their streamers far across a sky so full of stars it seemed to hold the radiance of a thousand nights in one. The brilliant beams went wheeling round, starting into sudden silhouette the towers and turrets of some castle in the clouds, until we seemed to see there the last scene of the *Gotterdämmerung*—the flaming Valhalla itself.

And so, on Tuesday night, after four days of unbroken sea, came our first sight of land. A dark rugged shape silently came into view on the port side and as silently passed on into the darkness; we were off the coast of Newfoundland, in Belle Isle Straits, and somewhere in the darkness on our right were the shores of Labrador.

Daddy used to take us into the chart room to follow the course of the voyage, and the following day there was a great deal of map consulting to be done, for during the next twenty-four hours we were out of sight of land again, passing through the Gulf of the St. Lawrence until the coast of Anticosti appeared. Somewhere about 4.30 a.m. we heard the engines stop, strange lights flashed across the porthole, and ghostly clanking and shuffling sounds told us that the pilot had come aboard and the mail bags were being put off for Father Point, Rimouski.

And when on Thursday morning we looked through our portholes they had indeed become

> "Magic casements opening on the foam
> Of perilous seas, in faery lands forlorn."

We were in the wide waters of the St. Lawrence, and the sheer loveliness of it all left us literally limp and breathless. In vain one tries to picture in cold print the wistful beauty of the scene; one is soon saying, with Shelley, "These words are ineffectual and metaphorical. Most words are so—No help!"

The shores each side were still far apart, though we were more than five hundred miles from the open Atlantic. To the north rose dark rugged hills that held the glint of distant waterfalls; thickly wooded slopes, purple pine forests reaching away into the dim regions beyond. And strangely enough, although the far-off coast was full of the charm and mystery of an unknown land, there was yet a curious feeling of "coming home"; it had a look of England, and of Welsh hills rising in the misty background.

Gradually the shore drew in towards us, and little islands and rocks came into sight, tiny villages and settlements, little white farms and cottages with bright red roofs, tiny beaches, each with its own miniature pier and toy lighthouse of red and white, large green-shuttered country houses in tree-fringed clearings, with lawns coming down to the water's edge, half-hidden gardens, with splashes of brilliant colour among the maple foliage: everywhere an atmosphere of indescribable peace and content.

Now the red and white roofs cluster more closely; the villages are growing, each one has its own church, and the slender spires flash into silver silhouette in the sunlight as we approach. Slowly the *Duchess* swings round a bend of the great river, and again one is held entranced by the new sight. Green fields wander down into the water; there are no banks, it almost seems the water is in flood, and just rising gently where it will. Everywhere are the typical thatched farms and out-buildings, with groups of haystacks dotted here and there.

We saw many a green isle, hardly half-a-mile square, with perhaps two or three haystacks and half-a-dozen apparently stranded cows; evidently this was all quite in order, though the idea of collecting a cow in a boat sounds a little Heath Robinsonian. Still, anything seemed possible that morning, and we remained spell-bound on the sun-deck while the luncheon bugle blew unheeded on the decks below. The villages were becoming towns, other boats passing, and our siren sending out sharp warning blasts. And then into the distance came the beautiful Isle of Orleans and the towering landmarks of old Quebec, where high on the hill-side stands the famous *Château Frontenac*, most picturesque of Canadian Hotels, against the grim slopes of the Heights of Abraham.

Many of the passengers were disembarking here, and those of us who wanted to go ashore during the three hours in dock had also to sort ourselves out for passport inspections and landing cards. Within half-an-hour we were most of us through, and hurrying down the gangway to set foot for the first time in Canada!

* * *

CANADA

Quebec—Montreal—Cabled news of W. E. Alldritt's death—Première of *Humpty Dumpty*, London, Ontario; Wee Georgie Wood, Hal Bryan, Dan Leno, jun., Fred Conquest—Montreal to Toronto—Royal York Hotel— Lake Ontario—*Humpty Dumpty* at the Princess Theatre, Toronto—To Niagara Falls with Georgie Wood—We cross into the United States—The pantomimes are launched on their 17,000 mile tour—The last night in Toronto.

Travelling has become so simple over there, and distance means so little, it is hard to realise that the Province of Quebec alone is nearly half the size of Europe!

We were slightly bewildered by the traffic of the dockyard— motor cars, horse carts, porters' trucks and trains all on the same level, crossing and intercrossing with much clanging of bells, in an apparently suicidal and yet perfectly orderly manner. There was only one thing to do, from the point of view of both time and safety: we took a taxi. Did we say safety? Never have we known such a journey. Hurled from side to side as we lurched round corners, or tore up the narrowest possible cobbled streets (1 in 3 at least), streams of good-humoured oaths and imprecations in French following on all sides, we felt we might run up the side of a house at any moment with the greatest ease. We began to get used to it as we passed other flying taxis bearing more of our friends on similar expeditions, and at last, by way of the Lower Town— mediaeval Quebec of the cobblestones, of quaint dormer windows, roof-to-roof bridges and picturesque ramparts—we found ourselves in the residential streets of the Upper Town where large houses lay back among beautiful lawns and gardens, all open to the road, giving a wonderful effect of freshness and space. And then to Battlefields Park, on the historic Plains of Abraham, where the guns lie rusting in the turf, and where once Wolfe stood and looked down on the St. Lawrence unfolding mile upon mile; then on to the *Château Frontenac* for tea in the gay verandah to the strains of a Strauss waltz.

Back to the boat in another terrifying taxi, and on board in time to lean on the gangway and see them shooting the mails as we waited for the others to come aboard.

It was seven o'clock and nearing sunset as we began the next stretch, and we adjourned once again to the sun-deck to await the great Quebec bridge. It was an awe-inspiring moment as the towering mass of steel slowly came upon us—it seemed utterly impossible that we could pass safely underneath. It was actually above us, and the first funnel clear, and then our eyes fled to the mast, rising higher still—it must surely be snapped like a matchstalk. Yet we glided beneath with more than fifteen feet to spare.

After dinner we anchored for the night in the river, near the dark shores dotted with twinkling lights, the boat motionless on the still waters. . . .

We woke next day to misted river banks, very close in now, looking hazily unreal in the cold light of the morning, before the sun had touched the colours in the farms and fields. Now it might have been our own Severn, very little wider, save that down the centre a line of tree-buoys marked the course, swaying strangely in the current. There was so little movement that a putting green was fixed on the top deck, and the click of balls went on intermittently until within an hour of landing.

By 11 o'clock we were approaching Montreal bridge—and soon the huge dock yards and grain elevators were in sight. Surrounded by our hand luggage, we foregathered for the last time at Muster Station C, in the few remaining deck chairs, there to make farewells, and, no less difficult, take our last leave of the ship. At last we managed to tear ourselves away, and passed down the gangway.

And at the very moment that we stepped ashore, a uniformed messenger came up to Daddy, saluted, and handed him a cablegram. It was from Birmingham, England—and it brought the news of the sudden death of our old friend Mr. W. E. Alldritt, one of his directors, whom, as accountant and auditor, he had left in almost entire charge of affairs at home, including the wind-up of the change-over of the Royal.

A tragic situation! Not only the loss of a valued friend and colleague, but another immediate and great responsibility in the knowledge that there was now no guiding hand at the helm in England.

Add to this the fact that the first night of the pantomime, which should have opened at Montreal, at the very last moment had had to be transferred to London, Ontario—for the simple but conclusive reason that the Montreal theatre had the week before gone over to the talkies, contracts apparently meaning nothing—and you may picture the position.

Once through the Customs, we made our way through the streets of this, the farthest inland ocean port in the world, to the Mount Royal Hotel. Daddy, from the first moment of his arrival, went into conclave with the Press, and only emerged in time to give us a few last hurried injunctions before bidding us farewell, and departing in a burst of telephone calls and the midnight train for London, Ontario. We three remained at Montreal during the next week, while the work of actual send-off and production was going on.

The Canadian newspapers, meanwhile, were making a great feature of "*The Philip Rodway Pantomime Company, Birmingham, England,*" and Daddy, as the Pioneer of Pantomime, became a figure of singular significance. Mr. S. Morgan-Powell, of the influential Montreal *Daily Star*, was writing on September 9th:

"In order fully to appreciate meeting Mr. Philip Rodway, the present managing director of the Theatre Royal, Birmingham,

England, who arrived in Montreal, Saturday, for a few days' visit, one must also understand the significance of his position in the theatrical life of England.

"He represents one of the oldest branches of theatrical history, in being the contemporary head of an institution that has been one of the main arteries in the body of things histrionic for a century and a half. The history of the Theatre Royal is the history of theatrical life from the last quarter of the eighteenth century up to the present day."

Here came a brief résumé of that history, and then:

"It is easy to see what a heritage of tradition fell to the lot of Philip Rodway when he became the active head of such an institution. Gordon Craig, that great artist of the theatre, who so recently complained that the entrance of business men into the ranks of theatrical producers was endangering the art of the theatre, would find Mr. Rodway a man after his own heart. He has been steeped in the world of the theatre since his youth, and has brought to his managership of the Theatre Royal, since 1904, not only a thorough knowledge of production, and a splendid appreciation of dramatic art, but also his gifts as a writer of pantomime. . . .

"Mr. Rodway has devoted his talents to bringing pantomime back from a mere disconnected series of vaudeville turns to the fairy story, where comedy is never left out, nor romance obscured. He is a thoroughly interesting individual to meet, and his knowledge as well as his appreciation of the theatre is a joy to discover, and brings one the realisation that if the future of the theatre is to be in the hands of such capable producers as he, we need have no fear of its deterioration."

Then followed an interview with Daddy, in which he commented upon the noteworthy fact that the children of Quebec are not allowed to attend the motion pictures while under sixteen years of age. It seemed that the pantomime would happen along at a very opportune time, when the children would be eager for just such merry and interesting theatrical entertainment as this. "The theatre is the place to foster that love of the whimsical and the fantastic in the hearts of children. They need more of this wholesome fare to stir up their young minds to lovely imaginings," he said.

"Mr. Rodway went on to speak of his belief that the theatre

of to-day is threatened by one outstanding evil, and that is the sin of commercialisation. 'There is a greater desire to be amused with any type of fare, since the great war, than ever before, but it is up to producers to bring the audiences back to a proper appreciation of real art in the theatre. And I thoroughly believe that there is no art greater than histrionic art at its best,' he concluded in his earnest, quiet way, that is impressive as well as reassuring for those who fear the preservation of the drama when it is handled by so many modern producers whose only aim is to make money."

And in the stop press of the same edition, we three, miles away in Montreal, read the latest news:

"GREAT SUCCESS IN LONDON

LONDON, ONT., SEPT. 9TH. (SPECIAL TO THE *Star*)—

The Philip Rodway Extravaganza *Humpty Dumpty*, which opened its Canadian tour on Saturday night in this city, proved a sensational surprise to a capacity audience. It is one of the largest musical attractions ever seen in the Dominion, and in addition to being a most elaborate spectacular production it contains a large company whose individual members reveal an exceptional array of talent. The applause at the close was in the nature of an ovation, and Mr. Philip Rodway, who was present, expressed himself as delighted with the first Canadian reception."

We had long trunk calls to Daddy every night, and were kept well in touch with what was going on, until he should be ready for us to join him for the Toronto send-off. The London papers duly arrived, and again the notices were wonderful, column after column, full of enthusiasm. As Georgie Wood has told us since, "We had a marvellous Press; right through the tour the newspaper men showered almost extravagant praise on the productions." An English pantomime was a new and original subject, and the journalists let themselves go.

"For more than a hundred years," they said, "the British public has attested the perennial popularity of the Christmas pantomime, and it does seem strange that not until the present time have Canadians had a real opportunity of seeing this form of entertainment at its best, and enjoying its wholesome merriment.

"In *Humpty Dumpty*, Philip Rodway's delightful musical pantomime extravaganza, which opened at the Grand Theatre on

Saturday, London theatregoers were happily introduced to an institution which has been dear to hearts of old and young in the old land for a century or more, and it was a case of love at first sight. Local playgoers went hardly knowing what to expect. They had been told that *Humpty Dumpty* was 'a fairy tale with music that will prove most enjoyable to people of all ages,' a statement which illustrates beautifully the British penchant for understating the merits of the case.

"For *Humpty Dumpty* is far more than a 'fairy tale with music.' It is, in some of its gorgeous scenes, a cross-section of Fairyland itself, with a definite plot running through it, gloriously reminiscent, in some of its whimsicalities, of Sir James Barrie's immortal *Peter Pan.*"

Others compared its charm with Lewis Carroll's *Alice in Wonderland*, and added that many of the catchy lyrics and melodies would not have come amiss in a Gilbert and Sullivan opera.

May we give just one of the notices, or part of it, verbatim, as it will offer some idea of the general enthusiasm, and perhaps recall memories of that historic pantomime which had had its birth in England in 1925.

"It opens with the crash of the ancient egg from the top of the wall. Humpty Dumpty emerges to mingle in a world of mortals, including a very jolly monarch and his court, and many fairy-tale characters of our childhood days. . . . The succeeding scenes are superbly staged, full advantage having been taken of the opportunity to use the quaint old English costumes which adorn the pages of the illustrated favourites of childhood.

"One scene is laid in Neptune's abode at the bottom of the sea, and for sheer beauty of effect has seldom been equalled in productions seen here. Equally beautiful in an entirely different way is another scene representing a Scottish moor. It was a real triumph of stagecraft, and an admirable setting for the appearance of practically the whole company dressed in Highland costume, in which authentic clan tartans were displayed to wonderful advantage. Nothing to approach it has been seen here since *Rob Roy*. . . . The closing scene in the Hall of Lace was a revelation of what can be accomplished in novelty of setting and costume.

"Wee Georgie Wood, prince of comedians, dominates the play and yet steals no thunder from his talented contemporaries . . .

his wit, gaiety, and charm are internationally famed. There is
something very fine, very stimulating in the delicacy of Georgie's
understanding, which makes his child impersonations far more
important than the ordinary stage offerings. He has retained in
manhood a very delicate and sympathetic appreciation of child
psychology, of the doubts and the wisdom, the laughter and the
gravity of childhood. Which is perhaps why children love him,
and why his sparkling nonsense is without cynicism, his pithy
quips without venom.

"An easy second in the affections of youthful members of the
audience was Fred Conquest, who enjoys the reputation of being
England's leading pantomime animal and bird impersonator.
First as Squeak, the penguin, and later as Chum, the dog, he
gave an impersonation which for sheer drollery could hardly
be excelled . . . he did not belie his name—he made a real conquest.

"Dan Leno, jun., in the rôle of Martha, Humpty's 'wished
for' mother, is immense. He is a comedy artist of a type definitely
robust, but never slapstick, and his turns are inimitably funny.

"Of a different order, yet scarcely less telling, is the wit of Hal
Bryan. As King Half-a-crown, he proves himself a pastmaster
of whimsical nonsense. Florence Hunter, playing the Scottish
Prince, is lovely and regal, whether in her silver kit or in Highland dress, or in the half dozen other fascinating costumes which
fall to her lot. Maisie Weldon is a charming Princess Elaine,
and Sid Smith, as prime minister, seems to have stepped directly
out of the pages of Shakespeare's *Hamlet*—he is Polonius to the
life. John Harcourt, as a troubadour, has several opportunities
to display the qualities of an excellent baritone voice. . . . The
chorus show the results of good training, etc., etc.

"Altogether the production provided three hours of wholesome
entertainment, and left one hoping that Empire free trade, when
it comes, will include provision for the importation to Canada
of many more productions of the calibre of *Humpty Dumpty*."

So many of Daddy's ideas and views were appearing in the
various Canadian papers that it may perhaps be as well to
mention one or two or them.

"Philip Rodway, of Birmingham, England, has been writing
and producing pantomimes for more than twenty years, and it is
his opinion that this art of dressing up nursery rhymes for the
stage, of putting life and motion into the stories, is a perennial

interest with each generation of children, and that so long as there are children in the world there will be pantomimes.

"Two decades of work amidst the atmosphere of the pantomime in England have taught him that there is nothing so real and so hugely enjoyable to the child as a good pantomime, and few things so restful to the adult as the fantasy and illusion that are part and parcel of the presentation of fairy stories in the form of pantomime.

"When the curtain fell at the end of the first performance he found time to talk on pantomime and its place in the education of the child, which is a hobby of his.

"If fairy stories and children belong to each other, and Mr. Rodway is certain that they do, then pantomime, which is a kinetic fairy story, belongs to children and childhood. And by the sequence of relationship, what interests the child interests the mother, and in most cases the father, too, so that the pantomime becomes a family affair.

"Just as fairy stories carry a moral and are built around the idea of presenting a moral in a form that can best be absorbed by a young mind, so the pantomime, beneath its superficial fun and frolic, its clowning and harlequinade, adorns its tale with a moral. In the case of *Humpty Dumpty*, the moral is that happiness is to be gained only by answering the call of right and duty. Humpty Dumpty does the thing that is right at the end. He surrenders what appears to be his happiness in order that those he loves may find theirs, and in so doing finds an El Dorado of well-being for himself. In the case of *Mother Goose*, the story which the company will play on their trip back from the coast, the moral is that contentment is more to be sought and held than riches or material wealth.

"'Unless we can inculcate these good ideas into the minds of our children, the outlook for the next generation is devastating,' said Philip Rodway. 'Perhaps I am old-fashioned, but I would rather have my own children brought up, in the theatrical sense, on a good fairy story pantomime than on all this screen and talkie stuff. . . .'

"'Human desire to see a human ideal made manifest is the basis of pantomime,' declared the producer. 'To the child it appears the natural way of life, and as such he enjoys it. To the adult it may appear the reflection of a happy dream impossible of accomplishment. To both the child and the adult, however, the appeal must stir in the blood, just so long as the one is a

N I

simple, trusting nature, and the other remains a rather disillusioned mind with the glamour a little dimmed by its experience.'"

Among other things, of course, appeared Daddy's "opinion of Canada." He was impressed with its "orderly prosperity," but since so far he had visited only a few of the great cities he was wisely hesitant about offering criticism of such a vast area. "I have seen Montreal," he said, "an old world metropolis of great charm, and this London of yours, a smaller city, but one of extraordinary beauty and appeal. I know of no city I have ever visited of the same size which made such a strong first impression on me as this London. It is spacious and busy, without being nervous, and from appearance, evidently a city of homes." The report went on:

" 'There is much in common between our London and your London,' continued the prominent Englishman. 'You have your Piccadilly, your Thames river, your Pall Mall; and many other familiar names greeted my eyes as I scanned a map of your city. I hope to be able to spend more time in it on one of my future Canadian trips. . . .' "

Meanwhile Mother and we two were spending an intensely interesting few days in Montreal. The Canadian people are extraordinarily charming and hospitable—we found it so wherever we went. French influence in Montreal is very noticeable, though less obviously so than in Quebec, and the further West one goes the less apparent does it become.

Mount Royal itself sounds perhaps the keynote of the city; the beautiful hill which dominates the town, and from which Montreal itself derives its name. At the very top, a landmark for miles around, rises an immense cross, at night lit up by thousands of electric bulbs, marking the place of one raised there four hundred years ago by Jacques Cartier, the first white man to visit the spot. From the lookout we saw an almost endless panorama; city, river and lake, villages and farmlands, even glimpses of the Laurentian mountains in distant Quebec and the Adirondacks in New York State. Near the top one may chance to stumble across a strangely quiet and very beautiful garden, perhaps two or three miles square, yet so sheltered by trees that it is easily missed, a Garden of Sleep, where lie some of the most impressive tombs imaginable, each one a miniature chapel—it might well be a corner of the Valley of the Kings.

In the city itself we found many fascinating places: the beautiful Notre Dame Church on Place d'Armes, the quaint old Château Ramezai, one-time residence of the governors, famous McGill University, with its shady greens, lying in the shelter of the mountain, the residential suburbs, Westmount, Outremont and the others, and the busy shopping centres.

In due course we left Montreal and went on to Toronto for the opening night of the pantomime. The nine hours' railroad journey to the "place of meeting" (literal translation of the Ancient Indian *toronto*) lies through some of the most beautiful country imaginable. We start, not from a platform, but from a level track, right among the towering trains, and climb into the coach with the help of a high foot-stool and unlimited West Indian porters.

From the swing arm-chairs of the parlor-car we see the country spread out like a relief map; between the towns, which are few and far between, comes the first suggestion of the "wide open spaces"—we run through mile upon mile of the loveliest natural scenery, wild and lonely and utterly untouched, where every colour seems accentuated; dark fir trees, grey rocks, and little bright green islands in the brilliant blue of lakes.

At intervals we come upon a lonely halt, miles from anywhere, just a solitary wooden shack, with a board nailed to a post to tell its name—*Green Valley*, or *Echo*, and the bell over the engine clangs once or twice (for all the world the self-same sound of some little village church), as we pass on, perhaps into a rocky cutting, or sheer on to the shores of a lake. One marvellous effect we saw—a terrific thunderstorm of dense black clouds and silver rods of rain—over as suddenly as it began, and clear blue sky again.

The most attractive place from which to watch is the observation car at the back of the train, where one takes chairs out on to the little open-air platform, under the awning. Everyone gets indescribably dusty—but nobody minds. Dust on these journeys is so well understood that, immediately on leaving the station, the coloured parlor-car attendants parade with clothes brushes, and large brown paper bags into which with beaming smiles they pop whatever hats or lighter possessions they see in the luggage racks.

Toronto at last, and we were immediately besieged by an army of "red caps," as these dusky porters are called. Slightly bewildered, we heard yet another voice at our elbow, "Carry yo' bag, lady?" in what appeared to be the best West Indian style; turning, we were delighted to discover Dr. Healey Willan, who at once took charge of things and guided us safely through the spacious halls of Union station to the newly opened Royal York Hotel, where Daddy, free for a few brief minutes, awaited us.

The Royal York claimed to be the largest hotel in the whole of the British Empire, and had only been opened a month or two when we were there in the September of 1929. At night the upper half of the twenty-eight stories of gleaming white limestone was cleverly illuminated, so skilfully floodlit that from afar it seemed a castle in the clouds.

The windows of our rooms looked right across Lake Ontario, with its busy flying- and speed-boats. Just across the bay, far removed from the rush of the city, though little more than a mile away, lies a group of beautiful islands, where we visited some of the most attractive summer residences (summer only, because in winter the stretch of water is frozen over, and all communication with the mainland cut off). Here are Avon backwaters and winding lagoons, grassy tree-shaded walks and sandhills, boathouses and bathing beaches, and endless river craft, while on the centre isle is the Royal Canadian Yacht Club, famous as the largest freshwater yacht club in the world.

On all sides one is greeted with extreme courtesy, but they have an extraordinarily different way of doing things over there; a disconcerting habit of altering all the theatrical printing, from posters to circulars, so that the first thing Daddy saw when he arrived in London, Ont., was a bill announcing *The "Humpty Dumpty Revue."* Above all, there were the difficulties experienced with the various unions. Briefly, the company had to travel a union duplicate of every member of the staff: another musical director, another property master, another electrician, another carpenter, and so on, and when one considers that the minimum salary was about 60 or 70 dollars a week (£15 to £17 in English money) it is easy to understand that the expenses must have been much in excess of the original estimate.

However, there was no doubt whatever as to the artistic success of the productions, and here again, in Toronto, Daddy was enthusiastically welcomed and acclaimed by Press and Public alike as the world-famous producer of English panto-mimes. Fêtes and receptions were arranged in our honour, and throughout the tour the first nights of production were very great occasions, attended by all the social rank and fashion for miles around.

* * *

The pantomime ran for a fortnight at the Princess Theatre, Toronto, while the city was experiencing the almost tropical heat of its Indian Summer. The thermometer was right up beyond 80 in the shade all the time, and Daddy had to take poor Fred Conquest out of one of the scenes, or he would have suffocated in his dog's disguise. It was glorious, though too hot to expect a packed house night after night, but in spite of it *Humpty Dumpty* did remarkably well, and paved the way for the tremendous success of the return visit with *Mother Goose*. These pantomimes were quite different from anything Canadian audiences had seen. As one of the critics wrote:

"It is not extravagant praise to acclaim *Humpty Dumpty* as one of the most thoroughly attractive and enjoyable performances ever presented here. Our best musical productions of the comedy sort come from England; the English have a flair for the particular kind of stagecraft which results in unforced fun and healthy nonsense. In these days of sound effects which are chiefly noise, of blaring orchestration and intricate and not altogether lovely dances, the text, melodies, and dance numbers of *Humpty Dumpty* come as a delightful relief. And the most English thing about it is the perfect finish and aplomb of the whole piece."

And Daddy himself said: "I have seen something in Canada which I never saw in England—members of an audience walking out of the theatre after a matinée and going straight round to the box office to book for a succeeding performance."

Meanwhile, of course, we were exploring Toronto: the Canadian National Exhibition Ground, where is held the greatest annual fair in the world, a fine shore road leading to it—land which was reclaimed from Lake Ontario less than ten years ago; the beautiful University, once again the largest in the British Empire, and part of which is the famed Hart House; the Conservatory of Music, Yonge Street and the shopping centres. . . .

One not-easily-forgotten afternoon we went to the Toronto Military Hospital. An old friend of Daddy's and Mother's, whom for years they had not seen, had read in the newspapers of the pantomime's visit, and immediately written off to Daddy. Out of the brilliant sunshine, into the cool stillness of the wards, past row upon row of beds, quiet room after quiet room, here and there a man sitting in a wheel-chair, and ninety per cent. of the cases—hopeless. A Canadian Military Hospital—*more than ten years after the finish of the war*—with a grim waiting-list of those who had but little longer to live, and from which every week a few more names would be struck off.

The meeting with poor Fred Albutt was a sad one; for years he had been dragging out a wretched existence from one hospital to another, and had finally been sent here—to die.

Snapshot by Phyllis

IN THE SPRAY OF NIAGARA FALLS
Mother, Lois, and Georgie Wood

HOMEWARD BOUND
On board the "Duchess of Richmond." The St. Lawrence River

They could hardly trace in the worn outline the face of the old schoolfriend they had known so well in bygone days. Less than two months later we heard of his death.

Georgie Wood's uncle, Mr. Walter W. Bamlett, lives in Toronto, and it was in his car, with Georgie, that we motored to Niagara Falls. Through the beautiful lakeside suburbs, Sunnyside, Roseland, and the rest: Holiday Camps, Honeymoon Camps, fascinating little huts perched in the branches of trees, with step-ladders attached; through the very Scotch Hamilton, and then into the fruit-growing districts of the Niagara Peninsula, where mile upon mile of vineyards and peach orchards loaded with ripe fruit line the road. Little "hot-dog" stalls also appear at intervals on the roadside, and more than once we stopped to try these typical spiced sausages—which were so hot that an entire basketful of peaches soon followed them.

As we drew nearer we could hear the roar of the falls, long before they came in sight, and the air was full of spray more than half a mile away. And then—the wide, white promenade of Niagara town itself, with the thundering waters of the American cascade before us, and the sweep of the Canadian Horseshoe Falls to the right.

New York State, U.S.A., lay just on the other side of the great bridge, and we decided to go over there for lunch, as our first visit to America. Alas! We very nearly had that lunch in jail!

It appears that to be allowed to pass the precincts of the American border, one must either have a special permit, taking ten days or more to obtain, or be a bona-fide Canadian subject by virtue of having lived there at least six months.

Having but a couple of hours to spare, we could hardly wait ten days for a permit, so, encouraged by Georgie and his uncle, we decided to chance it, and headed by Mr. Bamlett, who was the only authentic Canadian among us, sailed bravely across the bridge. At the far end the Customs Officials lay in wait. Mr. Bamlett was through; Georgie, with a superb bit of acting and a couple of words was through, and when we felt we were safe, the official, following up the usual question "How long have you been in Canada?" (to which we glibly replied, "Oh, let me see, about eight or nine months,") suddenly pounced on Lois and shot out:

"Say, what boat did you come over on?"

Poor Lois, thankful to have one question to which she might reply truthfully, answered at once:

"*The Duchess of Atholl.*"

That did it. How was she to know that the C.P.R. liner *Duchess of Atholl* was the newest and latest of the four sister ships, and had in fact been launched less than two months since? Georgie, with great presence of mind, kicked her gently and reminded her that of course she meant one of the *Mont* boats—"the *Montcalm*, wasn't it?"

It was no use. In ominous tones we were told to stand on one side. For the next five minutes some gruelling cross-questioning went on, and even now, looking back on it, we cannot for the life of us see how we ever got off. Presumably some very strong "arguments" must have been put forward on our side. Incidentally, Lois blushed so much that Georgie Wood afterwards said to Mother, "I thought you said your daughter was a good actress!"

Our way back across the bridge after that expensive lunch was simpleness itself. Apparently anyone may *leave* America, and anyone may *enter* Canada. The officials at the Canadian end were charming, and literally welcomed everyone over there with open arms.

We were lucky enough that day to see another marvellous effect—a brilliant rainbow arched across the falls, unreal in its beauty. Georgie took out his ciné-Kodak and made a colour film of it. The little *Maid of the Mist* beckoned to us in vain—we had to start back to be in time for the evening performance.

* * *

Having safely launched the pantomimes on their trans-Canadian tour, Daddy knew that he must get back to England. Business reasons connected with Mr. Alldritt's sudden death made his presence essential. It was a great disappointment to him, as to all of us, and Georgie Wood, writing to us since, says:

"I feel, as I did then, that if it had been possible for P.R. to accompany us throughout those five months, we should have done even better business, and we certainly would have been much happier because of the love certain of us had for him, and the confidence he inspired in all.

"'Why,' you might ask, 'would his being with you personally have helped to increase attendances? He did not appear personally.'

"'No,' I answer, 'but the social side is important in the Dominions and Colonies, and the fact that he was frequently asked for makes me feel that it would have helped a great deal—furthermore, his keen business sense would have, I think, saved thousands of dollars.'"

We must be brief indeed with the rest of our Canadian chronicle, for, like the genie in the Arabian Nights, it could go on expanding to infinity, while we emulate the fisherman and vainly try to coax it back and put the stopper on. We must take a flying leap into the midnight express for Montreal, when from our drawing-room sleepers we watched the lights of Toronto slipping away from us into the darkness.

But one thing more of Toronto, and that was an incident, both alarming and amusing, which took place on the very night of our return to England. Three of Daddy's most important principals were arrested and taken off to police headquarters immediately after the fall of the curtain! Mother, Lois and I had been in the theatre as usual that night, watching the performance, and were waiting for Daddy in the foyer afterwards when he appeared, looking very worried, and told us he was afraid we might not be able to sail. Hal Bryan has since given us the details, and we will let him tell it in his own words.

"This is how it happened. Dan Leno, jun., Fred Conquest,

and myself had each bought a bottle of whisky, and had to pay five dollars for a liquor permit before being able to purchase it. The said whisky was bought especially for that particular night just to toast the Guv'nor and wish him bon voyage, etc., which we did, each in our own dressing room, and naturally after the little ceremony was over the bottle of whisky was left standing on the dressing table in full view of anyone who happened to enter the room.

"Suddenly, while the show was in progress there was a great commotion backstage; a crowd of plain-clothes federal agents surged through the stage door and took possession of the theatre, making a thorough search of every dressing room.

"Needless to say, as I was actually on the stage with Fred Conquest and Dan Leno, jun. at the time, they did not have to search far, for in each of our rooms they found a bottle of whisky, and when we came off from the scene we had been doing we found standing outside each room a burly federal agent, who followed us in and arrested us for having, as they termed it, a broken bottle of liquor in our possession in a public building.

"They were perfectly decent and agreed to wait until the show was over before taking us away, so for the rest of that night we worked under the eyes of the law, and immediately the curtain fell we were put into a police car and whisked off to police headquarters, and there charged with our terrible crime.

"We, of course, were entirely ignorant of the fact that it was strictly illegal to have liquor, if it had been opened at all, in a public place in Canada, which excuse we pleaded but to no purpose, and we were kept there until our manager came and arranged our bail, which amounted to eight hundred dollars.

"They released us after that had been paid and we were told to be at the law courts next morning at 10 a.m. for our case to be heard.

"We engaged an attorney to plead for us, but it was no use and the judge fined us a hundred dollars.

"We paid the attorney 10 dollars each, and we had paid 5 dollars for the liquor permit, and I think it was 5 dollars for the whisky, so with the hundred dollars fine you can reckon it cost each of us just over 50 dollars, ten pounds in English money for a bottle of whisky out of which we had had only two drinks.

"The thing that annoyed us even more than the fine was that they wouldn't give us the whisky back. Oh no! That went away with the federal agents and we never saw it again."

Georgie Wood's succinct observation on the same incident. "Random Jottings. Toronto. Members of the company arrested for one half bottle of whisky being found in a dressing room, whereas they could have had cases of whisky in their hotel room trunk because that *trunk* was legally their residence."

You may imagine Daddy's state of mind as we entered the midnight express for Montreal, having to leave with the possibility of his principals spending the night in jail, but there could be no question of delay.

*   *   *

HOMEWARD BOUND

We four (Daddy, Mother, Lois and Phyllis) return to England on board the *Duchess of Richmond*.

Our boat sailed at nine a.m., and so we found ourselves next morning having breakfast on board the *Duchess of Richmond* in surroundings strangely familiar, for the four sister ships, though identical in design, naturally differ in little details, and it is a weird feeling to come suddenly upon a well-known lounge and find it has apparently suffered a sea-change since we left it, and become blue and silver instead of green and gold, or to make our way confidently to the gymnasium to find the bicycles where the horses ought to be.

We cast off within the hour, though moored still to the quay by thousands of coloured streamers. This time it might have been a different journey, for we saw by day the coast that coming we had passed by night. In brilliant sunshine we lay back in our deck chairs and watched the silver spires of the St. Lawrence slipping backward every hour. We anchored outside Quebec after dinner the first night, at the exact spot where the ill-fated *Empress of Ireland* went down on May 29th, 1914. (Daddy's old friend Laurence Irving—son of Sir Henry and brother of the famous H. B.—had been on board, and both he and his wife, Mabel Hackney, were drowned, together with several of his company. They had been touring *Typhoon*, a play which had fascinated Mother when they played it at the Royal only a few months before.)

The little lamp-lit tender came chugging up and drew in alongside, full of importance and mailbags, to take off the pilot and bring out a dozen or so more passengers. The moon was rising as we passed the Heights of Abraham, with the brilliant windows of the *Château Frontenac* high on the terrace; a thousand lights of city and harbour were reflected in the water—it was as if the stars had fallen. (I might mention that my attempt at a time exposure of "Quebec by night" resulted in a really remarkable picture of night; unfortunately there was no sign whatever of Quebec.) We lost sight of land on Monday morning, when Belle Isle went by, but the wide Atlantic seemed as calm as the St. Lawrence—*seemed*, because smooth though we found it, quite a number of people appeared on the last day whom until then nobody had seen.

Life-boat drill we now viewed almost with condescension—so much so that we took no notice whatever when the warning sirens sounded, and it was only when the deck steward suggested that he was sure the captain would like us to put on our life jackets, that we strolled through to the lift and nonchalantly rang the bell. When the lift attendant informed us severely: "This lift's been under water for the last ten minutes," we began to realise the solemnity of the occasion, and when, arriving at our cabins, we found our steward in a state of complete despair, everyone else having gone up on deck—he himself not able to leave his post until all his charges were safe—we were genuinely contrite.

This time, instead of five hundred Canadians and Americans returning from their summer holidays of a tour of Europe, there were now less than a hundred of us, (mostly young doctors and professional men coming over to take up posts in England,) so that by the first evening one knew practically everyone on board. The time passed all too quickly; there were the usual deck games and tournaments, fancy dress dances, impromptu concerts in the minstrels' gallery, and ghost stories round the fire until three o'clock in the morning.

By mid-day Friday we were in sight of land; beautiful

misty islands, rugged and grey, unutterably lonely and re-mote—Ireland on one side, Scotland on the other. They seemed to hold far more the strange grandeur of a foreign land than the quiet welcome of our own England. Then round the Mull of Kintyre, with Ailsa Craig in the distance, grim and aloof, and past the Isle of Arran.

Daddy was as spellbound by these mountainous shores as we had been by the wide waters of the St. Lawrence, foreseeing possibilities of transformation scenes in pantomimes yet to come. We watched him, as he leaned against the rail, puffing thoughtfully at his pipe, and knew just how much he would be planning and devising, transferring to imaginary full sets the poetic splendour of the picture. And we were reminded of Beverley Nichols' brilliant pen-portraits in *Are They the Same At Home?* where he tells us of Seymour Hicks:

"We were in the same boat, bound for Australia, and I was coming on deck as we steamed out of Naples at dusk. The ship was moving very slowly, and Hicks, for once in a way, was not moving at all. He was silhouetted against Vesuvius . . . the ship glided on, Seymour remained rapt, then suddenly he turned.

"'That,' he said, 'is one of the best back-cloths that Harker ever painted.'"

On up the Clyde to Greenock, and there the tender came out to take ashore more than half our fellow passengers. It was nearly dark by the time the luggage was stowed and the last passenger safely off, and the remaining few of us hung over the rails and waved good-byes as the tender sounded a sad little siren and apologetically put off for the misty grey roofs of Greenock. That night for the first time our fog-horn was sending out signals every three minutes, and we danced to a very pronounced roll, crossing over again to Ireland. We put in at Belfast just at midnight, and Daddy called us on deck to watch yet another little tender come up out of the blackness and make off with two more of our passengers.

We were in the Mersey early the next morning, and the pale

sunlight and mist that lay over the city as we docked at Liverpool seemed to sound an echo of the St. Lawrence.

Then, with the departure of the boat-train and most of our fellow passengers, we made for the North Western Hotel to await our own train. So smooth and still had been the sea that (quite unintentionally, I believe) we had broken the record for the crossing.

Everything looked exactly as on the day we had left—the mid-morning matter-of-factness of the streets, the quiet lounge in the hotel. Almost we felt that Canada and the Atlantic had been a dream. . . .

* * *

STORIES OF THE TOUR

Georgie Wood's reminiscences—And Hal Bryan's—The itinerary—Moose Jaw and Medicine Hat—Through the Rockies to Vancouver—Première of *Mother Goose*—The last curtain at Montreal on January 18th, 1930.

Far from a dream, however, for during the next two or three months news was continually coming over of the pantomime's tour through the Rockies to Vancouver, and of the return journey with *Mother Goose*. Many and varied were the experiences of the company, playing as they did big theatres of the standard of Winnipeg and Saskatoon one week, and picturesque one-night stands like Medicine Hat and Moose Jaw the next.

One of the most amusing situations, and one which recurred time and again, arose out of the children's difficulty in understanding why the principal boy should be a girl, and the dame a man. Georgie Wood, in his inimitable way, recounts the following dialogue:

"Conversation Overheard:

Fond Parent. Now, Junior, this is a real English pantomime, just like your grandad used to take father to see.

Junior. Did grandad like taking you to these pantomimes?

F.P. Of course.

Jr. You're getting a kick out of bringing me, ain't yer, pop?

F.P. Aren't you, father. Really, Junior!

Jr. O.K., Pop—er—father.

F.P. This is the sort of entertainment we always looked forward to every year in the old country.

Jr. Why is it called a pantomime? I thought that was some kind of play where nobody speaks?

F.P. So it is, but this is pantomime also, Junior.

Jr. Why?

F.P. Because it's—er—because it's called *Mother Goose*.

Jr. Who's Mother Goose?

F.P. Dan Leno, junior.

Jr. Who is Dan Leno?

F.P. This isn't Dan Leno, this is Dan Leno, junior.

Jr. I don't get yer.

F.P. Dan Leno was the great comedian my father took me to see, but this is Dan Leno, junior.

Jr. Sure. This is the guy your father took you to see.

F.P. No, Junior, that was Dan Leno but this is Dan Leno, junior.

Jr. (*confused*). Yeah! This is another fellow of the same name?

F.P. Yes, his son, Junior.

Jr. Whose son?

F.P. The son of Dan Leno.

Jr. His little boy?

F.P. Well, no, he's a man now.

Jr. You said he was Mother Goose?

F.P. So he is.

Jr. Well, that's a woman, ain't it?

F.P. Not in a pantomime. Hush, Junior, it's starting now.

Jr. (*whispers*). Why are they all calling that girl Robert?

F.P. She's the principal boy.

Jr. You said Wee Georgie What's-his-name was.

F.P. No, he's the star.

Jr. What, that girl with the stick in her hand?

F.P. No, she's the fairy.

Jr. Why is the principal boy a girl and the old woman a man?

F.P. Never mind now, eat your candy.

Jr. Who's this one called Jack?

F.P. That's Wee Georgie Wood, Mother Goose's little boy.

Jr. Why isn't he a girl like Robert?

F.P. Because he's supposed to be a little boy.

Jr. Well, ain't he a little boy?

F.P. No, he's a man.

(Junior gives up trying to make it out, and is prepared to feign great enjoyment because his Fond Parent's delight is so obvious, when he is raised to a pitch of excitement by his father nudging him and saying: "The Goose is coming."

The music plays softly . . . the lights are dimmed . . . the Goose enters . . . the magic of the impersonation is destroyed by a small voice which penetrates the stillness with "Is that an ostrich?")

F.P. Quiet, Junior, that's the Goose.

Jr. That's not a real goose.

F.P. No, he's wonderful.

Jr. Is it a man?

F.P. Yes, Junior.

Jr. But why do they call the Goose Priscilla if it's a man???

. . . The show has reached the scene of the laying of the golden eggs. Junior has captured from his father the spirit of pantomime . . .

Jr. Oh, I like this.

Later, at home

F.P. Junior, why did you eat your candies first and then forget to take your Syrup of Figs?

Jr. I was playing at Pantomime!"

Here are some more of Wee Georgie Wood's "Random Jottings" of the Canadian Tour:

On arrival in Canada. John Roker, P.R.'s dance arranger (who has gone ahead with the English dancers and the theatre staff), greets the company at Toronto: "You are to proceed to London immediately." Consternation of most of the company, until they realise he means London, Ontario.

In Vancouver. A packed matinée—*Humpty Dumpty*—the ship scene. The princess has just told me that she doesn't love me. . . . I sigh and address the audience:

"Of course she doesn't—nobody loves me."

A little girl of six or seven cries out:

"Never mind, I love you, Humpty Dumpty."

I step forward and assure her that this being so I care nothing for princesses and such! The incident was the subject of a most gracious leading article in the *Vancouver Daily Province*.

In Victoria, B.C. The Armistice service and the march of most of the crowd to our pantomime after passing the Cenotaph. The emotional effect of that particular performance, and generally, on the Old Country people over there.

In Prince Albert, Saskatchewan. The audience of Indians and trappers "parking" their guns as they check their hats and coats in the cloakroom.

In Montreal. Smashing success at end of tour, with phenomenal business. Telephone calls to P.R. in Birmingham, England, to discuss suggestion that Shubert Brothers present his pantomime in New York.

Georgie Wood tells us that the "high spots" of the tour were:

> Calgary (both times)
> Medicine Hat (oddly enough)
> Vancouver (second time)
> Victoria (towards the end of the run there).

"It was so often the case that our last night was tremendous, the public having only just discovered that we were giving them the real thing.

> Toronto (on our return visit and to the proper
> theatre at the proper time of the year with
> *Mother Goose*).

Montreal was a phenomenal success, partly due, perhaps, to the law preventing children from going into cinemas in Quebec Province under the age of sixteen. At any rate, they flocked into the theatre whenever a children's show was announced."

Wherever they went, the pantomimes, so typically English, awakened old enthusiasms and loyalties in our countrymen abroad. As one very tangible proof of this, there was the mail-bag of 1,200 letters which Georgie Wood brought home with him, to answer each one individually. They were not only representative of every type and class, they were full of memories of life in every part of the "Old Country," and in some of them the writers went back to old music hall days and the famous songs and personalities of long ago.

One of the most touching was from a pupil of the Montreal school for the blind, in praise of *Mother Goose*, and written in Braille. From Oak Bay, Victoria, comes the rather pathetic

OI

note: "A few lines of thanks from a grown-up child. You cannot possibly realise the happiness that *Humpty Dumpty* gave to, at any rate, two homesick English people, whom you transported, for a few all too short hours, across the sea and back through time to our native land."

From Brockville, Ontario: "I know of nothing that will restore more quickly the legitimate theatre to the position which it should occupy in Canada than the frequent presentation of English offerings of this type. . . . There will always be a warm welcome awaiting such ventures . . . throughout an entertainment-starved population."

A little boy in Cloverdale wrote of the joy it gave Canadians to see a real English performance. "It will show us the way they do things in the 'Old Country'—which we think is the best country in the world."

It almost seemed that the old music-hall tradition survives with greater virility among British folk overseas than here at home. Another interesting point was that, wherever they went, whenever they dropped into dialect, whether Yorkshire, Irish, Scottish, Welsh or Cockney, they always awakened a response in some section of the house and, strangely enough, Yorkshire was the most popular of all.

There was a firm conviction all over Canada "that no one can do a pantomime like Mr. Rodway, of Birmingham," and that "the name of Rodway stands for everything that is worth while in Pantomime." Some of the prairie folk who travelled tremendous distances to see the pantomime evidently felt the same thing about it. One man, for instance, actually travelled from McAdam, in New Brunswick, to Toronto, for his Christmas night-out—a distance of about 700 miles each way.

Hal Bryan has some interesting things to tell us.

"What a stupendous undertaking that Canadian tour was, and what joy Philip Rodway's two pantomimes brought to the many thousands of people in Canada from the 'Old Country,' many of whom had not seen a pantomime for twenty-five years.

"Those of us who were chosen to go on that trip have the very happiest recollections, and whenever we meet each other we still talk about the grand times we had out there under the Guv'nor's management.

"I suppose it was quite the most ambitious and certainly the largest touring company that ever visited Canada from the Old Country. Pantomime, too, was an unknown quantity out there, so much so that I remember our Canadian representative, Mr. Bert Lang, strongly advised Mr. Rodway not to bill the shows as pantomimes, but rather as musical shows, for the reason that pantomime, to the Canadians, meant purely a show done in pantomime, with no word spoken."

He tells us of the itinerary—Toronto, London, Hamilton (the Scotch city which literally went wild with enthusiasm over the Highland scene in *Humpty Dumpty*), Brantford, Guelph, North Bay, Fort William; then an all-night and all-next-day train jump to Winnipeg, Manitoba. At that lovely city in the middle west of Canada the company did even more excellent business, then on to Prince Albert and so to Regina, Saskatchewan.

"Regina," says Hal Bryan, "is the headquarters of the famous Canadian Mounted Police. The 'Mounties' are a fine lot of men, and we were taken all over their barracks and riding grounds and met a number of them personally.

"Major Grahame was the manager of the Grand Theatre. What a charming fellow he was, and what a splendid time he gave us in the two days we were with him.

"From there we went on to the busy little city of Saskatoon, and then another long train journey to Moose Jaw, just a one night stand for us, but a great event for the people living within a radius of fifty or sixty miles. It was quite a common thing to hear that a whole family had driven in from their farm, a distance of sixty or seventy miles, to see our shows.

"Moose Jaw to Medicine Hat, quaint names and quaint places, with quaint characters peopling them, as for instance one old man in Medicine Hat who handed me a very big laugh:

"I was sitting in the stalls, watching the stage crew hang the scenery, when a very old man with a white beard came and sat down beside me. For a long time he stayed there without a word being spoken, and then he said, in a dear, quivery old voice:

" 'Has the conductor come yet?'

"I replied that no doubt as there was to be a band rehearsal he would soon be here. Another long pause, and then from the old gentleman:

" 'Aye, there'll need to be one, I'm telling you;' at which remark I became interested.

" 'Are the musicians bad here then?' I asked.

" 'Oh, I wouldn't call 'em bad, but I wouldn't go so far as to say they was good neither.' After another pause he suddenly pointed to a dilapidated old double-bass fiddle.

" 'I've just been getting the dust out of that, ready for to-night,' he confided.

"A horrible thought crept into my mind. 'You don't mean to say you actually play that yourself, in the band?'

" 'Well, I'm playing it to-night, though I shall need a bit of practice—you see *I haven't touched it for twenty years!*' "

Now hundreds of miles from their starting point, having passed through the States of Ontario, Manitoba, and Saskatchewan, the company arrived at Lethbridge, Alberta, where they began to see definite signs of the old Canada. "Old Indian chiefs and their squaws, cowboys, tough-looking storekeepers, and frame houses, all just as I had often pictured it for myself, especially after reading a Jack London story," says Hal Bryan.

Thence to Calgary, right in the centre of the oil fields of Canada, where the Prince of Wales has his ranch, and where the company were taken out to see the actual oil wells, many of which were producing thousands of barrels a day.

"Alas," adds Hal, "the only one in which I am personally interested, in that remarkable Turner Valley, has not yet to my knowledge produced half a barrel, so let us hasten away from there, and after three days at Edmonton, still in Alberta, get aboard our sleeping car directly after the night show and start our long trek to Vancouver, British Columbia."

This was the one particular train jump to which they had all been looking forward—the journey through the famous Canadian Rockies, and Georgie Wood here tells us a story of Jack Riches ("Uncle Jack, the best property master I ever knew; you could order anything from a realistic imitation of a bunch of carrots to a chest of drawers that turned itself into a complete kitchen, and Uncle Jack would have it ready in record time"). Well, Jack used to say "I've come over here specially to see these Canadian Rockies." He lived for the sight of them.

Now it so happened that the weather as they went through westward was atrocious—a dull day with lashings of mist and rain. Georgie Wood turned to Jack and said:

"Look at it, Jack—you've got to admit it's beautiful scenery."

"Maybe," said Jack, "but the lighting's rotten!"

Vancouver, of course, is a wonderful city; an important shipping port, thoroughly cosmopolitan, and a splendid town for show business. From there it is a short sea trip over to Millionaires' Island, *i.e.* Victoria, B.C. Here they played *Humpty Dumpty* on the Monday, Tuesday, and Wednesday, and on the Thursday opened with *Mother Goose* for the first time in Canada, and made a terrific success of it.

On their way back they again took in Regina, Saskatoon, Edmonton, Calgary, etc., and so to Winnipeg, getting into Toronto on Wednesday, 18th December, where the advance bookings were exceptionally large, and for the whole two weeks' Christmas season they were packed to the doors, playing *Humpty Dumpty* one week, and *Mother Goose* the second, at the Alexandra Theatre.

A quick return visit to London, Ontario, then on to Hamilton, Brockville, and Kingston before going to Montreal, Quebec, for their last week in Canada. A beautiful city in which to finish the tour, where the business proved to be enormous, and the audience most enthusiastic.

Artistically, the pantomimes' Canadian tour was an unqualified success; financially, the unexpected expenses were very great. As already noted, the trade union rules were apparently never-ending; for instance, when reaching some theatres it was found that even the heavy extra staff already carried was still not sufficient for union requirements, and that yet more additional men had to be engaged, at sixty or seventy dollars each per week. The salary list was tremendous, and again, there were theatres in which even if capacity was played, a profit could not be made against the heavy expenses. Prince Albert and Medicine Hat were typical examples.

Bigger than anything, perhaps, was the cost of moving the gigantic productions from place to place. Playgoers who remember *Humpty Dumpty* or *Mother Goose* in Birmingham will recollect the tremendous and intricate scenic effects in each pantomime. When one realises that this scenery had to be moved week by week, and sometimes oftener, together with nearly a hundred personnel, wardrobe, etc., a clearer idea of this stupendous project can be gained. Compare the simplicity of the paraphernalia of Drinkwater's *Bird in Hand* company which immediately followed the pantomimes at many of the theatres, then remember that the prices of admission were naturally the same.

"I feel, too," says Georgie Wood, "that in P.R.'s absence it became nobody's business to keep down casual expenses. For example: when we arrived at Guelph, we were told we must be out of the train by 4 a.m. Naturally we protested, and eventually, after some inquiry, one of the management told us he had fixed things for us to stay on board until 8 o'clock. We were very gratified, but later I discovered this had only been fixed at a cost of I don't know how much to P.R. As we were all getting jolly good salaries, it ought to have been up to each of us, at our own expense, whether we stayed aboard or not. This was only one of many instances where costs mounted up without check.

"On the tour one of the most loyal champions of the Rodway traditions," he goes on, "was Jack Riches. He would always burst out protestingly against anything which he regarded as breaking away from them. As thus: 'You can all say what you've a mind, but the Guv'nor wouldn't have had these goings on. 'Props' don't mean anything, I know, but I'm going to have my way this time.' "

Two more of Georgie Wood's observations with which everyone was in agreement: that the tour suffered greatly from the lack of one captain and one captain only (P.R.'s guiding spirit having been needed even more urgently in England); and, above all, that it was a thousand pities he could not cash in another year on the reputation he earned on his first visit.

And Hal Bryan concludes:

"We rang down the curtain on our Canadian tour on Saturday night, January 18th, 1930, in Montreal, and so came to an end one of the happiest and most interesting trips, our only regret being that the grand man who had made the tour possible, Philip Rodway, was not able to be with us to see how splendidly we finished up."

CHAPTER 39

(1929-30)

The Silver Wedding—P.R. at laying of foundation stone of Shakespeare Memorial Theatre—His *Heraldry of Shakespeare* manuscript legacy—The new Covent Garden Opera Company—*Turandot*—*The Damask Rose*—1930 Season—Sir Frank Benson's farewell—P.R.'s views on a National Theatre—His lecture to the Rotary Club—Grave tidings—The night before the operation—Afterwards—*Frederica.*

*"*Soft in the summer air hovers and lingers sweet shadowy music in melody clear,*

Low, laughing gurgle of wandering waters, murmurous magical song of the weir;

Here in the hush of the dreaming meadows, lost in the long grass warm and still,

Steals just the sleepiest quivering sigh of the riotous rushing beyond the old mill;

Comes but a breath of the sound of its singing, yet all the fair countryside thrills to its call,

As lulled in the lilt of the rapturous river-song, over this green world a spell seems to fall."

On July 11th, 1929, at Harvington, Daddy and Mother celebrated their silver wedding—a perfect summer's day, the counterpart of that earlier one a quarter of a century before. He had asked her if the anniversary might take place in the quiet country surroundings which held for him the greatest charm in the world—which had lent their wedding an unusual beauty—and she was very happy that this should be so; he planned, therefore, that they should re-visit the beloved village in the Vale of Evesham, and, most important of all, enter the little church together at the self-same hour that they had been married twenty-five years before.

On the anniversary morning Daddy gave Mother a beautifully wrought brooch of diamonds, which he had chosen with great care some weeks earlier; she gave him a writing-desk set in mother-of-pearl, also chosen in the depths of secrecy at Liberty's in London. As a climax to all this mystery, before we drove off in the car, we took them,

---

Weir Song, Harvington, 1927. Phyllis.

WHERE PHILIP RODWAY FISHED: THE AVON, HARVINGTON

Specially painted by S. Towers, R.C.A.

Exhibited at the Royal Birmingham Society of Artists, Spring, 1934

accompanied by Nip, down the garden to show them our secret for them both; a stone sundial, with the inscription in old English letters

"I count only the sunny hours"

Old English lettering trips us all up, so we were not altogether surprised when Daddy took the opportunity of translating this as "I count only the funny hours."

Before they came out to the car we had tied inside a silver horseshoe which had been sent them for luck, and so we set off on our drive along the quiet country roads to Harvington. At the appointed hour we entered the church, and they walked up the aisle together.

And Time stood still; they were back in 1904. . . .

Out into the sunshine once more, and then through the cherry orchards to the mill beside the weir, that beautiful spot so full of happy memories and present happiness. . . .

"Stillness awhile, with the wash of the weir like a chord low and
   long-sustained, holding the fields,
And meshed in its music, each soft little summer sound merges and
   mingles, and melody yields.
Blue as the summer skies, two little butterflies, fragile and slight
   as the frailest of flowers,
Over the spires of the mist-white meadowsweet, dance into sight for
   a second, while showers
Of faëry notes are beginning to fall, where a skylark climbs high in
   the cloudless air,
Till flight upon flight, and phrase upon phrase, he and his song are
   vanished there.

"The drone of a bee looms loudly and fails, as over the clover heads
   gaily he sails,
And suddenly near comes the cry of a coot, from some break in the
   bank where the willow herb veils
His dim reedy nest. Now close by my hand, a tiny bronze beetle of
   brilliant sheen
In a forest of grass blades rambling, stumbling—slips, and is lost
   in the infinite green.

How still it is here!—yet were you to move where the sunlit bend of
the river gleams
You'd break on the full flood and flash of its falling, wonder of
thunderous clear-shining streams.

"No stillness breathes there, but ear-filling sound, for sheerly and
headlong the bright waters hurl
Their free-flowing glory in storming cascade, and out from the edge
of the eddy and swirl
Fling wide a network of lacy foam, that ever wavers and ever
spreads,
Melting its mesh, but to weave it once more on the translucent
surface, where silvery threads
Fashion faint intricate patterns of delicate curve and design, and
the slim rushes sway
With the swing of the deep-running current, as in the swift stream
of the mill-race it speeds on its way.

"Then gently is checked its wild frolic and chuckle, the glad rush is
changed to a steadier flow,
As smoothly and softly it moves and meanders through many a
meadow where green banks lean low,
By many a backwater, hid in a half-light of overhung branches and
intertwined reeds,
Past pebble-paved shallows, where swift-darting minnows flash
bright in the sun and fly back to the weeds,
Through old broken lock gates, where feathery grasses grow high
'mid the wheels that but seldom are moved,
And a little down-stream by a clear-shadowed ford, and a willow-
hung way where the cart tracks are grooved."

We followed the little lane back to the car, and so to
Evesham, and the Crown Hotel, where Daddy had ordered
a special surprise luncheon in a private room; exactly the
same menu as their wedding breakfast, the same lovely
white lilies decorating the table and filling the room with
their beauty and fragrance. Afterwards we all wandered
down the green slopes of the river gardens, before slowly
motoring on to the Fish and Anchor, where the ford crosses
the river to Harvington again.

We drove home in the evening light with the sun still

shining, to find more silver-wedding presents awaiting. Daddy did not go down to the theatre, so after supper we sat in The Woodlands garden until the stars came out, and there was the golden moon behind the big fir tree.

And they talked, and our thoughts wandered back to the weir, and the mill on the Avon—the river that had threaded its willow-hung way through the happiest days of their lives.

> "*And the way of the willow trees leads to a lane, a little lane winding*
> *in leafy content,*
> *Where blue-eyed forget-me-nots cluster with ladysmocks slender in*
> *faintest of opal-hues blent,*
> *Where sudden and strange as a swift little heartache, dreamful and*
> *sweet as dim bird-song at dawn,*
> *Indefinable, ever elusive, the spell-weaving scent of the river is borne,*
> *While all pervading as mists of the morning that over the shimmering*
> *meadows appear,*
> *Still through the willow trees shyly and wistfully wanders and*
> *whispers the voice of the weir.*"

Season 1929*

With New Year's Day, 1929, there began the last ten weeks or so of Philip Rodway's greatest epoch. For ten years he had driven the Royal and the Prince of Wales Theatre in double harness—driven them without hesitation, through, over, or round many obstacles. Now he was on the point of becoming once more a one-theatre man, and leaving behind him the Theatre Royal, his spiritual home and constant delight for over thirty years.

In friendly rivalry to his *Old King Cole* at the Royal, during January was *Oh, Kay!* at the Prince of Wales Theatre. This was a musical comedy written by Guy Bolton and P. G. Wodehouse, with lyrics by Ida Gershwin and music by George Gershwin. Norah Blaney was the heroine and Jay Laurier the extremely amusing chief comedian, while Paul England, Eddie Childs, and Sopha Treble were others in the cast.

A sequence of light shows followed in February, while on March 4th, the last week of Philip Rodway's dual responsibilities, the Prince of Wales was occupied by *Charivaria*, an entertainment blending the delights of the Chauve Souris with the inconsequentialities of the Co-optimists. Dorothy Dickson, Joan Clarkson, Claude Hulbert, Billy Bennett, and Reg Palmer had leading parts.

The new conditions, of course, made the booking for the Prince of Wales Theatre extremely difficult. The syndicate had naturally the first claim on most of the big touring attractions. To-day, indeed, they have such an extensive system of bookings in conjunction with other concerns that the few independent theatres can but seldom secure shows of outstanding merit.

In 1929, though the position was difficult, P.R.'s personal influence was such that he could always rely on such distinguished actor-managers as Sir John Martin Harvey, the Terrys, and Matheson Lang to play in the theatre which he

---

Old King Cole and the Canadian tour form a pantomime cycle which runs concurrently with this season of 1929.

controlled. The Stratford Festival Company, the Macdona Players, the Irish Players, the British National Opera Company (soon to be succeeded by the Covent Garden Opera Company), and other organisations gave his seasons a definite artistic and intellectual quality, while there were several "first nights" of importance to be staged under his management.

The Birmingham Grand Opera Society appeared for a week in May, giving *La Gioconda* under the baton of Appleby Matthews, with Jack Bierman as producer. The principals on the first night were Mabel Smith (Gioconda), Paul Eugene Vacher (Alvise), Eva Tollworthy (Laura), Marion E. Smith (La Cieca), Charles Gellion (Enzo), Oswald Rogers(Barnaba), T. A. Charge (Zuane), and Leslie Williams (Isepo).

After a week in which P.R. had the theatre beautifully re-carpeted and decorated, the Stratford Company came for their annual fortnight, with George Hayes, Wilfred Walter, Dorothy Massingham, Joyce Bland, and Mary Holder in the leading parts. Again Birmingham gave only half-hearted support, and the Macdona Players, who followed, found the city as frigidly indifferent as ever to Mr. Shaw. Their programme included *Misalliance* for the first time in Birmingham, with Leah Bateman as Lena.

On July 2nd, 1929, P.R. attended the laying of the foundation stone of the new Shakespeare Memorial Theatre at Stratford-upon-Avon. May we mention here that in his will he left to the Memorial Theatre his manuscript book, *The Heraldry of Shakespeare* (by his brother Alfred, the heraldic expert). We ourselves took it over afterwards, and gave it into the hands of Mr. Bridges Adams. The building was then still hardly completed, and "Bridges" unwrapped from its tissue-paper the key of his new desk to lay the book carefully inside—"This is the first thing to be put in," he said to us. When we visited the theatre this summer we were told that of all the treasured volumes there this is the most valued; hardly a day passes but its assistance is sought in clearing up some point, for there is not a character in the whole of the plays which, entitled to armorial bearings, has not its coat of arms within.

Daddy's brother was one of the great authorities of his day upon the subject of heraldry. We recall a certain actor-manager who had put on a brilliantly colourful play, in one of the scenes of which a number of coats of arms were displayed. "There," he said with pride, "What do you think of that?" "Well," replied Alfred, "it's all very effective, but nine of them are wrong and the rest never existed!"

In this July P.R. inaugurated at the Prince of Wales a short twice-nightly season, following the practice which had for years enabled him to avoid a summer vacation at the Royal. On this occasion, in conjunction with Macdonald and Young, he put up several of the most popular musical comedies—*Rose Marie*—*No, No, Nanette, etc.*—and found his enterprise reasonably well rewarded.

The big event of the year was the production of Ashley Dukes' *Jew Süss*, the dramatisation of Leon Feuchtwanger's great novel. This was seen on September 9th for the first time on any stage, with Matheson Lang as the hero, Frank Harvey as Karl Alexander, Felix Aylmer as Weissensee, Bromley Davenport as Remingchen, Joan Maude as Magdalen, and Peggy Ashcroft as Naemi, her first part of importance.

Distinction was also brought to the theatre by such a presentation as *The Lady with the Lamp*, in which Gwen ffrang-con Davies, Nadine March, Murray Carrington, and Neil Porter did splendid work. Dennis Neilson-Terry, reviving *Typhoon*, revived also memories of Laurence Irving in a great study, while his parents, Julia Neilson and Fred Terry, played at the Prince of Wales Theatre a week later, for the first time in all their long association with Birmingham.

A side-light on some of the business difficulties on P.R.'s shoulders at this time may be seen by the extraordinary general meeting which he caused to be called immediately upon our return from Canada. His first news on landing on the other side in September, had been of the sudden death of Mr. W. E. Alldritt, who, as liquidator, had been in charge of the final proceedings in connection with the change-over of the Theatre Royal. Daddy had to cut short our stay in Canada, leaving his biggest venture to continue on its way, while he returned to take over affairs at home. It was necessary formally to appoint another liquidator in place of Mr. Alldritt, and Mr. George H. Sawyer, of Messrs. Sharp, Parsons & Co., was elected to take over.

November brought the opening visit of the new Covent Garden Opera Company. It will be remembered that with the collapse of the B.N.O.C. and the non-fruition of other enterprises, the authorities at Covent Garden, who have steadily upheld opera in London for generations, came to the rescue and organised a tour of opera in English.

On this visit Puccini's *Turandot* was given for the first time in Birmingham. It proved to be a lavish and brilliant pro-duction on a scale which, as one of the critics observed, "reminded people of the great Christmas shows associated with the name of Philip Rodway." In fact, at the end of the second act, one heard it described as a high-brow panto-mime, and the phrase was not altogether inapt. Odette de Foras sang the Princess to the Stranger Prince of Francis Russell; other leading parts were taken by Frederick Davies (the Emperor), and Noel Eadic (Lui). John Barbirolli, who conducted with deep insight into the complexities of the score, gained a great personal triumph.

Another of the personal attractions was Sybil Thorndike in *Madame Plays Nap*, in which she was supported by Lewis Casson and a fine company. A visit from the Diaghileff Russian Ballet, and several of the latest Edgar Wallace plays, brought the season up to Christmas, when *The Damask Rose* was presented for five weeks.

This beautiful production by Robert Courtneidge was a romance of Poland, woven around the music of Chopin. It had been arranged by G. H. Clutsam (the maker of *Lilac*

Time from the airs of Schubert), and many of the song-settings were exquisitely lovely, notably the soft chorus which opened the second half, *Oh, Night Enchanting*. Wilma Berkely and John Morel were two delightful singers, and Amy Augarde and Walter Passmore played together perfectly—musical comedy acting at its most polished. Tom Shelford, Nancy Lovat, and Billy Spurling did their best with the comedy side, which unfortunately was not strong enough to carry *The Damask Rose* to the success it deserved, when it went to the Savoy a few weeks later. In Birmingham, however, scenes of extraordinary enthusiasm marked the last performance— the audience remained in their seats for fully twenty minutes after the final curtain, demanding speech after speech, and the principals, Robert Courtneidge and Philip Rodway all had to say a few words of appreciation for the splendid support.

We remember that this season re-started the fashion for wearing flowers at the theatre at night; we all loved having sprays of real damask roses on our evening frocks. (Mother tells us that in her young days she always wore a rose in her hair at the theatre.)

And Daddy had a quaint little idea as a publicity "stunt" to help the play along; a notice was put in the personal column of the *Birmingham Post*—"Will you be in the foyer of the Prince of Wales Theatre at 7.15 to-night? I shall be wearing a damask rose.—Q." Also he had beautiful damask roses made and given away at each performance as a souvenir posy or buttonhole—a very charming idea which pleased everyone.

Season 1930

In the spring of 1930, soon after a visit by the Covent Garden Opera Company, Sir Frank Benson made his last appearance on the Birmingham stage, and P.R. was able to arrange a pleasant ceremony to mark the farewell performance in *The Merchant of Venice*. It was carried out in happy vein by the then Lord Mayor, Alderman M. L. Lancaster,

PHYLLIS AND LOIS

From a painting by Bernard Munns, R.B.S.A.

Exhibited at the Royal Birmingham Society of Artists, Autumn, 1933

who went on the stage during an interval in the performance on the last night, delivered a little oration in praise of Sir Frank's outstanding services to the classic stage, and conferred on him a huge laurel wreath in token of Birmingham's admiration. "We recognise," he said, "that you have always supported the best tradition of the stage, and that your company has for many years been the nursery of some of the greatest actors who have ever appeared on the English stage."

Sir Frank, in a touching reply, said the evening's ceremony would be an everlasting memory to him. "Not only to-night, but on all the nights of the week, you have made our visit very pleasant, and to me this seems to foreshadow a continuance of my friend Philip Rodway's work in making this spacious and friendly theatre a great municipal institution.

"I, for one, believe firmly that what is national and municipal in the recognition of dramatic art should come in the informal way we have experienced to-night, rather than with any set purpose or sealed parchment bonds."

During the next few weeks there were some very fine bookings at the Prince of Wales, with Sir John Martin Harvey in *Rosemary*, Stanley Lupino and Laddie Cliff in *Love Lies*, and the D'Oyly Carte Opera Company. The Macdona Players, headed by George S. Wray and Leah Bateman, came for three weeks, and the Stratford-upon-Avon Festival Company, with Fabia Drake as their most important recruit, for a fortnight.

The Shakespeare Birthday Celebrations on the 366th anniversary were held as usual on April 23rd, and P.R. attended the luncheon at Stratford-upon-Avon. It may be interesting to-day to recall that about this time the question of building a National Repertory Theatre, to be regarded as a Shakespeare Memorial Theatre, was much in the air, and a week or two later, when the committee set up to inquire into the possibilities presented its report, P.R. was one of the first to be asked to express his views.

"As I see the scheme at the moment," he said in the *Birmingham Mail* of May 30th, "the intention is to erect, as the best of national

PI

memorials to Shakespeare, in the capital of the Empire, a theatre which in all essentials is to be a repertory theatre. I notice immediately that one of its objects is set out, almost condescendingly, as intended—'to keep the plays of Shakespeare in its repertory.' Indeed it almost appears as if the presentation of Shakespeare will again be left almost entirely to the much-derided commercial Theatre.

"Then again, I note in the aims of the scheme, a suggestion that the National Theatre Company should give performances in other towns of Great Britain and the Empire. Here I might point to the constantly overlooked fact that the 'commercial' provincial theatre has probably done as much in the cause of real drama as anyone. Again and again we in Birmingham have given plays of Shakespeare by the Stratford-upon-Avon Festival Company, when certain loss, and a heavy one at that, is bound to be our portion at the end of the engagement.

"The same applies to performances of Shaw's plays and others, and it seems to me that the new touring organisation that might spring into being, with the weight of State aid behind it, would come into conflict with the already existing stalwart managers and players who have pluckily combined to supply our needs in this direction for so long.

"Furthermore, in the objects set out there is mention of an effort 'to prevent recent plays of merit from falling into oblivion.' There again the scheme is bound to encounter those who are already wholeheartedly devoted to such a cause. We have a case in point at my old theatre, the Royal, this week. . . . My own view is that if there is to be a National Repertory Theatre it would be better to call it so and leave the reference to a Shakespeare memorial as a motive out of it entirely. . . . The Stratford Memorial Theatre can never be ousted in my affections by a theatre which would be presenting plays of all kinds and character."

*   *   *

P.R. did not often give a discourse in public. Knowing as much as any living man about most theatrical subjects— more than almost anybody else about some—he had a horror of anything savouring of theatricality or self-advertisement in his personal or his family life.

The address which he gave to the Birmingham Rotary Club at the Queen's Hotel, Birmingham, on May 5th, 1930, was probably the longest and most formal oration he ever made to a "lay" audience. It must have been with considerable difficulty that the club officials secured his name for their list, but once he had agreed to speak he went ahead with all his wonted attention to detail. The President, Mr. H. Ernest Plater, was in the chair, and there was an unusually large attendance.

"A great meeting," the official organ, *Rotaria*, described it. "The subject was Pantomime, on which Philip Rodway ranks as our greatest authority." Here is a more or less complete transcript of P.R.'s address, which was given important columns in all the Birmingham papers:

"I think Pantomime, over which pessimists have annually sung a dirge for several years past, will always remain successful if managers will only present it as a genuine fairy tale, making the fun a natural outcome of the story, instead of substituting a series of disconnected turns which have no relation to each other or to the main theme. . . .

"Pantomime originally was an art practised by the mimes or clowns—the art of mimicry in dumb show. Its form to-day is of course tremendously different from that of the plays from which it derived its name!

"It was not until the beginning of the 19th century that Pantomime in England took any very definitely settled form. As an entertainment it was much esteemed in the 19th century. Dickens, for instance, wrote: 'I was brought up from remote country parts in the dark ages of 1819-20 to behold the splendour of Christmas Pantomime and the humour of Joe (*i.e.* Grimaldi), in whose honour I am informed I clapped my hands with great precocity.'

"Fielding describes Pantomime as 'a most exquisite entertainment,' and William Archer, thirty years ago, uttered the perfect appreciation of the ideal Pantomime when he said 'It should charm the senses, stimulate the imagination, and satisfy the intelligence. It should be an enchanting fairy-tale to the young, to the old a witty, graceful, gently satiric phantasmagoria. The nursery folk-lore in which it finds its traditional subject blends the graceful with the grotesque.'

"Birmingham has played a very large part in the history and development of Pantomime in England, for since 1840* a

*Harlequin and the Silver Shield.

pantomime has been presented annually at the Theatre Royal. For many years, too, there was tremendous local rivalry with the Prince of Wales Theatre, though the Royal's record was, of course, by far the longest. No other city has pantomime traditions equal to those of Birmingham.

"Notabilities whose names have figured in Birmingham pantomime casts of the past include Edmund Kean, who played Harlequin in 1809; Grimaldi in 1808; and Sir Squire Bancroft, in *The Great Gosling*, in 1861. On Boxing Day, 1791, there was a performance of *Robinson Crusoe; or Friday turned Boxer*, in the course of which a sparring match took place between Man Friday and the celebrated bruiser Mr. Mendoza, from London.

"The Harlequinade was definitely dropped in Birmingham as an annual feature in 1892; I revived it for one season in 1906, with George Robey as Clown—and the small boys of the period promptly reached for their hats, saying reproachfully, 'Pater, what *are* you giving us?' Pater, years earlier, had laughed at it, but Filius knew neither Clown nor Pantaloon, nor wanted to.

"Gone are the political allusions, and, I think, most wisely so. Most of you remember such songs as *Three Acres and a Cow*, with patter in satirical reference to current politics and politicians. Gone are the songs of the *Champagne Charlie* type, popularised by George Leybourne; gone the 'Jingo' songs, which added another word to our vocabulary, exemplified in *We don't want to fight, but by Jingo if we do.*

"These were the days of the *lions comiques;* the gentlemen who wore elaborate evening dress, red-lined capes, and the indispensable red handkerchief, with which they made great play in the dramatic passages, and set the feminine hearts of the period all aflutter. Gone the war references, dropped by general consent early in the great war; gone, too, the transformation scene in its old form as a detached item, though it has crept back as a finale to the first half.

"In the old days one good song could pretty well *make* a pantomime. Take *Where did you get that hat?*, *Two lovely black eyes*, *Tar-rar-rar-boom-de-ay*, and *A bicycle made for two* as examples. In the pantomimes of twenty or thirty years ago, moreover, there was always a topical song, generally connected to a catch-phrase such as 'Yes, I don't think,' and there was a definite place for a ballad of either the patriotic or love type.

"Many of these songs still linger in the theatre-goer's memory, whereas who to-day can remember the popular song of, say, two years ago? And I don't suppose anyone wants to. Songs of sentiment such as *Comrades*, *The Miner's Dream of Home*, *The Ship I Love*, have remained in our minds for thirty years or more. So have the love songs—*Just a Song of Twilight*, *In the Gloaming*, and so on. Why is the modern song so soon forgotten? Probably because the modern song writer sacrifices everything to rhythm. Sentiment matters little so long as there is a strong accent on the first beat of every bar. The modern composer appears to rely on constant repetition to catch the sense of movement which most of us unconsciously possess, whereas the old-time composers relied on real tune and sentiment for their results. The wireless, the gramophone, and the dance band, by their pitiless persistent repetition of a melody, jazz it out of one's mind and memory in no time.

"Let me say something about the immense amount of work entailed in producing a big pantomime. We have about ten days in which to fuse a hundred people, and our success depends mainly on this process being more or less complete by the first night. The producer must bid 'Good-bye' to the outer world during this intensive period while he is giving shape to his ideas. On the evening before the dress rehearsal things appear so chaotic that successful production seems hopeless. When principals and chorus are brought to rehearse on the stage together for the first time, nervousness makes its appearance. Lines rehearsed perfectly in corridors and dressing rooms refuse to come. Artists develop stage-fright. The artistic temperament crops up. Passing phases, fortunately! And it is often the artist who rehearses least smoothly who gives the best show before the public. When orchestral rehearsals start we plunge into pandemonium, with the musicians getting their parts into order, and the chorus hard at it on the other side of the iron curtain. At the first 'all together' rehearsal the orchestra are the nearest approach to an audience the principals have had—and if the orchestra laugh at a comedian's joke it may safely be left in. The front of the theatre is tenanted only by the 'Wood family'—the professional term for the original rows of empty wooden seats—and it is while performers are rehearsing to 'The Woods' that a producer needs all his tact.

"Once a comedian drawing £300 a week came to me just before we started the first stage rehearsal and said 'Oh, Mr. Rodway, I do feel so funny.' To which I replied 'That's exactly what I've been waiting and hoping for.' I have known dress rehearsals, incidentally, start at 6.30 one evening, and go on until 6 next morning without being completed. . . ."

After his address, the vote of thanks was proposed by Rotarian Bache Matthews, then manager of the Birmingham Repertory Theatre. He claimed to have seen almost every Theatre Royal pantomime since his infancy, and he thought that Philip Rodway ought to publish his reminiscences as a means of helping to preserve the special traditions of this form of art.

Rotarian Canon Stuart Blofeld, Vicar of Edgbaston, who seconded the motion, said that the clergy would be lacking until it realised to the full the great benefit for good to a man's body, mind, and spirit which came from the stage, which formed an essential part of the life of the individual. Personally, he had never missed a "Royal" pantomime since he came to Birmingham. He thought definite plot and character-drawing much preferable to the disjointed revue-like efforts one so often saw.

In the same issue of *Rotaria* the Editor, Mr. W. Unite Jones (a noted Birmingham journalist and a lifelong friend of P.R.'s), wrote:

"What a fine address we had from Philip Rodway, of the Prince of Wales Theatre! It is rather difficult to avoid linking the Theatre Royal with his name, so intimately was he bound up with its destinies.

"I remember Philip Rodway when he was acting manager of that Theatre, and the youngest acting manager in England too. . . . He has established himself as the greatest authority on pantomime in the world, and we shall all eagerly await his promised address on how a Royal pantomime was received in Canada."

(This last had reference to a prospect held out by P.R. in acknowledging the vote of thanks—a hope which his fatal illness made it impossible for him to fulfil.)

Our purpose here is neither critical nor controversial. The reputation and success of the Philip Rodway pantomimes stand as a monument to their pre-eminence, and what has happened since he ceased producing at the Theatre Royal has increased, not reduced, the dimensions of that monument.

*   *   *

PHILIP
RODWAY.   HARRY RUSHWORTH.

Reproduced from "The Midlander"

June, 1930

On May 27th, 1930 (a Tuesday—every momentous event in Daddy's and Mother's life happened on a Tuesday), Daddy was told he would have to undergo a very serious operation. It seems one of the mysteries of fate that a man who had led an active and athletic life, with never a day's illness, should suddenly come up against such a crisis. Yet those who knew him best realised that the last two years had been very strenuous ones for him, and might well have thrown him out of the even course of his existence. The work incidental to the transfer of the Theatre Royal, quite apart from his own personal feelings on the matter, was arduous and worrying in the extreme, and almost on top of it came the physical strain, coupled with the mental anxiety, of the Canadian venture.

He took the blow wonderfully quietly, with no complaining; just a quiet putting of affairs into order. That done, he asked for a few days to spend with us before he entered the nursing home.

Mother, both before and after the operation, was a host in herself. By the small things of life apt to be distracted, in the big things she is as steadfast as a rock and never failed us for an instant.

Thus the two of them prepared for a short fortnight of— almost—holiday with us, and each day we set off on a tour of his favourite villages: Knightwick, Pershore, Harvington; just such a pleasant detour as he had chosen on their silver wedding anniversary, but with what different emotions. They both had a wonderful power of control, and it was hard to believe that an immoveable anxiety lay always at the back of their minds. So we spent the time till June 18th together, and Daddy had at last a short experience of home life proper. The Sunday before his operation was so happy and peaceful; surely everything could not fail to go right the following Tuesday?

*   *   *

His old friend W. H. Savery of the Stratford Festival Company (which was playing at the Prince of Wales at the time) has written to us:

"The night before he went in for his operation, he withdrew into his office and had a heart to heart talk with just one or two of those to whom he had given the rare gift of his friendship. How can I express what I felt at being invited to join him at such a time? Until then, perhaps, I had not fully understood that we had been friends for 25 years—friends in the deepest sense of the word.

"That night we had the most personal talk we had ever had. It was not about his coming ordeal (of which he had a certain nervous and wholly understandable dread), but of Theatre in general, our work at Stratford, and elsewhere, in particular.

"After his operation I was one of the very few whom he asked to visit him at the nursing home as soon as he was able to receive callers. Weak as he was, he was mentally the old P.R., with his mind on Theatre. His interest had at once reverted to the work he had done, the work he hoped to do. . . ."

He came through the operation well because of his fine constitution, and appeared to be on the road, if a slow one, to recovery. No advice was too much trouble for him to take, and he trod the difficult path with the greatest courage imaginable. Later, as his convalescence progressed, he spent a few quiet days fishing at Olton Mere, where we accompanied him. Also, he had at last what had been denied to him in his business life, weekday evenings at home. Now he came home soon after eight, and sometimes before his early retirement to bed, we gathered round the piano while Mother played the *Florodora* melodies and *The Lily of Laguna*, and Daddy his favourite *Cloches de Corneville*. Nip basked in the radiance of his master's unexpected returns—seven Sundays in a week made it a very heaven for him.

By the end of August he had more or less taken up his old routine at the theatre, and on September 3rd, as chairman of directors, he presided as usual at the annual meeting of shareholders. His speech struck a note of quiet confidence, and, despite the fact that the past year had been one of the worst commercially in the history of the British Drama, he was able to recommend a dividend of $12\frac{1}{2}$ per cent. on the accounts for the period ending that June. To a great extent, as he pointed out, they were commencing a new business at the Prince of Wales, because the conditions under which the theatre was now run were totally different from the conditions which obtained when they ran both the Theatre Royal and the Prince of Wales Theatre. He added that Mr. (now Sir) F. H. Pepper, an original shareholder in the Theatre Royal Company, had joined the Board on the death of Mr. Alldritt, and had rendered invaluable service at a particularly difficult time.

P.R. announced fine bookings for the autumn: Pavlova and her *corps de ballet* opened a week's engagement on October 6th, and other personal attractions included Hamilton Deane in *Frankenstein*, Julia Neilson and Fred Terry in *Henry of Navarre*, Irene Vanbrugh in *Art and Mrs. Bottle*, Godfrey Tearle in *Slings and Arrows*, Sybil Thorndike in *The Squall* (with a special matinée of Ibsen's *Ghosts*), a fortnight of the Covent Garden Opera Company, and the delightful musical comedy *Blue Roses*, with George Clarke, Roy Royston, Vera Bryer, and Jean Colin. And then—*Frederica*. This was a beautiful adaptation by Adrian Ross, to the music of Franz Lehar, of a German play concerning the romantic attachment of Goethe for Frederica Brion. It brought to Birmingham Lea Seidl, a charming and talented Viennese actress, whose rendering of Frederica lingers in one's mind as a most exquisite performance.

CHAPTER 40

Season 1931

Spring, 1931—St. Valentine's Day: Lois' and Charles' wedding—*The Good Companions*—Leon Salberg—Autumn bookings—The future of the Theatre: P.R.'s optimism—Finale.

In the early spring the D'Oyly Carte Opera Company held us in their customary spell at the Prince of Wales Theatre. We travel through their delightful season to the last day's performance on February 14th—*The Mikado*. And with it

> *"Brightly dawns our wedding day;*
> *Joyous hour, we give thee greeting!*
> *Whither, whither art thou fleeting?*
> *Fickle moment, prithee stay!"*

How we wish we could have the red-letter days of life again, with dear ones alive and well once more around us. Saint Valentine's Day dawned as golden as that lovely wedding day of July 11th, twenty-six years before. A deep, clear, blue sky, so sunny that we remember looking up and feeling that its brilliance must wane. But it never did, till the sun set. Looking back on the unlooked for, almost un-hoped for, perfection of that day, it seems akin to Daddy's unexpected gift of health for the space of the twelve hours. Little though we realised it at the time, it was to be the last public function he attended. It was not many months since his operation, and, doubtful as to how he would stand the strain, we had suggested a very quiet reception after the wedding. Unexpectedly, he would not hear of it, and enjoyed supervising the list of two hundred invitations and the menu for the "breakfast."

It was a day of great happiness, one for which to be very thankful. The dear little church, with its old-world charm, and the blue and white flag, fluttering "Like my *Humpty Dumpty* castle scene, Lois," as Daddy said as we drove up to the gates; the bridesmaids waiting there with their golden baskets of daffodils, their picture frocks and hats of the same

WEDDING SCENE FROM "THE MIKADO"

with

Derek Oldham, Bertha Lewis, Sir Henry Lytton, Darrell Fancourt, Leo Sheffield

FEBRUARY 14th, 1931

sunny shade; the interior of the church glowing with its masses
of spring blossoms, daffodils, blue irises, and pillars greenery-
entwined. On the way from the church door to the altar
on Daddy's arm, he and I may have paced it with the
measured tread I had previously imagined, but certainly
neither of us had planned to whisper to each other all the
way up the aisle to mask our nervousness. Neither of us
knew what we were saying, nor heard what the other said,
but it calmed us amazingly, as did the beautiful words of
Canon Blofeld.

After the ceremony at Edgbaston Old Church, we came
out into the brilliant sunshine and stepped under the awning,
where the sergeants of the 7th Battalion Royal Warwickshire
Regiment stood as guard of honour.

Twice only during that day did Daddy become ruffled.
It was inevitable—when the photographs were taken, once
at the church, once at the Botanical Gardens! No one in
the world could have disliked posed photographs more than
he. An occasional snapshot, taken when the subject was
unaware, was just permissible, but this standing in a row he
heartily detested; consequently our wedding photographs
have nearly all got that "Get-it-over-as-quickly-as-possible"
look on our faces. It is certain that the camera men were as
agitated as we were. In vain did Harold Baker plead "I've
waited two hours for this picture—can't you spare me just
two minutes?"

The reception was held at the Botanical Gardens, so full
of happy memories for us all; the Saturday garden parties
for the convalescent wounded soldiers, which Daddy had
organised during the war, the twenty-first birthday party,
and the pleasant days of his own convalescence. Daddy's
and Mother's guests for the "twenty-first" party and the
wedding naturally included the same friends, and they were
as rejoiced as we were to see him so well after the illness
which had occurred in the intervening year.

At the reception and wedding breakfast, Daddy was in

his very best form. Everyone who heard it has remembered
his speech, and they still talk of it as one of the most entertaining he ever made. It was to be his last; but that day we
were all radiant—and it seemed to be the forerunner of so
many happy times. After a brilliant opening he passed on to the
form of rhymed couplets, (a lyric form he and Tom Townson
delighted in working out together). Nonsensically these
introduced or punned on the name of every wedding guest
there, and almost literally brought down the house. Literally,
because as this was the Botanical Gardens there were parrots
and cockatoos and even monkeys half-hidden away among
the palms, and the laughter so roused a baby monk that he
too applauded and shook his bars till the hall rang.

In Daddy's inimitable way, with the minimum of effort,
he soon had every guest holding up a hand in turn as his or
her name was read out. We give the verses below, as so many
of his friends have asked for them. Of course, it is the way
lines are, theatrically speaking, "put over," not the intrinsic
value of the lines themselves, that counts, but they do reveal
his versatility and keen sense of humour even if they cannot
reveal his charm.

OUR GUESTS

A most distinguished gathering before me I espy—
A *Greatbach* of celebrities who've come from far and nigh,
Of officers we've many here, and one is *French* they say,
And when they smoke the pipe of peace these *Boyes* select a *Clay*.

We've got some splendid *Parsons*, and we've seen one tie the *Knott*,
We've also got a *Sailman* and a *Simmonds*, but no Yat.
I clearly see the *Thompsons* with their daughter; how they need her;
If brigands held her at a *Price*, we soon would shout "They've
    Freda."

We've *Nicolsons* and *Willisons* and other sons galore,
The *Davidsons* and *Harrisons* and *Wilkinsons*, and more;
The *Watsons* and the *Robinsons* are here to share our laughter,
We'll let our voices ring on high and reach the tallest *Rafter*.

Besides the sons we've got the tons, the *Billingtons*, I mean,
St. Johnstons, and the *Moretons*, yes, they're all upon the scene,
The *Harveys* came via New Street, but it's not "The Only Way,"
They might have come by other *Rhodes*, as *Cecil* used to say.

Then *Hubbard* to the cupboard went and found the cupboard bare,
The *Blofeld* Mother *Hubbard*, she'd not even *Pepper* there;
She struck the *Wall*, got several *Knox*, no longer could she hustle,
In falling she upset the *Coles* and made the curtain *Russell*.

A *Waterhouse* is not the place in which to house a *Cutler*:
Sir Waters house is perfect, they've a charming *Lady Butler*.
Lois the level of my wit: says *Ethel*, *Phyllis* glass up,
And give a *Philip* to his wit, so all your glasses pass up.

If *Deeley Rose* to take a shot at cricket, we'd applaud her,
And we've got a *Frederick Hobbs* to mount the score for the recorder,
If both should try stone-*Wall*ing we would have to change the
    wicket,
For it *Helps* a lot to get some fun for the *Price* of county cricket.

Discussing "slings and arrows" once, *Miss Baily*, of the College,
Said "Arrows may be very *Swift*, but *Slingsby* full of knowledge."
I now can mention *Smith* and *Jones*, the *Trubshaws*, yes, and *Walter*,
It's *Heaven* not to pun on them, for punning makes me falter.

With *Vernon* and with *Gibson* every line becomes more bafflin':
The *Keelings* wink as if to say—the only rhyme's *O'Loughlin*.
May good luck *Shepherd* in this year—a *Goodyear*, none shall rue it,
If to your joy there's any bar, well, you must up and *Hewitt*.

To *Garner* in a few more names won't take a brace of shakes,
And that brings me to Shakespeare, "As You Like It," and to
    Jaques;
Charles Kingsley's "Water Babies" lets me introduce you *Grimes*,
And when I've mentioned *Bradley* I have got a line that rhymes.

My *Levy*ty in going on will not prevail much longer:
My *Viggars* slowly giving out, your *Curtis*y is stronger;
I've still to say *Crump*, *Coley*, *Milne*, a quee*R odway* is mine,
And so with *Daniels* I will end, for the sake of Auld *Langs* Syne.

There is a modern magic which *does* enable us to live these hours again—a magic which would have been a miracle in the early ages, but is to us a commonplace. At the time it all seems hardly necessary—here is the day itself, how can the colours ever fade? But though the outlines remain, little by little the details slip away. It is thanks to the thoughtfulness of two friends* that we have a living pictorial memory of the whole wedding. They brought their Pathé-cinés and faithfully filmed the proceedings from the beginning.

To-day as the reel revolves on the projector, so too revolves the wheel of time. We see once more the guests arriving in the sunlight, and stepping from their cars under the striped awning leading to the church. Then the bridesmaids, next the bride's mother, and now the bride and her father. We catch a glimpse of their faces as they pass under the lych gate to the porch. There is a touch of artistic unreality in the effect of the bride's ivory velvet train as it sweeps and glistens in a silver cascade, and finally disappears with a swirl of the cloudy tulle veil into the darkness of the church porch. The bridesmaids are a discreet mingling of winter and spring, with their daffodil velvet jackets over organdie picture frocks.

And now the guard of honour, eight sergeants of the 7th Battalion the Royal Warwickshire Regiment, stand to attention as the bridal party come out of church, and are snapped by various press cameras. The bride and groom start the procession to the Gardens in their car, white ribbons fluttering, followed by the bridesmaids: Phyllis, Peggy Slingsby, Hilda Deeley, and Gwen Simmonds, with the best man, Norman Boyes. Then we see the bride's mother and father step into their car, she holding her bouquet of carnations and lilies against her bronze velvet dress. They look so happy, and so many letters have come since saying "We shall always think of you both together as you were at Lois's wedding."†

The smiling guard of honour sails away to the Gardens

*Miss Kellett and Mr. Goodyear.

in its bus, taking the curve past Edgbaston Park Road in a fine flourish. The next scene revealed by the magic of the turning film is at the Botanical Gardens, with flowers everywhere and rows of smiling waitresses ranged by the tables laid ready for the breakfast. The camera transports us then to the stage at the end of the ballroom, where Phil Brown's *Dominoes* are seen tuning their instruments. All is set for the reception.

Below the stage, at the edge of the dance floor, a sweep of the lens shows us the wedding presents. These have been formed into little scenes—a standard lamp behind a fireside chair and a monk's stool, on a richly coloured Persian rug; a bookcase, laden with books, and with lalique bowls on its polished surface.

We watch the reception, and know a bitter-sweetness as faces now lost to us pass laughing in front of the lens. We can almost hear the lilt of the waltz the band is playing. Now the wedding breakfast is being served, and there is the toastmaster, the faithful Sears, preparing the cake for the bride to cut. She appears to be in some difficulties with the bridegroom's sword. . . .

Then the camera isolates for us the speech-makers. First we can see Mr. Sydney Vernon, in a characteristically humorous and charming way proposing the health of the bride and bridegroom. Then the groom responds to him—it is obvious that there stands one lawyer replying to another, their sentences are so beautifully balanced! We do not need the spoken word to show us that, for we can see it by their actions as they turn first to the right and then to the left of their audience. But were the spoken word audible we should hear the bridegroom at the close of his speech saying that ever since childhood he had been thrilled by the Philip Rodway pantomimes, and the words "Rodway Production"—a hallmark in the theatre world—had conjured up for him, young and uninitiated as he then was, something rather special;

---

†"I shall always keep in mind that picture I have of you and your husband at Lois' and Charles' wedding—a vision of great love and happiness. Anne O'Loughlin."

but never did he in his wildest moments imagine that one day he would have a Rodway Production for his very own!

Mr. W. R. Trubshaw now proposes the toast of the host and hostess. There is Daddy rising to reply, and we can see the audience laughing as one by one their hands shoot up in answer to their names. . . .

There is Prof. J. L. Robinson, an old friend of the family, proposing the health of the bridesmaids, and the best man replying. Then we see the chief bridesmaid, Phyllis, proposing an unexpected but singularly appropriate toast, "St. Valentine," and we all drink willingly to the dear old saint.

So, with our glasses raised, with dancing and laughter and farewells yet to come, we will leave the reception; and offer our best wishes, in the kindly expression of Charles Lamb, to all those who still have an affection for old legends and "who are content to rank themselves humble diocesans of old Bishop Valentine and his true Church."

At night bridesmaids and groomsmen went on to a theatre party given for them and members of the family by Daddy and Mother. The D'Oyly Carte Opera Company was finishing its season that night with the happy Japanese wedding play, *The Mikado*. Company and audience alike seemed in a celebration mood: Sir Henry Lytton as Koko, incomparable Bertha Lewis as Katisha. Those who saw her that night will always remember it, for it was the last occasion on which she graced the Birmingham stage. A short while afterwards she was fatally injured in a tragic motor smash which robbed the theatre of a most gracious presence and a voice which will echo in our memories whenever Sullivan's sweet music is played. It has been said "one loses voices— until one hears them again." Of most voices this is true, but never will the rich melody of Bertha Lewis's voice pass from the hearts of anyone who had the infinite pleasure of listening to her.

Frederick Hobbs, the D'Oyly Carte manager and a personal friend of Daddy's, had sent as his wedding present an antique silver filigree spoon, and we may well conclude with the charmingly appropriate Gilbert and Sullivan tag which was tied on to the handle:

> *"When a merry maiden marries*
> *Sorrow flies and pleasure tarries!"*

*   *   *

The finest musical comedy team of the day, headed by Laddie Cliff and Barry Lupino, visited the Prince of Wales twice within two months or so, first in *The Love Race* and next in *The Millionaire Kid*. Another fine cast, in *Lavender*, included Eileen Moody, Walter Passmore, Amy Augarde and Chili (now Dorothy) Bouchier (the film star).

The last new production with which Philip Rodway was personally associated was *The Good Companions*, which was given for the first time on any stage at the Prince of Wales Theatre on April 14th. Julian Wylie, who presented the adaptation of J. B. Priestley's famous book, had a splendid send-off, and abundant publicity was given by P.R.'s newspaper friends. Dramatised by the author in conjunction with Edward Knoblock, the play necessitated sixteen scenes and a very large cast, the chief figures in which were Edward Chapman (Oakroyd), Edith Sharp (Miss Trant), Adèle Dixon (Susie Dean), and Anthony Hankey (Inigo Jollifant).

One of the photographs taken at the time shows Julian Wylie, Philip Rodway, and Leon Salberg in conference. Among P.R.'s closest friends in his own profession was Leon Salberg, chief proprietor and manager for nearly twenty-five years of the Alexandra Theatre. We could not possibly have sent this memoir to press without a few words from Mr. Salberg, who has contributed the following reminiscences:

"From the time I entered the business in 1911 Phil was a friend in the truest sense. In my earlier days as a theatre manager he repeatedly volunteered to help me to his utmost, and with him that was no empty offer. I looked on him as my guide through intricate paths—a guide who never failed me.

"He was the most honourable man in the theatrical world. His word was his bond, on which you could rely implicitly.

Though we were rivals in one sense, in another we were colleagues. Our work never clashed except at pantomime time, and then, while our competition was vigorous and healthy, we always used to avoid unnecessary clashing. By frankly comparing plans and notes, we were able to ensure that the public got the greatest possible diversity in the two productions, because neither show duplicated the special features of the other.

"In our business one does not often share confidences with the opposition on such vital matters, but in Phil the most complete trust could be reposed. We both knew that it was to our mutual advantage for the city to have two successful pantomimes, but beyond that there was the deep regard which made it unthinkable for either to dream of 'doing down' the other.

"As he progressed, I continued to receive lots of help and information from him. At his zenith, of course, he knew much more about pantomime than I did, yet even then he was not above taking notice of any suggestion or idea which struck him as sound. About pantomime, in fact, his ears were always open, his mind always receptive.

"When Phil Rodway died we lost one of the whitest men in the business, and I personally lost one of my dearest friends. His influence for good on Birmingham's entertainments was immense, and the city owes him a great debt of gratitude for his uncompromising stand against everything calculated to discredit her proud reputation."

The Good Companions was followed by the Birmingham Grand Opera Society, with *Cavalleria Rusticana* and *I Pagliacci*, and *Carmen*. Among their stars were Eva Tollworthy, Mabel Cliffe, Marion E. Smith, Stanley Wilcox, Oswald Rogers, Georgette Bleckley, Mae Element, James Doherty, Leslie Williams, Geoffrey Dams, and Alex Shanks, with Harold Gray as their new conductor. This, by the way, was another of the societies of which Philip Rodway was a vice-president; in this case together with Dr. Adrian Boult, Sir Thomas Beecham, Sir Granville Bantock, Mr. Percy Pitt, the late Colonel E. W. Blois (for so long the director of the D'Oyly Carte Opera Company), and Mr. Leslie Heward (the distinguished director of the City of Birmingham Orchestra).

George S. Wray, Leah Bateman, and Wilfred Lawson

MRS. PHILIP RODWAY

played the leads in the Macdona season of Bernard Shaw, and Dorothy Massingham, Gyles Isham, Hilda Coxhead, Randle Ayrton, and Roy Byford with the Stratford Festival Company.

This was the Stratford Company's seventh and last season in Birmingham under Philip Rodway's management. During all these seven seasons they were directed by Mr. W. Bridges Adams, that brilliant young producer whose association with the Stratford Festival ended, at least for the time, a few months ago. "Bridges" was in Daddy's inner circle of friends, and it is a great pleasure to us that he should have sent, for inclusion in this memoir, the following appreciation:

"To-day, when what may be called the chain-store influence is rapidly making itself felt even in the world of popular entertainment, it is refreshing to remember the stoutly independent individualist, the old-time provincial manager. A personality in his own town, he was no less redoubtable when he came to London to see the new plays and make his pencillings for next season. His own pronounced tastes, his stern sense of responsibility to his own public, made him a man to reckon with. He had his standards and ideals, both artistic and ethical, and he stuck to them; he was not to be imposed upon, and he would not buy a pig in a poke. Personal management is fast disappearing, elbowed out by syndicates and the mechanised drama, and the theatre and all who care for it are the worse for its going.

"Such a man, and in the first rank of the best of them, was Philip Rodway. He directed his two large theatres with a sure personal touch which was apparent alike in good times and bad. In days when the decay of character in our profession was universally lamented, here was the real thing, unobtrusive, firm, pervading. To the visiting manager the Royal and the Prince of Wales meant Philip Rodway.

"Among many memories of him, shared by many people—for surely no man had a greater faculty for turning business acquaintance into friendship—perhaps these stand foremost: his integrity, sincerity, and simplicity; his fairness in driving a bargain; and his generosity in interpreting its terms; his understanding of human nature at its queerest, which Heaven knows is sometimes necessary in our line of country; his solicitude for the happiness and well-being of all who visited his theatres, backstage and front, which

invariably made him play host as well as manager; his sense of
humour and gift for a good story.

"His qualities found yearly their supreme expression in Birmingham's saturnalia, his famous Pantomime. I saw enough of the
tender care he lavished on it to realise that there was in Philip
much of the creative artist.

"All who knew him, and miss him, will welcome this book.

"W. BRIDGES ADAMS.

"Shakespeare Memorial Theatre,
    "Stratford-upon-Avon.
        "1934."

*   *   *

The annual meeting on September 2nd, 1931, received
special attention in the Press, and was the subject of leading
articles and much approving comment. P.R., in his address,
expressed himself as a confirmed optimist as to the future of
the theatre. He had weighed things up very carefully, and
envisaged all the possibilities of the situation, and even so,
and in face of tremendous opposition and the trying times
they were going through, his confidence remained unshaken.

"All through the years," he said, "I have steadily refused
to join the band of those who will have it that the theatre is
dead. The theatre was said to be dead when I first entered
this profession as a boy in my teens! It is, of course, apparent
that the economic conditions, the shortage of money, bad
trade, and the reduced spending power of the public have
their effect upon theatre attendances, and I think the next
period will probably show no improvement in this respect,
but if one can present a first-class dramatic or musical
entertainment in a first-class manner in comfortable surroundings the public are always ready to respond."

In a congratulatory leading article the *Birmingham Mail*
complimented P.R. on his successful stand.

"The theatre," it said, "gave fresh proof of its vitality when the
shareholders of the Prince of Wales Theatre Ltd. met to vote
themselves the highly satisfactory dividend of 12½ per cent. as the
result of a year when theatrical business had generally been considered exceedingly difficult. Moreover they had the added pleasure

of listening to a thoroughly optimistic speech from the managing director, to whom the success achieved was, they knew, principally due. The circumstance is all the more noteworthy since too often the strains of pessimism have emanated from leaders of the business who ought to have known better than to run down their own profession, and by announcing its early demise administer to themselves the severest of all condemnations. The truth is that, as in all other undertakings, the success of the theatre depends fundamentally on *the personal equation. Where the men responsible know their business, the theatre flourishes: where they do not, it quickly gets into difficulties.*

"This success of the individual touch is all the more significant because not so very long ago one of the bogeys on the theatrical horizon was the power of the 'trust' or 'ring' to crush out all competition, to blot out local individuality, and to standardise theatrical amusement. . . . Like the extinction of the drama itself, that has not happened, and to judge from the list of attractions Mr. Rodway was able to announce for the coming season, it is not likely to do so. . . ."

When the once-nightly season was resumed, Anne Croft (with whom were Sara Allgood, Tom Shale and Horace Percival) came to the Prince of Wales in her first venture into management, a revival of *The Chocolate Soldier.* Revivals, much in the air then and since, were also typified by *Florodora* (with George Graves) and *The Geisha* (with the D'Oyly Carte favourite, Leo Sheffield). Hughes Macklin took Frederick Blamey's place as Schubert in the next return of *Lilac Time,* while Violet Vanbrugh and her daughter Prudence came in *After All,* Sybil Thorndike in *Saint Joan,* and Martin Harvey in *The King's Messenger.*

The Birmingham and Midland Operatic Society, hitherto playing at the Alexandra Theatre, provided a second week of amateur endeavour in the winter. This was *Miss Hook of Holland,* produced by F. Maxwell-Stuart, stage-managed by H. Gordon Toy, and conducted by Dr. Gordon Anderson. Reginald Poole played Mr. Hook, and Reginald Boardman, Simon Slinks; others in the cast were Evelyn Thomason (Miss Hook), Alfred Butler (the Bandmaster), Alec Dawkins

(Captain Paap), Jack Smith (Schnapps), and Lilian Haslam.

The Covent Garden Opera Company made a brilliant finish to the regular season, and on Boxing Day P.R. was able to present a new departure for the Christmas season—a five weeks' visit of the D'Oyly Carte Opera Company.

This brings us to the close of 1931. Almost till the end of the year Daddy had been carrying on with infinite courage and hope. The following quotations from the Press will show how bravely he tried to maintain the impression that nothing was wrong, and how he strove to keep invalidism at bay:

> "In spite of his illness, he was the same cheerful and courteous personality, with the same unruffled temperament right up to his last appearance at the theatre. He was as smiling as ever, till his illness gradually overcame even his fighting spirit.
>
> "He had a special microphone installed in his private room at the Prince of Wales, so that he could follow what was going on on the stage. . . ."

So from his private office he and Mother, he with hope and she with fear, heard for the last time together the gay music of *The Chocolate Soldier*, *The Geisha* and *Florodora*, which they had first heard together thirty years before.

PRINCE OF WALES THEATRE, BIRMINGHAM

Present day

PHILIP RODWAY

Outside Prince of Wales Theatre, 1931

In the garden by the river, Pershore-on-Avon

Mother and Daddy

CHAPTER 41

THE CURTAIN FALLS

When one reads Lamb's essay on his retirement, a lump rises in the throat, almost a sob of relief that any man can have the joy of saying, at 50, and of the remaining years of his life: "*I have worked taskwork, and have the rest of the day to myself.*" And the eyes fill at the thought of those who, too, "have worked taskwork," but . . .

"*The rest of the day to myself*"! How expressive a phrase! Those few treasured evening hours after a day's work is done; those treasured years when, after a good life's work, one dreams of sitting back and reviewing the past, and revelling in the quiet. Not severed entirely from work, but having the freedom to do the things one likes best. For that is the only time which a man can properly call his own, that which he has all to himself. The rest, though in some sense he may be said to live it, is other people's time, not his.

This biography has told of fishing and river holidays, but even those days were mostly seamed with telegrams and 'phone calls. So often on these brief holidays had 'Daddy said: "One day I'm going to have more time to do the things I like; I'll take your Mother our long-promised trip to Madeira; there's no hurry—we'll get it all in one day." The pathos, the tragedy, of the "one days" in life that never come; the hours that are going to be so happy that never strike!

In the early spring of 1930, when he was only 53, came those first insidious signs of the illness which was to prove fatal. He combated it very bravely. It awoke him still more to the realisation of how many of the good things in life he had put on one side for his work, of how rarely he had allowed himself to relax. *Now* he said: "When I get better I'll always come away with you for holidays, instead of staying behind. I want to have more time for reading and for going through my books. I've an idea for a Fairy Play for children which I want to write and produce at the Prince of Wales. As soon as I'm better we'll really enjoy ourselves." That even this poor pleasure, this slight happiness in anticipation, was not denied to him was solely owing to the heroism of Mother; for she alone knew that the first diagnosis of his illness had not been complete, that he should have been operated on earlier, and that, therefore, recovery was well-nigh impossible.

These two last years were, at any rate, not last years to him, thanks to Mother. They were difficult, hard times, which, he said bravely, he would get over. We can still hear him saying: "It hasn't got me down yet—I'm going to fight it." She alone knew that no amount of courage, nothing indeed short of a miracle, could give them both those longed-for years.

There are heroic actions from the beginnings of time to the present day, but heroism can go no further than that of a wife who sees her loved husband slipping away from her into the other world, and takes on herself the burden of bearing it alone. Hope was not only essential to Daddy's peace of mind, but it gave him the strength necessary to fight the illness. She allowed no word of its extreme serious-ness to trouble his faith and his hope. Until almost the very end she kept her self-imposed silence even with us. Sympathy eases the heart in trouble, as nothing else can, but she denied herself even this relief to save us pain and to prevent any inkling slipping back to him.

As a public figure, Daddy himself did not want his illness made much of, and he always tried to appear better than he was. It was his wish that we said as little about it as possible.

For many months Mother acted a rôle to their friends, because it was the only way to spare Daddy the torture of knowing what she knew—that his dream-days could never be fulfilled. By the end of January it was evident that the tragedy was drawing to its close. To Daddy's eldest sister, on February 1st, Mother wrote the following letter:

The Woodlands,
Edgbaston.
February 1st, 1932.

My dear Laura,
Thank you so very much for your kind and sympathetic letter this morning.

I am very, very anxious about poor Phil. You would, I know, do anything you could for my dearest husband, but the doctors at the nursing home have not been allowing anyone to see him except us. I doubt now whether he knows when we are there.

This gradual fading out may be merciful, but oh, Laura, it is heartbreaking.

He has been so brave, so patient, and tried to keep his illness quiet, and told us we must go on normally, which has made everything more difficult.

The bottom seems to be dropping out of my world; I think my heart is breaking.

With love,
Ethel.

Even before the letter arrived on February 2nd, Daddy was already passing away. He had lapsed into an unconsciousness from which he never woke. In his last conscious moments he had written a little letter to Mother; only three lines in pencil, in his usual beautiful hand, a little fainter and larger than usual. In these three lines we can read the whole volume of their mutual love and heroism:

My dearest girl
It's because as always I love you so much that I am praying to be spared to make you all happy.

Always the same
Philip

"Why continue? You may *hear* the curtain rustling down."

CHAPTER 42

February 5th, 1932

"But I have only gone through three acts, and not held out to the end of the fifth. You say well; but in life three acts make the play entire. He that ordered the opening of the first scene now gives the sign for shutting up the last; you are neither accountable for the one nor the other; therefore retire well satisfied, for he, by whom you are dismissed, is satisfied too."

The end
of the twelve books of the Emperor Marcus Aurelius Antoninus, 177A.D.

It is difficult at this distance to realise the change which came over us on the morning of the funeral; to capture the feeling of consolation, of sadness transmuted into something nearer to understanding, which came to us. After the tragedy of his illness, and with the memory that in February exactly a year ago, the flowers, the hymns, and the bells had been for a wedding, we had dreaded this day as sounding the last note in the saddest music in all our lives. Instead, as if by a miracle, a new chord was struck—of such unearthly beauty that sorrow for him seemed impossible, and sorrow for ourselves would have been wrong. It was as if we saw at last "clear shining after rain." Throughout the morning the flowers were coming, all bearing witness to the affection and esteem in which he was held . . . from the great floral feathers of the Prince of Wales, the Royal's crown, or that perfect model of a little stage, with tiny footlights fashioned from the bells of hyacinths . . . to the bunch of daffodils "In memory of my kind master from Silver." There was so much love and honour inscribed on the cards, such glory in the flowers themselves, that it was impossible to feel cast down. On every side there was praise of him, till sorrow was transfigured and there was no more need for tears.

As if to prepare the way, eight of the flower-laden cars led the funeral procession, instead of following it, each one radiant with a single colour, all white, all purple, or all gold.

And even as we moved off from The Woodlands, a curious feeling stole over us of someone other than ourselves directing it all, approving the order, the dignity, the beauty—for there *was* beauty. We had no doubt who that someone was. It was as if his spirit were with us still, quietly supervising, with his old power and energy. So complete was this impression that at any moment we expected to see him, to hear his voice.

Months later, with a throb of recognition, we found when reading Ellen Terry's memoirs that she had had the same experience at Irving's funeral. The parallel was so exact, the recognition so instantaneous, so like reading one's own words, that we cannot but give the quotation:

"How terribly I missed that face at his own funeral! I kept on expecting to see it, for indeed it seemed to me that he was directing the whole most moving and impressive ceremony. When the sun burst across the solemn misty grey of the Abbey, at the very moment when the coffin, under its superb pall of laurel leaves, was carried up the choir, I felt it was an effect which he would have loved.

"I can understand anyone who was present at his funeral thinking that this was his best memorial. . . ."

and there were many on February 5th who said the same of Philip Rodway, when in the little country churchyard of Northfield a thousand voices rose in the still air with "*The day Thou gavest, Lord, is ended. . . .*"

Never more shall we come up from the river, when the owlet light is come, and along the darkening lanes dim hedges glow with the pale stars of dog-roses. But there is consolation in the fact that though things change, they pass in a perpetuity of beauty. The stream remains though it does not stand still—the stream of lovely things that change, watched by loving eyes that change. And we place our trust within the hope that what is written "from the heart, may find its way to the heart again."

Finale

"Others among his family and his associates," writes Mr. H. F. Harvey, editor of the *Birmingham Mail*, "have dealt adequately with Phil's work in the theatre, but as an old friend one may be forgiven for adding a few words of personal tribute to his high ideals in this regard.

"His own creative work was, of course, in the field of pantomime, of the history and tradition of which he was a careful student. His knowledge and thoroughness were shown in the meticulous care with which he preserved at least the main lines of the old story which was his theme, and his faithfulness to tradition in the matter of both dressing and incident. Withal he had, as have most men who make any notable achievement in their day and generation, a thorough-going faith in himself. He had a fine sense of colour and of stage effect, as was evidenced in the many beautiful productions for which he was responsible. Some of us thought that he concentrated too much on this aspect of pantomime, and that he lost something of that old-time spirit of boisterous fun and laughter which was associated in our minds with this form of entertainment. Sometimes we told him so, but he was never convinced, and, after all, his pantomimes were conspicuously successful with the public, so that his judgment was probably right all the time.

"He was gifted with an extraordinary memory, and could be a most entertaining companion. Many an hour have I spent chatting with him in his private office, while the play which I had gone to see went forward to its destined end. At these times one saw Philip in his most intimate moods. But in the last few years of his life, when illness had set its grip upon him, the 'call boy's' summons became less frequent, and one realised, with a sense of sadness, that he was shutting himself off more and more from his friends. His visits to his old haunts, the Midland Club and the Press Club, became more rare, though he was always assured of the warmest of welcomes, until at last the final word went round, and we knew that we should never chat, or jest, or play again with the man whose friendship had always been a great joy and privilege."

EPILOGUE

By SIR FRANK BENSON

Sir Frank Benson, the distinguished Shakespearean actor, and founder of the famous school and company of actors which bear his name, sends us a most courteous letter in which he says:

"I enclose a very inadequate summary of my pleasant work with Philip Rodway. It will always remain among the treasured recollections of my career. I wish I could have made my notes more worthy of the very fine man he was."

We feel it is peculiarly appropriate that, in 1934, Sir Frank should be speaking the *Epilogue* to this memoir, for just ten years ago, in the December of 1924, it was he who spoke the *Prologue* at the Theatre Royal's 150th Anniversary Performance.

Always closely connected both as friends and in their love of the stage, it was in October, 1898 (as is told in the preceding pages), that Philip Rodway organised the first Shakespeare subscription season for Sir Frank, and the Benson company was the last but one to play in the old Theatre Royal in 1902. So the years bring us to the Christmas of 1924, when he was invited by P.R. to speak the original lines written by Samuel Foote for the opening of the first Theatre Royal in 1774. In March, 1930, under the auspices of Philip Rodway, Sir Frank made his farewell to the Birmingham stage.

And to-day the curtain comes down on *Philip Rodway, and A Tale of Two Theatres*, with the words of the great tragedian:

"When I was lucky enough to secure an engagement at the Lyceum Theatre with Sir Henry Irving and Ellen Terry in his elaborate production of 'Romeo and Juliet,' I was informed by the leading members of that very strong cast he had collected, that it was no good my staying on in London playing such parts as Paris, Claudius, etc. Instead I was advised to go into the Provinces, join a stock company and be put thoroughly through the mill.

"This advice, coming from such artists as Meade, Howe, Terris, Fernandez and their comrades, decided me to start on the road to serve a novitiate in the midst of the old traditions of the stage. Among those theatrical centres which preserved the memories of Garrick, Siddons, Kean and the Kendals, the Birmingham theatres played an important part.

"*The Theatres Royal and Prince of Wales preserved and upheld an all-round standard in every department of our craft. To this workshop, school and picture gallery with its complete equipment of scenery, properties, library, etc., Philip Rodway in due course succeeded.*

"*In association with his management, I was delighted to find myself engaged in producing some of Shakespeare's masterpieces with a company which included among others such names as Ainley, Asche, Weir, Rodney and a goodly band who have made a place for themselves in the annals of the stage.*

"*I at once realised that Philip Rodway was engaged in a larger and more important position in carrying out the work that I myself was attempting. Scenery, music, properties and all things necessary for stage production were carefully provided and polished under his active and unceasing superintendence. All the time there was a sympathetic encouragement; an understanding assistance for the visiting actors. I was much impressed by the clear grasp he had of the requirements of the audience, and those playing for him. With all his gentleness and courtesy, when necessary he was exceedingly quick and decided in action,—a rare mixture of poetry and practicality.*

"*Philip Rodway will remain an outstanding example of all that the manager of an important theatre should be, as an artist, a citizen, and a friend.*

"*With gratitude and affection I shall always remember the kindness and the help that he gave me in my work.*

"*Frank R. Benson.*"

APPENDIX

APPENDIX

"Mr. Inshaw." Page 7.

In these early days our great-grandfather, Councillor Inshaw, was carrying on business as an engineer, and had acquired what subsequently became known as the Steam Clock Music Hall, in the façade of which he inserted the face of a clock worked by steam, which gave the house its name. A lecture hall connected with the house was also equipped with all kinds of ingenious mechanical contrivances and working models, which for many years afforded interest to large numbers of people in a day when scientific education was less plentiful than it is now.

He fitted up an electric clock in the turret of Aston Hall, which is there to this day, and which found many admirers, including the Prince Consort and the late Earl of Beaconsfield.

Numerous anecdotes are related of "Mr. Inshaw coming to the rescue in difficult circumstances with the application of his mechanical ability. On one occasion he was on his way to Derby, to give his evidence as an expert in a case of considerable importance to the metal trades. He travelled in the same train as the judges and the counsel for both sides. Suddenly, without any apparent reason, the engine stopped and refused to move, and the judge and his learned followers recognised the prospects of the trial having to be postponed. The guard, knowing Mr. Inshaw, asked him to see if he could remedy the defect, and, after an urgent request from the judge, he consented to don some of the driver's clothes and to creep under the locomotive, where he made an investigation, finding that one of the eccentrics had shifted. It was soon remedied, and Mr. Inshaw received the thanks of the Midland Railway Company. . . . "

While returning from Ireland on one occasion, where he had been on engineering business, he found among his fellow-companions on board the *Cambria* the novelist Charles Dickens, to whom he predicted the ship's breakdown before they arrived at Liverpool. And his words came true, for not only was there a breakdown, but Mr. Inshaw had to take charge of the boat until it arrived at its journey's end. For his services he received a testimonial from the passengers, headed by the signature of Charles Dickens.

Another interesting episode occurred at the launching of the *Great Eastern.* Mr. Inshaw was present, and after witnessing the unsuccessful attempts to put her into the water, he suggested the

R I

use of hydraulic presses. These were ordered from Birmingham, and soon overcame a difficulty which at one time had seemed unsurmountable.

In addition to taking a part in the building of the Municipal Buildings, Councillor Inshaw also constructed a large portion of the machinery used in the erection of the Town Hall. He was an active and prominent member of the Mechanical Institute in Newhall Street, and frequently exhibited his models there and carried away prizes for them. Having laid down large paper mills for several firms in the vicinity of Birmingham, he established the Aston Manor Paper Mills, which have now an extensive connection both at home and abroad.

It was he who made the immense balloon, in the shape of a screw, which was sent up from Aston Hall on the occasion of the pyrotechnic display given by the then Mayor, Mr. Joseph Chamberlain, on the occasion of the laying of the foundation stone of the Council House.

In 1821, aged fourteen, he lit his father's house with gas, the heat from the retorts also being used for driving a steam engine. He was particularly interested in the construction of locomotive engines, and numbered among his intimate friends George Stephenson, who on many occasions consulted with Mr. Inshaw, especially as regards the construction of locomotive wheels.

He was a member of the Town Council, sitting for the Ladywood Ward, subsequently becoming an active member of the Baths and Parks Committee and of the Aston Local Board. Not satisfied with his experience of travels by land and sea, he travelled by balloon from the old Vauxhall Gardens to Ross, in Herefordshire.

His inventions were continuous. Having dealt with steam, gas, and electricity, he studied photography, and his family possess some of the finest positives that were ever produced in the days of the wet process. Moreover, he could claim the honour of being the engineer over the first locomotive made in Birmingham.

. . . *"the figure of her grandmother." Page 31.*

THE SAMPLER

It was just about dusk that the old Sampler began to murmur to itself—a sweet, faded whisper in a rather tired voice, but meticulously correct and mindful when necessary of its "Misters" and "Ma'ams." All the other pieces of furniture in the room stopped any tendency to creaking (their way of expressing restlessness), out of

respect and reverence for her age—for age in furniture always does
call forth respect, unless its companions be the over-modern bric-à-
brac, which sees nothing in tradition. And so to Samplers, even
feminine Samplers, antiquity is something of which to be most
proud. They were very quiet and attentive, for this was her hour.
Every chair and table, picture and stool, can of course choose some
time out of the twenty-four hours to express itself, and that is why,
if you wake at midnight, you hear such a rustling and a movement
in your room, such as you never hear in the daytime; the window
a-rattling, and the bookcase door and rafters a-creaking. For the
most part the furniture naturally chooses for its own the time when
mortals are, or ought to be, asleep. But midnight was far too late
for the Sampler to be awake (it was "not proper," felt the Victorian,
and truth to tell, she was always sleepy by 8.30).

She was talking, like all very old ladies, more to herself than to
anyone else. Now, when a Sampler wishes to speak it first repeats
its theme, its little verse; this is its "open-sesame" into the world outside its frame; it may repeat this several times before it has found
enough strength to proceed, for all Samplers are delicate creatures
and have not the stamina of, for example, a dower chest. Hark!

> "I envy no one's birth or fame
>   Their title, train or dress,
> Nor has my pride e'er stretch'd its aim
>   Beyond what I possess.
> I ask not, wish not, to appear
>   More beauteous, rich or gay—
> Lord make me wiser every year
>   And better every day."

EMMA HARFORD, Aged 8 years, 1830.
(She spoke the name with a sigh, as a tribute to memory.) This
little poem had become the very being of our Sampler, and consequently a more quiet, modest or gentle old lady it would be hard
to find. She was a particularly well-bred and distinguished character too—for the average A B C D E, 1 2 3 4 5, could of course only
create a humble undefined kind of personality, in comparison.

We will not listen too intently while she rehearses her motto;
instead, let us notice how the little tapestry houses, worked into the
delicate canvas, face each other as erect as ever, with their red walls
and blue doors, and grey curls of smoke from their chimneys; the
squirrels (are they squirrels?) are eating their scarlet nuts as vora-
ciously, and the little dogs are frisking as gaily as on the day when
their mistress stitched their tails at that charmingly impossible angle

to their bodies. The two robins which sing beside the houses (Heaven forfend that they should alight—as they are almost twice the size) are a little faded, but the whole is still perfectly neat; the old lady has spring-cleaned the houses and brushed the dogs once every year for the past 100 years.

Between some tapestries and their original owners, nothing exists but dislike and a wearied recollection, but this Sampler was beloved by its little worker. Each small stiff fruit tree round the edge was traced with loving care—and eight years of age is not very old to stitch such fine embroidery. But although she loved her work, the motto was rather too negative for even this child of eight. She didn't want to be more beauteous, rich or gay, but oh, she felt such a longing for adventure. The little verse which grew under her quick fingers seemed to ask of her a passiveness she did not possess, and, as if to justify her longings, it was recollections of such adventures, many years after, that the Sampler, so meek in personality, treasured most; never forgetting the memory of the happy day when she felt her mistress place the last stitch in her fabric, and knew she was to take a real part in the world at last.

When memories flash across the mind of a house that has weathered the centuries, its rooms are again filled—even for us—with the ghosts of bygone days. How much more of its history does it convey to its friends and inhabitants—the oak beams and the settles, and the gleaming brass upon its walls?

When a tallboy is put up for auction in an alien saleroom, the scene where it has felt its most intense experience may build itself up around it again. How much more easily can the Sampler, in the stillness and the half-light, with shadows from the fire already beginning to flicker across the carved rafters, find self-expression and dwell again on the days that are gone? Partly by whispers, but more often by scenes that shine against the faded tapestry, its history is being pieced together. And that evening all the furniture listened and looked. For though almost always it was the same story, they did not tire.

*　　　*　　　*

It is a late afternoon in the autumn of 1830—and the little girl of eight in the silver grey poplin dress is once more running to show her work, completed at last, to her mother. "See, see, Mama, I have finished my Sampler!" How it is praised! and how the bosom of the newly-born Sampler swelled with pride!

"And you have done something that will last—perhaps even a

great-granddaughter* will look at this one day and admire your industry," concludes her mother.

For a moment the child thinks soberly and happily of her mother's words, and tries to peep into the future ("—what if her beloved Sampler should really be seen by?—"); but then she skips off again, singing in the pleasure of the moment.

* * *

Eight years slip by like a second in the Sampler's mind, and it hangs again over its mistress's bed in the boarding Academy for Young Ladies at Bromsgrove. Emma Harford, schoolgirl of sixteen, is laying one hand on the frame and bidding it good-bye—there is no one else to whom she dare say it—before she slips out, without bonnet or shawl, to meet her lover. He is waiting for his bride at the corner of the road in his high gig, and he whirls her away to the little Church to be married. But first he must pull up in the market town to buy her a bonnet and shawl. . . .

The Sampler sighed, and then, as she recollected the sequel—how unceremoniously she, and the few other possessions, had been bundled away home in disgrace by the Governess—she shuddered with distaste.

* * *

Rough winds are shaking the little timbered cottage and blow on through the dark green woods beyond. Ireland's moors stretch out on the other side. In the room upstairs the Sampler sees itself once more hung precariously on the whitewashed wall beneath the sloping roof (the fine embroidery and ornate framing are out of place above the rickety cottage furniture—but it could never be left behind). Emma Harford has fled up to her room with her three-months old baby in her arms and her little daughter clinging to her skirts. Her arms encircling and protecting the children, she waits with fast shut door, beneath the Sampler, listening to that mad scampering below. More dangerous, at the moment, to the life of the tiny baby than the wolves which kept them awake by night howling in the forests; more frightening to the little girl; and yet only the keeper's ferrets, escaped from their wooden pen, and loose in the room below. Only? Though they are small in size, the mother knew there is no animal more vicious. They kill for killing's sake, . . . and the baby had been lying sleeping in its cradle by the hearth. But the children are safe now in their retreat, and how best can she soothe and quieten them till their father's return? (How happy was

---

*Lois.

the Sampler to recall her part.) The little daughter's favourite song, set to an old lullaby tune, of the Sampler on the wall, and the brown roofed houses, comes to her mind, and softly she begins. It was not till an hour later that the outer door, with its skins of bats, and feathers of owls, and pelts of the smaller forest animals, stretched tight and nailed upon its woodwork, was opened, and the capture quickly made. And when he found them, the children were sleeping soundly on the white bed beneath the Sampler, and the mother, bending over them, had still the song on her lips.*

*   *   *

The Sampler is tired. It is almost ready now to lean contentedly back against its wall, and doze. It dimly sees itself in the back of the two-wheeled jaunting car, jolting along the road to Dublin: it is being brought back to England with its mistress and her family; the past is fading, but it knows itself to be treasured by the little daughter of the low-storey'd Irish home; and knows itself to be treasured by her daughter's daughter's daughter. "It's all come true! for everyday her great-granddaughter looks at me, and every day admires anew her industry. I have been privileged to carry her name through a century. 'I envy *no one*'s birth or fame'" whispers the Sampler proudly, as she drifts into her sleep again.

Berry Hall. Page 112.

Berry Hall, Solihull, had been the residence of Mr. and Mrs. Henry Gillott, Mother's uncle and aunt, of the famous family of pen-makers.

Mrs. Gillott died when only twenty-eight years old, and, heart-broken, her husband died exactly a week later.

She was the baby in the Irish Cottage in *The Sampler* story, and her sister, the little girl "clinging to her mother's skirts," was mother's mother (and our grandmother Brown).

"Italian extemporal comedy." Page 227.

The figure of Harlequin, conventional character who held place for many years in English pantomime, stepped out of the Italian "masked comedy," itself an adaptation of the *fabulae atellanae* of ancient Rome. His many-coloured costume was a survival of the traditional attire of the Roman "Mimi"—the black skull-cap and mask the counterpart of shaven head and sooted face. The different

---

*The true facts—as retold by her great-granddaughter, Lois Harford Rodway, when the Sampler came into her possession a hundred years later, in 1930.

coloured lozenges each had their own meaning; black signified "Hate," red "Passion," blue "Love," and yellow "Jealousy"—and these became the connecting links between the scenes of the *Commedia del Arte*, as implied by the actions of *Arlecchino* (Harlequin).

From the old Italian popular comedy, too, there came to pantomime "the lean and slippered pantaloon, with spectacles on nose and pouch on side," owing his name to the favourite Venetian saint San Pantalone.

*   *   *

The evolution of pantomime itself may be traced back to the dim ages, when, in the primitive stages of civilisation, we see it beginning to express itself in sacrificial rites and war dances; through the Indians and Egyptians it comes, developing artistic forms; from the Greeks and their chorus-accompanied dramas; and from the Roman *pantomimus*, for the development of which they even had a special school, and which was a species of spectacular play, with scenic effects and distinguishing masks, much on the lines of the modern *ballet d'action*.

One of the first producers of pantomime in England was John Rich, lessee of the theatre then established in Lincoln's Inn Fields, who in 1717 produced a pantomime of *Harlequin executed* (in rivalry with the Theatre Royal in Drury Lane). It was probably the keen competition existing between these London theatres which, in 1723, with the production of the harlequinade *Dr. Faustus* at Drury Lane, gave pantomime its firm footing on the English stage.

INDEX

INDEX